D0894090

★ NEW ENGLAND STUDIES ★

Edited by John Putnam Demos, David Hackett Fischer,
and Robert A. Gross

FRANCIS J. BREMER
*Congregational Communion: Clerical Friendship
in the Anglo-American Puritan Community,
1610–1692*

EDWARD BYERS
The Nation of Nantucket

DANIEL P. JONES
*The Economic and Social Transformation of
Rural Rhode Island, 1780–1850*

JOHN R. MULKERN
The Know-Nothing Party in Massachusetts

RICHARD RABINOWITZ
The Spiritual Self in Everyday Life

CONRAD EDICK WRIGHT
*The Transformation of Charity in
Postrevolutionary New England*

Congregational Communion

CLERICAL FRIENDSHIP
IN THE ANGLO-AMERICAN
PURITAN COMMUNITY,
1610–1692

Francis J. Bremer

Northeastern University Press

BOSTON

Northeastern University Press

Library of Congress Cataloging-in-Publication Data

Bremer, Francis J.
    Congregational communion : clerical friendship in the Anglo-
American Puritan community, 1610–1692 / Francis J. Bremer.
        p.   cm. — (New England studies)
    Includes bibliographical references and index.
    ISBN 1-55553-186-5 (alk. paper)
        1. Puritans—New England—Clergy—Psychology.   2. Puritans—
England—Clergy—Psychology.   3. New England—Church history—17th
century.   4. England—Church history—17th century.   I. Title.
II. Series.
BX9358.B74   1994
285'.9'097409032—dc20   94-5620

Designed by Richard C. Bartlett and Ann Twombly

Composed in Fairfield by Coghill Composition, Richmond, Virginia.
Printed and bound by Maple Press, York, Pennsylvania. The paper is Maple
Eggshell, an acid-free stock.

MANUFACTURED IN THE UNITED STATES OF AMERICA
98 97 96 95 94   5 4 3 2 1

To

CHRISTOPHER HILL

MICHAEL MCGIFFERT

ALDEN VAUGHAN

Exemplary Scholars, Generous Friends

CONTENTS

	List of Maps	ix
	Preface	xi
PROLOGUE	As the Soule of Jonathan to David	3
ONE	The Cambridge Connection	17
TWO	A Whole Chain of Many Links	41
THREE	United for Reform	63
FOUR	A Spider of Divers Threads	81
FIVE	A Light upon a Hill	103
SIX	Blessed Work of a Publique Reformation	122
SEVEN	These Polemick Times	151
EIGHT	The Time When Church Is Militant	174
NINE	The Bread of Adversity, the Water of Affliction	201
TEN	For the Nation and the Interest of Christ	220
	Epilogue	253
	Notes	259
	Index	331

Maps

England   18
Cambridge Colleges and Churches, 1600–1630   22
East Anglia: Heartland of the Congregational Communion   44
New England   106

Preface

THE PURITAN LEGACY and the debate over its meaning lie at the core of the American experience. It has been emphasized by those who seek to place New England at the moral center of American history and criticized by those who complain that disproportionate emphasis on the region has eclipsed the contributions of other Americans. The Puritan colonists of New England have been awarded the credit for much that is good in the American dream and assigned the blame by some who see the past as a nightmare. After hundreds of scholars have plowed up the field and after thousands of books, theses, and articles have been harvested, we are no closer to consensus than we were earlier in the century when Vernon Parrington wrote to damn the Puritans and Samuel Eliot Morison sought to praise them. Indeed, recently some scholars have called into question the relevance of the preceding labor by suggesting that there was no such thing as a Puritan movement![1]

Yet, no dramatic closure of the debate is likely. The residents of early New England were a people who grappled directly with questions that resonate through the ages to our own time—the conflicting demands of self and community and the dividing line between liberty and license. They were also men and women of faith whose religious outlook strikes a chord with many contemporary Americans. Forty years ago Perry Miller, one of the most influential students of Puritanism, wrote that the New England colonies were an "ideal laboratory" for studying "the relation of thought or ideas to communal experience." Miller explained this by reference to the relatively small size of the population, its homogeneous character, and its relative isolation. Yet, the subject has proved as elusive as quicksilver spilled on a lab table. In the past four decades scholars chasing it have been drawn into examinations of topics as diverse as material culture and Reformation theology, and fields of inquiry such as literature and demography. Every attempt to channel the flow has only revealed new currents and set loose new tributaries.[2]

Amidst this ever-expanding field, *Congregational Communion* returns to the concern identified by Miller as central to his own work—the relationship between social experience and the shaping of belief. The experience of grace and the sense of being born again have long been accepted as being at the heart of the Puritan self-definition. I wish to draw attention to how in the process of conversion some English men and women shared in a godly communion that heightened their spiritual sense of election, provided them with friends to share their burdens, and opened them toward processes of shared responsibility. The doctrine of the communion of the saints, which has been of great importance throughout the history of Christianity, assumed a new meaning and urgency in seventeenth-century England. For most Puritans the doctrine became experience, and this was especially true, I will argue, for those clergymen who became Congregationalists first in practice and then in a denomination.

By focusing on this experience and the consequences of such communion, I hope to demonstrate afresh for those who need convincing that there was such a thing as Puritanism and to offer suggestions as to its character at a particular stage of its evolution. Attempts to fix the nature of the movement by delineating a Puritan mind have foundered on the failure of such models to predict behavior in Tudor-Stuart England and over the dynamic character of Puritan thought. Increasingly, scholars have spoken of a Puritan movement or character. My use of the term *Puritan* fits into that interpretive mold in that I focus on the experience of regeneration that brought men and women together in a godly communion, simultaneously binding them to each other and distancing them from contemporaries who did not share the illumination of grace. But I am also arguing that this experience confirmed for Puritans the truths of Calvinist theology and moved them toward forms of polity that emphasized the participation of the godly. Communion was important not only as an experience that generated friendship but as a force that influenced the shaping of ideas.

I hope to persuade readers that godly conference and communion formed a nexus in which social, spiritual, and theological impulses merged in a way that produced new ideas and innovative practices. I wish to explore a dynamic in which similar dispositions and common circumstances brought individuals together, leading to shared experiences and relationships that in turn influenced the shaping and spreading of beliefs. The lives and words of the saints attracted others to the communion where in turn they were exposed to communal experiences, setting the process going again as the movement spread through time and space. This Puritanism was dynamic and changing. Its roots preceded the starting point of this study and its history proceeded past the closing date of this study. *Congregational Communion* is a study of a portion of the Puritan story. The communion described was a concept that bound together all saints, laymen as well as ministers. But my primary concern is the importance of the experience for clergymen and in particular those who became Congregationalists. At various points I incorporate others into the story because of their interaction with the Congregational clerical network, and at such times I have suggested some of the broader implications of the sense of communion.

A few words are in order about my use of the term *Congregational*. I believe that we hinder our understanding of the early seventeenth century when we impose denominational categories on those whom we seek to understand. Yet, I found that within the overall Puritan movement there was a closer sense of agreement on issues and a greater similarity of temperament among those clergy, on the one hand, who would eventually become Congregationalists and those, on the other hand, who would eventually choose the Presbyterian path. I argue that the former had experienced godly communion in a way that led them to trust more in the redeemed nature of godly saints, whereas those who would become Presbyterians feared lay influence and cherished order in life. I have chosen the term *congregational* to refer to the former, frequently referring to a "congregational communion" so as to emphasize the spiritual, social, and emotional ties that united these men and to downplay the denominational implications.

The congregational communion is a significant one, for it represented the view of the majority of the Puritan clergy who came to America as well as of the English Dissenting Brethren. But this story could and should be paralleled by studies of similar religious networks. Kenneth Fincham has analyzed the Jacobean episcopate. Philip Gura's work has pointed to connections among radical sectarians, and historians have long been familiar with the trans-Atlantic dimensions of the aptly named Society of Friends. A study of trans-Atlantic friends who preferred presbyterian church systems would be a valuable complement to this study. So whereas I have focused on one particular network of the godly, I want to demonstrate as well that in the decades prior to 1640 the experiences that set them apart from fellow Puritans were nothing compared to the ties that bound them to the broader movement. On many issues this cluster of friends saw eye to eye with other Puritans. It was only as the chances of implementing religious reform grew that the importance of the issues dividing Puritans became evident. Strains within Puritanism then became more severe and the result contributed to the formation of institutional, denominational groupings.[3]

This study adopts a trans-Atlantic approach and seeks to focus on the ties that united congregational friends who, to borrow the words of John Winthrop, "though . . . absent from each other many miles, and had our employments as farre distant, yet . . . ought to consider ourselves knitt together by this bond of love." The story starts in England but evolves to follow the Puritan hegiras to the Netherlands and to New England. But just as those who migrated did not abandon England, so will I retain a broad focus that incorporates the exiled friends into the English story so that the tale remains one.[4]

In introducing a book that examines the influence of friends on each other's ideas it would be especially churlish not to thank those who have read various drafts of chapters and of papers in which I tested my interpretation. For their encouragement and advice I wish to thank Alden Vaughan, Christopher Hill, John Morrill, Michael McGiffert, Timothy Breen, Stephen Foster, John Murrin, Harry Stout, Sargent Bush, Alison Olson, Richard Johnson, Philip Gura, Alan Macfarlane, Jeremy Boissevain, Patrick Collinson, Hal Worthly, Raymond Cunningham, Richard Gildrie, George Selement, Carol Berkin, Pat Bonomi, Richard Brown, Timothy Sehr, Irene Brown, Daniel Richter, Dennis Downey, Edwin Schock, Martin Wood, Tom Webster, David Hackett Fischer, and Marlene Arnold. Though they have not read any portions of this work, I was encouraged in my pursuit of the Puritans by the studies of Margo Todd, Barbara Donagan, Jacqueline Eales, Ann Hughes, and Carol Schneider, which paralleled some of my own perceptions of the social context in which the English clergy labored. Their insights convinced me that I was on the right track. The collegial support of the Millersville History Department and Deans William Pearman and Christopher Dahl has always been appreciated. Thanks also are due to John Weingartner, Ann Twombly, and the staff of Northeastern University Press.

Grants and fellowships from the National Endowment for the Humanities, the American Council of Learned Societies, the American Philosophical Society, and the Millersville University Academic Research Committee provided opportunities to conduct research far and wide. As a Fulbright Fellow at Wolfson College, Cambridge University, I benefitted from the friendly welcome offered by the scholars in the Tudor History and Early Modern British History seminars. Librarians at the Bodleian Library at Oxford University, the Cambridge University Library and the college libraries, the British Library, the Suffolk Records Office at Bury St. Edmunds, the Norfolk Record Office, the Guildhall Library, the Public Record Office, the Royal Commission on Historical Manuscripts, Dr. Williams's Library, the Massachusetts Historical Society, the Connecticut Historical Society, the American Antiquarian Society, the Essex Institute, Columbia University, Union Theological Seminary, and the inter-library loan staff of Millersville University (especially Mrs. Bonnie Jolly) have made this study possible by providing me with access to the materials without which it could not have been written.

My family has supported me through many years of labor on a project in which they have little interest. I have always been touched by that support and by the sacrifices they have been willing to make. The loving communion of which I am a part with Bobbi, Heather, Kristin, Megan—and now Keegan —means more to me than I can ever express or acknowledge properly.

July 1993

CONGREGATIONAL COMMUNION

PROLOGUE

As the Soule of Jonathan to David

THE YEAR 1643 was a time of both hope and fear for John Cotton and other New Englanders anxiously awaiting the latest news of England's Puritan Revolution. Each ship's arrival drew their thoughts to the world from which they had departed, but to which they remained emotionally, intellectually, and spiritually engaged. It had been in England that Cotton formed the spiritual friendships that were to shape his career. In the hall of Emmanuel College, Cambridge, in the vicarage of St. Botolph's parish in Boston, Lincolnshire, and elsewhere in his native land, Cotton had worshiped, fasted, and exchanged advice with fellow saints in a godly communion that gave its members material aid, emotional comfort, and spiritual nourishment. The bonds of love that knit them together had survived when some members left for other parts of England, some for the Netherlands, and others to New England. Sustained by correspondence and buoyed by each other's prayers, they had maintained their unity as they continued to labor for the proper reformation of England's church.

Like other New England clergymen, Cotton had sacrificed much when he came to America to share in the creation of a society designed as a model for England's reform. He had given up the grandeur of St. Botolph's for a simple, wooden meetinghouse, and the comforts of civilization for the hardships of a frontier. More important, he lost face-to-face contacts with cherished friends who remained behind. Thus, the first news of the English conflict stimulated hopes for the triumph of reform, but also raised fears for the fate of friends caught up in the dangers of war.

Patience was difficult. News took months to reach America, and when it did the deluge of reports included rumors, fears, and outright lies. Which communications were reliable? How could the colonists identify and support the advocates of true reform? For Cotton and his fellow clergymen the answer was to trust the English friends whose spiritual friendship had sustained them in the past. With few exceptions the colonial clergy were tied to the English advocates of congregational forms led by Thomas Goodwin and Philip Nye, both of whom had recently returned to England from the Netherlands. Isolated from the struggle, impatient for news, and eager to assist, many New Englanders also considered returning home. And in 1643, Cotton, Thomas Hooker, and John Davenport were invited to join the Westminster Assembly, the gathering of clergy called by the Long Parliament to lay the foundations of a new state church. Cotton was eager to participate, but friends on both sides of the Atlantic dissuaded him. Hard as it was for New Englanders to understand, with victory in sight the unity of the reformers had begun to dissolve. Factions rent English Puritanism, and those who shared Cotton's views were unlikely to triumph at Westminster. His friends agreed that the leaders of New England Puritanism could best support the congregational cause of Goodwin and his fellow Dissenting Brethren from their posts in the New World. Responding to the needs of their English friends, the colonial clergy would use their decade-long experience in church reformation to provide a stream of advice on the proper ordering of state and church. Beginning in the early 1640s, treatise after treatise was dispatched to the motherland from the lofty heights of the colonial City on a Hill.

One of the more important products of this effort was Cotton's *Keyes of the Kingdom of Heaven* (London, 1644). In that treatise he essayed to explain the fundamentals of the congregational way of church government practiced in New England and espoused in England by close friends and allies. Cotton had known Thomas Goodwin since the time they were fellows at Cambridge University. Goodwin had introduced him to Nye, and Cotton had corresponded with both in the decade since he had left England. These two friends arranged for the publication of *Keyes of the Kingdom* and prefaced it with a statement affirming their attachment to the New Englander's views. As revolution and civil war gave way to the Commonwealth and then the Protectorate, colonial clergy continued to rely on such English friends for news, trusted them in their efforts to advance the common cause of reform, and assisted them through prayer and advice. Englishmen such as Goodwin would continue to espouse the New England Way as their own, advance its acceptance in England, and defend it and its colonial advocates against Presbyterian and sectarian critics.

*   *   *

In 1688 Increase Mather found himself in London burdened with a task every bit as challenging as that undertaken by John Cotton a generation earlier. New England's liberties had been curtailed and its privileges stripped away by the revocation and seizure of colonial charters and the creation of the Dominion of New England. The Boston clergyman had journeyed to England to petition King James II for a redress of colonial grievances against the Dominion's governor general, Sir Edmund Andros. Mather was no stranger to England, having first traveled there in the 1650s as a young Harvard graduate eager to share in the restructuring of the Commonwealth. There he had formed new friendships and had been more fully integrated into the congregational communion. It had been three decades since he had left England amidst the collapsing dream of the Puritan Revolution and returned to Massachusetts. The Restoration and its aftermath had brought significant ebbs and flows in English political and religious life; yet, Mather was familiar with those changes. Throughout his American career he felt pulled toward England and maintained an extensive correspondence with his friends there. When he returned to England in 1688 some of those friends would bring him to the attention of the king and aid him in pressing his cause. When King James was toppled in the Glorious Revolution and replaced on the throne by William and Mary, other friends of the Boston Puritan would help him gain access to the new regime. Mather credited much of his success in the negotiations for the new Massachusetts charter of 1691 to the intercession of those friends of his and of New England.

In both of these episodes spiritual communion between colonists and English clergymen played a key role. Knit together by the thread of grace and a legacy of shared experiences, members of this communion formed a network of friends who were determined to maintain their unity as they labored together to advance the reform cause. Brought together by shared doctrines or temperament, the Puritans of early Stuart England formed a fellowship of faith that set them apart from their peers. This is not to say that no non-Puritan nor even anti-Puritan cliques and groupings existed, for they undoubtedly did. But those who were perceived as Puritans felt themselves to be members of a special community—a communion of saints, a fellowship of the elect, a godly people. Regardless of whether entrance was purchased by grace, subscription to doctrine, social alienation, or economic drives, membership in that community was a profoundly important social and religious experience. The fellowship and love that sprang from it were among the "fruits of conversion." Connections with godly friends were clearly more important to those believers than to their contemporaries. This study investigates the significance of that communion for a particular group of Puritans and how it shaped their attitudes and actions. As was true of John Bunyan's

Pilgrim, so too for members of the congregational communion the advice and comfort of fellow saints made it possible to persevere in trying times.[1]

Friendship among the Puritans was given a depth many non-Puritans could not relate to because it was a spiritual as well as a social relationship. This seems to have been especially true of those who became part of a congregational communion based on a recognition in each other of the light of saving grace. The godly were no mere group of drinking associates, but a communion of the elect. Friendship was a bond valued by all Englishmen, but for the Puritan it was also a duty. For some Puritans it went even further and was one of the defining characteristics of their religious life. Bunyan's Greatheart described the obligations of such communion in *The Pilgrim's Progress*: "You must needs to along with us; we will wait for you, we will lend you our help, we will deny our selves of some things, both *Opinionative* and *Practical*, for your sake; . . . we will be made all things to you, rather than you shall be left behind." As the Reverend Paul Baynes expressed it, "the communion of the saints must be a point of practice, as well as an article of belief." Richard Sibbes, one of the foremost Puritan clergymen of the early seventeenth century, warned that God was angered "when there is not that sweet communion of saints among them to strengthen one another in the ways of holiness. . . . When there is not a beauty in their profession to allure and draw on others to a love and liking of the best things." In a 1640 sermon recorded by Robert Keayne, John Cotton urged the residents of colonial Boston to "Covet Societie with faythfull friends, the benefit is very greate, they wil be as Cruches." William Bridge stressed the importance of such ties when he asserted, "when a man is my friend, not only his Power is my friend, his Love is my friend, his Purse is my friend, . . . his sword is my friend."[2]

One of the most affecting descriptions of such communion is to be found in a letter from Governor John Winthrop to Sir William Spring, a lay friend in Suffolk. As he prepared to leave England and friends such as Spring, Winthrop was keenly aware of what he was about to lose. Describing their relationship, the governor wrote that "I embrace you and rest in your love, and delight to solace my first thoughts in these sweet affections of so deare a friende. The apprehension of your love and worth togither hath overcome my heart, and removed the veil of modestye, that I must needes tell you, my soule is knitt to you, as the soule of Jonathan to David: were I now with you, I shall bedewe that sweet bosome with the tears of affection." Such depth of feeling was characteristic of the relationship between saints. Like Winthrop, John Cotton used the Old Testament account of the love between David and Jonathan as an analogy for his own communion with John Preston. And John Owen defined "communion" as "the natural sharing of those good things which delight all those in that fellowship. This was so with David and Jonathan. Their souls were bound together in love." The scriptural story helped them to define what they experienced, just as their experience gave new meaning to their reading of scripture. And for Winthrop, "if any Embleme may expresse our Condition in heaven, it is this Communion in love."[3]

A short time after writing to Spring, Winthrop counseled his fellow immigrants on the importance of maintaining such ties in their New World communities and of retaining their love for English friends. Although most analyses of "The Modell of Christian Charity" focus on Winthrop's development of the structural and utopian aspects of community, the sermon contains lengthy discussions of the nature of the love and communion that should knit the saints together. Winthrop describes the communion between the souls of fellow saints as "like Adam when Eve was brought to him, shee must have it one with herselfe, this is of my fleshe (saith shee) and bone of my bone; shee conceives a great delighte in it, therefore shee desires neareness and familiarity with it: shee hath a great propensity to doe it good and receives such content in it, as fearing the miscarriage of her beloved shee bestowes it in the inmost closett of her heart; shee will not endure that it shall want any good which shee can give it." Those traveling to Massachusetts were leaving behind godly friends, but a trans-Atlantic communion should be maintained because (still using the analogy between the soul and Eve) "if by occasion shee be withdrawn from the Company of it, shee is still lookeing towardes the place where shee left her beloved; if shee heares it groane shee is with it presently, if shee finde it sadd and disconsolate shee sighes and mournes with it; shee hath noe such joy, as to see her beloved merry and thriving; if shee see it wronged, shee cannot beare it without passion; shee setts noe boundes of her affections, nor hath any thought of reward, shee finds recompence enough in the exercise of her love towardes it." Later, Winthrop again invokes the relationship between David and Jonathan as a model for godly communion.[4]

Winthrop was not alone in talking lyrically about the experience of communion. Robert Coachman called it "the most pleasant dew and sweet ointment." Thomas Brooks explained that "Love to the saints, for the image of God stamped upon them, is a flower that grows not in nature's garden." Expounding on this love that made the lives of the saints a *Heaven on Earth*, Brooks described such spiritual communion as "a love for the image of God that is stamped upon the soul." Turning to Scripture, he wrote that this "true love is like to that of Ruth's to Naomi, and that of Jonathan's to David, permanent and constant." Brooks highlighted the egalitarian implications that would sustain congregational beliefs. While recognizing the integrity of the individual, Brooks emphasized the importance of community, pointing out that this love united all the godly, "the meanest as well as the richest, the wealthiest as well as the strongest, the lowest as well as the highest. They have all the same Spirit, the same Jesus, the same faith; they are all fellow-members, fellow-travellers, fellow-soldiers, fellow-citizens, fellow-heirs, and therefore must they all be loved with a sincere and cordial love."[5]

When Puritans spoke of community or communion, "they did not mean," as Stephen Foster has pointed out, "the truism that society consists of more than a collection of atomized individuals, they meant Communion in the sacramental sense. Love was a kind of socialized Eucharist." The religious experience of God's grace in conversion gave a new identity to the individual by emphasizing his or her personal rebirth, but also provided the elect with a new social identity as a member of the communion of saints, bound by love to fellow believers. Communion was thus at the heart of an experience that both evoked and mediated between concepts of personal and corporate identity and responsibilities. In many ways they were adapting for their own uses elements of late medieval spirituality that had flourished in England, and especially in East Anglia. Eamon Duffy, in his masterful study of "traditional religion" in fifteenth- and sixteenth-century England, has argued that scholars who "emphasize the growth of individualism" in the spirituality of the period have neglected the equally important "unitive and corporate dimension of the Blessed Sacrament" laid out in the sources and reflected in the practices of the time. These emphases were especially evident in the "unity and fellowship of the Corpus Christi gild," which was viewed as "one aspect of the mystical body of Christ." "Only in that unity," according to Duffy, "can anyone be a member of Christ, and all the natural bonds of human fellowship, such as the loyalty and affection of one gild member for another . . . is an expression of this fundamental community in Christ through the sacrament." The communion of saints found in the Puritan conventicles of the sixteenth and seventeenth centuries evokes echoes of the guilds of the earlier era and hints at a redirected spirituality adapting to a new age and circumstances and modified by new theological beliefs. Rooted in such a fertile pietistic tradition, the communion of saints was a concept that assumed a special meaning for the reformers, distinguishing them from the ungodly masses whom they sought to uplift. And the Puritan clergy, who sought not only to preach but to live such fellowship, were the living model for communion among all saints.[6]

This communion of saintly friends was a source of emotional, spiritual, and material support—a force for cohesion and an inspiration for new directions. "The greatest evidence that we have a delightful, loving fellowship with someone is that we share our most intimate secrets with that person," wrote John Owen. And, more so than was the case for other Englishmen, Puritan friendships were capable of surviving geographical separation. The literacy that was characteristic of Puritans allowed them to maintain friendships over distances, even across oceans. As John Winthrop Jr. expressed it in a letter written in 1650, "Surely not the least we learn from correspondence is that though separated by an entire hemisphere, friends may yet from time to time, so to speak, talk and, though far long and absent from one another, may yet nourish a mutual friendship." It helped far-flung Puritans to hear of distant events and this in turn influenced their perceptions of such developments.[7]

      This study focuses on the godly communion of seventeenth-century Puritans. Though rooted in descriptions by the saints of what such fellowship meant to them, it has also been influenced by an understanding of the nature and meaning of friendship drawn from the insights of contemporary anthropology and psychology. Although the narrative will reveal that the intensity of feeling between the saints went beyond what many call "friendship," studies of ordinary friends can provide suggestions as to how such relationships are formed and how they can be identified. Studies of social networks can be particularly suggestive. Of course, the social-scientific investigations to be discussed are studies of our times and not the seventeenth century, yet they can be useful for those who would better understand the past. Relationships such as kinship and friendship in our society may parallel those in other societies removed in time. Similarities may be found between modern theory and seventeenth-century prescriptive literature. To the extent that an analysis of past realities shows those injunctions to have been followed, the facts will validate the application of the theory and the theory can then serve further to illuminate the reality.

Whereas its origins can be traced to metaphoric uses of the word *network* to designate "webs" of kinship and other ties of affinity in the works of R. R. Radcliffe-Brown and others, modern network theory was initially formulated and used by John Barnes and Elizabeth Bott in the 1950s. Some American sociologists began using the concept in the 1960s, but to date it has been most widely employed in British and European circles with anthropologists such as J. Clyde Mitchell and Jeremy Boissevain effectively articulating the theory and employing it in their studies. My research has been guided by an understanding of network theory, but I should make it clear that limitations of evidence do not allow for actual network analysis such as would precisely define the scope of the network, the density of its clusters, or the precise significance of transactions. In the text that follows, the clergy identified as "congregational" should be considered members of the network, and in the course of the narrative many of the ties that united them are documented. Undoubtedly, many others were members of the network and additional linkages existed which are now lost to us. In recent times, as Barry Wellman has explained of network analysis, "Some have hardened it into a method, whereas others have softened it into a metaphor." Given the limitations of the seventeenth-century sources, this study gravitates toward the latter end of that continuum.[8]

Network analysis, as defined by Boissevain, is "first of all an attempt to reintroduce the concept of man as an interacting social being capable of manipulating others and being manipulated by them. The network analogy indicates that people are dependent on others, not on abstract society." The researcher focuses upon the social relations connecting a given individual to others. Some members are known to one another directly, whereas some are known through information revealed by intermediaries. In other words, every person has direct linkage to some members of the network and indirect contact with others. These latter are "friends of friends." Taken together, these connections represent a social environment that influences a person and through which he influences others. "It is," writes Boissevain, "the reservoir of social relations from and through which he recruits support to counter his rivals and mobilizes support to attain his goal." In an extreme form, as described by Charles Wetherell, this form of analysis "rest[s] on the dual premises that the structure of a social system is determined by the relations, not the individual attributes, of its members and that the pattern of these relationships governs behavior."[9]

Within a network there exist certain "clusters" or areas where there is a higher density of contacts than in the web as a whole. In the trans-Atlantic Puritan network American clergymen and their English counterparts constituted separate clusters. Individuals who belonged to more than one cluster, such as John Cotton or Increase Mather, played an especially important role as brokers who held the various clusters together as a network. Remembering that such links are transactional, that is, bridges connecting individuals through action, the researcher must seek to examine the content of the transactions, the traffic that crosses the bridge. Until this is established the network exists only as a potential source of influence on members. People can, of course, be tied together in a variety of ways and perform different services for each other. A contact that is based on a single-role relationship, such as being schoolmates, is often referred to as being single stranded. If maintained over time, many such relationships become multistranded as the individuals involved befriend one another and begin sharing more of their lives and thoughts. Boissevain points out that "where a many-stranded relationship exists between two persons, there is greater accessibility, and thus response to pressure, than is the case in a single-stranded relation" and that "where multiplex relations exist they will be more intimate (in the sense of friendly and confidential)."[10]

Friendship, indeed, is what ties networks together and yet friendship, one of the most basic of all human relations, is also one of the least studied. It is difficult to define, in part because the word *friend* is used in everyday speech to cover a wide range of social contacts from intimates to casual acquaintances. For purposes of this study friendship will be used as meaning a relationship between two individuals that is maintained over time and that satisfies mutual needs. Friends in English and American culture are "persons with whom one has shared interests, experiences, and activities" and who are "also seen as supportive, dependable, understanding and accepting; in short . . . as people 'one can count on.' " The relationship is instrumental, yet also affective. In cases where friends share an intense religious experience which they identify as signifying a spiritual rebirth into a communion of saints, that affection is very strong, the experience defining them as an elect group separate from others.[11]

To understand how friendships produce, sustain, and mobilize networks, attention must be paid to how they are formed and to their connections with attitudes and behavior. Friendship, to begin with, is an achieved relationship as opposed to kinship, which is ascribed. It develops from social contact with those encountered in daily living. The more such contact one has with an individual, the more opportunity there is to assess the acquaintance as a potential friend. Friendships are most likely, therefore, between people who see a good deal of each other—neighbors, kin, schoolmates, and workmates. Acquaintances become friends when they share certain attitudes. As one psychologist has observed, "To like one another and to be alike have the same root in Old English. It is not surprising then, that a similarity-leads-to-liking hypothesis is the most general statement about the effects of another's perceived cognitions and feelings." Friendship can be based on similarity in personality, but attitudinal congruence seems to be a stronger force. Indeed, it can be argued that the closer two people are in their views regarding things they see as important the more likely they are to be friends. In the seventeenth century Lady Brilliana Harley pointed to the significance of shared religious experience when she wrote in her commonplace book that friends are "those that are of the same religion, affection and disposition." And her husband, Sir Robert, wrote that "religion . . . makes friends at first sight." The explanations for this vary, but most are tied to the concept that when individuals share each other's views, their acceptance of each other serves to reinforce their beliefs and to increase their self-esteem. An important point to remember, however, is that the similarity that contributes to friendship is *perceived* similarity, and that individuals often jump to conclusions about another person's views based on the context in which they encounter the person.[12]

What works in a setting between two individuals works in the formation of friendship cliques or networks as well. Similarity is functionally important to people in that the more one associates with those who share one's views the more those views seem justified. Such social reinforcement is especially important for ideas, such as religious beliefs, that do not lend themselves to empirical verification. Individuals join with those who reflect their own attitudes and beliefs. This is not to say that ideas develop for purely social reasons, nor is it to deny that some individuals mount ideological challenges against groups to which they belong. Nevertheless, most people are more comfortable with their ideas when the opinions are shared by associates. Thus, members of networks, and particularly of clusters within networks, are likely to share a common outlook. The stronger the social and communications ties are within the network, the greater the likelihood that the network will be effective.[13]

Attitudes not only are the basis for many friendships, but can be influenced by such relationships. According to Peter Berger, "One of the fundamental propositions of the sociology of knowledge is that the plausibility, in the sense of what people actually find credible, of views of reality depends on the social support these receive. Put more simply, we obtain our notions about the world originally from other human beings, and these notions continue to be plausible to us in a very large measure because others continue to affirm them." One tends to accept the friend of a friend in order to preserve the nature of the original tie. New ideas are greeted with more openness and enthusiasm if introduced by a friend. And the greater the interaction and affection between individuals, the more their views will become similar.[14]

Studies dealing with the diffusion of innovations reveal the importance of friendship networks. Preestablished social contacts facilitate the dissemination of news, and the advocacy of a new idea or procedure by friends guarantees the innovation a thoughtful reception and improves its chances of being adopted. The more integrated the group, or the more dense the network, the more rapid the rate of diffusion will be. The reasons for this are related to the dynamics of friendship. People are more likely to accept innovations if they like and trust the innovator; indeed, attitudes toward the innovator shape one's perception of the new idea. If an individual is perceived as a fellow saint, trust will normally follow. Boissevain contends that when a potential conflict exists because a new notion challenges established views, "persons will attempt to define the situation and to align themselves in such a way that the least possible damage is done to their basic values and their important personal relations." It will be seen that when English Congregationalists accepted cooperation with Baptists and urged a similar policy on colonial friends, the colonists responded at first by claiming that colonial Baptists were different from the English variety. By maintaining this position they denied that the advice was appropriate to their situation, thus enabling them to maintain their opposition to the colonial Baptists without condemning their friends across the Atlantic. As Tim Harris has observed in his study of London crowds of the post-Restoration era, "Research has shown that a person exposed to views hostile to the ones he already holds is likely to subconsciously misunderstand them, or interpret them in a way which confirms his existing prejudices." In other situations what can occur is a process of "funnelling" or "straining towards symmetry," whereby interaction between members of the network produces a convergence of opinion. Such was the normal result of interaction between the English and American wings of congregational Puritanism, even—eventually—on the issue of tolerating Baptists.[15]

Innovators, generally those who exert a leadership role in the network by virtue of their intellect or charisma, frequently also serve as the network's brokers. As such they maintain positions in more than one cluster of the network and seek to mediate among them, facilitating diffusion of the innovation and preventing schism. Such leaders are also responsible for ultimately enforcing conformity when the group's preferences become clear. They exert pressure on deviants to accept new standards and definitions of orthodoxy. The network expels those who refuse the orthodoxy, sacrificing them to the network's need for validation of its beliefs through consensus. Members of a network generally conceive their adherence to group norms as being closer than it actually is because it is socially important for them to believe so.[16]

Tying these insights together, we can build a model of behavior that can be used to examine the relationships among trans-Atlantic clergy in such a way as to illuminate some of the reasons for the beliefs adopted and the actions taken by English and American Puritans during the crises of the seventeenth century. And inasmuch as concepts drawn from the social sciences can draw our attention to the structure of friendships, it is equally important to capture the emotional intensity and religious feeling that bound Puritan saints together. I have tried to minimize my use of terms such as *broker* and *cluster* because they may suggest merely instrumental categories and draw the reader's attention from the spiritual and social essence of the particular network we are investigating.

Puritans, brought together in spiritual communion, formed a subculture that was set apart from the larger society. This study begins in Cambridge, where the beliefs and experiences of some students drew them together in bands of godly brethren. Friendships were formed, prayers were shared, and beliefs refined. Leaving the colleges on the Cam to serve in the church placed the clergyman in a world in which he no longer had such contacts on a daily basis. Participation in combination lectures, travel for conference with friends, and extensive correspondence became means to retain the spiritual support that had invigorated his encounters with university friends. Sustaining these friendships gave the minister a support system and helped him to keep step with his fellow saints in resistance to Laudian initiatives.

The clerical communion also became the mechanism for mobilizing support for the cause of Protestantism abroad and the reform of the church at home. Friends were active in raising funds for Palatinate refugees, for the Feoffees for Impropriations, and for other causes. When official pressure led some ministers to emigrate, the strength of friendship ties preserved unity among members of a congregational community dispersed throughout the Netherlands, New England, and the mother country. This unity was a factor in determining New England's continuing involvement in the evolution of Puritanism in the 1630s and its support of the Puritan Revolution and the Protectorate of Oliver Cromwell. Those who had experienced the equality of godly communion in religious exercises at Emmanuel College and elsewhere in Cambridge, who had labored together under threat of episcopal deprivation in the 1620s, and who had endured together the dangers of emigration were more inclined than some of their peers to trust in the brotherhood of saints that was at the core of Congregational polity. Their experience of communion confirmed the lessons regarding church order that they found in scripture and church history and sustained them in their effort "to live ancient lives."

The interaction of the Congregational clergy of England and New England is a story that has never before been thoroughly explored. The narrative of colonial contributions to the cause of the Dissenting Brethren is clear evidence of the error of those who maintain that New England lost interest in and sympathy for English Puritanism. John Cotton and his fellow colonial divines energetically lent their support to the cause of Thomas Goodwin and English Congregationalism. Focusing on that continuing communion and cooperation also helps shed light on the conservative nature of English Congregationalism, which was far less tolerant than often described.

The combined Congregational effort to reform England died with the Restoration, but the clerical communion survived and was reinforced by new immigration to the colonies. In the remaining decades of the seventeenth century friends across the Atlantic continued to influence each other, pray for each other, and tender each other material aid in times of suffering. New Englanders' connection to their English friends kept them involved in the broader Christian world and inhibited tendencies toward provincialism. It also gave them contacts to use in advancing colonial interests. The network was important to Increase Mather as it had been for John Cotton. For their part, English Congregationalists found in New England a beacon of hope for the eventual triumph of their cause.

The congregational communion was a network of friends united by a shared faith and common principles. But at its heart was a personal recognition of fellowship in the communion of saints, a love and confidence rooted in shared religious experience and nourished by common challenges. It retained its vitality for as long as most members of the network were known to each other in face-to-face and soul-to-soul encounters. The saints, according to John Owen, "have intimate, spiritual, heavenly joys, because their fellowship is a fellowship of love with the Father." "True friendship," wrote the Puritan vicar George Gifford, "is in the Lord, knitte in true Godliness," and, one might add, the apprehension of godliness in one another. When the time came that Congregationalists on opposite sides of the Atlantic were known to each other only by repute, the nature of the network would change and the trans-Atlantic communion would evolve into an imperial interest group. That marks a transition to a different story. In the seventeenth century friendships were a flame of faith that gave warmth and comfort, and communion was a light that many hoped would illumine the world. For John Cotton and others the spark was kindled and first fanned in the colleges of Cambridge in the fen country of East Anglia.[17]

CHAPTER ONE

The Cambridge Connection

In 1612 CAMBRIDGE UNIVERSITY included sixteen colleges. Over two thousand scholars immersed themselves with varying intensity in studies designed to polish young Englishmen for rule in the secular sphere or prepare them for a career in the church. Gentlemen and the sons of both gentry and wealthy merchants came from all over the realm to the halls along the river Cam. In chapel and lecture hall, at meals, and at study as well as walking in the quads, the various residents of the Cambridge colleges made the acquaintance of youth from other regions and classes. In some cases they shared little other than their common college experiences. In such instances time would erase these ties as classmates would lose touch with one another. But when college brought together two youths who discovered that they shared beliefs, attitudes, opinions, and hopes, friendship could become an alliance that was a lifetime commitment to mutual aid and cooperation. Such friends could call upon each other in the halls of Parliament, the corridors of Lambeth Palace, or the frontiers of colonial America. At Cambridge clerical friendships were formed which became the basis of a congregational communion that would influence the seventeenth-century history of England and New England.

From the first stirrings of the Reformation the colleges at Cambridge and at Oxford reflected the religious dissension in the realm. The seeds of reform that had been planted during the reign of Henry VIII had flowered under Edward VI, only to be threatened by the Catholic reaction

TUDOR
ENGLAND

.... County boundaries

Miles

0   40   80

under Mary Tudor. The scorch marks on the walls of Balliol College, Oxford, bore mute but eloquent testimony to the Protestant martyrs burned there in the Marian persecutions. When Queen Elizabeth again committed England to the Protestant camp, there were many in the realm who believed that the orthodoxy of the Church of England was but a halfway house on the road to true reformed religion. Such Puritans would labor from the accession of Elizabeth to the death of Oliver Cromwell one hundred years later to purge their land of popish corruption and to erect in England a new Jerusalem. The universities were a major battleground in this contest for the soul of English Protestantism, with Puritans and their opponents struggling to influence aspiring preachers and thus shape the beliefs of all Englishmen.

It has been claimed that the importance of the Puritan faction at Elizabethan Oxford was greater than has been commonly acknowledged. In the 1570s and 1580s Laurence Humphrey made Magdalen College a center of reformed influence. Though eventually criticized by some of the more extreme Puritans for what they perceived as his temporizing, Humphrey developed close contacts with divines in France and Germany as well as in Switzerland. He maintained an extensive correspondence with these continental leaders and hosted them on their visits to England. The vitality of Oxford reform was weakened, however, by the imposition in 1581 of a statute requiring all students over the age of fifteen to subscribe to the Thirty-Nine Articles of the Church of England—a requirement never made a condition of matriculation at Cambridge. Additional attacks on Puritan influence followed, such as Archbishop Bancroft's requirement that all fellows at Oxford wear the surplice at Sunday services. The Puritan faction was still strong enough in 1606 to get the young William Laud disciplined for being "popishly affected," and during the brief presidency of John Harding (1608–10) Magdalen recovered its status as a center of Calvinistic reform. But the matriculation statute was a serious discouragement to potential undergraduates. The absence of such a requirement at Cambridge, its location in the traditional East Anglian heartland of English religious reform, and the presence there of prominent Puritan leaders such as Perkins, Cotton, Preston, and Sibbes made the colleges on the Cam the more important center of reform in the early seventeenth century.[1]

Puritanism at Cambridge had strong roots in the Elizabethan period. One of the more significant developments at that time was the foundation of Emmanuel College in 1584 by Sir Walter Mildmay. Mildmay, who had been raised in Essex and educated for a time at Christ's College, Cambridge, wished to create a school that would provide the nation with reformed preachers. His effort was supported by other sympathetic members of the nobility as well as Puritan clergy such as Walter Travers and Thomas

Cartwright. Mildmay chose his former college tutor, Laurence Chaderton, as the first master.[2]

Chaderton was one of the most zealous defenders of Calvinism to be found in England. He had distinguished himself among the reformers by his defense of predestinarian teachings against the Arminian preaching of the Lady Margaret Professor Peter Baro. Under Chaderton's leadership the fellows of Emmanuel did not wear traditional caps and gowns. The regular days of fast of the Church of England were not observed in the college. The chapel faced north rather than east, parts of the Prayer Book were omitted in the services, communion was received sitting around the table, and fellows dispensed with the use of the surplice. The college statutes required the master and fellows to oppose "popery and other heresies and errors."[3]

Meanwhile, William Whitaker advanced the Puritan cause as master of St. John's. Samuel Ward made Sidney Sussex a center of Calvinist orthodoxy so that Laud would later describe it as one of the nurseries of Puritanism. The chapel of Sidney Sussex was unconsecrated and fellows gathered around a plain table. Ward would eventually retreat in his support of Puritan positions on discipline and organization, but he never wavered in his doctrinal Calvinism, which he espoused not only at Sidney Sussex but as Lady Margaret Professor of Divinity after 1623.[4]

Despite their very real importance, the Calvinists of Cambridge would gradually become an embattled minority. In 1616 the king ordered the chancellors of the universities to enforce the due observance of religious worship. Subscription to the Thirty-Nine Articles was required to take a degree. Thomas Goodwin later described his years as an undergraduate in the late 1610s as a time when "the noise of the Arminian controversy . . . began to be every man's talk." And as the party of William Laud rose in influence, reports on Cambridge Puritanism were solicited by the archbishop and royal injunctions issued to restrict the movement. By 1629 John Winthrop, who had studied at Trinity, Cambridge, complained that the two universities were "so corrupted . . . most children are perverted, corrupted, and utterly overthrown by the multitude of evil examples and [the universities'] licentious government."[5]

But during the early decades of the seventeenth century the university experience was especially important to the leaders of the reform faction. The orthodox Anglican clergy were sustained throughout their careers by the formal structure of the Church of England and encouraged by its hierarchy. For those who chose the path of opposition, informal networks of friends and colleagues were all they had to support them in their work. And, for many, the friendships that they depended on were forged in the universities. Although the congregational communion that fought for the New Jerusalem in old and New England came together through a variety of circumstances, university friendships were significant factors in its formation. One can select almost any year and identify students and fellows conferring at Cambridge who in later years would still cooperate in a pursuit of common goals.[6]

The year 1612 provides one such assemblage, a coming together of men who would play key roles in the history of Puritanism on both sides of the Atlantic. At Emmanuel College John Cotton towered over Puritan Cambridge as he later would over Puritan Massachusetts. In 1606 he had been awarded his master's degree and named a fellow. By 1612 he was at the height of his influence; later in the year he would leave to become vicar of St. Botolph's in Boston, Lincolnshire. The master of Emmanuel was Chaderton. William Sandcroft (BA 1601, MA 1604) was another Emmanuel fellow. Thomas Hooker had been granted his Emmanuel BA in 1608 and was then chosen the Dixie Fellow at the college, a post he held until 1618. John Yates was a fellow, while Hugh Goodyear was nearing the completion of his undergraduate studies. The John Ward who would later preach in Norwich and share a lectureship with Yates received his BA in 1612. John Wilson, who had left Cambridge in 1610, returned in 1612 or 1613 and remained for a time at Emmanuel. Thomas Pierson had just left to accept a living from Sir Robert Harley. These and other reformers worked, dined, and prayed together. They came to know and trust one another, and if later there was to be some rivalry between them, as with Cotton and Hooker, they would nevertheless work together in the common cause of reform.[7]

Although Emmanuel held the reputation of being the nursery of the Puritan movement, Puritans could be found elsewhere at Cambridge as well. Those who resided in the same college hall had greater opportunities to meet and befriend those of similar outlook, but examples of cross-college friendships and gatherings are abundant. Closer to the river than Emmanuel, between the Cam and the High Street, was another center of Puritan sympathy—Trinity College. There, in 1612, could be found Charles Chauncey, who had matriculated in 1610, and Thomas Welde, in his second year of studies. These two and the Emmanuel Puritans often found themselves together at Trinity Church, halfway between the two colleges, listening to Richard Sibbes, fellow of St. John's College, who was lecturer at Trinity Church from 1610 to 1615. Others who might have gathered to hear Sibbes preach included John Preston, a fellow at Queens' College and Samuel Fairclough, an undergraduate at that college; Samuel Skelton, who was to receive his BA from Clare in 1612; John Allin, who was in his first year at Caius; Joseph Mede, the famous millenarian who was a fellow of Christ's College; the future regicide Miles Corbet, a student at Christ's; John Wheelwright, who would receive his BA from Sidney Sussex in 1614; and Francis Higginson, whose Jesus College MA would be awarded in 1613. Waiting in the wings were men such as Samuel Whiting, Anthony Tuckney,

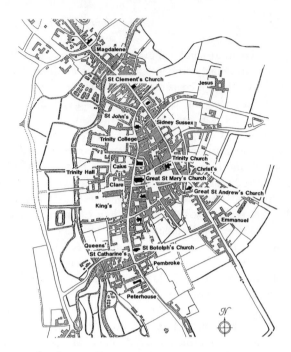

Cambridge College and Churches, 1600–1630

PARTIAL LIST OF PURITAN MEMBERS OF COLLEGES

Caius: John Allin, William Greenhill
Christ's: William Ames, Thomas Goodwin, William Leigh, Joseph Mede, William Pemberton
Clare: Samuel Skelton
Emmanuel: Simeon Ashe, Nathaniel Barnard, William Bridge, Thomas Brooks, Jeremiah
Burroughes, Adoniram Byfield, William Chaderton, Samuel Clarke, John Cotton,
Hugh Goodyear, Thomas Hill, Thomas Hooker, Isaac Johnson, Stephen
Marshall, Nicholas Morton, Thomas Pierson, John Preston, Nathaniel Ranew,
Nathaniel Rogers, William Sandcroft, Thomas Shepard, Sydrach Simpson,
Edward Sparrowhawke, Samuel Stone, John Stoughton, Zachariah Symmes,
Anthony Tuckey, John Ward, Samuel Whiting, John Wilson, John Yates, John
Yonge
Jesus: John Eliot, Francis Higginson
King's: William Gouge, John Wilson
Magdalene: John Knowles, Richard Vines
Pembroke: John Beadle, Francis Brewster, Edmund Calamy
Peterhouse: John Norton
Queens': Thomas Ball, Samuel Fairclough, George Fenwick, Martin Holbech, Thomas Mott,
John Preston, Samuel Winter
St. Catharine's: John Arrowsmith, Thomas Goodwin, John Knowles, Nicholas Price, Richard
Sibbes, William Strong
St. John's: John Arrowsmith, Henry Jessey, Matthew Newcomen
Sidney Sussex: John Wheelwright
Trinity College: Charles Chauncey, Hugh Peter, Thomas Welde

PARTIAL LIST OF PURITAN PREACHERS

Great St. Andrew's: William Perkins
St. Botolph's: John Preston
St. Clement's: Laurence Chaderton
Trinity Church: Thomas Goodwin, John Preston, Richard Sibbes

Hugh Peter, John Beadle, and Thomas Goodwin—all of whom would enter Cambridge colleges in 1613.

The year 1620 offers another chance to see young Puritans in a proximity conducive to the formation of lasting friendships. John Preston was still a fellow at Queens' while Charles Chauncey had become a fellow at Trinity and Anthony Tuckney a fellow at Emmanuel, but otherwise the names are different. Thomas Goodwin had just been chosen a fellow at St. Catharine's College. John Knowles matriculated as a pensioner at Magdalene in 1620, as did John Norton at Peterhouse. Martin Holbech was studying with Preston at Queens'. Thomas Mott, whose sermons John Winthrop would attentively follow in Suffolk later in the decade, matriculated at Queens' in 1620 and three years later transferred to Emmanuel. Henry Jessey had started his studies at St. John's in 1619, the same year in which John Eliot matriculated at Jesus College. Edmund Calamy commenced BA from Pembroke, while John Beadle received his MA from that college. Richard Vines was a student at Magdalene. William Leigh entered Christ's in 1620. George Fenwick was at Queens' and Francis Brewster at Pembroke. Among those preparing for the MA and at least occasionally at the university were William Greenhill of Caius, John Arrowsmith of St. John's, and Hugh Peter of Trinity. Emmanuel in 1620 lived up to its reputation. Chaderton still presided as master. Samuel Whiting appeared in 1620 to receive his MA. Two other future New Englanders were finishing the same degree—Isaac Johnson and Nathaniel Rogers (both MA 1621). Nicholas Morton (whose son George would be a prominent Puritan leader of the post-Restoration period) had succeeded Hooker as Dixie Fellow. Among the undergraduates were three of the Dissenting Brethren of the 1640s—William Bridge (BA 1623), Jeremiah Burroughes (BA 1621), and Sydrach Simpson (BA 1622). Stephen Marshall, Nathaniel Ranew, Edward Sparrowhawke, Adoniram Byfield, John Yonge, Thomas Hill, and Zachariah Symmes were also undergraduates. Sir Harbottle Grimston had entered in 1619. Thomas Shepard was admitted in 1620, as was Samuel Stone. A few years later Thomas Brooks entered Cambridge.

In 1612, 1620, or any other year, prospective leaders of English and American Puritanism could come together in a variety of ways and circumstances. Whereas students of Puritanism have long pointed to the formative influence of Cambridge studies on various famous preachers, they have directed their attention to the curriculum and, on occasion, to the role of famous lecturers such as Hildersham, Chaderton, Ames, and Preston. But college was not simply a place for pouring the nectar of Puritan thought into receptive vessels. The interaction of tutor with pupil, of student with student, and of fellow with fellow generated social forces and spiritual exchanges with equally important consequences. To begin to understand how some Cambridge Puritans were integrated into a spiritual communion requires knowledge of the various types of contact that went on and the environment in which the contact took place.[8]

Most university students were young, although there were exceptions such as Richard Mather, who had been active in the ministry before entering Brasenose College, Oxford. Of 107 future New Englanders whom Samuel Eliot Morison identified as having studied at British universities, 45 were admitted to a college before they were seventeen, while another 24 were seventeen years old. The new student was part of an influx large enough by pre-seventeenth-century standards, but small compared to what we are accustomed to. Emmanuel, for instance, admitted 56 students in 1612 and 62 in 1620. Less than two-thirds of those admitted stayed for degrees, so those who resided for more than two years were likely to become familiar with most of the other members of their college. The average number of matriculated students at Cambridge in any given year in the 1620s was about 420.[9]

Familiarity was made more likely by the scope of university life, and because we are investigating the circumstances that brought men into communion we should examine the rhythms of that life. An Oxford bias was undoubtedly present when the diarist John Evelyn described seventeenth-century Cambridge as a "town situated in a low dirty unpleasant place, the streets ill-paved, the air thick, as infested by the fenns," but the reality was that neither university town was very imposing. The total population of Cambridge in the 1620s did not far exceed eight thousand, with over one-third of that number being directly involved in the academic life of the university. The center of life for the student was his college, which was a residential foundation. At the heart of each college was the hall. A large room with a dais at one end where fellows dined at meals, the typical hall was also used for lectures, disputations, and the occasional stage play. Elsewhere in the quadrangle of college buildings was the chapel, where worship alternated with academic lectures. A library containing folios and valuable books was to be found in one of the buildings. Most of the space around the quadrangle was given over to chambers. No building was more than four stories high. Each staircase typically opened to two chambers per floor, each containing sleeping quarters for three or four, one of them a fellow or graduate student. Partitioned off from the common sleeping area in the chamber were small, individual studies or carrels. The master had private quarters, the lodge, which were connected to the hall. A parlor, or combination room, was a gathering place for the college's fellows, frequently connected to the hall and the lodge.[10]

The residents of such a college fell into a number of categories. The master was the head of the college. Instruction was carried on by twelve to twenty fellows, some of whom also held offices such as dean, bursar, and so on.

Undergraduates were fellow commoners, scholars, pensioners, or sizars. Pensioners (or commoners) paid the established fees, whereas scholars had their expenses remitted by the college and sizars were given a fee reduction in return for waiting on table and performing services for fellows and fellow commoners. Fellow commoners paid twice the usual fee, dined with the fellows, and had many of the same privileges of the latter group. [11]

The academic year was divided into three terms. Michaelmas term began on the 10th of October and ran until the 16th of December. Hilary or Lent term extended from the 13th of January to the second Friday before Easter. Easter or midsummer term started on the eleventh day after Easter and continued until the Friday after commencement, which was held on the first Tuesday in July. The course of studies followed by students during this academic year can perhaps best be understood by first describing the types of formal academic exercises that might be prescribed and then the way in which they fit into a daily routine. Lectures were given by professors or lecturers and were delivered either in the public schools of the university (open to all students) or in the private confines of the college. The declamation was an assigned set speech of a few hundred to a few thousand words delivered by a student and designed to show rhetorical skill as well as mastery of the topic. It could be assigned for delivery in either the college or the public schools. These could be very polished performances, and some of John Milton's student exercises were eventually published. The university also required undergraduates to appear four times in disputations in the public schools. Disputations in the college were a more frequent and less formal form of instruction, but in either case a student defended a given proposition while another student objected to it and one of the tutors—in colleges often the head lecturer—served as moderator. The topics were often casuistical, giving aspiring clergymen the opportunity to practice advising each other in cases of conscience. [12]

The central figure in the student's life was the fellow assigned as his tutor, who served as both teacher and guardian. As expressed by one contemporary, a fellow was expected to show "the insignia of a painfull life, joyned with holiness and sobriety, after which the younger sort may march." The master would commonly appoint a number of the college's chambers to the supervision of a tutor, who would assign rooms to the students under his supervision. Much of the student's education would take place in the tutor's chambers and there students would gather every night for prayers. As one undergraduate at Trinity recalled, his tutor was "careful of me, inquired of what company I was acquainted with, sometimes read lectures to us, prayed with us in his chamber every night, and . . . was a generous savoury Christian." Laurence Chaderton, according to his contemporary biographer, "took much pleasure also, and bestowed great pains, in his work with his pupils in college, among whom was William Perkins." Of John Cotton it was said that "by his School-stratagems he won the hearts of his Pupils both to himself, and to a desire of Learning: they were to each other as the prophets, and the sons of the Prophets: his Pupils were honourers, and lovers of him: and he was a Tutor, a Friend, and a Father unto them."[13]

For those of Puritan inclinations opportunities to grow in faith and grace were especially important. Students from all colleges could attend the lectures of the university's Regius Professor of Divinity and the divinity acts in the public schools. Most colleges made provisions for the study of theology, though Emmanuel, Cambridge, placed a greater emphasis on such studies than others. It was the duty of the dean or catechist at Emmanuel (a post held at different times by Cotton and Hooker) to expound on some article of the Christian faith for an hour each Saturday in addition to regularly supervising theological disputations. The Order Book of Emmanuel called for a regular system of "prophesying" for the edification of all members of the college. The importance of this exercise can hardly be overestimated. "Because it is necessarye that every mynister should be able to teache sound Doctrine by the true interpretation of the Word, and to confute all contrarye errours," the order provided for "mutuall conference of such as being very studious and of good towardness in learning" and who had decided on "the profession of divinitye." "All that come to this conference are to begyne the bible, and to proceed to the end therof, conferring of so much at one time as shall convenyentlye serve for the finishing of the whole once in two yeares." In their discussions the participating members of the college were to pursue and utilize knowledge of Hebrew and Greek, logic, rhetoric, ancient history, and the writings of earlier commentators. All members would participate as congregational equals, regardless of their academic standing. The exercise would also be a forum for "disputation [of] all the principall questions in controversie betweene us and the Papists and other heretics." Here men such as Chaderton, Preston, Hooker, and Cotton shared in each other's spiritual growth and came to appreciate the value of a communal search for truth rather than a hierarchical dispensation of it. As a result of such communion some of these divines would be more ready than most of their contemporaries to trust the practice of prophesying in English conventicles and New England congregations.[14]

Less regular sessions of the same sort were to be found at other colleges, and informal religious discussion groups of fellows and students were commonplace. Prayer groups were important means of experiencing the ecstasy of shared grace and expressing one's piety. One critic complained in 1636 that the prayers of some Puritan students in their tutors' rooms in Trinity College were "longer and louder by far at night than they are at chapel in the evening." Such members of the university regardless of status shared in a spiritual communion that combined respect for the individual saint with an emphasis on the community of belief. The sermons preached in the colleges and in the churches of Oxford and Cambridge were also forms of religious education and inspiration. Many took careful notes on these sermons and closely followed religious debates carried on from pulpit to pulpit over the course of many weeks. A pious student had ample opportunity to slake his thirst for the word. A Sunday in 1620 described by Symonds D'Ewes began with a sermon in his college chapel, which he followed with attendance at the university sermon at Great St. Mary's, then a sermon in a parish church, afternoon catechizing, and an evening of reviewing sermon notes. William Gouge "was not once absent (neither morning nor Evening) from the publicke and solemn worship of God in the Colledge performed twice every day, for the space of nine whole years together. He [also] read fifteen Chapters in the Bible every day." These experiences were also shared with godly friends and became an additional bond of the family of the faithful.[15]

The official daily routine of college life began as early as 5:00 A.M. when the members of the college would gather in chapel for morning prayer and a homily. Following breakfast in the hall students would proceed to their regular course of college or university studies. For many this meant meeting with other students in the tutor's chamber to progress in a subject from the reading of an introductory text to the discussion of controversial aspects of the discipline. Dinner in hall at 11:00 A.M. or noon was often followed by participation in or attendance at college or school disputations. A free period was followed by supper, after which some students engaged in a review of the day's lessons with their tutor. At Emmanuel under Chaderton prayers were said in the tutors' rooms at 8:00 P.M. and the college gates were locked at 10:00.[16]

The academic routine brought students and fellows regularly together, and the social life of the university reinforced these contacts. It was rare for anyone in the college, even a fellow, to have a room to himself. Up to four students shared a room, usually on the same staircase as their tutor. They provided their own coals or turves for heat, though the college rooms were hard to keep warm and many probably adopted a regimen similar to that of a sixteenth-century student who ran in the St. John's courtyard for a half hour before retiring "to get a heat on their feet when they go to bed." Dining in hall was designed to promote collegiality. Early statutes of the university restricted students to their colleges, but they had been relaxed by the seventeenth century. A student like William Gouge was unusual, but his experience shows the significance of the small social world of the college. According to his biographer, Gouge "during his first three years . . . kept the College so close, that he lay not one night out of the walls thereof; and at the three years end he was admitted Fellow, and went to visit his Friends." The shared experiences that shaped friendship were certainly not all spiritual ones. Most students were often to be found accompanying their friends to town and frequenting taverns such as the Rose and Mitre and the Dolphin. Though "puritans" were expected to exercise moderation, the diaries of Thomas Shepard and others show that they sometimes failed. Of course, conversation over a brew was possible within the college walls as well. Emmanuel had its own alehouse and also a "parler" or combination room for the fellows at the east end of the hall. [17]

Various forms of physical recreation were allowed by the statutes, and others, though prohibited, were also popular. A form of football was played in the Cambridge college courts and gardens by many students. A spacious green behind Queens' College was a popular location for these contests in the 1620s. Games against teams of townsfolk were not supposed to be played, but were. John Wheelwright, who played football, was also noted for his wrestling. The distinguished master of Emmanuel, Laurence Chaderton, was not above wrestling even in his maturity. Thomas Hooker's familiarity with the sport can be implied from an image he later used in one of his sermons: "God deales like a Wrastler, first catches hold then comes in, and at last throwes a man upon his back, makes him yeeld and confesse." Though forbidden because of the risks of drowning, students did swim often in the Cam. Various sports were played on the nearby Hogmagog Hills, and of course young gentlemen hunted and indulged in other pastimes of their class. Most of the colleges had enclosed tennis courts similar to that of Emmanuel, which had a gallery and a canopy-type roof. Bowling was also very popular in the early seventeenth century, with thirteen of the sixteen colleges at Cambridge having a bowling green, some of which were very elaborate. Symonds D'Ewes reported that he and his friends also repaired to the bowling greens for "jumping, running and pitching the bar." About a mile from Cambridge was a green that was an "ordinary place of recreation for all sorts," with a nearby cottage that provided refreshments. [18]

The social aspects of recreation are evident from the D'Ewes diary. The young student formed a close friendship with one of the fellows of his college. On one occasion the two played tennis at Christ's College, after which they dined outside the college with another fellow. The three lingered over their meal, enjoying the conversation. Because the weather was very hot, "no one had any great will to go to study," and so D'Ewes and his friend retired to the latter's chambers to play chess and discuss some books they shared an interest in. [19]

Not all student extracurricular activity was approved. In addition to breaking the rules against swimming, undergraduates often remained in town after their college gates were locked and were cited for returning late and climbing over walls. Smoking, though frowned upon by many, was widespread among students. But few violations of the decorum of college life were quite like that noted by Samuel Ward, who confessed to his diary in 1596 an "adulterous dream" prompted by "the grievous sinnes in Trinity Colledg, which had a woman which was [carried] from chamber to chamber on the night time."[20]

Life in the small world of a seventeenth-century university and the even smaller world of an individual college encouraged the development of close friendships. Young men who shared chambers, studied together, and played together came to know and dearly value some of their acquaintances. John Knowles, for instance, shared a room with Richard Vines at Magdalene, Cambridge, in the 1620s. They discovered shared ideas and interests and became close, lifelong friends. Zachariah Symmes likewise developed a close friendship with his chambermate, Jeremiah Burroughes. Samuel Whiting shared a chamber with Anthony Tuckney; their tutor was John Yates. When such contacts included an awareness of shared grace they not only made university life richer, but became the basis for a network of friendship which helped determine the course of English and American Puritan history.[21]

Exposed to one another by the daily routine of life at Emmanuel, William Bridge, Jeremiah Burroughes, and Sydrach Simpson became friends and were soon traveling into the countryside to hear noted Puritan preachers. Thomas Hooker and William Ames were together at Cambridge from 1603 to 1610 and developed a strong mutual friendship and respect. According to Cotton Mather, Ames claimed that "though he had been acquainted with many scholars of divers nations, yet he never met with Mr. Hooker's equal, either for preaching or for disputing." Nathaniel Ward befriended Bridge and Thomas Ball at Emmanuel. Robert Rich, later the second earl of Warwick, attended Cambridge with his friend from Eton College, William Gouge. The two were constantly together and associated with John Preston and Thomas Hooker, with whom they would actively work in later years. Thomas Shepard, later the son-in-law of Thomas Hooker, met Hooker's future Hartford colleague Samuel Stone when they were both pupils in Hooker's alma mater. The lifelong friendship of Thomas Gataker and Richard Stock began at Cambridge. Thomas Welde and Hugh Peter, who would work as a team representing Massachusetts in England in the 1640s, first befriended each other as students at Trinity, Cambridge, in the 1610s. Differences in status were not barriers to friendship. Many years later, when William Gouge eulogized the earl of Warwick, he was thinking of the close relationship they had begun in school when he reflected that with friends, "though in sundry respects they be unequall, yet unequall things to them become equall." Simon Bradstreet entered Cambridge as a sizar to Lord Rich, and Thomas Hooker acknowledged a spiritual debt to his sizar and friend Simeon Ashe.[22]

The Cambridge relationships formed by Rich are but one example of the importance of the college experience in providing a setting where friendships could develop between men preparing for the ministry and those who later might become their patrons and protectors. Sir Symonds D'Ewes arranged for his brother Richard to be admitted to St. Catharine's Hall in 1632 when Richard Sibbes was master because it was his "chief care to have him religiously and virtuously educated." There the young D'Ewes was supervised by "a very religious tutor," John Knowles. During the course of Sibbes's mastership sons of Sir Nathaniel Barnardiston, Sir Robert Brooke, Sir William Masham, and Sir Gilbert Gerard were also enrolled at St. Catharine's. John Preston gained a reputation as "the greatest Pupil-monger in England in man's memory" as a result of his success in attracting as students the sons of influential men—among them the young Sir William Roberts, two sons of the earl of Warwick, and a son of the earl of Lincoln. One of the opportunities the university experience provided aspiring preachers was the chance to learn how to deal with and form friendships with the gentry. [23]

University figures already recognizable as Puritan leaders often took a direct hand in drawing likely prospects to the movement. In some cases the powerful personality of such an individual could draw someone with no previous tendency toward Puritanism into the fold. The most famous of these incidents formed a spiritual genealogy as Richard Rogers taught Paul Baynes, who converted Richard Sibbes, who converted John Cotton, who in turn converted John Preston, who along with Sibbes was instrumental in the conversion of Thomas Goodwin. When a student of nineteen, Goodwin transferred from Christ's College to St. Catharine's. There he met Nicholas Price, who shortly thereafter left to accept a parish at King's Lynn. Though at first Goodwin fought against Price's message, as he did against the influence of Sibbes and Preston, he was drawn to attend the Wednesday and Sunday sermons preached by Price at King's Lynn. Following Goodwin's conversion the two men grew closer and before Price died in 1619 he suggested Goodwin as his successor. William Perkins converted William Ames and Richard Blackerby at Cambridge. In all these cases discipleship became the basis for or reinforced friendship, and influence was soon a two-way street. [24]

More common than the drama of conversion was the case of a noted Puritan reaching out with advice to befriend and influence a likely youth. At Queens' College John Preston expended great efforts on his students. He would "reade unto them & direct their studyes [till] he found himselfe much abridged of his owne tyme and was constreyned to take up tyme that should have bin bestowed on his body." Preston also used his friendship with "many eminent & Godly ministers, as Mr. Dod and Mr. Hildersham, who would come often to his chamber, and . . . he would get them many times to goe to prayer with his pupils." Shortly after the young Samuel Fairclough came to the attention of Preston, the fellow invited Fairclough to join in prayer and discussion with a group of Cambridge scholars. From these sessions Fairclough developed strong friendships with Preston, Arthur Hildersham, and William Perkins. John Wilson had a similar experience. Befriended by William Ames, Wilson soon made his rooms at King's College a center for Ames and other Puritans to confer, study Scripture, and pray. This type of gathering was a tradition at Cambridge. In the 1570s and 1580s John Carter, Laurence Chaderton, Ezekiel Culverwell, and other young Calvinist divines gathered in each other's rooms for sessions of prayer and Scripture study. The young Thomas Goodwin became a protégé of Richard Sibbes. Sibbes also saw special promise in John Norton and urged him to accept a university fellowship. William Strong was a favored student of Sibbes's at St. Catharine's. Laurence Chaderton had been William Perkins's tutor. Richard Roberts, who became one of the ecclesiastical Triers during the Protectorate, studied under Perkins. Samuel Clarke, the biographer of eminent Puritans, was a student of Thomas Hooker's at Emmanuel. Clarke, in his biography of his friend William Gouge, noted how Gouge "did not only ply his own studies, but used also to send for others whom he observed to be ingenious and willing, and instructed them in the Arts, whereby he was a great help to many, and brought them also to be better proficients." Thomas Hooker tutored Jeremiah Burroughes. Thomas Ball and Samuel Winter became students of John Preston while Samuel Ward was tutored by William Perkins. Ward confided to his diary that among God's blessings upon him, none was greater than that "he selected me from my brethren to come of Cambridge, as that I came to his Colledge, and that in Mr. Pirkins tyme, as that he hath continued me here so long, kept me from evill company, [and] brought me backe when I was in the Countrey." Matthew Newcomen, later one of the Smectymnian critics of the establishment, matriculated at St. John's in 1625 and became friends with John Knowles, who was then a fellow at another college. Thomas Shepard later recalled how God had brought him "to the best place for knowledge and learning, viz., to Cambridge, and there the Lord was not content to give me good means but the best means and ministry and help of private Christians, for Dr. Preston and Mr. Goodwin were the most able men for preaching Christ in this latter age." Not all students were quick to accept such influences. John Stoughton recalled that his tutor, William Sandcroft, had for a time called him his worst pupil because he neglected his prayers.[25]

The university not only saw the formation of spiritual friendships, but provided opportunities for such relationships to bear fruit. Communion was important not only as a means of renewing one's sense of God's caress but as a linkage that contributed to reform. The master and fellows of a Cambridge college were the governing body of the institution. Together they shaped the course of the college. Fellows likewise joined with their counterparts in other colleges to advance reform. Occasionally Puritans switched colleges in order to take up a post of greater usefulness. John Knowles left Magdalene to become a St. Catharine's fellow when Richard Sibbes was master there. Another fellow and protégé of Sibbes at that college was Thomas Goodwin. In fact Goodwin, along with John Arrowsmith, played a key role in securing the election of Sibbes as master in 1625. In 1621 John Preston was chosen to succeed James Ussher as Professor of Theological Controversies at Trinity College, Dublin. Preston was tempted, but "communicated with my friends, to whom in such cases I resign myself, which hath also been my practice formerly, as Dr. Chaderton . . . Mr. Dod and Mr. Sibbs, who think my stay here [at Queens' College, Cambridge] will be most advantageous to the Church, and will not yet permit a remove." Preston's ties with his friends were such that he trusted them with his future. Accepting their judgment that his services were needed at Cambridge, Preston remained. He delayed answering Ussher while waiting to see how serious John Cotton's current problems with the authorities would become. If Cotton had been silenced, Preston intended to suggest his name to Ussher. Since Cotton's danger passed, Preston suggested Hooker be appointed, though nothing came of it. Shortly after this exchange, Preston's friends managed to secure his election as master of Emmanuel. In 1626 Ussher sought to persuade Richard Sibbes to leave Cambridge and become provost of Trinity College, Dublin. Sibbes declined, citing "the judgment of my friends here [which] is for my stay, considering I am fixed already, and there must be a call for a place," and that if he left it was unlikely that he would be replaced by another Puritan.[26]

Election of a master was an event that often clarified and tested friendship alliances. In addition to the example of Sibbes's selection as master of St. Catharine's, an election at Christ's and two elections at Emmanuel in the early seventeenth century also revealed Puritan friendship alliances at work. Christ's College had begun to achieve a Puritan reputation when Laurence Chaderton was a fellow from 1568 to 1577. In the following decades Richard Rogers, Arthur Hildersham, William Perkins, and William Ames were among the members of the college. It was while at Christ's that Perkins had preached against the practice of kneeling to receive the eucharist. In the early 1600s the college became a center of opposition to Archbishop Bancroft. When the mastership became vacant in 1609, the king agreed to allow the fellows a free election, but suggested four candidates whom he considered conformable to the established church. The fellows, however, chose William Pemberton, a Puritan who had become a fellow in 1602. It was reported that the election had been influenced by "a conventicle held of divers of that faction, not only assembled from other colleges in Cambridge but out of the country adjoining, and that [Henry] Jacob, a notorious minister of London for faction and disquietness, carried a great hand amongst them." In this case the efforts of the network were thwarted, for the king—probably at Bancroft's urging—acted to overturn the choice and establish Valentine Cary as master. "Woe is me for Christ's College!" wrote Samuel Ward, for "surely he will be the utter ruin and destruction of that coll!" In fact, Cary did soon drive William Ames from the college, though a core of Puritan fellows persevered into the following decade.[27]

In 1622 the advanced age of the master of Emmanuel, Laurence Chaderton, was a source of concern for Puritans. Discussion concerning possible successors led to a plan to ensure a Puritan presence in that post. Procedures for electing a master called for posting notice of a vacancy for seven days if any fellows were absent. Timing his announcement when all eleven fellows were in residence, Chaderton announced his resignation on September 25, and on October 2 the fellows elected John Preston to the post. Before other interests even knew of the vacancy a fellow had ridden to London to arrange for the official letters of appointment from the king. As Matthew Mead wrote to Sir Martin Stuteville, "Never did I believe till now I see it experienced, that as many as 12 could keep counsell a week together, and fellowes of a college too! Who would have thought but there would have bin a Judas among 12?"[28]

When John Preston died in 1628 many again feared that a royal mandate would place an enemy of reform in the lodge. Within days of Preston's death Nathaniel Ward wrote to William Sandcroft to persuade him to allow his name to be advanced for the post. Ward hoped that Sandcroft would seek the advice of friends at Thomas Hooker's regional clerical conference and assured him of Hooker's support and that of John Cotton. Sandcroft had been a fellow at Emmanuel at the same time as Hooker and Cotton and he had been the tutor of Sir Nathaniel Rich. William Bridge worked with Ward in raising support. Ward indicated that Sandcroft had "the votes of all that heare of it and shall have their prayers" and informed the candidate that there were "friends powerfull with his Majesty and the Duke" that would support his candidacy. The earl of Warwick, Robert Rich, lent his considerable influence to Sandcroft's election. Ward also solicited the support of Sir Henry Mildmay. The efforts of these distinguished alumni and friends, combined with the politicking of Anthony Tuckney and others at the university, had the desired effect and Sandcroft was elected. The fellows of the college urged him to accept, writing that "we not only earnestly desire you, but in Christ chardge you to accept of this our call; if you fayle us the Colledge sinkes certainly, and way will be made for a mandat[e] to our undoing." Sandcroft did accept and guided Emmanuel into the 1630s.[29]

At the same time the assassination of the duke of Buckingham vacated the chancellorship of the university. The earl of Warwick sought to get the position for his brother, the earl of Holland. Holland, a courtier with strong connections to the French-born queen, who was a Catholic, nevertheless had a Puritan chaplain and cultivated Puritan support. Richard Sibbes, William Sandcroft, and other members of the Puritan network who had influence at Cambridge were enlisted on his behalf, and Holland's election was secured. In another contested election Puritan fellows at St. Catharine's outmaneuvered their opponents to elect Ralph Browning master in 1635. But the godly did not always win. Puritan efforts to elect Richard Holdsworth master of St. John's in 1633 led to a bitter dispute with two rival "masters" for nine months until the king imposed a "compromise" that was a defeat for the reformers.[30]

Along with the various masterships, key posts of influence were the lectureships at the major Cambridge churches. The experience of observing a noted preacher was an essential part of the preparation of godly youth for the ministry, but the sermons did more than provide models of pulpit style. From time to time they were the occasions for major attacks on vice and heresy. It was a 1609 sermon on the evils of card-playing—"one might as well abuse word or sacraments or oaths as play at cards"—and lotteries preached by William Ames at the university church of Great St. Mary's that caused "great fire here and smoke abroad," and led to Ames's being deprived of his academic degrees and forced from Cambridge. In 1624 Charles Chauncey of Trinity was forced to retract criticisms of church practice he had made in a sermon earlier in the year. In 1632 Nathaniel Barnard of Emmanuel was called before the High Commission for a sermon at Great St. Mary's in which he attacked Laudian practices. Two years later William Strong of St. Catharine's was forced to retract statements he had made from the pulpit. Many Puritan students such as Thomas Goodwin had attended Trinity Church to hear Richard Sibbes, "whose preaching was plain and wholesome." Indeed, the number of students who neglected the university sermons at Great St. Mary's to hear Sibbes preach at the same time at Holy Trinity was a bone of contention that contributed to his departure from the lectureship. Preston later assumed that post and the student element in the pews swelled again. When Preston died the fellowship exerted itself to secure the post for Thomas Goodwin and succeeded. Other pulpits offered similar opportunities. William Perkins had preached regularly at Great St. Andrew's and Preston had held forth at St. Botolph's, Cambridge, before being chosen to preach at Trinity. Laurence Chaderton preached for almost fifty years at St. Clement's. Sermons delivered in the college chapels could also gain a following. In their introduction to Thomas Hooker's *The Application of Redemption* (London, 1655), Thomas Goodwin and Philip Nye indicated that Hooker had first preached that cycle of sermons in the Emmanuel College chapel. Preston's divinity lectures at Queens' attracted so many auditors from other colleges and from the town "that the fellows, for the crowd and multitude, could not get through & come to chapple to their places," so that the vice-chancellor was appealed to and outsiders banned.[31]

Elections to college positions and lectureships were critical because of the rise of an anti-Calvinist spirit in England which was reflected in the universities. The publication of William Perkins's *A Golden Chain* in 1590, with its supralapsarian doctrine of absolute predestination, had symbolized the dominance of Calvinist teachings at Cambridge at the time. But such extreme Calvinism was prompting a reaction throughout reformed Europe. At Cambridge the first challenge was mounted by William Barrett, a chaplain at Caius, in a university sermon preached in April of 1595. Influenced by the views of Peter Baro, the Lady Margaret Professor of Divinity, Barrett criticized the teaching of unconditional predestination. The Consistory Court of the university was strongly Calvinist and forced Barrett to recant. It was his appeal of this decision that led Archbishop Whitgift to issue his strong Calvinist interpretation of Anglican orthodoxy, the Lambeth Articles. Barrett left Cambridge in 1597, going abroad and eventually becoming a Catholic—a fact that was not lost on his opponents. Meanwhile, in 1596, Baro preached against the view of limited atonement contained in the Lambeth Articles, which led to his defeat when he sought reelection to his professorship. He retired to London.[32]

The Calvinist dominance of university teaching and preaching continued into the early decades of the seventeenth century, though the tide of anti-Calvinism was rising outside the universities. While the English position at the Synod of Dort seemed to commit the church to orthodox Calvinism, influential factions were soon seeking to undermine that stand. In 1615 John Yates, then a fellow of Emmanuel, found it necessary to publish *God's Arraignment of Hypocrites* as a defense of William Perkins against the Dutch theologian Jacob Arminius, who had attacked Perkins's views in his *Examen Modestum* (Leiden, 1612). In 1619 Arminianism was an issue in a Cambridge election. James Beale was advanced by Bishop Andrewes, among others, as a candidate for master of Pembroke. Beale was accused of Arminianism by Ralph Brownrigg and others, who were counterattacked as Puritans. Andrewes's influence prevailed and Beale was elected. In July of 1622, "in the face of the whole commencement assembled, Mr. Lucie . . . preached a sermon totally for Arminianisme, wonderfully boldly and peremptorily," according to Matthew Mead. This was the period which Thomas Goodwin later referred to when he wrote how Arminianism was the divisive issue that everyone at the university argued about. While Calvinism was still in the ascendancy, as noted by Sandcroft's election at Emmanuel and the choice of Thomas Bancroft to head Caius in 1626, the anti-Calvinist element in the hierarchy did exert itself to get Matthew Wren elected at Peterhouse in 1625, despite the initial opposition of most of the college fellows.[33]

In June of 1626 Bishop Richard Neile—one of the key leaders of the anti-Calvinist element in the church—wrote to the Cambridge authorities to convey a royal proclamation prohibiting public airing of the predestinarian debate. At about the same time Neile, Wren, and Beale engineered the election of the duke of Buckingham as the university's new chancellor in a contest decided by a slim, four-vote margin. Though Buckingham had earlier been a patron of John Preston, his involvement in the discussions regarding Richard Montagu, which he hosted at York House early in 1626, showed clearly that he had moved into the other camp. Whereas these developments represented a shift in power at Cambridge, Samuel Ward and others continued to oppose Arminian views and the Puritan forces were able to get the less objectionable earl of Holland chosen chancellor when Buckingham was assassinated in 1628.[34]

The shift evident at Cambridge was seen at Oxford as well. And while anti-Calvinists such as John Pullen and John Willington advanced their views with impunity at the universities in the 1630s, Nathaniel Barnard was made an example of for defending Calvinism. Barnard, a graduate of Emmanuel who was a lecturer at St. Sepulchre in London, preached at Great St. Mary's in Cambridge on May 6, 1632. He claimed that England had departed from God's worship, citing Pelagian doctrines and Catholic ceremonies and superstitions that he said had made their way into the church. He specifically criticized Charles I's Catholic queen as a source of these evils. After he had been interviewed a number of times before the university Consistory Court, his case was handed over to the High Commission and he was imprisoned. In 1634 William Strong was stripped of his degrees and banished from the university for stating that Laud had sinned against the Holy Ghost and that "Hell was fuller for one" when the Arminian head of Trinity, Leonard Mawe, died. In that same year Samuel Ward expressed concern over the support given to John Tourney of Pembroke when he preached against the doctrine of justification by faith.[35]

The universities remained a battleground over doctrine and practice until the outbreak of the civil wars. In 1629 William Laud advocated the reform of "Emmanuel and Sidney Colleges . . . which are the Nurseries of Puritanism." Preparatory to a planned visitation that was never conducted, Laud in the 1630s received reports that the Emmanuel chapel was not consecrated and that services there were not conducted in accordance with the prescribed forms. At Sidney, Samuel Ward shared with his friend and fellow Calvinist William Bedell his concern over the new trends, but like the masters of Emmanuel he remained true to his beliefs and practices. Yet elsewhere the tide of anti-Calvinism rose, and new and elaborate rituals were introduced into worship. In the eyes of one undergraduate, Peterhouse under John Cosin became "noted above all the Towne for Popish superstitious practices." And

Joseph Mede, observing those practices from Emmanuel, wrote of Cosin that he "was a most audacious fellow and I doubt scarce a strong Protestant, and takes upon him impudently to bring superstitious innovation into our church." When he became vice-chancellor of the university, Cosin exercised his authority to reform other colleges and spent large sums at the university church of St. Mary's to restore the choir screen and doctors' stalls, decorate the altar, and install new altar rails. University Puritans who bemoaned such developments were thrown on the defensive in their support of Calvinism. Fighting a rearguard action, they came closer together.[36]

Whereas the universities were a primary stage for this struggle, they were not the only place where the fight was carried on. Fellows at Cambridge regularly sent promising students for post-baccalaureate study with former colleagues who had taken pastoral posts. Cotton and Hooker were but two of the many former Cambridge fellows who ran Puritan finishing schools, providing intensive preparation for the MA and integrating them into the congregational network outside the universities. Arthur Hildersham had been one of many "godly and learned young men" who studied with Richard Greenham at Dry Drayton. One of the most important of such "seminaries" was run by Alexander Richardson in his home at Barking, Essex. Richardson had been denied a Cambridge fellowship because of his extreme views, but retained many friends at the university. Among those who studied with him were William Ames, Thomas Hooker, Charles Chauncey, and John Yates, who later said of Richardson, "We follow in his footsteps." Long after Richardson had died the manuscript notes from his lectures were circulated by his former students and "most generally prized." At Ashden, Essex, Richard Blackerby, excluded from a parish post by his extreme Puritanism, devoted twenty-three years of his life to giving board and instruction to young men such as Samuel Fairclough and Samuel Stone. Fairclough had traveled there on the recommendation of Samuel Ward. At such a school an aspiring clergyman was able to study divinity and humane learning and also apprentice by occasionally preaching in nearby villages. Stephen Marshall was associated with Blackerby's seminary, possibly when Fairclough was there. Charles Offspring presided over a seminary at St. Antholin's in London. Hugh Peter studied at Thomas Gataker's seminary in Rotherithe. Gataker had a number of foreign students as a result of his close contacts with the Dutch Reformed congregation in London. Indeed, Wilhelm Thilenius, who became minister of the Dutch congregation at Austin Friars in London in 1624, was one of them. Gataker himself traveled to the Netherlands in 1620 and was a good friend of Willem Teelinck, the influential minister of Middelburg, some of whose works Gataker arranged to have published in England. It is possible that Peter developed friendships with some of the clergymen he would later encounter in the Netherlands. Certainly Gataker would have provided an introduction to Teelinck, whose sermons Peter attended in Middelburg and whose commitment to English Puritan divines Peter commented on. Among other English students there were Joseph Symonds and Thomas Young (who would later tutor John Milton). Jeremiah Burroughes, John Beadle, and Nathaniel Rogers studied under Thomas Hooker at Chelmsford. John Dod taught students at Canon Ashby in Northampton. John Ball conducted a seminary near Newcastle in Staffordshire, as did Thomas Taylor in Surrey and John Rogers in Dedham. John Preston, while master of Emmanuel, regularly sent promising protégés to study with John Cotton. Among those who traveled to Boston, Lincolnshire, were Thomas Hill (later master of Trinity, Cambridge, during the Interregnum), Samuel Winter, John Angier, and Anthony Tuckney. Cotton also attracted students from the continent. Maximilian Teelinck, later pastor at Flushing in the Netherlands, was the son of Middelburg's Willem Teelinck, Gataker's friend who had studied with Perkins at Cambridge and been called to the ministry through the efforts of Dod and Hildersham. Maximilian studied under Ames at Franeker and then traveled along with his son-in-law to Boston, Lincolnshire, where he studied with Cotton for three years. John Rulice was recommended to the university of Cambridge by the king of Bohemia. He studied with Preston at Emmanuel and was sent by Preston to live and learn with Cotton in Lincolnshire.[37]

Such private schools, frequented by students preparing for the MA or apprenticing for the ministry, rarely contained more than two or three students at a time. Friends when they came together, or sharing a common friend, the master and his pupils were in a situation where close social and spiritual bonds were likely to develop. The influence of such teachers was powerful. Daniel Rogers initially found that he could not "come into the presence of Mr. Blackerby without some kind of trembling upon him, because of the Divine Majesty and Holiness which seemed to shine in him." Samuel Fairclough combined his studies under Blackerby with preaching in neighboring towns. John Cotton fully incorporated his pupils into the life of his household. Every morning and evening they gathered with his family and servants for Scripture readings and prayer. Sabbath observance began on Saturday evening and ended with a psalm and prayers after Sunday supper. Living as a student in the Cotton household, John Angier formed lasting friendships not only with Cotton but with his fellow pupils Anthony Tuckney, Thomas Hill, and Samuel Winter. Samuel Fairclough married the daughter of Richard Blackerby. John Cotton introduced Samuel Winter to the woman he married and John Angier married Ellen Winstanly, Cotton's niece. Such unions added ties of kinship to the already strong bonds of friendship.[38]

Yet another tie to the universities was formed by grammar schools maintained by graduates of the colleges. These Puritan clergy identified promising students, helped prepare them for college, and recommended them to friends at Oxford and Cambridge. Nicholas Morton, having laid down the Dixie Fellowship at Emmanuel to become pastor of the London parish of St. Saviour's, Southwark, in the late 1620s, was instrumental in getting the young John Harvard into Emmanuel. William Gouge, having left St. Paul's school in London, had spent three years at "a Free-school in Felsted in Essex, where he was trained up three years under the publick Ministry of his uncle Mr. Ezekiel Culverwell," and then went on to matriculate at King's College in Cambridge. The earl of Warwick, whose ancestor had founded the school, appointed Martin Holbech as head on the recommendation of John Preston in 1627. Holbech, a friend of Thomas Shepard, ran the school from 1628 to 1649, instructing Samuel Rogers and four of the sons of Oliver Cromwell, among others. Thomas Hooker and John Eliot would also become noted as teachers as well as preachers.[39]

Young scholars still studying at the university frequently traveled through the surrounding countryside to attend services conducted by divines such as Cotton. Encouraged by the university friends of these luminaries, the students made the acquaintance of preachers who had previously lived for them only in college legends. Jeremiah Burroughes, William Bridge, and Thomas Goodwin traveled together to listen to John Wilson. John Shaw was converted to Puritanism by the preaching of Thomas Welde three miles from Shaw's student lodging at Cambridge.[40]

John Rogers drew many students to his sermons at Dedham, among them William Bridge and Jeremiah Burroughes. Thomas Goodwin in his later years related to his friend John Howe that "Being in the time of his youth a student at Cambridge, and having heard much of Mr. Rogers of Dedham in Essex, purposely he took a journey from Cambridge to Dedham to hear him preach on his Lecture day, a Lecture then so thronged and frequented that to those that came not very early there was no possibility of getting room in that spacious large church." On that occasion Rogers preached on the subject of the popular neglect of the Scriptures, stirring the congregation with an imaginary dialogue in which he alternated in voicing the views of God and the people. Such preaching elicited strong emotional responses. Goodwin told Howe that the congregation was "deluged with their own tears, and he told me that he himself [Goodwin], when he got up and was to take horse again to be gone, he was fain to hang a quarter of an hour upon the neck of his horse weeping, before he had power to mount, so strange an impression was there upon him and generally upon the people, upon being expostulated with for their neglect of the Bible." Oliver Heywood, writing a biography of his friend John Angier, who had "lived a season in Mr. Rogers house," likewise testified that "multitudes of people flocked from the parts adjacent [to hear Rogers], and his plain preaching was blessed with a large harvest." Heywood added further examples of Rogers's pulpit style, citing "some expressions and gestures he used, [which (in the late seventeenth century when Heywood wrote)] would now seem indecent; yet the gravity of the man, and general reverence people had for him, rendered them not only not offensive, but sometimes very effectual; his taking hold with both hands of the Canopy of the Pulpit, and roaring hideously, to represent the torments of the damned, had an awakening force attending to it." For students and recent graduates, attendance on the sermons of leading Puritan preachers offered lessons in effective preaching and initiated contacts that would often prove invaluable in later years. And those sermons also stirred emotions that intensified the individual's sense of communion with fellow saints.[41]

Many young clergymen such as John Owen traveled to London, where they could sample the sermons of a variety of preachers. Ann Hughes has described Thomas Dugard's journey to London after he received his MA from Sidney Sussex, Cambridge, in 1633. He browsed in bookshops, attended sermons by Gouge, Davenport, Byfield, and others, and "looked up important ex-fellows of Sidney, presumably to inquire after vacant posts." One such ex-fellow was Thomas Gataker. Dugard frequented his sermons, "dined with him often and was introduced by him to the second Lord Brooke," who would later offer Dugard a benefice.[42]

College ties were not the only glue holding the Puritan network together. But, then as now, the university was a turning point for young lives, a place where men formulated their ideals, set their goals, and made friendships to last a lifetime. Even after a student graduated or a fellow departed he was likely to be drawn back to the Cam periodically, particularly for commencement festivities. For the clergy who are the focal point of this study, the spiritual communion of which they partook at the universities became the driving force that united them in a network of mutual support. From Cambridge and from Oxford as well, a band of friends came forth dedicated to the task of reforming the English church and advancing the cause of international Protestantism.[43]

CHAPTER TWO

A Whole Chain of Many Links

WHEN THE PURITAN student had finished his studies at Cambridge or Oxford he left the relatively safe confines of the university to enter a world of considerable risk. Trained to preach and minister to needy souls, he was also committed to advocacy of a point of view that was officially discouraged and on occasion persecuted by the established authorities of his church. The monarch and the nation's leading bishops had never condoned Puritan influence in the universities, but in the colleges along the Cam and the Thames the young dissenter had been part of a communion of friends and fellow saints, a subculture that shielded its members from the sense of isolation many of them would face in confronting their parishes. Away from college, in the 1620s and later, they would find themselves standing alone, the target of traditionalists in the pews and of the bishop in the local see.

The Puritan cleric's college education set him apart from the flock to which he was to minister, but his nonconformity could further alienate him from the cultural consensus in the community he was to serve. The very fact of being united with fellow saints in spiritual communion marked those who were so blessed as separate from the mass of their contemporaries. This sense of isolation was part of the price paid for being a Puritan. The layman John Winthrop explained the situation in which the nonconformist often found himself: "There is least companie, and . . . those which doe walke openly in this way shalbe despised, pointed ayt, hated of the world, made a byword, reviled, slandered, rebuked, made a gazing stock, called Puritans, nice fooles, hypocrites, hairbrained fellows, rashes, indiscreet, vain glorious, and all that is naught." Accentuating this sense of separateness for the clergyman was the fact that he often differed from the members of his congregation in life-style, dress, and even speech. Often confronted by hostility, the Puritan cherished the reinforcement he received from his friends, whether those friends were laymen or clergy, patrons or colleagues. He felt a sense of community only "with fellow saints, the group of notable 'private christians' with whom he would hold voluntary house meetings on Sunday evenings."[1]

Yet if the professionalism and nonconformity of the young Puritans generated a sense of distance from the general lay society, it led to an intensified awareness of their identity in a spiritual fellowship. Friendship became a central relationship, communion with saints gave meaning to their lives. General college connections were not enough; what counted was the degree to which university or other experiences had led to affection grounded in a shared experience of grace. Though Jeremiah Burroughes and Edmund Calamy had both graduated from Emmanuel and both assumed posts at Bury St. Edmunds at about the same time, they were never close and never assisted one another. Jesper Rosenmeir, however, has described the friendship between John Cotton and John Preston as being for Cotton "the living image of the relationship in the Trinity. Of course, Cotton and Preston felt that their mutual affection only partially contained the divine element, but even though their expression was but in part, it did truly reflect the love that was communication and communion." Preaching a few years after Preston's death, Cotton expressed his belief that Preston's spiritual presence was still strong among his friends.[2]

Communion was one term used by many Puritans to identify this coming together with a friend for mutual aid. *Conference* was another, and "by conference," according to Richard Sibbes, "God works strangely many times." It was, in his view, a "sanctified means." Jonathan Mitchell, in "A Letter . . . to his Friend" appended to *Discourse of the Glory* (London, 1677), urged: "If you had a friend with whom you might now and then spend a little time, in conferring together, in opening your hearts, and presenting your unutterable groanings before God, it would be of excellent use: Such an one would greatly strengthen, bestead, and further you in your way to Heaven. . . . Oh! the life of God that falls into the hearts of the Godly, in and by gracious Heavenly Conference. Be open hearted one to another, and stand one for another against the Devil and all his Angels." This mutual love was the work of the Spirit, its product was the communion of saints. According to William Gouge, conference, or communion, was the most important means of dealing with "weighty matters," because one had "not only our help, but also the help of others." Such counseling with friends was a key element in Puritan decision making and a process that both helped the individual and also reinforced the "support network" of the clergy. "We were," wrote John Winthrop of such communion, "all much quickened and refreshed by it."[3]

The fact that Puritan dissent could continue to exist and even grow in the face of official disapproval was due to the peculiarities of the English church structure. There were about two thousand parishes in England at the beginning of the seventeenth century. A parson was instituted in his parish by a bishop, but he was chosen by the patron of the living (the person or institution possessing the advowson right). In the majority of parishes the advowson was held by a lay person, a corporation, or the parish itself. When such an individual or group had Puritan leanings an opportunity existed for the placement of a dissenting clergyman. Certainly this was frowned upon by the church hierarchy, but a bishop was legally bound to institute a patron's choice unless the person chosen was grossly scandalous in character or knowledge. Not until the rise of William Laud to archbishop of Canterbury would the hold of patrons on these livings be seriously challenged. In the meantime, though many lay patrons were not Puritan, the activities of those who were—such as the gentry families of Rich, Barrington, Fiennes, Barnardiston, and Russell—made a major contribution to the growth of the Puritan movement.[4]

Lectureships had developed as a means of supplementing the preaching that could be expected from a parish incumbent. A clergyman would be engaged to preach on a regular basis without having to assume any other clerical functions. Since much Puritan nonconformity involved methods of administering the sacraments, lecturers had less occasion to provide the authorities with clear justification for their removal. Individual and combination lectureships were supported by gentry, town corporations, and parishes. Here, too, a situation existed where Puritan patronage could find places for Puritan clergy. Finally, the dissenting cleric might find employment as a household chaplain with one of the gentry families.[5]

Ministers did not limit their friends to fellow ministers. To identify all lay members of the network is impossible, but in certain cases where laymen performed critical roles linking the network together and sustaining its activities it is appropriate that they be included. It is also important to realize that the experience of religious renewal and recognition of that grace in others united laymen and clerics in spirit and communion as fellow and equal saints. Such fellowship could make a peer befriend a clergyman of lesser status, and it could also explain a pastor's willingness to share the keys of church authority with a congregation of lay saints.[6]

Patronage was one of the most significant means whereby laymen supported the Puritan movement. Robert Rich, the second earl of Warwick, was one of the most energetic of the lay supporters of religious reform. He was a powerful

East Anglia: Heartland of the Congregational Communion

and influential nobleman in East Anglia and held the advowson rights to twenty-four livings. His Puritan leanings dated at least from his experiences at Emmanuel College, which he had entered in 1603. He had a strong appetite for sermons, traveled frequently to hear favorite preachers such as Thomas Hooker, and had a room built overlooking the Gray's Inn chapel so that he could hear his "special friend" Richard Sibbes. He kept a close interest in the Puritan position at Cambridge, as demonstrated by his contributions to the election of William Sandcroft as master of Emmanuel and his own brother as vice-chancellor of the university. But the more important field for his patronage was in the appointment of Puritans to clerical livings. His close friends William Gouge, John Preston, and Richard Sibbes often influenced his selections. Shortly after he assumed his title he appointed Hugh Peter to a living in Rayleigh, Essex. He installed Obadiah Sedgwick at Coggeshall when John Dod passed away in 1639. He gave Thomas Hooker's former student Samuel Clarke a post as his chaplain and later found him a lectureship. Warwick's nephew, Sir Nathaniel Rich, also had a Cambridge background, and both visited and corresponded with William Sandcroft, the master of Emmanuel. He appointed Nathaniel Ward to Stondon Massey in 1624. When Ward was deprived and left for New England, Rich appointed Anthony Sawbridge to Stondon Massey. Sawbridge moved there from a living in Hadleigh, where Warwick replaced him with Ward's son John. In 1635 the earl placed William Munnings, a cousin of both Nathaniel Ward and John Winthrop, in the living at Good Easter. In 1639 another Ward relation, also Nathaniel Ward, received a living in Hawkewell from Warwick. Edmund Calamy received a living at Rochford from the earl in 1637. In the following year Warwick employed Jeremiah Burroughes (in trouble with the authorities) as a chaplain in his household. It was Warwick who appointed Martin Holbech master of the grammar school at Felsted, acting on the recommendation of Preston, who had taught Holbech at Queens' College, Cambridge. Thomas Barnes, a friend of Lord Horace Vere, was a lecturer in Warwick's parish of Great Waltham. Only five of the many appointments he made were not Cambridge men and ten clergy holding his livings between 1619 and 1658 were graduates of the earl's alma mater, Emmanuel.[7]

The Barringtons were clients and friends of the earl of Warwick and like him were noted as patrons of Puritan clergy. Among those whom they appointed to positions was Ezekiel Rogers. John Preston preached at a lectureship at Hatfield Broad Oak maintained by Sir Francis Barrington. James Harrison, the regular lecturer at Hatfield Broad Oak, corresponded frequently with Lady Barrington and she stood as godmother for his son. When he solicited funds from her to relieve some distressed Puritans in Ipswich she responded generously. Thomas Barrington's brother-in-law, Sir

William Masham, employed Roger Williams and John Norton as chaplains. Thomas Welde received his living at Terling, Essex, from Robert Mildmay, another friend of Warwick and the Barringtons. John Haynes, another lay friend of Puritan clergy and later governor of Connecticut, lived but a short distance from Warwick's manor of Inworth.[8]

Although the intensity of the ties between clergymen and patrons varied immensely, some of the friendships formed clearly transcended class differences. Friendships between clergy and their patrons were perhaps facilitated at this time by the fact that the clergy had come to be recognized as "honorary or pseudo-gentry." But it is clear that communion leveled social distinctions. John Tombes, the vicar of Leominster in Herefordshire, was a friend to Sir Robert Harley. George Griffiths was also close to the Harleys and would maintain a correspondence with Lady Brilliana Harley after he moved from the area. Arthur Hildersham was on familiar terms with the Barringtons. Lady Joan Barrington entertained not only Hildersham but John Preston at Hatfield. Henry Jessey was entertained by Brampton Gurdon at Assington Hall. Richard Sibbes, while master of St. Catharine's, spent time between terms visiting friends such as Sir Robert Brooke; Sir William Masham wrote of a dinner he had enjoyed at William Prynne's chambers in London at which Sibbes was present. On a more somber occasion John Dod journeyed to preach to and console Sir Francis Barrington when that Puritan grandee was in the Marshalsea prison in 1627 for his opposition to the forced loan. When Roger Williams offended Lady Barrington with some candid advice, Sir William Masham interceded with her on Williams's behalf, saying of the clergyman, "a good man is a good friend." Thomas Gataker came to preach at the wedding of Sir Robert Harley and Brilliana Conway. Such friendship between social unequals was common enough to attract the attention of enemies of the Puritans, who denounced it as socially disruptive, objecting to the lay lords "clapping [the clergy] on the back, and . . . setting them at the upper end of the Tables."[9]

Whereas Puritan clergymen often found support from private patrons, others were extended positions by parishes and corporations. Thomas Hooker, whose first living came from the hands of Mr. Francis Drake (a distant kinsman of the Elizabethan seafarer), was appointed lecturer at St. Mary's in Chelmsford, Essex, by the parish authorities of that church. Jeremiah Burroughes served for a time as a parish lecturer at Bury St. Edmunds. Parishioners made the choice of John Carter to be curate and then vicar at St. Peter Mancroft in Norwich. John Davenport was chosen vicar of St. Stephen's on London's Coleman Street by that parish's vestry. The alderman and mayor of the borough of Boston, Lincolnshire, extended the call to John Cotton to be vicar of St. Botolph's church.[10]

In some of these cases, though the call came from a lay individual or group, the clergyman owed his selection to the recommendation of clerical friends. Thomas Hill recommended an Emmanuel College friend to Sir Robert Harley. John Dod suggested Thomas Hooker to Mr. Drake. Samuel Stone received the lectureship funded by Dr. Wilson on the recommendation of Thomas Shepard, who had previously held it and who was a native of Towcester, where the lecture was being resettled. Samuel Winter was "put into the living of Cottingham, where it was said that he was first known by his assistance in preaching to Ezekiel Rogers, who went to New England." Laurence Chaderton suggested Thomas Hooker to the corporation of King's Lynn for a pulpit there, though Hooker turned the offer down. William Gouge owed his call to St. Anne's Blackfriars to Arthur Hildersham. John Rogers of Dedham probably urged John Yates's call to the pastorate of St. Andrew's in Norwich. Thomas Hooker suggested Jeremiah Burroughes for the post of lecturer at Bury St. Edmunds. Thomas Pierson suggested possible tutors for the children of Sir Robert Harley. One who served occasionally in that post was Richard Blinman. As one contemporary noted about aspirants for London pulpits, "if any man . . . had letters testimonial from Patriarch White of Dorchester, Mr Cotton of Boston, or the like . . . this man was a choyce plant, and fit for their soyle."[11]

Fortunate though these and other Puritans were to find private or corporate patronage, they all found themselves in a vulnerable situation. The pews of churchgoers to whom they would preach would contain both radicals and traditionalists. As Patrick Collinson has shown in his studies of Elizabethan religion, and other scholars have demonstrated for the Jacobean era, lay radicals were often critical of clerical conformity with practices they considered impure. Awareness that his efforts to retain his living might be branded a sinful sellout must have been a source of anxiety for many a Puritan clergyman. The pews of most English churches, however, also contained parishioners who had a sincere attachment to the forms and liturgy of the Anglican Church and who would be quick to report any deviancy from those practices to the ecclesiastical authorities. Ministers were vulnerable to pressure from both extremes of the religious spectrum. Most Puritans who found themselves called upon to answer to a bishop for their preaching or practice owed that ordeal less to the efficient supervision of the diocesan authorities than to being reported by traditionalists in their own parish. John Cotton and Francis Higginson were but two of the many clergymen who suffered when parishioners raised complaints about their Puritan innovations.[12]

The bonds of communion generally protected the clergyman from open criticism from fellow saints, yet the Puritan preacher frequently found himself in a very public position with no one in his parish who could or would fully empathize with him. He was trying to satisfy his patron, his congregation, his conscience, and his God. He believed, of course, that he was a member of an international body of saints united by God's grace and Christian love. "The same thread of grace is spunne thorow the hearts of all the godly under Heaven," was the way the Reverend William Hooke expressed it. But such a community was rather too abstract to offer much of a sense of comfort. It was natural for the clergyman to seek the company of personal friends who shared the same faith and were undergoing the same types of trials, to seek their advice, and to solicit their prayers and moral support. So within the broad network of the communion of saints clerical friendship had a special importance. Friends made at university or elsewhere thus assumed a new and important role in the life of the clergyman. By conferring with them he was better able to place his problems in context, learn and reflect upon alternative responses, and feel the reassurance that came from being part of a group and knowing that others shared his predicament. [13]

Such reaching out to friends occurred in a variety of ways. For a limited number of Puritan ministers who were members of combination lectures such contact was regular and frequent. A group of lecturers was engaged to preach in rotation. Members of the combination would usually attend each other's sermons and meet afterwards. The Reverend John Ley, writing in the early 1640s, recalled the informality that could characterize such gatherings: "Our sermon ended, and some of us invited to a place of convenient repose, the rest of our Tribe . . . resorted unto us, every man accompanying his acquaintance and so making as it were a whole chaine of many linkes." Dinner might be at the home of one of the clergy or at an ordinary where they had reserved a separate room. This sharing of a communal meal evoked images of the eucharistic supper shared by Christ with his disciples and was emblematic of the clerical communion. Over dinner and wine they would discuss the subject of that day's lecture, matters of religious or political controversy, difficulties they were experiencing in their pastoral ministry, or any other matter of professional or personal concern. It was a communal experience with intellectual and social stimulation reminiscent of university days. One of the reasons expressed for combination lectures in the Diocese of Norwich was the "increase of love and acquaintance amongst preachers." [14]

One of the more famous of the combination lectures was at St. Antholin's church in London, where four or five clergymen were usually employed in the 1620s. At five in the morning the church bells would summon the Puritan faithful to prayer and psalm singing and the lecture at six. The organizer of this exercise was the rector, Charles Offspring and among the lecturers in that decade were Thomas Foxley, Zachariah Symmes, and John Archer. To the northeast a group of "trustees for the religion in Norwich and Norfolk" organized a lectureship. They had purchased the living of St. Peter Hungate for William Bridge and Bridge used his network contacts to develop a lecture at nearby St. George's Tombland. Among those who were involved in the early 1630s were Jeremiah Burroughes, William Greenhill, Robert Peck, Matthew Swallow (John Arrowsmith's curate), Robert Johnson, John Carter, and Thomas Walker. Lectures were on Friday, and following the sermon the clergy gathered for supper and talk. Greenhill and his "most intimate friend" Burroughes were also involved for a time in a combination lecture in the market town of Mendlesham in Suffolk. The Bury St. Edmunds exercise had been started by Elizabethan Puritans and remained important even during the early period of Wren's supervision of the diocese. Not until 1636 was Archbishop Laud convinced that it had been appropriately "regulated."[15]

Lectureships held by a single clergyman rather than a group in combination also brought neighboring ministers to listen and socialize. Such positions were common in the church and often filled by Puritans. Between 1603 and 1629 there were seventy-two lecturers active in forty-three Essex parishes, with fifty-nine identifiable as Puritans. In Suffolk Samuel Fairclough preached a regular Thursday lecture at Kedington. The audience frequently included as many as twenty fellows and students from Cambridge. A lectureship that had been established at Colchester in 1564 was generally held by a noted Cambridge divine who preached on Sunday afternoons, Wednesday forenoons, and on festivals, fasts, elections, and other special occasions. Among those to hold the post were William Ames, William Eyre, William Bridge, and John Knowles. For some, single or combination lectureships were a way of easing the transition from university to parish. The St. Antholin's lecturers, for instance, were usually serving in their first professional position. For others whose views on administration of the sacraments and other matters made it difficult for them to secure or keep a parish, lectureships offered access to a pulpit from which to reach the laity. In still other cases such as at St. Stephen's Coleman Street in London a lectureship offered a minister who had a parochial living a way of broadening his outreach while supplementing his income.[16]

Another occasion for bringing members of the network together was the formal gathering of Puritan ministers in regional clerical associations. Members came together to discuss doctrinal matters, to seek advice on points of contention with their congregations, and to serve as a clearinghouse for ecclesiastical livings. The most famous such conference or association was the one that met at Dedham from 1582 to 1589. The minutes of the group indicate the members discussing general strategies for spreading the gospel, specific issues of the day, methods of pastoral counseling, and practical concerns such as what to do if suspended for nonconformity. Richard Rogers, a member of another East Anglian classis, provided a personal link with the Puritan movement of the seventeenth century. In 1582 another gathering of sixty East Anglian clergy was held at Cockfield, Suffolk, to discuss what might be tolerated and what rejected in the Prayer Book. University fellows attended that session and occasionally hosted others, such as a conference at the master's lodge of St. John's College in Cambridge in 1589, where Laurence Chaderton was an active participant. The authorities suspected such groups of acting as Presbyterian classes, of being a church within a church, and were rigorous in dealing with them. But while the last so-called presbyterian conference was held in London in 1589, such conferences continued in other forms into the Stuart Age.[17]

The Reverend John Bois, Greek scholar and longtime fellow of St. John's, Cambridge, organized a form of clerical seminar when he assumed the pastoral post at Boxworth, near Cambridge. About a dozen like-minded ministers took turns hosting Friday-night get-togethers for dinner, study, and discussion. William Bedell was a strong Calvinist whose identification with the Puritan network faded in the years after he became provost of Trinity College, Dublin, but whose views even then were generally in sympathy with moderate Puritanism. While a fellow of Emmanuel College he helped organize a circle of preachers in the Cambridge area. The group included Thomas Gataker, Samuel Ward, and Samuel Clarke, and its members exchanged views on theological and professional issues while also serving as a placement service for university graduates by gathering news of vacancies and recommending candidates. Richard Rogers of Wethersfield recorded the communion of yet another group of East Anglian clergy who regularly got together so that "we fasted betwixt our selves, to the stirringe upp our selves to greater godliness . . . and then we determined to bringe into writing a direction for our lives, which might be both for our selves and others." Fasting was a common means by which each clergyman humbled himself and whereby the conference attendees as a whole put aside worldly distractions to bring themselves to higher levels of communion with God and with each other. Samuel Clarke wrote that in a similar gathering of preachers in the Wirral "love by frequent society was nourished and increased, so that all the professors, though living ten or twelve miles asunder, were intimate and familiar as if they had been all of one household." Arthur Hildersham was the key figure in another such ministerial association, centered on Ashby-de-la-Zouche, which included his close friend William Bradshaw. In the 1620s a group of up to twelve Puritan clergymen in London met regularly, among whom were John Preston, Richard Sibbes, Hugh Peter, John Davenport, and Thomas Goodwin. There were similar exercises in Essex, Lincolnshire, Yorkshire, and Lancashire.[18]

The Chelmsford conference in the 1620s was hosted by Thomas Hooker who had come to Chelmsford in 1626, in part to be near John Rogers. He settled close to the manor house of John Haynes and was soon hosting monthly meetings of local Puritan clergy that included Thomas Welde and Hugh

Peter. When he left his living at St. Mary's he resettled nearby at Cuckoos Farm in Little Baddow, making the farmhouse a school with the encouragement of John Newton, the local vicar, and Sir Henry Mildmay, the local magnate. Hooker hired John Eliot as his assistant and continued to host monthly clerical gatherings at the farm. A contemporary critic reported that Hooker's "private conference . . . hath already impeached the peace of our church more than his public ministry. . . . Our people's pallet grows so out of taste that no food contents it but of Mr. Hooker's dressing." Like similar conferences, the gathering hosted by Hooker was often approached by patrons for recommendations of clergy for ministerial posts.[19]

Visits to hear a friend preach and to talk with him afterwards were frequent occurrences in the lives of many members of the network, and such socializing could include laymen as well as clergy. The nourishment of spiritual communion could flow as readily between two saints who met alone as in a conference of many. William Perkins was famous for his hospitality to young clergy who came to him for advice. William Ames paid a visit to John Preston at Cambridge shortly after the death of James I. The diary of Thomas Dugard reveals that where parishes were close together, as in Warwickshire, clergy got together on an almost-daily basis. John Cotton's friendship with Arthur Hildersham flourished because the latter's vicarage at Ashby-de-la-Zouche was close enough to facilitate frequent contact. Samuel Whiting and Samuel Skelton ministered in other nearby parishes and also became close friends of Cotton's. Jeremiah Burroughes, William Bridge, and Thomas Goodwin traveled together to hear John Wilson on a number of occasions when that clergyman preached along the Essex–Suffolk border in the 1620s. Burroughes and Greenhill journeyed together to London to hear the great preachers of the city. The earl of Warwick frequented Thomas Hooker's sermons at Chelmsford, John Preston visited John Cotton in Boston at least once a year, and many other clergymen traveled to Boston, for—as Samuel Clarke wrote—"in that Candlestick the Father of Lights placed [Cotton] this burning and shining Light." Following his sermons Cotton led visiting clergymen in discussions. At Dedham John Rogers's sermons drew many fellow clerics such as George Phillips as well as Cambridge students. Thomas Goodwin later recalled how he and other students (including Bridge and Burroughes) would ride to Dedham "to get a little fire." Thomas Hooker often came to hear Rogers and the older clergyman invited Hooker to preach *The Faithful Covenanter* (London, 1644) at Dedham. William Gouge frequented Richard Sibbes's sermons at Gray's Inn, as did the earl of Warwick, Sir Gilbert Gerard, John Pym, and Solicitor General Sir Henry Yelverton.[20]

The young John Rowe often traveled to London to hear Gouge and Richard Stock. He was far from alone in his attendance on Gouge, of whom his friend and biographer wrote that "great was the confluence of hearers which in former times not onely from all parts of this famous City, but of many parts of *England*, frequented his Lectures at *Black-fryars* (for so great was the flame of his pains, that he heated those who sat a great way from it) and when the godly Christians of those times came to London, they thought not theire business *done* unless they had been at Black-fryars Lectures: and great was the benefit which many godly people, and young Ministers professed that they (then) reapt from his labours." Stephen Marshall, Daniel Rogers, and Thomas Hooker were likely present when James Harrison delivered a lecture at the Barringtons' in 1626. Daniel Rogers was a guest preacher at John Winthrop's Groton Manor on a number of occasions. Samuel Fairclough's Thursday lectures attracted area clergy and Cambridge students. John Shaw, in later years one of the foremost lecturers in Yorkshire, remembered the influence Thomas Welde had on those who came to hear him in the Cambridge area. On leaving Cambridge in 1624 Henry Jessey "begg'd the Lord to place him in Essex, near Suffolk, or in Suffolk near Essex, in regard that he had sometime been there and heard famous Preachers, and found many precious Christians." His prayer was answered, for he spent the next nine years in the Assington household of Brampton Gurdon, from which he traveled often to be with clerical friends. Among those with whom Jessey got together were Thomas Goodwin and Philip Nye. Richard Rogers frequently visited Ezekiel Culverwell. Thomas Dugard traveled to Staffordshire in 1634 to visit Thomas Ball, whose catechism he used and admired. Having read Richard Rogers's *Seven Treatises*, John Wilson rode often to Wethersfield to hear that famous divine preach and accepted a living at Sudbury so that he could be near Rogers.[21]

Thomas Shepard stayed at the home of Jeremiah Burroughes and probably preached at Mendlesham during his stay. Burroughes often rode to Chelmsford to hear Hooker and to attend the ministerial conferences held there. Kenneth Shipps has explained that "Every week young ministers came to Chelmsford to use Hooker's extensive library, to hear Hooker's lectures, to fast and confer with their 'Oracle in cases of Conscience and Divinity.' At the end of the week these young men returned to 'broach on the Sundaies' what Hooker had brewed." In addition to Burroughes these sessions were frequented by Thomas Shepard, John Beadle, Hugh Peter, Nathaniel Rogers, and Thomas Welde, among others. The earl of Warwick was sometimes there. Samuel Rogers traveled to hear Hooker and Thomas Shepard. Richard Sibbes took John Davenport's pulpit to preach two sermons at St. Stephen's Coleman Street in 1629. Oliver St. John, William Lenthall, William Prynne, and William Sheppard—all of whom would play key roles in the coming of the Puritan Revolution—were among those who regularly attended John Preston's sermons at Lincoln's Inn in 1622. They later attended the sermons of Joseph Caryl, who succeeded Preston in 1623. Symonds D'Ewes recorded a typical Sabbath of sermon gadding in London in May of 1623: "In the morning I went to Blacke Friers where Mr. Gouge did well, in the afternoone to St. Andrewes and heard a good sermon and lastlye to Lincoln's Inn to the new built Chappel, but had not the good fortune to hear Mr. Preston himselfe." When resident in London Sir Robert Harley attended St. Mary's Aldermanbury to hear Thomas Taylor or St. Stephen's Coleman Street to listen to Davenport's sermons. When Charles Chauncey preached, according to one hostile informant, "the whole tribe of God flocked thither," including Lord Say and Sele. A hostile contemporary account claimed that "they had their mutuall intelligence throughout the Whole Kingdome, and . . . they had their Emissaries . . . or Scouts to give notice when men of their Tribe preached; so that not any one of their Ministers, could come to London from the farthest parts of England, but found entertainment in the City; for whose randevouz a Widow (whom Alderman Pennington married) kept an Ordinary in White Fryars, where many of them lodged in Doctor Prestons dayes." All such encounters between friends provided opportunities for sharing common experiences, discussing common problems, forming new friendships, and reinforcing old ones.[22]

When a student or clergyman traveled with a friend to hear a sermon or visit another colleague, the journey itself could become an occasion for the exchange of confidences and advice. Riding from Cambridge to the home of Richard Greenham in September 1587, Richard Rogers discussed his spiritual state with Ezekiel Culverwell. At another time Rogers recorded "a most sweet journey with mr. Cu[lverwell] 2 dayes, and much time bestowed in the way about our christian estat, of godes mercy in our calleing to the fellowsh[ip] of the gospel, of the true testimonies of fayth, and of the great comfort which by continuinge herein doth come unto godes people." In his life of John Angier, Oliver Heywood recounted that when the young Angier was boarding with John Cotton he would frequently accompany Cotton on trips. The older man took advantage of these rides through the countryside to talk with Angier, letting the landscape and the weather serve as points of departure for observations he wished to make. The diary of the Suffolk clergyman John Rous reveals an individual who traveled often within East Anglia and spent much of his time exchanging news and gossip with fellow clergy.[23]

In some of the country's larger churches a clergyman might have the good fortune to have a colleague of similar viewpoint who would quickly become a friend. Samuel Winter was an assistant to Ezekiel Rogers at Rowley in the mid-1630s. Anthony Tuckney was associated with John Cotton at St. Botolph's for a few years. John Davenport informally assisted at Thomas Taylor's church of St. Mary's Aldermanbury in 1617. After 1638 Peter Sterry joined Simeon Ashe as chaplains to Lord Brooke.[24]

For all Puritans, but especially for those too far apart to meet regularly with old friends, correspondence became a major means of keeping the network vital. Official surveillance was not what it would become after the Restoration, and William Gouge evidently felt that the carrier of a letter to Sir Robert Harley could be trusted when he described Archbishop Neile as "the disturber of our peace that busie-body Neale." But much such correspondence was destroyed lest if fall into the wrong hands and compromise the author. When Thomas Cartwright yielded to the urgings of John Field and answered young Arthur Hildersham's request for advice on the study of divinity he urged Hildersham to let no one know of his letter, "or els let it smell of the fyre." Given the odds against any single personal letter surviving destruction or simple loss, the volume of correspondence between clerical friends is impressive. Jeremiah Burroughes, for instance, wrote John Cotton in 1631 to send news and solicit assistance, explaining that "you and my tutor Hooker I especially rely on for counsel under God" and desiring "to be remembered to Mr. Angier if he be with you." In that same year Nathaniel Ward sent Cotton news of his problems with Bishop Laud. Hugh Peter, having relocated in the Netherlands, exchanged news with John Phillips at Wrentham and also corresponded with Thomas Hooker. Alexander Whitaker corresponded with William Gouge, John Ward wrote to William Sandcroft, and John Preston often exchanged letters with Arthur Hildersham. Thomas Hooker and John Cotton exchanged views about migrating to America. Samuel Clarke remembered that Cotton "answered many Letters that were sent him far and near, wherein were handled many difficult Cases of Conscience, and many doubts cleared to great satisfaction." One young clergyman wrote to Cotton in 1625 asking for advice on whether it was lawful to publicly pray for friends by name (yes, Cotton responded), to play cards (no), to pick valentines in the form of a lottery (no), and to engage in mixed dancing (yes). Thomas Goodwin corresponded in the 1630s with John Davenport (his "dear friend," according to Cotton Mather) and John Cotton. When Cotton came to Massachusetts and Davenport was still in London, the New Englander wrote to his English friend. Cotton also wrote to Hugh Peter in Rotterdam. William Greenhill and John Preston wrote to each other in the years just before Preston's death. When Laud's agents arrested Dr. John Stoughton and seized his papers they found correspondence with many prominent Puritans including John White, Henry Whitefield, Israel Stoughton, James Cudworth, John Wilson, John Winthrop, and Stephen Marshall. Stoughton also corresponded with William Sandcroft. Thomas Hooker wrote to Richard Mather urging Mather to migrate to New England. Jeremiah Burroughes wrote to his friend Zachariah Symmes after Symmes had settled in Massachusetts.[25]

Samuel Ward's correspondence in the Bodleian Library contains exchanges on political news, ecclesiastical gossip, and the changing scene at the universities. Among his correspondents were William Bedell, Richard Sibbes,

Thomas Gataker, and John Preston. Laurence Chaderton's papers contain numerous letters from clerical friends soliciting his views on whether they should conform to innovations in church practice. Samuel Clarke recalled that William Gouge, "By reason of his ability and dexterity in resolving Cases of Conscience . . . was much sought unto for his judgement in doubtful cases, and scruples of Conscience . . . by divers Ministers . . . both in the City and Country, sometimes by word of mouth, and others sometimes by writing." In 1629 copies of a book by William Prynne were distributed through the network to William Bridge, Thomas Ball, Anthony Tuckney, Samuel Ward, and Stephen Marshall, among others. Correspondence helped clergy and laymen put local events in a national and international perspective, but it was not limited to weighty issues. Friends exchanged gossip, asked about each other's families and fellow acquaintances, and performed services for each other. Bedell and Samuel Ward of Cambridge, both of whom were avid gardeners, sent each other seeds and plant graftings. Perhaps the best expression of what such correspondence could mean is to be found in a letter from Ezekiel Rogers to Lady Barrington in 1626. Rogers, who had been seriously ill, explained that "though I have had more need of letters & comfort from my friends, then benefitt to write, yet now so soone as I am a little recovered I long to be talking (at least in paper) with those, with whom sometime I have had sweete communion."[26]

Lay leaders of the reform movement were, of course, also part of the correspondence chain, playing a variety of functions. John Winthrop, who had brought Puritan clergy to Groton Manor to preach, received letters from clerical friends such as Nathaniel Ward, Ezekiel Culverwell, John Wilson, William Ames, and Henry Jessey. Nathaniel Rich exchanged lengthy letters on current affairs with Samuel Ward, the master of Sidney Sussex, among others. The earl of Lincoln received considerable information from and regarding lay and clerical leaders in New England during the early 1630s and shared it with his friend John Cotton. Lady Mary Vere corresponded with John Preston, William Ames, John Davenport, and the chaplains of the English volunteer regiments in the Netherlands, one of which was commanded by her husband. Lady Joan Barrington corresponded with William Hooke, Ezekiel Rogers, and Roger Williams, among others. Another function laymen would play was to provide a letter drop. Thus, for instance, when Henry Jessey was without a settled living he instructed his correspondents to direct letters for him to Henry Overton's bookshop in Pope's Head Alley in London, where he would periodically pick up his mail. This was more than a convenience, since it also served to shield the residence of a radical clergyman from the eyes of the authorities.[27]

Whether they came together face to face or through correspondence, Puritan clergymen found in such friendships the type of support they needed to persevere in their nonconformity. Continuing contacts with each other also enabled them to expand their communion, and in many cases the friends of their friends became their friends as well. John Winthrop introduced Thomas Hewson to Henry Jessey. William Bridge introduced Thomas Shepard to the Mrs. Corbet who would later assist Shepard. While a member of Sir Matthew Boynton's household Henry Jessey became friends with Sir Richard Saltonstall, Sir William Constable, and Philip Nye. Divinity students sent by John Preston or others to study at the home of a friend also would fall into this category if that recommendation resulted in friendship.[28]

The records abound in references to friendships of which details are not provided. Thus, although we are told by contemporary sources that John Norton and Thomas Shepard were friends in England in the 1620s and that Samuel Clarke knew Richard Mather, we are not sure when or how they first met, when and how often they got together, or the details of how they benefitted from that relationship. Nevertheless, many examples of friendship at work can be elicited and they provide insight into what friendship could mean for members of the network. Through the 1620s and 1630s and beyond Puritan friends aided and advised each other, remembered each other in their wills, cooperated in publishing projects, sheltered one another, and labored together in the cause of English reformation.

Friends in need often received help from members of the network. Thomas Hooker used his influence in 1627 to obtain a lectureship for Jeremiah Burroughes at Bury St. Edmunds. John Knowles recommended Matthew Newcomen to succeed John Rogers in the lectureship at Dedham. Arthur Hildersham suggested William Gouge for a vacancy at St. Anne's Blackfriars. Thomas Hill gave advice on appointments to Sir Robert Harley. John Cotton interceded with his friend Lewis Bayly, the bishop of Bangor, to arrange the ordination of John Angier without Angier making the required subscription. John Preston used his influence at court to secure the release of Arthur Hildersham and his restoration to his living at Ashby-de-la-Zouche. Colonel Edward Harwood, a Puritan and one of the commanders of the English volunteers in the Netherlands, interceded with Prince Maurice to get William Ames appointed to the faculty of the University of Franeker when the Puritan divine was forced to leave England. Henry Whitefield was able to warn his friend John Stoughton of danger from the authorities in 1634. William Bridge received offers of lectureships at Colchester and Norwich through the efforts of William Gouge and Richard Sibbes. Thomas Goodwin recommended John Arrowsmith of St. Catharine's College for a lectureship at King's Lynn. Samuel Fairclough initially turned down the living at Barnardiston because he did not want to stand in the way of his friend Thomas Welde, who was also under consideration. When Thomas Shepard was evading the bishop's agents Ezekiel Rogers arranged for him to be sheltered in the home of Sir Richard Darley. Richard Rogers and Ezekiel Culverwell covenanted together to watch over each other and help each other lead godly lives. Similarly, in 1646 Ralph Josselin recorded in his diary that "upon an apprehension of the weaknesse of my owne spirit, I made serious covenant with a deare friend to be a help to mee in the way of god, and to watch over my heart." Sometimes what was most important was not the help itself but the assurance such gestures gave that one was part of a community of friends that was also a communion of saints.[29]

In the 1620s and 1630s influential Puritan gentry were often best placed to offer material assistance to members of the network. When the bishop of London initially vetoed John Davenport's call to the parish of St. Stephen's Coleman Street, Davenport was able to call upon the intercession of Lady Mary Vere and her brother-in-law Sir Edward Conway to gain reversal of that decision. Lady Vere, who was also a close friend of John Preston and William Ames, later took care of the Davenports' son John when the parents left England in 1637, keeping the child with her until they were able to arrange his subsequent passage to New England. John Maidstone assisted George Phillips to migrate to New England. Lady Joan Barrington gave financial assistance to Stephen Marshall, Arthur Hildersham, Richard Blackerby, Thomas Hooker, and Nathaniel Ward, among others. The earl of Warwick was notorious for aggressively shielding members of the network from the church authorities. When John Wilson was suspended and imprisoned Warwick obtained his release and a relaxation of his suspension. When Hugh Peter was placed under arrest for sedition (he was said to have declared the damnation of Queen Henrietta Marie in a fast sermon preached at Warwick's request) the earl was initially unsuccessful in securing his release, but did eventually obtain his freedom on bail, which the earl posted. He informed his "loving friend Mr. Peter" that he was his "asshured friend & Patron" and assisted the clergyman to skip bail and flee to the Netherlands. Warwick, the earl of Holland, and the earl of Manchester all sought to prevent Jeremiah Burroughes's deprivation in 1637, but to no avail. Warwick then sheltered Burroughes for several months. The clergyman's sermon "Courage in Evil Times" was probably preached in Warwick's house in 1638 to a group that included Oliver Cromwell and John Hampden. The ties between Burroughes and Warwick were strong enough that when the earl was taken ill in London about this time he sent for Burroughes to be with him. When John Stoughton was summoned to appear before the High Commission Sir Robert Harley accompanied him.[30]

When Thomas Hooker finally came to the unfavorable attention of Bishop Laud his clerical and lay friends both rallied to his cause. Stephen Marshall, Thomas Welde, and Nathaniel Ward were among forty-nine ministers of

Essex (seven of whom were former members of Emmanuel College) who sent a petition to Laud on Hooker's behalf, but it was ineffectual. The earl of Warwick intervened to try to have Hooker excused from appearing before the Court of High Commission. When that too failed Warwick had one of his tenants post Hooker's bond. Meanwhile Hooker was soliciting advice from friends as to what course to follow. He conferred with Richard Sibbes, John Rogers, and Thomas Welde. In company with John Cotton and Roger Williams he rode to the earl of Lincoln's estate to talk with members of the New England Company who were meeting there in July of 1629. Having decided to forfeit his bond and not appear to place himself in the hands of the authorities, he again was aided by Warwick. The earl hid Hooker for a time on one of his estates, helped him to escape to the Netherlands, and provided for Hooker's family until they could join him. On his arrival in the Netherlands Hooker took up residence with his friend Hugh Peter until he could find a position. Later, when he secretly returned to England in order to embark for Massachusetts, he was sheltered by his friend the Reverend Samuel Stone in Towcester.[31]

The earl of Warwick's flouting of the authorities to help Wilson, Peter, Burroughes, Hooker, and others was dramatic but not exceptional. Though evidence of such illegal interventions would, for obvious reasons, be hard to find, similar cases can be documented. Katherine Redich described Arthur Hildersham as her "bosom friend" and she and her husband frequently shielded him. Henry Whitefield at various times sheltered John Cotton, Thomas Hooker, Philip Nye, and Thomas Goodwin. The earl of Lincoln took in Samuel Skelton when he lost his living. The earl of Holland secured John Stoughton's release from prison in 1635. Returning from Massachusetts to get his wife, John Wilson stayed with Nathaniel Rogers. The earl of Huntingdon was noted for aiding Puritan clergy. When John Cotton and his wife were seriously ill, the earl of Lincoln brought them to his estate to be cared for. When Cotton was suspended for his nonconformity Lincoln again aided him. Then, traveling to London, the fugitive was sheltered by his friends Thomas Goodwin, John Davenport, and Philip Nye. For a time Cotton took refuge with Henry Whitefield in Ockley, County Surrey, where Thomas Hooker and Davenport secretly visited him. When John Stoughton was brought before the High Commission, Sir Robert Harley accompanied him "and earned the 'favors' of the archbishop for his efforts." The earl of Lincoln successfully intervened on behalf of Anthony Whiting when he was cited for nonconformity. In 1637 Jeremiah Burroughes and William Bridge, having been silenced by Bishop Wren and taken refuge in the Netherlands for a time, returned to England in disguise. They landed at Yarmouth to smuggle books and letters into the country. The two clergymen were sheltered by

Miles Corbet, a friend of John Winthrop who would later sit in the Long Parliament and eventually be executed as a regicide.[32]

The extent of network aid to members in trouble can perhaps best be appreciated by focusing on the experience of one young clergyman, Thomas Shepard. The youthful Shepard had been converted at Cambridge by John Preston. He later recorded in his autobiography his thanks to God for having exposed him to the influence of Preston and Thomas Goodwin while he was a student there. In the mid-1620s he began to lodge with Thomas Welde and his family in Terling, Essex. He attended the meetings of the Chelmsford conference and became a close friend of Thomas Hooker, whose eldest daughter Shepard would later take as his second wife. The conference recommended Shepard for a lectureship at Earls Colne. There he made converts of the leading family of the community, the Harlackendens, who would always support their clerical friend (and his successor Ralph Josselin). Richard Harlackenden would later become an officer in the parliamentary army; his brother Roger would emigrate to Massachusetts with Shepard. Shepard's nonconformity eventually brought him to the attention of Bishop Laud. Thomas Welde, Daniel Rogers, Nathaniel Ward, Stephen Marshall, and Samuel Wharton gathered at Braintree to discuss Shepard's situation and offer their advice. Deciding to take a stand, Shepard (accompanied by Welde) confronted Laud and was silenced. Despite the risk of further penalties the clergyman began an underground preaching ministry that ended only with his departure from England in 1635. During this period Sir Richard Darley and his brother Henry made £20 a year available toward Shepard's support. Shepard was sheltered by various friends, staying for a time with Edward Collins, who would emigrate to Massachusetts and whose clergyman son, John, would return to England in the 1650s to help carry the reform standard. Shepard next took refuge with William Bridge at Yarmouth. The wife of Sir John Corbet, a friend of Bridge, offered Shepard use of a house she owned in Bastwick. He stayed there for half a year, accompanied by Roger Harlackenden, who "paid all the charge of housekeeping." Leaving Bastwick, Shepard stayed with Jeremiah Burroughes in Norfolk and then with additional friends in London while waiting to sail for Massachusetts.[33]

Less dramatic, but equally important, was the assistance in the form of counsel that members of the network provided each other, whether it was Thomas Hooker's advice to Simeon Ashe on preaching ("Sim, let it be hot!") or whether it dealt with such important questions as conformity and emigration. John Dod commended Sibbes on the latter's sermon on Canticles that he had sent Dod in manuscript. Like his tutor William Perkins before him, and like other Cambridge fellows, Samuel Ward was frequently asked for advice on theological issues. Thomas Gataker wrote to ask Ward's views on the revision of one of his manuscripts. Francis Tayler requested that Ward review a treatise on the "faith of the Church of England." Other clergy turned to Ward to borrow books. Though Ward would remain loyal to the king at the outbreak of the civil wars, during the decades when the religious lines in England were drawn between Calvinists and Arminians, Ward was seen as a spokesman at the university for the Puritan viewpoint.[34]

The ties of communion led friends to extend each other advice, aid, and comfort. Thomas Dugard reviewed his friend Daniel Evans's maiden sermon to the Warwick Castle lecture the day before it was delivered. John Cotton influenced Henry Whitefield toward Congregationalism. Thomas Hooker exerted a strong influence on the religious views of Thomas Shepard, John Eliot, and many others. John Wilson would not accept a call to a church in Sudbury until he had received the advice and support of his ministerial friends. Hugh Peter late in life recollected how in the 1620s, when in a troubled state because of a "sense of sinful estate," he traveled to Essex and was calmed and brought to a state of inner peace by the "love and labours of Mr Thomas Hooker." On a more practical level, Nathaniel Rogers decided against wearing the surplice during services after consulting with Hooker. Francis Higginson was converted to nonconformity by Hooker and Arthur Hildersham, and John Beadle traced his Congregational views to Hooker. While they rode to the 1629 meeting of the New England Company, Hooker, Cotton, and Williams discussed the question of to what degree they should conform to church practices they disapproved of. In 1632 Cotton conferred with Philip Nye, John Davenport, and Thomas Goodwin on the same issue of conformity. Goodwin and Davenport sought to keep Cotton from trouble by urging him to conform to various practices. They hoped he would then be able to continue as a force for reform in England, but by then the Boston clergyman felt that there was no turning back from the course that had brought him under the scrutiny of the authorities. Conformity was more and more difficult as the Laudian movement began to control the church. As the four friends wrestled with these issues Nye, Goodwin, and Davenport were persuaded to follow the risky path being walked by Cotton. Nye had a manuscript of "all the conferences . . . [with] Cotton upon this subject," which probably circulated among other members of the network. Soon they followed Cotton's example in leaving England and they continued to correspond with and be influenced by Cotton. Robert Baillie later blamed Cotton for Goodwin's continued drift toward Congregational practices, claiming that Goodwin "was brought by his [Cotton's] Letters from New England to follow him unto this step also of his progress."[35]

In addition to his discussions with Goodwin and Davenport, Cotton sought the advice of other friends—including John Dod—regarding where he could best serve the Lord if he were forced to leave England. Cotton was among many who solicited such advice as they contemplated the long voyage to the

New World. Thomas Hooker discussed emigration with friends in Chelmsford and the surrounding area. John Davenport consulted with Cotton and Thomas Goodwin on moving to New England. John Dod, the Puritan patriarch who encouraged Cotton and others to embark on their errand into the wilderness, reassured the wife of John Wilson when she came to him with fears about following her husband across the Atlantic.[36]

John Angier, who had lived with John Cotton and married Cotton's niece, considered migration to New England in the 1630s. He traveled to Lancashire ("Lancaster" on the map on p. 18) to visit his wife's connections and there met Richard Mather. Mather invited Angier to preach at Toxteth Park and shortly thereafter Angier was offered a clerical post at nearby Ringley. He discussed his situation with his friends in Lancashire and with Cotton and decided to accept the position rather than emigrate.[37]

The association of clergy in this network of friends was a major stimulus to scholarship and publication. Friends not only encouraged each other to undertake such efforts but assisted in the task of bringing works to press. William Ames translated into Latin William Bradshaw's *English Puritanism* (London, 1610) and later arranged for the posthumous publication of Paul Baynes's *The Diocesans Trial* (London, 1621). Simeon Ashe, who had been a friend of Thomas Ball's from their student days at Cambridge, published some of Ball's sermons after his death. Ball and Thomas Goodwin had worked together to edit the Cambridge sermons of their friend and colleague John Preston as well as a collection of Preston's *Sermons Preached Before his Majestie* (London, 1630). Richard Sibbes and John Davenport combined to perform the same labor of love on Preston's Lincoln's Inn sermons. Davenport was said to have been particularly close to Preston. Thomas Pierson edited sermons of William Perkins for posthumous publication. Thomas Goodwin and John Cotton issued several editions of sermons preached by Richard Sibbes. After Sibbes died in 1635 Goodwin combined with Philip Nye to bring out a collection of Sibbes's sermons. Hugh Peter prepared some of William Ames's works for publication. John Yates eventually edited some of the works of his friend Jeremiah Burroughes.[38]

A related service was offered by clergymen who wrote a preface to introduce the work of a friend to the reading public. Cotton wrote a note "to the Godly Reader" for Arthur Hildersham's *Lectures Upon the Fourth of John* (London, 1629). William Ames wrote the preface to Paul Baynes's *Diocesans Trial*. Thomas Hooker contributed the preface to William Ames's *A Fresh Suit Against Human Ceremonies in God's Worship* (Amsterdam, 1633) and to John Rogers's *The Doctrine of Faith* (London, 1629). Hugh Peter wrote a preface to Ames's volume on the Psalms. These and other such efforts would become more common as the civil wars opened greater access to the press for Puritans in the 1640s.[39]

Whereas the preceding paragraphs have focused on publications in the sense of printed manuscripts, it should be pointed out that some of the most important "publications" were circulated in manuscript. John Dury's commentary on Colossians, responses of Hooker and Davenport to John Paget, the manuscript reviewing the discussions between Cotton and his friends regarding the limits of conformity—these and many other such items, most of which do not survive, were passed from friend to friend in the network. The same was true of sermon notes, which were circulated clandestinely until it became possible to print them in the 1640s and 1650s.

As members of the older generation of the Puritan network passed away they left testimony to their friendships in their wills. In requests for a close friend to deliver a funeral sermon, in their choice of executors, and in their naming of beneficiaries they recorded the ties that bound them as friends to former teachers, students, and colleagues. William Perkins named Laurence Chaderton as one of his executors. John Preston named Richard Sibbes, John Cotton, Peter Bulkeley, Thomas Hooker, and John Dod as beneficiaries. Richard Sibbes remembered John Pym in his will. Most of his clerical friends had left England when this inspirational figure died, but he named as executors noted Puritan gentry including Sir Nathaniel Rich and Sir Nathaniel Barnardiston. Isaac Johnson, the grandson of Laurence Chaderton who had migrated to New England with John Winthrop, remembered Chaderton and John Cotton with personal gifts and left "the advowson and right of patronage of the Rectory and Parish Church of Clipsham" to be administered by Cotton, Richard Bellingham, and Thomas Dudley. Among the executors he named were John Winthrop and John Hampden. Lady Katherine Barnardiston willed money to Stephen Marshall to distribute to needy clergy and to John Dury in support of his efforts at Christian union. The earl of Warwick's second wife left monetary legacies to Samuel Wharton, John Beadle, and Daniel Rogers.[40]

Additional insight into friendship bonds can be found at the deathbeds of Puritans and in their choices of whom they chose to preach their funeral sermons. John Wilson and John Knowles were present at the death of John Rogers. On his own deathbed years later Wilson expressed his belief that "I shall ere long be with my old friends Dr. Preston, Dr. Sibs, Dr. Taylor, Dr. Gouge, Dr. Ames, Mr. Cotton, Mr. Norton, my Inns of Court friends and my consort." Clearly such occasions called for remembrance of friends current and past. John Dod delivered John Preston's funeral sermon. John Knowles performed the same service for John Rogers and Matthew Newcomen for Samuel Collings. Thomas Gataker eulogized his friend Richard Stock in *Abraham's Decrease* (London, 1627), which was dedicated to Sir Henry Yelverton, who had been a member of Stock's congregation. Samuel Ward of Ipswich preached a memorial sermon in honor of John Carter in 1634. Hugh

Peter preached the service for William Ames, and Richard Sibbes asked that William Gouge preach at his funeral.[41]

Such occasions also illuminated the connections between lay and clerical members of the network. John Preston died at the home of Sir Richard Knightley (a relation of the Barnardistons and Hampdens) and when Thomas Ball and Thomas Goodwin prepared Preston's *Golden Sceptre* (London, 1638) for posthumous publication they dedicated it to Knightley, to whom they referred as a special friend of the dead divine. Samuel Fairclough's *The Saints Worthiness and the World's Worthlessness* (London, 1653) was a funeral sermon for Sir Nathaniel Barnardiston. Richard Sibbes preached the funeral sermons for Sir Thomas Crew and for Thomas Sherland. Thomas Goodwin's *A Fair Prospect* (London, 1658) was a funeral sermon for Lady Judith Barrington. Such examples could be multiplied many times, though not all such efforts were published. The members of the network called on their own to commemorate their departed loved ones.[42]

Through such everyday patterns of concern expressed, assistance given, and ideas exchanged, the Puritan network sustained, strengthened, and expanded itself. A broad Puritan network emerged that united clergymen with lay men and women and Presbyterians with Congregationalists. Within this larger movement a network of congregationally inclined ministers had its own distinctive existence. Included in it were ministers such as John Cotton, Thomas Hooker, Thomas Goodwin, Jeremiah Burroughes, Thomas Welde, and others whose friendships and communion had taken root at Cambridge and flowered through the activities of conferences, combination lectures, and correspondence. Thomas Shepard would echo the type of sentiment shared by many when he gave thanks to "the God that carried me into Essex from Cambridge and gave me the sweet society of so many godly ministers, as Mr. Hooker and Mr. Wells [Welde] and Mr. Wharton, Mr. Beadle, and Mr. Burrows [Burroughes], etc." Friends, kin, colleagues—in these and other roles Puritan clergy and their lay supporters developed a system for survival. But the goal of the Puritan movement was not merely survival. The main purpose of the network was to nurture the reform of England and in the 1620s it would develop a number of initiatives directed to that end.[43]

CHAPTER THREE

United for Reform

ALTHOUGH lectures, conferences, correspondence, and similar forms of interpersonal exchange helped to extend the clerical communion, the historically significant role of the network was in sustaining clerical unity and mobilizing support for the major Puritan crusades of the time. Whether in organizing aid for Protestants abroad, raising money to buy livings for Puritan clergymen at home, or planning settlements across the Atlantic, Puritan clergymen called upon their friends. These were among the matters discussed at conferences and in correspondence. Experience in such endeavors tested and reinforced old ties and provided the opportunities for the formation of new ones.

As far back as one can trace their reform movement, Puritans had identified with the cause of international Protestantism. But in the ways in which they developed and expressed this viewpoint, Puritans helped define their movement and give it purpose. Their vision of history centered upon a conviction that England was an elect nation chosen by God to lead his saints to universal triumph in the battle against the anti-Christian legions of the pope. As John Milton expressed it, "When God is decreeing some great work of Reformation to be done, what does he then but reveal himself as is his manner first to his Englishmen." William Bradford expressed the same sentiment when he wrote that "England was the first nation to which the Lord gave the light of the gospel after the darkness of popery." Nurtured on the writings of John Foxe and other exponents of England's mission, Puritans were responsive to the idea that the thousand-year rule of the saints was imminent and that they had been chosen for a crucial role in inaugurating it. Yet they were crusaders not merely for a reformed England but for a reformed Christendom. They identified with and supported what they often referred to as "the best reformed churches throughout Christendom." When John Cotton preached that "all the Saints in Christendome have but one king," he was echoing the Geneva catechism's explanation of the word *catholic* as used in the Creed: "This word means that as there is but one Head of the faithful so they ought all to be united in one body."[1]

The internationalism of the Puritan faction was probably due in part to the experiences abroad of some of the early reformers. Though the Marian exile was the most famous such exodus to continental refuge, both before and after the reign of Queen Mary English nonconformists found havens in the reformed centers of Europe when crackdowns on dissent forced them temporarily from their native land. In the seventeenth century members of the network would likewise feel comfortable on the continent—from William Ames, Thomas Goodwin, and Hugh Peter in the first decades of the century to Matthew Mead and John Howe in the 1670s and 1680s. Various connections between reformers and continental Protestants were also forged in England. Dedicated Calvinists in the English church maintained contact with Reformed and other "stranger" churches in London, some of which served foreign merchants and diplomats. Other such congregations were exile communities whose flight from their native lands was testimony to the threat of the Catholic Counter-Reformation. Additionally, some young continental clergymen traveled to England to study under John Cotton and other English reformers.[2]

Recognizing a tie to other reformed churches, Puritans historically endorsed efforts to heal the divisions in Protestant Christendom. Irenic leaders had sought various types of Protestant union during the reign of Elizabeth. In the seventeenth century the leading advocate of such union was John Dury. By far his greatest English support came from within the Puritan network. Richard Sibbes, John Stoughton, Stephen Marshall, Richard Holdsworth, John White, John Davenport, Samuel Ward, Thomas Goodwin, Thomas Taylor, Cornelius Burgess, Adoniram Byfield, Sydrach Simpson, and Philip Nye all gave Dury assistance. Nye and Davenport were singled out as "forward, earnest and judicious in the work" in correspondence between Dury and his close ally Samuel Hartlib. These members of the network signed his petitions, led their congregations in prayer, recommended Dury to their friends, and in some cases donated funds for his cause. In later decades these clergymen and others within the network would continue to support Dury's plans for Protestant union.[3]

As they hoped to bring Protestant churches together, English Puritans were also committed to soliciting English support for continental Protestants in their struggles against Catholic foes. One of the dominant themes of seventeenth-century English history was an ongoing and intense anti-Catholicism. Many Englishmen viewed their time as one in which the climactic struggle between Christ and Antichrist—Protestant and Catholic—was being waged. This perception was not the monopoly of Puritans but was to be found among all who identified as Puritans, and it firmly colored their views on international news and domestic politics. In the 1620s the Puritans had two pressing foreign concerns. They watched with anxiety the fortunes of the Protestant cause in the Thirty Years' War and they followed with concern Spanish threats to the continued independence of the Netherlands.[4]

The Thirty Years' War began as a struggle between the Catholic Archduke Ferdinand and the Calvinist Frederick, Elector of the Palatine, who was the son-in-law of James I. Ferdinand was chosen king-elect of Bohemia in 1617. When he moved firmly against Protestant dissidents he sparked a revolt in Bohemia. The state's Assembly repudiated the earlier election and chose Frederick as king. Ferdinand, who became Holy Roman Emperor in 1619, responded by using his full resources in an effort not only to suppress the Bohemian revolt but to crush Protestantism throughout the empire.[5]

The cause of Frederick of Palatine was supported by many Englishmen; for Puritans it became identical with the cause of international Protestantism. As the conflict expanded it assumed an almost cosmic significance. Here was Armageddon, where the forces of good and evil were arrayed against each other. But whereas Londoners attempted to stage an illumination in celebration of Frederick's accession to the Bohemian throne, James I officially denied any prior knowledge of his son-in-law's move, and "pronounced [it] rash." The fate of the Palatine soon came to involve the security of the Netherlands. Spain supported Emperor Ferdinand and in return was granted permission to cross imperial lands to launch an attack on the Netherlands when the Spanish-Dutch truce expired in 1621. Five days after the truce with Spain had expired the Dutch welcomed Frederick and Elizabeth to The Hague and within a month an alliance was signed between the two Protestant states. The Dutch also allied themselves with the Protestant king of Denmark.[6]

None of these developments was sufficient to stem the Catholic tide. In the summer of 1622 Spanish forces under Ambrogio Spinola laid siege to the key Dutch fortress of Bergen op Zoom and imperial forces under Count Tilly virtually completed the conquest of the Palatine. Catholic forces massacred the English defenders of Heidelberg. A small garrison of English volunteers at Frankenthall represented the last Protestant foothold in Frederick's former lands. King James, attempting to negotiate the marriage of the prince of Wales to the Spanish infanta, ignored his son-in-law's plight, ordered the

English to withdraw from Frankenthall, and allowed the Spanish to recruit English subjects to fight in their regiments in the Palatine.[7]

Support for Frederick and Elizabeth and for the Dutch cause became a distinguishing mark of the Puritan movement in England and won the dissenters the sympathy of other internationally minded Englishmen. The international orientation of the Puritan clerical brotherhood had created numerous links with Reformed divines on the continent such as Middelburg's Teelinck as well as with leaders of the foreign churches in England. Continental clergymen such as John Rulice, Jonas Proost, and Wilhelm Thilenius had studied under members of the network. Cesar Calandrini, later preacher at Austin Friars, corresponded with John Davenport, Hugh Peter, Thomas Gataker, and other Puritans. Such contacts were both sources for news regarding the trials of continental Protestantism and further reason for Puritan sympathies for that cause. In contrast to the ongoing refusal of James I, and later Charles I, to involve England and royal flirtations with Spain, Puritans applauded Count Mansfield when he came to London seeking support in 1624, praised Christian IV of Denmark when he intervened to rescue the Protestant cause in 1625, and gave thanks when Gustavus Adolphus of Sweden sought to redeem the cause following Christian's defeat. They mourned the death of Frederick in 1632 and continued to support their princess, Elizabeth of Bohemia. They drew sharp contrasts between Protestant champions such as Christian and Gustavus and their own monarchs, who offered Spain an alliance and established diplomatic contacts with the papacy.[8]

Members of the Puritan network worked in concert in a number of ways to advance the Protestant cause. Fast days—a practice adopted from the Reformed churches on the continent—were observed in many English congregations as they sought God's aid for the Protestant forces. Members of the network used their pulpits to voice a chorus of concern in an effort to waken the English public and government to the crisis. "Shall the members of Christ suffer in other countries, and we profess ourselves to be living members, and YET NOT SYMPATHIZE WITH THEM?" asked Richard Sibbes. "Let us," he urged on another occasion, "consider with what hearts we entertain those doleful and sad reports of foreign churches." "When we can hear of the estate of the church abroad, the poor church in the Palatine, in Bohemia and those places, . . . when we hear of those things and are not affected it is a sign we have hollow and dead hearts." "We forget the misery of the church in other places," he chided, informing his congregation that "they pray and call upon us, as farre as Heidleberg, as farre as France, that we would take notice of their afflictions." Sibbes refused to despair at the bad news from the continent. "For the present state of the church, we see how forlorn it is, yet let us comfort ourselves that Christ's cause shall prevail," for, as he believed,

"Christ and his church, when they are at the lowest, are nearest rising; his enemies at the highest are nearest a downfall." Sibbes constantly reminded his listeners that the cause of reform abroad should be England's cause. Preaching about the continental Protestants, he claimed that "they and we make but one body. That member that hath not a sympathy with the body, it is but a dead member. Therefore if we be not affected with the presence of God with the armies abroad, we are dead members."[9]

John Preston, in sermons preached at the royal court as well as elsewhere, echoed the same sentiments. "Are we infatuate and see nothing?" he asked in the 1620s. "Doe we not see the whole bodie of those that professe the truth besieged round about through Christendome; at this time are not present armies not only stired up, but united together and we disjoyned to assist them; are not our Allies wasted; are not many branches of the Church cut off already, and more in hazard. In a word . . . have not things been long going downhill, and are now hastening to a period?" Preston used this type of refrain frequently, trying to alert England's leaders to the distressed state of reformed religion and criticizing the king's pro-Catholic foreign policy. In frequent touch with clerical and lay members of the network, Preston was looked to for leadership by his friends on account of his influence for a time with the duke of Buckingham and Prince Charles. In addition to raising these concerns in his sermons, Preston also worked behind the scenes to advance the cause. On one such occasion he provided some of his noble friends with arguments against the proposed Spanish match.[10]

William Bridge, preaching in exile to a regiment of English volunteers in the Netherlands, urged them to "pray for all the Churches, pray for Germany, the first place of reformation, pray for Holland, your hiding place, and in all your prayers forget not England, still pray for England." Thomas Hooker, in a sermon preached in 1626, lamented that "the fire of God's fury hath flamed and consumed all the country round about us; Bohemia, and the Palatinate, and Denmark"; and in that same year Hugh Peter told a London congregation that "God hath wept over England. Come Lord," he urged, "knock one more and enter. . . . Has thou dealt so with Bohemia & the Palatinate? Bow & buckle our harts at last." Preaching to the members of the London Artillery Company, John Davenport told them that "the distress of our brethren abroad should quicken us to the use of all means, whereby we may be enabled to help them. If a neighbours Oxe, or Horse be in a ditch, we will even runne to helpe it out, saith our Saviour: much more if his house be on fire; most of all, if the danger be of the losse of their Countrey, of Religion, Families, lives and all." Military efforts were an important means of tendering aid (and many Englishmen volunteered), but not the only one. "In Ecclesiastical Histories we read," preached Davenport, "of an Army of Christians . . . [who] by prayer they obtained, that God scattered their enemies." Prayers had served the Protestant cause in England in "that *Mirabilis anno*, in 88, when the prayers of God's people prevailed to raise the winds, which scattered that *Invincible Armado*." Prayer was like other weaponry: "the more exercise, the more skill; the more courage, the better successe."[11]

Both John Cotton and William Gouge read apocalyptic significance into the struggle, linking the banishment of Reformed ministers from Heidelberg to the departure of a righteous remnant before divine judgment. Gouge and Thomas Hooker drew lessons for England from the Protestant reverses on the continent. Unless England reformed, she too would face divine retribution. In a sermon preached in November of 1626 Hooker asked, "Why may I not say . . . that the Lord hath an eye unto me [England] above all the rest . . . when the fire of God's fury hath flamed and consumed all the country round about us?" A few days later Hooker's friend Hugh Peter drew the same lesson for a London congregation. "How God hath wept for England," he told his countrymen. Thomas Gataker warned that if England did not "help and releeve" Protestants abroad "the Curse of Meroz may light upon us; we and ours may be destroyed; the destruction threatened them may be inflicted on us." Not only did such sermons evoke the type of prayers that Davenport called for, but in uniting Puritans in a prayerful barrage they solidified the movement and heightened its members' sense of community in a shared enterprise.[12]

Corresponding with one another, listening to each other preach, gathering to discuss the plight of international Protestantism, these clerical friends tuned their pulpits to a common pitch and thundered forth against the failure of England to assume her proper role in history. For some, prayers and sermons were not sufficient outlets for their concern. English volunteers fought for the Palatinate, for the freedom of the Netherlands, and with French Protestants in that country's wars of religion. Certainly not all were Puritans, and many who fought had no religious interest in the struggle. But among those who would later fight under parliamentary standards in England's civil wars, Thomas Fairfax, Philip Skippon, and George Monck saw service in the Thirty Years' War. Sir Horace Vere commanded English volunteers in the Palatinate and then in the Netherlands. Sir Edward Harwood, whose brother would later be a member of the Massachusetts Bay Company, was another colonel of English volunteers. Theophilus Clinton, the fourth earl of Lincoln and a friend of John Cotton's, considered leading troops to the continent in 1626 and summoned Thomas Dudley, his steward, to join him. Dudley, who had himself fought in France as a volunteer in that country's wars of religion, stopped in Cambridge to discuss the matter with John Preston. Advice from Preston, Dudley, and other friends persuaded Clinton to postpone his plans, but in 1629 he took the field under Mansfield in command of three hundred English volunteers.[13]

Clerical members of the network as well as laymen served the cause. When war broke out in the Germanic states William Ames was chaplain to Sir Horace Vere on the continent. Later Obadiah Sedgwick held that post. William Bridge preached to English troops serving in the Netherlands. John Preston visited Elizabeth of Bohemia at The Hague in 1622 and offered his services as her chaplain. Hugh Peter left the congregation he served in Rotterdam to join the English volunteers in the defense of Bergen op Zoom in 1631, later writing a ten-page account of the defense, *Digitus Dei, or Good Newes from Holland* (Rotterdam, 1631). Peter also served as chaplain to Colonel Harwood's troops in the siege of Maestricht and in 1632 visited the Swedish army in Germany, where he saw the "Lion of the North," Gustavus Adolphus.[14]

Puritans in Parliament used their influence in efforts to shift the king and persuade him to send more than volunteers to the support of the beleaguered Protestants. Members of the clerical network were energetic in fostering such parliamentary initiatives. Using sermons, petitions, personal contact, and correspondence, they reminded their lay friends and patrons of their responsibilities to God. Many members of Parliament listened to the sermons of Richard Sibbes, John Preston, and Joseph Caryl at the Inns of Court in the 1620s. The Privy Council made every effort to restrain criticism of government policy, taking action to discourage public attacks and inhibiting opposition correspondence by intercepting and examining letters. Yet considerable correspondence exists to show clerical influence on parliamentary Puritans. The largest such collection to survive is in the letters of Sir Robert Harley. Harley exchanged news and views with numerous clergymen, including William Gouge, Thomas Taylor, John Stoughton, and the rector of his home parish, Thomas Pierson. Sir Nathaniel Rich exchanged lengthy letters with Samuel Ward, the master of Sidney Sussex, and others. The earl of Lincoln corresponded with John Cotton. Among the clerical correspondents of the Barringtons were Ezekiel Rogers, Roger Williams, and William Hooke. The Samuel Ward papers in the Bodleian Library contain extensive correspondence on political concerns such as the Thirty Years' War.[15]

Stirred by reports from friends in the front lines and from other sources, Puritan clergymen organized to raise funds for the defense of the Palatine and the relief of refugees from the advancing Catholic forces. Shortly after an appeal from foreign clergy was read to a consistory of Dutch churches in England meeting at Austin Friars, Richard Sibbes, John Davenport, Thomas Taylor, and William Gouge composed a circular letter on behalf of the cause. The letter told of "the lamentable distresse of two hundred and forty godly preachers with their wives and families of about foure score, desolate widows and sundrie thousands of godly private persons with them cast out of their home, out of their callings and Countries by the furie of the merciless papists in the upper Palatinate." The authors "desire all godly Christians . . . as fellow feelinge members of the same body of Jesus Christ to commiserate their pr[e]sent want and enlarge their harts and hands for some present and private supply for them till some publique manes (which hereafter may be hoped) may be raised for their reliefe, assuringe themselves that whatsoever is cast unto heaven and falleth in the lapp of Christ in his members shall return with abundant increase in the harvest." "We know," they assured potential donors, "a sure and safe way, whereby whatsoever is given, shall undoubtedly come to their hands to whom it is intended."[16]

The letter circulated to members of the network and to lay patrons of Puritanism. Clerical friends such as Hugh Peter and Francis Higginson and laymen such as Isaac Johnson and Isaac Pennington supported the drive. Raising funds to aid needy brethren was a way in which the saints came together in a demonstration of their communion with each other and with the objects of their charity, and it would always be an important activity of the network. A substantial amount was raised by the Reverend John White in Dorchester. In addition to raising money, clergymen like John Cotton sheltered and trained refugee ministers from the war zones. John White took one refugee, John Rulice (a former student of Cotton's), as his curate and another whom he sheltered married the clergyman's niece. More than £1,750 were collected in a brief period. Contributions came from seventy-four parishes. The activities of the ringleaders soon came to the attention of William Laud, newly elevated to the see of London. The fact that the subscriptions for the relief of the Palatine were more forthcoming than payments of the king's forced loan was only one reason for Laud's disapproval of the project. The new bishop had previously commented adversely on the Puritan attachment to Elizabeth of Bohemia and her cause and had recommended against any government relief effort for the dispossessed Protestants. Seeing the effort of Davenport and his friends as subversive of government policy and a challenge to established church authorities, he ordered the four signatories to appear before the Court of High Commission where they were reprimanded and ordered to desist. Despite Laud's reluctance, the government did initiate its own royal collections for the cause and Gouge, Davenport, and other members of the network exerted themselves in the fundraising efforts, the first of which realized £3,700 and the second £5,908.[17]

For the members of the Puritan network and their lay allies, the struggles to free the Palatinate and to purify their native land were related parts of the one task of establishing a reformed Christendom. They believed that England had been chosen by God to lead the cause of international Protestantism and they felt an urgent need to purify the Church of England. This concern became more pronounced in the 1620s when it seemed to many Englishmen that Calvinism was being undermined at home as well as attacked abroad.

The reaction against Calvinist rigidity that was evident in the late sixteenth century in the English universities had continued to gain momentum, yet the official complexion of the English church had remained firmly Calvinist. Between 1579 and 1615 more than thirty-nine English editions of the Geneva Bible were published with predestinarian catechisms bound with them. The Irish Articles of 1615 and the Scottish Confession of 1616—both approved by King James—reflected a strong Calvinist stand, and the Lambeth Articles were perceived as a true, if unofficial, statement of England's creed. The delegation that James sent to the Synod of Dort in 1619 joined in the condemnation of Arminian errors, and in the early 1620s two of those delegates—George Carleton and John Davenant—were elevated to bishoprics. But the tide began to shift shortly after Dort.[18]

In 1622 James issued directions to the clergy prohibiting "popular" preaching on "predestination, reprobation, or the . . . irresistibility of God's grace." Though not as restrictive as later directives, this prohibition seemed to indicate a shift on the king's part. Indeed, it prompted rumors that the king was ready to convert to Catholicism. The man most responsible for moving James in this direction was Richard Neile, the archbishop of York. Neile and the Durham House group he gathered around him became the first organized opposition to English Calvinism. For the first time since the accession of Elizabeth theological issues rather than quarrels over discipline, liturgy, and government began to polarize English Protestants.[19]

Neile and those who shared his views were quickly branded Arminians by their foes, but they were not significantly influenced by the writings of Arminius. The use of the label points to the fact that they shared with the Dutch theologian a desire to modify reformed teachings, and Nicholas Tyacke's use of the term *anti-Calvinist* is more accurate. These Englishmen drew on patristic writings to advance an interpretation of Church of England teachings that allowed greater scope for free will and falling from grace, and emphasized sacraments over preaching the word as an aid in achieving grace. Stressing the "beauty of holiness," they sought to revive ceremonies that the Church of England had long since dispensed with. They emphasized the liturgical calendar at a time when Puritans were seeking to rid the church of special days of celebration, including Christmas. They stressed the importance of episcopacy and downplayed the identification of the papacy with Antichrist.[20]

Accused of Arminianism and Pelagianism by staunch Calvinists, the Durham House group also aroused fears of a restoration of Catholicism. Whereas Neile, William Laud, and other leaders of the faction were by no means Catholic, their views of the sacraments and ceremonies were closer to Rome than to Geneva. Indeed, under Laud the English church ceased to proclaim the pope to be Antichrist. Neile and his supporters were gaining influence in

England as the Thirty Years' War inflamed fears of Catholic reaction, and they achieved a dominant position in the church under Charles I. John Ward wrote of the "artifices of the Prelates for the adultering of the Doctrine of the Gospel, by Arminianisme and Popery, the introducing of Innovations, for the blending and polluting of the publike worship and ordinances of God; the corrupting of the manners of the people." Contributing to the movement's identification with Catholicism were the actions of Charles's queen. The negotiations for a Spanish match, which had aroused great hostility among English Puritans, had failed, but they were followed by Charles's marriage to the French Catholic princess Henrietta Marie—a union that was just as unpopular. John Preston had preached against the match. Thomas Hooker alluded to it by reference to Malachi 2:11–12: "An abomination is committed, Judah hath married the daughter of a strange God, the Lord will cut off the many that doeth this." Hugh Peter publicly prayed that the new queen "would forsake the Idolatry and superstition wherein she was and needes perish if she continued in the service." The queen, of course, did not abandon her faith, but rather became the center of a protected Catholic clique at court. The duke of Buckingham's mother converted to Catholicism and Catholic peers achieved greater influence. The tolerance of the mass at the same time that crypto-Catholic elements were being introduced into the Church of England made it inevitable that the anti-Calvinism of Neile and Laud would be connected in the popular mind with popery.[21]

The influence of the anti-Calvinist faction became evident in the controversy that erupted around Richard Montagu in the mid-1620s. Montagu, a former fellow of King's College, Cambridge, published *A New Gagg for an Old Goose* in 1624. In it he denied that Calvinism was the official creed of the Church of England, labeling absolute predestination, and unconditional perseverance in particular, as merely the private views of some wrong-thinking clerics. John Yates and Nathaniel Ward, both graduates of Emmanuel, prepared a petition that was submitted to Parliament in 1625 and presented to the Commons by John Pym. Pym was the brother-in-law of William Hooke and, according to Conrad Russell, the "gravest crime in Pym's political calendar was that of destroying the purity and the unity of true religion." Montagu, meanwhile, had defended himself against his critics in *Appello Caesarem* (1625), explicitly repudiating the authority of the Synod of Dort and labeling the Calvinist element in the church "Puritans." Yates responded with *Ibis ad Caesarem* (1626) and Henry Burton, Bishop Carleton, and Ezekiel Culverwell likewise entered the lists as critics of Montagu.[22]

William Laud, with whom anti-Calvinism would come to be most closely identified, was bishop of St. David's in 1624 and was in the process of replacing John Preston as the cleric to whom the duke of Buckingham looked for advice. In December of that year, as the Montagu controversy was beginning, Laud drew up a paper, "Doctrinal Puritanism," for the duke in which he identified Calvinists as Puritans. Shortly after the succession of Charles in 1625 Laud provided Buckingham with a list of leading clergy, each identified with either an "O" for "orthodox" or a "P" for "Puritan." As the new regime took shape the Calvinist element in the church—including many who were not Puritans—was excluded from ecclesiastical committees and the king intervened with Parliament to protect Montagu.[23]

Two major efforts were made to suppress Montagu's views in 1626. Pym and Francis Rous (the intellectual leader of the Calvinist gentry) led the attack in Parliament. A subcommittee of Parliament branded Montagu's views as repugnant to the teachings of the Church of England and similar to popery, but Charles dissolved Parliament before both houses could act on the report. On another front Puritan peers including Warwick, Brooke, and Say pressured Buckingham into presiding over a conference where the issues could be debated. Bishop Thomas Morton and John Preston developed the attack on Montagu's views at the York House conference, but the outcome made it clear that Buckingham and the king sided with the anti-Calvinist faction.[24]

The rise of anti-Calvinism tended to sharpen the lines of division in the church. The boundaries of Puritanism are very difficult to establish prior to 1625. Members of the network shared a commitment to Calvinist theology and reformed worship, but were willing to compromise in the early decades of the century because the establishment was equally committed to Calvinism. Even a generally recognized leader of the network such as John Preston cannot be labeled a Puritan if one uses a definition that specifies nonconformity as part of the essence of Puritanism. Though Preston and others were dissatisfied with much in the church, the general troubles facing international Protestantism made them willing to adopt a united front with bishops such as Abbot on many issues. John Davenport best expressed this view in a letter to Alexander Leighton just before the Montagu controversy erupted.

> When we duely Consider the distresses of the Reformed Churches in these days, we shall soon conclude with him that sayd, Non sunt litigandi ista sed orandi tempora [these are not times for disputing but praying]. . . . Were it not better to unite our forces against those who oppose us in Fundam[en]tals then to be divided amongst ourselves about Ceremonialls? Who can, without sorrowe, and feare observe how Atheisme, Libertinisme, papisme, and Arminianisme, both at home, and abroad have stolne in, and taken possession of the house, whilest we are at strife about the hangings and paintings of it? . . . How much better would it beseeme us to combine together in an holy league against the common Adversary.[25]

The success of Neile, Laud, and their supporters in capturing the king's ear and gaining control of the church made such compromise impossible, for what now divided the Puritan clergy from the establishment was fundamentals. Moreover, the fact that Laud's ceremonial innovations were part of his anti-Calvinist package made compromise over ceremonies less palatable. Samuel Ward in 1625 kept a special fast and recorded as "motyves to fasting and publick humiliation: 1. the fear of encreasing of popery, by the permission of the new Queen and her followers for to have their chappell, etc." Looking back over this period from a later perspective, Ralph Josselin noted as "certaine remarkable things that fell out in my remembrance: 1. The marriage of P. Charles K of England etc: to a papist, with so many indulgences to her religion . . . [and] 2. The strange carriage of things in England, a protestant state, wheeling in points of doctrine, in ceremonyes towards popery, and in prosecuting orthodox men of the ministry and otherwise." A few years after having explained his reasons for conformity to Alexander Leighton, Davenport was expressing a far more militant stand: "In a time of *feares* (as the case now stands) . . . men should be like the *Roman Triary*, that would chuse to dye in the fight, rather than to preserve their lives by flight."[26]

The fight to preserve the Calvinist basis of the Church of England for which Davenport and others began to gird themselves achieved one of its earliest successes in the activities of the Feoffees for Impropriations. In 1625 twelve Puritans in London came together to form this unincorporated association. Four members were clergymen: Richard Stock, the rector of All Hallows; Richard Sibbes, then a preacher at Gray's Inn; Charles Offspring, the rector at St. Antholin's; and Davenport, the vicar of St. Stephen's. William Gouge, rector of St. Anne's Blackfriars, was chosen to replace Stock when the latter died early in 1626. The other eight Feoffees were laymen: lawyer John White (the Winthrop family attorney), Samuel Browne (a kinsman of Oliver Cromwell), Ralph Eyre, Christopher Sherland, and merchants John Gering, Richard Davis, George Harwood (Colonel Edwards's brother), and Francis Bridges. A thirteenth member, Alderman Royland Heylin, was added later. Sir Thomas Crew, Speaker of the House of Commons in 1623 and 1625, filled a later vacancy. Samuel Aldersy, a member of Davenport's congregation and brother-in-law of Charles Offspring, was the group's treasurer. The design of the group was to remodel the church from within. The Feoffees solicited funds with which they could purchase church impropriations and advowsons. They appointed curates and lecturers to the livings they then controlled, supplemented the income of other established lecturers (such as those at St. Antholin's), and helped support ejected ministers. Samuel Clarke, one of their supporters, reported that they "met very frequently, and spent much time, and pains in consultation about that business. . . . Their designe was to plant a learned and painful Ministry,

especially in Cities, and Market Towns in several parts of the Kingdom."
With anti-Calvinist teaching on the rise this task assumed a greater importance than ever.[27]

In his analysis of the Feoffees' success Christopher Hill has concluded that
between 1625 and 1633 £6,361.6s.1d was recorded as contributions to the
group. The head of the vestry of St. Stephen's, who described Davenport as
his "good friend," contributed £100 and the recorder of Northampton donated
£400, but most contributions were smaller. The Feoffees acquired real estate
in fourteen counties, and in 1633 they possessed thirty-one church properties
and patronage in eighteen counties. Hugh Peter referred to the effort as "that
famous, ancient, glorious work of buying in impropriations" and claimed that
"40 or 50 preachers were . . . maintained in the dark parts of this kingdom."
Their success generated imitation, with similar groups organized in communities such as Norwich. William Bridge acted as an agent of the Feoffees in
establishing a combination lectureship in Norwich. Twelve residents of that
community organized themselves as "trustees for the advancement of religion
in Norwich and Norfolk." They raised £200, which they sent to "our proto-
trustees in London" who paid Bridge £20 per year to supplement his living at
St. Peter Hungate. The Norwich group also established criteria for supporting
preachers, insisting that they be university graduates and Calvinists. Lancashire merchants living in London pursued a similar course in supporting five
or six ministers in their native county. John Shaw was one of a number of
Puritan clergy placed in a Devon lectureship by merchants born in Devon and
living in London.[28]

Many members of the network were involved with the Feoffees in soliciting,
donating, or receiving funds. William Greenhill was supported by the Feoffees in a lectureship at London's Woolchurch. Thomas Foxley, Zachariah
Symmes, and John Archer—all of whom later migrated to New England—
preached at St. Antholin's when that lectureship was affiliated with the
Feoffees. That affiliation was established with the understanding that lecturers would be at the London parish for six years, after which they would be
placed elsewhere and replaced with new, young clergymen. In line with this
understanding the Feoffees placed Foxley, Symmes, and Archer in other
livings when their apprenticeships ended. Hugh Peter was supported at St.
Antholin's for a time by the Feoffees, attended some of the meetings of the
association, and solicited funds on their behalf. George Hughes was maintained by the Feoffees as lecturer at All Hallows Bread Street in London.
William Prynne was a major supporter of the effort, as was Sir Robert Harley.
Among those whose connection with the group was likely, if unrecorded, was
John Winthrop, who was a friend of a number of the Feoffees.[29]

Certainly the activities of the Feoffees were perceived as a threat by the
church authorities. When the lawyer John White had occasion to appear

before Laud on a separate matter, the bishop established that White was one of the Feoffees and then attacked him as "an enemy of the Church, an underminer of religion." Laud proceeded on this occasion to denounce "this work of his and his fellow-Feofees [as] mischievous to the Church and Destructive to Religion," and he warned that he would "see him and his fellows shortly called to Account for it, and stop them from proceeding in that work." On another occasion Laud referred to the Feoffees as "a cunning, under a glorious pretence, to overthrow the Church Government, by getting into their power more dependency of clergy than the King, and all the Peers, and all the Bishops in all the kingdom had."[30]

The counteroffensive against the Feoffees was initiated by Peter Heylyn, a fellow at Oxford's Magdalen College, in a sermon preached at the university church of St. Mary the Virgin on July 11, 1630. This was Act Sunday—the middle of the degree pageantry—and Heylyn was assured a large and distinguished audience. His account of how he came across the Feoffees and how he perceived their activities, though biased, nevertheless sheds considerable light on the operations of the Puritan clerical network at this time.[31]

Heylyn was in the habit of "resorting . . . to a Town in Glouchestshire, where one of these new *Lectures* had been founded" by the Feoffees. He soon found that the new lecturer installed "was one of notorious Inconformity, found upon further search to have been hunted from one Diocese to another." His investigations led him to an awareness of a conspiracy "to set up stipendiary Lectures in all or most Market-Towns, where the people had commonly less to do, and consequently were more apt to Faction & Innovation than in other places, and of all Market-Towns, to chuse such as were Priviledged for sending Burgesses to the High-Court of Parliament." "What are those intrusted in the managing of this great business?" he asked. "Are they not the most of them the most active and the best affected men in the whole cause, and Magna Partium momenta, Chief Patrons of the Faction? And what are those whom they prefer? Are they not most of them such as must be serviceable to their dangerous innovations? And will they not in time have more preferments to bestow, and therefore more dependencies than all the Prelates in the Kingdom?" Heylyn was convinced that there was a network of Puritan clergy who were seeking to gain control of state and church. He accused them of holding "constant conferences . . . at all publicke meetings and assemblies; here, at our sister universitie, at the great cittie," using such occasions and locations so "their resorte from all corners of the land may be less suspected." Such gatherings of clerical friends were held "to receive intelligence, to communicate their counsailes, and conforme their partie." The Feoffees were but the latest and most dangerous activity whereby they hoped to make "themselves so strong a partie, that the maine counsailes of the state are crossed or carried by them."[32]

Heylyn sent a copy of his sermon, along with supporting information he had gathered, to Laud. He received preferment for his efforts and the material he provided was used in the preparation of a bill introduced in the equity side of the Court of Exchequer in the Easter term of 1632. The Feoffees were accused of behaving like a corporation without having received letters patent and of holding property without the sanction of the crown. William Lenthall, later Speaker of the House of Commons in the Long Parliament, was principal counsel for the defendants. Robert Holborne, who would shortly gain additional notice as John Hampden's attorney in the Ship Money case, assisted Lenthall. Citing both technical breaches of the law and concern that the Feoffees were involved in "introducing many novelties of dangerous consequences, both in church and commonwealth," the judges confiscated the group's funds and suppressed their activities.[33]

There is some dispute as to how grave a threat the Feoffees posed to the church establishment. In theory, of course, their activities had the potential of securing Puritan control of a substantial number of clerical posts. William Prynne, who was noted for occasional exaggeration, believed that if left alone the Feoffees would "in all probability have purchased in most of the great Towns & noted Parishes Impropriations of England in Lay-mens hands, where Preaching was most wanting, and meanes to maintain it." Some historians believe that they were far from reaching their potential when their activities were brought to an end. The government, however, was concerned about the political as well as the religious implications of such a development. The involvement in the Feoffees of parliamentary figures such as White and Crew with clerical leaders such as Sibbes and Davenport was but one of the many signs of a growing fusion of parliamentary and Puritan dissent. Members of the Puritan network were politically active and many were friends with prominent members of the Lords and Commons. They not only drew upon the patronage of such lay leaders, but used their pulpits and influence to help advance the political fortunes of the Puritan movement. Parliament increasingly seemed the best and only hope to reverse the nation's foreign policy and its drift towards Arminianism. In his prosecution of the Feoffees, Attorney General Noy made a special point of charging the group with having emphasized the placement of clergy in boroughs that had representation in Parliament.[34]

The use of the pulpit to influence elections was neither a new development nor one monopolized by the Puritans, but members of the network had become adept at it. In 1604 Lord Rich had sought the election of Sir Francis Barrington as one of the knights of the shire despite the earl of Suffolk's opposition to the candidacy. Arthur Hildersham joined Barrington's household for a time and preached frequently prior to the election, which Barrington won. Heylyn, whose uncle was both a member of the Feoffees and a

London alderman, accused the Feoffees of seeking to influence elections. Henry Sherfield, Sir Thomas Fanshaw, and Christopher Sherland (himself a Feoffee) were supported by the network and chosen to sit in the 1626 Parliament, where all three were outspoken in the attack on Montagu. John Davenport supported Sir Roger Townshend, a Norfolk MP, to whom the clergyman referred as having "strong complyance with the best affected patriots in parliament." In 1628 Puritan clergy were very active in supporting candidates who shared their views on what was wrong with England. Samuel Ward of Ipswich had always "been influential in securing the election of an unbeaten string of county puritans as knights of the shire." In 1628, when Sir Edward Coke decided to sit for Buckinghamshire instead of taking the Suffolk seat he had also won, it was Ward who "eliminated any opposition to Sir William Spring's special election." Also in 1628 John Wilson, lecturer at Sudbury, supported Sir Francis Barrington as "the Best of those worthy Zelots and patriots," and Samuel Fairclough supported Sir Nathaniel Barnardiston's candidacy.[35]

Clerical electioneering in cooperation with Puritan peers would be even more noticeable in the elections for the Short and Long Parliaments, coming as they did at a time when the Puritan cause seemed truly desperate. The election of Nathaniel Stephens from Horsely in the Cotswolds was credited to support generated by Puritan clergy. Thomas Ball mobilized backing for Sir Gilbert Pickering. Matthew Newcomen was active in Dedham electioneering. Peter Heylyn received reports from his informants in Gloucestershire that named eleven clergymen working to elect Puritans to Parliament. "Factious Nonconformists" were accused of claiming that the king's candidate in Sandwich was inclined to popery. The earl of Warwick was at the center of Puritan electoral efforts in Essex. A defeated candidate for election to the Short Parliament complained to the authorities that the earl "made good use of his Lord-Lieutenancy, in sending out letters to the captains of the Trainbands . . . which brought many to his side." Furthermore, "Those ministers who gave their voices for my Lord of Warwick, as Mr. [Stephen] Marshall and others, preached often out of their own parishes before the election." When a citizen was arrested for verbally abusing Nevil, the earl allowed the offender to be released on bail. On election day "Mr. [Daniel] Rogers, being a silenced minister, coming into the Sessions' House, they made room for him to sit down, and give him ease by my Lord of Warwick's command." Among those chosen for the Commons over Nevil were Sir Francis Barrington and Sir Harbottle Grimston for the county seats, Sir William Masham and Grimston's son for Colchester, and Sir Henry Mildmay for Maldon—all Warwick candidates and all men with ties to the clerical network.[36]

The pulpit also continued to be used for political purposes other than electioneering as clergymen worked to influence government leaders and citizens. John Preston preached at Barrington Hall to the group of nobles considering means of pressuring Buckingham and the king to repudiate Montagu (the York House conference was the unsuccessful outcome of the resulting effort). John Wilson was jailed for "seditious speeches" against the forced loan and he was not alone in opposing compliance. Throughout Essex resistance to the loan was greatest in areas where Puritan preachers were most active. In December of 1626 Bishop Montaigne reported to Buckingham that "there is rumour of a private fast that was kept on St Andrew's Day last. . . . This only is confessed—that the Earl of Warwick did desire Mr Peters, one of the preachers, to preach that day out of his own church in Christ Church which he did, and, besides, Peters confesses that Sir Robert Harley of the Mint, told him that there were divers who would take the opportunity of the many sermons preached that day to humble themselves to Almighty God in a holy fast." Through such means Puritan clergymen continued to stir up general concern about the state of the nation—there is "sin enough in the Court, city, country, university to take away peace and prince," warned Hugh Peter in 1626.[37]

These efforts did show some results. Supporters of Calvinism led the attack on Montagu in 1626 and were even stronger in 1628. The House of Commons impeached Montagu in that year and censured another anti-Calvinist, Roger Manwaring. In January of 1629 the House voted that "the matter of religion shall have the Precedencie over all other Business" in that session. The Committee on Religion began to receive evidence from a variety of sources, many of them members of the clerical network mobilized for that purpose. Thus, for example, Oliver Cromwell transmitted information sent to him by the Reverend Thomas Beard. Sir Roger Phelips communicated charges from Stephen Marshall, on the basis of which Phelips concluded that "two sects are dangerously crept in to undermine King and Kingdome, if not now prevented, the one ancient Popery, the other new Arminianisme." For most Puritans the two seemed intertwined. If Laudian innovations were not themselves Catholic, they were conducive to popery. Early in 1629 the House passed resolutions concluding with the statement that "here in England we observe an extraordinary growth of Popery." The resolution pointed to an increase in the number of Catholic recusants, "a bold and open Allowance of their religion, by frequent and public resort to mass, in multitudes, without control, and that even to the Queen's Court." Another sign of the growth of popery was "the subtle and pernicious spreading of the Arminian faction; whereby they have kindled such a fire of division in the very bowels of the State, as if not speedily extinguished, it is of itself sufficient to ruin our religion: by dividing us from the Reformed Churches abroad, and separating amongst ourselves at home by casting doubts upon religion professed and established." Previously the House had taken another swipe at Laudianism by voting to observe its fast days in St. Margaret's rather than the Abbey church so as to avoid the "copes and wafer cakes" used at the Abbey. [38]

Measures such as these helped persuade Charles to dissolve Parliament. But the House had a last point to make, and as the Speaker was forcibly held in his chair the members approved a final resolve on religion. Anyone who sought "to extend or introduce Popery or Arminianism or other opinions disagreeing from the true and orthodox Church" would be considered a "capital enemy . . . [to the] Kingdom and Commonwealth." This was an empty gesture, however. Leaders of the parliamentary opposition were jailed and the other members returned to their homes not realizing how long it would be before Parliament would meet again. The king's failure to aid the French Huguenots only reinforced Puritan gloom. William Greenhill wrote to Lady Joan Barrington that the peace with France allowed the pope to send a bishop and eight priests to England. Such rumors and fears would continue to spread in the 1630s, fueled by William Laud's efforts to purge the Puritan clergy from the pulpits of the land. Clergy found new needs for friends as they sought to adapt to an ever-worsening situation and to chart the new strategies that would be necessary not just for the victory of reform but for their very survival. [39]

CHAPTER FOUR

A *Spider of Divers Threads*

THE 1630S WERE a time when the Puritan movement was on the defensive. The rise of the anti-Calvinist faction to power changed the nature of the English church. For the first time men in power had the determination as well as the ability to harry Puritans out of the church. Members of the clerical network would face unprecedented pressure to conform. They would need all the support they could get from their friends as they had to choose between two painful options that confronted them—deprivation and persecution at home or exile in the Netherlands or the New World. More and more they needed to rely on those with whom they enjoyed spiritual communion for advice and comfort. And as they came together in communion in private meetings with clerical friends and in congregational conventicles with lay saints, they became more dependent upon one another and more sharply defined in contrast to other Englishmen.

William Laud's rise to influence was rapid and he soon eclipsed his mentor, Bishop Neile, as the leader of the anti-Calvinist element in the church. As a royal chaplain he had accompanied King James on the monarch's visit to Scotland in 1617 and had antagonized his hosts by wearing a surplice at a funeral. In 1621 he was installed as bishop of St. David's; five years later he was promoted to the bishopric of Bath and Wells; in 1627 he was named to the Privy Council, and in 1629 was elevated to bishop of London. He had been promised the archbishopric of Canterbury as early as 1626 and, though he had to wait until 1633 for that vacancy to occur, he was clearly the leading religious adviser to Charles I as early as February of 1626, when he preached a strong anti-Puritan sermon to the king's second Parliament.[1]

In every post he held—including chancellor of Oxford University, which he assumed in 1630—Laud worked to establish episcopal authority. He was far less tolerant than most bishops when it came to dealing with failures to observe prescribed liturgical practices. He was suspicious of unbeneficed preachers and in 1629 sought to end the practice of replacing catechizing with afternoon sermons. He required that all preached sermons be preceded by a reading from the Prayer Book and that those delivering sermons be appropriately vested. He insisted that the placement of altars be determined by the ordinary, which was perceived as an effort to return communion tables to where altars had stood in the days of Catholic worship. He wanted altar rails restored and believers to bow to the altar on entering and leaving the church. He wanted communicants to kneel to receive the sacrament. He restored crucifixes to churches and favored the use of other religious images. Laud reissued King James's *Book of Sports* and ordered that it be read from pulpits. On his urging the king prohibited preaching on disputed theological points, but the edict was primarily enforced against Calvinists. Laud departed from traditional English attitudes in his refusal to depict the pope as Antichrist and in his lack of sympathy for the stranger churches of foreign Protestants on English soil.[2]

Laud's followers were no more identical in their views than their Puritan opponents were. The ritualism of John Cosin, the dean of Durham who referred to services as the "mass," was greater than Laud's. Richard Montagu actually believed reunion with Rome was possible, whereas Laud—who was evidently offered a cardinal's hat if he would engineer such an event—did not seek a return to Catholicism. By the 1630s Laud's attitude toward predestination was more moderate than that of most of the anti-Calvinists. But Laud, Neile, Montagu, and their allies were agreed in their determination to control Puritan dissent.[3]

Clergy began to be suspended or deprived of their livings for refusing to wear vestments, for omitting parts of the Prayer Book in services, and for failing to read the *Book of Sports*. Diocesan visitations became more rigorous and when Laud gained the see of Canterbury he became the first archbishop in a century to order metropolitan visitations. On such occasions the authority of the diocesan bishop was temporarily suspended as the archbishop or his commissioners inquired into the state of religion and the practices and beliefs of the clergy of the diocese. The Court of High Commission was commonly used to prosecute nonconformists, and on some occasions dissidents such as William Prynne were brought before the Star Chamber at Laud's instigation.[4]

Clergy such as Richard Sibbes, William Gouge, John Preston, and John Cotton had made a science of skirting the edges of conformity. They were part of a church that had flaws but which they sought to reform. They had rejected the strategy of the Separatists. "Must we therefore separate for Ceremonies, which many think may be lawfully used?" asked Richard Sibbes of Thomas Goodwin. "Admit they be evils, must we make a rent in the Church for Ceremonious Rites, for circumstantiall evils? That were a remedy worse than the disease." Members of the network had accepted some practices they disapproved of and quietly evaded some that troubled them more, all the while developing rationales for their limited nonconformity. For the most part bishops had been willing to put up with such practices to keep these forceful preachers in the pulpit. Indeed, it was reported that when confronted with militant young clergy who would not sufficiently conform, Bishop John Williams would send them "to his old collegiate Dr. Sibbes, or Dr. Gouch [Gouge], who knew the scruples of these men's hearts, and how to bring them about, the best of any in the city of London." As archbishop of Canterbury (1611–1633), George Abbot had taken steps against outspoken critics such as William Ames, but had been willing to accept "intermittent ceremonial conformity" from most Puritans and reinstated clergymen such as Dod and Hildersham to their livings after the death of James I.[5]

An example of the type of accommodation that had been worked out before the rise of Laud is to be found in a letter of John Cotton to the bishop of Lincoln. "The truth is," Cotton admitted, "the Ceremonyes of the Ringe in Marriage, and standing at the Creede are usually performed by myselfe: and all the other Ceremonyes of Surplice, Crosse in Baptisme, Kneeling at Communion are frequently used by my fellow-Minister in our Church, and without the disturbance of the People." Cotton offered an excuse why one of the prescribed rituals was not employed: "It is true indeede, that in Receyvinge the Communion, sundry of them do not kneele: but . . . it is not out of any scruple of Conscience, but from the store and multitude of Communicants, which often doe so thronge one another in this great Congregation, that they can hardly stand (much lesse kneele) one by another." A similar argument was advanced by John Davenport for failure of communicants to kneel in the crowded congregation of St. Stephen's Coleman Street. Davenport, of course, had firmly expressed himself in the 1620s on the importance of not allowing such matters to shatter the church's united opposition to the enemies of Calvinism. Whereas the bishops of England agreed on that paramount objective, they were willing to accept explanations such as these from a Cotton or a Davenport.[6]

Charles I and William Laud, however, were not willing to tolerate such evasions and compromises. Those who failed to adhere rigorously to the church's rituals and orders were to be hounded with a greater intensity than ever before and the burden of proof was placed on them to demonstrate their conformity. Such rigidity puzzled a clergyman like William Gouge, who wrote to Laud to defend his "guiltless soul" against accusations that had been leveled against him. He trusted that Laud would "not entertain a report against a minister without proof, nor censure him till he hath spoken what he can for himself." He had "never heard that any have been deprived but such as utterly refused to conform." But new policies and new standards of conformity were now to be introduced. The greater emphasis on ceremonial observances and liturgy went hand in hand with new views concerning predestination. Clergymen like Gouge became increasingly uneasy as the intent of the new regime became evident. Works by William Perkins which had been valued by bishops of England were prohibited from being sold in the archdiocese of York in the early 1630s. Diocesan visitations began to scrutinize clerical practices more closely. The position of the Puritan clergy was made more difficult now by demands of them not merely for total conformity to usages that had been on the book but largely as dead letters, but for conformity to new practices introduced by Laud. One of the focal points of the deepening quarrel was the manner in which believers received the eucharist. Puritans wished to receive the bread and wine sitting, preferably while gathered around a table, because this emphasized their view of the sacrament as a collective meal commemorating the Last Supper, which united believers in communion and symbolized their union with Christ and with each other. Recognizing this, the authorities worked harder to restore altar rails and to insist on reception while kneeling.[7]

Visitations were the primary means of identifying Puritans and soliciting evidence against them. As early as 1614 Bishop Neile's visitation articles—the points to be investigated in every parish—showed a strong concern for ferreting out Puritans. Such an approach became commonplace. The articles prepared by John Cosin in 1627 for the visitation of the West Riding of Yorkshire showed little concern for moral lapses (the traditional reason for such supervisory visits) and concentrated on matters such as kneeling for the sacraments, failing to wear the surplice, omitting the sign of the cross in baptism, marrying in private houses and without a ring, failing to adhere to the prescribed lessons, neglecting Rogationtide parish perambulations, and using catechisms other than the standard version in the Prayer Book. Laud's own visitations included these points and also inquired whether each parish had " 'a decent communion table' with silk and linen coverings that was protected from unholy use." He made his detestation of Puritans clear. Approached during his 1632 diocesan visitation by a delegation from Colchester seeking approval of William Bridge as town lecturer, he exploded, "I scorn to be so used. I'll never have him lecture in my diocese."[8]

No matter how rigorous the visitation, it was not always possible to prove a case against a recognized Puritan. Sir Nathaniel Brent, vicar general responsible for the metropolitan visitation of the Diocese of London in 1637, was frustrated in his efforts against Stephen Marshall. "Mr Marshall of Finching-field," he reported, "is held to be a dangerous person, but exceeding cunning. No man doubteth but that he hath an inconformable heart, but externally he observeth all. I could not prove upon him omitting of the blessed name of Jesus . . . nor anything else concerning the ceremonies of the Church." Sometimes the supporters of a Puritan clergyman worked behind his back to save him from trouble. Prior to a scheduled metropolitan visitation, John White of Dorchester was urged by his bishop and by local supporters to read the *Book of Sports* so that parishioners could attest that it had been read in their church. When he refused, the churchwardens arranged for his assistant to read it in the church on a Friday morning when no one was there. White, who was willing to take a stand on the issue, was furious, but the visitors had one less charge they could substantiate. When the churchwardens of Terling, Thomas Welde's parish in Essex, were questioned about a sermon preached there by Hugh Peter, they responded that they had not known Peter had been suspended, they did not know who had invited him, and they had not even known he was to preach until he entered the pulpit.[9]

Visitors might be evaded or misled, but they would come back. Laud and his bishops also used spies and the Court of High Commission to root out evidence of nonconformity. Laud received a report in 1630 of a "foul" sermon by Philip Nye preached in St. Michael's Cornhill. Another London informant reported in 1637 "against Mr. Goodwin, Mr. Genoa, Mr. Byfield, Mr. Simmonds," and that "many communion tables in the city are not railed in, and some are placed in the middle of the church." In 1635 John Stoughton's study was searched and the papers and letters found there used in his trial before the High Commission. The pressure on Puritan clergy, even those who escaped initial inquiry, was intense. Archbishops Neile in York and Laud in Canterbury insisted that their bishops exert themselves in the cause. John Williams, the bishop of Lincoln who feuded with Laud for most of a decade, was noticeably ineffective in curbing dissent, but this only added to Laud's case against Williams himself, who was suspended by Star Chamber and sent to the Tower in 1637. The success of the new campaign varied from region to region, but nowhere did it completely fail. As Peter Heylyn, serving as one of Laud's chaplains in the 1630s, explained it, "The people . . . when they found . . . that they had lost the Comfort of their Lecturers and their Ministers began to shrink away at the very name of Visitation."[10]

The attack on the Puritan clergy was carried forth most energetically in the Diocese of Norwich under Bishop Matthew Wren and then, when Wren was transferred to Ely in 1638, by the new bishop of the diocese, Richard Montagu. Wren's articles of visitation struck at churchwardens and clergy alike. In addition to checking on kneeling at communion, using the surplice, and other disputed rituals, Wren asked specific questions about the placement of the altar. When a House of Commons committee later investigated his episcopate it concluded that because of Wren's actions "both ministers and tradesmen were driven to fly to Holland and new England." The estimate of one scholar that Wren's innovation and visitations led more than three thousand to leave Norfolk in the 1630s is probably an exaggeration, but the bishop's impact was certainly widespread. Samuel Rogers expressed the apprehensions of many young clergymen when he wrote in December of 1636 that "the Church of God [is] held under hatches, the walls of Jerusalem beaten down: poor Suffolk and Norfolk lying desolate by that cursed, wretched Wren." A month after Rogers's lament William Prynne's *News from Ipswich* (1637) appeared in print. Prynne castigated Wren, Laud, and Wren's aides such as Clement Corbet (former master of Trinity Hall and chancellor of the diocese) as criminals whose actions threatened Protestantism and the rule of law. For his intemperate attacks on authority Prynne was condemned by the Star Chamber to life imprisonment, branding, and a further cropping of his ears (it was not the first time Prynne had run afoul of the government).[11]

Leaders of the clerical network found it increasingly difficult to reconcile their beliefs with what was demanded of them if they were to keep their livings, and many were thus deprived of their posts. Among those suspended and deprived by Wren were Thomas Allen, who was accused of disregarding the bishop's injunctions, failing to have his congregation kneel to receive communion, and holding services late on Sunday afternoons to attract believers from other parishes. The bishop also deprived John Allin and William Bridge. Wren dissolved the combination lectureship at Mendlesham where John Symonds, Jeremiah Burroughes, and William Greenhill were among the lecturers. Like Wren, Bishop Piers of Bath and Wells was energetic in suppressing extraparochial lectures.[12]

Clergy throughout the nation were deprived for various reasons. William Bridge lost his living at St. George Tombland for failure to restore altar rails in his church. That was also the critical charge against Charles Chauncey in 1635. The ecclesiastical commissioners in the Diocese of Peterborough found Chauncey guilty of "opposing the setting up a rail about the communion table in the church of Ware with a kneeling bench affixed, and of inveighing against such rail, saying it was an innovation, a snare to men's consciences, superstitious, a breach of the second commandment, an addition to God's worship, and such like." Others likewise suffered for opposing changes in the physical appearance of the church. Some were deprived for refusing to move the communion table; others, like Henry Jessey, for removing a crucifix from the church.[13]

Failure to wear a surplice, also one of the charges against Chauncey, was another common ground for loss of a living. Nathaniel Rogers was dismissed as a curate in Bocking, Essex, for refusing to wear the surplice and failing to use the sign of the cross in baptism. John Knowles was presented for conducting a burial service in his cloak without a surplice and for failing to read prescribed homilies as well as for other offenses. Peter Saxton was another clergyman suspended for not wearing a surplice.[14]

Refusal to read the *Book of Sports* from the pulpit presented problems for many in addition to Dorchester's John White. Simeon Ashe, William Gouge, Samuel Ward of Ipswich, John Beadle, Thomas Allen, Ezekiel Rogers, Joseph Glover, and Henry Whitefield were all subject to ecclesiastical discipline for that offense. Aside from those who were suspended for failing to read the book, many saw the handwriting on the wall and left their livings. Reflecting from the vantage point of 1659, Hugh Peter believed that "had not the Book for Encouragement of Sports on the Sabbath come forth, many had staid."[15]

It was more difficult to deprive clergymen for what they said as opposed to their actions, but it was not impossible. As early as 1621 Nathaniel Ward had heard "a strong rumour that all lectures are to be dissolved or discharged." John White of Dorchester was prosecuted before the High Commission for preaching against Arminianism and the new ceremonies. Marmaduke Matthews was suspended for a sermon against the observance of saints' days. John Wilson was reported for having preached that "Popery and treason are nearly allied, all Papists being bound to take the part of the Pope against their Sovereign." Laud believed that "the puritan William Gouge's criticisms of the sins of the prince reveal him as anti-monarchical and therefore heretical." George Burdett, who had been in trouble for failing to bow at the name of Jesus and other offenses, lost his living for ridiculing the sermons of the vicar in the town where he lectured.[16]

Lectureships, which had been relatively free from episcopal supervision, came under new scrutiny. In 1629 Laud was instrumental in gaining the issuance of "royal instructions" which required afternoon sermons to be turned into catechizing sessions, and he insisted that lectures were to be preceded by divine services conducted in proper surplice and hood. The effect of this was to prompt a major crackdown on the lectureships. Some historians have been misled by the fact that there was no significant decline in the number of lectures. But, as Patrick Collinson has shown, bishops such as Wren, Montaigne, Neile, and Laud himself labored to regulate and reform the lectureships, successfully removing suspect preachers and replacing them with those who were both complaisant and orthodox.[17]

Many Puritan clergymen survived the effort to eject them. Sympathetic churchwardens were an obstacle to successful prosecutions. Gentry supporters used their influence to protect clergymen and offered new posts to those who had been suspended. Subterfuges such as that arranged by the Dorchester churchwardens sometimes worked. Stephen Marshall managed to outwit his opponents and hold his living. The earl of Warwick gave Edmund Calamy a living at Rochford when he lost his lectureship at Bury St. Edmunds. Warwick also sustained a weekly lecture at his country seat despite opposition. Simeon Ashe, deprived of a living in Staffordshire, was given the post of chaplain by Lord Brooke. Living under threat, these and other clergymen rallied to one another, relied on the support of their lay patrons, and endured the troubled times of the 1630s.[18]

Other clergymen resigned their livings to avoid prosecution for their beliefs and practices. Thomas Goodwin surrendered his lectureship at Cambridge in 1634. John Carter left his curacy at St. Peter Mancroft in Norwich, where, Chancellor Clement Corbet wrote, "he intends to turn schoolmaster. He will do more mischief in that course than he has done in his snuffling practices in the Church." Sydrach Simpson, who had been charged by Laud with a breach of the canons in 1635, resigned his post in 1638. When John Cotton was called before the High Commission he left St. Botolph's in Boston and emigrated. John Owen left Oxford around 1637 because of the anti-Puritan measures being imposed at the university. Thomas Hooker was allowed to leave his position quietly rather than have popular sentiments stirred up by the trial of the well-regarded preacher. William Hooke resigned his living in the face of strong harassment in the mid-1630s. Martin Holbech tried to save Thomas Shepard from Laud's wrath when the archbishop quarreled with Shepard's friend Thomas Welde, taking Shepard away before Laud could deal with him. But Shepard soon abandoned his living. When Laud was elevated to archbishop, John Davenport—who had clashed with the prelate over aid to the Palatinate and over the Feoffees—saw the handwriting on the wall and left St. Stephen's.[19]

Davenport and the parish of St. Stephen's offer a valuable case study to illuminate how the situation of Puritan clergymen was changing in the period. St. Stephen's was one of the most important of the six London city parishes that had the right to choose their own vicars. The parish had a strong Puritan tradition. Thomas Wilcox, one of the coauthors of the Elizabethan *Admonition to Parliament*, had lived there. John Dod was vicar from 1597 to 1609. When Davenport was called to the living in 1624 he had not yet received a degree, though he had studied at Magdalen College in Oxford. He had lectured and officiated at Thomas Taylor's church of St. Mary's Aldermanbury and had then served as a curate and lecturer at St. Lawrence, Jewry, also in the city. At St. Lawrence he had become widely known and appreciated as a forceful Calvinist preacher.[20]

Davenport's reputation for extreme views threatened to prevent his installation at St. Stephen's, but he was able to secure the intervention of powerful allies. He had befriended Lady Mary Vere, wife of Sir Horace, and her brother-in-law Sir Edward Conway, the secretary of state. Conway was noted for his support of the English ministers in exile abroad, had intervened to protect Preston at Cambridge, and had shielded London clergy from episcopal scrutiny on other occasions. Patrick Collinson has suggested that Conway's son-in-law Sir Robert Harley also urged the secretary of state to take an interest in Davenport's case. Both Lady Vere and Conway interceded on his behalf with George Montaigne, the bishop of London. Though a firm Calvinist, Davenport stressed his conformity. "If by a puritan is meant one opposite to the present government; I profess . . . the Contrary," he wrote to Conway. He claimed that while at St. Lawrence he used the sign of the cross in baptism, wore the surplice, and read the Book of Common Prayer. A few days later the secretary wrote to Archbishop Abbot—himself a strong Calvinist—recommending Davenport as an "eminent and well deserving light in the Church," and one who not only conformed but persuaded others to do so as well. Montaigne still had doubts and wrote to Conway that Davenport was "a factious and popular preacher [reported] to draw large assemblies of common people." But the bishop finally allowed himself to be persuaded by Davenport's friends and agreed to install him.[21]

Shortly after being settled at St. Stephen's, Davenport wrote the letter to Alexander Leighton in which he expressed his belief in the importance of avoiding controversy over nonessential ceremonial matters so as to maintain a united Protestant front against popery and Arminianism. He finally received his degree, in the process demonstrating again his strong Calvinism in his defense of the negative position "on the question of whether the regenerated could finally fall from grace" in his Oxford disputation. Davenport was moving in a strongly Puritan environment. He conferred often with clerical friends such as John Preston, Richard Sibbes, and William Gouge. In his parish were many leading Puritan laymen, including Owen Rowe, Thomas Barnardiston, the printer Henry Overton, Robert Eyre, Samuel Aldersy, Sir Richard Saltonstall, and Nathaniel Eaton. Francis Bright, who later migrated to New England, was Davenport's curate. Matthew Craddock was married at St. Stephen's.[22]

Davenport's concern for Calvinist orthodoxy and international reform led him to join with his friends in organizing relief for Palatinate refugees and in establishing the Feoffees for Impropriations. His confrontations with William Laud as a result of these efforts tended to radicalize him and it is clear that by the late 1620s and early 1630s he had begun to abandon some of the prescribed forms of worship. In 1630 Timothy Hood, who had occasionally served as his curate, leveled a variety of charges against Davenport. He was accused of dispensing with reading the Litany of the Saints, failing to use the surplice, and administering communion to parishioners who sat in their pews. Baptism at St. Stephen's was concluded with the formula "I sign thee with the seal of the covenant" rather than with the sign of the cross. Once again Davenport had to defend himself before William Laud. In his lengthy reply to the charges he denied some, tried to excuse others (the church was too crowded for any other method of distributing communion), explained others as being common usage in neighboring churches, and attacked Hood's character.[23]

There was not sufficient evidence for the authorities to proceed against Davenport at that point, but he knew it was only a matter of time. As early as 1628 he had written to Lady Vere that "I expect ere long to be deprived of my pastoral charge in Coleman Street." Davenport did not believe in separatism and he still counseled others to hold on to their livings if possible. When John Cotton journeyed to London in 1632 he, Davenport, and Thomas Goodwin wrestled with the problems of how far one could in good conscience conform. The three were close friends and shared many views. In 1633 one of Laud's agents reported that "Mr Cotton of Boston hath convinced Mr Damport and Mr Nye, two of the great preachers of the citty that kneeling at the sacrament etc is plaine Idolatry, and that for that reason Mr Damport hath absented himself every sacrament day which is once a month since Christmas." Cotton had found it impossible to stay at St. Botolph's and when Laud became archbishop, Davenport knew his own days were numbered. He left St. Stephen's and journeyed to the Netherlands.[24]

The rules had changed and Davenport was not the only one-time conformist to find himself a nonconformist. Some older clergymen were unable to adapt to or understand what was happening. In Brent's report of the metropolitan visitation of 1637 he cited "one Mr. Harrison, a lecturer where Sir Thomas Barrington dwelleth, [who] prayed and preached above three hours in the time of the fast, and curtailed the prayers set out by authority. He is a very old man and seemed to be very sorry for what he had done." But the more common result of the Laudian persecution was to further unite the Puritans and alienate them from the new establishment. John Davenport, writing from Amsterdam in 1634, expressed the sentiments of many of those who had been forced from a loose conformity by the Laudian initiatives. "The particulars wherein I have changed, are no other than the same, for which many worthy ministers, and lights eminent for godliness and learning have suffered the loss of theyre ministry and liberty; some whereof are now in perfect peace, and rest, others are dispersed in severall countryes, and some yet live in England as private persons, who were and are loyall and faythfull subjects to theyre soveraigne, and have witnessed against heresyes, and schisme and against all sectaryes."[25]

Faced with pressure to conform and the aggressive use of visitations, clergymen turned to friends for advice and support. One of the most significant consequences of the Laudian repression was that in driving Puritan clergy from their positions within the church the bishops deprived them of regular interaction with mixed congregations and forced them into exclusive religious involvement with fellow saints. Future Congregationalists became accustomed to trusting the judgment of godly laymen as exercised in informal gatherings. Involvement in conventicles and clerical conferences heightened bonds of spiritual communion and nurtured the spirit of resistance to innovation. Clergy encouraged one another to stand firm and gave each other the comfort of godly support. In effect, Laud's policies radicalized the Puritan movement, and especially those in congregational communion.

Clerical friends gathered in private to fast and pray together and to discuss the threats they faced. Thomas Hooker counseled Nathaniel Rogers against wearing the surplice. Nathaniel Ward discussed with John Cotton the problems he was having with bishops. Cotton, Davenport, and Thomas Goodwin discussed among themselves the limits of conformity. Cotton had several similar discussions with Hooker and with Roger Williams. Thomas Dugard discussed his situation with Charles Chauncey. Thomas Welde and Thomas Shepard sought the advice of clerical friends before they confronted Laud. John Angier consulted John Cotton about whether he should accept a ministerial post in Ringley, Lancashire. Cotton was also in touch with Arthur Hildersham and Samuel Winter. Nathaniel Ward wrote to Cotton about his confrontation with Laud. The correspondence of Samuel Ward of Cambridge and John Stoughton contains many exchanges of advice on the issue of conformity. Such correspondence could be dangerous if intercepted or seized (as was the case with Stoughton's papers). Much was destroyed by recipients. To minimize the threat of discovery various subterfuges were employed. One method was to use an unsuspected intermediary to transmit materials. One letter seized by the authorities when they acted against Stoughton was intended for that clergyman and contained messages for Thomas Goodwin and Sydrach Simpson. Commencing "Dear Doctor," it had, however, been sent to Lady Elizabeth Cleere in Coleman Street. A letter from Hugh Peter in the Netherlands to John Phillips in Wrentham was seized by the authorities. A note in Laud's hand reads, "This is a copy of a letter which I intercepted at Yarmouth." It was copied and then allowed to reach Phillips. "I had hoped," wrote Laud, "to receive his answer but the right reverend Phillips was too crafty." Face-to-face encounters carried less risk and those gathered at combination lectures, at university commencements, and at other gatherings of clergy discussed the same issues.[26]

Many of these discussions included weighing the options open to those who were forced from or deprived of their livings. Some clergymen sought, at least initially, to continue their work in England. Thomas Shepard moved from place to place seeking to preach to the faithful while evading the agents of the High Commission. Thomas Goodwin worked underground from the time of his resignation from Trinity Church, Cambridge, in 1634 until he finally left England at the close of the decade. These and other clergymen relied on the network of clerical and lay friends for refuge, as did those who needed shelter while completing plans for emigration. And among the options discussed by these friends, leaving England increasingly seemed the only way to continue preaching God's word.[27]

At the time of the York House conference, when it had become obvious that he had lost his influence at court, John Preston had considered emigrating to Basel, Switzerland. Nathaniel Ward went abroad to serve as minister to an English merchant congregation in Elbing in the Holy Roman Empire. But most Puritans who crossed to the continent took up residence in the Netherlands. Ever since the Dutch revolt that nation had held an important place in the hearts of English Puritans, and there many exiled reformers had found refuge. Thomas Cartwright, Henry Jacob, and a variety of Elizabethan nonconformists and outright Separatists had settled there temporarily or permanently. Robert Dury had ministered in Leiden. Hugh Goodyear had completed his studies in Leiden after receiving his BA from Emmanuel. While in Leiden he had lodged with another expatriate, Alexander Leighton. Exiles found employment ministering to fellow exiles or to congregations supported by the English Society of Merchant Adventurers, or as chaplains to English troops in the Low Countries. Such contacts were at the heart of the Puritan exile community in the Netherlands.[28]

In 1621, prior to the rise of the anti-Calvinist tide, eleven English and Scottish ministers in the Netherlands had persuaded James I to authorize the establishment of a classis after the model of the Dutch and French Reformed Churches to help them maintain order among their congregations. Though some Presbyterians and all Separatists refused to acknowledge the classis, its supporters, led by John Forbes, succeeded in gaining Dutch as well as English approbation of the organization. This gave them considerable scope to develop church practices such as they had long advocated in England. The classis itself would prove supportive of congregational rights and some of its members in the late 1620s and early 1630s—such as Hugh Peter and Thomas Hooker—would receive the approbation of the classis for practices that would later become features of the New England Way and of English Congregational Independency.[29]

The Dutch classis offered the promise of security to Puritans imperiled by the activities of the Laudian repression. In the Netherlands such clergymen would encounter former friends and teachers who had been victims of earlier spates of persecution. One such exile was William Ames, who had become a center of controversy at Cambridge earlier in the century for refusing to wear the surplice in college chapel and preaching strongly against what he perceived as the vices prevalent in the university community. In 1610, two months after Valentine Cary, a bitter enemy of Ames, was chosen master of

Christ's, Ames left the college. Denied a license to preach in England, he had journeyed to the Netherlands, where he was appointed chaplain to Sir Horace Vere. Pressures upon Vere from the English authorities forced Ames to surrender that post in 1619 and further English intervention denied him an appointment to the faculty of the University of Leiden. But Colonel Edward Harwood interceded with Prince Maurice of Orange and obtained for Ames the theological chair at the University of Franeker in 1622. Nathaniel Eaton and John Bastwick studied under Ames at Franeker and Thomas Parker and Hugh Goodyear were close friends with whom he met frequently. With the Laudian reforms, more English friends joined Ames in the Netherlands.[30]

Hugh Peter fled to the Netherlands in the winter of 1627–28 and presented himself to Ames to gain that divine's assistance in finding a living. An effort was made to get Peter associated with John Paget's English church in Amsterdam. Paget had been a curate in Chesire and had served as chaplain to one of the English regiments on the continent. In Amsterdam he had accepted the Belgic Confession of Faith and affiliated himself with the Dutch Reformed Church instead of the English classis. In most respects Paget's views represented those of the English Puritan mainstream, but on two points in particular he would divide from Puritans of the congregational communion. He emphasized ministerial authority within the congregation to a degree that some English exiles would find unacceptable, and he came to believe that religious order required that individual congregations be subject to higher authority. Leaders of the classis would engage in a long struggle to gain a foothold in Paget's church. The attempt to place Peter there was one of their early efforts, and it failed. Peter did obtain a ministerial post on an island near Franeker, but he had trouble collecting his salary. After he made a brief return to England in 1628 Ames helped him secure a post as proctor at the University of Franeker.[31]

In 1629 Peter was called to minister to a congregation supported by the English Society of Merchant Adventurers in Rotterdam. He would remain there until he left the Netherlands for New England, though he did take brief leaves to serve with British volunteers in the defense of Bergen op Zoom, to travel to the camp of Gustavus Adolphus with John Forbes, and to serve as Colonel Edward Harwood's chaplain in the campaign against Maestricht. As pastor of the English church at Rotterdam he was active in the attempts of the classis to influence Paget's church, and worked to secure the publication of Puritan tracts and to smuggle them into England. Even efforts that did not succeed reveal the efforts of the network. In 1634 Samuel Hartlib received news from Nathaniel Ward in New England of a plan to "stir up Hooker [and] Cotton to publish their Medita[tions]" by sending them "all to H Peters in Roter[dam] qui can cause them to be printed." Peter also reorganized his church on Congregational principles. In 1633 he gathered his congregation anew, drawing up a church covenant and admitting to the sacraments only those who would subscribe to the covenant. Emphasis on the communion of saints had led to an effort to restrict communion to the saints in a step that was significant for future Congregational practice. The new-formed congregation then called Peter to be its pastor and he was instituted as such by the laying-on of hands by John Forbes and other classis members. That summer William Ames joined the church to serve as Peter's copastor. The two planned to establish a Congregational college in the city, a project warmly endorsed by the Rotterdam authorities. But Ames's death in the fall of 1633 put an end to such plans and Peter himself left the Netherlands within a year of his friend's death.[32]

In the spring of 1631 Thomas Hooker left England a few steps ahead of the episcopal pursuivants and journeyed to the Netherlands. He took up residence with Hugh Peter in Rotterdam while awaiting installation as John Paget's colleague in Amsterdam. The prospect of this position had developed when a Congregationalist faction in the Amsterdam church had invited Hooker to be Paget's assistant. Paget had bristled at the irregularity of the proceedings and was suspicious of Hooker's doctrines. The Presbyterian proposed twenty questions Hooker would have to answer satisfactorily to be admitted to the church as one of its officers. Hooker prepared his "Twenty Answers" while still residing with Peter. He also consulted with other friends. At least five handwritten copies of his answers were prepared, one of which he sent to John Davenport in London. Among the points Hooker insisted on, and which Paget rejected, were the right of a congregation to call its ministers, the lack of authority of a synod or classis to overturn the decisions of a congregation, and the right of laymen to preach or prophesy. Paget presented the questions and Hooker's responses to the Dutch classis of Amsterdam to which the church belonged. The Dutch ministers decided that Hooker "could not with edification be allowed hereafter to preach to the English Church in this city." Aided by Forbes and the English classis, the elders of Paget's church persisted in their efforts to install Hooker, refusing to concede defeat until rebuffed by the South Holland Synod. Meanwhile, Hooker had joined Forbes as his assistant.[33]

The controversy in Amsterdam was one of a number of disputes in the English religious community in the Netherlands that served to focus attention on the extent to which some exiled churchmen were developing an ecclesiastical order that differed not only from Anglican orthodoxy but from the practices of the exiled Presbyterians and Separatists as well. The arrival of William Boswell as the new English ambassador in August of 1632 signaled trouble ahead for these proto-Congregationalists. Boswell had earned a reputation in England as an agent of William Laud skilled at ferreting out Puritan nonconformists. He would devote a major portion of his attention in the Netherlands to reducing the English churches there to conformity with English practice. He was aided in this effort by the embittered John Paget and by Stephen Goffe, a staunch supporter of orthodoxy despite the equally pronounced Puritan leanings of other members of his family.[34]

Working closely with Laud, Boswell arranged for the English government to enjoin the Merchant Adventurers from employing any preacher censured in England for nonconformity. This was followed in 1633 with an order that the Adventurers not employ any minister without the approbation of the king. John Forbes was eased out of his position and died in 1634 while making preparations to move to New England. Boswell's second objective was to force the chaplains serving the English regiments to conform, a goal that he initially fell short of achieving, though he did make things more difficult for Puritans so employed. Finally, the ambassador worked to gather information that would justify Charles I in withdrawing royal authorization for the English classis and to induce the Dutch States General to also rescind their approval of the group. With the assistance of allies such as Paget and Goffe, Boswell showered the English and Dutch authorities with evidence of contention among the English congregations, of blatant innovations such as the covenant of Peter's church, and of the activities of the English exiles in publishing and smuggling Puritan propaganda into England. The English Privy Council finally responded by placing all clergy employed by the Merchant Adventurers and all chaplains serving English regiments overseas under the jurisdiction of the bishop of London. Threats to reduce monetary aid to the Dutch in their struggle against Spain finally persuaded the States General to require the exiled clergy to conform to the church of their homeland.[35]

A new controversy in Paget's church played into Boswell's hands. The same Congregational elders who had invited Hooker had gone on to consider Thomas Welde (rejected by Paget and the classis) and Samuel Balmford and then had extended a call to John Davenport to join the aging Paget as copastor. Davenport had left England in the winter of 1633 to avoid action against himself (Stephen Goffe reported back to England that "Mr. Damport . . . came over disguised in a grey suit and an overgrown beard"), but he had not actually been deprived of his living and so claimed to be eligible for the Amsterdam post. Unlike Hooker, Davenport was willing at this point to recognize and join the Dutch classis to which the church belonged. After considerable attacks on Davenport's conformity to English practices were forwarded to the Amsterdam authorities by Boswell, Goffe, and others, the magistrates allowed Paget to confront Davenport with the same twenty questions given Hooker earlier. Though Davenport's answers were more conciliatory than Hooker's and the leaders of the Dutch classis held hopes for a compromise, that hope was eventually dashed. As in Hooker's case, the controversy disrupted the English religious community and underlined the unorthodoxy of the English classis, which supported Davenport as one of its last actions before being brought under the authority of the bishop of London.[36]

Boswell's efforts did not succeed, however, in bringing an end to Congregational practices in the Netherlands. After Davenport was denied an official post in Amsterdam his supporters met at his lodgings for weekly "catechizings." In October of 1634 between eighty and one hundred believers were attending these services, and the Dutch authorities in the city prohibited Davenport from any preaching. Samuel Eaton, a friend of Davenport's, came to Amsterdam at this time and organized a small church among Davenport's supporters. Meanwhile Hugh Peter brought Davenport to Rotterdam as his assistant. There Davenport began a drawn-out pamphlet controversy with Paget that would echo down into the polity disputes of the 1640s. What was clear in these squabbles was that Hooker, Peter, Davenport, and their friends were trying to shape a Congregational system of local autonomy that was as anathema to Paget and those inclined to Presbyterianism as it was to Laud and his bishops.[37]

In June of 1635 Peter, who had become a primary target of Ambassador Boswell, left the Netherlands, but the church he had nurtured continued to assert an independent spirit. Thomas Allen and Samuel Eaton both preached there when in Rotterdam. Davenport, shortly before he left the Netherlands, welcomed to the congregation a group of refugees driven from Norfolk by Bishop Wren. Among these newcomers was William Bridge, who accepted the church covenant and an invitation to preach, as did John Ward and Sydrach Simpson. Ward was chosen as pastor with Bridge and Simpson as teachers. They renounced their Anglican orders and were ordained anew by the congregation.[38]

Friends and colleagues in the congregational communion occasionally found their relationships strained by disagreements when they first had total freedom to order a church as they thought proper. Such a dispute temporarily divided the new leaders of the Rotterdam church. Simpson believed in the appropriateness of lay prophesyings at all religious services, whereas Bridge denied the right of laymen to ask questions after the sermon on the Sabbath. When the disagreement could not be resolved, Simpson withdrew and formed a congregation of his own. Ward, who shared Simpson's views, was ousted by the remnant of the original congregation and then joined Simpson. Bridge meanwhile was joined in 1638 by Jeremiah Burroughes, who arrived in Rotterdam and accepted the post of teacher in the congregation. Though their relationship was seriously strained by these events, Bridge and Simpson would heal their differences when they returned to England at the outbreak of the civil wars.[39]

Ambassador Boswell had concentrated his efforts on forcing the Merchant Adventurers to impose conformity on the churches under their jurisdiction. A few groups of English merchants operated in the Netherlands independent of that organization, and in the early 1630s Philip Nye joined one such group in Arnhem as their minister. A few years later he was joined by two other nonconformist divines, his friends John Archer and Thomas Goodwin. The "new light that did shine forth in the Candlestick of Arnhem," as Robert Baillie would sarcastically describe it in later years, was a form of Congregationalism, but it was not new with the Arnhem church. Congregational autonomy was an idea, not always fully shaped, that had been developing within an important cluster of the Puritan clerical network for decades. It was rooted in the experience of communion, which brought born-again saints together in mutual love and unity. It was implicit in the conferences at Emmanuel College under Chaderton and Preston. Experiences of godly communion shaped the way many ministers read scriptural accounts of the structure of the apostolic church. Ministers such as Ames, Cotton, Davenport, and Goodwin made such Congregational interpretations explicit as they sought to preserve enough parish autonomy to reject false forms of worship while denying the separatist solution of departure from a national church. St. Stephen's Coleman Street, with its right to choose its own vicar, was obviously hospitable to such views, and it is clear that Davenport was a proto-Congregationalist in the 1620s. John Cotton and other members of the network had organized special prayer groups—congregations within the parish—for the godly members of their churches. Many of these ideas began to flower in the Netherlands.[40]

The controversies centering on the Amsterdam church focused on polity and the nature of church membership. When John Drake became pastor of the English church at Middelburg in Zealand in 1623 on William Ames's recommendation, he organized his church with a congregational covenant. Drake later supported Hooker and Davenport on the question of restricting baptism to the children of members. When Drake died in 1642 he was succeeded by Peter Gribius, a Dutchman who had been a student of Ames at Franeker, had studied and lived with John Cotton in England, and maintained the congregational tradition started in his church by Drake.[41]

Hugh Peter reorganized the Rotterdam church as a covenanted congregation. The Scottish Presbyterian Robert Baillie charged that Congregationalism was something Peter "seemeth he also learned by Mr. Cotton's Letters from New England." The timing of events casts doubt on that explanation, but Peter had discussed such ideas in England with friends such as Hooker, Goodwin, and Davenport, and with Ames in Franeker. Congregationalism was an idea that gave form to the experience of godly communion and it was spreading throughout the network. In his life of Samuel Fairclough, Samuel

Clarke reported that this clergyman admitted to communion only those who publicly owned the baptismal covenant he had drawn up. The Dutch experience of some of these clergymen would help them refine their notions, as would the comparable experiences of the Puritans who went to America. The Arnhem church, presided over by Goodwin and Nye, not only employed a covenant but limited membership to the "truly godly." In a letter to John Goodwin, Thomas Goodwin defended the use of a conversion narrative for admission to that church. It was reported that when Sydrach Simpson was admitted to the Rotterdam church he was required to give "a profession of his faith, and a confession of his experience of the grace of God wrought in him." This could have been the practice at Rotterdam when Hugh Peter was pastor, prior to his departure for New England. When John Quick journeyed to the Netherlands he found that covenants were a common feature in the English exile churches. Views would continue to be exchanged between friends in England, New England, and the Netherlands. The colonial experience may have shaped some of the later experiments in the Netherlands, just as it would later influence some churches in England. But the Dutch experience was also considered by New Englanders as they shaped their church system, just as knowledge of the quarrels in Amsterdam and developments in New England would lead other groups of Puritans to agree on the need for a degree of discipline and order that would draw them toward Presbyterianism.[42]

The vitality of the network under circumstances of dispersal was maintained by frequent correspondence that overcame the physical separation of its members. John Forbes kept John Stoughton abreast of news from the English congregations in the Netherlands and Stoughton spread that news to other friends in England. Hugh Peter corresponded from Rotterdam with John Phillips in Wrenthan. Thomas Hooker corresponded with John Cotton while the former was in the Netherlands and Cotton still in England. Hooker also exchanged news and views with Arthur Hildersham. Faced with Paget's questions, Hooker sent a draft of his answers to John Davenport. As one of Hooker's biographers has pointed out, that document was probably a topic for discussion when Davenport, Cotton, Thomas Goodwin, and Nye were meeting in London in 1633 to grapple with questions of conformity and church organization. In the late 1620s, when Davenport was at St. Stephen's, the English clergyman corresponded with Samuel Balmford, Obadiah Sedgwick, and other friends in the Low Countries. On one occasion in 1635 Balmford traveled to England to visit his mother and carried a letter for Davenport on his return. Hugh Goodyear had a number of English correspondents, and William Bridge maintained contact with English friends after he moved to the Netherlands. Correspondence between John Dury and Samuel Hartlib makes reference to manuscripts that do not survive in which John Cotton and Thomas Goodwin deal with the issue of bowing at the name of Jesus, quite possibly an exchange between the two friends such as the ones Robert Baillie would later allude to.[43]

In addition to sending letters, exiled Englishmen smuggled thousands of Puritan books and pamphlets to their friends back home. In 1633 Boswell reported on the appearance of "a book wholly directed against the ceremonies of the Church of England" written by William Ames, printed in Amsterdam, and being sent to England. "Peters . . . was a great venter of them, as passengers go for England." Various methods were employed to ship them into the country. In the case of the Ames volume, Boswell reported that "copies were immediately sent from Amsterdam to London, to the stationers of the Marygold, in Paul's Church Yard, to be passed for white paper, and so never looked into." Printing false title pages was another method frequently employed.[44]

Members of the network sometimes returned to England in person to visit friends and family. Samuel Balmford was seized and detained five weeks by the High Commission when he left his Dutch refuge to visit his elderly mother in England. But others made the journey with more success. Thomas Allen, having gone to the Netherlands, returned to confer with William Carter at Cambridge. Often clergymen would resort to disguise. John Davenport returned to England in 1636 preparatory to sailing for New England. A government informant reported that "he goeth in grey like a country gentleman." Jeremiah Burroughes and William Greenhill landed at Yarmouth in 1637. They came disguised as soldiers and smuggled copies of "*Dr. Batwick's Library*" into the country. By personal visits and correspondence the members of the Puritan network maintained their ties of friendship, a web of mutual influence described by their enemy William Boswell as "a spider of divers threads, uneven, very much entangled."[45]

Goodwin and Nye remained in the Netherlands until the events of the early 1640s drew them back to England. But the survival of the Arnhem church in the late 1630s was exceptional. Most Puritan reformers reluctantly gave up their hopes of remodeling English worship from a Dutch base. Many began to look across the Atlantic for a new opportunity of combining refuge with a chance to renew their efforts at reform.

Puritan clergy and laymen had long been involved in some of the corporations formed to establish English colonies overseas. In 1623 a group of west country Puritans that included the Reverend John White and John Humfry (the son-in-law of the earl of Lincoln) had organized the Dorchester Adventurers. The goal of the group was to make money through the establishment of fishing outposts on the New England coast, though they also hoped to spread the gospel to the Indians. The enterprise never achieved the success envisioned by its promoters, but by the later years of the decade some of the investors, John White in particular, began to perceive another future for the outposts. With many Puritans deprived of their livings in England, White believed that the New World might offer nonconformists a safe refuge from which to assault the establishment with prayers and writings on behalf of reform. White, Humfry, and other members of the Dorchester Adventurers arranged the transfer of the company's land to a new corporation, the New England Company for a Plantation in Massachusetts Bay. Organized by Humfry, Sir John Yonge, and John Endecott, among others, the company received a patent from the earl of Warwick on behalf of the Council for New England on March 19, 1628. Hugh Peter was among those who invested in the company. This awarded them land in the heart of New England for the purpose of establishing a colony.[46]

In June the company dispatched John Endecott to assume the governorship of the settlers originally sent over by the Dorchester Adventurers. His instructions were signed by John Venn (a future MP and regicide), Matthew Craddock, George Harwood, John Humfry, George Hewson, Hugh Peter, John White, and seven others. It seems clear that at this point the establishment of a clearly Puritan society was being considered. To strengthen the legal status of the colony John White the lawyer prepared a petition for a royal charter that would confirm the company's grant. Six days before the dissolution of Parliament, on March 4, 1629, the New England Company was transformed by the grant of a royal charter into the Governor and Company of the Massachusetts Bay in New England.[47]

At about the same time another group of Puritans was involved in the organization of the Providence Island Company. Formed in 1630, this company's leadership was drawn from the foremost ranks of the Puritan political opposition to crown policies. These Puritan gentry sought to establish a base on Providence Island, off the coast of Central America. They perceived it as an advance base for an English Protestant assault on the papist fortress of Spanish America. Anticipating Oliver Cromwell's "Western Design" of the 1650s, it was, like Cromwell's policy, an expression of the same spirit of Puritan internationalism that generated concern in the network about the state of the reformed faith in Germany and the Netherlands.[48]

Almost to a man, the investors in the Providence Island Company were affiliated with the clerical network. Although not all members of the company attended all its meetings, the sessions held in Gray's Inn Lane and elsewhere gave those present ample opportunity to promote not only overseas settlement but the political and religious reform of England. The Puritan opposition to the Ship Money assessments was planned in large part at meetings of the company in 1637 and 1638. Among the clergy sent to the New World by the company were Arthur Rous, younger brother of Francis Rous and step-brother of Pym, and a Mr. Ditloft, who was a refugee minister from the Palatinate.[49]

In March of 1632 the earl of Warwick, who in addition to involvement with Providence Island was then serving as president of the New England Council, deeded a tract of land in what would become Connecticut to a group called the Saybrook Adventurers. Six of the eleven proprietors were also members of the Providence Island Company and all were committed to Puritan reform at home and abroad. The patentees chose John Winthrop Jr. to establish and govern the settlement. No clergymen were to be found among the directors of the Providence Island or Saybrook companies (though Philip Nye assisted with the secretarial work for the latter), but their influence was felt and William Greenhill would later comment on the close connection between the Providence Island enterprise and the Feoffees.[50]

At the time of the reorganization of the Massachusetts Bay Company there were approximately 110 members of the corporation. A number of those individuals had been active in the Feoffees—including John Davenport, George Harwood, the lawyer John White, Samuel Browne, Richard Davis, John Archer, and Hugh Peter. Members of the clerical network, including John Cotton, Thomas Hooker, and Henry Jessey, were active in the deliberations of the company. The clerical network became one of the primary means of reaching out for broader support of the enterprise. John Davenport's friend and parishioner, the London merchant Theophilus Eaton, invested in the company. Another supporter was Owen Rowe, a vestryman of St. Stephen's who later signed the death warrant for Charles I. The Darleys, patrons and friends of Thomas Shepard, were members. Another member, Sir Richard Saltonstall, would be associated with Thomas Goodwin, Philip Nye, and John Archer in their exile congregation at Arnhem, as would Bay Company members John White and Thomas Andrewes. Thomas Dudley was a friend of John Cotton who had earlier been influenced by the ministry of John Dod and Arthur Hildersham. Isaac Johnson was the grandson of Laurence Chaderton and was another friend of Cotton's. John Venn had been a parishioner of Richard Stock, the clerical Feoffee who died in 1626. William Pynchon was a family friend of the Reverend John White. A variety of laymen who had been active as patrons of the Puritan movement and of individual clergymen were also members of the company, including Sir William Spurstowe, Sir Robert Crane, Samuel Vassall, Charles Fiennes, Sir William Brereton, and Sir John Yonge. The first governor of the company was Matthew Craddock. Craddock had been married in St. Stephen's Coleman Street and one of his daughters later married Thomas Andrewes. He was connected by marriage to other leading Puritan families such as the Spurstowes, and his cousin was wed to John Endecott.[51]

Members of the network were involved in the choice of the first clergymen whom the company dispatched to the colony. John Cotton discussed potential candidates with Isaac Johnson. One of his suggestions was William Ames, who would later consider moving to Massachusetts, but who was still effective in the Netherlands. John Davenport and the Reverend John White were also consulted. An interesting indication of the international perspective of the founders is their offer of a clerical living in America to John Dury, who was then in Elbing. Dury, still involved in his irenic efforts in Europe, declined. The result of these and other deliberations was the company's decision to send Samuel Skelton and Francis Higginson. Skelton was well known to Cotton. A Cambridge BA in 1612, he had received his MA in 1615. Skelton was the rector at Sempringham from 1615 to 1620 and subsequently served as chaplain to Cotton's friend and protector, the earl of Lincoln. Francis Higginson was also a Cambridge graduate (St. John's BA 1609, MA 1613). He had been influenced in his nonconformity by Arthur Hildersham and Thomas Hooker and had worked with Davenport and his associates in the campaign to succor the refugees from the Palatinate. The two clergymen found themselves in a situation in which they had total freedom to translate Puritan theory into practice. The innovations they introduced—like those of some of the Puritan congregations in the Netherlands—seemed radical and dangerous to some whose imaginations were curbed by the requirements of compromise imposed by their decision to remain in England. John Cotton could not initially accept some aspects of the Congregational polity introduced at Salem and wrote to his friend Skelton for an explanation. Cotton expressed his fear that Skelton was allowing himself to be drawn toward Brownist errors, but future correspondence with friends in the colony eased his fears sufficiently so that he later migrated and became the leading advocate of a system he had initially mistrusted.[52]

While Skelton and Higginson (who died in August of 1630) were giving flesh to Puritan theory, developments in England were reshaping the character of the colony. In the summer of 1629 leaders of the company, including a new member, John Winthrop, met to consider Matthew Craddock's proposal to transfer the seat of government for the enterprise to the New World. The charter did not stipulate that the document be kept in England. At a meeting in Cambridge, twelve leaders of the company—including Winthrop, Dudley, Humfry, and Saltonstall—agreed to journey to Massachusetts and settle there. Since Craddock was not prepared to make the move at that time he was replaced as governor by John Winthrop in October 1629. Preparations were hastened for a large-scale migration the following year. In these formative months of its development, the Massachusetts experiment was but one hope of Puritans. Yet, as chances of success in England and the Netherlands waned, the importance of New England waxed. The hopes of Endecott, Winthrop, and others who had made their commitment by 1629 came to be shared by a growing number of Puritans not only in America but in the mother country as well.[53]

CHAPTER FIVE

A *Light upon a Hill*

THE PURITAN REFORM QUIVER contained many arrows as the 1620s drew to a close. Some clergymen chose to remain in England and to continue their advocacy of Calvinism, in the pulpit if possible but in the underground church if necessary. For others emigration offered a chance to live their faith free from Laudian persecution and also to come together in congregations of believers that were both an inspiration to their brethren in England and bases for dispatching aid and advice back home. The Netherlands attracted many members of the congregational communion and other Puritans as well. The Dutch states were close to England, offering the opportunity of secret visits to friends and relatives at home, but when Charles I's government succeeded in getting the Dutch authorities to crack down on the English congregations, many exiles began to consider New England. Some members of the network who had gone to the Netherlands moved again to New England—Hugh Peter, Thomas Hooker, and John Davenport for example. Many others who had considered the Netherlands as a refuge thought again and came to the New World. The colonies that developed in New England in the 1630s were looked upon by many Puritans on both sides of the Atlantic as both a refuge and a source of inspiration and aid.

Many who voyaged to the west did so for reasons that had little directly to do with religion. Disruptions in the clothing trade and other economic troubles, dissatisfaction with local government, neighborhood quarrels, and various other nonreligious factors influenced different emigrants. Families who considered migration were unquestionably influenced by the decisions of neighbors and friends. John Cotton would later acknowledge that "sundry elder and younger persons . . . came over hither not out of respect to conscience, or spiritual ends, but out of respect to friends." Unraveling the reasons for the "Puritan hegira" is a complex task, and it should never be forgotten that even in the most Puritan regions of England only a minority of the saints left their homes, and of them a majority may have gone to destinations other than New England. But those who did journey to New England, if not driven by religious motives, must have been willing to live in a Puritan society. There is no doubt that the lay and clerical leaders of the enterprise espoused as their goal the creation of godly communities. Between the sermons preached by their promoters and the challenges brought by their enemies, the character of the "Bible Commonwealths" became very clear early in their history.[1]

Among the leadership two types of considerations seem to have motivated those who considered coming to America. One goal was refuge. Many clergy were finding it difficult to retain their positions in the face of Laud's offensive, but a belief was also spreading that England was to face a judgment from the Lord. Just as God had corrected the chosen people of the Old Testament, so the new Israelites could expect divine wrath when they continued to break God's law and reject the role he had assigned them. Englishmen had ignored the warnings God had given them. "He hath smitten all the other Churches before our eyes, and hath made them to drinke of the bitter cuppe of tribulation, even unto death," wrote John Winthrop. "We sawe this, and humbled not ourselves, to turne from our evill wayes, but have provoked him more than all the nations rounde us: therefore he is turninge the cuppe towards us also, and because we are the last, our portion must be, to drinke the verry dreggs which remaine." The 1620s had been what William Hunt has characterized as a "decade of disaster" with military defeat, plague, bad harvests, a depression in the cloth trade, and other problems that gave rise to a spate of sermonic "Hoseads" warning the nation of further judgments to come. Richard Mather, Thomas Hooker, and many other leaders of the movement were persuaded that if England did not change her ways, God's wrath would sweep the nation. When Charles dissolved Parliament in March of 1629 it seemed to many that one of the last hopes for reform, perhaps *the* last hope, had been snuffed out.[2]

There was always an element of defensiveness that went with such explanations. Were Puritan emigrants deserting their homeland, their friends and associates—seeking their own safety with no thought for those who stayed behind? Members of the network were troubled not only about what others would think and say but about whether they were indeed acting in a cowardly fashion. Clergy and laymen entered many conferences to seek advice from their friends, and most decided that "the rule of Christ to his Apostles

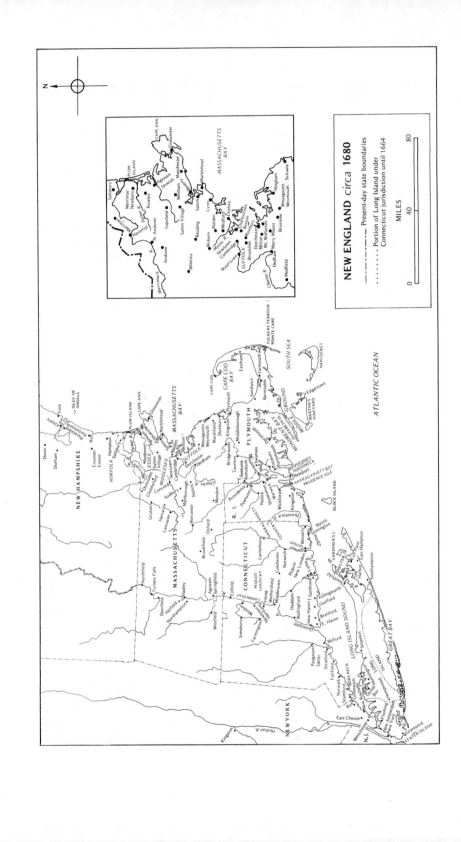

NEW ENGLAND *circa 1680*

––––––– Present-day state boundaries

·········· Portion of Long Island under
Connecticut jurisdiction until 1664

MILES

0   40   80

and Saints, and the practice of God's Saints in all ages, may allow us this liberty as well as others, to fly into the Wildernesse from the face of the Dragon." John Cotton, having discussed emigration with Dod and others before journeying to the new Boston—"remember," he later wrote, "that we consulted as many private individuals as we could, conspicuous for their sincere and pious witness"—was ready to deny charges later brought against the colonists. "It is a serious misrepresentation," he complained, "unworthy of the spirit of Christian truth, to say that our brethren, either those [in] . . . the Netherlands or those exiled in New England, fled from England like mice from a crumbling house, anticipating its ruin, prudently looking to their own safety, and treacherously giving up the defence of the common cause of the Reformation. Blame was not attached to Elijah that once for fear of Jezebel he fled into the wilderness (1 Kings 19) nor to those pious witnesses, who in the days of Mary took themselves to foreign parts in Germany or Geneva." John Norton echoed these sentiments when he wrote that "it was not a flight from duty" but a desire to find "a more opportune place for the profession" of the truth. Cotton remembered that some who were consulted agreed to join in the movement, whereas others were "satisfied with our decision to leave, on the ground that it was an actual necessity not only for us but for the peace of the church."[3]

But the saints' departure was not merely for self-preservation. Like the Marian exiles to whom Cotton alluded and like similar reformers in England's past, the colonists justified their exile as a means of bearing witness to the truth. John Winthrop's pledge that Massachusetts "shall be as a City on a Hill" was a reflection of a widely shared belief that the saints were called to lead exemplary lives, to offer "a manifest attestation to the truth, by open professions against Corruptions of Worship in use, for the necessity of reformation of the Church." Congregations of Puritan saints—pious, dedicated, worshiping in accordance with God's will—would exemplify in their congregational practices the communion of saints. It was "for England's sake," according to Edward Johnson, that "they are going from England to pray without ceasing for England." Cotton recalled that he and his friends "came to the judgement that by the free preaching of the word and the actual practice of our church discipline we could offer a much clearer and fuller witness in another land than in the wretched and loathsome prisons of London, where there would be no opportunity for books or pens or friends or conferences."[4]

The colonists believed that God had called them to provide such an example. Thomas Welde attributed the ministers' migration to the "hand of Providence." John Brock gave credit to "the Lord," who "heard me to open a Way for us to leave England & to get the Society of a beloved Christian" commonwealth. Thomas Shepard and John Allin attributed the colonization of New England to "the Spirit who gives various gifts, and all to profit withall [and] in such times doth single out every one to such worke, as hee in wisdom intends to call them unto."[5]

New Englanders were taken to task by some of their friends who accused the colonists of exaggerating the importance of their settlement. Lord Say and Sele complained to John Winthrop about the colonists' self-identification as the new Israelites. The colonists did believe in their role as models. Edward Johnson used a variant of Winthrop's image when he told his fellow settlers, "you are to be set as lights upon a Hill more obvious than the highest mountain in the World." "From New England," he wrote, "God's presence shines upon many parts of the world." But both Winthrop and Johnson were drawing upon a traditional imagery of giving witness. In the reign of Elizabeth, Colchester, in Essex, was a "town, for the earnest profession of the gospel became like unto the city upon a hill: and as a candle upon a candlestick gave light to all those who, for the comfort of their consciences, came to confer there, from divers places in the realm." William Ames had referred to William Perkins as an inspiration to those who knew him, who "for many yeares held forth a burning and shining light, the sparks whereof did file abroad into all corners of the land." Many individuals and churches in England, the Netherlands, and New England would be so labeled in the seventeenth century. Not only was the light of the gospel believed to shine from Massachusetts and her sister colonies, but it was expected to shine from there as a comfort and inspiration to all Christians. Samuel Rogers, writing in England in 1636, reflected that "the more I have of God the more I sigh after New England, and the more I think of that, I think I find more of God." The same enthusiasm can be found in the writings of laymen ranging from London artisans to country squires. "He who doeth good in any one place," wrote John Winthrop, "serves the church in all places."[6]

Although the early colonists did not claim to be the only hope for mankind, there was at the time some widely shared sense of the New World's being destined to be the site of a religious renewal, and this probably influenced how some came to view New England. George Herbert, not a Puritan, captured this notion in his poetry with this image: "religion stands on tiptoe in our land / Ready to pass to the American strand." That image recurs in the writings of some members of the Puritan brotherhood. According to David Corkran, "William Twisse recorded that many divines thought the Gospel was fleeing westward, and Twisse himself wondered for a time if the English American plantations might not become the New Jerusalem." Richard Sibbes preached that "the gospel's course hath hitherto been as that of the sun, from east to west, and so in God's time may proceed yet further west." Among the forty-three charges leveled by the authorities against Samuel Ward of Ipswich was one that he had preached that true religion was traveling west. In 1634

Thomas Goodwin expressed his regrets that there were "few good English books. The best th[ings] are kept in mens studies in Ms so that . . . those which Cotton only had done were worth all that were ever printed." He reported that James Ussher "counseleth all good books [i.e., manuscripts] to be bought up and sent into some parte of America for preservation," since the Laudian authorities "would labor to root out all the godly men and their books." Such notions may have helped persuade the early emigrants that God favored their enterprise. Later these ideas would contribute to the development of a clearly articulated concept of New England's uniqueness.[7]

Edward Johnson and his contemporaries believed themselves to be "the forerunners of Christ's army," but not the whole force. Eventually this sense of mission would become more exclusive. Propelled by the inner dynamics of colonial history and the failure of Puritan reform elsewhere, New England's image would become that of the only hope of reform. The myth of *the* City on a Hill would evolve from the belief in being *a* City on a Hill. In the first decades of settlement the colonies were perceived as one candle among many, but they nevertheless felt compelled by that role to fashion truly reformed institutions and to offer their prayers and advice to their friends overseas.[8]

The hope of living in a society where they "might enjoy Christ & his Ordinances in their primitive purity" and participate openly in godly communion with each other attracted many Englishmen to the shores of the New World. Whereas not all or even most members of the network migrated, many did and their friends generally supported their decision. Douglas Horton has estimated that in the 1630s approximately 21,000 Englishmen migrated to New England, with over two-thirds of that number settling in Massachusetts and most of the others in the sister commonwealths of New Haven and Connecticut (the former settled by John Davenport and his supporters, the latter by Thomas Hooker's followers). Clergymen such as Cotton, Hooker, Edward Norris, Thomas Foxley, Zachariah Symmes, John Archer, and John Wilson supported the enterprise from their pulpits and eventually joined it. John Angier considered going to New England, but on a farewell visit to his wife's relatives in Lancashire (where he met and befriended Richard Mather) he was persuaded to stay and accept a ministerial post at Ringley. In 1635 Henry Jessey turned down a first call to be pastor of the London congregation previously served by Henry Jacob and John Lathrop because "he had another place in his eye, viz., New-England." He was persuaded to change his mind and stay, but he, like Angier and others who persevered in England, remained fervent supporters of the colonies. William Ames died before embarking for New England, but his wife and children arrived in Massachusetts in 1637. Criticizing the Dissenting Brethren—Thomas Goodwin, Philip Nye, William Bridge, Sydrach Simpson, and Jeremiah Burroughes—Thomas Edwards in the 1640s recollected that though none of those Congregationalists had made the journey they had all, "as you may remember some of you told me," intended "to go to New England" from their first refuge in the Netherlands. "One of you," wrote Edwards, "marrying a wife in reference to your going to New England" and changing plans when she died. "Another of you, having sent over goods before (and in particular) books, where he meant to follow after. (I have a very bad memory if these things be not so.) A third (namely Mr Simpson) when he desired his dismission from that Church at Rotterdam, he alledged that as a cause, that he was intended for New England." Though none of these went, they were in close touch with friends in the colonies. Samuel Ward of Ipswich was another who never made the journey, though he encouraged others to do so.[9]

Erecting a model society was a difficult task. None of the colonial magistrates had extensive experience on the level of the stage that they would be expected to act on. Few of the clergymen who came to the Bay Colony had had the opportunity to conduct church worship with no other consideration than fulfilling God's will. Puritans of all varieties were thrown together and forced to hammer out a consensus. The task of delineating the bounds of orthodox theory and practice strained talents and tempers. Given the importance they placed on the consensual reinforcement of spiritual communion, it is not surprising that conferences among friends and various formal and informal gatherings of leaders became essential to developing new systems. The colonists recognized, as John Norton put it, that God had sent them to New England to encourage "a fuller inquiry after . . . his holy ordinances." The need to develop viable structures was paramount. Their prior experience of godly communion provided the key. According to Norton, "the event soon shewed the wisdom of God . . . the people in a short time understanding that faith in practice, which by dispute they could not in a long time attain unto." In the New World the Puritans were free to institute proper observance of the Sabbath, including abstinence from sports and pastimes and gathering for worship. Sabbath worship, explained Thomas Shepard, was a time "of special fellowship and sweetest mutual embracings . . . a whole day, that there may be time enough to have their fill of love in each other's bosom before they part." The loving communion of which he wrote was enhanced by the architecture of the meetinghouses, where there were no chancels or altar rails to separate the clergy from the saints.[10]

The 1630s were thus a time of challenge and compromise in New England. In the realm of government popular representatives frequently opposed the plans of the magistrates and the scope of magisterial power. From the debates that ensued a rough consensus emerged over the respective rights of the magistrates and the populace—the mixture of aristocracy and democracy that Winthrop, Cotton, and later New Englanders came to view with pride. That consensus having been reached, questions about political structure declined in significance after 1640. A similar pattern unfolded in the realm of religious affairs. The greater freedom of the New World opened new possibilities, and differences soon appeared among men and women who had viewed one another as saints in England. The majority of the Puritans who came to the Bay Colony in its early years became committed to congregational autonomy, and in a society that rejected the authority of both bishop and presbyter the informal processes of friendly consultation became essential if any orthodoxy was to evolve. The communal support provided by the network was an experiential foundation that contributed to the acceptance of the congregational idea.

The legacy of clerical consultation and communion that members of the network brought with them from England proved invaluable in New England. Faced with the need to develop a uniform religious system in spite of an attachment to the autonomy of each individual congregation, the clergy were forced to depend on informal means of working toward consensus. Trust shaped by social cohesion would make easier the task of achieving religious uniformity. Just as they had in their motherland, clergy traveled the roads in New England to hear colleagues preach and to assemble in open meetings reminiscent of English prophesyings. Public lectures, the days of which varied from town to town, were also occasions for clerical leaders to gather over a meal, renew friendships, and discuss matters of common concern.[11]

Most of those who gathered in this fashion already agreed as a result of conferences in England on what were seen as fundamentals of the faith. Discussion in New England helped to solidify their common ground as friendly exchanges moved discussants toward symmetry. Where consensus could not be achieved, "they sought to accommodate personal differences for the sake of what they called 'unity and verity.' . . . While in accommodation of their differences clerical consensus lost a clarity of detail, it gained strength from a commonly held if necessarily generalized point of view." The experience of spiritual communion led the clergy to value the faith of the individual as well as the cohesion of the group. Members of the congregational network sought consensus on essentials while respecting differences on nonessentials. On occasion a friend did stray too far, and in such a case peer pressure could be used to bring the individual back into the unity of the group, as when John Eliot chided a colleague, "brother, learn the meaning of these three little words, bear, forbear, forgive." Eliot asserted and his colleagues almost all agreed that "the Lord Jesus takes much notice of what is done and said among his ministers when they are together," and this belief gave an authority in practice to gatherings of clerical friends that such assemblages did not have in law. Circulating sermon notes was another traditional means of securing a common viewpoint. Practiced by friends in England, it was renewed in the colonies. Thus, friends who had informally worked together to effect reform back home stepped naturally into the same role in the new England. Their experience of communion and the trust and the procedures such experience engendered convinced them that such informal means were sufficient to maintain the unity of the various congregations.[12]

As the "Bible Commonwealths" grew in population and attracted growing interest from abroad, such clerical gatherings became more regularized. The importance that the clergy placed on godly communion as a means of spiritual and emotional sustenance is clear in the "Modell of Church and Civil Power" prepared by a group of Massachusetts clergy. In that document gatherings of the religious elders were justified by "1. Need of each others helpe, in regard of dayly Emergent troubles, doubts, and controversies. 2. Love of each others Fellowship. 3. Zeale of Gods glory out of a Publique Spirit to seek the welfare of all the churches abroad, as well as their own at home. . . . 4. The great blessing and speciall presence of God upon such Assemblies hitherto. 5. The good respect the Elders and Brethren of Churches shall have abroad hereby, by which Communion of love, others shall know they are disciples of Christ." In the mid-1630s the ministers of the Bay Colony came regularly to Boston to listen to John Cotton's weekly Thursday lecture and afterward met privately for refreshment and talk at John Wilson's home. Later, Boston merchant Robert Keayne would make provision in his will for a room in the Town House for ministerial meetings, a library there, and refreshments for the clergy. Similar gatherings of the Connecticut clergy occurred in the Hartford home of Thomas Hooker. In the long run such informal gatherings of friends were more conducive to congregational consensus than the better-known synods and assemblies of the seventeenth century, and it was the sense of spiritual brotherhood reinforced and the agreements reached in these gatherings that produced the unity that facilitated the work of the synods.[13]

Of course, not all the friendly persuasion that could be mobilized succeeded in curbing the divergent tendencies present in Puritanism. The free air of the New World allowed for a degree of experimentation and open expression that had not been possible in England, and some immigrants—most notably Roger Williams and Anne Hutchinson—would not accept the religious consensus that was emerging. In Williams's case, one of the critical differences that alienated him from his former friends and made accommodation impossible was his suspicion of informal clerical gatherings. Together with his Salem associate, Samuel Skelton, Williams boycotted the ministerial meetings and thus placed himself outside the clerical community.[14]

The ideas of a Roger Williams, an Anne Hutchinson, or others like them helped set the agenda for clerical assemblies, forcing the gathered ministers to clarify their own views, to strive toward defining a consensus and delineating the boundaries of acceptable dissent. In their response to such challenges the fellowship of friends became even closer, and some clergy revised their previously expressed views to sustain unity with their clerical brethren. The classic example of this concerns John Cotton. Inclined toward what would later be labeled hyper-Calvinism, Cotton was less fearful of antinomianism than of Arminianism. His emphasis on grace inspired Anne Hutchinson in the development of her views. The resulting controversy led to polarization and a definition of orthodoxy that threatened to leave Cotton outside the fold. Ultimately, conferences with friends led him to define a place within the orthodox consensus that he could live with. He not only participated in the church trial of Anne Hutchinson but defended the actions taken against her. Later he would try to win John Wheelwright (who had been banished along with Anne Hutchinson) back to the Bay church's viewpoint.[15]

Even while the Puritans of New England kindled the spark they hoped to fan into a beacon to illumine the world, they maintained contact with their brethren overseas. Letters, books, and travelers moved between England, the Netherlands, and the colonies, sustaining ties of friendship and extending aid and advice. Keeping friends in their thoughts and prayers and corresponding with them became means of sustaining communion in the absence of face-to-face contact. During the late 1630s John Davenport and twenty-four others sent John Dury a pledge of monetary support for "the godly endeavors of some reverend and well affected brethren" organized by Dury to aid the reformed cause. News was one of the most important commodities carried on the ships that plied the Atlantic and the North Sea, but rumors and false reports were mingled with accurate accounts. Trust in the source of news was essential if clerical and lay leaders were to understand their world and deal with it.[16]

Maintaining unity with friends across the Atlantic would prove more difficult than sustaining a consensus in the Bay Colony. Deprived of face-to-face contact, friends had to explain themselves and combat rumors about their shifting perspectives in letters that were subject to loss or interception. Indeed, the first news of the religious practices of the Bay Colony that had been received in England had threatened the survival of trans-Atlantic unity by raising English fears that the Salem settlers had drifted into separatism.

Recent scholarship, by turning away from earlier attempts to interpret Puritanism from the perspective of later denominations, has provided considerable insight into the actual attitudes of reformers toward issues of church governance and can help us understand the unease that threatened to divide English and American Puritans. "Presbyterian" and "congregational" beliefs in the sixteenth and early seventeenth centuries were not what they would become later, and for a time the two were close enough that the inevitability of a split was not evident. Carol Schneider in particular has done much to overthrow the view that presbyterianism and congregationalism in the early seventeenth century "constituted at the time a pair of preemptive and holistic categories." Discarding the dualism explicit or implicit in much previous historiography, we find instead that, as Stephen Brachlow expresses it, the Puritans' "programmes for reform were not always so fully developed as to provide easy classification. Instead, they were subtly textured enough to suggest several organizational possibilities." Scholars such as Schneider and Brachlow have found congregational passages in Cartwright and Travers and presbyterian elements in the writings of Ames and Perkins. Most members of the movement believed in the importance of both the individual congregation of saints and of the larger community of the faithful. Depending on whether at a particular moment they were trying to differentiate themselves from conservative episcopal opponents or radical separatists, Puritan polemicists might emphasize one or the other of these elements.[17]

Elizabethan and Jacobean Puritans pursued the goal of reformed congregations of disciplined believers. They tended to emphasize the importance of these congregations being led by ruling elders that included a pastor, teacher, and deacon. These ruling elders were considered to be a presbytery and for many of the Elizabethan "presbyterians" what they meant by presbyterianism was rule of a congregation by that congregation's elders. Because the circumstances in which they found themselves offered greater prospects for local and regional than for national reform, reformers often identified as the founders of English Presbyterianism frequently were asserting the integrity of the individual congregation as a true church. Authors such as Baynes, Travers, and Cartwright denied that any particular church had power over another. Although these and other reformers did at times claim more authority for supracongregational bodies—such as on the issue of whether final appointment of a minister required approval of the congregation or a body of ministers—they always held an important role for the congregation.[18]

The views of "presbyterians" such as Cartwright contained much that would be acceptable to those later classified as "congregationalists." The overlapping evident in their writings between concerns for local liberty and for order can also be found on the other end of the Puritan spectrum. Separatism derived from the left wing of the Puritan movement, and amidst that left wing emphases on congregational rights were often tempered by a desire for uniformity. Whereas their circumstances precluded the need for a well-developed theory of intercongregational relations, most of those who have been labeled Separatists as well as Non-separating Congregationalists strove toward unity with like believers through informal means "formed through a web of mutual friendship and shared religious experience of godly life in the midst of an unregenerate and unreceptive world." William Ames and William Bradshaw accepted the legitimacy and value of synods, though limiting their authority to giving advice. Henry Jacob likewise accepted the value of synods to "maintain a reasonable level of unity between particular churches." All of these "congregationalists" were also willing to accept the intervention of a godly magistrate to maintain order in cases where the informal pressure of ministers and synods was not sufficient.[19]

Although the potential for disagreement was always there, quarrels over where to define the line between congregation and synod were not likely to arise in a situation where most Puritans conformed to the structure of the episcopal national church. Indeed, their efforts to distinguish themselves from the Separatists who did break away served to bring the conforming Puritans closer together. But the events of the 1620s and 1630s began to erode that uniformity and bring to the fore some of the fault lines in Puritan thought. One of the first divisions, as we have seen, came when a growing number of Puritans found conformity increasingly distasteful. Their rejection of conformity and movement to the Netherlands and later New England cast an implied judgment on those who continued to conform. At the same time, the mere fact of locating in the freer air of Arnhem or the new Boston removed the most forceful reasons for having to conform and led to experiments in church structure that surprised and troubled conforming Puritans back in England. The debates that resulted—some of which took the form of exchanges between New Englanders and English Puritans later published in the 1640s—in some cases signified an English effort to reach an understanding of the new practices. Some English clergy also expressed displeasure at the tendency of the emigrants to see the new reformed structures as essential rather than a matter indifferent, for that undercut the legitimacy of their own conformity. Other concerns were based on fears that the colonists were moving too far toward congregational autonomy in ways that threatened to become separatism, and that within the new-formed congregations the balance of power was shifting too far toward the visible saints and away from the ruling elders. Though not opposed to church covenants, some English critics were disturbed by the colonists' insistence that only by owning a covenant could one be entitled to church privileges. The reordination of clergy in the colonies called into question the validity of the Anglican orders of English friends, and Richard Bernard wrote to remind the colonists that "Ministers have power over the people by the word of God . . . and not by mens engaging themselves by Covenant."[20]

Brought to the fore by the opportunities to create new churches, the potential of these issues to divide Puritans would grow stronger when the chance for church reform in England dawned in the 1640s. Already by the 1630s, however, the example of reformed churches in the Netherlands and in New England made many Englishmen question the compromises they had long lived with, triggering impulses toward purity that threatened to disturb the order of the church and alienating those clergy who were suspicious of lay initiatives. The lines of fissure were ideological but paralleled and were in part shaped by lines of social exchange. Members of Puritan clusters who had met informally in the previous decades tended to share similar sentiments and move together toward congregational or presbyterian priorities. Although some friendships across clusters were strained and would eventually break, what is remarkable is the extent to which members of network clusters would make the same choices on the new issues of conformity and church governance brought to the fore in the 1620s and thereafter. One element of this erosion of Puritan unity was a division between the New England colonists and some of those left behind. But the concerns that English clergy such as John Ball had about New England they had about the congregations in the Netherlands as well. The issues raised by Ball and his friends in letters to New England were the same ones he raised in a conference with Thomas Goodwin that was arranged by Lord Say and Sele and John Pym.[21]

The way in which this progress toward a more pronounced congregationalism often took place is illustrated in the life of John Cotton. Cotton had been moving in the direction of congregational practice since his participation in the prophesyings at Emmanuel College. He had read the works of Ames, Baynes, and others regarding church government, and he had discussed their views with friends in his days at Cambridge. Though he may not have met John Robinson, he was familiar with him as a "man I reverence as godly and learned." And though he rejected the separatist direction in which Robinson had gone, Cotton himself organized a covenanted group of believers within his Boston, Lincolnshire, parish with whom he experienced godly communion. Having tried to follow a congregational path without veering into separatism himself, Cotton was taken aback in 1630 with the news from Massachusetts that his friend Samuel Skelton had refused the sacraments to a number of emigrants on the grounds that they were not members of a recognized, particular, covenanted church. Among those so treated were Isaac Johnson, Thomas Dudley, and William Coddington—all members of Cotton's English church. Cotton wrote to Skelton requesting an explanation and arguing that these members of English churches were true Christians and should be accepted as fellow believers. Though the full range of correspondence does not survive, the news from New England obviously prompted a new discussion on the meaning of a true church among Puritan clergy on both sides of the Atlantic (Cotton's letter to Skelton, for instance, survives in the form of a copy written out by Richard Mather in Lancashire). These exchanges, along with discussions of the experience of friends in the Netherlands such as Hooker and Davenport, moved Cotton and others further toward acceptance of the notion of a covenanted congregation. Fearful in 1630 that New England might be moving too close to a separatist stance, Cotton and other members of the network gradually joined in the shaping of a nonseparatist congregationalism that became established as the "New England Way." His surviving letter to Skelton, combining concern for the welfare of friends in the colony with the initiation of a dialogue on religious matters, and his sharing of this exchange with friends in England are indicative of the way in which members of the network were striving to retain fellowship in the face of rapidly changing circumstances. Trust in the judgment of his friends and a willingness to give them the benefit of the doubt meant that Cotton and others like him kept an open mind, exchanged further views, and were finally persuaded to move further down the road to congregationalism.[22]

John Winthrop and other lay leaders wrote to their English brethren in April 1630 assuring them that they were not rejecting their native land or the good of her churches, but during the years that followed, reports of the emerging church order highlighted the ways in which the colonists had freed themselves from the compromises forced on those who had stayed in England. The New Englanders allowed lay prophesying, rejected the liturgy of the Book of Common Prayer, restricted membership to those who gave evidence of regeneration, and allowed congregations to choose and ordain their ministers. By restricting the eucharist to member saints who gathered around a communion table to share bread, they made the sacramental meal a visible sign of the spiritual communion of saints within the congregation. It became, as E. Brooks Holifield has expressed it, "a monthly sign of the love that the . . . members had for each other." They stressed the need to heal all conflict with neighbors; such breaches weakened the bond of communion and had to be healed in preparation for the eucharist. Communal singing was mandated because, according to Holifield, "it enhanced love and mutuality within the community." Indeed, the sacramental practices and liturgical patterns that emerged in New England were keyed to the congregational emphasis on a communion of member saints and the importance of communal Christian activity.[23]

It is not surprising that English Puritan questions about New England continued and eventually caused some significant divisions between colonial clergymen and former friends who would not follow the American Puritans down the path to Congregationalism. Simeon Ashe and John Ball were two of the signatories of a letter from English clergymen to colonial friends in the late 1630s in which former unity in England was recalled and the colonists were asked to explain or repent what many at home refused to see as anything but rank separatism. Cotton, who was then in Massachusetts, wrote a conciliatory response, but Ashe and Ball remained suspicious and would side with the Presbyterian party in the polity debates of the 1640s. Although they knew and respected New Englanders such as Cotton and Hooker, they were more closely knit to friends who shared with them a greater concern for order. Ball, Ashe, and clerical friends such as William Rathband and Robert Nichols met regularly in the 1620s and 1630s at the home of Lady Margaret

Bromley in Shropshire, where they reinforced each other in beliefs that would lead them to espouse Presbyterianism in the 1640s. English complaints about the colonists' "upstart opinions" continued. The Reverend Richard Bernard of Somersetshire sent two copies of a manuscript criticizing colonial practice to the Boston clergy in 1636 and the colonists approved a response two years later. Both John Davenport and Cotton answered a discourse on prayer by Ball in which the Englishman took the colonists to task. Criticisms of the new churches in the Netherlands and in New England came not only from future Presbyterians. Thomas Goodwin (who had met with Ball, Ashe, Rathband, and others in an unsuccessful attempt to persuade them to join him in rejecting set forms of prayer) was taken to task by the future sectary John Goodwin for adopting separatist practices in the Arnhem church. But what is remarkable is not that some English Puritans rejected the new light, but that so many in England trusted their exiled friends, sought their explanations, and were persuaded by their views.[24]

Correspondence knit trans-Atlantic friends together and friendship smoothed their acceptance of new ideas. Cotton corresponded with friends in England and the Netherlands after he moved to Massachusetts, as did many other clergymen, including John Davenport, Thomas Hooker, Nathaniel Ward, Thomas Welde, Thomas Shepard, William Hooke, and Hugh Peter. Hugh Goodyear, Thomas Goodwin, and Philip Nye in the Netherlands were also heavily involved in the trans-Atlantic clerical correspondence chain. Letters were also often written by exiled clergymen to former patrons and other gentry in England. The earl of Lincoln, Lord Say and Sele, the Barringtons, the earl of Warwick, and the Veres all received numerous letters from Puritans abroad. All such communications were handed around to other friends. Occasionally such letters would be read at gatherings of the saints, thus communicating the news and views from New England to a wider circle and endorsing the communication as well.[25]

As had always been the case, correspondence between clerical friends was a means to exchange personal and public news, to offer advice, and to transmit other forms of aid. It also called distant friends to mind and kindled recollections of shared communion. Paul Seaver has shown the importance that Nehemiah Wallington placed on his friendship with the New Englander James Cole despite their separation by the Atlantic. Letters from Geneva, Leiden, and elsewhere on the continent communicated news of the fortunes of the Protestant forces in the Thirty Years' War and of the English churches in the Netherlands and Germany. New Englanders were also interested in their friends in England and eagerly perused letters from home. They followed the news of Laud's further persecutions of the faithful and offered refuge and livings to English clergymen such as John Stoughton and John Angier.[26]

Correspondence was also one of the media through which members of the network discussed questions of church polity. Cotton, Thomas Goodwin, Davenport, Nye, and others had been moving toward notions of congregational decision making while in England. The freedom they experienced as members of churches free from episcopal control in the Netherlands and in New England nudged them further down this path. Edging their way along, they sought advice from one another. Hooker sought Davenport's views during his quarrel with Paget. Hugh Peter had received news of some church practices in Massachusetts at the time he was drawing up the covenant for the Rotterdam church. Cotton's correspondence was perceived by contemporaries as especially influential in shaping emerging congregational views. Robert Baillie, the Scottish advocate of Presbyterianism, labeled Cotton "the great instrument of drawing to it [congregationalism] not only the thousands of those who left England, but also by his Letters to his friends who abode in their Countrey [England], made it become lovely to many who never before had appeared in the least degree of affection toward it." Baillie also identified Cotton as having communicated his views to Thomas Goodwin and others in Holland. Another critic of the Congregationalists, Thomas Edwards, made the same charges. "One of you (more especially)," he wrote, "was so engaged in his thoughts of one of the Ministers of New England . . . that he said 'there was not such another man in the worlde againe': which Minister, after his going into New England, and falling into the Church-way there, and sending over Letters, began the falling off" of others into the Congregational way. In the 1640s Goodwin, Nye, Burroughes, and the other leading English Congregationalists readily acknowledged this debt to their colonial friends.[27]

The success of the colonists in developing a godly society excited the New Englanders and also their friends overseas, stimulating requests for further news of the "Bible Commonwealths" and stirring further immigration. John Davenport later revealed that when he was in the Netherlands he had received letters from Cotton and the news "that the Order of the Churches and the Commonwealth was so settled, by common consent; that it brought to his mind, the New Heaven and New Earth." Henry Jessey and Samuel Rogers were two of the many English clergymen who expressed an eagerness for more news about the New England churches. Richard Mather made a copy of a letter from New England in which it was argued that the Sabbath began at sundown on Saturday. Jeremiah Burroughes wrote for advice on procedures for being dismissed by a congregation in order to accept another living and Cotton, despite "a long continued feebleness" from an illness that required him to dictate his answer to another "friendly hand," provided guidance.[28]

Some of these exchanges became important statements of New England's position, which were printed in England through the agency of friends. When John Ball's *Friendly Trial of the Grounds Tending to Separatism* (London,

1640) was first circulating in manuscript it was, John Cotton recalled, "much briefer than that which since is put forth in print. That brief Discourse a religious Knight sent over . . . with desire to heare our judgement of it. At his request I drew up a short Answer, and sent one Copie of it to the Knight, and another to Mr. Ball." Cotton's answer was later printed as an answer to Ball's publication. Thomas Shepard's *Certain Select Cases* (London, 1648) was a letter answering questions about spiritual health and offering pastoral advice to a friend. A 1637 set of *Thirty Two Questions* regarding colonial practices was answered in 1639 by Richard Mather. Occasionally such exchanges could develop into protracted debates. A *Letter of Many Ministers in Olde England . . . Concerning Nine Positions* in 1637 was answered by John Davenport, which prompted John Ball to write A *Trial of the New Church Way* (London, 1640), to which Thomas Shepard and John Allin responded with A *Defence of the Answer* (London, 1648).[29]

Tracts prepared in the 1630s were often not published till later because of English censorship, but they did circulate in manuscript and had considerable influence. By the end of the decade colonial practices were well enough known that when the popular Monmouthshire rector William Wroth was deprived of his living in 1639 he organized an underground gathered church "according to the New England pattern." As has been seen, not all English Puritans admired colonial practices. Within the broader reformed network many rejected the New England pattern as being too close to the separatism that most Puritans had consistently rejected. Though many were undecided, others were persuaded to support the colonial views, and the factional clusters that were to clash in the 1640s and beyond were beginning to be identifiable. At the heart of the emerging congregational movement was a band of close friends centered on Cotton, Davenport, Hooker, Goodwin, Nye, Peter, Burroughes, and Bridge.[30]

Though correspondence largely replaced face-to-face encounters as a means of exchange between trans-Atlantic Puritan friends, it did not do so entirely. Some New Englanders returned to Europe for brief stays in the 1630s, meeting with friends and potential emigrants there and laboring to explain what their New England Way was all about. John Wilson, pastor of the church in the new Boston, made a number of journeys to England to arrange for his wife to join him and also to wrap up other family business. On one such trip in 1636 he spent time with Daniel Rogers, who had been suspended by Laud in 1632. Wilson shared a bed with Rogers's clergyman son, Samuel, who was enthusiastic about the news from New England. Two years later Samuel Rogers was at the Barringtons' home at Hatfield, where a group had assembled to meet with another New England visitor. He recorded in his diary how "my heart [is] rejoicing in the Word, good company, and heart leaping at New England. A friend came from New England with good news." At Hatfield the young Rogers discussed the colonies and the possibility of moving there with the unnamed New Englander, with Sydrach Simpson, and with others.[31]

New Englanders sought to advance the cause of reform not only by their advice and their example but also by their prayers. Prayers were viewed as spiritual weapons, "murtherers that will kill point blanke from one end of the world to the other," and the colonists deployed those weapons on behalf of reform in England and the advancement of the Protestant cause in the Thirty Years' War. The colonists observed numerous days of fast on which all the citizens gathered in churches to join in communal prayer for special intentions. According to Lewis Bayly, the purpose of such observances was that "we may escape the judgement of the Lord: not for the merit of our fasting (which is none) but for the mercy of God, who hath promised to remove his Judgements from us, when wee by fasting doe unfainedly humble our selves before him." Popular among English Puritans, fast days were frowned upon by the authorities there. In the colonies and in the Netherlands the observance of such days was more frequent. Coincident with the great migration to Massachusetts, the king of Sweden, Gustavus Adolphus, had entered the Thirty Years' War as the Protestant champion. English Puritan William Gouge described Gustavus as a "defender of the true religion, another Cyrus, the Lord's Anointed, whose right hand the Lord hath holden to subdue nations before him." This Swedish intervention temporarily turned the tide of the struggle.[32]

In the fall of 1631 Gustavus swept through northern Germany. He crushed the imperial forces at Breitenfeld on September 17, lifting the threat that a Catholic order might be imposed through the empire. New Englanders received word of the victory from the first ships to arrive from Europe in 1632 and on June 13, 1632, the colonists celebrated with a public day of thanksgiving held in the churches of the Bay Colony. A few months later, on September 27, the colonists gathered in their churches to thank the Lord for the triumphant entry of the Swedish army into Munich. In sermons preached throughout New England Gustavus was praised as a David opposed to the emperor, depicted as Saul.[33]

The death of Gustavus in his great victory at Lützen in November 1632 turned the course of the war again. New Englanders mourned his loss and for the remainder of the decade fast days in the colonies called for prayers for the "miserable state of the churches in Germany." Coupled with that decline in the fortunes of continental Protestantism was the putting down of "faithfull" ministers by the English bishops and the advance of popish ceremonies and doctrines in their homeland. Fast days were observed to marshal prayer for the success of the faith in both Germany and England.[34]

By the mid-1630s prayers were also being solicited to ensure the future of the colonies themselves. Complaints about New England had led to an investigation of Massachusetts by a special commission appointed by the king in 1633. In the following year the investigating committee was reconstituted under the chairmanship of William Laud and granted extensive new authority. The trans-Atlantic network became an important source of information for the colonists as they sought to assess and respond to the mounting threat against them. The fortification of Boston harbor was hastened and the colony's trainbands began to drill more regularly. As concern about this external threat peaked, the colony became bitterly divided in a debate over religious images sparked by John Endecott's action in cutting the cross from the ensign used by the Salem trainband. Although many leaders agreed with Endecott in theory, they feared that news of his action would prompt more charges of treason against the colony. Endecott was censured and friends in England were provided with arguments to counter any such charges that might arise.[35]

The colonists responded to rumors that a governor general was being dispatched by preparing to resist. But the Laud commission was unable to carry out that design and turned instead to cutting off future migration to the colonies. Passengers traveling to New England or to the Netherlands were required to provide "a testimonial of conformity and a certificate of no tax debts, and of loyalty to the Crown, the certificate bearing the signature of two local justices." After 1637 clergy seeking to emigrate were required to have proof of their conformity signed by the bishop of London and the archbishop of Canterbury. Further restrictions were attempted in 1638 on the grounds that "His Majesty well knowing the factious disposition of the People (or a greater part of them) in that Plantation, and how unfit and unworthy they are of any support or countenance from hence." It seemed that just as Laud had succeeded in reducing the effectiveness of Puritanism in the Netherlands, he would succeed in the colonies. Indeed, in 1638 the Massachusetts authorities were ordered to surrender their charter.[36]

In April of 1638 a general fast was observed in the Bay Colony to seek God's aid in removing this threat. Within two months John Winthrop was recording in his journal that the troubles the king faced in Scotland had left Charles I and his advisers with neither the heart nor the leisure to concern themselves with New England. And indeed, as further news of the fighting in Scotland was received from their friends at home, the colonists began to hope that events in England would mean not only an end to colonial fears but the long-hoped-for reformation of the English church and state.[37]

CHAPTER SIX

Blessed Work of a Publique Reformation

A<small>LTHOUGH</small> M<small>ANY</small> Puritan clergy and laymen left England to build new communities in places such as Arnhem and Hartford, the majority of the godly remained in England. The events of the 1630s seemed to bear out the predictions of Hooker and the others who had foretold a time of judgment approaching for England. The tax policies of the government, the continuing crackdown on the Puritan clergy, growing fears of Catholic influence, the long personal rule following the dissolution of the 1629 Parliament, and new policies toward Scotland and Ireland would all propel England toward a decade of civil conflict that would transform the nation's political and religious life. This was a struggle that would involve not only Puritans who had remained in England but their brethren who had left in the preceding decades.[1]

The political crisis of the early 1640s was the culmination of over a decade of personal rule marked by quarrels over Ship Money, the forced loan, and other royal policies. Intertwined with the political concerns of Charles's subjects were a variety of fears for the Protestant character of the church. Catholicism seemed to be on the rise with the growth and assertiveness of the Catholic element that surrounded the queen, the series of papal envoys who were welcomed in England, the increase of Catholic conversions among members of the nobility, and renewed rumors of the promise of a cardinal's hat for William Laud should he bring England back to the papal fold. The relocation of Dutch Arminians in Catholic Antwerp raised further suspicions about the tendencies of Arminian views. The anti-Calvinist faction's ascendancy in the church seemed more pronounced, if only because of the departure of some of England's leading Calvinist divines for the Netherlands and New England. Puritan ministers such as the young Essex clergyman John Owen shared with friends concerns about rising Arminian influences on the local level.[2]

The initiative that sent England down the road to conflict was the king's decision in 1637 to impose a form of the Anglican Prayer Book on his native kingdom of Scotland. The Scots defied their king with a protest from the General Assembly and public subscription to a religious manifesto, the Scottish National Covenant, first presented to the people in Greyfriar's churchyard in Edinburgh and eventually sworn to by most Scots. Challenged, Charles raised troops to enforce his will, but he was stymied by the Scots in the First Bishops War in 1639. Needing more troops than he could raise on his own resources, the king was forced to call a parliament. Puritan clergy were among those electioneering for members who would bring about reform of the people's accumulated grievances. For many, religion was a foremost concern, perhaps the most important issue in the elections. Certainly religion was among the areas in which the new Parliament demanded changes of the king, refusing to grant the monarch revenue until he had dealt satisfactorily with their demands. John Pym linked the introduction of altars, pictures, and crosses in the churches with a drift toward Rome and placed reformation of the church ahead of civil issues such as ship money on his agenda when he addressed his fellow members.[3]

Faced with such demands, Charles dissolved what would become known as the Short Parliament after three weeks and proceeded to take measures that would only deepen the growing rift with his subjects. He ordered the studies of Pym, the earl of Warwick, John Hampden, Lord Say and Sele, and other critics of the government searched for seditious papers (including correspondence from New England). Convocation, which always met concurrently with Parliament, was, despite many protests, continued in session after Parliament was dissolved. Under Laud's leadership the assembled churchmen adopted a new set of canons that required altars to be railed, mandated that clergy preach the doctrine of the divine right of kings, and required all clergy to swear an oath that the current structure of the church existed "as of right" and that they would make no effort to alter it. Charles, who had been urged to fight the Scots by the papal emissary George Con, appointed the Catholic earl of Arundel commander of his forces and negotiated for the use of Spanish mercenaries. Rumors began to circulate that an army of Irish Catholics raised by the earl of Strafford (the king's Irish deputy and principal adviser) would be used against the Scots. Yet Charles was unprepared when Alexander Leslie led his Scottish army across the Tweed and into England on August

20, 1640. Defeated at Newburn, Charles appointed commissioners to negotiate with the Scots. The invaders agreed to halt their advance temporarily for as long as they were paid a daily subsidy. To keep them at bay Charles needed money, and he was forced to call a parliament which he would not be able to easily dismiss.[4]

What would become known as the Long Parliament opened on November 3, 1640. Eight days later Strafford was impeached, eventually to be executed by act of attainder. William Laud was impeached in February of 1641 and lodged in the Tower of London. Demands for redress of grievances, fueled by popular pleas such as the Root and Branch Petition, would culminate in the Grand Remonstrance presented to Charles by Parliament in November of 1641. Alongside the complaints of constitutional infringements by the king were charges with strong religious overtones. He was blamed for the fact that in his reign the Catholic "party began to revive and flourish . . . [and] retained a purpose and resolution to weaken the Protestant parties in all parts . . . to make way for the change of religion which they intended at home." Charles was criticized for the "peace with Spain without consent of Parliament . . . whereby the Palatine's cause was deserted," and for the policy that "the Puritans, under which name they include all those that desire to preserve the laws and liberties of the kingdom, and to maintain religion in the power of it, must be either rooted out of the kingdom with force, or driven out with fear."[5]

Among those who had been rooted out or driven from England's shores, interest in these events was intense. Were these developments the harbingers of a dreaded judgment or the heralds of a new day of reform? Close by in the Netherlands, the Congregationalists of Arnhem and elsewhere grasped eagerly at news from their native land. Further away, in New England, news was scarcer, often months old, and frequently unreliable. But in these circumstances the network once again proved its value. Friends made the effort to inform their brethren abroad, and friends were relied on to inform accurately and interpret developments wisely.

The year 1639 had brought news to New England of the Bishops War and the difficulties of the king. In February of 1640 the colonists learned of the calling of a parliament as well as news of the continued fighting in Germany. The worries of English friends were clear: "Evils are feared." "At present many men are worried and concerned about what is to come." Some of those chosen to sit in Parliament were known friends of New England and a few, such as Matthew Craddock, were actually members of the Massachusetts Bay Company. One of those new MPs, Sir Nathaniel Barnardiston, confided his concerns for the future to his friend John Winthrop, expressing his wish that Winthrop and others who had gone to New England were home to help in the trials to come. Another correspondent feared "sad timmes," which seemed to be borne out when news came of the dissolution of the Short Parliament, the arrest of some members, and the seizure of papers belonging to opposition leaders. Whereas one correspondent took satisfaction from the fact that "the lower house of Parliament stood very strongly for the privilege of the subject and the Re-establishment of Religion," another wrote, "not knowing whether in these troublesome times it will please God that I'll long have life or liberty to write again."[6]

The colonial reaction to these events showed the same mixture of fear and hope as was felt by Englishmen, with fears for friends predominating as word was received of the dissolution of the Short Parliament and of the canons adopted by convocation. Roger Williams expressed concern that there would be a "general and grievous persecution of all Saints," whereas William Bradford prayed that "the Lord be merciful to them, and us, and teach us to make that use thereof that is befitting so sade a condition." In May of 1640 the Massachusetts authorities appointed the 23d day of July as a "day of public fasting and humiliation" for their troubled homeland. In Taunton, the Reverend William Hooke preached a sermon—"New Englands Teares for Old Englands Feares"—which in its title as well as in its content captures the colonial sentiments in the summer of 1640.[7]

"The good fortune and prosperity of New England," according to Hooke, "produces a joy which is however tempered by the prospect of civil strife in England." Urging his listeners to "lay aside the thoughts of all our comforts," he asked them to "fasten our eyes upon the calamities of our brethren in old ENGLAND, calamities, at least, imminent calamities dropping, swords that have hung a long time over their heads by a twine thread, judgements long since threatened as forseene by many of God's messengers." Given the prospect of strife in "a Countrey well knowne to you, where you drew your first breath, where once, yea where lately you dwelt, where you . . . have many a deare friend and Countrey-man and kinsman abiding, how could you but lament and mourne?" "War," he claimed, "is a malum complexum, a mixt misery." But such a judgment—"the last of God's Stroakes upon them that will take no warning"—was deserved. England had been blessed—"never was there a Land, I think, since Christ and his Apostles left the World, so richly blest in converts"—and that special place it had in God's affection "heighteneth its Sinnes above the Sunne, and makes it more sinfull then any Land at this time in the whole World, insomuch, that we cannot but yeeld that there are no warres that Englands sinnes have not deserved." Hooke called upon the colonists to pray for England so that she might emerge from these afflictions to resume her proper role in history. *New Englands Teares* was printed in England in 1641 through the aid of "a worthy member of the House of Commons," probably Hooke's friend and in-law Oliver Cromwell. It appeared in three printings that year and became one of the earliest interpretations that the nation's woes were a judgment that called for repentance and religious reform. In New England other fasts were held in the summer of 1640 as the colonists prayed that "the Lord in mercy so order and dispose as what is amis may be reformed, and his name may be glorified."[8]

Fears and tears turned to hope as the news in 1641 indicated the strength of the reform cause in the Long Parliament: "There is an act passed to have a Parliament every third year. . . . The Lieut of Ireland is now on trial. . . . It is reported that the Bishops shall have no more voice in Parliament." "We have put his grace of canterbury in the tower and if our St Peter keeps the keys his grace is like to cool his shins before his gets in [from] this cold weather for we speak only of his confusion and unpardonable sins." "All non conformists are suffered to preach and . . . Altars are some of them puld upp, Surplusses and communion books some torne, the communion tabls brought downe into the bodye of the church." "The Bishopp wrenn had thought to have flowen but his wings weare to short." "The deputie was latly beheaded and C[a]nterbury who hath benne an enymie to god and good men is likly to suffer." "The ministers shalbe noe more subject to the bishopps." "The convocation which presumed to sit after Parliament was broken up is fined severly to pay the Scots." English friends communicated their hopes that "we may once see christ set up as lord and King of his church, and enjoye his ordinances in greater purity than our eies ever sawe or beheld," and these views helped shape colonial perceptions.[9]

Throughout the international Puritan community the belief spread that a true turning point had been reached. Thomas Goodwin, Philip Nye, and other members of the network in the Netherlands returned to England to aid in the reform cause. Samuel Eaton of New Haven, who had returned to England to defend his estate against a legal challenge, decided to remain and preached a sermon in Chesire early in 1641 advocating the abolition of episcopacy. Other New Englanders began to consider a return to their native land.[10]

This enthusiasm within the Congregational network was fanned by a spirit of millennial expectancy. Whereas such speculation was occasionally offered by Stephen Marshall and other Presbyterians, it was charged by Robert Baillie and other contemporaries and has been accepted by most modern students of the subject that millennial zeal was most commonly found among the Congregationalists. The English tradition of millenarianism drew on Augustine and on John Foxe, but was largely shaped by Thomas Brightman in the Elizabethan age. Sir Henry Finch, who graduated from Christ's College, Cambridge, published *The World's Great Restauration or the Calling of the Jews* in 1621 with the help of William Gouge. While a member of the Cambridge community Finch was influenced (as were many members of the network who studied by the Cam in the 1610s and 1620s) by Joseph Mede, who was a fellow of Christ's College. A respected authority on the subject, Mede wrote *Key of the Revelation,* which circulated in manuscript for over fifteen years before it was published posthumously in 1643. Richard Sibbes included hints of millenarian views in his sermons during the 1610s and 1620s, and William Perkins viewed the growing decline of faith as a sign of the last days. But the dramatic events initiated by the First Bishops War were the inspiration for some of the key works in the Congregational millennialist canon.[11]

John Archer's *The Personal Reign of Jesus Christ upon Earth* (1642), William Bridge's *Babylon's Downfall* (1641), Jeremiah Burroughes's *Moses His Choice* (1641), and Thomas Goodwin's *Exposition upon the Revelation* (1639) and *A Glimpse of Sions Glory* (1641) were all originally delivered early in the crisis from Dutch pulpits. All the ministers except Archer shortly thereafter returned to England. For Goodwin and Archer especially, "the nature of Christ's millennial kingdom of the true (spiritual) saints was future, literal and personal." The events of the times were signs that "the hope of all ages would soon be consumated." God's people in reformed churches would usher in the kingdom of Christ. The implicit antimonarchism in this view would eventually make it easier for Congregationalists to accept the necessity of regicide. But their millenarianism did not imply support for an egalitarian social upheaval, and when the millenarian movement took a direction in the 1650s that seemed to threaten the social order, many Congregationalists drew back from it. Still, in the early 1640s, Congregationalism and millenarianism were closely associated.[12]

While Goodwin and others were preaching of the last days in the Netherlands, their friends in America were expressing similar expectations. Indeed, it is easy to see how the speculations between Cotton, Mede, Goodwin, and others at Cambridge early in the century contributed to interpretations of the events of the 1640s. John Cotton's *Powring Out of the Seven Vials* (1642) was preached in Boston in the late 1630s and his *Exposition upon the 13th Chapter of the Revelation* (1655) was a series of sermons delivered early in 1640. These were not the only millennial sermons preached by Cotton. Robert Keayne's sermon notebook records Cotton in 1640 preaching that "the time is fulfilled, the Time of Christ's Cominge, the time of the accomplishinge of the prophecies Concerninge Christ Jesus. . . . The kingdom of heaven is at hand."[13]

John Davenport preached a series of sermons on Canticles in which he followed the millennial speculations of Brightman. Brightman's influence was also evident in Thomas Hooker's introduction to his *Survey of the Summe of Church Discipline* (1648), and the Englishman's interpretation of the scriptural prophecies was cited by Thomas Shepard in his sermons. The group-sponsored *Letter of Many Ministers,* prepared by the area's clergy, observed of the times that "churches had still need to grow from apparent defects to purity, and from reformation to reformation . . . till the Lord hath utterly abolished Antichrist." John Eliot would become one of the leading colonial prophets of the imminence of the millennium. Nathaniel Rogers, in an open letter to the Long Parliament, expressed his belief that "Antichrist will not downe with ease, nor the woman bring forth the man-child, that should rule all nations with a rod of iron . . . without the painfull throwes, and blood sufferings of many Martyrs." "Truly sir," he continued, "our eyes are looking up, waiting and hoping, that the Lord is doing some great work by you in these dayes. . . . You know what great things are expectd of a long time from the *Revelation* and I hope some of them are at the doore." Richard Mather wrote of the changes in England as the forerunner of "new Jerusalem come down from heaven, as a Bride adorned for her Husband, the Lord Jesus Christ." Such speculations so permeated the Congregational communities of New England that laymen such as Robert Keayne began to keep notebooks to analyze the biblical prophecies and Lieutenant Roger Clap named his new-born son Wait "because he did suppose the fall of antichrist was not far off."[14]

Like their friend Goodwin, Cotton and the New Englanders saw the millennium as literal and temporal. The seven vials were symbolic of stages in the fall of the papal Antichrist and events were moving rapidly toward a fulfillment of the prophecies. Cotton believed that the pouring of the fourth vial included the actions whereby England had been delivered from the Armada and Gustavus Adolphus had struck blows for the Protestant cause in the Thirty Years' War. The pouring of the fifth vial would be the destruction of the English episcopal system by Parliament. In the decades to come the prophecies would be fulfilled as the nations of Europe renounced Catholicism (sixth vial) and God's saving grace eradicated the darkness left by popery (seventh vial). His reading of the Scriptures heightened his sense of the importance of English events and the role Congregationalists in New England and elsewhere would play in furthering the change.[15]

Early in 1642 reform turned to revolution in England. Charles, pushed further by Parliament, ordered the impeachment of leaders of the Commons and on January 4 entered the House with troops to seize Pym, Hampden, and three others. The five members, alerted in advance, had taken refuge in Davenport's old parish of St. Stephen's Coleman Street. Six days later the king left London, and when later attempts at reconciliation failed Charles raised his standard at Nottingham on August 22. The civil wars had begun.[16]

Parliament sought an alliance with the Scots, whose army was still poised on England's northern border. Those named to negotiate for the English included Sir Henry Vane (former governor of Massachusetts), Sir Henry Darley (an original member of the Massachusetts Bay Company), Sir William

Armine (MP for Lincoln and a friend of John Cotton), and the clergymen Philip Nye and Stephen Marshall. In the Solemn League and Covenant to which the two sides agreed, England pledged to preserve the Church of Scotland and to reform the church in England "according to the Word of God, and the example of the best Reformed Churches." What that meant exactly would prove open to debate. There is no question that the Scots believed that it called for creation of an English presbyterian system modeled after the Scottish kirk. But Nye is claimed to have written to his fellow Congregationists denying that the Covenant committed England to a Scottish model and Vane, Darley, and Armine are likely to have agreed with that assessment.[17]

Religious reform, stipulated as a priority in the Solemn League and Covenant, had not been neglected in the previous months. Early in November 1640 the Commons had formed a Grand Committee of the Whole House for Religion which met each Monday under the chairmanship of John White, the lawyer who had been active in the Feoffees for Impropriations. After a few meetings a subcommittee was established with authority to receive and act on petitions complaining about local clergy. More than eight hundred such petitions were received in the first few months. Also, in December of 1640 Isaac Pennington presented the petition to the Parliament calling for the abolition of episcopacy "with all its dependencies, roots and branches." Impetus for religious reform existed in the Parliament, but prospects for change were slim for as long as the bishops sat in the House of Lords. While debate over the Root and Branch Petition continued into the summer of 1641, pressure from the Puritan provinces mounted and in many localities citizens took reform into their own hands as they tore down altar rails and crosses and moved altars. The abolition of the Court of High Commission by Parliament did betoken the dismantling of the ecclesiastical courts that had been used so effectively against Puritan preachers, but failure to replace them with any alternative system of discipline provided a setting for large numbers of radical preachers to take to streets and pulpits. Early in 1642 the bishops were stripped of their votes in Parliament. The chance then existed for directed reform, but the nation's leaders would have to work hard to catch up to the movements in the streets.[18]

The conflict of the 1640s has often been called the Puritan Revolution and that term is regaining favor as historians are recognizing again the importance of religion in the struggle. It would be misleading, however, to think that all who rebelled were Puritan or that all Puritans rebelled. Certainly many prominent Puritan clergy were at best ambivalent about whether to fight their king. Samuel Ward at Cambridge did not support Parliament in the opening stages of the war, was imprisoned, and soon died. The elderly John Dod expressed his dismay at events in a letter to Lady Vere in 1642. Most

Puritans did see the hand of God in Parliament's actions and looked forward to a reform of the church and state, but the opportunity to change the church would bring to the forefront in England the divisions hinted at in the earlier disputes regarding Puritan congregations overseas.[19]

The Grand Remonstrance presented to Charles I in 1641 had called for the reform of the church through the convening of a synod of English ministers "assisted with some from foreign parts, professing the same religion with us." The following April Parliament began to select potential ministers for such a gathering, but when a bill was introduced for that purpose in May the king refused to approve it. The proposal at that time was for the divines to be selected from the various shrines by the parliamentary members and for the assembly to be advisory, with Parliament having the final say on reforms. By the spring of 1643 Parliament was ready to act on its own. An ordinance of June 12 called for an assembly that would include 30 members of Parliament serving as "lay assessors" and 130 divines, with 40 being sufficient for a quorum.[20]

As with the proposal of the previous year, the members were nominated by members of Parliament. Some of those selected never took their seats. Among those declining were about twenty clerics who supported the king and the established episcopal structure. It was suggested that "brethren who have suffered in the cause" and were abroad also be invited. The New Englanders John Cotton, John Davenport, and Thomas Hooker decided not to journey to England to participate. But it appears that all those chosen—including those who stayed away—were committed Calvinists. Excluded were not only radical preachers from outside the Calvinist mainstream, John Goodwin, for example, but also outspoken Presbyterians such as Thomas Edwards and extreme Congregationalists such as Henry Burton. Clearly the hope was that middle-of-the-road Puritans could sidestep the disagreements that had arisen over the practices of the churches in the Netherlands and New England and achieve a quick church settlement.[21]

The failure to achieve a mutually acceptable settlement has often obscured the degree to which most who would later be designated Congregationalists and Presbyterians wished for such an agreement and sincerely worked for it in the period before 1644. Although I have focused primarily on the group of clerical friends who would emerge as leaders of Congregationalism, a map of the entire Puritan network in the early decades of the seventeenth century would show other clusters of friends, such as the connections between John Ball, Simeon Ashe, William Rathband, Thomas Langley, and others who would come to be labeled Presbyterians. In discussing life at Cambridge and the struggles for reform in the decades before the civil wars, one finds extensive evidence of cooperation and assistance extended across the entire Puritan network. In hindsight it may be suggested that within the broader movement there were those who together with Cotton, Thomas Goodwin, and their friends were perhaps more mystical in their faith and more concerned with purity, whereas those who gathered in proto-Presbyterian clusters emphasized outward signs of faith, order, and discipline a bit more strongly. Cotton and his friends had learned to trust fellow saints to the point that they believed laymen who were of the elect could exercise power wisely and that fellow clergymen could be trusted to maintain religious consensus through clerical communion and conference. Those who chose the Presbyterian way were less willing to extend such trust to fellow saints and insisted that clergy must have power within congregations and presbyteries over them. Such different emphases and temperaments may explain why some clergy felt more comfortable with some friends than others, developing multistranded ties that would lead their cluster as a whole toward either Presbyterian or Congregational conclusions. But even though it is helpful to label such groups as Presbyterian or Congregational, most of these men had friendships with those in other clusters, were long aware of what divided them, and even when they began to draw apart regretted that such a division had to come to pass. The disputes that had flared up in Paget's Amsterdam congregation, the conference between Ball and Thomas Goodwin, and the exchanges regarding New England practices had shown the potential for disagreement and highlighted the issues over which such divisions might arise. But united in their commitment to Calvinist theology and to the overthrow of the Laudian establishment, both sides were eager to downplay what divided them.[22]

Shortly after the return of Thomas Goodwin, Philip Nye, and the other Congregationalists from the Netherlands, they struck an agreement with the spokesmen for English Presbyterianism. These men might have had differences, but they knew each other, had attended school together, worked together in the cause, and thought well of one another. Meeting at the home of Edmund Calamy in Aldermanbury late in 1641, Congregationalists and Presbyterians pledged themselves neither to speak nor write, nor take any other action against the views of the other side. At the same time both groups pledged themselves to work against episcopacy and the spread of sectarian views. This spirit of accord was reflected in a number of publications in the early 1640s. *The Beauty of Church Government in a Church Reformed,* which suggested how the church models of New England *and* Scotland might be reconciled, issued from this clerical coalition. *An Answer to a Book Entitled An Humble Remonstrance* (London, 1641) was written by "Smectymnuus," an acronym for Stephen Marshall, Edmund Calamy, Thomas Young, Matthew Newcomen, and William Spurstowe. They argued that episcopacy was not divinely mandated and espoused presbyterianism without, however, addressing the "question whether there should be congregational presbyteries, or classical presbyteries, or synodical assemblies—or what the relation of these might be." In short, it evaded the questions that would eventually divide the orthodox Puritans. The Scottish Presbyterian Robert Baillie identified Jeremiah Burroughes, Thomas Goodwin, and their friends as authors of *The Petition for the Prelates Briefly Examined* (London, 1641). This attack on episcopacy was commended by Baillie, prefaced by his Presbyterian colleague Alexander Henderson, and contains evidence that the Congregationalist authors had prepublication access to the works of the Presbyterian Smectymnians. Thus, the clergymen who had agreed to the Aldermanbury accord were able to cooperate effectively against their common foes. At the time when the Assembly of Divines convened this alliance was holding firm.[23]

The Westminster Assembly was convened on July 1, 1643, with a sermon by its presiding officer, or prolocutor, William Twisse. Sixty-nine members were in attendance. Within the first week the Reverends John White of Dorchester and Cornelius Burgess were chosen as assessors to assist Twisse. The Assembly was organized into three standing committees to address its major tasks, which were the preparation of a theological confession of faith, of a directory of worship, and of a new organizational structure for the church. Through the summer months almost all of the attention of the divines was focused on theological issues, with work proceeding on revision of the Thirty-Nine Articles to emphasize the clear Calvinist orthodoxy of the Church of England. Congregational clergymen such as Thomas Goodwin made important contributions as they worked closely with and were part of the Assembly majority on these issues.[24]

With England's subscription to the Solemn League and Covenant, the character of the Assembly changed, for added to the membership were Scottish commissioners who sat not as members in the same sense as the English participants, but as representatives of the kirk and state of Scotland charged with seeing that England carried out the religious obligations taken on in the Covenant. George Gillespie would be the most vocal of the Scottish commissioners, ably seconded in debates by Alexander Henderson and Samuel Rutherford. Robert Baillie, the fourth member of the delegation, did not speak in the Assembly sessions but was active in its committees and outside the halls. The membership of these Scots on the Committee of Both Kingdoms as well gave them added influence by bringing them into direct contact with leaders of the English Parliament.[25]

With the arrival of the Scots the Assembly began to devote more time to the issues of governance and worship, which would come to divide the Puritan reformers. Initially, the Scots held out hope for bringing the whole Assembly over to their brand of Presbyterianism. Baillie had been in England when Thomas Goodwin and his fellow exiles returned from the Netherlands and he had established contact with them. "All the English ministers of Holland, who are for New-England way, are here now," he reported to Scotland. He found that "they are all in good termes with us: Our only considerable difference will be about the jurisdiction of Synods and Presbyteries. As for Brownists, and Separatists of many kynds, here they mislyke them well near as much as we." Baillie found the Congregationalists to be "learned, discreet, and zealous men, well seen in cases of conscience." "We expect," he wrote, "no small help from these men to abolish the great Idol of England, the Service-Book." He expressed the belief that "it were all the pities in the world that wee and they should differ in anie thing," but differences would begin to divide the two groups late in 1643.[26]

For their part, Goodwin and his associates had to have recognized the possibility of differences. Their willingness to join with English Presbyterians in an accord to mute discussion of ecclesiology was a major concession, because the Scots were not part of that agreement and had no hesitancy in addressing the Parliament and the English public about the importance of Presbyterian forms. Given this situation, it is worth speculating on the reasons that the outstanding Congregationalists in New England chose not to return to England. In early September of 1642 John Winthrop recorded in his journal that "there came letters from divers Lords of the upper house, and some 30 of the house of commons . . . to Mr. Cotton of Boston, Mr. Hooker of Hartford, and Mr. Davenport of New Haven to call them to England . . . to assist in the synod there appointed, to consider and advise about the settling of church government." Among those who extended the invitation were the earl of Warwick, Lord Say and Sele, Thomas Barrington, Arthur Haselrig, Oliver Cromwell, Nathaniel Barnardiston, Henry Darley, Oliver St. John, Miles Corbet, and Isaac Pennington. Initially, the magistrates and elders of Massachusetts considered the call to be from God, and Cotton and Davenport expressed an eagerness to accept. But soon, according to Winthrop, "came other letters from England" that led them to change their minds. Among those writing were Thomas Welde and Hugh Peter. Welde, who had been John Eliot's colleague at Roxbury, and Peter, the pastor at Salem, had been sent to the mother country in 1641 as emissaries of Massachusetts. They were charged with, among other things, furthering the work of reformation and had established contact with their Congregational friends in the London area. Their advice to Cotton, Hooker, and Davenport was that the colonial leaders stay in New England. Though none of the letters alluded to by Winthrop have survived, it is likely that Goodwin, Burroughes, and other correspondents of the colonists were also in touch and proffered the same advice. If Cotton and his colleagues returned to sit in the Assembly they would be expected to abide by the same accord whereby their English friends had agreed not to publicly advocate the Congregational way. In such a case, who would speak for Congregationalism and counter the rising Presbyterian tide? Based in New England, Cotton and his brethren were free to expound and defend the cause, and during the remainder of 1642 and beyond the argument over Congregational polity was sustained in print between the Scots on the one side and the New Englanders on the other. English Congregationalists adhered to the Aldermanbury accord and kept quiet themselves while soliciting colonial tracts and arranging for their publication. Accepting the advice of their English friends, the leaders of the network in New England accepted their role as the primary exponents of the system.[27]

The division that began to fragment the Assembly of Divines did not initially lead to a clear Presbyterian–Congregational polarization. Scholars who have carefully studied the records of the debates are unanimous in noting the absence of hard-and-fast lines of division in the fall of 1643. George Yule has argued that there were "at least five types of Presbyterian polity discernable," ranging from the system in place in Scotland at one end of the spectrum to the decentralized form advocated by Thomas Goodwin and his allies on the other end, and that on given issues different alliances would form. Robert Paul has similarly claimed that the majority in the Assembly in 1643 was committed to neither the Scots' model nor that of New England. In the ensuing debates given individuals might agree on one issue and find themselves on opposite sides on the next question.[28]

On one fundamental question everyone at the time seemed in agreement. All parties in the Assembly espoused the ideal of a national church. In June of 1643 William Carter had tried to reassure moderates, Presbyterians, and Puritan episcopalians that Congregationalists did not deny union with their godly brethren in the parish churches. "By Baptisme," he argued, "we . . . are united to Christ and one to another, by mutuall covenant, if not actuall and formall, yet virtuall and interpretive, and thereby made members of particular visible Churches, nationall and cogregationall." In November the question of whether the Church of England as then instituted was a true church arose more specifically in the debate on whether admission to the Lord's Supper could be limited. Whereas it was evident that the Congregationalists did not wish to recognize all parishes as true and all chuchgoers as saints, they were even more concerned to assert their faith in a national church and make it clear that they were not Separatists. Philip Nye tried to downplay any disagreements and William Bridge declared that "I thinke that there are true churches & parochial churches in England[,] many & many hundred." For their part, the moderate Presbyterians Calamy and Marshall accepted, according to Rosemary Bradley, "that the concept of a national church did not exclude a semi-separatist definition of a loose federation of autonomous congregational bodies."[29]

There were, however, divisions over other issues. The compilation of a new Directory of Worship was entrusted to a subcommittee that included the four

Scottish clergymen, four English Presbyterians—Stephen Marshall, Thomas Young, Herbert Palmer, and Charles Herle—and Thomas Goodwin. Philip Nye was added through Goodwin's efforts. On the issue of whether the reading of the lectionary should be limited to ordained clergymen, Herle and Palmer joined Goodwin and Nye in seeking that limitation, though the committee report extended the right to all who intended being ordained. The Scots wished communion distributed at the table to successive groups of communicants. Palmer, Herle, and Marshall agreed with Congregationalists that elements blessed at the table could be carried to where the communicants sat in pews or seats. Marshall was eventually won over to the Scots' position on this, though the final decision was a compromise that permitted "the communicants" to "orderly sit about it, or at it." On other issues of worship the Scots were not pleased by what Marshall had drafted on preaching and with Palmer's draft statement on catechizing.[30]

On other occasions the Congregationalists and the Scots were allied against the English Presbyterians and the Assembly's uncommitted majority. One of these issues was the selection of pastors. Initially both the Scots and the Congregationalists wished to preserve a role for the congregation to choose or (in the case of the Scots) to approve of a pastor. But the English Presbyterians (strongly reminiscent of their concerns about New England practices in the 1630s) were fearful of popular control in religious matters and sought to invest new presbyteries with the powers of the former bishops. On another issue the Scots and the Congregationalists stood together in their belief that a congregation should have two clergymen when possible—a pastor and a teacher. Robert Baillie praised the Congregationalists as "very able men" and applauded their stand. In the debate over the office of ruling elder, Thomas Goodwin and his friends found themselves siding with Baillie's party and in this case with many English Presbyterians against delegates who saw this as an unwanted departure from the traditions of the English church.[31]

As late as December of 1643 there was no pattern of opposition between the Congregationalists and the Presbyterians of either England or Scotland. Although Goodwin, Nye, and their friends consistently espoused the practices and beliefs that had evolved within the Congregational communion as a result of experiences in England, the Netherlands, and New England, they usually found themselves supported by or allied with some other elements in the Assembly. But the pattern of shifting alliances began to change in that month. As evidenced by their views on the choice of pastors, a majority of the Assembly was deeply concerned about populist forces in the church. The growth of unchecked sectarianism outside the Assembly accentuated these fears. Members of the Assembly began to talk of measures to force all Englishmen back into the parish churches. A proposal was introduced on December 22 calling on Englishmen to refrain from gathering new churches.

When an attempt was made to amend this to require the disbanding of already gathered churches the Congregationalists reacted strongly and were able to defeat the motion. But in turn they agreed to support the original measure and signed the *Certain Considerations to Disswade Men from Further Gathering of Churches in the Present Juncture of Time,* which was published the next day. In doing so Goodwin, Nye, Burroughes, and the other Congregationalists showed their continuing commitment to orthodoxy, their opposition to the sects, and their hope of reaching an acceptable solution to the issues facing the Assembly. The majority at Westminster, however, was moving toward the Scots, convinced that a Presbyterian structure was more likely to lead to religious order and a suppression of the sects. The effect of this realignment first became evident in the debate over ordination begun in January of 1644.[32]

On January 17 the Assembly received a committee recommendation that "preaching presbyters are only to ordain." This recommendation indicates that in the committee representatives of both English Presbyterians and those who favored a reformed episcopacy had concluded that a Presbyterian settlement offered the best chance of controlling the sects. The Congregationalists fought for the right of a congregation to ordain its own clergy, but were defeated. Implicit in the decision was a Presbyterian concept of the relationship of individual congregations to a national church.[33]

Both sides saw the division that was coming and labored to prevent it. Philip Nye emphasized how much the Congregationalists agreed with the Presbyterians, pointing out that "were the government of Scotland laid before us, he and his party would come nearer to it in many things than divers of this Assembly will do in other things." Robert Baillie invited Thomas Goodwin "to dinner, and spent an afternoon with him verie sweetly. It were a thousand pities of that man; he is of manie excellent parts: I hope God will not permitt him to goe on to lead a faction for renting of the kirk." George Gillespie likewise viewed the Congregationalists as brethren and wished to have them in his church. But Gillespie also knew that his faction now had the votes to carry the Assembly toward Presbyterianism and he and his allies were firmly convinced that their way was necessary for the spiritual health of the nation.[34]

The key issue on which the two sides would not be able to agree was the role of synods in the church, and this moved to the fore in February and March. The Congregationalist position was precisely that of the New Englanders. As reported by one of the Assembly's members, "Mr Nye did confess . . . as that they held classical and synodical meetings very useful and profitable; yet possibly agreeable to the institution of Christ. But the quare is in this, Whether these meetings have the same power that 'eclesia prima', or one single congregation has?" "Mr Nye," he continued, "would strive a middle way betwixt no interest and jurisdiction, and prove that those t[w]o notions of power and jurisdiction are separable. . . . So our debates here are of authority, but not of jurisdiction." Whereas each congregation had the power to manage its own affairs, there was an obligation for individual congregations to consult with others in church assemblies and synods. In cases where an individual or a congregation strayed from the truth, other congregations or a synod could intervene. Indeed, said Jeremiah Burroughes, "it is their duty to send for them . . . but it is not their power." Synods could censure and advise but not compel. If erring parties refused to accept advice others were to withdraw from their fellowship.[35]

On February 14 Thomas Goodwin made an important speech in which he argued that discipline in the church, like the preaching of the word, must be centered on the individual congregation. As the debate continued Bridge and Goodwin both tried to distance themselves from the Separatists by emphasizing that within the self-governing congregation the influence of the elders should normally be paramount. Gillespie recognized that the Congregationalists "differ so far from the Brownists that they hold the people, without the officers, cannot excommunicate," but the Congregationalist position was still unacceptable to the majority. Not having had the same experience of clerical and congregational communion, they did not trust in the ability of congregational polity to control error. The debate was allowed to continue and early closure rejected only, according to one observer, "that we might not seem cruel to our brethren abroad," presumably Goodwin's allies in New England and the Netherlands.[36]

Related to the dispute over relations between congregations and synods was the question of the role of the state. The Presbyterians sought a national church with full power unto itself to enforce its will and beliefs. The Congregationalists, as was the case in New England, limited religious jurisdiction to persuasion and relied upon the civil power of the magistrate to safeguard the faith from unacceptable error.[37]

From some perspectives the area of disagreement between the two sides was very small—Baillie himself acknowledged that the Congregationalists "avow a dependencie, and that by divine command, on all the neighbour churches; only denyes a superiority of jurisdiction of any church or synod over another church"—but it was enough to make Congregational acceptance of the emerging national church impossible. Would the leaders of that church at least give them the liberty to pursue their own way in congregations that accepted all aspects of the national establishment except the authority of synods? That became the new goal of the Goodwin group, and when they sensed that their clerical brethren would be unaccommodating, they appealed over the head of the Assembly to the Parliament it reported to.[38]

The Congregationalists must have recognized from the start that they might have to go beyond the Assembly, and they would have likely been confirmed in the necessity of that step after Alexander Henderson's "A Sermon Preached to the Honourable House of Commons . . . December 27, 1643" made it clear that the Scots would not accommodate them. A week later *An Apologetical Narration* was registered and in late January copies were being distributed both in and outside the Assembly. The tract was signed by Thomas Goodwin, Philip Nye, Sydrach Simpson, Jeremiah Burroughes, and William Bridge, the five of whom became known as the Dissenting Brethren. The position they espoused was strongly supported in the Assembly by William Greenhill, John Phillips, William Carter, and Joseph Caryl, while others frequently voted with them on various issues. Outside the Assembly Hugh Peter, Thomas Welde, and others quickly endorsed the document.[39]

An Apologetical Narration was not a plea for religious liberty. The authors maintained that they would never have addressed Parliament "if in all matters of Doctrine, we were not as Orthodoxe in our judgements as our brethren themselves." The Dissenting Brethren would subscribe to the Westminster Confession of Faith and to the Directory of Worship, but they could not in conscience accept the authority of synods over individual congregations. They sought the right to order their own affairs as they had been allowed to do over the previous few years. To bolster their case they specifically drew upon the fact that they merely advocated the right to order themselves as the New Englanders—"godly men of our own Nation, and among them some as holy and judicious Divines as this Kingdome hath bred; whose sincerity in their way hath been testified before all the world, and wil be unto all generations to come by . . . transplanting themselves many thousand miles distance, and that by sea, into a Wildernes, merely to worship God more purely."[40]

The reaction to *An Apologetical Narration* was explosive. Presbyterians had believed that in the end the Congregationalists would accept the judgment of the Assembly majority. Surprised, and feeling betrayed by the violation of the Aldermanbury accord, they lashed out at the Dissenting Brethren in sermons and in print. Sectaries saw in the arguments of the Apologists a platform that they could perhaps use in seeking their own toleration. As the debate on the value of religious liberty reached new heights in Parliament, in the press, and around the campfires of the army, the Congregationalists were steadily forced toward an uneasy alliance with sects with whom they shared little but the common goal of independence from a Presbyterian authority.

The term *Independent* became the label for the opponents of Presbyterianism in the 1640s. None were more eager to employ it than the Presbyterians, who, branding all their enemies with a label that was meant to imply insubordination and anarchy, hoped to gather to themselves all who were concerned with order. But was there an actual Independent party in the sense of a group that shared common beliefs and coordinated strategies?

Probably not. Historians have had to distinguish between "Independents" in Parliament and religious "Independents," in part because clearly not all of the Parliament men of that faction shared the ideals of religious Independency. But the idea of "religious Independents" as a group also needs correction. Those whom the Scots labeled Independents certainly agreed that they did not want a Presbyterian national church such as existed in Scotland. But some believed in a national church whereas others rejected the concept. Despite the charges of their enemies, not all Independents believed in a general religious toleration. Congregationalists were bound to each other by communion, to the sects by convenience. Historians who have assumed that Independency stood for religious liberty have misread the facts and have distorted the reality of the period.

Despite being labeled Independents by their enemies and cooperating with some sectarian leaders on some measures, the English Congregational leaders were never advocates of toleration per se. In 1644 Thomas Goodwin had, as Robert Baillie admitted, "undertaken a public lecture against the Anabaptists." Baillie reported that when it was proposed that an Anabaptist "admonition" be read to the Westminster Assembly, "Goodwin, Nye and their party [were] by all means pressing the neglect, contempt and suppressing all such fantastic papers." In 1645 Joseph Caryl encouraged Parliament to "find and discerne the limit-stone, between liberty and libertinisme, between the humours of men, and their consciences." In *England Plus Ultra* Caryl was more explicit, writing that "whatever . . . is an errour or heresie, let all the penalties which Christ hath charged upon it be executed to the utmost." Jeremiah Burroughes recorded that "there is a great outcry against toleration of all religions, & we are willing to join against such toleration." Also in 1645 Thomas Goodwin claimed that "if any man think I am pleading for liberty of all opinions, of what nature and how gross soever, I humbly desire them to remember that I only plead for the Saints." Burroughes similarly tried to correct the record in a defense of his views against Thomas Edwards in 1646: "I did not preach for a universall, an unlimited toleration of all Religions, of all things, as both my selfe and others are very sinfully reported to do. . . . For my part, as I never was, so I am now not for a toleration of all things, nay I should be loath to live in England if ever it should be here."[41]

The Congregationalists wished to see a national church in which all who joined in the fundamentals of Calvinist faith should be free to worship, even if they differed on matters such as the proper authority of synods. As they understood it, this was in accordance with the practice of the best reformed churches such as those in the Netherlands, where Congregationalists and Presbyterians coexisted, and in New England, where those inclined toward Presbyterian views of pastor-congregation relations were tolerated within a Congregational establishment. But it was in the political interests of extreme

Presbyterians to exaggerate the views of the Dissenting Brethren and by so doing alienate them from the support of all moderate Puritans.

The goal of the Presbyterian majority was clearly expressed by Robert Baillie. "We hope," he wrote, "shortlie to get the Independents [Dissenting Brethren] put to it to declare themselves either to be for the rest of the Sectaries, or against them. If they declare against them, they will be but a small inconsiderable companie; if for them, all honest men will cry out upon them for separating from all the Reformed Churches, to joyne with Anabaptists and Libertines." It was in their interests to lump the Congregationalists with the sects. The principal Presbyterian propaganda works of the next few years—Baillie's *Dissuasive from the Errours of the Time,* Thomas Edwards's *Gangraena,* and John Vicars's *The Schismatick Sifted*—identified Congregationalists with the radical sects while blaming the Congregational system in old and New England for the rise of the erroneous opinions. While seeking to discredit the Congregationalists by linking them with the radicals, the Presbyterians also sought to use that linkage to discredit the limited accommodation which the Dissenting Brethren claimed was all they wanted. A *Letter of the Ministers of the City of London,* prepared by the Presbyterian leaders in the capital, argued that to "grant to them [the Dissenting Brethren] and not to other Sectaries who are free born as well as they, and have done as good service as they to the publicke (as they use to plead) will be counted injustice and great partiality; but to grant it unto all will scarce be cleared from great impiety." In addition to discrediting the views of their opponents, the Presbyterians sought to destroy their character. Vicars not only accused the Congregationalists of breaching the Aldermanbury accord, but charged that Philip Nye had deceitfully obtained the signed document from Calamy and had either destroyed or hidden it. Edwards charged that even prior to the issuance of the *Apologetical Narration* the Congregationalists had broken the accord by publishing defenses of their polity by others, "especially some books from out of New England, and particularly of Mr. Cotton's."[42]

Though the Presbyterians tried to paint the Congregationalists with the same brush used to describe the extreme sects, that characterization was false. It was denied not only by the Congregationalists but by their purported allies. The leading spokesmen for a broad religious liberty were willing to cooperate with the Apologists on some common goals, but they denounced the limited position taken by Goodwin and his colleagues in the *Apologetical Narration.* William Walwyn told of how, when that tract appeared, he "did with gladness undertake the reading thereof, expecting therein to find such general reasons for justification of themselves, to the world, as would have justified all Separation. . . . But finding contrary to that expectation that their Apology therein for themselves and their Toleration was grounded rather upon a Remonstrance of the nearness between them and the Presbyterians, being one in Doctrine with them, and very little differing from them in Discipline," he was very disappointed. In fact, Walwyn found the references made to the Separatists by the Dissenting Brethren to be "the worst sort of calumny." Roger Williams, John Goodwin, and other sectarian leaders were similarly critical of the Dissenting Brethren, though that did not prevent the two groups and their parliamentary supporters from using each other's aid to deflect a Presbyterian settlement.[43]

As the debate over religion spilled into the public arena, events of significance continued to occur in the Assembly and the Parliament. For the members of Parliament the primary task before them was winning the military struggle against the king. They were concerned with the reform of the church, but there was no more consensus over religion in Parliament than in the Assembly. Clearly some supporters of Presbyterianism in the two houses, especially among peers, were concerned with order. Many MPs, however, were friends of New England and its church practices. English Congregational clergymen were invited to preach to Parliament in numbers far exceeding their importance in the country at large. In addition to members who may have sympathized with Congregationalism and a few who may have held sectarian sympathies, there were others inclined to oppose Presbyterianism because it impinged on what they believed to be the religious authority of the civil magistrates. Some of this element were Erastians, others probably supporters of a reformed episcopacy. Beyond all these groups there were in the Parliament, as in the Assembly and in the nation, many who wanted reform but were committed to no particular program. Also complicating the search for a new religious order, especially for the last group, were the military imperatives. If the support of the Scots and their army was vital early in the conflict, by 1644 a growing sectarian element in the English army had to be accommodated. As Baillie expressed it, "The politick part in the Parliament . . . are resolute to conclude nothing in the matters of Religion, that may grieve the sectaries, whom they count necessarie for the time."[44]

Early in 1644 a meeting was held between the Scots' commissioners, three of the Dissenting Brethren (Goodwin, Burroughes, and Bridge), three moderate English Presbyterians (Marshall, Palmer, and Richard Vines), and three members of Parliament (Lord Wharton, Sir Henry Vane, and Oliver St. John). The purpose was to explore the possibility of accommodation, which all nine of the English discussants seemed to desire. The Scots hoped that a decision would be reached that would lead to unanimous recommendations from the Assembly, but they held the upper hand in the Assembly and their military contribution was needed by Parliament. Any decision would have to be on their terms. In March the group was constituted as an official Committee of Accommodation. The Congregationalists conceded a good deal. Among the points they agreed to were that presbyteries were lawful, had power to determine doctrine, could require congregations to account for errors in practice or doctrine, could admonish those who disturbed the peace of the church, and could urge congregations to withdraw from fellowship with a recalcitrant congregation. But though they accepted a large role for presbyteries, they could not concede *jure divino* power of such bodies. Many members of the Assembly may have been willing to accept the proposed agreement, but the Scots were not, and they had the votes.[45]

The Assembly's march toward a Presbyterian system continued through the spring and summer of 1644. Though Marshall, Vines, Herle, William Rathband, and other moderate Presbyterians supported some of the positions taken by the Dissenting Brethren, the latter group was fighting a delaying action and was gradually being alienated from the majority. The defeat of Congregationalism seemed inevitable. Throughout this difficult period the Congregationalists were sustained by the bonds of friendship that dated back to their experiences in the 1620s and 1630s. They engaged in godly conference and communion, aided one another, and worked in concert both in and out of the Assembly. A loose system of organization was developed by 1644 to maintain the unity of Congregationalists, and they were encouraged by the support of their friends abroad.[46]

One of the problems that continued to beset all Englishmen at this time was how to determine exactly what was happening. Sifting truth from rumor was more difficult than usual between 1640 and 1642. This was especially true for those separated by the ocean from the scene of events. As Massachusetts Governor John Winthrop expressed it, "indeed it was so usual to have false news brought from all parts, that we were very doubtful of the most probable reports." Friendship played a key role in the exchange of news, with reports from friends accepted far more readily than those carried by strangers. Memories of shared religious experience, of communion, were the foundation for trust. And trusting in the love they bore each other, colonists relied on trans-Atlantic friends to provide accurate news, sound advice, and helpful prayer.[47]

Based on what they learned from their English friends, the colonial clergy supported the parliamentary cause, hoped for religious reform, and shaped their own strategies for advancing Congregationalism. The colonists rejoiced when they "heard of that which might have been the work of many yeares, such a Parliament once chosen and assembled; such liberties granted unto it, such acts done by it . . . against enemies of God, Religion, Church, State, such tall cedars felled, etc." Concerned when war broke out—"the mart of all commodities, made the shop of artillery; the garden of pleasure, the stage of warre"—they supported the cause of Parliament. They criticized the king's recruitment of "Papists, Atheists, Neuters and mongrell Protestants." They reacted angrily against the uprising in Ireland with "those blood-thirsty sons of that scarlet-whore" executing "cruell rage, that cries to heaven." They approved the Solemn League and Covenant, but reminded Parliament that the important thing was not "that it is made with the Scottish, but that its made by them and you with the great God of Heaven." They approved and encouraged Parliament in its actions against the king. "Feare not," Nathaniel Rogers wrote to England's leaders, "but let your hands be strong, you fight the battels of the Lord. . . . He shall bind up your soules in the bundle of life, but the soules of the Cavaliers shall be slung out as out of the midst of a sling." And William Hooke urged them to "bee strong and of a good courage, bee not afraid, neither bee dismayed; for the Lord your God is with you whithersoever you goe."[48]

English friends continued to beseech their colonial correspondents for prayers: "Pray for England, for if ever Mother had need of daughter's help it is now"; "England stands in need of New England's strong Cries unto the Lord in regard to Church and Commonwealth"; "We need not stir you up to pray for us, of whose forwardness that way we rest so well assured." "Prayers are the Soules Ambassadors," the Puritans believed, "sent to Heaven to negotiate great things with God for us, and they will do what they are sent about."[49]

The colonists believed that prayer was a weapon as potent as any firearm. "Churches of praying believers," wrote Thomas Cobbett, "are terrible as so many Armies with Banners, as so many thundering Legions." Preaching on a day when believers throughout New England had gathered to fast and ask God's aid for their friends in England, William Hooke said, "I cannot but look upon the Churches in this Land this day, as upon so many severall Regiments, or bands of Soldiers lying in ambush here under the fearn and brushets of the Wilderness." While some of God's forces engaged the enemy on the battlefields of England, the colonists had been "sent . . . to lye in wait in the wildernesse, to come upon the backs of Gods Enemies with deadly Fastings and Prayer, murtherers that will kill point blanke from one end of the world to the other."[50]

This was the second fast-day sermon Hooke preached, the occasion being but one of many such days on which the colonists prayed for England. Fasts were held "for our native countrey," and "for the good success of the parliament." The hope of Ezekiel Rogers that "the Lord Jesus be mercifull to poore England" was widely shared. In Massachusetts these were called on specific occasions by the General Court or by individual congregations. In southern New England this practice became regularized. In Connecticut in January 1644, "The Courte taking the state of our native Country into consideration have Ordered that there shall be monthly a day of humiliation kept through the Plantation according to the course of our neighbors at New

Haven." Fast days for England continued during the remainder of the decade and into the 1650s, increasingly interspersed with days of thanksgiving to celebrate the evidence from England that the prayers of the saints had been answered. English friends believed such prayers were important and asked for them. The colonists believed that God would answer their prayers and hastened to comply. And those Englishmen who sided with the king charged the colonists "with schism and faction for fasting and praying for the affliction of their brethren in England."[51]

New Englanders were not content just to pray. Early in 1641 the leaders of the Bay Colony began to consider sending a mission to England, owing in part to the economic impact that the English events were having on the colonies. As John Winthrop explained it, "The parliament of England setting upon a general reformation both of church and state, the Earl of Strafford being beheaded, and the archbishop (our great enemy) and many others . . . imprisoned and called to account, this caused all men to stay in England in expectation of a new world, so as few coming to us, all foreign commodities grew scarce, and our own of no price." Given this situation, "The general court . . . thought fit also to send some chosen men into England, to congratulate the happy success there, and to satisfy our creditors of the true cause why we could not make so current payment as in former years we had done, and to be ready to make use of any opportunity God should offer for the good of the country here, as also to give any advice, as it should be required, for the settling right form of church discipline." Not everyone was convinced of the wisdom of this course. But some of the colony's English friends had written to Winthrop urging that the colony "send over some to solicit for us in the parliament, giving us hope that we might obtain much," and so the court decided to proceed.[52]

Chosen to represent Massachusetts were the Reverends Hugh Peter and Thomas Welde and the Boston merchant William Hibbins. The agents were able to placate the colony's creditors and obtained some forms of economic aid for the colonies. They succeeded in raising funds for an ironworks being established in New England by John Winthrop Jr. and secured some relief from customs duties. Welde received £100 from Lady Ann Moulson for support of Harvard, the donation funding the college's first scholarship. The two clergymen also solicited other contributions of money and books for the school. Samuel Hartlib, a friend of Peter's from the 1620s, was one of the Englishmen who helped them in this. Peter also developed a scheme whereby the homeless children of Irish Protestants would be sent as laborers to New England. The agents received Parliament's approval for the scheme, though they were able to raise only £875 and transported only about two dozen youths.[53]

In conjunction with their efforts to get aid for New England, Welde used materials furnished him by John Eliot and others to publish *New England's First Fruits* in 1643. Though it contained information on the climate and way of life of the colonists, the prime thrusts of the volume were a discussion of Eliot's success in bringing the gospel to the Indians and information on the founding and early years of Harvard. The book was well received and probably contributed not only to English interest in those projects but also to the acceptance of Harvard degrees when graduates began to arrive in England.[54]

From the start of the mission the two colonial clergymen devoted considerable efforts to the cause of religious reform. Working with former friends in the ministry, they did all they could to advance the New England Way. Peter traveled widely, journeying to the army in Ireland in the summer of 1642 and visiting former associates in the Netherlands on behalf of the cause in 1643. For a time he became one of the most popular and influential preachers in the army. Welde, who visited Archbishop Laud in the Tower to "demand of him recompence for all the wrongs he had done," sought to aid the cause by working with the Apologists and publishing materials on the New England Way.[55]

Publishing treatises that explained and defended Congregational Puritanism was seen as a significant way for New Englanders to advance the cause of reform in the motherland. The colonial clergy believed that their example and advice had brought things to the point already reached. According to John Cotton, Englishmen who had remained home "upon our departure grew more inquisitive into the cause of our voluntary exile, and there upon, more jealous of corruptions at home in the Worship of God, and in Church-Discipline; more sensible of the burden and danger of Episcopall tyranny and consequently more ready to follow . . . in rejecting and shaking off Episcopall usurpations." Having helped inspire the conflict, the colonists were bound to the parliamentary cause. "For what hath England said to us of late?" asked William Hooke, answering on the nation's behalf that "if the Papists, Prelates, and Atheists be too strong for us, then you shall help us; and if at any time the enemy be too strong for you, wee will help you." English friends who offered a preface to one of Thomas Shepard's treatises believed that "God gave life to New England to quicken Old." The colonists would show "our affection to this blessed work of a publique Reformation, of the Nation in generall, and the particular Churches or Congregations of the Land in particular . . . not only by here by our daily prayers for it," wrote Shepard and John Allin, "but also we have given some testimonies thereof by private Letters, and the publique motions of some of God's eminent servants among us." One of those eminent servants was John Cotton, who told his fellow colonists that it was their task "to wrastle with God, that they [Englishmen] may not perish for lack of knowledge, nor mistake a false Church for a true."

"Great pity were it," he concluded, "that they should want any light which might possibly be afforded them."[56]

The dissemination of New England views in the 1640s was a continuation of the sharing of such advice in the 1630s, but with censorship breaking down in England, friends of the New England Way rushed the treatises into print to give them a wider circulation. Those members of the Congregational network who were in England were the key figures in this effort for, as Roger Williams accused them, it was the goal of Thomas Goodwin, Philip Nye, and the others "to persuade the Mother Old England to imitate her Daughter New England's practice." In the late 1630s John Ball and other English nonconformists had addressed a series of questions to the New Englanders regarding concerns they had about the direction the colonists were taking. John Davenport had been deputed to respond and his *Church Government and Church Covenant Discussed in an Answer to the Elders* was published in London in 1643. Hugh Peter saw his friend's work through the press and added his own preface, in which he pointed out that "Presbytery and Independency (as it is cal'd) are the ways of worship and Church fellowship, now looked at, since (we hope) Episcopacy is crossed out." New Englanders and their English Congregational allies "are much charged with what we own not, viz. Independency," he continued, "when as we know not any Churches Reformed, more looking at sister Churches for helpe then ours doe, onely we cannot have rule yet discovered from any friend or enemy, that we should be under canon, or power of any other Church; under their Councell we are." Ball responded in a tract that Simeon Ashe and William Rathband published in 1643 with the relevant previous communications, *A Letter of Many Ministers in Old England . . . Together with An Answer . . . and a Reply*. Ball's reply alone appeared in 1644 as *A Tryall of the New Church Way in New England and Old*. This particular debate concluded with Thomas Shepard and John Allin's *A Defence of the Answer . . . Against the Reply . . . by Mr. John Ball* (London, 1648).[57]

Two other sets of questions about the New England Way had been sent to the colonists in the late 1630s, one by a group of Lancashire Puritans and another by the Reverend Richard Bernard. Richard Mather responded to Bernard in *An Apologie of the Churches in New England for Church Government* (London, 1643) and to his fellow Lancashire divines in *Church Government . . . an Answer to Two and Thirty Questions* (London, 1643). Both of these were seen to press by Peter. In 1644 William Rathband attacked Mather's views in *A Brief Narration of Some Church Courses Held in Opinion and Practice in the Churches Lately Erected in New England*. Thomas Welde rushed into print to defend the colonial churches. Explaining that, since he was a former colonist, "few or none are here [who] have had more experience of New England 'church-courses' than myself," he published *An Answer to W. R.* (London, 1644). Mather himself took advantage of Rathband's attack to prepare a magisterial "Plea for the Churches of Christ in New England." This six-hundred-page explanation of Congregationalism never saw print, though Joseph Caryl gave it his imprimatur and it is likely that it circulated in manuscript. In a private letter to a friend in England, Mather complained that Rathband had brought "forth such sour fruit in his old age & that he should dishonor his hoary head in the last act of his life . . . at 3000 mile distance & to draw out the supposed divisions of our Churches who never saw as much as the tops of our chimnies or the shadowes of our trees."[58]

In addition to his questions for the colonists, John Ball published a defense of set forms of prayer. This was the issue that Ball had debated earlier with Thomas Goodwin and Philip Nye, with the two Congregationalists rejecting the set formulas as contained in the official liturgy. John Cotton responded with *A Modest and Cleare Answer to Mr Ball's Discourse of Set Formes of Prayer* (London, 1642), and Thomas Hooker also explained the colonial position in *A Briefe Exposition of the Lord's Prayer* (London, 1645).[59]

A matter that would concern the Assembly of Divines and the entire Puritan community was the subject of infant baptism. The Englishman John Spilsbury attacked the practice in *A Treatise Concerning the Lawfull Subject of Baptism* (London, 1643). Thomas Hooker responded in *The Covenant of Grace Opened*, which circulated in manuscript before being posthumously published in London in 1649. Richard Mather also wrote an "Answer to Nine Reasons of John Spilsbury." This circulated in manuscript, but unlike Hooker's treatise it was never published. John Tombes sent John Cotton a defense of Baptist views, which the colonial clergy assigned to Thomas Cobbett to answer. Cotton dispatched a manuscript copy of Cobbett's *Vindication of the Covenant and Church Estate of Church Members* (London, 1643) to Tombes when it was ready. New England's George Phillips had earlier written a justification of infant baptism in response to questions from Nathaniel Briscoe. This response circulated widely in England in manuscript. When Thomas Lamb published a *Confutation of Infant Baptism* (London, 1643), which attacked some of Phillips's positions, Phillips responded with *A Reply to a Confutation of Some Grounds for Infant Baptism* (London, 1645). A striking fact about these works is that they were slower to reach print than works on other subjects, which might be accounted for by the fact that English Congregationalists were developing an understanding with some English Calvinist Baptists and did not want works from their American friends disrupting that alliance.

John Cotton was widely perceived as one of the international leaders of

Puritan Congregationalism and there was great interest in his views. In 1641 *A Copy of a Letter of Mr Cotton of Boston* was published. In 1642 there appeared *The Churches Resurrection, The True Constitution of a Particular Visible Church*, and one of his millenarian works, *The Powring Out of the Seven Vials*. In 1644 *The Keyes of the Kingdom of Heaven* was published. *The Way of the Churches of Christ in New England* and *The Covenant of God's Free Grace* both appeared in 1645.

Thomas Hooker was second only to Cotton in the estimation of his Congregational friends in England and the Netherlands. Hooker's *The Christians Two Chiefe Lessons* was published in 1640. Copies of sermons he had preached in England were among other works published in the early 1640s. *The Danger of Desertion* (London, 1641) and *The Faithful Covenanter* (London, 1644) were series of such sermons that addressed the nature of England's relationship with God. Hooker also became involved in one of the key debates of the decade. In 1643 the moderate Presbyterian Charles Herle authored *The Independency on Scriptures of the Independency of Churches*. Richard Mather and William Thompson, who knew and appreciated the Englishman, prepared *A Modest and Brotherly Answer to Mr Herle*. Samuel Rutherford brought a sharper tone to the debate when he responded with his *Due Right of Presbyteries* (London, 1644). Mather prepared *A Reply to Mr Rutherford, or a Defence of the Answer to Herle* (London, 1647). Thomas Hooker was also answering Rutherford in his *Survey of the Summe of Church Discipline* (London, 1648), which became one of the classic statements of the New England Way.

Thomas Shepard's *The Sincere Convert* (London, 1641) was printed from notes taken of earlier English sermons by a friend, whereas *The Sound Believer* (London, 1645) was a companion piece he sent for publication himself. Interest in all aspects of the New England Way ran high in the mother country, and John Davenport's *A Profession of faith Made at his admission into one of the Churches of God in New England* (London, 1642) answered questions about the process of Congregational church admission. Although most overseas interest was focused on religious practices, other aspects of life in the "City on a Hill" were also subjects on which the colonists felt they had something to offer—John Cotton published *An Abstract of the Lawes of New England* (London, 1641), for example. As the debate over church and state expanded and changed in the following years, the New England contribution would continue and change.

As noted before, the English Congregationalists, bound by the Aldermanbury accord not to promote their polity, relied on New Englanders' surrogates to spread the message for them. There is no question that Thomas Goodwin and his fellow Congregationalists played a key role in guiding the works of colonial friends into print. Thomas Edwards accused them of this in his *Antapologia* and the eighteenth-century New England Baptist Isaac Backus claimed that "the famous Dr. Thomas Goodwin ushered their performances into the world." In the case of treatises on faith and worship there was no need to do this surreptitiously. Philip Nye and Sydrach Simpson attested to one of Samuel Eaton's works. William Greenhill wrote an epistle, "To the Reader," introducing Thomas Shepard's *Sincere Convert*. Shepard also entrusted the manuscript for *The Sound Believer* to Greenhill, "leaving it wholly with your selfe, whom I much love and honour, that you would add or detract any thing you see meet." Thomas Goodwin and Philip Nye wrote a preface to their friend Hooker's treatise on the Lord's Prayer. In the case of works on church government they maintained a lower profile, probably assisting Welde, Peter, and others in bringing treatises to print. Following publication of the *Apologetical Narration* any such constraints no longer existed. Goodwin and Nye guided Cotton's *Way of the Churches* into print, and from that point on the record of their assistance is clear.[60]

Not all the colonists were content to advise from afar. Cotton, Hooker, and Davenport were persuaded that they could best advance Congregationalism by remaining in New England, but many other colonists returned to the motherland. Although most American Puritans had come to view New England as their home, many felt the call to England. Emigration was heavy early in the 1640s and the loss of potential colonial leaders was noticeable. Seven of the nine members of Harvard's first graduating class (1642) went to England, as did at least fourteen of the twenty-four graduates from the next five classes.[61]

Some of those who journeyed eastward across the Atlantic did so because they were dissatisfied with New England. This included those like Hanserd Knollys, Robert Lenthall, Marmaduke Matthews, and George Burdett, who dissented from the rule of the saints; men like Edward Carlton, who were lonely and had never adjusted to the New World; and some who suffered from the slump in the region's economy in the early 1640s and sought new opportunities back home. But most who made the journey sought to carry New England's light with them so as to illumine their countrymen and inspire further reform.[62]

Among those who returned were many who sought to promote the Congregational cause. Hugh Peter and Thomas Welde were directly charged with that task by the Massachusetts General Court. John Phillips, who had preached in England previously and had married a sister of William Ames, returned to his former parish at Wrentham and was named to the Westminster Assembly. Others who returned in the 1640s to parishes in which they had previously ministered included Robert Peck and Thomas Waterhouse. Harvard graduates who quickly obtained clerical posts at this time included John Allin, Nathaniel Brewster, John Bulkeley, and John Welde. When the rupture between Congregationalists and Presbyterians divided the nation in the aftermath of the *Apologetical Narration*, these men and other New Englanders such as Samuel Eaton who came over became strong advocates of the Congregational Way.[63]

As the struggle between Presbyterians and Congregationalists began to assume an importance second only to that between the king and Parliament, New Englanders increasingly made their presence felt. Informed by friends of the nature and significance of English events, the colonists mobilized to help those friends and depended on them to channel their contributions most effectively.

CHAPTER SEVEN

These Polemick Times

AT THE TIME when the Dissenting Brethren issued their *Apologetical Narration*, the Scottish army had reentered England, the Scottish commissioners seemed to command a clear majority in the Assembly, and the imposition of a Scottish church order on England seemed inevitable. Five years later the king of England would be awaiting execution, Scotland had been occupied by forces of the English Parliament, and the anticipated dawn of a Presbyterian era had never materialized. The wheel had turned, and the Congregationalists, whose situation had seemed desperate in 1644, were the rising force in English religion.[1]

The struggle to define the form of England's church in the 1640s took place on many levels. Among the more important were the stages of the Assembly and Parliament, where legislation was shaped; the forum of the press, where clergy fought to persuade the public; and the congregations scattered throughout the land, where individual clergymen and their flocks worked to establish what they believed were proper reformed practices. The attempt by the nation's leaders to explore the possibility of accommodation that had failed early in 1644 had taken place essentially as an Assembly effort, though some political leaders had been involved. In September of that year, buoyed by the boost to English spirits and to his own reputation by the July military victory at Marston Moor, Oliver Cromwell persuaded Parliament to pass an accommodation order appointing a committee to "take into consideration the differences in opinion of the members of the Assembly in point of church government." This intervention of Parliament took the Scots by surprise. Meeting for the first time on September 20, the new Committee of Accommodation appointed a subcommittee of Assembly members, which soon brought forth a recommendation that stressed the unity of the Congregationalists and Presbyterians in most areas of religion. It provided that church government should be administered by county boards composed of local ministers and laymen who would be named by Parliament. This introduced an Erastian element that would have been acceptable to the Dissenting Brethren, but not to the Scottish Presbyterians. Following the capture of Newcastle by the Scottish armies the Presbyterian party was again riding high. The Scottish commissioners pressured Parliament into requesting the Assembly to produce proposals to curb antinomianism and Anabaptism and to order the Committee of Accommodation to suspend its deliberations indefinitely.[2]

Despite this setback, many still hoped that a formula for accommodation would be reached, and even the Scots in the Assembly continued to hope that the Congregationalists would eventually unite with them. The Dissenting Brethren continued to participate in the shaping of the Assembly's reports and the size of their group showed some growth. The core of the Congregationalist faction in the Assembly remained the five authors of the *Apologetical Narration*: Thomas Goodwin, Philip Nye, Jeremiah Burroughes, William Bridge, and Sydrach Simpson. Generally voting with them were William Greenhill, William Carter the younger, John Bond, John Green, John Phillips (of New England), and Joseph Caryl. William Strong was a Congregationalist added to the Assembly in January 1646. Peter Sterry and Anthony Burgess frequently voted with the Dissenting Brethren. Working with them outside the Assembly but as part of the Congregational clerical network were numerous other clergy, including returned New Englanders such as Hugh Peter and Thomas Welde. The Congregationalists in the Assembly accepted the Directory of Worship that was adopted in January of 1645. They shared in the development of the Confession of Faith. But in the debates on government they were in a minority, and their arguments were increasingly viewed by the majority less as contributions than as obstructionism. On April 4, 1645, stung perhaps by New England criticism that the majority was ignoring the position of the Congregationalists, the Presbyterian Matthew Newcomen proposed that "the Brethren of this Assembly, who have formerly entered their dissents to the Presbyteriall Government, shall be a Committee to bring in the whole Frame of their Judgements, concerning Church Government." Newcomen was willing to find a basis for accommodation with the Congregationalists.[3]

Though moderate English Presbyterians may have sincerely hoped that this strategy would produce unity, it was the plan of others to bury the Dissenting

Brethren. As Robert Baillie put it after returning from a visit to Scotland, the Apologists "have not much troubled the Assembly" because they were busy working on their platform. Furthermore, in his opinion, "The Assemblie purposes not to take it [the awaited Congregationalist statement] into publick debate, but to give it to some committee," where it could be ignored. The Dissenting Brethren labored at their task through the summer months, but found themselves in difficulties. A platform of church government would reveal precisely what limits they would place on toleration, and politically they were not willing, in the prevailing circumstances, to alienate their sectarian support in the army and in the country at large. Indeed, they might have come to suspect that this was the reason the Presbyterians were pushing for a statement. While the Congregationalists deliberated, the Presbyterian majority framed a system of church government and voted in July to send it on to Parliament.[4]

In September the Assembly began to push the Congregationalists for their statement, and in response on October 13 Sydrach Simpson read to the Assembly what was later published as *A Copy of a Remonstrance Delivered in the Assembly . . . Declaring the Grounds and Reasons of their declining to bring in to the Assembly their Moddell of Church Government* (London, 1645). The remonstrants complained that they had been treated unfairly by their colleagues, who had pretended to care about their views while not being prepared to give them serious consideration. They complained that the Assembly had refused them permission to bring in their proposals piece by piece as the new form of government was being proposed, though the Presbyterian system was being introduced piecemeal. Having insisted on a complete package, the Assembly had not waited for it before approving the Presbyterian system. The Assembly knew what they objected to—"the Presbyteriall government over many Congregations" and "the subordination of Synods." "Upon these considerations," they concluded, "we think that this Assembly hath no cause now to require a Report of us, nor will that our Report be of any use, seeing that *Reports* are for *Debates* and *Debates* are for *Results* to be sent up to the Honourable Houses, *who have already voted another form of government than what we shall present.*" Declining to tip their hand by presenting their plan to the Assembly, they were "resolved to wait for some further opportunitie, to improve what we have prepared."[5]

In essence, the Dissenting Brethren were again appealing over the Assembly to the Parliament, and that body responded by instructing the dormant Committee of Accommodation to resume its deliberations. But there was no longer any hope of bringing the alienated parties together. The Congregationalists affirmed their support for the Directory of Worship and the work being done on the Confession of Faith. They no longer asked to be accommodated within a Presbyterian church, but to be tolerated outside it, which perhaps shows a growing distrust of the Presbyterian majority. They desired recognition of congregational ordination, liberty for anyone to join a gathered church, and freedom of their congregations from Presbyterian discipline. According to Baillie, they "expressed their desyres for toleration, not only to themselves, but to other Sects." Some members of the committee still seem to have wanted to compromise, but the majority sentiment agreed with Baillie that if the Congregationalists received what they wanted, "this Church, will by law be given over to confusion." On March 9, 1646, the committee adjourned for what proved to be the last time.[6]

The Assembly continued to produce reports and Parliament gradually implemented a Presbyterian system, though not one based on the *jure divino* precept that had divided the Scots and Congregationalists. Classes began to meet in London in 1646. The Confession of Faith was adopted by Parliament in 1648, as was the Shorter Catechism. (Among the works that seem to have influenced the Assembly's catechism was Thomas Hooker's *An Exposition of the Principles of Religion* [London, 1645].) That same year the Presbyterian structure of government became law, but the new church was only a shadow of what the Scots had hoped for and the Independents had dreaded. In fact, many of those chosen to serve as "Presbyterian elders" in London and elsewhere were Congregationalists (and still others were Independents of various stripes) who would use their influence in the classes to accommodate some diversity of opinion. Nationally and locally the church was under greater lay control than its sister church in the northern kingdom. By their tactics of delay and their vigorous defenses of their position in public debate, Congregationalists had achieved their primary objective of a de facto toleration of their existence.[7]

The pamphlet debates over religion were far more heated than the verbal exchanges among the Assembly's opposing theologians. In what New England's Thomas Cobbett called "these polemick times," Presbyterian authors such as John Bastwick, John Vicars, and Thomas Edwards did not share the respect and affection that Assembly moderates such as Stephen Marshall held for the Dissenting Brethren. Their goal was to savagely attack the Congregationalists along with all the Independents, making no distinctions between the Apologists and the spokesmen of the most extreme religious views.

John Bastwick's *Independency not God's Ordinance* (London, 1645) was one of the first no-holds-barred attacks on the Independents. He identified the idea of toleration as springing from the devil and dismissed the Congregationalists' claim that they agreed with the Presbyterians in doctrine as serving only to conceal their true perfidy. He singled out Independency as the breeding ground of all other errors and justified punishment of heresy and blasphemy by death. Equally extreme were the views of John Vicars, who called Philip Nye the *"nimble-Agent* for their *Schismaticall Church-way"* and claimed that the Congregationalists were no different from the most radical sectaries, labeling the Dissenting Brethren as *"Sampsons Foxes,* fast tyed by their tails with destructive *Firebrands* of *Dissention, Division,* and *Confusion* between them, to destroy (as much as in them is) the *good-corn* of *Gods field."*[8]

Thomas Edwards was perhaps the most relentless opponent of the Independents. Like Bastwick, he viewed the idea of toleration as spawned by the devil and advocacy of the idea as sufficient proof of heresy. His *Gangraena* was an attack on "the errors, heresies, blasphemies in this Catalogue particularized . . . as, namely, Independents, Brownists, Chiliasts or Millenarians, Antinomians, Libertines, Familists, Enthusiasts, Seekers and Waiters, Perfectists, Socinians, Arians, Anti-Trinitarians, Anti-Scripturists, Sceptics, and Questionists." He never doubted the *jure divino* legitimacy of a strong Presbyterian order and, again like Bastwick, he believed that physical punishment was justified to purge the land of those who erred. Edwards presented the Scottish commissioner Robert Baillie with a copy of his *Apologia,* and Baillie approved of it. "Mr. Edwards," he wrote, "has written a splendid confutation of all Independents' Apologie." Baillie worked with "more than a hundred" ministers from the London area to "erect a weekly lecture for him [Edwards] in Christ's Church, the heart of the city, where he may handle these questions, and nothing else, before all that will come to hear."[9]

One of the tactics used by most of the Presbyterian authors, including Baillie himself in his *A Dissuasive from the Errours of the Time* (London, 1645), was to cite the early history of New England as proof that Congregationalism bred error. This involved demonstrating that John Cotton and the Puritan clergy in the colonies were but an American wing of the movement led by the Dissenting Brethren. Of course, Thomas Goodwin and his fellow Apologists admitted as much, but Presbyterian authors provided evidence to reinforce the connection. Edwards claimed that William Bridge and Jeremiah Burroughes had publicly acknowledged that "we agree with them of New England, and are of their Church-way." Edwards also claimed that the *Apologetical Narration* resulted from "many meetings and consultations both of writing letters into New England for their help and furtherance, and about what you should do, and how to order matters." The Presbyterian author of *An Antidote Against the Contagious Air of Independency* (London, 1644) referred to the Independents "come from Holland and America" as the cause of English divisions. Robert Baillie often referred to "that party, both from Arnheim, Rotterdam, and New England" and to "the English Ministers of Holland who are for the New England Way."[10]

Having proved to their satisfaction that the Dissenting Brethren were no different from the New Englanders, the Presbyterians attacked the colonial order. According to Baillie, "that which demonstrates the Genuine Nature of this Plant [Congregationalism], is its fruits in New-England, where . . . in a short time there, it brought forth such a multitude of grosse Heresies and Divisions, as did threaten not the Churches alone, but the Civil State also with a totall Ruine." Congregationalism as espoused by Goodwin and Nye became generally discussed in England as "the New England Way" and by discrediting the New Englanders, Presbyterians hoped to defeat the English members of the network. The result was to draw New Englanders and their experience ever more deeply into the English struggle.[11]

One of the first and most controversial colonial contributions to this stage of the debate was made by Thomas Welde. The New England agent had brought to England John Winthrop's manuscript account of the antinomian controversy and the banishment of Anne Hutchinson and her supporters. The manuscript was passed from hand to hand until 1644 when Welde decided to publish it. His purpose was to clear New England from the charge of generating error. *A Short Story of the Rise, reign, and ruine of the Antinomians, Familists & Libertines* (London, 1644) made a case that Welde must have believed would prove a valuable defense for English Congregationalists. The tract demonstrated that Anne Hutchinson had been influenced by radicals in England before she ever came to the colonies, so that her heresies were not the product of the New England Way. Indeed, the colonial Congregationalists had gathered in a synod and condemned her errors. The Boston church exercised its spiritual weapons in excommunicating the leading Hutchinsonians while the magistrates expelled those whose errors were deemed disruptive to the public peace. The message was clear: New England Congregationalism did not breed error but could control it as efficiently as any Presbyterian system could.[12]

Unfortunately, the publication of *A Short Story* was not the unalloyed blessing for the Dissenting Brethren that Welde had hoped it would be—or at least they found it politic to distance themselves from it. A year earlier, when there was hope for a Presbyterian-Congregationalist accommodation, the Apologists may have found the tract useful, but when it actually appeared, Thomas Goodwin and his brethren were reaching out for allies against the Presbyterians and *A Short Story* was an embarrassment. Not only was the news of Congregationalists' suppressing sects politically disruptive to Independent unity, but *A Short Story* depicted one-time Massachusetts governor Henry Vane in a very poor light, and Vane was a pivotal figure in the Parliamentary Independent party. Thomas Hooker, though an ocean away, realized the implications quite well and could only assume that Presbyterians "had a secret hand to provoke Mr Welde to set forth his 'Short Story' touching occasions here in Mr Vane his reign." Hooker was deeply suspicious of the Scots and also wrote that "I easilie see that the Scotch party do seriously set themselves to fortify their Presbyterian side, with the improvement of all means (I had almost said Jesuit-like) to weaken the proceedings and the persons of the contrary minded."[13]

One of those who took issue with Winthrop's *Short Story* was John Wheelwright, who had been banished as a supporter of Hutchinson. Believing that his views had been misrepresented both by the Massachusetts General Court and by Winthrop in the latter's account, Wheelwright or his son published *Mercurius Americanus, Mr Welds his Antitype, or Massachusetts great Apologie examined* (London, 1645). The primary goal of this work was to defend Wheelwright by distinguishing his views from Hutchinson's, and in the process the author was willing to condemn her errors. "As for Mrs Hutchinson," he wrote, "in spirituals indeed she gave her understanding over into the power of suggestion and immediate dictates, by reason of which she had many strange fancies, and erroneous tennents possest her." This tract, along with *A Short Story*, only fueled the arguments of those like Edwards who chose to claim that the "true story of New England is one of great heresies, etc., caused by Independency." Hutchinson, Wheelwright, Samuel Gorton, and other "radicals" were cited as evidence for his claims, and much of the ammunition used by Edwards and other Presbyterians came from New Englanders. In the case of Gorton, it was actually Roger Williams who provided the Presbyterians with information, when he gave Robert Baillie a paper describing some of Gorton's errors. A more understandable source was New England supporters of Presbyterian policies, such as the Reverend Thomas Parker of Newbury, who hoped that the rising Presbyterian tide would sweep over the colonies as well as England.[14]

As part of their attack the Presbyterian polemicists, whether discussing Congregationalism in old or New England, labeled it "Independency," hoping by that means to emphasize the connection they believed existed between the Congregationalists and the radical sects. Ideally, they hoped to stir conservative fears by highlighting the origin of vile heresies in Congregational New England. At the same time their discussion of colonial disputes was intended to sow seeds of dissension in the emerging English Independent coalition by providing colonial evidence that sects had little to hope for from a Congregational ascendancy. Thus, Thomas Edwards challenged the Dissenting Brethren's arguments for toleration by examples of New England intolerance. Here again, their goals were inadvertently being advanced by colonial writers, for the most outspoken opponents of New England Congregational intolerance were the victims of it, and none was more articulate than Roger Williams.[15]

Williams had been forced to leave the Bay Colony in the 1630s when he refused to desist from criticizing aspects of the emerging Massachusetts orthodoxy. He believed himself ill treated and took advantage of the new freedom of the English press to proclaim how he had been wronged. In 1644 he aided in the publication of *Mr Cotton's Letter Lately Printed, Examined and*

Answered and followed that with his *The Bloudy Tenent of Persecution, for cause of Conscience discussed, in a Conference between Truth and Peace* (London, 1644). These initiated responses from Cotton—*Master John Cottons Answer to Master Roger Williams* (London, 1647) and *The Bloudy Tenent, Washed, And Made White in the Bloude of the Lambe* (London, 1647)—to which Williams responded with *The Bloudy Tenent Yet More Bloudy* (London, 1652).

The Cotton-Williams debate may have been an embarrassment to the Congregationalists in the Assembly, but it was more than that. The exchange showed clearly the line of division between Congregationalists and leaders such as Williams. Whereas the Dissenting Brethren still sought a national church that would comprehend all, but only, orthodox believers, "Sundrie of the Independent partie," according to Baillie, "are stepped out of the Church, and follows my good acquaintance Mr Roger Williams" in seeking a more universal toleration. Stephen Marshall likewise noted that Williams had gone further than the Congregationalists in taking away from the magistrate his right and duty to suppress heresy.[16]

This, of course, was precisely the issue that divided the two colonists. Although many contemporaries and most historians have accepted Williams's depiction of the New England position as valid, Conrad Wright has correctly perceived the moderate tone of Cotton's writings. Cotton maintained a position virtually identical to that of the Dissenting Brethren—denying toleration to beliefs such as Catholicism and antinomianism that were believed to threaten the peace, to views that violated national standards of decency, and to practices that violated the law, while being willing to accept a diversity of views on matters of polity and nonfundamental religious beliefs. If this was not as liberal as twentieth-century sensibilities would wish, it was not as intolerant as Williams wished to portray it. Cotton sided with the claims of his friends Thomas Goodwin and Philip Nye that orthodox dissenters such as they ought to be accommodated or tolerated in a Presbyterian England. He rejected an extension of toleration to those "Dissenters in fundamentals, and that out of obstinacy against conscience and seducers, to the perdition of soules, and to the disturbance of civill and church peace," seeking to limit toleration to "only such Dissenters as vary either in matters of lesse weight, or of fundamentall, yet not out of wilfull obstinacy, but out of tenderness of conscience."[17]

Baillie and Marshall noted that Williams was taking a stand that not only attacked New England orthodoxy but distanced him from the English Congregationalist members of the Independent coalition. *An Attestation of our reverend Brethren of the Province of London* (London, 1648) distinguished among the Independents between "(O) some of them to be adverse in a great measure to such a Toleration as you might truely terme intolerable and abominable, which that Catholick Advocate and Patron (P) of all irreligious proposeth," identifying "O" as Jeremiah Burroughes and "P" as Roger Williams. The difference was one Williams himself acknowledged. Though he agreed with the Dissenting Brethren on the need to prevent a Presbyterian settlement, he attacked them for holding the same limited notions of toleration he had objected to in New England. In 1644 he published *Querries of Highest Consideration, Proposed to the Five Holland Ministers and the Scottish Commissioners* in which he attacked the authors of the *Apologetical Narration* for being no different from the Scots in their acceptance of a state church and the exercise of power to curb schism and heresies. In the *Bloudy Tenent* he lumped presbyters, prelates, and Congregationalist leaders together as sheltering under the civil magistrate's power, and in *The Bloudy Tenent Yet More Bloudy* he denied that there was much that he or those like him "may expect from the very *Independent clergie* themselves."[18]

Roger Williams was not the only New England dissident who was as uncomfortable with the English Congregationalists as he was with the leaders of the Bay Colony. Samuel Gorton had also been banished from Massachusetts for his heterodox views and in 1645 he journeyed to England to bring his case before the Parliamentary Commission for Foreign Plantations. In his testimony and through publication of *Simplicities Defense Against Seven-Headed Piety* (London, 1646), Gorton brought once again to the attention of Englishmen the intolerance of the New England Congregationalists. Plymouth Colony's Edward Winslow had been engaged by the Massachusetts magistrates to act as their agent in defense of the colony and he responded to Gorton's attack with *Hypocrisie Unmasked by the True Relation of the Proceedings of the Governor and Company of the Massachusetts against Samuel Gorton* (London, 1646).[19]

Even when answers appeared quickly, the charges against New England continued to be spread and exaggerated by those who had an interest in discrediting Congregationalism and the Independent movement to which the Congregationalists belonged. In his *Heresiography*, the Presbyterian Ephraim Pagitt reported that "in *New England* they perswade the Magistrates to kill all idolaters and Heretickes, even whole Cities, men, women, and children." To counter such attacks, Englishmen sympathetic with the colonies cautioned New Englanders "to be carefull of your practice there, for whatever you doe that may have the least shadow of severitie, is heightened here, and cast in your brethrens teeth." Henry Vane, who personally had reason to be aware of the treatment accorded dissidents in the Bay Colony, urged John Winthrop to deal with heretics more cautiously. Vane saw divisions in the Independent ranks playing into the hands of the Presbyterians and warned that "while the Congregational way among you is in your freedom, and is backed with power," the situation in England was different and New England intolerance would "teach its [Congregationalism's] opposers here to extirpate it and root it out."[20]

Despite such warnings, the colonial clergy continued to pursue their way, to defend it, and, increasingly, to strike polemical blows against the Scots and those who would impose an intolerant Presbyterianism on England. In appealing to the majority of their fellow Englishmen, Congregationalists had to demonstrate that their church polity could prevent or eliminate gross religious errors. Despite the risk of alienating allies among the sects, Congregationalists on both sides of the Atlantic spoke out against the more extreme errors of the times, and New Englanders claimed success in dealing with such heretics.

Dismissing the Presbyterian charge that Congregationalism bred error, Thomas Welde countered by admitting that "we have had 'division' amongst us," but claimed that "these 'divisions' were not caused by our church-discipline, but by certain vile 'opinions' brought us from England." Errors such as antinomianism and familism "and an hundred such like odd fancies," according to Thomas Shepard, "these Churches in *New England* have examined and publickly condemned, and sent to their grave, and have seen their burial." It was in England, not in New England, that such errors were uncontrolled, and Shepard argued that "the Familists and Antinomians . . . will prove (if not crusht) the scourge of that Land, and the most subtle enemies to the power of godliness, that *England* can have, as they were once amongst us." John Davenport was another colonist who saw England mired in an "hour of Temptation: wherein Satan the old Serpent . . . as it were rolling himself into a circle, reviveth old heresies under new names and pretexts: which . . . now appear in Troops; as if Satan were mustering up all his forces together for his last assault." John Cotton likewise complained that England, not the colonies, had to be "more zealous against the horrid blasphemies and heresies." Welde best expressed the colonial counterattack in his *Answer to W.R.* It was "under that government of ours which you call,—or rather, miscall,—'popular,' the very neck of 'schisme' and vile opinions, brought to us from hence, was broken," he pointed out, "when here, amongst you, where there is not such a government, they walk bolt upright amongst you, and cry aloud. You shall do better to lay aside this objection," he warned, "till a Presbyterian government have healed these sore breaches in these churches here!"[21]

Along with these attempts to clear themselves from the charge of breeding heresy, the colonists denied they were Independents in the sense in which the term was being used in England. Thomas Hooker rejected "the distasteful term of 'Independency,' " whereas John Cotton proclaimed, "Nor is Independency a fit name of the way of our churches." Regarding what separated the New Englanders and the Dissenting Brethren on the one hand from the Scots on the other, Cotton concluded, "I know none fitter than to denominate theirs Classical, and ours Congregational." In rejecting the name Independent (which their English friends also tried to discard), the New Englanders were trying to deny their affiliation not with English Congregationalism but with the radical inferences with which the Presbyterians had loaded the name.[22]

None of this meant that New Englanders accepted the other portrait being painted of them, in which they were depicted as narrowly intolerant of all who disagreed with them. Writing to his friend Hugh Peter in 1645, Thomas Shepard expressed his "feare [that] greater sorrowes [will] attend England if they do not seasonably suppresse and beare publicke witnesse agaynst such delusions which fill the land like locusts . . . and will certainly (if suffered) eat up the greene grass of the land." But in the same letter Shepard expressed a "desire to shew the utmost forbearance to godly men if for a time deluded" and remarked that "there may be some connivance for a time while 'tis tumultuous and while the wars call all spirits thither." Connivance was precisely the relationship of the Dissenting Brethren to their Independent allies and Shepard realized this. He even went so far as to concede that "the case may be such as a state may tolerate all, because of necessity they must, the numbers being so many and the hazard more," but in such a case the saints should labor to change the circumstances that gave rise to such a necessity.[23]

Shepard was unusual in admitting—even in private correspondence—that a broad toleration was something Englishmen might have to accept for the time. But all the New Englanders complained that the picture of colonial oppression being circulated in England was too extreme; that New Englanders themselves allowed some diversity under a broad umbrella of orthodoxy. Edward Winslow, for example, pointed to the willingness of the Plymouth colonists to accept into fellowship members of the French and Dutch Reformed Churches. More important, Winslow made much of the fact that the Massachusetts authorities had always tolerated the Reverends Thomas Parker and John Noyse of Newbury and the Reverend Peter Hobart of Hingham—all of whom subscribed to Presbyterian views of church government and imposed such a discipline in their own congregations. Even Baptists, it was claimed, despite laws against them, were not acted against "as long as they carry themselves peaceably." This is the image that the New Englanders portrayed in response to charges of religious disorder resulting from Congregationalism: vile heresies had been curbed, orthodox Reformed believers of various persuasions had been accommodated, and the region was at peace. Thomas Shepard waxed lyrical about it: "We wonder at God for our peace the Lord gives us in these parts," he wrote. "The reports of the divisions in *New England* are fables; the Churches are here in peace; the Common-wealth in peace; the

Ministry in most sweet peace; All our families in peace." Yet this was not enough, for "this peace giveth us no rest, while our deare England is in trouble, for which we would weepe."[24]

To help England it was not enough to refute attacks on the colonies. The clergy worked together to set forth the nature and the superiority of the Congregational Way. As had been the case early in the civil wars, this campaign often took the form of responding to Presbyterian tracts, though the works produced could for the most part stand alone. Production of the response was orchestrated by the colonial clerical network. John Cotton highlighted some of the key efforts in his own *Way of the Congregational Churches Cleared* (London, 1648), when he pointed out "that Mr Hooker hath written a large answer to Mr Rutherford; Mr Davenport, to Mr Paget; Mr Mather to Mr Rathbone; Mr Shepard and Mr Allin to Mr Ball; Mr Norton in Latin to Mr Apopoliz; myself to Mr Williams." The decision as to who was to take up which theological cudgel was often reached in conferences of network members. Thus, Hooker explained that his *Survey of the Summe of Church Discipline* was undertaken when "at a common meeting [of the clergy] I was desired by them all, to publish what I now do." The type of gathering in which such decisions were reached is described by John Winthrop in his journal entry for March 5, 1645: "The elders of the churches through all the United Colonies agreed upon a meeting at Cambridge this day, where they conferred their councils and examined the writings which some of them had prepared in answer to the said books [attacking New England religious practice], which being agreed and perfected were sent into England." Such conferences were common in the 1640s, as were ongoing exchanges of advice through correspondence. In 1647, for example, Samuel Stone wrote to Thomas Shepard about a work that would be an "Answer to Dr. Crispe" and said he planned to "take further advice." Shepard himself explained in the preface to his *Theses Sabaticae* that he was "desired by all the Elders in the Country, then met together, to commit them [the *Theses*] to publique view." Indeed, the foundation upon which the colonial arguments for Congregationalism rested was their confidence in the sufficiency of such godly communion, a confidence their opponents did not share and could not trust in.[25]

The publication of New England defenses of and explications of Congregationalism involved the efforts of more than just the members of the network in the colonies. Friends and allies in England who were members of the network played an equally significant role in seeing that these works appeared. English Congregationalists were the ones who sent Presbyterian and sectarian tracts to the colonies, who in some cases explicitly solicited colonial responses, and who in almost all instances saw to the printing of the New England tracts, often adding a laudatory preface. Thomas Goodwin and Philip Nye saw Cotton's *Keyes of the Kingdom* into print and prefaced it with an endorsement identifying it as an expression of "that very middle way (which in our Apology we did in the general intimate and intend) between that which is called *Brownisme* and the *presbyterial government* as it is practised." Hooker's survey was initially lost when the ship carrying it to England sank. His friends helped to prepare a new copy that was printed posthumously in England through the efforts of Thomas Goodwin, who acknowledged "the honour I bore to him, and love unto this cause my heart is in." Goodwin, Nye, and Sydrach Simpson spoke glowingly of Norton's *Answer to Appolonius* when they rushed it into print "because it takes up and defends not our side of the controversy . . . but, as we believe, the side of Jesus Christ." The point was, of course, that these friends saw no difference between the cause of New England, the cause of Congregationalism, and the cause of Christ. They sought a national church that would recognize the churches of all orthodox Calvinists and in which Congregationalists would be free to control their own affairs and to persuade others of the superiority of their way. The practice of their churches was virtually identical with that of New England in terms of standards and procedures for admission, methods of choosing church officers and of exercising discipline, and liturgical practices. Nathaniel Holmes introduced Cotton's *Way of the Churches Cleared* as "a true and terse history of the purer churches in later puddled times" and a "fair *additional* to the models (afore printed) of the church way," among which he listed without distinction colonial treatises by Mather, Cotton, and others and the works of English Congregationalists, including the *Apologetical Narration*.[26]

Perhaps no one expressed the English Congregationalist promotion of the New England Way better than William Greenhill. Introducing Thomas Allen's *A Chain of Scripture Chronology*, publication of which had been long delayed until Greenhill took it in hand, he placed the colonists in the context they often claimed for themselves: "When Moses, Daniel, and John were in suffering conditions, they had much light from God, and gave forth much Truth concerning the Church and the Times: and many of our reverend, learned, and godly Brethren, living through the iniquity of the Times driven into America, by looking up unto God, and by searching of the Scriptures, received and found much light concerning the Church and Times; and have made us, and Ages to come, beholding unto them, by communicating the same." New Englanders labored to bring a new dawn that would lift the darkness covering England; their English friends welcomed that light and sought to magnify it.[27]

Some of the more interesting exchanges in the debate that involved the trans-Atlantic network resulted from the efforts of Robert Baillie and others to isolate Congregationalists from the international Reformed community. Members of the Congregationalist network had always identified themselves with international reform, expressing that support through cooperation with the stranger churches in England, fundraising for Palatinate refugees, and prayers for Gustavus Adolphus and other Protestant champions. Those who had spent time in the Netherlands had made lasting friendships with clergymen there. But because of the concern Puritans in general had for the opinion of the "best Reformed churches," Robert Baillie labored hard to drive a wedge between the Congregationalists and the Reformed leaders abroad. In a letter to William Spang as early as 1643 he wrote that "it would be a great dashe" to the Congregationalists if the Reformed churches of Holland, France, and Switzerland would support the Presbyterian stand. The publication of Paget's resuscitation of the dispute in the Amsterdam church served his purpose well. But Baillie's major success was in providing Dutch theologians with materials that depicted colonial Congregationalism in a poor light and encouraging them to join the debate. In the prefatory letter to his attack on Congregational practices, William Apollonius recounted how "the Zealand brethren have therefore been pleased to assign to me the task of assembling a set of questions, especially from the writings of the exiled brethren in New England." His attack on New England threatened to isolate the Congregationalists from the Reformed community.[28]

The English Congregationalists turned to their New England allies for assistance, and a gathering of the clergy selected John Norton to undertake the task. Writing in Latin for an international audience, Norton produced his *Answer* in 1645. He defended New England practices regarding qualifications for church membership, the use of church covenants, the role of the congregation in church affairs, the nature of synods, and the practice of prophesying. John Cotton wrote a preface to the work, insisting that "no one despise this as the inelegant production of exiled and abandoned brethren . . . as long as it can be said of them, as Jehosaphat once said of Elisha, who was living temporarily in the wilderness of Edom: The Word of the Lord is with them." Thomas Goodwin, Nye, and Simpson arranged for its publication and applauded it because they found the work "speaks for a verdict, not for vanity. It attempts not to entrap the enemy with allurements but by sheer strength of argument to lead him captive into the camp of Christ."[29]

As it became clear that the system of church order that would emerge from the Westminster Assembly would be a Presbyterian one, some of the colonial clergy began to consider preparing an alternative statement. As Thomas Welde expressed it, "We hold it not unlawful to have a 'Platform' of church-government." Indeed, some apologized for not having set forth such an official compilation of colonial faith and order earlier. Shepard and Allin wrote, "We confesse we have been too slow in this service of Christ, not having to this day set forth an unanimous Confession of that Form of wholsome words which is Preached, received, and professed in these Churches of the Lord

Jesus." They were prodded not only by the dynamics of the English debate, but perhaps as well by a desire to strengthen their system against internal critics such as Peter Hobart, while countering any effort by Parliament to fill a perceived vacuum by imposing a Presbyterian settlement on the colonies. The Massachusetts General Court in May 1646 invited the churches of New England to send delegates to a synod that would set forth a formal statement of the New England Way. The call made reference to the fact that "divers of our Christian country men & friends in England, both of the ministry and others, . . . have sundry times out of their brotherly faithfulnes & love . . . earnestly by letters from thence solicited & called upon us that we would not neglect the opportunity" to issue such a document.[30]

The Cambridge Synod met on and off for two years beginning in September of 1646, its first sessions slowed by the fear of some churches that the calling of such a synod might mean that the region was moving too close toward Presbyterianism. In their final statement the New Englanders gave their "professed & hearty assent and attestation to the whole confession of faith (for substance of doctrine) which the Reverend assembly presented to the Religious & Honorable Parliament of England," thus reaffirming that Congregationalists shared in the faith of the Westminster Assembly's Presbyterian majority. But the essence of the work was a *Platform of Church Discipline* drafted by Richard Mather with a preface by John Cotton and published at Cambridge, Massachusetts, in 1649. This Cambridge *Platform* further justified the New England Way and presented it as an example for England. Copies of the *Platform* were sent to English friends and in 1653 Edward Winslow arranged for an English printing.

The cooperation between the two wings of the network remained strong as each side sought to advance the common cause. While laboring in the Westminster Assembly, the Dissenting Brethren and their allies also defended their position with sermons and tracts aimed at the broader Puritan community. In addition to what these works said about Congregationalism, their efforts show that they differed from their Presbyterian foes in their millenarian-inspired confidence in the possibility of perfection, in the greater role they gave to civil magistrates in the nurturing of the reformed faith, and in their willingness to accommodate a broader range of opinions on some practices for those who agreed with them on the fundamentals of faith.[31]

Distinguishing these English Congregationalists from the other groups in the Independent movement is made difficult by the fact that modern British Independent churches include the Dissenting Brethren as spiritual ancestors and foster the interchangeable use of the words *Congregational* and *Independent*. And, of course, it has been noted that it was in the interests of the Presbyterians after 1644 to promote the idea that all Independents, including the Congregationalists, were alike. They have thus been lumped with the more radical advocates of religious toleration both by contemporaries for whom such an identification was a label of reproach and by later generations who deemed it a badge of honor! But the fact is that the designation is inappropriate.[32]

It is certainly true that in the period 1644–1649 Congregationalists found themselves working with others who were likewise labeled "Independents." The need to save themselves from the consequences of a Presbyterian establishment dictated that tactic, for if the Presbyterians triumphed, then they had no hope of gaining any toleration. Forced to the left to find allies, they found themselves in company they were most uncomfortable with. Though they might work with these allies for specific goals, they consistently rejected being labeled with the same name. In the *Apologetical Narration* they complained, as did the colonial Congregationalists, that the "insolent title of Independencie was affixed unto us . . . which we abhor and detest." Hugh Peter protested that "we are much charged with what we own not, viz: *Independency*." Sydrach Simpson's *Anatomist Anatomized* was a defense of "the cause that is falsely called 'Independency.' " The Congregationalist author of the *Reply to A.S.* referred to "the Form of Church Government maintained by the Apologists; commonly called—*nomine ad invidiam comparato*—by the nickname 'Independency', by themselves 'Congregational.' "[33]

Aside from seeking the support of the moderate Puritan center by denying that they were Independents, the Congregationalists furthered that distinction by denouncing the major errors commonly associated with Independency. Jeremiah Burroughes accused the Presbyterians of categorizing as "Independents . . . such as would have no Government, as would have all Religion, all Blasphemies and Heresies tolerated, as would bee under no Laws." This was not the position of the Congregationalists. In the Assembly debate over antinomianism, Thomas Goodwin proclaimed, "I say I hate them as much as any." Thomas Hill urged Parliament to "put in caveats against *Arminian* errours" and to "put a value upon such Truthes as discover the dangerous errours of *Socinianism*." Burroughes advised the House of Lords, "For conivance at Blasphemie or damnable Heresies, God forbid any should open his mouth: those who are guilty herein against the light of nature, should be taken off from the face of the earth; and such as are guilty against supernatural light, are to be restrained and kept from the society of men, that they infect not others." Joseph Caryl regretted that "there are errours amongst us: and some very dangerous, destructive and damnable, perverting souls, and wasting the vitals of Religion," and urged that "whatsoever (I say) is an errour or heresie, let all the penalties which Christ hath charged upon it be executed to the utmost."[34]

Their firm rejection of universal toleration and their opposition to heresy distinguished the Congregationalists from many of their sectarian allies.

What distinguished them from the Presbyterians was their understanding of how to oppose error. In their written expressions of the mid-1640s, the English Congregationalists sounded remarkably like their colonial brethren. The first approach to error was persuasion. "The wound seems to be in the Understanding, and the Cure must lie there," stated Hugh Peter, who believed that "religion is to be taught, not forced. This I am sure, Conviction should go before Punishment." If an individual persisted in error in the face of having had the truth explained, then further steps would be necessary. But "what flaming sword is there in the hand of a Classical Presbytery to keep men out of errors, which may not be in a Congregation?" Sydrach Simpson asked. "In one congregation," he continued, "there may be as many presbyters [i.e., elders] as, from many congregations, make a classis: and why may they not do the self same acts? Their officers and office is the same, and therefore the promise of assistance is the same. And if the counsel and advice of other neighbour churches be required, a Congregation may have that as well, and perhaps sooner than a Classis can." This method was employed on more than one occasion, such as when Simpson's own congregation excommunicated Robert Norwood when he could not be persuaded of the error of his ways. Congregationalists accepted some diversity of belief, exemplified by the stand of Jeremiah Burroughes who, we are told, placed on his study door the motto "Variety of opinions and unity in opinion are not incompatible." He believed that it was a false dichotomy to say that either all views must be tolerated or only one. Communion meant recognizing the integrity of the individual saint as well as the harmony of shared love. But there were limits. Burroughes himself claimed, "the Devil must not be left alone, though he be got into mens consciences. God hath appointed no City of Refuge for him; if he flees to mens consciences . . . he must be fetched from hence." Within the fellowship of believers considerable leeway was given and friends sought to sway friends to their viewpoint. But once fellowship was broken, reaction was harsh. This was a lesson that Roger Williams and Anne Hutchinson had learned in New England and that Norwood and others were taught by the Congregationalist churches in England.[35]

When persuasion failed to end heresy, Congregationalists believed that the churches could employ only spiritual weapons such as excommunication. But such circumstances often required the intervention of the civil magistrate, who had the right and duty to discipline erring men or even erring congregations. As early as in the *Apologetical Narration* Thomas Goodwin and his brethren had asserted that the land could be kept from gross error "if the Magistrates power (to which we give as much and (as we think) more, then the principles of the Presbyteriall government will suffer them to yeeld) doe but assist and back the sentence of other churches against Churches miscarrying, according to the nature of the crime, as they judge meet . . . then without all controversie this our way of Church proceedings wil be everyway so effectual as their other can be supposed to be." Indeed, the greater reliance placed upon the magistrate by Congregationalists in old and New England was one of the key reasons that their system was opposed by the Scottish Presbyterians and that it found favor among a growing number of members of Parliament.[36]

One of the most articulate spokesmen for the Congregationalists' method of dealing with error in the late 1640s was John Owen. When the Westminster Assembly convened, Owen, an Oxford-educated Puritan clergyman, was "not acquainted with any one person, minister or other" of "the congregational way." In his support of reform he had "looked very little farther into those affaires than I was led by an opposition to episcopacy and ceremonies." In 1643 he published a treatise against Arminianism that, because of certain passages, led him to be labeled a Presbyterian, a designation he was then willing to accept. To better understand the other side of the debate and thus be better prepared to refute it, he read John Cotton's *Keyes of the Kingdom.* "Quite besides, and contrary to my expectation," as he later explained, "at a time and season wherein I could expecxt nothing in that account but ruin in this world, without the knowlege or advice of, or conference with, any one person of that judgement, I was prevailed on to receive that, and those principles which I had thought to have set myself in opposition unto." Owen became not merely an advocate of Congregationalism but a leader rivaled in stature in England only by Thomas Goodwin. The identification of his Congregational advocacy with the New England Way would be so close that one later English chronicler would label Owen "an Independent of New England," and Cotton Mather would include Owen's biography in the *Magnalia Christi Americana*, explaining that "he was by his intention, so much a New England Man, that a New English book affords no improper station for him."[37]

Owen's views on religious error paralleled closely those of Cotton in his writings against Roger Williams. "For my part," Owen wrote, "if by *Toleration* you mean . . . an universal *concession* of an *unbounded* liberty, or rather bold unbridled *licentiousness,* for every one to *vent* what he pleaseth, and to take what *course* seems good in his own eies, in things concerning *Religion* and the worship of God, I cannot give my *vote* for it." He was convinced that "God hath undertaken to found and establish Zion . . . [and] He will also give his people one heart, and one way." Yet until men were persuaded to that one way, "a peaceable dissent in some small things, disputable questions, not absolutely necessary assertions, deserves not any rigid censure, distance of affections, or breach of Christian community and amity." But *"waies and opinions"* that are *"false, erroneous,* contrary to sound doctrine . . . especially, if credibly supposed to *shake* any *fundamentals* of the common *faith"* must be opposed by the saints "with all their *strength* and abilities, in all *lawfull waies*, upon every just call, *to oppose*, suppresse and overthrow them, to *root* them up, and *cast* them out, that they may not as *noxious* weeds and tarres *overgrow* and choak the *good corn.*" Furthermore, "any doctrine *tending* undeniably in its own *nature* (and not by strained consequences) to the *disturbance* of the civil state, may be *suppressed*" and "such *heresies* or misperswasions as are attended with any *notorious* sin in practice . . . may be in their *authors*, more severely *punished*, than such *crimes* not owned and maintained do singly deserve." The weapons of first choice for dealing with religious error were the spiritual weapons of "admonitions, reproofs, mighty Scripture convictions, [and] evidencing of the truth, with fervent prayers to Almighty God." But when church courses failed, the task would fall to "the rulers in and of the world [who] shall exert and exercise their power in subserviency to the interest of Christ."[38]

None of these statements by Congregationalist spokesmen, no matter how opposed to the toleration of heresy, actually defines the line between orthodox diversity and unacceptable heresy, and it was this fuzziness that enabled the Independent coalition to hold together. "Independents" such as Roger Williams and John Goodwin believed in a much broader liberty. As the 1640s advanced, some of the sectarian leaders in the coalition proclaimed their suspicions of their Congregationalist allies. William Walwyn, for example, claimed that the Dissenting Brethren sought toleration only for themselves and justified that request by virtue of "the nearness between them and the Presbyterians." But just as the Congregationalists needed the support of the radicals, the sects gained some respectability from association with the Dissenting Brethren. As long as the Presbyterian threat appeared greater than what either group could fear from the other, their alliance held.[39]

While debate raged in the Assembly, the Parliament, and the press, the struggle for the souls of Englishmen was also taking place in the churches of the realm. From the start of the civil wars clergymen who had lived through the years of Laudian repression began to express their views more openly and to reshape the liturgical practices and ornamentation of their churches. They were joined in these efforts by ministers who had returned to England from the Netherlands or the colonies and who had gained parish posts or gathered new congregations. Some churches assumed the shape of Presbyterian parishes, others became centers of sectarian experimentation, and still others brought into practice the New England Way of Congregationalism. One of the first steps for Congregationalist clergy as well as for Puritans of other persuasions was what William Bridge called "purging and reformation," which required congregations "to pluck downe idolatrous crosses, to silence Organs, to abolish relickes of Popery, to scum off the filth of our Liturgies and Church-service, and to put away out of our *Cathedrals*, those bawling

Boyes, and drunken singing men." Beyond this, Congregationalists began to adopt practices formerly seen only in New England and in a few of the Dutch churches.[40]

One of the distinguishing marks of the English Congregational reforms was the limitation of church membership to the godly and the corresponding restriction of the sacraments to the members (though not denying others the opportunity and even the obligation to attend). In his *Hypocrisie Unmasked* New England's Edward Winslow had strongly urged adoption of this colonial practice and to some degree it seems to have been adopted in most churches with a Congregationalist pastor. Thomas Goodwin defended the practice in a letter to John Goodwin early in the decade and stated, "We find Confession with the Mouth of the Work of Faith in the Heart, a Means among others sanctified by God to make ones Grace evident and visible to others." Like New Englanders who made the same concession, Thomas Goodwin admitted that the congregation's decision to admit a believer "is not infallible Judgement; for Men may deceive us in our Applications of it," but he contended that "it is righteous Judgement, being squared by the Rule given us." Limiting membership in this way was easily adopted in gathered churches. In cases in which a Congregationalist clergyman assumed a parish living, the practice was far more controversial because restricting membership meant excluding some parishioners from the sacraments they had been accustomed to receive. Yet, John Owen did so in his ministry, Thomas Welde did so at Gateshead, John Phillips restricted membership at Wrentham, and many others did likewise. When Richard Baxter took over a parish at Acton where Philip Nye had ministered, he complained that Nye had limited access to the Lord's Supper to so few "that the rest were partly by this course (and other reasons) distasted." Thomas Brooks had to defend himself when members of his parish petitioned the Committee for Plundered Ministers against him for his restriction of baptism and the Lord's Supper. Stephen Ford published directions for admitting persons to membership which were virtually identical to the practices of the churches in New England.[41]

Another similarity with New England practice was the adoption of a church covenant to, as Joseph Caryl expressed it, "draw men into a friendly and holy communion, and converse with one another." This practice, and Congregationalism in general, was more widespread in East Anglia than elsewhere, but was to be found throughout the land. In London, at Stepney, a brief statement sufficed: "The church being constitute by mutual consent and agreement of Henry Barton and his wife, William Parker, John Odingsell, William Greenhill, and John Pockocke, in the presence of Mr. Henry Burton, pastor of a church in London, to walk in all the ways of Christ held out unto them in the Gospel, and having the right hand of fellowship given them by the aforementioned, and owned for a true Church of Jesus Christ, these were added unto them from time to time as followeth," with room in the church record for later admissions. The involvement of a neighboring church was typical in this as in other official ceremonies among the Congregationalists. The covenant of the Yarmouth church organized by William Bridge was more elaborate. The members began by promising, "we will for ever acknowledge and avouch God to be our God in Jesus Christ," and went on to pledge that they would endeavor "to walk in his ways and ordinances," to avoid being "polluted by any sinful ways, either public or private," and to "in all love, improve our communion as brethren, by watching over one another, and as need shall be, to counsel, admonish, reprove, comfort, relieve, assist, and bear with one another, humbly submitting ourselves to the Government of Christ in His churches." Godly communion prepared them for Congregationalism and godly communion was one of the fruits of such organization.[42]

One of the points that had divided the Dissenting Brethren from the Presbyterians in the Assembly was that the former followed New England practice in distinguishing between the pastor and teacher in congregations with two ministers. In the churches organized by the Congregationalists in England this was done when appropriate, with the congregation's members choosing or approving their ministerial officers. Those chosen would be ordained by the congregation in a ceremony involving representatives of neighboring churches. In Norwich, following a pattern familiar to anyone who has studied New England church practice, the process was begun when ten of twelve "whose hearts God stirred" organized themselves in November 1642. They decided to settle the church in Great Yarmouth and in June of 1643 William Bridge and ten others subscribed to the covenant they had drawn up and which is quoted above. In September the congregation chose Bridge as pastor and then proceeded to choose and install deacons and other officers, including ancient widows.[43]

There were other ways in which these reformed English churches reflected the influence of New England. Generally the congregations followed colonial practice in making marriage a civil rather than a religious ceremony. The Beccles church was one of a number that adopted the *Bay Psalm Book* for the musical parts of the service. Many of the English Congregationalists, including Owen, Nye, and Thomas Goodwin, believed in a regulated form of lay prophesying, though some New Englanders had reduced that practice after their experiences with Anne Hutchinson. The practice of formally dismissing and recommending to another congregation a member who was moving to a new area was also adopted from New England. This was done not only to aid the saint and to preserve the purity of membership but as an expression of unity in the Congregational community. Increasingly Congregationalists carried such letters when crossing the Atlantic as well.[44]

Congregations were autonomous, but were bound together by consultation between churches and by the type of ministerial consocation that had characterized the network from the start. John Owen was the center of a group of Congregationalist ministers who regularly met to discuss religious matters in Essex. Ralph Josselin's diary contains numerous references to meetings of these "divers honest christian friends . . . at conference," sometimes at his house, sometimes at Owen's, and occasionally elsewhere. As had been the case in earlier decades, these meetings were important to keep the movement in step, but also valuable for the lift to the spirits experienced by those gathering in fellowship. Thomas Welde organized a group of clergymen in the Durham area and the consocation there helped one member church to uncover a man believed to be a Catholic spy who had infiltrated the congregation. John Phillips became a recognized leader whose advice on church affairs was sought in meetings and through correspondence.[45]

The publication of the Cambridge *Platform* provided many English congregations with a guide and it was often quoted in the records of these churches, thus further cementing the identification of English Congregationalism with the New England Way. But in drawing these connections we should be careful to avoid depicting English Congregationalism as merely derivative from colonial practice. Many English churches were indeed influenced by New England tracts. Ralph Josselin, for instance, recorded in 1648 that he had "begun reading, and noting the principle things, out of 2 treatises concerning church government by Mr. Hooker . . . the second treatise by Mr. Cotton." Thomas Shepard's *Theses Sabaticae* helped to shape proper observance in England and left its mark. New Englanders continued to correspond with friends in England and to provide advice in response to questions. And many of the English churches were actually reformed by one-time colonists who had returned home, such as Welde and Phillips. But Congregationalism was not simply an American invention. The practices associated with the New England Way had evolved from the godly communion shared by the saints, from the discussions between members of the network in England in the 1620s, from the experiences of congregations in the Netherlands such as the Arnhem and Rotterdam churches, and from correspondence between Congregationalists on both sides of the Atlantic in the decade prior to the civil wars. Though the size and success of the American Puritan experiment made its light shine bright, it was not the only source of Congregationalist inspiration.[46]

From 1644 to 1649 Congregational practices were adopted by a growing number of churches, which came into closer communion as the larger Puritan network splintered over questions of church government. Clergymen such as Cotton, Hooker, Goodwin, Nye, and Peter had been involved in collegial forms of religious organization in their Cambridge colleges. They had participated in cooperative efforts to reform England in the 1630s. Of course some of the leaders of what became English Presbyterianism had similar experiences, but those Puritan leaders who became Congregationalists had spent much of the 1630s in exile, where they were able to develop congregational forms of government in which all the saints, clerical and lay, had a share. From these experiences and their shared reflections on them with friends, they developed a confidence in congregational authority and a belief that godly liberty and order were compatible, views that clergymen such as Marshall, Ball, Baxter, and Calamy could not share. The latter group remained convinced that order could come only in a system with hierarchical authority.

But the controversies in print and Parliament prevented a Presbyterian triumph. By the end of 1649 Presbyterian hopes had been dashed and around the campfires of the army there also appeared signs that the Independent coalition had outlived its usefulness and was beginning to crumble. When Philip Nye joined with army officer Henry Ireton in opposing the Leveller proposals for religious toleration during the army debates, one sectarian champion was prompted to publish *The Vanities of the Present Churches*. The anonymous author blames the Congregationalists for "a most destructive and persecuting disposition" since the recent time when they had "obtained much countenance from authority." The tract accurately foretells the path that England was about to follow in its religious struggle. In the decade following the execution of the king and the military defeat of the Scots, the Congregationalists would rise to a position of preeminence if not dominance in England. As they did so they would show less and less tolerance for the radicals such as John Goodwin who had been their allies in the Independent coalition of the 1640s.[47]

CHAPTER EIGHT

The Time When Church Is Militant

THE 30TH OF JANUARY IN 1649 was a turning point for all who had struggled over the political and religious reform of England, for on that day the king, Charles Stuart, was executed by order of a special tribunal that had tried, convicted, and sentenced him. The decade to follow saw Puritan leaders experimenting in finding a new and better way to govern the land and minister to the spiritual needs of its people. It would be a time dominated by Oliver Cromwell, and the religious group that rose to the greatest influence under his aegis was the Congregationalists. On both sides of the Atlantic friends labored to achieve the reform of England they had long prayed for and the trans-Atlantic unity of the network continued to be revealed in clerical reactions to the changing times. This optimism was reflected in the words of John Cotton: "Now is the time when Church is militant, Time hast'neth fast when it shall be Tryumphant."[1]

Connecting the regicide with the imminence of Christ's kingdom was common in Congregationalist preaching. Thomas Brooks had made such a connection even before the trial. John Owen told the House of Commons on the day after the execution that the tumult of the time was preparation for the coming of Christ's kingdom. Jeremiah Burroughes, in a treatise that was endorsed in a preface by his fellow Apologists, argued that God was "winding up and putting an end to the glories of the kingdoms of men." "Time is short," he wrote, "and life shorter . . . ; the end of all things is at hand." The greater disposition toward millenarianism among the Congregationalists may explain in part the prominent role they played in urging the army and the Parliament to try the king. On the other side, a number of prominent Presbyterians—including Edmund Calamy, Daniel Cawdrey, William Spurstowe, and Thomas Manton—signed a vindication of themselves from the murder of Charles I.[2]

New England reaction to the regicide duplicated that of the colonists' Congregationalist friends in England. Though the news initially shocked some—"King is beheaded! O Dreadful Judgement!" wrote John Brock—most who expressed themselves on the subject supported the action. News of the event was first heard in May, Roger Williams noting reports from ships recently arrived that "the King and many great Lords . . . are beheaded" and that "Mr Peters preached (after the fashion of England) the fun[eral] Sermon to the K[ing] after sentence, out of the terrible Denunciation to the King of Babilon." Writing later to John Winthrop Jr., Williams expressed no sorrow for the king's death, since he "breathed from first to last absolute Monarchy and Episcopacie" and "was guilty of much blood." John Hull marked the date in his diary as "a very solemn and strange act," trusting that "God alone can work good by so great a change." Henry Dunster not only accepted the necessity of the action but wrote to friends in Lancashire to let them know the New England view: "Truly wee are all one heart (I mean the body of the godly) with the parliament and Army, and see that Christ hath carried them beyond men and themselves in all they have (not so much chosen to do, as) by his impulse in a sort been driven to do." In a thanksgiving sermon preached in Boston late in 1650 John Cotton reviewed the causes and course of the civil wars, justifying the resistance to Charles as well as his trial and execution.[3]

English and American believers in the millennium thought that God worked through human agencies and thus they took special interest in the reshaping of England's political system during the 1650s, especially insofar as those changes affected the realm's religious life. The leadership of the Council of State and the Rump Parliament left much to be desired, and Cromwell responded to the advice of many and expelled the Rump in the spring of 1653. A nominated Parliament of the Saints that summer failed to fulfill the hopes of Cromwell and that attempt gave way to the establishment of the Protectorate with Cromwell as Lord Protector. Though this brought some degree of political stability it did not end further experiments. Puritan leaders argued over whether Cromwell should be crowned king, and the Lord Protector himself sparked controversy with his attempt to rule the localities through appointed major generals. As England's internal turmoil subsided, the Puritan state embarked on adventures overseas. Commercial rivalry was allowed to overcome religious affinity when the Commonwealth entered the first of the Anglo-Dutch Wars in 1652. Cromwell extracted England from that quarrel and implemented his own foreign policy, which was pointedly pro-Protestant and anti-Catholic, perhaps best expressed in his "Western Design" to drive Spain from the Caribbean.[4]

New Englanders continued to look eagerly for news from England, relying on reports from proven friends to help them sift fact from rumor and thus to understand the nature of the debates and changes in the motherland. Both before and after the execution of the king, New Englanders cast their lot with their English Puritan friends. When Oliver Cromwell became Lord Protector the Massachusetts General Court instructed its agent in England, John Leverett, to "take the first convenient opportunitie to . . . let his Highness understand how thankfullie we accept and at all tymes readilie acknowledge his Highness favour and clemencie towards us, and to assure him of our own reall and syncere affection towards his Highness and readines upon all occasions to be serviceable unto him to the utmost of our power and abilitie." John Cotton corresponded with Cromwell, to whom he conveyed his belief that "the Lord hath set you forth as a vessell of honour to his name, in working many and great deliverances for his people, and for his truth."[5]

New Englanders saw Cromwell as the agent of the Lord who would accomplish the goals they had long labored for. John Eliot, in dedicating his *Tears of Repentance* to Cromwell, struck a millennial theme. Claiming that "the Lord hath raised and improved you in an Eminent manner to overthrow Antichrist," he expressed his belief that "the design of Christ in these daies is double, namely, First, to overthrow Antichrist by the Wars of the Lamb, and Secondly to raise up His own Kingdom . . . by indeavoring to put Government into the hands of Saints, which the Lord hath made you eminently useful to do." Thomas Cobbett also saw the times as those in which "Satan being disturbed, and in a manner dethroned from his so large Dominions, possessed under him by his eldest son, the Great Antichrist," and he dedicated his treatise *Civil Magistrates Power* (London, 1653) to Cromwell. Others, including John Norton, also expressed their confidence in Cromwell by dedicating works to him.[6]

This trust in Cromwell predated his rise to power in the 1650s. He had attended Cambridge, was known to many of the East Anglian Congregationalists, and had supported Puritan colonizing efforts. It was reported that he had planned to migrate to Massachusetts had the Grand Remonstrance been rejected. His success in war and his attribution of that success to the Almighty recommended him to the American Puritans. A group of colonial clergy that included Peter Bulkeley, Thomas Cobbett, Samuel Whiting, and John Knowles wrote to Cromwell in 1650 congratulating the general for his success in Ireland and referring to him as "a glorious Instrument of the execution of his just vengeance upon those bloody monsters of mankind." They went on to "thankfully acknowledge this as a superadded mercy . . .

that by his grace he hath kept it in the frame of your heart amidst all the glorious victories which under God you have gotten, thankfully to ascribe the glory therof to him alone . . . as it hath not a little honoured you in our eyes; so have we looked at the same, as a speaking pledge that God will yet goe on to perfect his admirable work by you."[7]

It was shortly after this that John Cotton and Cromwell conducted an exchange of letters. Cotton endorsed Pride's Purge and Cromwell's part in the trial of the king. He expressed himself "fully satisfyed, that you have all the while fought the Lords battells, and the Lord hath owned you, and honoured himself in you." Cromwell responded by acknowledging Cotton as one "whome I love and honour in the Lord," asked for his prayers, and inquired, "How shall we behave ourselves after such mercies? What is the Lord a-doing? What prophecies are now fulfilling?" Cotton shared his millennial views with the Lord Protector, and Roger Williams later expressed his belief that "Mr. Cotton's interpreting the Euphrates to be the West Indies" had encouraged Cromwell in the development of his western design of conquering the Spanish colonies. Though such may not have actually been the case, Williams's belief illustrates the perspective from which many viewed the events of the time.[8]

New England's positive view of Cromwell was reinforced by reports of New Englanders who returned home and had contacts with the Protector. Cotton wrote approvingly to Cromwell that "I hear, by Mr. Desboroughs letter last night, that you have well vindicated yourself . . . by cashiering sundry corrupt spirits out of the army." John Haynes wrote to John Winthrop Jr. in 1652 that when an attempt was made to license a catechism that denied the divinity of Christ "Cromwell mainly opposed." John Leverett informed Massachusetts Governor John Endecott that on an occasion when one of Cromwell's advisers complained of "New England's rigidness and persecution, . . . his Highness was pleased to answer very much in favour of them, that they acted like wise men." John Wheelwright wrote to his former parishioners in New Hampshire of his private meeting with the Protector, reflecting that "all his speeches seemed to me very orthodox and gracious, no way favouring sectaries." William Hooke, who was related to Cromwell by marriage and became one of the Protector's chaplains on his return to England, wrote John Winthrop Jr. that Cromwell "is a godly man, much in prayer and good discourses, delighting in good men and good ministers, self-denying, and ready to promote any good work for Christ." In 1656 he was reported to have said of colonial action against sectaries that "they acted like wise men, and God had broken the designs of evil instruments."[9]

Whether views such as this accord with the judgment of modern scholars, they represented the image of Cromwell that was formed in New England. The reports seemed validated by the Protector's actions. Massachusetts was allowed to coin its own currency while Cromwell ruled England. Though New Englanders chose not to accept his invitations to resettle in Ireland or the West Indies, they acknowledged his good intentions. They noted the appointment of former colonists to positions of responsibility and the "great Respect shewn to Gods poor people from the highest Magistrate there." The colonists attributed to Cromwell the dispatch of Scottish prisoners to New England as servants. When Boston merchant William Franklin sought compensation for a ship seized by Prince Rupert he appealed to Cromwell and sought John Cotton's intercession with the general. Cromwell referred the matter to the Council of State, which recommended that Franklin be compensated with "some employment in the Customs House or in some other way suitable to his experience." On a larger scale, Cromwell responded to requests from New Haven and Connecticut for help against the Dutch by sending a military expedition under former New Englanders Robert Sedgwick and John Leverett to aid in a projected invasion of New Netherland.[10]

These and other evidences of his support led the colonial leaders to regularly acknowledge their support of Cromwell—"an anniversary acknowledgement of our obligation," as John Endecott called one such missive. When they "received the sad news of the death of the Lord Protector, Oliver Cromwell, a man of excellent worth," they would remember him as "one that sought the good of New England." New Englanders into the eighteenth century would name their sons Oliver with a greater frequency than did parents anywhere else in the English-speaking world.[11]

As they had in the 1640s, New Englanders wrote home in the 1650s to offer advice on the religious and civil reform of their native land. Thomas Cobbett's *Civil Magistrates Power* and John Eliot's *Christian Commonwealth* were among the treatises designed to offer political advice. Richard Mather's *An Heart-Melting Exhortation* was written as advice to his friends back in Lancashire. Edward Johnson justified the publication of his *Wonder-Working Providence of Sions Saviour in New England* by the argument that the colonial way should be the model for English reform.[12]

The strength of the Congregationalist network in England was enhanced during the 1650s by the return of former English clergymen from New England and by the integration into the network of numerous Harvard graduates who had journeyed to England after completion of their degrees. Recent historical studies have downplayed this return migration, one scholar offering the belief that "repatriation was in fact quite rare." This is not true. Numerous laymen returned to rebuild England, and the clerical migration was very significant. At the start of the conflict William Hooke had said that "when sometimes a New England man returns thither, how he is lookt upon, lookt after, received, entertained, the ground he walks upon beloved for his sake, and the house held the better where he is . . . neither is any love or hindrance held too much for such a man." In the 1650s things had not changed. Nathaniel Mather, having journeyed to England, wrote to a friend in Massachusetts, " 'Tis a notion of mighty great and high respect to have been a New-English man, 'tis enough to gayne a man very much respect, yea almost any preferment."[13]

Though the influx was not welcomed by most Presbyterians, it was cause for rejoicing for the Dissenting Brethren and their fellow Congregationalists. Whereas the most renowned New England divines, such as Cotton, Davenport, Hooker, Wilson, and Shepard, stayed in America, other ministers returned to churches that they had been forced to leave in the 1620s and 1630s, and others returned to England to take up new challenges. Not all the returnees became prominent, but many did and most provided support for Congregational reform. Robert Peck left Hingham, Massachusetts, to return to his rectorship in Hingham, England. Thomas James, who had preached at both Charlestown, Massachusetts, and New Haven, returned to England and ministered to a congregation at Needham Market, whereas Hugh Peter combined his representation of Massachusetts with the role of an army chaplain. Thomas Welde, who returned to the parochial ministry in the late 1640s as rector of St. Mary's in Gateshead, had frequent contacts with Jeremiah Burroughes and other leaders of the Congregationalist movement and was named one of the first Visitors of Durham College by Oliver Cromwell in 1657. Welde's brother John, another returning clergyman, became rector at Bildeston in Suffolk. Thomas Peter, Hugh's brother, returned to England and preached in Cornwall till his death in 1654. Nathaniel Norcrosse received his MA from St. Catharine's, Cambridge, in 1637, migrated to New England in the next year, and then journeyed home in 1650, where he became vicar of St. Mary's in Dover, Kent. Henry Whitefield went to the New Haven colony in 1637 and was the first pastor at Guilford. In 1650 he returned to England and accepted a ministerial post at Winchester. Giles Firmin was another Cambridge graduate who, after a stay in the colonies, became minister at Shalford, Essex. John Wheelwright returned to England in the mid-1650s. Francis Higginson Jr., who had served as a schoolmaster in Cambridge, Massachusetts, left the colonies to pursue his postgraduate studies at the University of Leiden, and then ministered to a congregation in Westmorland, England, where he preached and wrote against the Quakers. Samuel Eaton had left New Haven and returned to England to deal with family matters in 1640. When the conflict broke out he organized one of the first Congregational churches in the land at Duckenfield, Chesire ("Chester" on the map on p. 18). William Hooke left Davenport's New Haven to become one of Oliver Cromwell's chaplains and then master of the Savoy Palace.[14]

John Knowles, who had been a fellow at Cambridge in the 1620s and a respected member of the network, migrated to Massachusetts and assisted his friend George Phillips in the church at Watertown. He briefly labored to carry the Puritan gospel to Virginia, and then returned to England. He became a preacher at Bristol Cathedral and was in part responsible for the formation of a Congregational church there. Thomas Allen, another active member of the Puritan brotherhood in the early 1630s, had fled to the Netherlands in 1636 and moved to New England two years later. On his return to England in the early 1650s he was called as a municipal preacher in Norwich and in 1657 he was chosen pastor by the congregation meeting at St. George Tombland. Allen worked with William Bridge and John Phillips. Phillips had left his church in Wrentham, Suffolk, in 1638, but returned from the colonies four years later. He restructured his old parish along New England lines and became one of the respected leaders of Congregationalism in East Anglia.[15]

Further network connections can be seen through the career of Thomas Harrison. Harrison had spent time in New England and then, along with Knowles, had preached in Virginia. He married a cousin of John Winthrop. Returning to England, he succeeded Thomas Goodwin as pastor of a gathered church in St. Dunstan's in the east when Goodwin accepted the presidency of Magdalen College, Oxford. In 1653 Harrison met with the Lord Protector and he was one of a group of clergy that included John Owen and Philip Nye which convened to discuss the religious settlement. Four years later Harrison accompanied Henry Cromwell to Ireland as one of the Lord Lieutenant's chaplains and he also served as Congregationalist lecturer at Christ Church, Dublin. He then became a preacher at Chester Cathedral, where he added to the growth of Chesire Congregationalism, which had been initiated by Samuel Eaton.[16]

Established clergy were not the only ones who journeyed home to aid in the building of a Congregational England. A large number of the Harvard graduates of the 1640s and 1650s made the same decision. Benjamin Woodbridge, the first graduate of Harvard, returned to England and assumed a pastoral post in Newbury. Jeremiah Holland settled first near London, then accepted a living in Northamptonshire. Nathaniel Brewster was another early graduate who went to England. He ministered for a few years in Norfolk and attracted the attention of Oliver Cromwell. The Protector sent him to Ireland in 1655 with a letter instructing Charles Fleetwood to "use this Bearer, Mr. Brewster kindly. Let him be near you: indeed he is a very able holy man; trust me you will find him so." William Stoughton graduated from Harvard in 1650, completed an MA at Oxford, and then preached in Sussex. Henry Butler of the class of 1651 preached in Dorchester, England, till later ejected. He continued to preach illegally, was fined and imprisoned, but eventually was one of those nominated to succeed to the Dorchester, Massachusetts, pastorate on the death of Richard Mather. A number of members of the 1653 Harvard class went to England, including Edward Rawson (son of the Bay Colony's secretary), who preached in Kent; Nehemiah Ambrose, who settled in Lancashire; and John Stone, who ministered to a congregation in Sussex. John Sammes was chosen vicar of Kevedon in Essex in 1647 and seven years later became vicar of Coggeshall.[17]

The sons of many New England clergymen followed their fathers into the ministry and returned to England to preach. William Hooke's son John left Harvard in 1652 and was presented to the vicarage of Kingsworthy through the efforts of Cromwell. Edmund Welde journeyed home in 1650, accompanied Cromwell as a chaplain on the Irish expedition, and remained in that land as a Congregationalist clergyman in County Cork. Peter Bulkeley's son John was one of the early returnees, succeeding John Owen as vicar at Fordham and remaining in England as a physician after being ejected from that living in 1662.[18]

Most of these Harvard-trained clergy and other returnees mentioned thus far—as well as others such as John Birden, Henry Butler, John Haynes, Joseph Swinnock, Jacob Ward, and Henry Saltonstall—became integral parts of the network that knit Congregationalists together. Some became leaders of the movement who would help shape its growth in the following decades, for the return of colonial Puritans revitalized the network. Friends who had not seen each other for two decades—for example, Thomas Welde and Jeremiah Burroughes—found their relationships spiritually and socially revitalized. Mutual confidence was strengthened for those once again in face-to-face communion, and the trust that those still on opposite sides of the Atlantic had in each other was renewed when the migration brought eyewitness reports of friends long absent. Furthermore, ties of friendship and kinship facilitated the integration of new blood into the network. English friends and relatives of their parents helped the young Harvard graduates gain acceptance and clerical posts in the mother country, incorporating them into the family-like intimacy of the clerical communion. A new generation of Puritan Congregationalists would be immersed in the same types of communion, conference, and cooperative reform efforts that had shaped and reinforced clerical friendships for their fathers' generation.[19]

William Ames had died in the Netherlands while preparing to migrate to New England. His family made the journey and William Ames Jr. graduated from Harvard in 1645. He returned to England and joined with another former colonist, his uncle John Phillips, in gathering a Congregational church in Wrentham, Suffolk, where their families had lived earlier in the century. His name as well as his talents made Ames a respected member of the network. Leonard Hoar was another young member of the network who achieved prominence. After graduating from Harvard in 1650 he returned to England and continued his studies at Cambridge. In 1656 he was presented to a living in Wamstead, Essex, by Sir Henry Mildmay, but he eventually returned to the colonies when John Owen recommended him for the vacant presidency of Harvard. John Collins graduated in 1649 and journeyed to England four years later. He became a fellow of Pembroke College, Cambridge, but soon left to become one of the chaplains to General Monck and the Scottish Council. Lucy Downing, whose connections with New England remained strong, wrote from Edinburgh that "Mr Collins is a man very precious, and of eminent parts." Later he was elected a lecturer at St. Antholin's. After the Restoration he would be an important link connecting New Englanders with their English friends. John Allin, the son of the Dedham pastor of the same name, graduated from Harvard in 1643. He held a lectureship in London and then became vicar of Rye, making that Sussex town a model of New England reform so that it became known as a "City on a Hill." Comfort Starr (Harvard, 1647) returned to his mother country in 1650, where he became a Congregationalist minister at Carlisle, Cumberland, and an assistant to the Commission of Triers for the Four Northern Counties. He later ministered in Kent and Sussex, became active in Congregational decision making, and was one of the delegates at the Savoy Assembly. Like John Collins, he would be one of the brokers of news and assistance between the trans-Atlantic wings of the network in the decades after the Restoration. Ichabod and Isaac Chauncey, sons of the Reverend Charles Chauncey, both graduated from Harvard in 1651. Ichabod served as a clergyman in Dorset and was chaplain to Sir Edward Harley's regiment stationed at Dunkirk. After the Restoration he practiced as a physician in Bristol. Isaac was presented to a living in Wiltshire by Oliver Cromwell. After ejection he was pastor of a Congregational church in Andover until 1687, when he accepted a call to a congregation meeting in Mark Lane, London, where he preached until he was succeeded by his friend Isaac Watts in 1701. During the 1680s and 1690s he was one of the most respected Congregational divines in the capital.[20]

Perhaps the most important young divines to cross the Atlantic in this period were the sons of Richard Mather. Samuel, the eldest, journeyed to England in 1650. His New England connections secured him the post of chaplain to Thomas Andrewes, then Lord Mayor of London and a former member of Thomas Goodwin's Arnhem congregation. Mather became a good friend of Sydrach Simpson, who helped the young New Englander screen preaching requests. Along with Simpson and Robert Bragge, Samuel Mather journeyed with English commissioners to Scotland, where they preached on a number of occasions. He soon removed to Oxford, where he served as a chaplain at Magdalen College while proceeding to the MA degree. The president of Magdalen at the time was Thomas Goodwin, who came to have a great deal of respect and affection for Samuel Mather. In 1654 Philip Nye recommended him as a preacher to the Council of State in Ireland and he sailed for that land with Henry Cromwell, the Reverend Samuel Winter, and Stephen Charnock as well as his fellow New Englanders Nathaniel Brewster and Thomas Harrison. Over the next few years he preached regularly before Henry Cromwell. In 1656 he received a call to the ministry of St. Nicholas's Church in Dublin and was ordained in a Congregational ceremony presided over by Timothy Taylor, Thomas Jenner, and Winter. Winter, who had gathered that congregation and served as its pastor, was a protégé of John Cotton, and was well known to the New Englanders. Winter also served as provost of Trinity College in Dublin and involved Mather in the college as a fellow. John Owen was one of the college trustees. Among the students with whom Samuel Mather had contact were Thomas Jollie's brother John, Winter's son Josiah, and his own brother Increase Mather. At the time of the Restoration Samuel left Ireland to preach in Lancashire, where he had been born, but in 1662 he returned to Dublin, where he ministered for the remainder of his life.[21]

Nathaniel Mather followed his brother to England and accepted ministerial posts first at Harbeton and then in 1656 at Barnstable, both communities in Devonshire. He became friends with John Howe, who was the vicar at nearby Great Torrington. Mather became a member of the Devon Association—a clerical consociation—in 1655 and in 1657 was named an assistant to the Devon Commission of Triers. Throughout this period he was in frequent contact with fellow New Englanders such as Comfort Starr. After the Restoration he went to Holland and ministered to an English congregation in Rotterdam. When his brother Samuel died in 1671 he succeeded him in ministering to the congregation in New Row, Dublin. Driven from Ireland, he succeeded John Collins in the London Lime Street church, where he became a leader of orthodox Congregationalists in the latter years of the century.[22]

The Mather brother who would achieve the most fame was Increase. The youngest of the three, he left Boston in 1657. After a brief stay in London he traveled to Lancashire, where he "was very kindly enterteyned by my Fathers old friends and Christian acquaintances." In September he journeyed to Dublin, where he lodged with his brother Samuel while pursuing the MA at Trinity College. When he graduated in 1658 his fellow "scholars were so well pleased that they humm'd him, which was a compliment to which he was a stranger in New England." In Dublin he met and befriended leading Congregationalists such as Winter, Taylor, and Jollie and also made an impression on Henry Cromwell. Mather later recorded that "the Lord deputy was so respective as to send me word that I should not go to England for want of encouragement in Ireland while he was in power." But the offer of a ministerial position in England that Nathaniel and his friends had secured led him to leave Ireland. Back in England at the time of the Savoy Assembly he was introduced to and quickly befriended a number of prominent clergymen, including Nathaniel's neighbor John Howe. Howe had recently been chosen a chaplain to Oliver Cromwell and was kept on by Richard Cromwell when he succeeded his father as Protector. Authorized to appoint a curate at full salary for his parish at Great Torrington, Howe offered the post to Increase Mather. Preferring that post to the living he had been offered in Exeter, he accepted and took up residence nine miles from his brother in the winter of 1658–59. With the fall of the Protectorate, Howe moved back to Great Torrington. After holding a few temporary posts on Guernsey and near Thomas Jollie at Toxteth Chapel outside Liverpool, Increase returned to the colonies. His continuing correspondence with his brothers and with leading nonconformist clergymen whom he had befriended would serve him, his colony, and the Congregational cause in good stead.[23]

These New England clergymen as well as many others not named would labor with men like Thomas Goodwin and John Owen to create a reformed religious establishment in the 1650s. Though the Second Civil War and then the invasion of Scotland had made it clear that a Scottish Presbyterian–style system would not triumph in England, some echoes of the Congregational-Presbyterian debate of the 1640s did linger into the following decade. Daniel Cawdrey attacked the works of John Cotton and Thomas Hooker in his 1651 treatise *The Inconsistency of the Independent Way with the Scriptures and Itself.* Hooker had died in 1647 and his colleague Samuel Stone wrote *A Congregational Church is a Catholic Visible Church* (London, 1652) in his defense. Cotton died in 1652 before completing his own response to Cawdrey. John Owen was given the unfinished manuscript, which he completed and published with his own views as *A Defence of Mr John Cotton from the Imputation of Selfe Contradiction Charged him by Mr Dan: Cawdrey* (Oxford, 1658). Other New England works continued to be published to advance the Congregational Puritan cause, though few written in the 1650s were directly critical of Presbyterianism. William Greenhill and Samuel Mather collaborated in writing a preface to a 1652 edition of Thomas Shepard's *Treatise of Ineffectual Hearing the Word* and *Subjection to Christ in all his Ordinances and Appointments,* which were published as a single volume three years after the author's death. Christopher Scott, an English Congregationalist in Essex, edited and published Cotton's *Practical Commentary on the 1st Epistle of John* in 1656. William Pynchon, whose views on the nature of redemption had led him to challenge the restriction of church membership to visible saints, had left the colonies for England and carried on a pamphlet debate with John Norton, who defended the orthodox Congregational position. But for the most part it seemed, as Peter Sterry expressed it in 1652, that the "seed of God" in England had been spared not only from "the Romish Papacy" but from "the Scotch-Presbytery" as well.[24]

As the threat from the Presbyterian right diminished, the Congregationalists became more outspoken in their opposition to the radical views of their supposed sectarian allies. One of the early signs of this came at a London banquet to celebrate Cromwell's purge of the Levellers in the army, when Thomas Goodwin opened the festivities with a sermon. John Owen turned his pen to renewed attacks on the Arminian beliefs of some radicals. His *Doctrine of the Saints Perseverance* was directed against the views of John Goodwin. Owen also prefaced two works against John Goodwin written by George Kendall (a member, with Nathaniel Mather, of the Devon Association). In 1651 Thomas Welde was one of seven clergymen who complained to Cromwell that Captain Robert Everhard was preaching Arminian and Socinian doctrines to troops.[25]

Congregationalists were outspoken in their opposition to the growing Quaker movement. George Cockayn preached often against the sect. John Owen, as vice-chancellor of Oxford, ordered two Quaker female missionaries whipped and expelled from the town. William Bridge's Yarmouth church had a Quaker imprisoned after he had tried to address the congregation and "one of their Elders . . . violently threw him down over a high seat to the endangering of his life." Thomas Welde joined with some of his orthodox fellow clergy in the Newcastle area to publish two attacks on the Quakers— *The Perfect Pharisee under Monkish Holiness* (Gateshead, 1653) and *A Further Discoverie of that Generation of Men Called Quakers* (Gateshead, 1654). George Griffiths, Philip Nye, and Joseph Caryl were among those who sought to get James Naylor to retract his blasphemies, and the Congregationalist Major General William Goffe exercised his authority in efforts to suppress the sect.[26]

Another group with which the Congregationalists entered into conflict was the Fifth Monarchists, extreme millenarians whose belief in the imminence of the Second Coming led them to advance radical ideas that threatened orthodox views of order. Early in 1654 Thomas Goodwin, Philip Nye, Sydrach Simpson, and John Owen wrote a strong letter "to the Congregational churches" warning them against Fifth Monarchist views. William Bridge was involved in a 1656 meeting of all the Congregational churches in the area of Norwich to deal with the spread of the sect. Philip Nye became the chief opponent of the movement in London, while Owen, Thomas Goodwin, and others sought to purge the ideas from the universities.[27]

Though some sectarian leaders had feared such opposition from the earliest days of the Independent alliance, they bitterly reproached the Congregationalist leaders for what they viewed as old hypocrisy become new treachery. But the new vigor of the Congregationalist attacks on error opened up the possibility of support from Presbyterians. There had always been a group of moderate Presbyterians who had maintained close friendships with the Dissenting Brethren and who had labored to find a middle ground on which both sides could agree. Thomas Ball, who died before the two elements in the Assembly split apart, had certainly been one such clergyman. A friend of many of the Congregationalists, he had worked with Thomas Goodwin in the 1630s to edit some of the sermons of John Preston. Ball had been troubled by reports of some New England practices, but he had been willing to discuss these differences with the Congregationalists. Anthony Tuckney was another Presbyterian who had sympathy for the Congregational leaders. Tuckney was a cousin of John Cotton and had assisted the latter at St. Botolph's in Boston, Lincolnshire. One of the authors of the Shorter Catechism, he was well aware of the doctrinal orthodoxy of the Congregationalists and showed his moderation by arranging for the publication of Cotton's *Exposition upon Ecclesiastes* in 1654. Anthony Palmer, Richard Vines, Thomas Gataker, and Thomas Wilson supported the Congregationalists on some issues during the Assembly debates. John Dury, whose plans for Christian unity were consistently supported by the Congregationalists, wrote *An Epistolary Discourse* (London, 1644) in support of accommodating them within a Presbyterian system and dedicated it to Thomas Goodwin, Philip Nye, and Samuel Hartlib. Thomas Hill, who had studied under John Cotton as a youth, strongly supported union between the two groups. In a sermon preached in London in July 1645 he called for a healing of the division between the two groups and expressed his belief that the use of labels such as "Presbyterian" and "Congregationalist" were harmful in that they emphasized differences rather than the common ground shared by the two.[28]

The two most noted Presbyterian supporters of a middle way were Charles Herle and Stephen Marshall. Herle was personally close to a number of the Congregationalists on both sides of the Atlantic. His polemic exchanges with New Englanders such as Richard Mather were marked by mutual respect and a search for the truth. His friendship with Philip Nye allowed the two to tease each other during the Assembly debates, and he commented on one occasion, "I conceive it is part of our unhappiness when we are upon disputing we fall accomodating, and when accomodating then disputing." He was concerned that both sides be free to present their views, and thus he was the individual who licensed the *Apologetical Narration*, saying, " 'tis so full of peaceableness, modesty, and candour; and withall, at this time so seasonably needfull, . . . that however for mine owne part I have appeared on, and doe still encline to the Presbyteriall way of Church Government, yet doe I think it every way fit for the Presse." In his own published refutation of Congregationalism he accepted that the two groups were "brethren still, and . . . ready to rescue each other on all occasions against the common enemy." As for their differences, " 'tis but the better or worse way for the exercise of the same forme of discipline that is in question." When he succeeded William Twisse as the Assembly Prolocutor in July 1646 his selection was greeted with approval by the Dissenting Brethren.[29]

Stephen Marshall was another Presbyterian who had worked closely in previous decades with the men now identified as Congregationalists. His major sermons and writings in the 1640s emphasized the common goals of reform rather than the issues that divided the Puritan group. Like other moderate Presbyterians he had great personal respect for the Congregational leaders. He was especially close to Philip Nye, whose son John married Marshall's daughter. Marshall was prominent on all of the committees seeking accommodation in the 1640s.[30]

The efforts of these moderates gained them the suspicion of their more zealous brethren in the Presbyterian ascendancy. Robert Baillie criticized Marshall for seeking "a middle way of his own" and expressed dissatisfaction with Herle for being a "good friend" of the Congregationalists. But with the decline of the Presbyterian cause the moderates were in an excellent position to chart a common cause with the rising Congregationalists. Some die-hard Presbyterians refused to be reconciled to the new mood of cooperation. Thomas Edwards, of whom Jeremiah Burroughes said, "Bishop Wren was not more mischievous to the Prelacy, than he hath been to the Presbytery," moved to Amsterdam and settled in the congregation over which John Paget had presided. But the moderates were the ones who were able to take advantage of the new circumstances, blaming past differences with the Congregationalists on those who, like Edwards, "would not have tolerated who were not only tolerable, but worthy, instruments and members in the churches." Some clergy, such as Nicholas Lockyer, who had been assumed to be Presbyterians earlier now were labeled Congregationalists. Others, such as Stephen Charnock, were so firmly entrenched in the middle ground that contemporaries and historians alike found it difficult to agree on how to classify them.[31]

Examples of Congregational-Presbyterian cooperation became common in the late 1640s and through the 1650s. J. Sears McGee has found that even "amidst all their bitter quarrels [of the earlier period], one finds many references to a sense of kinship" and points to a 1647 engraving "which depicts 'a godly dissenting brother' clasping hands with 'a godly brother of the presbyterian way' and saying 'Let there be no strife between thee and me for we are brethren.' " Cuthbert Sydenham, a Newcastle Presbyterian, cooperated with local Congregationalists such as Thomas Welde, and Welde wrote a preface for Sydenham's *Hypocrisie Discovered* (Newcastle, 1654). Walter Craddock, whose uncle had been one of the early leaders of the Massachusetts Bay Company, wrote that "Presbytery and [Congregational] Independency are not two religions, but one religion to a godly honest heart." Thomas Goodwin wrote an introductory letter to the Presbyterian Reverend John White's *Way to the Tree of Life* (London, 1647). Joseph Caryl participated in the London Presbyterian Assembly. Giles Firmin, a former New Englander who is generally classified as a Presbyterian, not only sustained close relations with friends in New England but enjoyed a friendship with John Owen. John Howe is classified by one of his biographers as "indistinguishable from a . . . Congregationalist" and was reported to have worked with the Congregationalist leaders at the 1658 Savoy Assembly. John Angier, a former student of John Cotton, was a Presbyterian member of the Manchester classis, but an ally of the local Congregationalists as well. In 1656 the Presbyterian Exeter Assembly voted to associate with the area Congregationalists, "leaving all further differences to a brotherly and amicable debate." John and Thomas Jollie, Michael Briscoe, and Jeremiah Marsden were among the Lancashire clergy who signed terms of accommodation between county Presbyterians and Congregationalists. In some cases, as with London's St. Dunstan's in the east, it became impossible to classify a parish as Congregational or Presbyterian because its membership was evenly divided.[32]

One of the Congregationalists who worked hard to involve clergy of both persuasions in clerical conferences was John Owen. On the other side Richard Baxter labored to produce concord. In the preface to his *Church Concord* (London, 1691), a treatise in which he sought to establish the common ground on which the two groups could unite (and in which he cited John Norton in support of his views), Baxter described his work in this regard in the 1650s. "I attempted," he wrote, a "work of Concord in Worcestershire . . . for the willing Ministers Episcopal, Presbyterian and Independent to Associate." Not all the local clergy were willing and "as the Foreigners (Prelatists) and Popular called Brownist kept off, so but few of the rigid Presbyterian or Independent joined with us. . . . But the main body of our Association were men that thought the Episcopal, Presbyterians and Independents, had each of them some good in which they excelled the other two Parties, and each of them some mistakes: And that to select out of all three the best part, and leave the worst, was the most desireable (and ancient) form of Government."[33]

One of the early expressions of Congregational-Presbyterian cooperation came in the support both groups could unquestioningly offer to the conversion of the Indians in New England, a noncontroversial cause on which all could agree. In 1648 Ralph Josselin recorded in his diary how "the lord gave me to hear the newes of the Indians then looking towards Jesus Christ," and from that point on he and others would follow such news closely, relating it to reports of successful conversions in the Far East, and speculating on what such events might portend for the second coming of Christ. When *The Day-Breaking, if Not the Sun Rising of the Gospel with the Indians in New England* (London, 1647) was sent to England for publication it was rushed to press and prefaced by an open letter to Parliament signed by Presbyterians such as Stephen Marshall and Simeon Ashe as well as Congregationalists such as Thomas Goodwin, William Greenhill, and Sydrach Simpson. Parliament chartered the New England Company for the Propagation of the Gospel to aid John Eliot and others in their missionary efforts. Henry Newcome preached to raise money for the cause. Simeon Ashe, Ralph Josselin, Richard Lobb, and Henry Jessey were also among the many who raised funds, and Ashe introduced Henry Ashurst to the company's activities. In 1652 Henry Whitefield published a collection of letters from New England reporting progress in the work. Titled *Strength out of Weaknesse* (London, 1652), the volume was dedicated to Parliament in a preface signed by Whitefield, Ralph Venning, William Strong, Joseph Caryl, John Owen, William Greenhill, William Bridge, George Griffiths, William Carter, Thomas Goodwin, Philip Nye, and Sydrach Simpson.[34]

The real test of cooperation would come in the efforts to create a national church during the period of the Commonwealth and Protectorate. Even as the last, ineffectual steps were being taken to try to erect a Presbyterian church in 1648, Congregationalist clergy were mobilizing in support of the 1648 Parliamentary ordinance for punishing blasphemers and heretics. In fact, this was an early sign of Congregationalist defection from their sectarian allies. This ordinance, and the one that replaced it in 1650, bore a close resemblance to New England law in that it vested in the civil magistrates the responsibility for punishing not private belief but proselytization of error by preaching, writing, or teaching. Among the errors identified were questioning the existence or nature of God and specifically of Christ, denying that Scripture was the word of God, denial of the resurrection or the final judgment, believing in universal salvation, free will, and the adequacy of reason, and asserting that the Church of England was not a true church. According to a strict interpretation of its provision Antinomians, Quakers, Baptists, and other radical sects would have been outlawed.[35]

The Blasphemy Act, in its provision for greater magisterial supervision of religious matters, was more Erastian than the Presbyterian establishment that had been advocated by the Scots. This reliance on the civil authority was characteristic of Congregationalists in old and New England and was to be found in the writings of clergymen such as the Bay Colony's Thomas Cobbett and in works such as John Owen's *Righteous Zeal Encouraged by Divine Protection* and *Christ's Kingdom and the Magistrate's Power*, and Thomas

Goodwin's *The Constitution, Right Order, and Government of the Churches of Christ*.[36]

The rise of Congregationalist influence was clearly visible as the new regime began. In March of 1650 John Owen was named a preacher to the Council of State, responsible for offering daily prayers at council meetings and for preaching a weekly Friday sermon at their chapel at Whitehall. In the same year Owen, Joseph Caryl, William Carter, and Philip Nye were asked by the council to recommend candidates for army chaplains. Thomas Goodwin, Philip Nye, and Peter Sterry were appointed, along with John Milton and others, to organize the records of the Westminster Assembly. Hugh Peter, William Bridge, Samuel Petto, and Thomas Brooks were among others given responsibility by the Rump Parliament and the Council. The newly ascendant Congregationalists strongly influenced the 1650 Act for the Propagation of the Gospel in Wales.[37]

In 1652 the Council of State appointed Owen, Sydrach Simpson, and Nicholas Lockyer to advise them about sending godly clergy to Ireland. Owen had spent time in Ireland with Cromwell, had helped in the reorganization of Trinity College, Dublin, and had been named a trustee of the college in 1650. At about the same time as the council consulted with Owen, Cromwell sought the advice of Owen and Lockyer as well as Hugh Peter and other Congregationalists regarding the Irish church. A result of these deliberations was the appointment of men such as Samuel Winter, Samuel Mather, and, later, Stephen Charnock, Thomas Harrison, and Increase Mather as the nucleus of the new Irish church establishment.[38]

Another area where reformation was carried out by the appointment of Congregationalists to key positions was the universities. Thomas Goodwin and John Owen were among those named as Visitors for both universities and for schools such as Winchester, Westminster. The two Congregationalists became especially important figures at Oxford, which Puritans in general deemed more in need of a shake-up than Cambridge. Goodwin was chosen president of Magdalen College, whereas Owen was selected as dean of Christ Church and vice-chancellor of the university. The two also took turns preaching the Sunday afternoon sermons at St. Mary's. Owen helped to initiate a number of changes at Christ Church—stained-glass windows were removed, a Thursday lecture was established and opened to the university, and tutors were instructed to lead students in nightly prayer sessions reminiscent of those communal sessions presided over by Preston and other Cambridge fellows early in the century.[39]

Once again the universities became nurseries of Puritanism and a new generation of aspiring clergymen would be drawn into the network. John Thompson was a student at Christ Church when Owen was dean. Thankful Owen, Theophilus Gale, Moses Lowman, and John Howe were associated with Goodwin at Oxford. Reform touched Cambridge as well, where Sydrach Simpson was named master of Peterhouse in 1650, joining other Puritan heads of colleges. Oliver Heywood, Thomas Jollie, and Thomas Hill became close friends in the colleges by the Cam. As in the early century, the universities became magnets that attracted clergy in the region, drawing them for commencements and other formal occasions, but also for less formal gatherings in the rooms of fellows.[40]

A further demonstration of the prominence of the Congregational network came early in 1652 as the Rump Parliament responded to the publication of the Racovian Catechism of the Polish Socinian Churches. Ten clergymen— John Owen, Philip Nye, Sydrach Simpson, William Strong, John Dury, William Bridge, William Greenhill, Adoniram Byfield, Thomas Harrison, and George Griffiths—were chosen to meet with a parliamentary committee to prepare a condemnation of these anti-Trinitarian views which, as well as denying the divinity of Christ, also called into question the doctrines of the atonement and justification by grace. On the basis of their report, the Rump Parliament ordered that all copies of the catechism be burned and appointed another committee to consider how better to promote the true faith.[41]

The fourteen-member Committee for the Propagation of the Gospel, which included Oliver Cromwell, began its deliberations in February 1652. Envisioning the creation of a state church, the committee solicited recommendations from various clerical groups. One proposal was submitted to them by Edward Whalley, a Congregationalist army officer who was a cousin of Cromwell and brother-in-law of William Hooke. Signing the document were over twenty others, including Owen, Nye, and Simpson. Their proposal was based on experience gained from the effort to propagate the faith in Wales, and it was revised a number of times in the following months. One version was published as *The Humble Proposals of Mr Owen, Mr Tho Goodwin, Mr Nye, Mr Simpson and other ministers* (London, 1652). In addition to those named in the title, other signatories included Harrison, Bridge, Strong, and Greenhill. They called for supervision of a national church by two sets of commissions composed of both laymen and clergy. Local committees would examine and approve ministers and a national commission would have powers to eject from the pulpit and the schools those deemed unfit. Approved clergy would be supported by tithes. Sunday church attendance was to be mandated, even if believers would not be compelled to worship in parish churches. Though the initial proposals were unclear as to the criteria to be used in judging clergy, it was evident that with *The Humble Proposals* the Congregationalist authors had broken firmly with their former sectarian allies. The rupture was widened when on December 2, 1652, a new edition of *The Humble Proposals* was issued with the addition of "Principles of Christian Religion." The doctrines reflected a strong Calvinist orthodoxy. Among them were belief in the Trinity, justification by grace, the Scriptures as the revealed word of God, the incarnation, the resurrection, the necessity of forsaking sin, and the worship of God according to his will.[42]

These proposals brought forth a barrage of criticism from the sects, much of it led by Roger Williams. Williams attacked the Congregationalist plan in *The Fourth Paper* (London, 1652), *The Hireling Ministry None of Christs* (London, 1652), and *The Examiner Defended* (London, 1652). He also added an appendix attacking the scheme to *The Bloudy Tenent Yet More Bloudy* and probably authored the prefatory letter to Parliament denouncing the Independents that was included in John Clarke's *Ill News from New England*. For Williams, who was working in connection with John Milton and Henry Vane, it was clear that the English Congregationalists were trying to impose a New England–style intolerance on England. A version of *The Humble Proposals* that toned down the censorship of those who preached contrary to Christian principles was submitted to Parliament by the committee in February of 1653 but rejected by that body, some members feeling that the concessions to the sects went too far and others that they failed to go far enough. The Congregationalist blueprint, however, was not dead.[43]

In April of 1653 Oliver Cromwell used the army to dissolve the Rump Parliament. Inspired perhaps by the idea of a New England–style system in which only the visible saints exercised political power, the army officers sent letters to the gathered churches inviting them to nominate members for a parliamentary-style assembly. John Owen and William Bridge as well as other Congregationalists were involved in the process of nomination, but by the time 129 members gathered in the Nominated Parliament in July of 1653, the Congregationalists had begun to express concern about the representation in the body of extreme millenarians who believed in the imminence of the Fifth Monarchy. Just as the Presbyterians of the 1640s had found the millennial views of Thomas Goodwin and John Cotton alarming, so now the Congregationalists found the more extreme Fifth Monarchist views threatening to their hopes for a settled church. Philip Nye labored hard with the Presbyterian clergy of London to bring them into the fight, and the campaign against the Fifth Monarchists gave a clear expression to widespread Congregational-Presbyterian cooperation in London.[44]

Cromwell shared many of the same concerns and in October he called upon leading Congregationalist, Presbyterian, and Baptist clergy to consult with him. But the group—which included Owen, Nye, Harrison, Henry Jessey, and Stephen Marshall—failed to agree on a plan for a unified establishment. Owen, Goodwin, and Nye then worked with their supporters in the Parliament to introduce a plan similar to *The Humble Proposals*. A special committee reported the proposal to the assembly. This version called for the division of the nation into six administrative districts with three commissioners in each who would have the authority to settle godly ministers. In an attempt to gain support for the measure tentative suggestions of the commissioners were made, the list including Congregationalists such as Thomas Goodwin, Presbyterians such as Marshall, and Baptists such as Henry Jessey and John Tombes. Among the proposed lay commissioners were Arthur Barnardiston and Hezekiah Haynes. Nye helped organize a petition from the City of London in support of the plan, and Owen and Goodwin persuaded the Oxford convocation to congratulate the city for its petition. But the Parliament rejected the plan by a vote of fifty-six to fifty-four. Rebuffed in this effort, the Congregationalists joined with other moderates in pushing through a measure surrendering back to Cromwell the powers the Assembly had been granted. Whalley, William Goffe, and other Congregational army officers took measures to prevent the Fifth Monarchists from reconvening the Parliament. Owen, Goodwin, Simpson, and Nye composed a circular letter that denounced the Fifth Monarchists "if to no other end but to clere our selves before the Churches & the world, from any participation with them in that judgement and endeavour."[45]

Within days of the dissolution of the Nominated Parliament, Oliver Cromwell was installed as Lord Protector of England under the terms of an Instrument of Government that had been prepared by John Lambert and other army officers. Cromwell was empowered to govern by ordinance until the election of a Parliament in September of 1654, and with this authority he took steps to create a new religious system. Recent studies, especially by Blair Worden, have clearly shown that Cromwell's concept of toleration was not as far-reaching as often depicted. A Calvinist himself, he surrounded himself with orthodox Calvinist advisers—especially Congregationalists—and sought to move England back to a Calvinist consensus. In February of 1654 Cromwell began consulting Congregationalist friends as well as Presbyterian and Baptist leaders. On March 20 the first of the Protector's ecclesiastical ordinances was passed. This called for the appointment of thirty-eight commissioners responsible for examining and approving the qualifications of those proposed for religious benefices. Of the thirty-eight named, close to half were Congregationalists, including the clergymen William Carter, Joseph Caryl, Thomas Goodwin, William Greenhill, Nicholas Lockyer, Hugh Peter, Philip Nye, John Owen, Sydrach Simpson, William Strong, Thankful Owen, and Samuel Slater. Presbyterians were the next-largest contingent, with the moderates Stephen Marshall, Samuel Fairclough, Francis Rous, Obadiah Sedgwick, and Thomas Manton included on the commission. The small number of Baptists included Henry Jessey and John Tombes, both of whom were staunch Calvinists with a record of cooperation with the Congregationalists. The Cambridge connection was very evident, for of the Triers with university degrees twice as many came from Cambridge as from Oxford, with twelve graduates of Emmanuel College and another four from St. Catharine's.[46]

The inclusion of Baptists, even if in a small role, was indicative of the one lasting effect that immersion in the Independent coalition of the 1640s had had on the Congregationalists. Questioning of infant baptism had troubled the reform movement in the English church from the sixteenth century. Some of those who raised the issue were following what they saw as the logic of Calvinist emphasis on justification as the transforming event of entry into the brotherhood of the saints. Others were influenced by continental influences that were of questionable orthodoxy from the Calvinist perspective. Of course, the specter of Münster hovered like a cloud over those who advocated believer baptism, often obscuring the actual arguments being proffered.

The Baptist movement of the 1640s was a collage of many different groups, preachers, and beliefs. One segment of the picture was occupied by those who believed in free will and were perceived as "Arminian" in their attitudes toward human nature. These "General" Baptists, as they would come to be known, were viewed with hostility by orthodox Calvinists of all persuasions. The other major element in the movement were Baptists who were orthodox Calvinists differing from the Dissenting Brethren only in their rejection of infant baptism. Of these, some organized closed churches that would admit only fellow Baptists to communion, whereas others formed churches that were based on Calvinistic theology and Congregational practice and in which infant baptism was optional. Typical of this last type was Henry Jessey.

Jessey had been a member of the congregational communion in the pre–civil war decades. He had been an active supporter of the Massachusetts Bay Company. In the early 1640s Jessey—like Harvard president Henry Dunster—began to question the efficacy of infant baptism. In 1644 his London gathered congregation began to debate the issue. Praisegod Barebone was consulted, as were Jeremiah Burroughes and Thomas Goodwin. The Congregationalists advised that "the position taken [by the Baptists in the church] was held not out of 'obstinacy but tender conscience and holiness' so that the people concerned should be treated as church members in good standing until either they returned or grew 'giddy and scandalous.' " In that same year Thomas Goodwin, Nye, and other Congregationalists met with William Kiffin and other Calvinist Baptists and agreed to maintain communion between their churches. Hugh Peter participated in some of these conferences. Jessey himself converted to believer baptism in 1645, but this only reinforced Congregationalist willingness to accept and consociate with Baptists whose theology was orthodox. Many Congregational churches came to contain members who rejected infant baptism. Though this made some clergymen anxious, most Congregationalists continued to view Calvinist, or Particular, Baptists as the one group for whom they truly espoused toleration. And, for their part, Baptists such as Jessey and Tombes had more in common with the Hugh Peters and John Owens of the Congregationalist community than with the General Baptist mechanic preachers. They valued an educated ministry and they had experienced spiritual communion with Congregational leaders. Though Jessey and Tombes initially questioned some of Owen's proposals for church government—particularly the method of approving preachers—they joined the Congregationalists in denouncing the Fifth Monarchists and came to accept positions as Triers in the Cromwellian church.[47]

The willingness of Thomas Goodwin and his brethren to tolerate Baptists is often viewed as the cause of a fatal rupture between them and their New England supporters. This misconception has resulted in part from the unquestioning use of a later English criticism misdated to the 1640s and by a failure of scholars to distinguish between the different varieties of Baptists and how those different groups were perceived on both sides of the Atlantic. Just as it is incorrect to claim that English Congregationalists believed in toleration of all Baptists (they were critical of the Arminianism of the General Baptists), so it is erroneous to claim that New Englanders treated all Baptists harshly. Many New England opponents of infant baptism tended to be unorthodox in their views on the nature of regeneration and man's role in it, to be politically and socially radical, to question the need for a university-educated clergy, and to be intolerant of those who accepted infant baptism. In short, they were nothing like Henry Jessey and John Tombes. The anti-Baptist legislation enacted by the Massachusetts General Court singled out some of these areas of concern. The magistrates expressed their fear that "they who have held the baptizing of infants unlawful, have usually held other errors or heresies" regarding matters of faith, and "denied the ordinance of magistracy, and the lawfulness of making war." For these reasons, it was "ordered and agreed that if any person or persons, within this jurisdiction, shall either openly condemn or oppose the baptizing of infants" they would be subject to banishment. Proselytization was criminal rather than quiet doubts about infant baptism.[48]

New Englanders did, of course, use their pens to attack the spread of Baptist ideas. Thomas Hooker preached his sermons *The Covenant of Grace Opened* (London, 1649) in 1644 in answer to John Spilsbury's *Treatise Concerning the Lawfull Subject of Baptism* (London, 1643), and Richard Mather prepared an "Answer to Nine Reasons of John Spilsbury" in the mid-1640s. Thomas Shepard's *Church Membership of Children* (London, 1663) was actually prepared in the 1640s, and Thomas Cobbett's *Just Vindication of the Covenant and Church Estate of Children of Members as Also their Right to Baptism* (London, 1648) was another volley in this barrage. George Phillips wrote *A Reply to a Confutation of some grounds for Infant Baptism* (London,

1645) when Nathaniel Briscoe forwarded to him the views of English Baptist friends for his reaction.[49]

But much of the concern in these colonial tracts was directed against those who, as John Cotton put it, "plead against the baptism of children upon any of those Arminian and popish grounds." The fact is that Particular Baptists in New England were treated moderately. John Tombes and Henry Jessey continued to regard New Englanders such as Cotton, Wilson, and Winthrop as friends and continued to correspond with them. The treatment of Henry Dunster by the Bay Colony clergy when he espoused Baptist views was not much different from the consideration given Jessey by the Dissenting Brethren. And, as time passed in the colonies, magistrates became more tolerant of those who quietly rejected infant baptism without seeking to win others over to their views.[50]

This is not to say that treatment of Baptists caused no friction within the Congregational communion. New Englanders were not as exposed to Calvinist Baptists and sometimes did overgeneralize, giving themselves a reputation more extreme than they deserved and making it difficult for English Baptists such as Jessey to persuade their own followers to maintain union with the English allies of the New England Way. Politically, the Dissenting Brethren found that reports—especially exaggerated ones—of New England intolerance threatened their needed alliances of the 1640s. But though this was and would remain a problem the network had to work on, it never threatened either the trans-Atlantic unity of the Congregationalists or the colonial support for the emerging Cromwellian church.[51]

The union of Congregationalists, moderate Presbyterians, and Calvinist Baptists as the nucleus of that Cromwellian church continued as time progressed. In August of 1654 Cromwell issued an Ordinance for the Ejecting of Scandalous, Ignorant and Insufficient Ministers and Schoolmasters. This established thirty-eight local boards, each with an average of twenty-two lay commissioners and fourteen clerical assistants. These boards of Ejectors were primarily composed of Congregationalists, Presbyterians, and Baptists. Between them, the Triers and Ejectors worked to establish a Calvinist unity in the state-supported church. In judging the clergy who came before them, the commissioners placed great emphasis on the individual's experience of saving grace and on his orthodox theology. John Goodwin complained that "the triers made their own narrow Calvinian sentiments in divinity the choice to all church preferments." Even more telling was a comment from Richard Baxter, whose own theological orthodoxy would later be called into question. It was his opinion that the commissioners often "were too severe against all that were Arminians." By judging the appropriateness of all who hoped to be supported by state tithes, the Triers and Ejectors exerted considerable influence over the religion of the land. Cromwell would tell the first Protectorate Parliament that by means of his religious ordinances, "This government hath endeavoured to put a stop to that heady way . . . of every man making himself a minister and a preacher."[52]

During that first Protectorate Parliament an effort was made to further the religious settlement by defining the fundamentals of the Christian faith. After rejecting as too imprecise a proposal that fourteen of the old Thirty-Nine Articles be defined as a "confession of faith," Parliament named a committee of divines to devise a set of fundamentals. Among the members of the committee were Thomas Goodwin, John Owen, Sydrach Simpson, Stephen Marshall, Samuel Fairclough, and Henry Jessey. Their report essentially revived the Calvinist *Humble Proposals* of 1652. Some members of Parliament thought it was too conservative, whereas others considered it not rigid enough. The proposed list was rejected by Parliament in December, but although they were not officially promulgated, the fundamentals reflected the beliefs that the majority of Triers and Ejectors were employing as an ad hoc standard of orthodoxy.[53]

In the years that followed, the efforts of the Triers and Ejectors were supplemented by the work of ministerial associations and by the governing authority of the major generals appointed by Cromwell in 1655. Charles Morton was one of the organizers of a clerical association formed in Cornwall in September of 1655. The secretary of the group, he later brought the idea and the minutes book to New England. Writing a letter to his New England friend Henry Dunster, Newcastle's William Cutter described cooperation between Congregationalists and Presbyterians. These efforts as well as those described earlier were supported by New Englanders, who did everything they could to encourage this cooperation between English Congregationalists and moderate Presbyterians. Just before his death in 1652 John Cotton had completed *Certain Queries Tending to Accommodation and Communion of Presbyterian & Congregational Churches* (London, 1654). Edward Johnson's *Wonder-Working Providence* was intended for the edification of the "two sorts of persons in our Native Country, whom the Elders and Brethren here do highly honour in Christ, and prefer before themselves, namely the godly Presbyterian party, and the Congregational sincere servants of Christ." John Norton reaffirmed his friendship with former New Englander and moderate Presbyterian Giles Firmin in a letter in which he acknowledged that he thought "better of many Presbyterians" than of some of the sects with whom the English Congregationalists had earlier been identified, "for I distinguish between Independents and Congregational men."[54]

Though institutionalized cooperation among Congregationalists, Presbyterians, and Particular Baptists was increasingly common in the mid-1650s—both on state-appointed commissions such as the Triers and Ejectors and in self-organized consociations—the informal functioning of the Congregationalist network continued to flourish. In 1656 Samuel Eaton's former colleague Thomas Taylor, who was then pastor at Bury St. Edmunds, journeyed to Yarmouth to consult with William Bridge, one of the key brokers of the network in East Anglia. Bridge gave advice on the gathering of churches at Beccles, Godwich, Guestwick, and other communities. He helped train John Oxenbridge, Job Tuby, and others who served as his assistants before moving to their own congregations. Many friends such as Taylor visited him to seek his advice. He corresponded with national Congregational leaders such as Nye and Owen, who were his friends, and he helped publish and promote books by his friends. Such activities, reminiscent of the types of cooperation discussed in earlier chapters, remained an important part of the lives of Congregational brethren.[55]

The move toward conservative Calvinist orthodoxy was evident in the mid-decade in the actions taken against Roman Catholics and Quakers by the Second Protectorate Parliament and also in the actions of the major generals. These appointed magistrates were responsible for maintaining religious as well as civil order. Like the members of the church commissions, the men chosen as major generals by Cromwell reflected an orthodox Calvinist viewpoint and most would be categorized as Congregationalists. Indeed, of the eleven, Charles Fleetwood, John Desborough, James Berry, Edward Whalley, William Goffe, and John Lambert would later worship in a congregation gathered by John Owen that met in Fleetwood's home. Three of these six—Desborough, Goffe, and Whalley—as well as another one of the major generals, Hezekiah Haynes, had strong connections to New England.[56]

Despite the successes achieved by the Congregationalists, there was still no definition of orthodoxy. Yet another attempt to achieve this goal was incorporated as part of the *Humble Petition and Advice*, a program for constitutional revision presented to Cromwell in 1657. The most controversial element of the proposal, which divided the Congregationalists and which Parliament later deleted at Cromwell's request, called for making Cromwell king. Among the religious provisions in the document that was finally approved was a "desire that such as do openly revile" the clergy as established by the Triers and Ejectors, "or their assemblies, or disturb them in the worship or service of God, to the dishonor of God, scandal of good men, or breach of the peace, may be punished according to law." Furthermore, it was requested "that the true Protestant Christian religion, as it is contained in the Holy Scriptures of the Old and New Testament, and no other, be held forth and asserted for the public profession of these nations; and that a Confession of faith, to be agreed by your Highness and the Parliament, . . . be asserted, held forth, and recommended to the people of these nations." The mechanism for producing a confession was not stipulated and earlier efforts had failed. Though it is possible to see the Congregationalist Savoy

Assembly of 1658 as a means to produce such a document, the evidence of the intent behind this last major episode in Interregnum Congregationalism is unclear. [57]

In June of 1658 Henry Scobell, one of the lay elders of John Rowe's Congregational church that met at Westminster Abbey, who was also a clerk to Oliver Cromwell's council, sent a letter announcing that a "Meeting of the Elders of the Congregational Churches in and about London is appointed at Mr. Griffiths." George Griffiths was a preacher at the Charter House. It is likely that the meeting at his home saw some of the early planning for a national gathering of clergy. The following month some of these same clergy met with Congregationalists in and around Oxford following commencement, and over the summer Griffiths wrote to invite representatives of Congregational churches throughout the realm to gather in a synod at the Savoy Palace in London in late September. Responses were to be directed to Henry Scobell. The Savoy was a large building that had been erected in the Strand in the thirteenth century as a residence for the count of Savoy, the uncle of Henry III's consort. It had later served as a convent and a hospital and was used by Oliver Cromwell to accommodate members of his court. The Reverend William Hooke, John Davenport's former colleague in New England, had been appointed master of the Savoy and would host the visiting clergy. [58]

The Assembly convened on September 29 with about 120 churches represented by slightly fewer than twice that number of "messengers." Though there is no accurate list of representatives and few can be positively identified, those who are known to have been there include many of the leading members of the network. Thomas Goodwin, Philip Nye, William Bridge, William Greenhill, Joseph Caryl, John Owen, George Griffiths, Thomas Jollie, Thomas Gilbert, Cairns Helme, Isaac Loeffs, and John Stonestreet were among those who attended. Among former New Englanders who were definitely there were William Hooke, Comfort Starr, and John Knowles. It seems likely that Increase and possibly Nathaniel Mather were there as well. Though he is generally regarded as a Presbyterian, there are indications that John Howe sat in on the sessions. [59]

Thomas Jollie preached to the Assembly, which seems to have chosen Philip Nye as chair and George Griffiths as clerk. A committee consisting of Nye, Goodwin, Bridge, Caryl, Owen, and Greenhill was chosen to draft articles to be acted on by the full body. It took the Assembly but a few weeks to agree to a Declaration of Faith and Order. Dismissing what separated them from the Presbyterians as "differences between fellow servants," the Congregationalists asserted their strict Calvinist orthodoxy by essentially reiterating the theological stance of the Westminster Confession of Faith. On the question of polity, the Congregationalists explained that "what we have laid down and asserted about CHURCHES and their *Government*, we humbly conceive to be the *Order* which Christ himself hath appointed to be observed, we have endeavoured to follow Scripture-light; and those also that went before us according to that Rule, desirous of nearest uniformity with *reforming Churches*, as with our Brethren in *New England*, so with others that differ from them and us." The details—taking state connections for granted, spelling out the nature of Congregational church formation, discipline, and consociation, and distinguishing between tolerable and intolerable differences—owed much to the New England example in general and the Cambridge *Platform* in particular.[60]

Was this program intended as the blueprint for a national establishment? Oliver Cromwell is reported to have been consulted about the calling of the gathering. Scobell's involvement could have been in an official capacity. Edmund Calamy claimed that the Protector had ordered that Nye be chairman. The results of the Assembly were presented to the government "to countenance and propagate." But the question can never be answered with certainty because even while the Congregationalist ministers were nearing their greatest achievement, Oliver Cromwell—their patron and protector—died. It was the new Protector, Richard Cromwell, to whom Thomas Goodwin presented the assembly's results. The future of Congregationalism, of the Protectorate, and of English Puritanism was suddenly in jeopardy.[61]

CHAPTER NINE

The Bread of Adversity, the Water of Affliction

THE DEATH of Oliver Cromwell on September 3, 1658, changed the course of events in England. If the rise of the saints was attributable to providential design, then perhaps it was understandable for one of those close to Cromwell to respond to his death by wailing that God had spit in their faces. Not only was Congregational ascendancy within the Protectorate in question, but the survival of Puritanism was in jeopardy as well. Within four years Charles II would sit on the throne, countless dissenting clergymen would be ejected from their livings, and reformers on both sides of the Atlantic would be forced to reconsider what role God had actually cast them for. Once again the clerical network would be relied upon to sustain the unity of an embattled rather than a triumphant brotherhood.[1]

The Congregational ascendancy had never been clearer than in 1658. Thomas Goodwin had been close to Oliver Cromwell throughout his last illness, comforting the Protector when he needed to be reassured about the perseverance of the saints and witnessing the nomination of Richard Cromwell to succeed as the new Protector. Goodwin, John Owen, Joseph Caryl, and Peter Sterry were among the clergy who consoled the family in the weeks following Oliver's death. William Hooke, who wrote to John Winthrop Jr. that he was "holding my relation still to W[hite]:H[all], the same as in the late Protector's time," was undoubtedly also there. These clergy also conducted a fast in the household in remembrance of Oliver. John Howe retained his chaplaincy to the family and became close to Richard Cromwell. Sterry was reported to have prayed for the new Protector that God might "make him the brightness of the father's glory, and the express image of his person." The Congregational churches delivered a supportive address to Protector Richard. Thomas Goodwin preached at the opening of Parliament on the 27th of January and John Owen preached to the legislators a week later. The results of the Savoy Assembly were submitted to the new head of state with the expectation of his approval and support. But within a few months John Maidstone was writing to Connecticut's Winthrop that "the interest of religion lies dreadfully in the dust," and William Hooke was sharing his concern that "I know not what will become of us; we are e[v]ene at our witts end."[2]

The supporters of Oliver Cromwell's regime had begun to quarrel. Hooke revealed that "God's people . . . are divided in Councill, Parliament, militia [and] are slow to combine, & to endeavour speedy union, though it be the onely outward meanes visible, of our safety. Neither are the feares of God's people (for ought I see) suitable to the appearance of danger; nor such a spirit of prayer stirring as sometimes there was." Some of the divisions were attributable to personal jealousies and political ambitions. Many of those who had willingly lived in Oliver's shadow were less amenable to subordinating themselves to the less-experienced Richard Cromwell. From a religious point of view, some were distressed at the new regime's apparent shift toward Presbyterianism. Parliament showed little likelihood of adopting the Savoy Declaration, but listened to a variety of proposals commonly associated with Presbyterians. At the same time the leaders of the army also seemed to be losing influence in the government.[3]

Army officers who resented Richard or who had hoped to dominate his regime, and others who were dissatisfied with the new emphases in policy, began to meet at Wallingford House, the residence of General Fleetwood. It may be that they sought only to gain influence over Richard Cromwell rather than to oust him from power, but the dissolution of the Protectorate Parliament in April of 1659 was followed by the resignation of Richard a month later, after the Rump Parliament had been called back into session.[4]

Then, in October of 1659, a clique of army officers expelled the Rump Parliament and established a Council of State dominated by the army. This only served to further erode any vestige of legitimacy borne by those who sought to govern the realm. If the future was to be determined by sheer power, the man looming on the horizon was General George Monck, commander of the English forces occupying Scotland. Congregationalist leaders such as Owen and Nye worked with army and civil leaders to find ways to prevent Monck's intervention and, that showing little promise, the clerical leaders sought to protect their interests by dealing with him. Caryl and Barker, together with Monck's army colleagues Whalley and Goffe, carried a letter from the London-area churches to Monck, seeking to draw him out as to his intentions. His response indicated a respect for the Congregationalist leaders and their churches, but no guarantees. Messengers of East Anglian Congregational churches met in November and sent representatives to a larger gathering of Congregationalists in London in December. The gathered delegates reaffirmed their commitment to the Savoy Declaration and to the principles of parliamentary government. But these were not likely to be safeguarded by Monck and those close to him. Monck's forces brushed aside the minor opposition they faced, entered London, and restored the Long Parliament as it had existed before Pride's Purge.[5]

The restored Parliament dissolved itself after making arrangements for new elections. Negotiations with the exiled Charles Stuart led to his issuance of the Declaration of Breda, taking a conciliatory posture toward those of tender consciences. The Convention Parliament invited Charles to return and on May 29, 1660, he entered London. A year later a new legislature that came to be known as the Cavalier Parliament began to lay down the details of the Restoration settlement. Presbyterians such as Simeon Ashe and Richard Baxter for a time hoped that the new monarch would honor his father's 1647 commitment to establish presbytery, but that was not likely. Arthur Annesley, who had abandoned hope of a continued rule of the saints and cooperated in the restoration of the monarchy, helped persuade the new king to issue the Worcester House Declaration of October 1660, which was a gesture seeking to reconcile Presbyterians to the new order. But pressures for a more conservative settlement from Gilbert Sheldon, the new archbishop of Canterbury, and the other bishops were to prove more attractive to the newly elected, strongly anti-Puritan Cavalier Parliament. Presbyterian hopes of accommodation were soon dashed. Congregationalists had been divided over the turn of events that followed Monck's takeover. A few, such as Philip Nye and Thomas Brooks, had been willing to encourage continued fighting to preserve the republic. Some, like George Griffiths and Joseph Caryl, were willing to trust to the Lord and the Parliament to produce an equitable religious settlement. But most seemed to have been caught unprepared and left confused by the rapid reversal of their fortune.[6]

Politically, the restored monarchy struck a general note of conciliation in the early months of Charles's reign, though some—including those who signed the death warrant for his father—were excluded from the general pardon. Among those executed as regicides were Henry Vane and Hugh Peter. Some of those sought by the authorities fled to the Netherlands, though of these Miles Corbet and two others were lured back and put to death. Generals Whalley and Goffe and John Dixwell fled to New England, where they were sheltered for the remainder of their lives. One-time New Englander Hezekiah Haynes escaped treatment as a regicide, but was arrested for treasonable designs and released only after posting a sizable bond.[7]

The religious establishment was shaped more by the members of the Cavalier Parliament than by the king or his advisers. The high Anglican element preyed upon the fears of their fellow MPs, arguing that clear lines of authority in the church were necessary to purge the nation of the confusion and turmoil of recent decades. Early in its deliberations the House of Commons required all its members to take communion under the liturgical usage of the Book of Common Prayer. It was decided to restore the bishops to the House of Lords. This had important consequences, since bishops such as Durham's John Cosin would prove uncompromising in their opposition to any religious concessions to the saints. In December the Corporation Act required all mayors and other local officials to swear loyalty to the king and to receive communion in the Church of England.[8]

Efforts to rid the church of Puritans had begun soon after the return of Charles and his bishops. William Hooke was removed from the mastership of the Savoy, clergymen such as Owen lost their university preferments, and others lost livings controlled by the government and by Anglican peers. In April of 1662 Parliament passed an Act of Uniformity that required all beneficed clergy to swear their agreement to everything in the Book of Common Prayer and to seek reordination from a bishop if they had been originally ordained by presbyters or congregations. Clergymen were granted until August 24, St. Bartholomew's Day, to conform. In all, more than two thousand clergy would be deprived of their livings in England and Wales during the first years of the new regime; they either left rather than conform or waited to be ejected. A large proportion of those who were ejected were in East Anglia, London, Devonshire, and Yorkshire.[9]

The actions of the Cavalier Parliament reflected the resurgent Anglicanism of many if not most Englishmen. In parishes where Puritan clergymen had been installed during the Interregnum, the laity often sought to anticipate the new laws. In August of 1660 close to three hundred parishioners of St. Giles, Criplegate, petitioned for the removal of the Reverend Samuel Annesley, who had been appointed to the living by Richard Cromwell in 1658. The parishioners of St. Paul's, Covent Garden, petitioned the bishop of London in January of 1661 to force Thomas Manton to use the Prayer Book service. Thomas Gouge was also a target of parishioners seeking use of the Prayer Book. On the other side, the vestry of All Hallows the Great appealed to the archbishop of Canterbury in December of 1660 that the Congregationalist Robert Bragge be allowed to continue in his ministry, testifying that he was "sound in Doctrine, & of a holy Conversation." But popularity did not matter. Bragge was ejected along with his fellow nonconformists in 1662. Speaking for all who refused to conform, Joseph Caryl explained to his congregation at St. Magnus, London, his refusal to take the oath: "The lips of the righteous know what is acceptable to God. . . . I hold fast my integrity, and my heart shall not reproach me as long as I live."[10]

Even as the Cavalier Parliament sought to drive the Puritan element from the church, there seemed some chance of deflecting or reversing that initiative. Edward Hyde, the earl of Clarendon, was not doctrinally committed to the Church of England. Though he believed in a clearly defined settlement, he was not averse to some form of comprehension if he could be sure that the subversive political tendencies of Puritanism could be curbed. James Stuart, the king's brother, was willing to consider tolerating those outside the church—including, in the long run, Catholics—though he was not in favor of comprehending groups such as the Presbyterians within the state church. Others around the king, such as Arthur Annesley, also encouraged some form of compromise and in the winter of 1662–63 King Charles agreed to submit a bill of indulgence that would have given some relief to the nonconformists. The willingness of Charles and some of his advisers to consider a degree of toleration was always tempered by their concern over order. The arrest and imprisonment of Haynes had been based on suspicions that he was implicated in a plot against the king. Major General Berry was kept in jail on similar suspicions from 1660 to 1671. A letter purportedly written by Major General Desborough in April of 1660 described a plot involving Henry Vane, Hugh Peter, John Owen, and others. Another alleged rising seemed to have more substance. In what became known as the Sowerby Plot, about thirty army veterans and clergymen met in the north in July 1660, presumably to plan an insurrection. Among those identified at the meeting were Thomas Jollie, Samuel Eaton, and Michael Briscoe.[11]

There was no element of uncertainty regarding Venner's uprising. Thomas Venner was a former wine cooper in Salem and Boston, Massachusetts. He had traveled to England in 1651 and became one of the leaders in a radical Fifth Monarchist conventicle in Swan Alley, off Coleman Street in London. Venner had led a rising against Cromwell in 1657 and had been jailed for two years. In January of 1661 he led a band of about fifty followers to conquer the world for Christ. Twenty-two Londoners were killed and the city terrorized before order was restored. Searches of suspicious persons in the aftermath of the rising failed to reveal a more extensive conspiracy, but did turn up items such as a few cases of pistols in the home of John Owen.[12]

Congregationalists were quick to disavow any role in the uprising, aware of the connection many Englishmen habitually made between New Englanders and Congregationalism. Indeed, one of the contemporary reports on the incident claimed that "we'll never deny his [Venner's] New England testimony . . . because such troublesome New Englanders [had caused England] . . . to smart for too long." Twenty-five clergymen, including Joseph Caryl, Thomas Goodwin, George Cockayn, Philip Nye, and George Griffiths, published *A Renunciation and Declaration of the Ministers of Congregational Churches and Publick Preachers* (London, 1661). They were willing to condemn the Fifth Monarchists—even making comparisons to Münster—but were not willing to allow the government to use the uprising as an excuse to curb their own religious exercises.[13]

Expressions of nonconformist strength, spontaneous outbreaks of violence, and reports of new plots all worked to strengthen the hands of those opposed to any accommodation. Two thousand mourners including Caryl, Bragge, and Thomas Brooks gathered for the funeral of the Fifth Monarchist and army veteran Wentworth Day after he died in prison. Rioting that included acts of iconoclasm was a common reaction to St. Bartholomew's Day and the ejection of popular nonconforming clergy. Later in 1662 the government claimed to have evidence of another plot. Philip Nye and Thomas Brooks were both accused of responsibility and it was rumored that Goffe and Whalley had returned from New England to lead troops. When Henry Jessey died shortly after his release from prison his dying words were that "the Lord would destroy the powers in being." Between four thousand and five thousand nonconformists followed Jessey's body to the grave in what authorities viewed as a troubling sign of the movement's strength.[14]

Troubles continued in 1663. Joseph Caryl was accused of preaching treason. There were reports of a plot centered in Dublin with Stephen Charnock implicated and reports that Henry Cromwell would arrive to lead the rebels. A rising was reported to have been planned for September 3. It was claimed that guns had been smuggled into the northern counties from New England and the Netherlands and that Thomas Jollie was one of the clergymen implicated.[15]

This ongoing background of protests, uprisings, and rumored plots helped the opponents of toleration to persuade Charles II to back down from supporting the bill of indulgence and also provided the rationale for more rigid measures. The new harshness was manifest in the Conventicle Act of 1664. Any individual attending a nonconformist religious meeting of more than five individuals would be fined £5 for one offense, £10 for the second, and in the case of a third violation would be fined £100 or transported to the tropical colonies for seven years. Those who failed to pay the fines would be imprisoned. In the following years more than two hundred dissenters, mostly from the London area, were transported. In 1665 Parliament passed the Five Mile Act, requiring all ejected clergy to swear an oath that they would not attempt any alteration of the government of church or state and stipulating that those who refused to take the oath be debarred from coming within five miles of where they had ever exercised their ministry or held a conventicle as well as from all cities, towns, and boroughs represented in Parliament. Taken together, this Clarendon Code ushered in a dark period for the nonconformists.[16]

New England had given open support to the Puritan Parliament and the Cromwellian Protectorate. The Restoration would bring the colonies into confrontation with a hostile home government and usher in a period of contention that would eventually culminate in the revocation of the Massachusetts Bay charter and the establishment of the Dominion of New England. As news of the Restoration reached the Americas, the Puritan colonies grudgingly recognized the legitimacy of the new regime, though the Bay Colony did have to be prodded to do so by the English authorities.[17]

Throughout the region colonists were divided over how to react to the new king. Merchants who had developed their own trans-Atlantic network of trading partners tended to welcome the stability the Restoration promised and favored a moderate, cooperative response. Many of the clergy and some of the lay leaders such as Massachusetts Governor John Endecott sought to distance themselves from the Whitehall government and assert a semiautonomous status as a commonwealth, yielding only grudgingly to English edicts and making it clear that resistance would be considered if interference became too great. Their policy would be to avoid contact with or cooperation with the royal government as much as possible.[18]

Preoccupied with the shaping of Restoration England and troubled by their fears of Puritan plots in the British Isles, Edward Hyde, earl of Clarendon, and his fellow administrators were not in a position to crack down on the colonies. Any interest in doing so was probably further tempered by a belief that any crackdown might be met with armed resistance. The New England colonies had a sizable militia. Many Cromwellian veteran officers had returned to the Bay and her sister colonies. And on a number of occasions in the 1660s the commander of the fort in Boston harbor was ordered to put his defenses at the ready. Prepared though they might have been to fight, the colonists were willing to avoid fighting if the price was minimal recognition of royal authority. Connecticut and Rhode Island both shored up their legal status by seeking and obtaining royal charters (Connecticut in the process absorbing the territory that had been the New Haven Colony). A royal commission to investigate colonial affairs in 1664 was received and eventually sent packing without having accomplished much.[19]

The autonomy which the Commonwealth faction in Massachusetts sought to preserve was precarious at best. As the royal government became more stable and secure it would be more likely to seek control over the colonies. The moderate faction within the colonies would grow in numbers and power in the decades after 1660. And the confidence of the Commonwealth clergy and laity would be shaken by divisions over religion and doubts about God's plan for them.

The events of 1658 to 1664 not only challenged the position the Congregationalists had achieved in both old and New England, but also raised questions about the role God had cast for them. The light that shone from their churches illumined an empty room, for the majority of Englishmen had lost interest in the Puritan experiment. Congregationalists were plunged from a confidence in their ability to reform not only England but the world into a fear for their survival as a saved if not saving remnant. Making the adjustment to these new circumstances more difficult was the loss of leaders suffered by the clerical network in the years surrounding the Restoration. In England Jeremiah Burroughes died in 1646, Stephen Marshall in 1653, William Strong and Thomas Gataker in 1654, Richard Vines in 1656, William Carter and Sydrach Simpson in 1658, Hugh Peter (executed) in 1660, John Phillips also in 1660, Thomas Welde in 1661, and Henry Jessey in 1663. In New England Thomas Hooker passed away in 1647, Thomas Shepard in 1649, John Cotton in 1652, Nathaniel Rogers in 1655, Peter Bulkeley in 1659, Ezekiel Rogers in 1660, and John Norton as well as Samuel Stone in 1663. Although many of those who had been active since the 1620s remained, the years at the turn of the next decade would take a further toll with the demise of John Beadle (1667), Thomas Brooks (1670), William Bridge (1670), William Greenhill (1671), Joseph Caryl and Thomas Allen (1673) in England, and John Wilson (1667), Richard Mather (1669), John Davenport (1670), John Allin (1671), and Zachariah Symmes (1672) in New England.[20]

The surviving members of the old congregational communion such as Thomas Goodwin, John Knowles, John Eliot, and William Hooke would deal with the challenges of the post-Restoration era in company with younger clergy such as the Mathers, Matthew Mead, Stephen Lobb, John Collins, and Thomas Jollie—men who had been integrated into the network during the struggles of the Interregnum. But the loss of so many experienced leaders was difficult to overcome and relatively untested clergy had a more difficult time gaining lay confidence in an era of troubles and confusion. Adding to the sense of crisis in this period was the genuine uncertainty felt by the clergy when it came to explaining why God had brought things to the state they were in.

In 1662 many of the Congregational and Presbyterian clergy in England preached farewell sermons to their congregations in anticipation of their departure on St. Bartholomew's Day. For the most part, these ministers focused on the need for the saints to persevere in their faith. "Go thy way blessed soul," urged Joseph Caryl, "eat thy bread with joy, though the world feed thee with the bread of adversity and though the world give thee nothing but the water of affliction. Yet let thy garments be always white; though the world clothe thee in mourning, and cease thee to prophesie in sack cloth with the Witnesses yet be of good comfort, O Lilly white soul, for God now accepteth thy works." Caryl warned his auditors, "If you defile your garments, Christ will pronounce another sentence, he will pronounce a sentence against you, he hath threatenings for those who defile their garments, in the place of rewards for those who keep them clean." Others expressed similar views. Harvard graduate John Collins warned that a "luke-warm indifferent temper hath done the Church of God a great deal of mischief formerly; and if admittd now, will do you as much mischief again." In one of the few attempts to explain the reason that God had evidently turned his back on England, Collins suggested that the "luke-warm indifferent temper . . . hath been one of the sins which the Lord at this day is judging & punishing his poor people for, that our zeal hath been so hot against one another for meer circumstances, and so cold when we are like to lose the substance: that our contentions rise so high in matters hardly any moment, & our spirits work so low when they are to gain the great things for which Christ suffered." Communion with fellow saints would heal differences among the elect and be the means of rekindling a fervent faith.[21]

By pointing to quarrels over insignificant differences and lack of attention to the essentials as sins for which the saints were being punished, the clergy hoped to draw their flocks back to true communion and orthodoxy. But they also sought to comfort the faithful, pointing to the fact that it was often the lot of saints to suffer. This, of course, would be a point developed in the great nonconformist literary works by Bunyan and Milton. It was the message from the pulpit in the 1660s. "The sum of all," Collins preached, "is to beg that you would be Valiant for the Truth of Christ; that whatever hath been delivered to us, that you would struggle might and main by all Christian courage, by argument, practice, prayer, by suffering, rather than let go those truths that God hath taught you by his faithful Ministers." "Do not complain of the worst condition that the providence of God shall cast you into," Matthew Mead counseled, "in this it may be You shall suffer hard things, but remember, so long as thy soul is secure, never complain of hard things." Indeed, "when . . . we must either run through sin or sufferings, then I may safely conclude, that Christ called me to suffer, & in this cause we may expect the peace & sweetness of his presence."[22]

Similar views were expressed by John Davenport in a series of sermons preached in New Haven and published in England through the efforts of William Hooke and Joseph Caryl. In *The Saints Anchor-Hold, In All Storms and Tempests* (London, 1661) the New Haven clergyman admitted the "frustration and disappointment" of those who, "when they have given up their names unto Christ, looked for peace, prosperity, and good dayes, but find troubles, crosses and afflictions of various kinds." But it was wrong to despair, and perhaps it had been arrogant to assume that men had understood God's timetable for reform. The fact was that "God some times puts a long Date to the performance of his Promises." Indeed, looking at the international context that had concerned him since the 1620s, Davenport believed that when "we add the great advantages which the Popish party hath against the Protestant, and what posture the Protestant Churches are in, in respect to their mutual relation to each other, to oppose this combination of their enemies . . . it will become manifest that the Antichristian party had never so great advantage against the Churches of Christ, since the Reformation began, as now they have."[23]

Yet this was not cause for despair. There was a purpose, Davenport believed, to these new times of testing: "God's deferring of the rule of the saints is no empty space but a time of fitting his Church and People for the good things promised. While Physick is working, the time is not lost, though health be not recovered: For, when the sick humour is purged out, then comes health. . . . Time waiting is not a meer staying God's leisure, but a continuing in a gracious inoffensive course, till the good waited for be attained." Though millennial speculation would not be as common in the latter decades of the seventeenth century, those such as Davenport who did return to these themes would see the trials of the 1660s and 1670s in terms of the prophesied slaying of the witnesses—a time of suffering before the dawn of God's triumph.[24]

The encouragement they gave to their followers was to persevere, but the leaders of the Congregational network seem to have had no clear program for further reform. The following decades would mark a return to the earlier forms of network activity: binding together the communion of the saints through sharing ideas, prayers, and meetings; extending material assistance to those in need; and campaigning to achieve limited objectives. Some successes would be recorded, but the network of the Restoration era was not as well integrated as had been that of the pre–civil war decades. The Interregnum had brought to the fore issues that divided one-time friends—the dispute between Congregationalists and Presbyterians, dissension over the appropriateness of infant baptism, differences concerning the bounds of orthodoxy, and the relationships between laity and clergy and church and state, to name but a few. Efforts begun in the 1650s to draw orthodox friends back into union would continue in the following decades, but frequently fail just when they seemed on the verge of success. In New England the quarrel over extending baptism to the children of those who were not visible saints—the Half-Way Covenant dispute—created bitter feelings that inhibited the sense of clerical brotherhood. It was also less common for members of the new generation to be bound to their congregations by experiences of godly communion and shared grace. The debate over the Half-Way Covenant centered on the problem that fewer and fewer believers had experienced the spiritual ecstasy that enabled them to join in communion with fellow saints. Additionally, when one considers that though trans-Atlantic Congregationalism had grown in numbers, fewer members were personally known to counterparts across the sea, the degree to which the Congregationalists succeeded in recovering unity was remarkable.

Persecution tended to force English dissenters together. The threat to Congregationalist clergy was greater following their expulsion from the Church of England than it had been in the 1620s and 1630s. Thomas Jollie was arrested on at least six occasions for violations of the Conventicle Act and the Five Mile Act and took to preaching "from a staircase to people gathered in his sitting room, separated by a door which was cut in two and hinged, thus providing a pulpit while Jollie was preaching but a shutter which could quickly be closed to hide the preacher should the meeting be disturbed." Other expedients employed by dissenters included preaching on horseback in a wood and providing members of a congregation with bread and cheese to give the assembly the appearance of a party rather than a religious service. John Flavell preached from a rock in the Kingsbridge estuary at low tide. The Stepney congregation of William Greenhill and Matthew Mead worshiped in a concealed attic above the meetinghouse. Congregations frequently met late at night, even at three o'clock in the morning. But as the government spy system improved, the best chance for members of a conventicle and their ministers to avoid imprisonment was to post sentries to give the alarm when the authorities approached. Clergymen adopted various other expedients to escape detection. Nathaniel Mather wrote to his brother Increase, "I spake with one lately come from London who told mee that he was on occasion with about 40 Non Con Ministers, all in strange disguises; few or none of them daring to be seen in the streets, so as to bee known, & concealing also their lodgings." Yet, despite these precautions, in London alone in the 1680s almost four thousand different nonconformists were charged with attendance at conventicles.[25]

Disregarding the best efforts of the authorities to enforce the provisions of the Clarendon Code, Congregationalists like other dissenters managed to sustain an active life of worship. Persecution drove them closer together as it had in the days of Archbishop Laud, and godly communion once again became the nourishment upon which their religious efforts depended. For most of the 1660s Congregational clergy ministered, often in conjunction with one or more friends, to conventicles that numbered as few as several dozen to as many as several hundred. Often a clergyman was involved with more than one conventicle. Thus, in 1669 William Bridge shared in the ministry of a conventicle of about thirty in Wattesfield along with William Ames Jr., while he was also associated with Samuel Petto in a Yarmouth conventicle of more than four hundred. In the Stepney parish in London where he had ministered with Jeremiah Burroughes, William Greenhill was joined by Matthew Mead in ministering to one conventicle that met by Greenhill's home next to the parish church. That gathering often numbered close to five hundred, and the two Congregationalists also preached to a conventicle of about three hundred in Meeting House Alley in Wapping. In the same Stepney parish their friends John Collins and Nicholas Lockyer ministered to a congregation in Bell Lane by Spitalfields. John Loder and Philip Nye shared the pastorate of a congregation in Silver Street in London. Thomas Harrison and Joseph Caryl were ministers to a conventicle in Leaden Hall Street. On occasion a group of clergymen would join together in a combination lecture similar to those that had attracted Puritan clergy in the 1620s. In 1669 one such combination in the London area, in Hackney, included Peter Sterry, Philip Nye, Thomas Goodwin, George Griffiths, Thomas Brooks, John Owen, Thomas Watson, and William Bates. George Griffiths was also reported to be associated in a combination near the Guildhall with Owen, Thomas Goodwin, Matthew Barker, and George Cockayn.[26]

During times when the government was energetic in prosecuting dissenters, conventicles might shift their meeting places. Some congregations sought to avoid detection by meeting at different locations on different days. The conventicle led by Thomas Allen in Norwich in the late 1660s met at the home of one of its members, a grocer, for Sunday services and met on other days at the home of other members. Clergymen sought to hide the place not only of their religious gatherings but also of their dwellings. John Owen, despite his early access to Clarendon and other powerful connections, was at certain times so "harried from place to place that he seriously considered the advisability of leaving England." Thus, as Nathaniel Mather reported, many ministers ventured forth in disguises and tried to conceal their lodgings. An example of this type of effort to evade the authorities can be seen in a letter from William Hooke to his friend and former colleague John Davenport. Writing in 1663 he explained, "I am not, at present, where I was, when you wrote last to me, yet in the same Family, but in a place of some privilege." Aware of the danger of his correspondence being intercepted, Hooke was not going to be more explicit. He wrote that "the bearer heereof may, perhaps, tell you, if need be," but Hooke was willing to drop a series of hints he hoped his friend would understand—his host was married to "the daughter of one to whom Mr. Aldersey was Uncle, with whom, they say, you were well acquainted." A gentleman also lived in the house who was a courtier, a scholar, an "Episcopal," but with a very "anti-Episcopal" wife.[27]

Such circumlocution was common, as was the attempt to find lodgings with laymen who might not draw as much attention from the spies employed by the government. But from the reports of these agents and other records one can gain some sense of the location of the clergymen and their tendency to congregate in communities where they could be sustained by spiritual communion with their friends. In the London area the Congregationalists were concentrated in the northern and eastern quarters of the city and its suburbs. An important cluster of friends resided around Moorgate. Just north of the city wall, in the vicinity of the Bunhill Fields where many of them would later be buried, lived John Owen and Anthony Palmer. Thankful Owen and Philip Nye lived a few streets away in Cherry Tree Alley, as did Thomas Goodwin on Bone Hill. Just south of the city wall from Moorgate was Coleman Street. Henry Jessey lived in Swan Alley, off Coleman Street, and John Winthrop Jr. had lodgings there while seeking the Connecticut charter. George Griffiths lived a few blocks east of Coleman Street, and George Cockayn and Matthew Barker dwelt on Soper Lane just to the south. Barker preached near St. Clement Eastcheap, which was a few blocks to the east and part of the same neighborhood, extending within the walls between Moorgate and Bishopsgate. Lime Street, where Thomas Brooks lived (and where Nathaniel Mather would later live and preach) and Little Eastcheap, where John Knowles preached, were within a short distance of St. Clement.[28]

Exiting from the city from Bishopsgate and traveling to the north would take one to the new neighborhoods around Spitalfields, where William Hooke lived for a time, as did the Presbyterian Samuel Annesley. The northern and eastern suburbs were developing rapidly in the Stuart era and many Congregationalists found residences in these new neighborhoods. The next gate to the east of Bishopsgate was Aldgate and that would be the normal way to travel into Stepney parish where William Greenhill, Matthew Mead, and others lived and preached. Along an arc extending from Spitalfields in the north to the river just south of Stepney were hamlets such as Bethnal Green, Hackney, Ratcliffe, and Wapping, where members of the network could be found. North from Moorgate a journey of a few miles would take a traveler to Newington Green, which would also be an important center of Congregationalist activity. All these clusters were close enough to allow friends to see each other frequently, to listen to each other preach, and to gather to consider crises facing the network.

Newington Green was also the location of some of the new and important dissenting academies. The test oaths required by the government drove the nonconformists from the nation's universities. Never again could there be a Congregationalist communion at Cambridge. Driven by their concern to provide an educated clergy, the dissenters had to create their own alternative educational system by founding academies that were often run by ejected fellows of the universities. Theophilus Gale, who had been a fellow at Thomas Goodwin's Magdalen, Oxford, during the Commonwealth, was active in educational ventures after the Restoration. He tutored two of the sons of Lord

Wharton, taking them abroad for study on one occasion. He opened an academy at Newington Green in the mid-1660s. When he died he left his personal library to Harvard College. Gale was succeeded in his teaching post by Thomas Rowe. Some of the academy's students were supported by the Common Fund after it was established. Graduates included Isaac Watts and the clergyman-historian Daniel Neal. Charles Morton, another Oxford graduate of the Owen-Goodwin era, opened another academy at Newington Green in 1675. It came to be considered one of the best. Included among the amenities were a garden, a bowling green, and a fish pond. On the academic side, it reflected Morton's interests by having a laboratory and a science curriculum that probably excelled that of the university colleges. Among the graduates were Daniel Defoe and Samuel Wesley.[29]

Samuel Craddock conducted a school for a brief time in Suffolk, where his pupils included Edmund Calamy and Timothy Goodwin. In the 1670s, however, the authorities began to crack down on the academies, harassing Edward Veal enough that he gave up his school at Stepney in 1680. Government hostility contributed to Charles Morton's decision to migrate to New England. In that case Stephen Lobb stepped in to fill Morton's shoes for a time and in general the academies did continue. In fact, Timothy Jollie, the son of Thomas, opened an academy in the late 1680s, which he named Christ's College. Testimonials from individuals such as Calamy and Defoe give hints at the importance of the educational and social experience for a new generation of dissenters.[30]

The London-area Congregationalists maintained contact with friends elsewhere in England, such as William Bridge and Thomas Jollie, with clergy in Ireland, such as the Mathers, and with friends overseas. As in the early decades of the century, some members of the network fled to the Netherlands while still others journeyed to New England. These movements actually revitalized the trans-Atlantic communion, giving it an Indian summer by placing abroad personal friends of those who had stayed behind in England, friends who not only could and would communicate with friends in England but would help to explain the English scene and its actors to those abroad.

Nicholas Lockyer, who had studied at Emmanuel, Cambridge, in the 1630s, had been a Trier during the Protectorate, and was provost of Eton from 1659 to 1660, migrated to Holland during the Restoration. He preached to a church in Rotterdam in the mid-1660s, returned to England, but fled briefly again after publishing a tract against the Conventicle Act. He came home for a final time and died in London in 1685. Matthew Mead spent time in the Netherlands in the 1660s and became closely involved with members of the Dutch government, including William of Orange. He was in England for much of the following decade, but returned to Utrecht in 1682 after being implicated in the Rye House Plot. Thomas Gouge, who had received part of his schooling in Holland, ministered to an English congregation in Amsterdam in the 1670s. Hugh Goodyear, who had moved to the Netherlands during the Laudian persecutions and remained in Leiden till his death in 1661, was succeeded in his pastorate by Matthew Newcomen. John Quick preached to the English Reformed Church in Middelburg in the early 1680s and reported that of the twelve pastors in the town six were "strict Puritans and my particular friends." Robert Bragge and Nathaniel Taylor visited the church at Utrecht and preached. Nathaniel Mather was an assistant in the Rotterdam church from 1663 to 1671. Immediately after the Restoration he had written of his own plans to his brother Increase, who was still in England, and informed him that Urian Oakes at St. Catharine's, Cambridge, could give Increase information on how to journey safely to the Netherlands, should he choose to. Increase returned to New England, but corresponded with friends in the Netherlands as well as those in England. Ichabod Chauncey, Thomas Woodcock, and John Howe also ministered to congregations in the Netherlands. It was when Howe was preaching at Utrecht that he befriended William of Orange.[31]

Large numbers of refugees also invigorated the New England wing of the Congregationalist network in the years after the Restoration. In addition to those such as Increase Mather who were returning to familiar surroundings, numerous clergymen were coming to what was to them truly a new world. Thomas Gouge's son Edward settled in Boston. Ministers who came to New England around the time of the 1662 ejections included Thomas Gilbert, John Oxenbridge, James Allen, Thomas Thornton, Thomas Walley, and Nicholas Woodrop. The migration started even before the return of Charles Stuart. As the Puritan regime had begun to crumble, John Maidstone had written to John Winthrop Jr. asking for "advice, by the next opportunity, concerning friends here, what encouragement persons may have, if times press them, to transport their families to New England." As the Clarendon Code was imposed, the number of emigrants increased. Increase Mather, back in the colonies himself, wrote to John Davenport in June of 1662 of a ship that had carried forty Englishmen to Boston and that "many men of considerable quality & Estate . . . have a desire to come into this Country, if they may have incouragement from hence. Capt Pearce is coming with 2 or 300 passengers." Davenport heard similar reports from his English correspondents and wrote to another friend that same summer that "there is great talke of many Ministers with theire Congregations comeing over the next yeare if roome can be found for them." Thomas Goodwin was one "who had come over now if his wife had not opposed it," according to Increase Mather.[32]

There was no lack of encouragement—colonial churches in this period often preferred English divines to Harvard graduates for pastoral posts—but it was not always easy to make the journey. Eleazar Mather reported the case of a "Mr Bartlett of Bidiford & his son [who] were shipt for N E: but an Oath was imposed upon them afore they could get out of the harbor, & that stopt them, for they chused rather to dye in prison than take it." Often evasion was called for, since the government was wary about allowing an increase in the number of disaffected colonists. For the most part, however, the government did less to stop the flow than to monitor it, keeping close track, for instance, of the activities of the English merchant John Harwood, who was active in smuggling dissenters abroad.[33]

Many who came would achieve prominence in the New World. Edward Taylor was only eighteen at the time of the Restoration. Blocked from a ministerial career in England, the future poet left his native land in 1668, graduated from Harvard in 1671, and accepted a call to the pulpit in Connecticut. James Allen had been educated at Magdalen, Oxford, during the presidency of Thomas Goodwin and was a good friend of the older clergyman. Coming to New England, he was ordained teacher of the First Church of Boston in 1668 and was one of the leaders of New England Puritanism in the following decades. He became a friend and ally of John Davenport. Together with John Oxenbridge, another new arrival from England, he worked to persuade the colonists to moderate their treatment of Baptists.[34]

Charles Morton had played a prominent role in English Puritan affairs. He had studied at Oxford during the time when Owen and Goodwin dominated the university. James Allen was a contemporary and friend there, as was the New Englander William Stoughton. Morton was a member of a clerical association in Cornwall in the 1650s and secretary of the group. He settled in the London area after the Restoration but lost most of his possessions in the Great Fire. He then opened his academy at Newington Green. In 1685 he inquired about sending his nephew to Harvard. Correspondence with Increase Mather, whom he had met years earlier in England, led him to migrate, accompanied by Samuel Penhallow and some of his other students. Morton became pastor of the church at Charlestown and was active in the affairs of Harvard. He was one of the organizers of the Cambridge ministerial association and an outspoken opponent of the Dominion of New England.[35]

Samuel Lee was another of Goodwin's students at Magdalen, Oxford, and served as a fellow of Wadham College from 1648 to 1657. He was associated with Theophilus Gale in a Congregationalist conventicle in Holborn and then moved to Newington Green in the late 1670s, where he was reunited with Morton, who had been a close friend at Oxford. He sailed for New England in the same year as Morton and became pastor of a congregation in Bristol, Rhode Island, maintaining contact with Morton and conducting an active correspondence with the Boston merchant and magistrate Samuel Sewall.[36]

New England attracted many soldiers and other lay supporters of the

Cromwellian regime. The disaffected Samuel Maverick complained to Clarendon of the "many seditious factious persons" migrating to the colonies. Some, such as William Jones (son of one of the executed judges of Charles I), became respected civic leaders, and others such as Peter Sergeant (a nephew of Henry Ashurst) became prosperous merchants with important English contacts. But the ones who attracted the most attention then and later were the regicides. The story of their reception provides a fascinating insight into the way Congregational friends would protect fellow saints.[37]

In August of 1660 John Davenport wrote to John Winthrop Jr. of the arrival in Boston of "Commisary General [Edward] Whalley, Sister Hooke's brother [Jane Hooke, William's wife], and his son-in-law, who is with him, is Colonel [William] Goffe, boath Godly men, and escaped pursuite in Engl narrowly." The two veterans had arrived in Boston on July 27, and they had indeed barely escaped arrest and execution as regicides. They carried with them testimonial letters from the Reverends John Rowe and Seth Wood as well as other English clergy. The two Cromwellians were well received in Boston: Governor John Endecott embraced them, entertained them, and wished that more like them would make the journey to the colonies. On August 9 Goffe recorded in his journal that they "went to Boston Lecture, heard mr. Norton on Hebr. 2.16. went afterwards to his house, where wee wr Lovingly Entertained, with many Ministers, and found great respects from them." The two must have carried letters attesting to their Congregational church membership in England, for they were allowed to receive communion in the Boston church. On the fifteenth of the month they saw an old friend they had known decades before in England: "Sup't at mr Chauncey's, the good old Servant of the Lord, still Expressing much affection, & telling us, he was perswaded the Ld had brought us into this country for good both to them and our Selves."[38]

But Whalley and Goffe were under sentence of death from the king's government—Davenport had commented at the time of their arrival that they had narrowly escaped—and orders were received that the colonial officials should apprehend them. Having first made sure that the two men were safely on their way to New Haven, Governor Endecott empowered two newly arrived royalists, Thomas Kellond and Thomas Kirke, to search for and seize the fugitives. But despite the efforts of Kellond and Kirke, and of those who tried later on—Springfield's John Pynchon tried to capture them and the royal agent Edward Randolph maintained an interest in finding them long after they in fact had died—the two regicides were successfully protected by their friends. John Davenport took them into his home in New Haven in April of 1661 and then moved them from place to place in that area over the following months. In October of 1664 Whalley and Goffe took up what would be their final residence in Hadley, where they were looked after by the Reverend John

Russell. Despite rumors in England that tied them to Oliverian plots, they never left the Massachusetts frontier.[39]

Richard Saltonstall, who had known them in England, visited Whalley and Goffe in 1672 as he prepared to travel to the mother country. He left them £50 for their support and carried messages to their friends back home. John Leverett, back from England and serving as governor of Massachusetts, visited his old army comrades as well. Increase Mather visited the pair and, along with John Davenport in the colonies and William and Jane Hooke in England, was a key figure in the correspondence network that allowed the two exiles to write to their families and friends in England, generally in code. Whalley died in 1674; Goffe probably survived until 1678. Legend would claim that Goffe was the mysterious "angel of Hadley" who appeared among the settlers to rally them against an Indian attack during King Philip's War—a legend that Nathaniel Hawthorne would draw upon in developing his tale of New England's "Grey Champion."[40]

The network was kept together by correspondence such as that maintained by Whalley and Goffe, but evidence of these communications is not as extensive as historians would like. The government intercepted mail and seized private papers, putting at risk those who committed strong views to writing. Not all Congregationalist clergymen were radicals, though the government tended to regard them as such. Some of the resulting difficulties in sustaining correspondence are clearly revealed in the *Mather Papers*. "There is no fault in any person but my self that you have not recd L[ette]rs from mee," wrote Samuel Baker to Increase Mather, explaining that "I judged it prudence to keep silence." Joshua Churchill wrote to Mather in 1684 apologizing that "I cannot say, such & such give you their service; they would have done it, had they known of my writeing, or could I walk abroad (which I dare not, warrants being in severall hands for my apprehending)." A letter written by William Hooke to John Davenport in 1663 was seized, along with letters from a Major Thompson. "Newes here a prohibited commodity," wrote Samuel Craddock, and Samuel Petto explained to Mather, "I doubt not but you had information by persons which came over, *viva voce*, what condition we are in that live in Old England, both as to civill & religious liberties, & I must still refer you to such information for your satisfaction. I think it not expedient to write anything concerning it."[41]

Various methods were used to evade the efforts of the government to intercept letters. William Hooke sent letters concealed in packets of books. William Goffe's letters to friends in England were occasionally bound into a book or notebook. Trusted intermediaries concealed letters on their persons or in their effects and carried them between correspondents, as Richard Lawrence did for Yarmouth Congregationalists and George Thorne for those in Weymouth. Some letters were written in code. Adopting a false identity could deflect interest, and so William Hooke wrote to William Goffe in 1663 that "you may know mee hereafter by D: G: Letters are so often broke up that many are loath to write their names." Another ploy was to rely on friends with connections. Thomas Cobbett wrote from Massachusetts to Nathaniel Mather in Ireland, but sent the letters to John Hill, a friend of Cobbett's employed in the Treasury at Whitehall, who then enclosed Cobbett's letters in a packet he mailed to a Mrs. Bridge who was a member of Mather's Dublin congregation. Such precautions might seem humorously excessive were there not ample evidence of letters being intercepted and dissenters imprisoned.[42]

To further protect themselves many English clergy had their letters directed to third parties. John Allin had letters sent addressed "to Mr Charles Cooke, Turner at the Plow and Harrow, in little Eastcheape, London . . . with two round dashes with the penn over *London*"—those marks indicating that the letter was meant for Allin rather than Cooke. A year later he was asking that letters be sent to a Mr. Edward Burtt "with the old distinction over *London*," because he had been "forced to a suddaine remove" from his former residence. Jonathan Heyes at the sign of the Brewers in Turnbull Street, London, was the intermediary in the correspondence between Thomas Jollie and Increase Mather. Jonathan Tuckney had mail directed to John Whiting. When Increase Mather was on his charter mission to England in 1688 he recorded in his diary a whole list of letter drops and accommodation addresses for correspondence with his English friends. This form of misdirection was important, as was the reliance on known carriers of messages, because the government-run postal service could not be trusted, especially after May of 1663, when all postmasters were forced on pain of dismissal to prove their conformity to the Church of England. But nothing the government tried worked, and as late as 1681 Edward Randolph was futilely urging the government to do more to cut off the correspondence between the "factious parties in old and New England."[43]

And so, scattered by changes in government and the imposition of the Clarendon Code, the Congregational clergy sought to retain their sense of communion—through personal contact when possible, by correspondence when that was all that was available. United as brethren but unsure of what the future held for them, they would confront the challenges of the coming decade.

CHAPTER TEN

For the Nation and the Interest of Christ

In the decades that stretched from the Restoration to the Glorious Revolution, English nonconformists were restive under the pressures of the Clarendon Code. Congregationalism began to assume the character of a denomination and clergymen had to deal with the new realities of religious pluralism. The Dissenting community included a radical underground whose plots against the government seemed to justify government fears of the political implications of religious nonconformity. That connection would emerge forcefully in the crises of the Popish Plot, the Exclusion Crisis, the Rye House Plot, Monmouth's Rebellion, and finally the Glorious Revolution. In America, New England Puritans would share the fears of their English friends and suffer their own trials when the Stuart-imposed Dominion of New England seemed to threaten both the civil and religious practices of the colonists. In these times of shared danger, trans-Atlantic friends would once again cooperate in any effort to achieve religious unity and the protection of their common faith.

English Congregationalists had to deal with a variety of issues resulting from their exclusion from the state church, in particular with the question of what stance they should take relative to that church and to the society that surrounded them. As they struggled to structure their own denomination, they had to assess the desirability of cooperation with other Dissenters. In dealing with all these problems, they came to rely upon the advice and assistance of their friends in the Congregational communion.

The effect of the Clarendon Code was to drive the Congregationalists from the church. Few had shared Presbyterian hopes for comprehension, and their belief that innovations in the restored church smacked of popery only confirmed them in their separation. John Owen was especially critical of what he perceived as the drift of the new Anglicanism from orthodox Calvinist standards. Jonathan Tuckney felt the same, writing to John Cotton Jr., "It is the wonderfull mercy of God to his people . . . that we are not overrun with popery; for doubtless that is the desire & design of sundry (too many) of our great ones." Yet, some laymen sought to avoid the civil disabilities of the test acts by attending parish worship as well as Congregational services. Though such occasional conformity was not the inflammatory issue it would later become, it was an issue the clergy often discussed in the decades following the Restoration and it was one on which clergy in the Congregational communion came to accept a diversity of opinion. Philip Nye resisted the fact that there would no longer be a national church and held to the old nonseparating notion of reform from within. He believed that in addition to worshiping in conventicles, it was a "Duty that we and our Families frequent also (as we have Liberty and Opportunity) the more *Publicke* and *National* Ministry." Thomas Goodwin distinguished between parishes in which the majority were godly believers and the pastor a worthy minister and those "where ignorance and profanenes overwhelm the generality" and the clergyman was scandalous. In the former case it was lawful to participate in the same way as a Congregationalist abroad might join in the worship of foreign reformed churches, but in the latter case even occasional conformity was unacceptable. Owen opposed the practice entirely, as did William Bridge, who went further than most in threatening to excommunicate members of his church who attended parish services.[1]

The legal status of Congregationalists and other dissenting sects would be modified on a number of occasions in the decades after the Restoration. In March 1672 Charles II used the royal prerogative to issue a Declaration of Indulgence suspending all of the ecclesiastical penal laws and allowing Dissenters to worship publicly if their clergyman and meetinghouse were licensed. Charles had been trying to gain nonconformist support and had freed some Dissenters from prison preparatory to his March edict. Though more than 1,600 clergymen did seek licenses, their response was not uniformly enthusiastic. Many were politically opposed to the exercise of prerogative powers by the king regardless of how good the cause. Some feared that the information on clergymen and their meeting places obtained in the licensing procedures could later be used against them. For those few who still longed for comprehension, the act of being licensed as a dissenting clergyman represented crossing a religious Rubicon. But, most important, Protestant dissenters were suspicious that the king's plan was a Trojan horse designed to open the doors to the toleration of Catholics and they were reluctant to pay such a price for their own relief.[2]

The reaction of the bishops and the high Anglican lords was quick once Parliament met again. In February of 1673 the House of Commons voted that the king had no authority to suspend the penal laws without parliamentary approval and the king bowed to the mounting pressure by withdrawing the declaration a year after it had been issued. Charles shifted directions, allying himself with the high Anglican party. Any question of how the government viewed the licenses granted in 1672 was eliminated with their official withdrawal in February 1675. Yet the brief window of opportunity had given the Dissenters a valuable respite, providing them with an opportunity to organize more effectively and build greater strength.[3]

Having been separated from the institutional national church, it was imperative for Congregationalists to find their own means of retaining uniform beliefs and practices. The family-like ties of communion bound them together and formed a hedge against outside influence. The methods of informal association that had served them so well in earlier decades were used to implement the principles of consociation called for in the Savoy Declaration. It is clear that some form of Congregationalist clerical association existed in the London area during the period, perhaps a continuation of the group that had assisted in the planning for the Savoy Assembly. Their renunciation of Venner's uprising was published as a declaration of the "Congregational churches and public preachers of the said Judgement, living in and about the City of London" and implied some organization of the group. In 1663 William Hooke wrote to John Davenport that he had "met last summer in a meeting of several ministers (I suppose between 12 & 20 of them) who are pleased to admit me to be among them," which indicates that membership in the association was not open to all. Hooke's brief description of a meeting indicates that the group acted like the old clerical prophesyings, with certain members preaching and being exposed to questions. Thomas Jollie's papers reveal evidence of a similar clerical association in the north to which Jollie and Samuel Eaton belonged, and there were undoubtedly other such groups in East Anglia and other Puritan strongholds. Such sessions were important for the spiritual and emotional sustenance they provided as well as for their role in shaping a new denominational order.[4]

There seem to have been no "national" synods or assemblies in the decades after the Restoration, but the London consociation appears to have served the function of coordinating the efforts of the regional groups, by advising them (and the churches in New England) and by welcoming messengers from the other groups. On occasion these assemblages could resemble a national assembly. Thomas Jollie recorded a number of visits to the London clergy in his notebook and he seems to have been acting as a messenger from his local association. In 1675 he mentions how "a meeting in and about London was called; something was begun upon as to the encouraging of suffering churches and candidates."[5]

The community of churches that these assemblies tried to encourage was reinforced by the traditional participation of neighboring congregations in the installation of new pastors. In the London area Owen, Caryl, Griffiths, and Collins assisted in the ordination of Matthew Mead as pastor of the Stepney congregation after the death of William Greenhill in 1671. Owen also assisted in the installation in 1674 of Thomas Cole as pastor of the congregation meeting at Cutler's Hall in Cloak Lane. John Langston, who was William Hooke's assistant for much of the 1660s, became pastor of a congregation in Ipswich and was installed by a number of neighboring clergy, including Samuel Petto. Petto was also involved in the ordination of Thomas Milway at Bury in 1674. The records of the Yarmouth congregation show similar activities involving that church and its neighbors in the Norwich region.[6]

Churches also cooperated in recommending individuals to a congregation in the community to which that person was moving. Thus, for example, the First Church of Boston in Massachusetts voted that "our brother Mr. Richard Hutchinson 2nd according to his Desire by letters was Dismissed to the Church of Christ whereof Mr. Thomas Goodwin is pastor with the Consent of our Church." By means of such formal actions and also by simple letters of private recommendation from clergymen, Congregationalists were able both to attest to their unity in faith and also to aid each other in maintaining the orthodoxy of their separate churches.[7]

Congregations and consociations also exchanged advice on issues that confronted them. When the church in Norwich was confused over the distinction between the offices of pastor and teacher they sought advice from others, including Thomas Goodwin and John Owen. Both responded and referred Robert Asty, who was considering a call to the Norwich ministry, to the New England model. Goodwin suggested that Asty "may see this opened at large by Mr. *Cotton* in the *Way of the Churches* of New England." Owen similarly advised, "I know no difference between a pastor and a teacher, but what follows their different gifts; the office is absolutely the same in both; the power the same, the right to the administration of all ordinances every way the same; and at that great church at Boston, in New England, the teacher was always the principal person; so was Mr. Cotton and Mr. Norton." Owen was also asked to advise about the admission to the Watesfield, Suffolk, church of a woman who had experienced grace but had never been baptized. Nathaniel Mather advised Thomas Jollie's church on questions of accommodation. Jollie himself gave advice on matters of church organization to the nearby congregation at Walmsly. George Griffiths and John Owen wrote to Francis Holcroft's Cambridge congregation regarding what they felt was an ill-advised excommunication of two members. Sometimes advice was personal, as when John Collins advised Matthew Newcomen about whether the latter should accept a call to a pulpit in the Netherlands.[8]

Advice was solicited from and offered by consociations as well as by individual clergy. George Moxon had ministered in the 1640s to the Springfield, Massachusetts, church. William Pynchon, a leading magistrate and member of that church, had been censured for the expression of heterodox views on the atonement in his *The Meritorious Price of Redemption* (London, 1655). Moxon had left the colonies in 1652, perhaps in part because he was suspected of sharing in Pynchon's views. In 1674 he was ministering to a church in Chesire and his views were brought before "the Messengers of the Associated Churches in the adjacent parishes of Yorkshire, Lancashire and Chesire" that "owned the Declaration of Faith and Order 12 of 8 Mo 1658 at the Savoy as theirs." The assembled clergy considered the "Case of Moxon . . . who dissents from the doctrine of the churches declared by the said confession in certain points concerning the Satisfaction of Christ. The brethren Mr. Briscoe and Mr. Birch to confer with him." The same meeting considered an application by Oliver Heywood's congregation to be admitted to the consociation and resolved to have their secretary, Thomas Jollie, solicit John Owen's opinion on the appropriateness of an appeal to the king for relief from the new wave of persecution that followed the revocation of the Declaration of Indulgence.[9]

Because Jollie's records of that particular association have survived, we have some idea of the functioning of such a group. In addition to the types of activities described above, members engaged in communal fasts and prayers as well as other joint spiritual exercises. The consociation often sent Jollie to London to seek advice from the national leaders of Congregationalism. When a question arose in 1682 regarding whether ordination to the ministry need be public, Jollie sought advice from his New England friends and journeyed to London "to consult with several of greatest note in the ministry." He arrived in the capital after "narrowly escaping the soldiers sometimes." Letters to Jollie from the colonies were directed to a friend of his in London and "it was a speciall providence that I there mett with a letter from N. E. Mr. Mather." This "gave me advantage in my debate with some who did something oppose, but soon yielded." The London clergymen he met with also showed an interest in a plan the northern consociation had advanced for an "accommodation and association of evangelicall reforming churches," and Jollie believed that this "converse at London gave me some advantage to make some alteration for the better in my draught thereof." On other occasions Jollie's kinsman Nathaniel Guillym, who was a member of Nathaniel Mather's Lime Street congregation, carried papers from Jollie to the area clergy and forwarded their responses.[10]

Despite the disabilities imposed on them by the Restoration settlement, English Congregationalists and other Dissenters remained engaged with the great issues of their day and found means to influence events. The period was one in which nonconformists were concerned with the decline of English morality, especially as evidenced in the court of Charles II. They complained about the spread of brothels, the incidence of drunkenness, and other signs of moral decay. These worries overlapped with a growing concern over a resurgent Catholic threat. The Catholic influence at court extended from the king's council chambers to his bedchambers, where he dallied with Catholic whores. The government seemed intent on a pro-Catholic, pro-French foreign policy—and there was enough evidence of this even without knowledge of the secret Treaty of Dover. The king's brother, James Stuart, was a Catholic and it seemed likely that he would succeed to the throne. James displayed an eagerness to advance fellow Catholics, and appointed one as governor of his proprietary colony of New York. His marriage to an Italian Catholic only heightened concerns. Catholics became the scapegoats for many of the reverses suffered by England. The Great Fire of London was said to have been started as a result of a plot hatched in Paris.[11]

Responding to these concerns, English Congregationalists and other Dissenters sought to influence events through various means. Prayer was still a respected weapon—Samuel Mather assured the readers of his *Testimony from the Scriptures Against Idolatry* that "when Saints pray, God will hear," and that "there is no standing before the Prayers of the Saints." But other tactics were used as well. At various times some of the more militant Dissenters were drawn into plots of armed insurrection, though the number of Congregationalists actively involved in this was small until the 1680s. More common were efforts to sway the government by supporting the election of sympathetic MPs and by influencing members of the houses of Parliament. Even amidst the general enthusiasm for the Restoration, the united efforts of Congregationalists, Presbyterians, and Baptists were able to secure the election of two Congregationalists (Sir William Thomson and William Love) as well as two Presbyterians in the London city elections of 1661. Throughout the land there would be many municipalities and boroughs where Dissenting clergy were involved in local elections, developing an influence that would contribute to the emerging Whig party when parliamentary elections were held again. Even the hostile Cavalier Parliament contained peers such as Wharton, Anglesey, Orrery, and others who were connected to dissent by ideology and friendship. Clergy urged them to use their influence on behalf of the reform of the nation and toleration for dissent. John Owen and members of the London clerical consociation were especially active in this regard, their influence noted and strongly condemned by Anglican critics such as George Vernon. The use of lobbying, pamphleteering, and petitioning was not new to these clergy, and it would become more developed in the 1670s as the earl of Shaftesbury emerged as the Whig champion.[12]

Occasionally Dissenter frustration with the course of events led to outbursts of violence, especially in London. Tim Harris has argued that the Bawdy House Riots of 1668 were one such reaction to the religious and secular policies of the court, and the first pope-burning procession in London was a reaction to the marriage of James Stuart. Whig leaders could use such signs of popular discontent to pressure the government, and that strategy was especially evident when the hysteria unleashed by Titus Oates's revelation of a "Popish Plot" was used to fuel efforts to exclude James from the succession. During the resulting Exclusion Crisis anti-Catholic feelings ran unchecked. Oates's claim to have uncovered a plot to kill King Charles spawned numerous other rumors: French troops would aid a newly crowned James in the massacre of Protestants and imposition of papacy on England; Catholics in the colony of Maryland were using Indians to kill Protestants; the fire that had recently destroyed much of colonial Boston had, like the London fire, been set by Catholics.[13]

The government was also ready to see plots everywhere. An interesting example of network activity that came under suspicion involved fundraising being conducted by John Knowles and others in the 1660s. Ostensibly, members of the clerical network such as Owen, Thomas Goodwin, and George Griffiths sought, along with Knowles, to raise funds for the relief of dispossessed Polish Protestants. As much as £1,000 may have been raised. This appears to have followed on an earlier effort to assist Protestants exiled from the Piedmont and resembled the efforts of Richard Sibbes, John Davenport, and other clerical friends to raise money for Palatinate refugees in the 1620s. But, as in that earlier case, officials suspected that the funds raised were to support those opposed to the government. One official asked "whether or no these Polonian fugitives are not . . . the English rebels in Holland and the Low Countries," and the surviving evidence does not exclude such a possibility.[14]

The defeat of exclusion and the collapse of Shaftesbury's fortunes in the early 1680s meant the end of hopes that substantive reforms could be achieved through Parliament. Whig political leaders were accused of involvement in the Rye House Plot, leading to the execution of some and the flight of others to the Netherlands. Matthew Mead, Stephen Lobb, John Owen, Ichabod Chauncey, and George Griffiths were among the Congregational clergy accused of complicity and forced into hiding. A new crackdown on dissent began, making the early 1680s one of the worst periods for Dissenters. Government actions to strip corporations of their charters threatened the political base of what Whig strength remained. Increasingly, more Dissenters began to become radicalized, seeing armed resistance as a legitimate response to a secret popish conspiracy against the Protestant faith and the ancient constitution. [15]

Such fears were heightened by the accession of James II in 1685, leading some Dissenters to gamble on Monmouth's Rebellion. Although many Congregationalists, including Thomas Jollie and Matthew Mead, disapproved of the effort to replace James with the illegitimate Protestant son of Charles II, others did support the uprising. Axminster's Reverend Stephen Towgood called Monmouth "a deliverer for the nation, and the interest of Christ." John Owen, Robert Ferguson, and Ichabod Chauncey supported the rebellion. But the hopes of the rebels were destroyed at Sedgemoor and the new king was not generous to his foes. The troops of Percy Kirke and the tribunals of Judge Jeffreys sought to crush forever the spirit of resistance. More than two hundred were executed in the Bloody Assizes, including Alice Lisle, the mother-in-law of Harvard's Leonard Hoar; her crime was harboring fugitive rebels. [16]

English friends kept colonial Congregationalists informed of events in the mother country and shaped American perceptions of those events. As one colonist expressed it, "You had need to lift up your hearts to God, when you are about to read your letters from our native Country, to give you wisdom, and hearts duly affected, that you may receive such intelligences as you ought." As the Puritan regime was crumbling, John Hull's receipt of English news led him to lament that "ther reformation, purchased by so much war and blood, should be given up again to heretics and papists." A few months later, "We heard of the bishops; and with them the old formalities of surplice, etc, were begun to be practised again in our native land." In 1662 William Hooke was providing further news of the dismantling of Puritan influence: "The Savoy hath beene the place of meeting of men Diametrically contrary to those that met there, & made the confession." With St. Bartholomew's Day come and gone, Hooke reported, "The Ejected Ministers in this Land are . . . in a very low & poor condition." "Great & strict inquisition, search & watching there hath been in the City upon the Lord's days, to find out private meetings, by soldiers, constables & officers. . . . Multitudes have been surprised & forthwith carried to prisons. . . . Many have died in imprisonment, & been even stifled through thronging together, & want of air, & necessary helps, etc." Continuing a long letter, Hooke told the cautionary tale of one clergyman who had conformed to the new order, "read the service with a disturbed spirit, & was so smitten in it, that he took to his bed, & died," and another who, "going to conform . . . , fell thereon from his horse & his heart fell upon a stone . . . & he dyed." John Allin dispatched news of special relevance to the colonies when he reported in September 1663 of the "2 frigattes preparing to goe with Commissioners to New England." The colonists were also informed of the judgments of fire and plague that had been visited upon England.[17]

The new decade opened with a lament from an English friend that "Prophanes is . . . through the land. We are not the better either for judgments, which have been tremendous, nor for mercys which have been oblidging to repentance." Robert Atkyn expressed the same concern over the fact that "we here are full of looseness & prophanes, debauchery & what not crying Synns. . . . Lycentiousness much more pleasing to the Generality of people then a strict holy course of Livinge." Hooke mourned over the fact that "God hath of late years taken away many of our able ministers." John Collins reported that "the parliament [in 1675] will one way or another give a great change to things . . . though I expect none good." Nathaniel Mather believed that there had been a "departure . . . of late in congregational men from old principles & practices . . . [and] Mr Nye not long before his death saw & much layd to heart what he saw of that kind." A year later, in 1677, William Hooke compiled a list of more than forty clergymen who had died in the past few years. Richard Blinman gave the colonists the bad news in August 1677 that "your Agents in London have not so good a Reception as is desired & that you will be like to lose your patent."[18]

The late 1670s saw the disclosure of the Popish Plot and the events leading to the Exclusion Crisis. The fears of English Congregationalists emerge clearly in their letters to New England friends. "There hath been a deep & generall design amongst the papists to involve us in confusion & blood," wrote Nathaniel Mather in December 1678, promising, "If wee live till spring I shall send by way of London; perhaps more largely." It was, as Samuel Petto reported, "the crying sins of the Nation & want of reformation" that "doth much threaten us with a storm of judgment." When the accused conspirators were brought to justice it seemed "that the first tidings you heard of Engl this year was not that Engl was drowned in a deluge of Protestant blood & wholly subjugated to the Power of Rome, is a miracle of Mercy." "As to publique matters wee are yet in peace, which is a great wonder & the Lord's owne doeing." Yet further rumors of French invasions, a crackdown on Scottish Presbyterians, and the tensions of the Exclusion Crisis kept English Congregationalists on edge. "The Lord seems to be threatening us with some unhappy intestine eruption & if it ever come, it is like to be with much violence & rage. Let us have your prayers," wrote Nathaniel Mather, who concluded, "Saw you but what our eyes see & heard you but what our ears hear, you would not, you could not be unconcerned for us. But I may not write how it is with us."[19]

The 1680s began with the failure of exclusion, the accusation of nonconformist leaders implicated in the Rye House Plot, and news from Thomas Jollie that "nothing [is] more fully designed, nor more probable to bee effected, than the destruction of Ld. Shaftsbury." The resurgence of royal absolutism was reflected in the news reported by Ichabod Chauncey that Edward Cranfield, "a very base Tory," had been appointed the new royal governor of New Hampshire. Other correspondents reported that the duke of York, James Stuart, was "at cort & of as great influence as ever" and "Nonconformists are generally, all over England, greatly persecuted all manner of ways." News soon followed of the threat to and then the revocation of the charter of London and then that "a *quo warranto* is gone out against your Patent in New England." Nathaniel Mather, commenting on loyal addresses to the king from Plymouth and Connecticut, instructed Increase on the emerging terms of English political discourse, writing, "you of Massachusetts are more whiggish, & your neighbors more toryish . . . to express it in the language of late in use." That summer of 1684 was a bleak one. "I cannot hear of any place in England where the Nonconformists are suffered to meet unmolested. . . . Nor is their case better but rather more difficult in Scotland. . . . At present I see no place that is like to be quiet, unless you in New England bee." But New England was far from quiet, for the Bay Colony charter had been revoked and the region reorganized into the Dominion of New England. The Restoration had finally come in full force to America.[20]

New Englanders, though troubled by English news and faced with a growing threat themselves from the new royalist regime, had continued to exercise a large degree of control over their own world in the aftermath of the Restoration. Belief that they were a remnant chosen by God to save all Christendom had previously given New Englanders a sense of confidence and optimism in their dealing with the outside world. But now when they envisioned themselves as a saving remnant, their attention was on the fact that they were the last small community of saints in a hostile and threatening world. This led in many cases to greater fears regarding innovations and more intransigence toward the agents of change. Communion was an increasingly defensive posture.[21]

Fearful that God would punish their transgressions as he had punished England's and concerned that they were beset by enemies, the colonists became overscrupulous. Calls to return to the standards of the fathers were prompted by fears of declension from those standards. The quarrel over the Half-Way Covenant, the inability of the government to deal effectively with growing numbers of Baptists and Quakers, the influx of immigrants motivated by a desire to partake of the region's economic rather than religious opportunities, the greater availability of imported luxuries, and the introduction of new fashions were all matters that concerned the colonial clergy. Thomas Shepard Jr. even noted that there were "pictures and images of Christ, of the

Virgin Mary, and other canonized popish Saints . . . sold in some shops,"
which he feared "may become an Introduction to Popery itself." The times
were changing at a time when change itself was looked upon as a betrayal of
the fathers.[22]

Yet the colonists continued to believe in their mission and continued to
support the international Reformed community. In 1659 John Norton composed a letter signed by forty-three colonial clergymen and addressed to John
Dury. The ministers expressed their hope that they and their posterity might
remain true to the religion of their founders and went on to express support
for Dury's advocacy of Protestant unity. John Davenport likewise held on to a
traditional internationalist perspective in the sermons published as *The Saints
Anchor-Hold*, placing the plight of New England in the general context of
reverses suffered by the Protestant faith throughout Christendom.[23]

"God forbid that after *New England* hath now shined twenty years and
more, like a *light upon a hill*, it should at last go out," wrote John Norton in
The Heart of New England Rent. If anything, as the surrounding world became
darker it was more important than ever before for the beacon to be pure and
bright. In his 1661 election sermon Norton reiterated his call for perseverance, explaining the failure of reform in England as the result of England's
failure to live up to her covenant with God. New Englanders must take heed
and live up to the terms of their own commission lest they wish to feel the
same punishment.[24]

This theme—that England's fate was a warning to New England—was
reiterated by others. In a letter written in 1665 Davenport expressed his
amazement at how blind some men were. "The next age will wonder," he
concluded, "at the Dedolency, and stupidity of this age, wherein soe few
discerne the signes of the times." Lest his correspondent be one of those who
were less than clear-sighted, he spelled the signs out, in the process showing
that millennial expectations had not been totally snuffed out among Congregationalists: "The witnesses that are now killed, shall rise shortly. Rome shall
be ere long ruined. Christ will take unto himself his kingdome, which hath
beene usurped by Brutish men the vileness of whose spirits hath appeared in
scattering the churches gathered unto Christ, in sylencing the faithfull
Ministers, in imprisoning and banishing the innocent, in corrupting Religion
with Antichristian superstitions [and] in killing sundry that deserved better
usage." Continuing to show his knowledge of English events, Davenport
pointed to signs that God was already beginning to punish those who had
deserted him. The Lord "god hath brought a double sword upon them, the
sword of the Angell in the noysome pestillence [the plague in London] . . .
and the sword of war [the second Anglo-Dutch War]." The message for the
colonists was clear. "N England allsoe hath cause to tremble, whose day is
comeing, if speedy repentence, and reformation prevent not, for our backslid-

ing, and changing our waies, from the ancient pathes." Here, of course, Davenport was arguing against innovations such as the Half-Way Covenant, and in general the recollection of New England's covenant with God would be a conservative force in these decades.[25]

Similar themes were expressed by other clergymen, including those of the younger generation. John Higginson's *The Cause of God* (Cambridge, Mass., 1663) was an election sermon that called for adherence to the goals of the founders. Jonathan Mitchell, in a 1667 election sermon, likened the situation of the colonists to that of the Israelites in the time of Nehemiah: "They were a small, weak and despised people. . . . They were beset round with Adversaries, and Ill-willers, and many Informers and Complainers there were against them. . . . Their Adversaries did labour to fright them with the Accusation of Rebellion. . . . There were Discontents and Divisions among themselves." But they continued in their work of reforming and rebuilding, erecting a new wall around the holy city. Echoing John Winthrop's message in the "Modell of Christian Charity," Mitchell reminded his listeners that "the eyes of the whole Christian World are upon you; yea which is more, the eyes of God and of his holy Angels are upon you." The following year William Stoughton, who had been in England in the 1650s, expressed his belief to the magistrates that New England's true interest was "*Foundation-work*; not to lay a new foundation, but to continue and strengthen, and beautifie, and build upon that which had been laid." The colonists were "surely the Lord's *first-born* in this Wilderness," for "God sifted a whole Nation that he might send choice Grain over to this Wilderness." Reverses had been suffered, but the faithful must persevere, for "God hath taken up great Expectations of us, and made great Promises to himself concerning us, and this has been, and is New-England's day and season of Probation."[26]

John Davenport preached to the Massachusetts General Court at the 1669 election and warned the colonists to "take heed and beware . . . lest he [God] remove the golden Candlesticks, and the burning and shining Light in them." Jonathan Mitchell had first used the phrase "errand into the wilderness" in his 1667 sermon. In 1670 Samuel Danforth, John Eliot's colleague at Roxbury, preached to the magistrates *A Brief Recognition of New England's Errand into the Wilderness* (Cambridge, Mass., 1671). Urian Oakes also used the phrase in 1673. Thomas Shepard Jr., preaching on Jeremiah 2:31 in 1672, also called on the civic leaders to keep the people to their mission: "Remember that a main design of God's people adventuring into this wilderness was for progress in the work of Reformation," he urged, "and that in the way of brotherly communion with the Reformed Churches of Christ in other parts of the world." "Let the Liberties of the Churches . . . be preserved and maintained," he exhorted them, "for the Church is a Light upon an hill: the people of God are to shine as lights in the world." Others were still watching and New England must be true. "The Interest of *New-England* was Religion, which did distinguish us from other *English Plantations*," was the message of Increase Mather as he warned of impending judgments in 1674. And in a later sermon, bewailing innovations such as the celebration of Christmas, he expressed his belief that "such vanities . . . are good no where; but in New England they are a thousand times worse."[27]

The colonists were encouraged to strengthen their godly commonwealths by friends overseas. Despite their own problems, English Congregationalists continued to be inspired by the New England example. John Westgate wrote to Increase Mather describing the colonial church in Boston as "a Beacon upon the top of a mountaine, being as it were a City in comparison to all other Towns." Joshua Churchill, who lived out his ministry in England, nevertheless believed that "if I could tread upon N. E. ground, I have often thought that I should fall down & kiss it." Samuel Craddock thought of the colonists as "a people that walk as religiously, & so agreeably to the rule of the word, that there are not so many thousand people together anywhere upon the globe of the earth (that we know of) that for the generality, live more Christianly, soberly, & righteously."[28]

On both sides of the Atlantic Congregational friends continued to rely upon each other's assistance to sustain and nourish their faith. As in the past, clergymen assisted each other in the publication of religious treatises that made their views available to a wider audience. John Owen edited a posthumous collection of Joseph Caryl's sermons and wrote prefaces to a large number of works by his friends, including Samuel Petto's *The Difference Between the Old and New Covenant* (London, 1674), William Bridge's *The Freeness of Grace* (London, 1671), Stephen Lobb's *The Glory of Free Grace Displayed* (London, 1680), Theophilus Gale's *The True Idea of Jansenisme* (London, 1669), Caryl's *The Nature and Principles of Love* (London, 1673), Thomas Gouge's *The Surest and Safest Way of Thriving* (London, 1674), and Elisha Cole's *Practical Discourse of God's Sovereignty* (London, 1678). When Nathaniel Mather was preparing an edition of his brother Samuel's "notes on the types" he included "an Epistle before it, by mee, & I think I will indeavor to procure another by Dr. Owen." Nathaniel would later edit Owen's *Two Discourses Concerning the Holy Spirit* (London, 1693). William Greenhill, John Yates, and William Adderley wrote a preface to an edition of William Bridge's works. John Rowe and George Griffiths were among those who published a posthumous collection of William Strong's sermons. Samuel Lee published a collection of Rowe's sermons in 1680. John Bunyan was very close to Owen and the Congregational leadership and George Cockayn prefaced Bunyan's last book, *The Acceptable Sacrifice*.[29]

The trans-Atlantic connection was evident in this pattern of assistance as well. John Owen wrote a preface to Increase Mather's *Some Important Truths About Conversion* (London, 1674). William Hooke and Joseph Caryl coedited John Davenport's *Saints Anchor-Hold.* Hooke and William Greenhill wrote prefaces to Increase Mather's *The Mystery of Israel's Salvation.* John Collins wrote an epistolary preface to Jonathan Mitchell's *Discourse of the Glory to Which God Hath Called Believers* (London, 1677). Nathaniel Mather wrote a preface "to the reader" for Davenport's *The Power of the Congregational Churches Asserted and Vindicated* (London, 1672). Occasionally New Englanders would arrange for colonial publication of works by their English friends. Thus, in 1679 James Allen saw William Bridge's *A Word to the Aged* through the Boston press.[30]

In addition to these and many other examples of friends helping friends present their views to the public, members of the network sent each other books they deemed worth reading. This was especially important in the trans-Atlantic context. Colonists learned of new English books of merit from their friends abroad, and relied on those friends to obtain and ship them copies. Samuel Petto, for example, sent new works by Owen, Thomas Goodwin, and others to Increase Mather. Diaries of various colonists reveal how familiar they were with the works of the leading English Congregationalists. After the press in Cambridge, Massachusetts, began to publish an increasing number of New England treatises, those productions were often sent to English friends. Increase Mather sent books to Owen, Jollie, Samuel Baker, Petto, Samuel Craddock, his brother Nathaniel, and many others. John Eliot was yet another of the many colonial clergy who sent books to English friends.[31]

Increase Mather played a particularly important role in the trans-Atlantic exchange of correspondence, advice, manuscripts, and books. His experience in England and Ireland in the 1650s had enabled him to befriend many of the men who would lead English Nonconformity in the post-Restoration era. His brothers remained in the British Isles, as did a number of his former Harvard classmates. In New England his pastorship of one of the Boston churches and his presidency of Harvard put him in the geographical and social centers of colonial life. No one else was as well placed to interpret English and American Congregationalists to one another, to facilitate exchange between them, and to introduce leaders of the movement's two wings to one another.[32]

Correspondence remained one of the key links that kept friends in communion. Just as New Englanders heard from English friends of the trials endured by Dissenters in their mother country, English Congregationalists heard of the treatment of Baptists and Quakers, the debate over the Half-Way Covenant, a destructive fire in Boston, the devastating Indian conflict called King Philip's War, as well as other occurrences. News of portents was also eagerly received. John Allin received a letter from his father in New England, from which he learned of an incident in which "was heard the noise of drumms, trumpets, neighing of horses, and clattering of armes about ii in the morning." Thomas Adams sent Thomas Jollie a report on the sighting of a comet. Furthermore, correspondence in both directions was filled with personal news of friends and relatives, of their health and safety, and of their deaths.[33]

Trans-Atlantic news spurred trans-Atlantic aid. A number of Congregationalist clergy, including some former New Englanders such as John Allin and John Knowles, were active in ministering to the London populace during the plague and in the aftermath of the Great Fire. Thomas Vincent's *God's Terrible Voice in the City of London Wherein You Have the Narration of the Two Late Dreadful Judgements of Plague and Fire* was reprinted in Cambridge, Massachusetts, in 1668. Increase Mather preached a sermon to raise contributions for the "poor saints in England" and "wrote letters to ministers in London about [the] Collections." John Davenport responded to a request from Jane Hooke by raising a fund for the assistance of English ministers who had lost their homes or otherwise suffered. Some of the funds sent to England were designated for any needy members of the ejected clergy, not just those who had suffered from the events in London. In 1666 John Eliot gave his annual salary from the New England Company to be disposed of for those ministers deemed needy by his English Congregational friends Joseph Caryl and Thomas Brooks. Such activities continued throughout these decades. In 1677 Samuel Wakeman wrote to Increase Mather from Connecticut that "it pleased God to stir up the spirits of some well affected persons amongst us to contribute somewhat to the reliefe of the distressed saints (ministers & their children in special) in the other England."[34]

Colonial crises brought English aid. From the time early in the century when members of the network had joined in the relief effort for the Palatinate, fundraising had been an important function of communion. It bound donors together in shared sacrifice and united recipients with donors in ties of loving charity. Members of Thomas Jollie's church heard of the Indian war and "were much affected with the desolations." John Westgate reported in 1677 how "the sad condition of N. E. (where some times I lived some years) have been much upon our hearts [and] we have had many solemne dayes of humiliation, & the 25 of January last we had a solemne day of thanksgiving, for the great deliverance we heard the Lord had given you. This was general among all the congregational churches in City & countrey round about, we sending one to another & agreeing to the day before hand." Thomas Bailey also testified to how there were "frequent & fervent remembrances of you, . . . the kingdom throughout, in country places as well as others." John Owen's congregation, that of John Collins, and others in London raised money as well as prayers for the benefit of the victims of war and those who had lost their homes in the Boston fire. Jane Hooke collected funds and

clothes for the distressed colonists. Relief also came from the Congregationalist churches in Dublin. John Wilson of Medfield sent Jane Hooke cranber-
ries as tokens of appreciation for those in the London area who had made
contributions. The first batch was so well received that Mrs. Hooke asked
Wilson if he could send more.[35]

English friends also became regular supporters of New England's college
and of John Eliot's missionary efforts. In 1659 the Massachusetts General
Court had appointed an English board of trustees to raise funds for Harvard.
The board was headed by the MP Nathaniel Bacon and included Henry
Ashurst, William Hooke, John Knowles, and Thomas Allen. In 1664 Thomas
Gilbert reported that "Dr. Owen with a New England gentleman were at my
house," and they offered him the presidency of the college. Though he
decided that "were I worthy that dignity I think I ought rather at present to
frame myself to sufer in Old, than to reign in New England," he appreciated
the offer and assisted the college in years to come. In 1672 a group of New
England clergy and magistrates wrote to the London-area Congregational
consociation seeking assistance in raising funds for new buildings and advice
on a new president. The English clergymen offered to raise what funds they
could and to encourage English Congregationalists to send their sons to
Harvard. They recommended Leonard Hoar, a 1650 Harvard graduate who
had just returned to New England that July, for the presidency, and he was
selected by the college authorities. John Collins, who was himself considered
for the college presidency on at least one occasion, was active in raising funds
for the colony. John Knowles solicited bequests. Many Englishmen, including
Theophilus Gale, Owen Stockton, and Robert Thorner, left money or books
to the college.[36]

English interest in the colonial missions, which had surfaced during the
Interregnum, continued into the post-Restoration decades and continued to
draw support from other than Congregationalists. The Ashurst family would
provide the leadership of the English Society for the Propagation of the
Gospel in New England for over sixty years. Though the work attracted
support from Presbyterians as well as Congregationalists, many of the latter
were involved, including Joseph Caryl, who was presented with a copy of
Eliot's Indian Bible in 1662 in appreciation of his efforts.[37]

On a more personal level, the network continued to serve the needs of
individual clergymen. Ministers gave lodging to friends and concealed them
from the authorities. They visited each other, watched over sick friends,
prayed with and consoled them at their deathbeds, preached their funeral
sermons, and remembered one another in their wills. As had been the case
for earlier generations, the relationship between fellow clergymen often went
beyond a simply professional one. When rooted in experiences of shared

grace, the friendship between ministers was a godly communion of great emotional and religious depth.[38]

Friends who had experienced such communion turned to one another for advice on how to deal with the shifting sands of their world, and their efforts were vital to the attempt to retain some uniformity within Congregationalism. Nathaniel and Increase Mather exchanged views over the nature of the deacon's office. When the Half-Way Covenant was proposed in New England the new form of membership was discussed by many clergymen in England. Thomas Waterhouse recalled one such meeting at which there was a discussion by a number of ministers who had been in New England earlier in their careers. Among others, Nathaniel Mather expressed disagreement with the colonial proposal, whereas Thomas Jollie was among those who favored it because of its potential to increase church membership. John Davenport engaged in exchanges with English friends regarding the Half-Way Covenant and cited some of them in his opposition to the innovation. John Owen shared his views on the Sabbath with John Eliot. William Hooke sent Davenport a copy of the Savoy Declaration for his reaction. Daniel Hemingway asked Increase Mather's advice regarding church practices. Thomas Jollie and Increase Mather exchanged views on requirements for admission to the Lord's Supper and on the association of churches of different denominations. A position paper on an unidentified matter of religious beliefs was prepared by Philip Nye and circulated among English Congregationalists and New England friends.[39]

English clergymen were as concerned as their colonial counterparts about moral declension on both sides of the Atlantic and they advised New Englanders how to deal with the situation. "The greater my love is to N. E. the more I am grieved at their failings," wrote the English Congregationalist Robert Mascall in 1669. Influenced by colonial reports of dissension and backsliding, Englishmen came to share the colonists' fear that the region faced divine chastisement. When that seemed to come in the form of King Philip's War and the Boston fire, they hoped the shock of those events would bring their American friends to their senses, and they were disappointed when it failed to do so. "I, with many others are grieved to heare, that so little Reformation hath been wrought by the awful dispensations of God to New E, & doe feare what will be the issue of them," wrote Richard Blinman. John Westgate echoed the same sentiments, stating that if a "general reformation . . . be accomplished, you are like to be a flourishing happie people, but if you faile in this, I fear . . . God have yet other Judgements for N. E. though the sword should be removed; one sad one I hear already you have met with in your town of Boston by fire."[40]

Westgate concluded that this "rod of the Lord . . . calls you to a thorough reformation." A more specific suggestion was offered by Thomas Jollie.

Writing to Increase Mather in February of 1678, he observed, "Wee must not only send up our prayers to heaven one for another, but second them with our counsells one to another, and to follow all with suitable endeavours. The advice I humbly offer for your awakening to duty in the reforming of your manifest evills and for preventing of threatening ruine is, that a Synod be gathered for that purpose." Jollie proceeded to draw on biblical precedents and to suggest the roles appropriate to laymen as well as to clergy in such a gathering.[41]

The advice of Jollie and others spurred Mather to prepare a petition signed by eighteen ministers and presented to the Massachusetts General Court in May 1679. The magistrates responded with a call for what became known as the Reforming Synod. A committee was chosen to draw up a report on the evils that had provoked God and on proposed remedies. That report, *The Necessity for Reformation* (Boston, 1679), was published by order of the General Court. The same committee, whose principal members were Increase Mather, Urian Oakes, and Samuel Willard, recommended that the synod accept as its own the Savoy Declaration of 1658. Mather and Oakes had been in England, and perhaps at the Savoy, when that statement was drafted. By urging it on their fellow colonists they sought, successfully, to reaffirm the trans-Atlantic unity of the Congregationalist movement.[42]

Friends in England received the news with hope. Jollie wrote that "concerning the business of your last Synod, I heartily beg for a good success thereof," and indicated that there was talk among the English clergy to do the same. Samuel Baker also testified to English approval and asked Mather to send additional copies of the synod's work. Nathaniel Mather congratulated the colonists on their effort and had special praise for his brother's role in the Assembly.[43]

None of this means that there were no strains on the network. The changing circumstances of Congregationalism in England called forth responses that were not always understood or accepted by colonial clergy. The most significant of such strains concerned the relationship of Congregationalists to the other denominations that had emerged from the ruins of the older Puritan movement. Both English Congregationalist cooperation with Baptists and suspicions of Presbyterians caused dissension with New Englanders that needed to be resolved.

The distinction between Calvinistic Particular Baptists and English Congregationalists had never seemed significant, and the relationship between the two groups had generally been close during the years of the civil wars and Interregnum. Indeed, there were a number of open-membership congregations that tolerated both supporters of infant baptism and believers in adult baptism. Some claimed that the Savoy Declaration allowed for *both* practices.

The Particular Baptists issued a confession of faith in 1677 that drew heavily on the Westminster and Savoy statements. John Bunyan was perhaps the most famous Baptist to be positioned on this mixed field. Theologically, Bunyan, John Tombes, Benjamin Keach, and similar leaders were as orthodox in their Calvinism as the most rigid Congregationalists. Bunyan's Bedford congregation viewed George Griffiths's London congregation as an acceptable place for members to worship on visits to the city and also an appropriate church to transfer membership to. Bunyan himself worshiped with Griffiths's congregation. He was also a close friend of George Cockayn and John Owen.[44]

The cooperation between these Baptists and the Congregationalists appeared to be in sharp contrast to the treatment accorded Baptists in New England. Though they had been willing to overlook the Baptist views of Harvard President Henry Dunster, the colonial authorities had shown little tolerance for poorly educated and less-articulate opponents of infant baptism such as Thomas Gould. During the 1650s lay Baptists had been harassed and pressured by the authorities in an effort to force them to conform. In 1663, as Gould later wrote, "God sent out of Old England some who were Baptists" and the newcomers joined with Gould and others to hold religious meetings. In 1665 nine of them decided to rebaptize each other and form a church. Those who were members of existing congregations were excommunicated. The members of this first Baptist church were fined and imprisoned, but to no effect. In 1668 it was decided to hold a debate with the Reverend John Allin of Dedham as moderator to persuade the Baptists of the error of their ways in separating from the Congregational churches. One of the things revealed in the exchanges, according to William McLoughlin, the foremost student of the colonial Baptists, was that "the Baptist position was so ambiguous and so poorly defined that its defenders frequently argued at cross purposes." Although Gould himself was willing to accept the sort of open-communion toleration exhibited in England by Congregationalists such as Griffiths and Baptists like Bunyan, other members of the church argued for separate-but-equal status, whereas yet others denounced the Congregational churches as corrupt. The Bay Colony magistrates determined that the Baptist position was on the whole schismatic and the General Court voted to banish them, but at this point a lack of unanimity in the colony became evident. Sixty-six citizens petitioned that the sentence be repealed. As events transpired, Gould and some of his followers went into semiexile on Noddles Island in Boston harbor, where they continued to conduct services for the next five years.[45]

This incident prompted intervention by English Congregationalists. In a letter addressed to the General Court of Massachusetts, thirteen clergymen of the London-area consociation—including Owen, Nye, Thomas Goodwin, John Collins, George Griffiths, Joseph Caryl, and Thomas Brooks—attempted to change the mind of their New England friends. The English clergymen began by reassuring the colonists that "we have and ever shall looke on all your concernments with the same regard and affection as our own. . . . We have constantly had reliefe of our trouble and Sorowes or an addition unto them as we have heard of your welfare and peace or of your feares and pressures." Acknowledging that they had no personal knowledge of the New England Baptists or their practices, and not wishing "any of the least Difference with persons whom wee soe much love and honour in the lord," they gingerly asked that the colonists reconsider their position. They reminded their friends that "it is known what indulgence wee stand in need of from them whose established laws and orders about the worship of god we Dissent from," and pointed out that although "we are sure you would be unwilling to put advantages into the hands of those who seeke pretence and occasion against our liberty and . . . now we cannot Deney but this in some measure hath beene Done." The English enemies of Congregationalism argued that those who would not tolerate others should not be tolerated themselves. Not only had the persecution of the Bay Colony Baptists been used against English Congregationalists, but "some of us have observed how much it hath turned to your Disadvantage, for those who are pleased with such severityes and would bee engaging in them towards us are utterly your enemies and Doe seek your extirpation from the face of the earth." They asked "whether under all these circumstances and sundry others of the like nature that might be added, if it bee not advisable at the present to putt an end to the sufferings and confinements of the persons censured amongst you and restore them to their former liberty."[46]

This was not the first or the only such plea by English Congregationalists. Robert Mascall, a cousin of John Leverett, also wrote in the spring of 1669, coupling his praise for New England—"your churches shall ever be to me as the gates of heaven"—with regret at that "sad thing that much effects us. . . to hear that you even in N England persecute your brethren; men sound in the faith; of holy life; agreeing in worship and discipline with you; only differing in point of baptism." Mascall reminded the colonists that "we here do love and honor them [Baptists], hold familiarity with them and take sweet council together. . . . In a word, we freely admit them into churches; few of our churches but many of our members are anabaptist. . . . This is love in England; this is moderation; this is a right new testament spirit."[47]

New Englanders were divided. Their intense debate over the Half-Way Covenant had given the question of baptism greater importance than it seemed to have in England. Opponents of that reform such as John Davenport often went so far in their opposition to watering down the sacrament that they were accused of harboring Baptist tendencies themselves. Supporters of the reform, having just extended the right of baptism, were insistent on the importance of the sacrament for infants. Clergy who returned from England after the Restoration not only did not have to be told of Congregational-Baptist cooperation, they had engaged in it. Yet some were reluctant to grant a greater latitude than was absolutely necessary.

It was against this background that English friends continued their efforts to influence colonial leaders. John Westgate, having first made clear that there were limits to what he was willing to tolerate by stating that he "dare not be an advocate to plead for the cursed Generation of Quakers," did "speak a few words about or in behalf of the Baptists." Some colonial leaders—particularly lay leaders such as Governor Leverett and clergymen such as James Allen and John Oxenbridge who had associated with Baptists in England—worked to liberalize New England practice, but others wavered. Both English and American members of the network feared a rupture in their friendship and seemed to have hoped for a reason that would excuse their different practices. The London clergy who had written in 1669 had admitted that they knew nothing about the Boston Baptists. Westgate, having said a word for tolerating the denomination, went on to qualify that. Even in England, he admitted, there were different kinds of Baptists: "Some, especially in London, that strain the principle of baptisme so high that they look upon all of us as unbaptised persons & little better than heathens & will not join in prayer with the most eminent of our congregational ministers . . . ; others amongst us are sober, moderate men . . . & these upon our occasional meeting we join hand & heart with, & call some of them out to pray with us . . . & we would not have the difference in Judgement between us make the least breach in affection." Finally, Westgate wrote, "We have a third sort (but they are not many & most of them at London) that take into fellowship those that are Godly & desire to joyne with them, though they come not to be baptized & walk lovingly together, making no difference between the one & the other."[48]

Increase Mather picked up on this distinction in his 1680 attack on Baptist principles, *The Divine Right of Infant-Baptism* (Boston, 1680). Explaining that "I do not . . . judge simple Antipedobaptists as Hereticks," he wrote, "I have known those of that way not only in *New England*, but in *England* and in *Ireland*, that I believe were sincerely Conscientious their error notwithstanding, [whom I] could imbrace with both arms, for I believe God hath received them." Mather's tract prompted a response by the Woburn, Massachusetts, Baptist John Russell. His *Brief Narrative* (London, 1680) denied that the colonial dissenters were a threat to order or any less worthy of toleration than their English coreligionists. Yet Russell was not willing to accept any claim for the value of infant baptism and he repudiated the belief that clergy must be university graduates. His treatise was prefaced by six English Baptists (none of whom was closely allied with Congregationalists). Samuel Willard answered Russell in *Ne Sutor Ultra Crepidam* (Boston, 1681), arguing that the colonists need not tolerate any group that denied that the established congregations of the region comprised visible saints. Mather prefaced this work with an epistle in which he again tried to demonstrate that the New England situation was different. Responding to the argument that "those of the Congregational way in *England, plead for Anabaptists liberty as for their own*," Mather admitted, "When I was in *England*, I did so myself; and if I were there now, I would do so again." But Mather opposed such liberal treatment of men like Gould and Russell because they did not remind him of Henry Jessey or John Tombes. In his opinion, that English Congregationalists "should plead liberty unto such practices, as our Anabaptists have been guilty of is not easie to believe." Thomas Cobbett hoped that Mather's epistle and Willard's book would make their English friends "so Abundantly satisfied as no more to plead for the toleration of such scandalous Anabaptists amongst us."[49]

Such protests did have some effect overseas, with Jane Hooke, for instance, writing that she had been glad to hear "how N. E. was wronged about their cruelty about the anabaptists." Yet English friends continued to seek some moderation of the colonial policy. They informed the colonists that days of fast and prayer for New England were "also kept by many of the Baptist congregations." Nathaniel Mather and others argued against the views of New Englanders and in some cases accused them of moving toward Presbyterianism. All this had an effect. Baptists were gradually accorded a form of de facto toleration and eventually a level of acceptance that would be symbolized when Increase Mather extended the right hand of fellowship during the ordination of a university-trained Baptist minister in 1718. In general, though there was some disagreement between the two wings of trans-Atlantic Congregationalists over how to relate to Baptists, the degree of discord has been exaggerated by most historians. The social pressures of English friends gradually moved the Congregationalists of old and New England toward a greater degree of agreement.[50]

If their own experience of cooperation with Baptists made the English Congregationalists more willing to cooperate with that denomination than their American friends, the opposite was true in regard to relations with Presbyterians. In this case the colonists were the ones who cooperated with the few New England Presbyterians so that the distinction between the two was often blurred, whereas some English clergy had reservations about cooperation.

Despite friction with colonial Presbyterians such as Hobart and Parker in the early decades of settlement, relations between the two New England groups had been amicable owing to the preponderance of Congregationalists and the efficient system of informal gatherings and occasional synods that had guaranteed order. As time went on the distinction between the two groups would become even less meaningful. The clergy became more concerned about declension and their own clerical status; the familial experience of communion that had linked clerics and laity was no longer as common, and ministers came to stress even more the importance of clerical organization and church discipline. Clergy were increasingly ordained by fellow clergy rather than by lay members of the congregation. Conversion narratives were likely to be given to the minister in private rather than to the congregation in public. Even the interior architecture of the churches changed in ways that eroded the sense of communion by implying distinctions between the preacher and the pewholders and also between the ranks of those laymen gathered to worship. Though some New Englanders were concerned about this drift, whatever differences existed between colonial Congregationalists and Presbyterians were becoming even less significant in the second half of the century.[51]

Many English Congregationalists and Presbyterians had learned to work together in the 1650s and such cooperation continued in the Restoration era. A lectureship was established in Hackney in 1669 where the Presbyterians Peter Sterry, Thomas Watson, and William Bates shared the pulpit with Congregationalists Philip Nye, George Griffiths, Thomas Brooks, and John Owen. In 1672 Richard Baxter and others contributed to a lectureship at Pinner's Hall in London. Bates and Thomas Manton were among the Presbyterian lecturers, John Owen and John Collins the original Congregational preachers. Cooperation between the two groups became common in many provinces in the 1660s, and by the 1670s believers of the two denominations worshiped together in places such as Northowram and Yarmouth. John Angier was claimed by both groups and indeed, when Dissenters were licensed under the Declaration of Indulgence, some—such as James Briscoe of Toxteth Park, Liverpool—were licensed as both Presbyterian and Congregational.[52]

There was considerable interest in clerical cooperation in areas where the two denominations were both strong. Thomas Jollie consulted Increase Mather on the subject in 1678, offering his own view that "the interest of Christ is very much concerned in the Association of Churches. . . . I have therefore this 28 yeares, according to my capacity, and as I have had opportunity, laboured to promote that affair, especially since the change I have looked on it as more needful every way; yea, more adviseable and feasible in some respects. I have therefore both in the Country and City endeavoured much, though effected little." That year saw a group of London laymen produce an *Essay for the Accommodation Betwixt the Ministers of the Presbyterian and Congregational Way*, which formed a basis for ongoing discussions in the years to come. Some London clergy drafted their own proposal a year or so later and a number of prominent ministers supported the idea of greater cooperation. John Owen's *Some Considerations About Union Among Protestants* (London, 1680) and Samuel Mather's *Irenicum: or, An Essay for Union among Reformers* (Dublin, 1680) were among these works. Mather specifically called for the extending of fellowship among Congregationalists, Presbyterians, and Baptists based on their shared theological orthodoxy and the small differences that divided them. Jollie was in London in 1682 to promote such efforts and received the support of Owen, John Faldo, and others.[53]

These efforts produced some increased cooperation regionally, but on the national level they were pushed to the background during the period of repression following the Exclusion Crisis. But even when the proposals circulated freely, not all Congregationalists were comfortable with the idea. Despite the arguments in his brother Samuel's *Irenicum*, Nathaniel Mather announced that although he favored "Consociation of Churches . . . for their mutuall helpfulness & advice & communion with one another and also for their combining . . . in Synods, as emergent occasions may require," he opposed more formally structured "combinations of severall churches that lye in a neighborhood into a body made up of them all, or of persons deputed from them all." Mather feared Presbyterian authority and believed that vesting power in such groups "hath been disowned by men of the Congregational way, & so by those that were at the Savoy, An. 1658."[54]

Behind the concerns of Nathaniel Mather and others was a growing suspicion of some Presbyterians. Some of this dated from the time of the Restoration, when Presbyterians themselves had been divided between "ducklings" who had been willing to throw in their lot with the Congregationalists and other Dissenters, and the "dons" such as Baxter who had sought comprehension within the new establishment even if it meant abandoning their former Puritan allies. Other factors also contributed to suspicions. Presbyterians tended to be wealthier and socially more prominent than Congregationalists. But most important, perhaps, was the doubt many English Congregationalist clergy had begun to have about the theological orthodoxy of their Presbyterian counterparts.[55]

Factors such as these that separated some English Congregationalists and Presbyterians were outside the experience that New Englanders had had with Presbyterianism. The American members of the network were often as perplexed by English Congregational failures to cooperate more fully with Presbyterians as those English friends were by the colonial difficulties with Baptists. Indeed, some New England Congregationalists established better relations with Richard Baxter than Baxter had with English clergymen such as Owen and Thomas Goodwin. But, as in the case of the friction over the Baptists, this was not allowed to bring the activities of the network to an end.[56]

As friends struggled to understand each other's points of view it was evident that the vitality of the Congregational communion was weakening. Fewer clergymen were united to trans-Atlantic friends by shared experiences of grace and shared labor in the cause of reform. Members of the rising generation knew their trans-Atlantic counterparts by reputation, but not through face-to-face and soul-to-soul contact. The circumstances of English and American Congregationalism were increasingly different and even friends had a difficult time understanding the challenge faced by coreligionists abroad. But the communion still existed, and as Puritans in old and New England faced a new threat of Stuart absolutism, friends once again rallied to each other's aid.

The long-threatened attempt to curb New England's autonomy began to take substance in the early 1680s. An emerging group of colonial moderates that included men such as Joseph Dudley and Richard Wharton cooperated with the king's agent Edward Randolph in building a case against the Bay and her sister colonies. The moderate faction in general consisted of men who were less committed to maintaining Congregational supremacy than to protecting their own economic and political interests. They had their own English correspondents in the corridors of Whitehall and the countinghouses of English merchants. Confident that by cooperating with the inevitable they would be able to shape the course of events, they assisted Randolph and counseled their neighbors to acquiesce to royal demands.[57]

The spirit of resistance was still shared by many New Englanders; it was part of their English identity. John Wilson's early poem on the Gunpowder Plot, *Song of Deliverance,* was reprinted at the time of the English Exclusion Crisis. Opponents of yielding to the king's authority cited the persecution of dissent that had occurred in Norwich when that East Anglian community had surrendered its charter. The example of the recently appointed royal governor of New Hampshire was also cited by those who urged resistance. In an address delivered to the citizens of Boston at the Town House in January 1684, Increase Mather announced that "we shall sin against God" if the charter were surrendered. He too cited English precedents, describing how "we hear from London, that when it came to [the revocation of that city's charter], the loyal citizens would not make a full submission and entire resignation . . . lest, haply, their posterity should curse them." "I hope," he concluded, "there is not one freeman in Boston that will dare to be guilty of so great a sin."[58]

News of the revocation of the Massachusetts Bay charter was followed by numerous rumors and the colonists, according to Randolph, were "struck with a panick feare upon the aprihention of Colonel Kirks coming hither to be theire governor." When that rumor proved false and the king placed Joseph

Dudley, "a gentleman borne among themselves," in charge of a provisional government, the charter government yielded and hopes were expressed that through Dudley they would "continue the government among themselves." This soon proved a vain hope. Sir Edmund Andros was named governor general of the Dominion of New England, a supercolony encompassing all the former Puritan settlements and expanded in a few years to include New York and East Jersey. There was to be no legislative assembly, town meetings were limited, land titles were questioned, taxes imposed without representation, and the Third Church of Boston was forced to share its meetinghouse with an Anglican congregation.[59]

Resistance to the Andros regime was often led by Congregationalist clergy, frequently those immersed in the trans-Atlantic network. For such individuals the Anglo-American world was one. During the period when reports of Monmouth's Rebellion were arriving, "not one Minister [in New England] op'ned his lipps to pray for the King, hoping that the tyme of their deliverance from monarchy & popery was at hand." Randolph, who made these critical observations, also reported that three of the men nominated for the Dominion Council had refused their seats in the "hope some providence like that of Monmouth's Rebellion may fall out wch will restore them to their former priviledges." He identified the Reverends John and Thomas Bailey, "great & daring Non Conformists" who had recently arrived from Ireland, as among those who "in the tyme of Monmouths Rebellion . . . animated the people Saying the time of their deliverance was at hand." Another target of Randolph's criticism was Charles Morton, "an Excommunicated Minister came heither from Newington Green." "The independent faction still prevails," he complained, "and persons of dangerous principles from England, Ireland and other places are here received and highly encouraged. . . . The independent ministers . . . have spoken treasonable words in their pulpits." Randolph advised the Whitehall authorities that "liberty of conscience will much obstruct the settlement of this place," and urged that "no minister from England be permitted to land without the licence of the General Governor & that he have power to licence or restrain from preaching publickly such as are already upon the place."[60]

Randolph's concerns were not entirely unfounded. In 1685 some colonists had urged rebellion, and in 1686 the reintroduction of the English flag with the cross of St. George sparked popular resentment. Samuel Sewall sought the advice of Increase Mather, who lent him a manuscript treatise against use of the cross in the flag, which had been written by John Cotton half a century earlier. Persuaded that the new flag was an idolatrous symbol, Sewall resigned his militia commission. Others also expressed their hostility to the innovation. In 1687 Morton, in a sermon preached to his Charlestown congregation, claimed that the old charter government, "the rulers of Jerusalem, were unjustly set aside," and that "it would not be long before God restored the ancient Magistrates." He was cited for sedition and ordered to stand trial.[61]

It was in light of these troubled conditions that Congregationalists on both sides of the Atlantic had to evaluate a new Declaration of Indulgence issued by James II in 1686. There was little question about the fact that in the hands of James this would provide an opening wedge for Catholic freedoms, and, as in 1672, some worried about the constitutional consequences of recognizing this exercise of prerogative powers. But the enmity between the high Anglicans and the Dissenters was such that many nonconformists were ready to welcome the relaxation of the penal codes. Richard Lobb, the brother of the Reverend Stephen Lobb and a relation of Nathaniel Mather by marriage, wrote to Increase Mather explaining the dilemma, "Our N. C. M. [nonconformist ministers] are very backward to make use of the liberty granted them," believing that "liberty is not granted us out of good will, but to carry on some evil designe." Yet Lobb's brother Stephen, who had earlier been implicated in the Rye House Plot, "hath gotten his pardon . . . and preacheth again to his own Congregation." Richard Lobb welcomed the declaration, standing with those who trusted that "the same God that inclined his Majesty to grant us the liberty, is able enough to protect us from all consequents." Thomas Goodwin had died in 1680 and John Owen in 1683. The remaining Congregationalist leaders were divided, but George Cockayn, John Collins, John Faldo, Samuel Baker, Isaac Loeffs, and Stephen Lobb were among those who in April 1687 presented James II an address signed by close to 150 Congregational laymen thanking the king for his indulgence. Others, including Griffiths, Mead, John Howe, and probably Nathaniel Mather, took an opposing stand and worked with those conspiring to place William of Orange on the throne.[62]

In the colonies, where the threat of Catholicism was much less real, the Declaration of Indulgence appeared in a different aspect to clergymen who had recently seen their own religious establishment called into question by Edmund Andros. The governor general published the Declaration of Indulgence in August 1687, but the colonists had already received the news from English friends. At a meeting of the Boston-area clergy in October, Increase Mather "moved that our churches . . . might thank the King for his declaration." A statement penned by Samuel Willard was adopted and Mather was selected to "go to London with this Address, who might there obtain an Interest in such NonConformists as have the king's ear." Mather saw a chance to use this opportunity to gain a redress of some of the colonial grievances. He probably also saw a return to England as a chance to defend himself against what his brother Nathaniel reported as "a letter of yours said . . . to be written to Mr Gouge of Amsterdam wherein you invite over Mr.

Ferguson [one of the Rye House plotters], telling him hee may be as safe as Goff & Whalley were." Increase had accused Edward Randolph of having forged the letter to discredit him, and suits and countersuits had resulted.[63]

Mather arrived in England in the spring of 1688. At Weymouth "many friends made me welcome who had some rememberd of me almost 30 years ago." As he journeyed toward London he stopped occasionally to visit with old friends. He found lodgings with Major Robert Thompson at Newington Green, where he had many clerical friends and acquaintances. Thompson was a veteran who had lost his leg in Cromwell's service and had been a member of the Council of State during the Interregnum. After the Restoration Thompson had been an object of surveillance and was suspected of complicity in various plots. In the months that followed Mather visited, dined, and conversed with friends such as Samuel Petto, George Griffiths, Joshua Churchill, John Loder, Stephen Lobb, and his brother Nathaniel.[64]

As one of the leading Congregationalist supporters of the Declaration of Indulgence, Lobb was a welcome figure at the court of King James. Through his intervention Mather was presented to the court and received a private audience with the king. The New Englander presented the colonists' thanks for the declaration and accused Andros of violating its spirit. Over the next few months Mather presented the king with petitions seeking protection of the colonists' religious rights, continued Congregationalist control of Harvard, recognition of property titles, and restoration of an assembly and town meeting privileges. In August James promised to issue a decree that would confirm property rights and freedom of worship.[65]

With the Glorious Revolution, the patterns of influence at Whitehall changed. The new monarchs, William and Mary, had their own coterie of advisers. Mather therefore turned to friends in the Congregational network who had closer ties to the new regime. Among the clergy Matthew Mead and John Howe were close to William. Henry Ashurst, Goodwin Wharton, John Hampden the younger, and other lay friends were also enlisted by the New Englander. The Dutch clergyman Abraham Kick, with whom Mather had corresponded for many years, was asked to intervene with the prince of Orange. Lord Wharton introduced Mather to Gilbert Burnet, who as bishop of Salisbury had shown sympathy to Dissenters, and Mather was able to persuade that churchman to intercede with the king on behalf of the colonists.[66]

News of the English revolt had led to an uprising against the Dominion of New England, the seizure of Andros, Dudley, Randolph, and other Dominion officials, and de facto resumption of the pre-Dominion political forms. The colonists justified this rebellion by placing it in the broader context of the fight for true religion, attacking popery, remembering the persecutions of Mary Tudor, and claiming that the Popish Plot of 1678 had persisted in the form of Dominion policies against Puritan faith. The new task for Increase Mather and his friends was to justify these events and seek the official restoration of the old charter governments. Mather was presented to King William in January 1689. In the following months he secured the king's endorsement of the provisional regimes in the colonies and succeeded in getting the Massachusetts charter included among those that were to be restored under the terms of a proposed Corporation Bill. At one meeting, according to Mather's later recollection, "Mr Mead, being with me, sayd to the King that Hee could not do anything more gratefull to his dissenting subjects in England than to be kind to New England in restoring them to their former privileges." Assisting English friends by preaching from their pulpits, Mather in return asked that they use their influence with persons in authority to further New England's cause. Though Parliament was prorogued before the Corporation Bill had its third reading and Mather failed in his effort to gain restoration of the old charter, what he did accomplish was considerable. He secured a new charter that guaranteed many of the Bay Colony's former privileges and he was allowed to nominate the first appointed royal governor. When he eventually returned to New England he carried with him a "Letter Written by Some of the Most Eminent Nonconformist Divines in London" attesting to his efforts to secure the colonists' interests.[67]

During his stay in England Mather also immersed himself in the religious affairs of English dissent. His personal friendships with clergymen of the Interregnum era and his stature as the foremost American Puritan gave him a significant influence with English Nonconformists. During the Glorious Revolution, Congregationalist and Presbyterian leaders had worked to maintain a united front both in opposing James and in seeking new freedom from William. Mather joined with Mead and Howe in an effort to bring the two groups into a more formal union. Others were also active in trying to revive the old "Essay of Accommodation." A group of Bristol clergymen which included Isaac Noble revised that earlier statement and subscribed to it in 1690. Noble was in contact with Thomas Jollie, who continued to support such a union. In London Mather, Howe, and Mead shelved the earlier plan and drafted a set of Heads of Agreement which were adopted by most of the city Congregational and Presbyterian clergy and inaugurated at a service at the Stepney meeting in April 1691 with Matthew Mead preaching on Ezekiel 37:19, "Two Sticks Made One."[68]

News of the agreement spread rapidly. Mead sent a copy to Thomas Jollie on March 17, pleased that he could "confidently assure you of an happy union between us. . . . The next week we shall make it publick. It causes great joy in the city." Mather also wrote to Jollie and other friends. The Heads of Agreement were adopted by the Congregationalist and Presbyterian clergy of Chesire in May, Devon in June, and other counties in the months that followed. Gloucester and the Lancashire churches voted to replace their earlier forms of union with the new agreement. Essex, Cumberland, and Westmorland clergy also joined the "Happy Union." Richard Baxter wrote to the "United Protestant Nonconformists in London" that "though I was, by the Confinement of decrepit Age, and pain, hindred from having any part, in the form or Contract of your Agreement . . . I greatly rejoice in your very attempt."[69]

The "Happy Union" brought clergy of the two denominations together in regular meetings that were labeled classes but only wielded the advisory powers Congregationalists granted to synods. Even so, not all Congregationalists supported the union. Increase Mather's own brother, Nathaniel, was among those who were reluctant to join with Presbyterians. Eventually such differences would sunder the union, but in the first years of the new decade it seemed that there was hope for a general Puritan unity once again. One of the first consequences of the Heads of Agreement was the creation of a Common Fund reminiscent of the former Feoffees for Impropriations, with lay and clerical managers raising funds to support clerical education and supplement ministerial salaries. Among the original clerical managers were the Congregationalists Isaac Chauncey, Matthew Mead, Nathaniel Mather, George Cockayn, John Faldo, Matthew Barker, and George Griffiths, and the Presbyterians John Howe, Vincent Alsop, Samuel Annesley, Daniel Williams, and William Bates. The meetings of the fund also brought together lay managers and others involved in the affairs of the city, and the sessions facilitated the shaping of political as well as religious strategies. More than a dozen of the fund's lay managers were elected to London offices in the years 1690–1693.[70]

The hope for a lasting interdenominational union was soon dashed. Indeed, the seeds of its dissolution were germinating even while the Heads of Agreement were being drafted. In 1690 Samuel Crisp republished the sermons of his father, Tobias. The volume was prefaced by a testimonial signed by six Presbyterians, a Baptist, and the Congregationalists Griffiths, Cockayn, and Nathaniel and Increase Mather. Richard Baxter attacked Crisp's views as antinomian in a sermon at Pinner's Hall, and the younger Crisp came to his father's defense in *Christ Made Sin* (London, 1691). Baxter had died in the interim, but one of his disciples, Daniel Williams, countered Crisp with his *Gospel-Truth Stated and Vindicated* (London, 1692). Williams attacked not only the Crisps but the Congregational evangelical preacher Richard Davis. When Davis visited London in 1692 in order to meet with the ministers of the "Happy Union," Williams publicly accused him of antinomianism. Williams marshaled Presbyterian support for his views; sixteen of his fellow religionists signed a testimonial endorsement of the first edition of *Gospel-Truth* and forty-nine more attested to the second edition.[71]

Six Congregationalists, including Griffiths, Isaac Chauncey, and Nathaniel Mather, signed a "Paper of Objections" attacking Williams for preaching Arminian doctrines of justification by works. Comfort Starr joined in the criticisms of Williams and his allies. Stephen Lobb sided with his fellow Congregationalists, though he tried to serve a healing role in his *A Peaceable Enquiry into the Nature of the Present Controversie Among Our United Brethren about Justification* (London, 1693). Referring to "the Differences between some of us" as one that he "would rather call a Contention only who should be most Orthodox," he recognized that the roots of the dispute went deep into the past. Yet he believed that though "some . . . esteem the Differences among us . . . to be such that the Two Poles may as soon meet, as their Doctrines be found in *Substance* the same," that in fact the argument was more over emphasis than substance. Lobb reported, "In my closest Converses with each Brother, He who seems to be most for the Exaltation of *Free Grace*, abhors nothing more than to give the Least Encouragement to an Elect person's Living in Sin. . . . And the other Brother, who so much presses the Necessity of Faith, Repentance, and a Holy Life, detests nothing so much as in any one Instance to Diminish the Glory of *Free Grace*." He also cited the fact that both sides attested to the doctrinal formulas of the Westminster and Savoy confessions.[72]

Yet even in this treatise Lobb had to admit that "it cannot be Denied but many in their Opposition to *Antinomianism*, have faln in with *Arminian*, etc and that Divers in running from *Arminianism* etc have plung'd themselves into the *Antinomian* Gulph, and that they who lend their Strength against the one Error, are in danger of being accused for Inclining too much towards the other." The quarrel between Williams and his Congregationalist foes echoed the dispute in earlier decades between Baxter, whom Owen had labeled Arminian, and Owen, who Baxter claimed "had written some Passages too near to Antinomianism." Caryl, Brooks, Gale, and Thomas Goodwin had earlier expressed fears that Presbyterians were drifting from Calvinist orthodoxy toward the shoals of Arminian and Socinian error. Nathaniel Mather and other Congregationalists who had questioned the Heads of Agreement had cited concerns about the views of some Presbyterians. Williams had brought these issues into the open and the result was the fracturing of the "Happy Union." In 1694 Williams was removed from the Pinner's Hall lectureship and along with fellow Presbyterians who left in protest established a rival lectureship at Salter's Hall. Nathaniel Mather, Stephen Lobb, and Thomas Gouge were chosen to fill the vacancies at Pinner's Hall. In 1695 the Congregationalists withdrew from the Common Fund and set up a separate Congregational Fund that was soon matched by a Presbyterian Fund. Though interdenominational cooperation continued in some of the counties, in the councils of the New England Company, and in a growing number of political enterprises, hopes of a national Puritan union were dead.[73]

Increase Mather had left England before the collapse of the Heads of Agreement and he carried the plan with him to the colonies. There he found that a regular meeting of ministers had already been organized through the efforts of Charles Morton. The Cambridge Association met every six weeks at Harvard. The extensive records of the meetings reveal the range of the clerical concerns: recommending that men should be ordained to teach where there were no churches; discussing (relevant to the founding of the Brattle Street Church) whether Scripture should be read in church without exposition; planning to aid Harvard; encouraging compilation of a church history of New England; considering (in August 1692) whether "the devils may sometimes have a permission to represent an innocent person"; and discussing the power of synods, the lawfulness of an individual's marrying the sister of his deceased wife, at what point loans became usury, and if it was lawful to eat blood and "things strangled."[74]

Increase Mather was an active member of the association and he hoped that similar groups would be organized throughout New England, but his involvement also bred opposition from supporters of Elisha Cooke's emerging "popular party," which blamed the Boston clergyman for the failure to regain the old charter. Many smaller rural churches were suspicious of the role of such associations, fearing that they would lead to a Presbyterian-style interference with the autonomy of congregations. Such fears had merit, for some clergymen did see consociation as a step toward authoritative synods, and the proposals of 1705, which called for such assemblies, sparked bitter opposition. Increase Mather himself evidently believed that the proposals went beyond the type of cooperation called for in the Heads of Agreement and practiced by the Cambridge Association. The Heads of Agreement were formally adopted as part of Connecticut's Saybrook Platform of 1708 and there they were interpreted to provide for a Presbyterian style of government. One of the last cooperative religious enterprises of Congregational friends, and the last significant effort to reunite the old Puritan groups, the union was not happy and its failure signaled the end of an era.[75]

Epilogue

INCREASE MATHER'S role in shaping the Heads of Agreement was the last significant example of the type of cooperative effort that had characterized the trans-Atlantic Congregational communion ever since the founding of the colonies. There would still be trans-Atlantic exchanges, but the old network was fading. The concerns of New England Puritans and English Dissenters continued to diverge. Debates in one community had little resonance or clarity for those on the opposite side of the Atlantic.

Issues were different in the new century, as were the clergymen. As Increase Mather and his friends passed away, few of their successors had experiences on both sides of the Atlantic. Those colonists who did journey to England (such as Benjamin Colman and Thomas Prince) spent little time there, met many clergy but made few close friends, and contributed nothing to the cause of English Nonconformity. New Englanders of the seventeenth century such as Cotton, Davenport, Peter, Hooker, Morton, and Increase Mather made contributions to English as well as American history. Their lives are to be found in the British *Dictionary of National Biography* as well as the *Dictionary of American Biography*. The same would not be true of the leading colonial clergy of the eighteenth century. At the same time, New England suffered the effects of growing cultural isolation. The fact that fewer individuals were active on both sides of the Atlantic meant that New England was removed from the mainstream of English intellectual life. Those who did make the journey to England were observers of the world of Nonconformity, not players in it.[1]

Links still existed, but they were different types of contact. Cotton Mather boasted of his many correspondents overseas, but they were contacts inherited from his father, men attracted by his works, or individuals whose attention he had solicited from afar. None were known to him personally, for Cotton never journeyed to England, nor did the leaders of English dissent cross the

Atlantic to America. Colman and Prince had traveled in England and met some of their overseas correspondents, but their letters give little indication of close relationships. The correspondence of their generation displays none of the interest in the personal lives of friends abroad, their families, and mutual friends that characterized the letters of Davenport, Hooke, and Increase Mather with their English friends. There is no sharing of everyday concerns and problems and no exchange of gifts. Few Congregationalists of this era experienced the mystical union with God and their fellow saints that seemed to characterize the conversion experiences of Puritans of the early seventeenth century. Indeed, the type of religious enthusiasm that had generated emotional bonds of communion was in disfavor. The experience of godly union that had united pastor to layman and clergyman to clergyman was rarely found among believers on either side of the Atlantic. Congregationalism was entering a new phase in which evangelical zeal was not encouraged. The ministry was becoming more professionalized and the emerging self-image of the clergy accentuated the gulf between pulpit and pew in place of the earlier emphasis on the communion of all the elect. The new links connecting clerical associates were ones of professional affiliation rather than spiritual communion.[2]

The reign of Queen Anne saw little meaningful contact between New England Congregationalists and their English brethren. English Nonconformists were increasingly preoccupied with the threat to their status posed by the rise of the Tories to power. The inflammatory attacks on dissent by the Reverend Henry Sacheverell and the hostility ignited by his prosecution led not only to the destruction of Nonconformist meetinghouses but parliamentary passage of the Bill for Preventing Occasional Conformity in 1711 and the Schism Act, which undermined the Dissenting Academies, in 1714. The English Dissenters worked to develop stronger political influence and the leadership of that effort was increasingly assumed by laymen of substance such as the Ashursts, Averys, and Barringtons, who were closely identified with the Whigs. Few of their particular concerns seemed relevant to the colonists. The perspective of English dissent was of such little concern to the Americans that many Bay Colony clergy supported the appointment of Joseph Dudley—who was politically tied to the Tory party—to be governor of Massachusetts.[3]

An example of the erosion of traditional trans-Atlantic Congregational relations can be glimpsed through some of the experiences of Cotton Mather. He was perhaps the most energetic of all his contemporaries in trying to maintain an international support group. Yet, try as he might, Mather failed to establish the type of close, trusting, sympathetic relationship with English Dissenters that his father had achieved. His failure to do so led to frustration, blunders, and embarrassment on more than one occasion. Increase Mather had, when in England on the charter mission, worked with the Reverend John Quick and preached to Quick's London congregation. Back in New England, Increase and Cotton prepared and saw through the Boston press Quick's treatise *Man's Claim unto the Sacrament of the Lord's Supper.* That connection with Quick served Cotton well, since the London clergyman was instrumental in publishing Cotton Mather's *Magnalia Christi Americana.* But the New Englander's later sailing was not so smooth. Seeking to have his "Biblia Americana" published in England after Quick had died, he found himself without any friends to steer it through to publication. He importuned numerous Dissenting clergymen, including occasional correspondents such as Thomas Reynolds, in an effort to stir them to action on his behalf, but to no avail. By 1714 he was complaining to Sir William Ashurst, "From the Dissenters I expect nothing." A year later he picked up on the same refrain, offering his opinion that "the Dissenters do not seem to overvalue literature," and that "a poor American must never be allowed capable of doing anything worth anyone's regarding."[4]

Mather did follow the news of the Salter's Hall debates with concern. He deplored the popularity of Arian views in some English quarters, but seemed uncertain as to how to relate to the English situation. Two of his correspondents, Isaac Watts and Samuel Browne, were part of the nonsubscribing minority tainted with the label of Arian sympathizers, and a prominent member of that faction was Lord Barrington, the brother of the new Massachusetts governor, Samuel Shute, whom Mather was eager to befriend. When the Bostonian did try to interject his views into the controversy, his lack of appropriate contacts again cost him. Two of the three works he wrote went unpublished. One of these did, however, circulate in manuscript and caused Mather great embarrassment. Lord Barrington felt that the colonial clergyman had been critical of him and accused him of having a "mercenary pen." Mather saw his relationship with Governor Shute threatened and hastened to disavow ever having hinted that Barrington was an Arian.[5]

If Mather failed to relate successfully to English Nonconformists, in his view they failed to understand New England. Although he congratulated the English Nonconformist historian Daniel Neal on his *History of New England,* he complained to others that Neal's account misrepresented many aspects of New England's past. He wrote of Neal that "it is plain that this my Independent brother, is (as too many honest men of that denomination are) a very weak and shallow man." Benjamin Colman, who had more contacts with latitudinarian Anglicans and Presbyterians of an Arian disposition than he had with Calvinist Congregationalists, shared Mather's views regarding Neal's *History.*[6]

When English Nonconformists established political lobbying groups— culminating in the organization of the Dissenting Deputies in 1732—the colonists would learn to utilize those formal lobbies to achieve some of the goals formerly pursued through the informal network of clerical friends. But no longer did the two wings of trans-Atlantic Puritanism march to the beat of a common drum. The networks of friends had passed, to be replaced by alliances of convenience and interest. The language they had shared was, for a time, forgotten. Yet the legacy they left behind was recognized by believers on both sides of the Atlantic and the idea of communion could eventually be revitalized. When revivalism rekindled the spiritual zeal of the early Puritans, saints in New England and in England would hearken back to that legacy. The language of the early divines would resonate again among those who experienced the new light of grace that had once brought Puritans into godly communion. During the time of the Great Awakening numerous pietistic works of English and colonial Congregationalists would be reprinted, and once again names such as Owen and Shepard would be familiar on both sides of the Atlantic. In that season of grace some sense of trans-Atlantic participation in a communion of saints was recaptured. But that is a different story. As for the hopes of the members of the original congregational communion, the new Jerusalems they had sought to build remained mere visions in the seventeenth-century skies.[7]

The communion uniting the early Puritans in spiritual love, which they likened to that between David and Jonathan, was a vital element in the evolution of Puritanism in the seventeenth century. Awareness of the nature and importance of communion can cast new light on familiar episodes in Puritan history. As the movement gained strength communion reinforced each individual's conviction of his election and sustained reformers in their advocacy of Calvinist principles. It provided them with the advice, comfort, and aid necessary to withstand the Laudian initiatives of the 1630s.

For those driven into exile, communion had continued to be of great importance. In places such as Arnhem and Salem, Rotterdam and Dedham, the fellowship of shared godly love united lay and clerical saints and led them to create new churches organized on congregational principles of shared authority. By limiting the Lord's Supper to those recognized as part of the communion of saints they made that sacramental meal a means of fueling the love between them and a sign of the underlying spiritual union that was the church. The congregational covenants they drew up memorialized the love that had brought them together and pledged them to walk in communion in the future.

But congregational communion not only united those in church covenant, it also created a network of clergy who strove for consensus; and that has been the focus of this work. Although they respected the image of God in each individual, the clergy believed in the importance of maintaining a unity of members in the spiritual body of Christ. Because they recognized no ecclesiastical authority superior to that of the individual church, the mainte-nance of order in Congregationalism relied on the informal mechanisms of conference and consultation. Ministers labored to follow the counsel of John Eliot to retain unity by learning to "bear, forbear, forgive." Their efforts succeeded because trusting one another was at the heart of the experience of communion.

The same striving for understanding and consensus bound New England clergymen to friends in the Old World. Distance could not erase the memories of spiritual communion such as those that bound John Cotton to Thomas Goodwin. Focusing on communion enables us to bring to the fore the ongoing unity of trans-Atlantic Congregational Puritanism throughout much of the seventeenth century. Confidence in trans-Atlantic friends helped Congrega-tionalists to respond in a unified manner to the challenges of the 1640s and the opportunities of the 1650s. The orchestration of colonial support for the Dissenting Brethren in the 1640s could not have been more effective if it had been directed by an all-powerful archbishop. Building on their success in warding off a Presbyterian ascendancy, English Congregationalists welcomed former friends such as William Hooke back from New England, and incorpo-rated into their communion friends of colonial friends such as the young Mathers. The rise of Congregationalism during the 1650s was achieved through the cooperative efforts of the trans-Atlantic clerical network.

Although the Restoration dashed the hope for a Puritan England, members of the clerical communion continued to assist one another locally and across the Atlantic, even to the time of Increase Mather's charter mission. The nature of the trans-Atlantic clerical community, however, was changing. Historical circumstances were pulling the two wings of Congregationalism apart. It became increasingly difficult for clergy on one side of the Atlantic to understand the situation of their friends on the other side. More important, the nature of trans-Atlantic friendships was changing. In earlier decades trust could overcome misunderstanding, but as the seventeenth century reached its close, more and more ministers knew their counterparts abroad by repute rather than through shared experiences of grace. They had not lived, prayed, or fought the Lord's battles together. They were united by interests but not by love, and interest alone was not as powerful a force of cohesion. Increase Mather was perhaps the last American Puritan of note to have ties of shared communion with English leaders. Cooperation in the new order of the eighteenth century would be a way of using allies across the sea to further local interests rather than the shared pursuit of a common international goal. Communion as it had sustained and shaped the Congre-gational Puritan clergy of the seventeenth century had passed; an era of religious history had come to an end.

Notes

Abbreviations

AASP   *American Antiquarian Society Proceedings*
AFR   *Archiv für Reformationgeschichte*
AHR   *American Historical Review*
AJS   *American Journal of Sociology*
APS   *Proceedings of the American Philosophical Society*
BIHR   *Bulletin of the Institute of Historical Research*
CH   *Church History*
CHST   *Congregational Historical Society Transactions*
CQR   *Church Quarterly Review*
CSM   *Publication of the Colonial Society of Massachusetts*
CSPC   *Calendar of State Papers, Colonial*
CSPD   *Calendar of State Papers, Domestic*
DAB   *Dictionary of American Biography*
DNB   *Dictionary of National Biography*
EAL   *Early American Literature*
EHR   *English Historical Review*
EIHC   *Essex Institute Historical Collections*
HJ   *Historical Journal*
HLQ   *Huntington Library Quarterly*
HMCR   *Historical Manuscripts Commission Reports*
HMPEC   *Historical Magazine of the Protestant Episcopal Church*
HR   *Historical Research*
HTR   *Harvard Theological Review*
JAS   *Journal of American Studies*
JBS   *Journal of British Studies*
JEH   *Journal of Ecclesiastical History*
JHI   *Journal of the History of Ideas*
JIH   *Journal of Interdisciplinary History*
JMH   *Journal of Modern History*
JRS   *Journal of Religious Studies*
MHS   Massachusetts Historical Society

MHSC   *Massachusetts Historical Society Collections*
MHSP   *Massachusetts Historical Society Proceedings*
NAS   *Original Papers of the Norfolk and Norwich Archaeological Society*
NEHGR   *New England Historical and Genealogical Register*
NEQ   *New England Quarterly*
PP   *Past & Present*
VCH   *Victoria County Histories*
WMQ   *William and Mary Quarterly, third series*

Preface

1. Vernon Louis Parrington, *Main Currents in American Thought, Volume One* (New York, 1927); Samuel Eliot Morison, *Builders of the Bay Colony* (Boston, 1930).

2. Perry Miller, *The New England Mind: From Colony to Province* (Cambridge, Mass., 1953), ii.

3. Kenneth Fincham, *Pastor as Prelate: The Episcopate of James I* (Oxford, 1990); Philip Gura, *A Glimpse of Sion's Glory: Puritan Radicalism in New England, 1620–1660* (Middletown, Conn., 1984); Frederick Tolles, *The Atlantic Community of Early Friends* (London, 1952).

4. John Winthrop Jr. quoted in Malcolm Freiberg, "The Winthrops and Their Papers," *MHSP*, 80 (1968), 70.

Prologue

1. Richard Cust and Ann Hughes, "After Revisionism," in Richard Cust and Ann Hughes, eds., *Conflict in Early Stuart England* (London, 1989), 22; J. Sears McGee, *The Godly Man in Stuart England* (New Haven, 1976), 205. McGee's chapter 5 is entitled "The Fruits of Conversion: Fellowship and Charity." The importance of private conference in *The Pilgrim's Progress* is drawn from Charles E. Hambrick-Stowe, *The Practice of Piety* (Chapel Hill, N.C., 1982), 151. See also A. S. P. Woodhouse, *Puritanism and Liberty* (London, 1951). On a more general level, Mary Fulbrook has pointed out the importance Christopher Hill has placed on the social context of ideas in "Christopher Hill and Historical Sociology," in Geoff Eley and William Hunt, eds., *Reviving the English Revolution* (London, 1988), 52.

2. Greatheart's speech is quoted in *Pilgrim's Progress, Puritan Progress* (Urbana, Ill., 1993), in which Kathleen M. Swain discusses the importance of the Christian community, particularly as set forth in the second part of *The Pilgrim's Progress*. Paul Baynes quoted in Paul Seaver, *Wallington's World: A Puritan Artisan in Seventeenth-Century London* (Stanford, Calif., 1985), 131; Sibbes quoted in McGee, *Godly Man*, 195; transcript of notes on John Cotton's 1640 sermon in Helle M. Alpert, "Robert Keayne: Notes of Sermons by John Cotton and Proceedings of the First Church of Boston from 23 November 1639 to 1 June 1640" (Ph.D. thesis, Tufts University, 1974), 176; William Bridge, *The Saints Hiding-Place* (London, 1647), 8.

3. John Winthrop to Sir William Spring, 8 February 1630, *Winthrop Papers*, six volumes to date (Boston, 1929–   ), II, 203–206; John Owen, *Communion with God*, abridged and edited by R. J. K. Law (Edinburgh, 1991), 2.

4. John Winthrop, "The Modell of Christian Charity," *Winthrop Papers*, II, 290–291.

5. Robert Coachman, quoted in McGee, *Godly Man*, 206; Thomas Brooks, *Heaven on Earth* (London, 1654; repr. Edinburgh, 1961), 248–249, 248, 251, 249.

6. Stephen Foster, *Their Solitary Way* (New Haven, Conn., 1971), 44; Eamon Duffy, *The Stripping of the Altars, Traditional Religion in England c. 1400–c. 1580* (New Haven, Conn., 1992), 92. Space does not allow a full treatment of the theological background of the concept of communion as employed by the Puritans.

7. Owen, *Communion*, 100; John Winthrop Jr. is quoted by Malcolm Freiberg in "The Winthrops and Their Papers," *MHSP*, LXXX (1968), 70. Paul Seaver has made a similar point in *Wallington's World*, stressing how literacy gave Puritans the opportunity to sustain friendships over distance by correspondence. Richard Brown, in his study *Modernization: The Transformation of American Life 1600–1865* (New York, 1976), correctly reminds us that "the idea of an intercolonial transatlantic network for written communications was modern, but its operation served only a portion of the colonial elite. Most people lived their whole lives without ever sending or receiving a letter" (p. 53).

8. Barry Wellman, "Structural Analysis: From Method and Metaphor to Theory and Substance," in Barry Wellman and S. D. Berkowitz, eds., *Social Structures: A Network Approach* (Cambridge, Eng., 1988), 20. See, for example, J. A. Barnes, *Social Networks* (Reading, Mass., 1972); Elizabeth Bott, *Family and Social Network* (London, 1957; 2d ed., New York, 1971); Jeremy Boissevain, *Friends of Friends: Networks, Manipulators and Coalitions* (New York, 1974); and J. Clyde Mitchell, *Social Networks in Urban Situations* (Manchester, Eng., 1969). Among the more sophisticated works that discuss technical methods of network analysis are Ronald S. Burt and Michael J. Minor, eds., *Applied Network Analysis* (Beverly Hills, Calif., 1983), and Ronald S. Burt, *Toward a Structural Theory of Action* (New York, 1982). There have been few attempts thus far to employ network analysis in the study of the seventeenth century. Three attempts to do so in the examination of small geographical regions are Alan Macfarlane, *The Family Life of Ralph Josselin* (Cambridge, Eng., 1970); Robert Lord Goodman, "Newbury, Massachusetts, 1635–1685: The Social Foundations of Harmony and Conflict" (Ph.D. thesis, Michigan State University, 1974); and Darrett Rutman, *A Place in Time* (New York, 1984). David Cressy employs some of the language of network analysis in *Coming Over: Migration and Communication between England and New England in the Seventeenth Century* (Cambridge, Eng., 1987). Barbara Ritter Dailey has recognized the importance of social networks for "radicals" in "The Itinerant Preacher and the Social Network in Seventeenth-Century New England," in Peter Benes, ed., *Itinerancy in New England and New York* (Dublin Seminar for New England Folklife Annual Proceedings, 1984, 37–48). Ann Hughes has identified Thomas Dugard's circle as a network and has identified the potential of that connection in protecting Puritans during Laud's ascendancy and its contribution to the effort to reform England in the 1640s. See Ann Hughes, "Thomas Dugard and His Circle in the 1630s—A 'Parliamentary-Puritan' Connexion?" *HJ*, 29 (1986), 771–793, and Cust and Hughes, "After Revisionism," 32–33.

9. Jeremy Boissevain and J. Clyde Mitchell, eds., *Network Analysis* (The Hague, 1973), viii; Samuel Leinhardt, ed., *Social Networks* (New York, 1977), xiii; Boissevain, *Friends*, 24, 27; Mary Noble, "Social Network: Its Use As a Conceptual Framework in Family Analysis," in Boissevain and Mitchell, *Network Analysis*, 7; Geert A. Banck, "Network Analysis and Social Theory: Some Remarks," in Boissevain and Mitchell, *Network Analysis*, 37; Charles Wetherell, "Network Analysis Comes of Age," *JIH*, XIX (1989), 646. See also Wellman and Berkowitz, *Social Structures*.

10. J. Clyde Mitchell, "Social Networks," *Annual Review of Anthropology*, 3 (1974), 289; Boissevain, *Friends*, 43, 30–32; John R. P. French, "A Formal Theory of Social Power," *Psychological Review*, 62 (1956), 181–194; Mark Granovetter, "The Strength of Weak Ties," *AJS*, 78 (1973), 1360–1380; Wellman, "Structural Analysis," 26–27, 37.

11. Donn Byrne, *The Attraction Paradigm* (New York, 1971), 24–25; Klaus Scherer, Ronald Abele, and Claude Fischer, *Human Aggression and Conflict* (Englewood Cliffs, N.J., 1975), 154; Ted Hutson and George Levinger, "Interpersonal Attraction and Relationships," *Annual Review of Psychology*, 29 (1978), 135.

12. Eric Wolfe, "Aspects of Group Relations in a Complex Society," *American Anthropologist*, 58 (1956), 1065–1078; Hutson and Levinger, "Interpersonal Attraction," 136; Steven Duck, "Tell Me Where Is Fancy Bred: Some Thoughts on the Study of Interpersonal Attraction," in Steven Duck, ed., *Theory and Practice in Interpersonal Attraction* (London, 1977), 7–8; Hutson and Levinger, "Interpersonal Attraction," 124; Byrne, *Attraction Paradigm*, 35, 36; François Lorrain and Harrison White, "Structural Equivalence of Individuals in Social Networks," *Journal of Mathematical Sociology*, I (1971), 71; Bernard Berelson and Gary Steiner, *Human Behavior: An Inventory of Scientific Findings* (New York, 1964), 327; James Davis, "Structural Balance, Mechanical Solidarity and Interpersonal Relations," *AJS*, 68 (1963), 443–463; G. L. Clore, "Reinforcement and Affect in Attraction," in Duck, ed., *Attraction*, 41; Icek Ajzen, "Information Processing Approaches to Interpersonal Attraction," in Duck, ed., *Attraction*, 53; A. J. Lott and B. E. Lott, "A Learning Theory Approach to Interpersonal Attitudes," in Anthony Greenwald, Timothy Brock, and Thomas Ostrom, eds., *Psychological Foundations of Attitudes* (New York, 1968), 81; Zick Rubin, *Liking and Loving* (New York, 1973), 139–140; Hutson and Levinger, "Interpersonal Attraction," 121, 125; Scherer, *Human Aggression*, 157; Berelson, *Human Behavior*, 327. The quotes from Sir Robert and Lady Harley are from Jacqueline Eales, *Puritans and Roundheads* (Cambridge, Eng., 1990), 61. See also John C. Turner, *Rediscovering the Social Group* (London, 1987).

13. Berelson, *Human Behavior*, 566; Steven Duck, *Personal Relationships and Personal Constructs* (London, 1973), 26; Scherer, *Human Aggression*, 156; Byrne, *Attraction Paradigm*, 267; Granovetter, "Strength of Weak Ties," 1367–68; Davis, "Structural Balance," passim; Wolfe, "Complex Societies," 15–16; Diana Crane, "Social Structure in a Group of Scientists: A Test of the 'Invisible College' Hypothesis," *American Sociological Review*, 34 (1969), 335–352.

14. Peter Berger quoted in Dewey B. Wallace, *Puritans and Predestination: Grace in English Protestant Theology, 1525–1695* (Chapel Hill, N.C., 1982), 191; Berelson, *Human Behavior*, 566–568, 328–330; Goodman, "Newbury," 31–32; Grano-

vetter, "Strength of Weak Ties," passim; Davis, "Structural Balance," passim; Byrne, *Attraction Paradigm*, 303; D. G. Jongmans, "Politics on the Village Level," in Boissevain and Mitchell, *Network Analysis*, 204; Ajzen, "Information," 70.

15. William Erbe, "Gregariousness, Group Membership and the Flow of Information," *AJS*, 67 (1962), 502–516; Bott, *Family and Social Network*, 327–328; Berelson, *Human Behavior*, 348; James Coleman, Elihu Katz, and Herbert Menzel, "The Diffusion of an Innovation among Physicians," *Sociometry*, 20 (1957), 253–279; Davis, "Structural Balance," passim; Alice Eagerly and Samuel Himmelfarb, "Attitudes and Opinions," *American Review of Psychology*, 29 (1978), 518; Boissevain, *Friends*, 50; Eagerly and Himmelfarb, "Attitudes," 520; Tim Harris, *London Crowds in the Reign of Charles II* (Cambridge, Eng., 1987), 97; French, "Social Power," passim; Dorwin Cartwright and Frank Havary, "Structural Balance: A Generalization of Heider's Theory," *Psychological Review*, 63 (1956), 277–293; Byrne, *Attraction Paradigm*, 38.

16. Rudo Niemeijer, "Some Applications of the Notion of Density to Network Analysis," in Boissevain and Mitchell, *Network Analysis*, 51; Boissevain, *Friends*, 148, 42; Byrne, *Attraction Paradigm*, 40; Berelson, *Human Behavior*, 336; Duck, *Personal Relationships*, 71.

17. Owen, *Communion*, 36; George Gifford quoted in Patrick Collinson, *The Religion of Protestants* (Oxford, 1982), 104; for Gifford see Alan Macfarlane, "A Tudor Anthropologist: George Gifford's *Discourse* and *Dialogue*," in Sydney Anglo, ed., *The Damned Art* (London, 1977), 140–155. Stephen Foster, "The Godly in Transit: English Popular Protestantism and the Creation of a Puritan Establishment in America," in David Hall and David Grayson Allen, *Seventeenth-Century New England* (Boston, 1984), 206.

Chapter One

1. Patrick Collinson, *The Elizabethan Puritan Movement* (Los Angeles, 1967), 129; John Morgan, *Godly Learning* (Cambridge, Eng., 1986), 232; C. M. Dent, *Protestant Reformers in Elizabethan Oxford* (Oxford, 1983), 82; Dewey Wallace Jr., "The Life and Thought of John Owen to 1660: A Study of the Significance of Calvinist Theology in English Puritanism" (Ph.D. thesis, Princeton University, 1965), 18; V. I. H. Green, *Religion at Oxford and Cambridge* (London, 1964), 112; Wallace, "Owen," 18, 19; Dent, *Oxford,* 73. Geoffrey Nuttall has commented on the preponderance of Cambridge over Oxford graduates among the first Nonconformists in the 1660s; see Nuttall, "The Emergence of Nonconformity," in Geoffrey Nuttall et al., *The Beginnings of Nonconformity* (London, 1964), 23.

2. Rebecca Seward Rolph, "Emmanuel College, Cambridge, and the Puritan Movements of Old and New England" (Ph.D. thesis, University of Southern California, 1979), 13, 18; Claire Cross, *The Puritan Earl* (London, 1966), 41; Richard Tyler, "The Children of Disobedience: The Social Composition of Emmanuel College, Cambridge, 1596–1645" (Ph.D. thesis, University of California, Berkeley, 1976), 158–159.

3. Rolph, "Emmanuel College," 4, 16, 100, 193; Morgan, *Godly Learning,* 248; Rolph, "Emmanuel College," 144.

4. Green, *Religion at Oxford and Cambridge,* 117–118; Morgan, *Godly*

Learning, 256; Mark Curtis, *Oxford and Cambridge in Transition, 1558–1642* (Oxford, 1959), 208; M. M. Knappen, ed., *Two Elizabethan Puritan Diaries by Richard Rogers and Samuel Ward* (repr., Gloucester, Mass., 1966), 44, 40.

5. *CSPD (1611–1618),* 411; Green, *Religion at Oxford and Cambridge,* 129; Wallace, "Owen," 43; H. C. Porter, "Catharine Hall and the Reformation, 1500–1650," in E. E. Rich, ed., *St. Catharine's College, Cambridge 1473–1973* (Leeds, 1973), 99; Hugh Kearney, *Scholars and Gentlemen* (Ithaca, N.Y., 1970), 94–95; Green, *Religion at Oxford and Cambridge,* 132; John Winthrop, "General Considerations for the Plantation of New England," *Winthrop Papers,* II (Boston, 1931), 115.

6. Collinson, *Elizabethan Puritan Movement,* 122, 127. The university experience could, of course, be important for those of other persuasions who formed friendships there. Hugh Trevor-Roper has emphasized the importance of Cambridge connections in the anti-Calvinist party in his *Catholics, Anglicans and Puritans* (Chicago, 1987), chapter two.

7. Information on college careers in this and subsequent paragraphs is drawn from J. A. Venn, *Alumni Cantabrigienses,* 4 vols. (Cambridge, Eng., 1922–1954).

8. For an examination of reform from the perspective of the development of ideas, see H. C. Porter, *Reformation and Reaction at Tudor Cambridge* (Cambridge, Eng., 1958). It should be pointed out that some Cambridge friends eventually parted company, but even in some such cases the influence of college friendships remained. It is likely that John Robinson's close association with Perkins and other members of the Cambridge Puritan network accounted for his willingness to maintain contacts with such friends after he became a separatist; see Timothy George, *John Robinson and the English Separatist Tradition* (Macon, Ga., 1982), chapter three, for an excellent discussion of Robinson at Cambridge.

9. Samuel Eliot Morison, *The Founding of Harvard College* (Cambridge, Mass., 1935), 61–62; Tyler, "Children of Disobedience," 294; John David Twigg, "The University of Cambridge and the English Revolution, 1625–1688" (D.Ph. thesis, Cambridge, 1983), 217.

10. E. S. de Beer, ed., *The Diary of John Evelyn,* III (London, 1955), 140; Harrison Francis Fletcher, *The Intellectual Development of John Milton, Vol. II: The Cambridge University Period, 1625–32* (Urbana, Ill., 1961), 13; David Masson, *The Life of John Milton,* vol. I (rev., London, 1881), 179; Robert Willis and John Willis Clark, *The Architectural History of the University of Cambridge,* 4 vols. (Cambridge, Eng., 1886), III, 297–298, 377, 308–312, 324–325.

11. Morison, *Founding of Harvard,* 82–86.

12. Masson, *Life of Milton,* I, 133–134; William T. Costello, *The Scholastic Curriculum at Early Seventeenth-Century Cambridge* (Cambridge, Mass., 1958), 31–32; Masson, *Life of Milton,* I, 261, 275; Costello, *Curriculum at Cambridge,* 14–15; Morgan, *Godly Learning,* 250; Von Victor Morgan, "Approaches to the History of the English Universities in the Sixteenth and Seventeenth Centuries," *Wiener Beiträge zur Geschichte der Neuzeit,* 5 (1978), 138–164; Fletcher, *Intellectual Development of Milton,* II, 56; Curtis, *Oxford and Cambridge,* 105, 144, 96–97; Jefferson Looney, "Undergraduate Education at Early Stuart Cambridge," *History of Education,*

10 (1982), 19, 16; Keith Thomas, "Cases of Conscience in Seventeenth-Century England," in John Morrill, Paul Slack, and Daniel Woolf, eds., *Public Duty and Private Conscience in Seventeenth-Century England* (Oxford, 1993), 39. See also Margo Todd, *Christian Humanism and the Puritan Social Order* (Cambridge, Eng., 1987), 54–56; Margo Todd, "Seneca and the Protestant Mind: The Influence of Stoicism on Puritan Ethics," *AFR*, 74 (1983), 182–199; and K. Charlton, *Education in Renaissance England* (London, 1965).

13. Curtis, *Oxford and Cambridge,* 7; student quoted in Twigg, "Cambridge," vi; Fletcher, *Intellectual Development of Milton*, II, 28; Curtis, *Oxford and Cambridge*, 114; Porter, "Catharine Hall," 98; quote regarding Cotton in William Dillingham, *Laurence Chaderton, D.D. Translated from a Latin Memoir of Dr. Dillingham* by Richard Farmer with an essay by E. S. Shuckburgh (Cambridge, Eng., 1884), 5; Morgan, *Godly Learning*, 287; Louis B. Wright, "William Perkins, Elizabethan Apostle of Practical Divinity," *HLQ*, III (1939–1940), 172.

14. Masson, *Life of Milton*, I, 262; Rolph, "Emmanuel College," 357; Costello, *Curriculum at Cambridge*, 110; Rolph, "Emmanuel College," 152; E. S. Shuckburgh, *Emmanuel College* (London, 1904), 46, 45; Morgan, *Godly Learning*, 250–251, 237–238; Rolph, "Emmanuel College," 178, 180; the order is found in Emmanuel College Mss. Col. 14, 1, the College Order Book, 3–8; see also Albert Peel, ed., *The Seconde Parte of a Register*, 2 vols. (Cambridge, Eng., 1915), I, 133–134.

15. Porter, "Catharine Hall," 97; Costello, *Curriculum at Cambridge*, 111–112; Porter, "Catharine Hall," 97; J. H. Marsden, *College Life in the Time of James the First* (London, 1851), 65, 76; William Jenkyn, *A Shock of Corn Coming in Its Season* (London, 1654), 33.

16. Masson, *Life of Milton*, I, 136; Curtis, *Oxford and Cambridge*, 110–112; Fletcher, *Intellectual Development of Milton*, II, 57–58, 28; Shuckburgh, *Emmanuel College*, 30–31; Rolph, "Emmanuel College," 185. A useful discussion of Roger Williams's life at Pembroke College can be found in chapter four of L. Raymond Camp, *Roger Williams, God's Apostle of Advocacy* (Lewiston, Penn., 1989).

17. Fletcher, *Intellectual Development of Milton*, II, 28; Masson, *Life of Milton*, I, 133; Rolph, "Emmanuel College," 160; Fletcher, *Intellectual Development of Milton*, II, 78; Porter, "Catharine Hall," 74; Rolph, "Emmanuel College," 165; Masson, *Life of Milton*, I, 138; Samuel Clarke, *The Lives of Thirty-Two English Divines* (3d ed., London, 1677), 235; Masson, *Life of Milton*, I, 138; Rolph, "Emmanuel College," 374; de Beer, ed., *Evelyn Diary*, III, 139; Porter, "Catharine Hall," 61.

18. John Venn, *Early Collegiate Life* (Cambridge, Eng., 1913), 121; Marsden, *College Life*, 94–95; Masson, *Life of Milton*, I, 139; Venn, *Collegiate Life*, 123–124; John Heard, *John Wheelwright* (Boston, 1930), 10; Kenneth Fincham, *Pastor as Prelate: The Episcopate of James I* (Oxford, 1990), 8, relates a story of Chaderton besting Archbishop Richard Bancroft when the two wrestled at Lambeth Palace; Thomas Hooker, *The Saints Guide* (London, 1645), 30; Shuckburgh, *Emmanuel College*, 24–35; Willis, *Architectural History of Cambridge*, III, 573–574, 571; II, 720; III, 567, 576; II, 720; III, 577; Marsden, *College Life*, 96–97.

19. Marsden, *College Life*, 40–42.

20. Rolph, "Emmanuel College," 201; Masson, *Life of Milton,* I, 139; Fletcher, *Intellectual Development of Milton,* II, 59; Knappen, *Two Diaries,* 111.

21. Walter Wilson, *History of the Dissenting Churches in London,* 4 vols. (London, 1808), I, 154; Morison, *Founding of Harvard,* 85–86; Cotton Mather, *Magnalia Christi Americana,* 2 vols. (New York, 1967 reprint of 1852 edition), I, 460, 502; Shuckburgh, *Emmanuel College,* 48.

22. Charles B. Jewson, "The English Church at Rotterdam and Its Norfolk Connection," *NAS* (Norwich, 1947), 335; Robert Paul, ed., *An Apologetical Narration* (Boston, 1963), 97–106; Sargent Bush Jr., *The Writings of Thomas Hooker* (Madison, 1980), 64, includes quote from *Magnalia;* K. W. Shipps, "Lay Patronage of East Anglian Puritan Clerics in Pre-Revolutionary England" (Ph.D. thesis, Yale University, 1971), 190, 355; Andrew Thomas Denholm, "Thomas Hooker: Puritan Preacher, 1586–1647" (Ph.D. thesis, Hartford Seminary, 1961), 26; Venn, *Alumni,* IV, 168, 360, 351; Clarke, *Thirty-Two Divines,* 249; Gouge quote in Barbara Donagan, "Puritan Ministers and Laymen: Professional Claims and Social Constraints in Seventeenth-Century England," *HLQ,* XLVII (1984), 98–99; Tyler, "Children of Disobedience," 111–112; Frank Shuffleton, *Thomas Hooker, 1586–1647* (Princeton, N.J., 1977), 25.

23. J. T. Cliffe, *The Yorkshire Gentry from the Reformation to the Civil War* (London, 1969), 101–102; Morison, *Founding of Harvard,* 85–86; Cliffe, *Yorkshire Gentry,* 101; Tyler, "Children of Disobedience," 76; D'Ewes quoted in Todd, *Christian Humanism,* 86; Austin Woolrych, *Commonwealth to Protectorate* (Oxford, 1982), 203; Rolph, "Emmanuel College," 264.

24. Irvonwy Morgan, *Prince Charles's Puritan Chaplain* (London, 1957), 40, 44; John Ball, *Life of the Renowned Dr. Preston, Written in the Year 1628* (London, 1885), 16; Shipps, "Lay Patronage," 307–309; Harry Lee Poe, "Evangelistic Fervency Among the Puritans in Stuart England, 1603–1688" (Ph.D. thesis, Southern Baptist Seminary, 1982), 125–126; Keith Sprunger, *The Learned Doctor William Ames* (Urbana, Ill., 1972), 11; Samuel Clarke, *The Lives of Sundry Eminent Persons in this Later Age* (London, 1683), 57.

25. Ball, *Preston,* 33–34; Clarke, *Eminent Persons,* 155–156, 157; T. W. Davids, *Annals of Evangelical Nonconformity in the County of Essex* (London, 1863), 611–613; J. Duncan, "Rev. Samuel Fairclough, 1594–1677" (typescript in Dr. Williams's Library), 2; Davids, *Nonconformity in Essex,* 166; Morgan, *Puritan Chaplain,* 17; Sprunger, *William Ames,* 17; Samuel Clarke, *A Collection of the Lives of Ten Eminent Divines* (London, 1662), 2–3; Sprague, *Annals of the American Pulpit,* I, 54; Ira Boseley, *The Ministers of the Abbey Independent Church, 1650–1660* (London, 1911), 44; Ian Breward, ed., *The Works of William Perkins* (Abingdon, Berkshire, 1970), 3; Rolph, "Emmanuel College," 26; W. Urwick, *Historical Sketches of Nonconformity in the County Palatinate of Chester* (London, 1864), 137; Clarke, *Eminent Persons,* 3; Cliffe, *Yorkshire Gentry,* 93; Clarke, *Thirty-Two Divines,* 236; Clarke, *Eminent Persons,* 95; Shipps, "Lay Patronage," 117; Geoffrey Nuttall, "John Cotton's *Keyes of the Kingdom* (1644)," *CHST,* 14 (1940–1944), 206; Tyler, "Children of Disobedience," 7; T. F. Merrill, *William Perkins* (Nieuwkoop, 1966), xvii; Ward in Knappen, *Two Diaries,* 119; Davids, *Nonconformity in Essex,* 381; Thomas Shepard, "Autobiography,"

in Michael McGiffert, ed., *God's Plot: The Paradoxes of Puritan Piety* (Amherst, Mass., 1972), 72–73; Shipps, "Lay Patronage," 199–200.

26. Porter, "Catharine Hall," 107; Wilson, *Dissenting Churches*, I, 154; Stanley Fienberg, "Thomas Goodwin, Puritan Pastor and Independent Divine" (Ph.D. thesis, University of Chicago, 1974), 4; Shipps, "Lay Patronage," 310; John Preston to James Ussher, July 1621, in James Ussher, *The Whole Works of the Rev. James Ussher, DD.*, 18 vols. (London, 1847), XVI, 371; Rolph, "Emmanuel College," 528; Richard Sibbes to James Ussher, 7 February 1627, in Ussher, *Works*, XVI, 453.

27. This paragraph is based on Stephen Bondos-Greene, "The End of an Era: Cambridge Puritanism and the Christ College Election of 1609," *HJ*, 25 (1982), 197–208. The quote from an anonymous critic of the Puritans is on p. 205 of that article; the quote from Ward is from Trevor-Roper, *Catholics, Anglicans and Puritans*, 49.

28. Ball, *Preston*, 82–85; Shuckburgh, *Emmanuel College*, 54–55; Curtis, *Oxford and Cambridge*, 47; Matthew Mead to Sir Martin Stuteville, in J. Heywood and T. Wright, eds., *Cambridge University Transactions During the Puritan Controversies*, 2 vols. (London, 1854), II, 312.

29. Nathaniel Ward to William Sandcroft, July 1628, in *NEHGR*, 37 (1883), 59; Shipps, "Lay Patronage," 188–189; Tyler, "Children of Disobedience," 255–256. Interest in college elections was widespread among Puritan alumni; Emmanuel College fellows quoted in John David Twigg, *The University of Cambridge and the English Revolution 1625–1688* (Woodridge, Eng., 1990), 28. John Rous, who received his MA from Emmanuel in 1607, made a number of references to college events in his diary (John Rous, *The Diary of John Rous*, ed. M. A. Everett Green [1866]), and Samuel Ward corresponded with Sir Nathaniel Rich regarding a disputed election to a fellowship (*HMCR*, 8, II, 50b).

30. Shipps, "Lay Patronage," 193–194. For Holland see Barbara Donagan, "A Courtier's Progress: Greed and Consistency in the Life of the Earl of Holland," *HJ*, 19 (1976), 317–353; Twigg, "Cambridge," 9–10.

31. Dent, *Oxford*, 205; Margo Todd, "Providence, Chance and the New Science in Early Stuart Cambridge," *HJ*, 29 (1986), 697–698; quote attributed to Ames in Charles Henry Cooper, *Annals of Cambridge* (Cambridge, Eng., 1845), III, 34; Margo Todd, " 'An Act of Discretion': Evangelical Conformity and the Puritan Dons," *Albion*, 18 (1986), 597; *Victoria County History of Cambridgeshire*, III (London, 1959), 196; Cooper, *Annals of Cambridge*, III, 166; Twigg, "Cambridge," 11; Poe, "Fervency," 55; Porter, "Catharine Hall," 95–96; *Victoria County History of Cambridgeshire*, III, 125; "Memoir of Thomas Goodwin," in John Miller and Robert Halley, eds., *The Works of Thomas Goodwin*, 11 vols. (Edinburgh, 1865), I, xxiii–xxiv; Richard Sibbes, *The Complete Works of Richard Sibbes*, ed. with memoir by Alexander B. Grosart, I (Edinburgh, 1862), cxi; R. Waterhouse, "Reluctant Emigrants: The English Background of the First Generation of New England Clergy," *HMPEC*, 44 (1975), 477; Dillingham, *Chaderton*, 12; George Williams, "The Life of Thomas Hooker in England and Holland," in George H. Williams et al., *Thomas Hooker, Writings in England and Holland* (Cambridge, Mass., 1975), 256; Ball, *Preston*, 39–42.

32. N. R. N. Tyacke, *Anti-Calvinists: The Rise of English Arminianism*

c. 1590–1640 (Oxford, 1987), 29–31, 35; Dewey B. Wallace, *Puritans and Predestination: Grace in English Protestant Theology, 1525–1695* (Chapel Hill, N.C., 1982), 67. Although Whitgift accepted the judgment against Barrett and issued the Lambeth Articles, this did not necessarily mean that he viewed Barrett's opinions from the same perspective as the heads of the college. Peter Lake has shown that the archbishop's anti-Catholicism was different from that of the heads; see Lake, "The Significance of the Elizabethan Identification of the Pope as Antichrist," *JEH*, 31 (1980), 161–178; see also John G. Hoffman, "The Puritan Revolution and the 'Beauty of Holiness' at Cambridge: The Case of John Cosin," *Proceedings of the Cambridge Antiquarian Society*, LXXII (1984), 94–95.

33. Tyacke, *Anti-Calvinists*, 21, 129–140, 45; Matthew Mead to Sir Martin Stuteville, 6 July 1622, in Heywood and Wright, *Transactions*, 309; Twigg, "Cambridge," 9. R. G. Blackwood has argued that Major General Ralph Asseton and other Lancashire parliamentary leaders were influenced toward Puritanism as a result of their Cambridge experiences; see Blackwood, "Parties and Issues in Civil War Lancashire," in J. I. Kermode and C. B. Phillips, eds., *Seventeenth-Century Lancashire* (1983), 118. A different perspective on the conflicts within Cambridge can be found in V. Morgan, "Country, Court and Cambridge University 1558–1640" (D.Ph. thesis, University of East Anglia, 1983), but see David Michael Hoyle, " 'Near Popery Yet No Popery': Theological Debate in Cambridge 1590–1644" (D.Ph. thesis, Cambridge University, 1991), especially 67–69, for a reasonable criticism of Morgan's classification of various individuals.

34. Tyacke, *Anti-Calvinists*, 48–49, 50–51.

35. Tyacke, *Anti-Calvinists*, 57, n.135; Heywood and Wright, *Transactions*, 403; Cooper, *Annals of Cambridge*, III, 252; Tyacke, *Anti-Calvinists*, 52–53; Twigg, *University of Cambridge*, 31.

36. Tyler, "Disobedience," 3–4; Rolph, "Emmanuel," 322; report to Laud quoted in Shuckburgh, *Emmanuel*, 36; Willis, *Architectural History*, II, 701; Ann Kibbey, *The Interpretation of Material Shapes in Puritanism* (Cambridge, Eng., 1988), 50; Todd, "Puritan Dons," 595; Hoffman, "Cosin," 95, 100–101; see also Hoyle, " 'Near Popery Yet No Popery,' " 132–143.

37. Collinson, *The Religion of Protestants*, 118–119; Morgan, *Godly Learning*, 296; Mather, *Magnalia*, I, 336; Keith Sprunger, "John Yates of Norfolk: The Radical Puritan Preacher as Ramist Philosopher," *JHI*, 37 (1976), 699–700; John C. Adams, "Alexander Richardson's Philosophy of Art and the Sources of the Puritan Social Ethic," *JHI*, 50 (1989), 232; Samuel Thomson, "To the Reader," in Alexander Richardson, *Logician's School Master* (1657 edition); Shipps, "Lay Patronage," 271; Collinson, *Religion of Protestants*, 119; William Hunt, *The Puritan Moment* (Cambridge, Mass., 1983), 110–111; Ole Peter Grell, *Dutch Calvinists in Early Stuart London* (Leiden, 1989), 58–59, 61; Clarke, *Eminent Persons*, 159; H. Smith, *The Ecclesiastical History of Essex Under the Long Parliament* (Colchester, n.d.), 21; Morgan, *Godly Learning*, 296–297, 297 n.125; Benjamin Brook, *Lives of the Puritans to 1662*, 3 vols. (London, 1813), III, 423; Shipps, "Lay Patronage," 353–355, 116–117; Clarke, *Ten Divines*, 85–86; Donald Come, "John Cotton, Guide of the Chosen People" (Ph.D. thesis, Princeton University, 1949), 132; Davids, *Nonconformity in Essex*, 583; Geof-

frey F. Nuttall, "English Dissenters in the Netherlands, 1640–1689," *Nederlands Archief voor Kerkgeschiedensis*, 58 (1978), 39; Morgan, *Godly Learning*, 295; G. H. Turnbull, *Hartlib, Dury and Comenius: Gleanings from Hartlib's Papers* (London, 1947), 14–15. Samuel Hartlib, who would become one of the linchpins of the correspondence network, was at Cambridge in the late 1620s and became close to Sibbes and Preston as well as many of the younger members of the network; see Charles Webster, ed., *Samuel Hartlib and the Advancement of Learning* (Cambridge, Eng., 1970), 6–8.

    38. Duncan, "Fairclough," 2–3; Come, "Cotton," 134; Davids, *Annals of Nonconformity*, 583; Dewey B. Wallace Jr., "The Image of Saintliness in Puritan Hagiography 1650–1700," in John E. Booty, ed., *The Divine Drama in History and Literature* (Allison Park, Penn., 1984), 31; Oliver Heywood, "Life of John Angier of Denton," *Remains Historical and Literary Connected with the Palatine Counties of Lancaster and Chester*, new ser., 97 (1937), 52; Morgan, *Godly Learning*, 297–298.

    39. Samuel Eliot Morison, "Biographical Sketch of Charles Morton," *CSM*, XXIII (1940), vii; Clarke, *Ten Divines*, 95–96; A. G. Matthews, *Calamy Revised* (Oxford, 1934), 270; Kenneth W. Shipps, "The Puritan Emigration to New England: A New Source on Motivation," *NEHGR*, CXXXV (1981), 85; Bush, *Thomas Hooker*, 4.

    40. Davids, *Nonconformity in Essex*, 166–167; John Shaw, "The Life of Mr. John Shaw," *Surtees Society*, LXV (1877), 124.

    41. Shipps, "Lay Patronage," 190; John Howe, *The Works of the Reverend John Howe* (London, 1834), VI, 493; Heywood, *Life of Angier*, 51, 50.

    42. Wallace, "Owen," 115; Hughes, "Thomas Dugard," 774.

    43. Collinson, *Religion of Protestants*, 118. Henry Jessey was one graduate who, after receiving his degree from St. John's, Cambridge, in 1623, "went on to keep Termes and the Commencements." [Edward Whiston], *The Life and Death of Mr. Henry Jessey* (London, 1671), 5. John Twigg, *Cambridge University*, asserts that "Puritanism as a cohesive national movement was to a large extent the work of university graduates, from Cambridge in particular, who carried a sense of fellowship and common cause out into the parishes where they became ministers" (p. 15).

Chapter Two

    1. David Underdown, *Revel, Riot and Rebellion* (Oxford, 1985), 29; Avihu Zakai, "Exile and Kingdom: Reformation, Separation and the Millennial Quest in the Formation of Massachusetts and its Relationship with England, 1628–1668" (Ph.D. thesis, Johns Hopkins University, 1983), 59–60; John Winthrop, "Religious Experience," *Winthrop Papers* (Boston, 1929–), I, 196; Collinson, *The Religion of Protestants* (Oxford, 1982), 105, 110–111. See also Ian Green, "Career Prospects and Clerical Conformity in the Early Stuart Church," *PP*, 90 (1981), 111. In his study *From Iconoclasm to Iconophobia*, The Stenton Lecture, 1985 (Reading, Eng., 1986), Patrick Collinson observes that "internalising in social relations and experience a morally austere and demanding version of Christianity . . . turned the doctrine of election into a principle of invidious exclusion and stimulated an unrelenting warfare between the elect and the children of perdition, accentuating that mentality of opposites and contrary correspondences which was so prevalent in early modern England" (p. 6). The ways in which the self-defining activities of the godly could divide Englishmen

and their communities have been touched upon in a number of recent works. See for instance Peter Lake's "Puritanism, Arminianism and a Shropshire Axe-Murder," *Midland History*, XV (1990), 37–64; Patrick Collinson, "Godly Preachers and Zealous Magistrates," in E. S. Leedham-Green, ed., *Religious Dissent in East Anglia* (Cambridge, Eng., 1991), 5–27; and Collinson's "The Cohabitation of the Faithful with the Unfaithful," in Ole Peter Grell, Jonathan I. Israel, and Nicholas Tyacke, eds., *From Persecution to Toleration* (Oxford, 1991), 51–76. John Stachniewski points out the sense of despair felt by those who accepted the premises of Calvinism but who could not believe they were of the elect in *The Persecutory Imagination* (Oxford, 1991). In the process he also adds to the picture of the bond that united those who believed themselves to be in the communion of saints.

2. Hunt, *The Puritan Moment*, 231; Collinson, *Religion of Protestants*, 114. Collinson, in *The Religion of Protestants*, argues for a clerical identity for all ministers in the Church of England. Although I agree that a sense of being a distinct "profession" was shared by a growing number of clergy regardless of factional persuasion, I believe that the Puritan clergy, and especially those in congregational communion, form a more self-conscious network than Collinson emphasizes. Shipps, "Lay Patronage," 316; Jesper Rosenmeir, " 'Clearing the Medium': A Reevaluation of the Puritan Plain Style in Light of John Cotton's A *Practical Commentary Upon the First Epistle Generall of John*," *WMQ*, XXXVII (1980), 588, 580.

3. Sibbes is quoted in McGee, *Godly Man*, 196; Jonathan Mitchell, *Discourse of the Glory*, 2d ed. (London, 1677), 285–286; William Gouge, *Commentary on the Whole Epistle to the Hebrews*, vol. I of *The Complete Works of William Gouge* (Edinburgh, 1856–1862), 206; Barbara Donagan, "Godly Choice: Puritan Decision-making in Seventeenth Century England," *HTR*, 76 (1983), 313; Winthrop quoted in McGee, *Godly Man*, 196.

4. See H. G. Alexander, *Religion in England, 1558–1662* (London, 1968), and Christopher Hill, *Economic Problems of the Church from Archbishop Whitgift to the Long Parliament* (Oxford, 1956).

5. See Paul Seaver, *The Puritan Lectureships* (Stanford, 1970). For another perspective on church lectureships see Patrick Collinson, "Lectures by Combination: Structures and Characteristics of Church Life in 17th Century England," *BIHR*, XLVIII (1975), 182–213.

6. Barbara Donagan, "The Clerical Patronage of Robert Rich, Second Earl of Warwick, 1619–1642," *APS*, 120 (1976), 394. Paul Seaver has shown how Puritan clergy could also bring together humbler laymen from different communities, the network functioning to place godly men and women in touch with members of other parishes who became their friends; Seaver, *Wallington's World*, 190–191. Some valuable points regarding the formation of networks of communication and influence among the gentry can be found in Joan Thirsk, "The Fashioning of the Tudor-Stuart Gentry," *Bulletin of the John Rylands University Library*, 77 (1990), 69–85.

7. Waterhouse, "Reluctant Emigrants," 481; Donagan, "Patronage," 405, 399; Sir Nathaniel Rich to William Sandcroft, 20 November 1633, *NEHGR*, 37 (1883), 59–60; Clive Holmes, *The Eastern Association in the English Civil War* (Cambridge, Eng., 1974), 19; Donagan, "Patronage," 410, 401; Shipps, "Lay Patron-

age," 184–185; Waterhouse, "Reluctant Emigrants," 481–482; Donagan, "Patronage," 392; Holmes, *Eastern Association*, 19; Donagan, "Patronage," 399; Hunt, *Puritan Moment*, 176, 184; Donagan, "Patronage," 397.

8. John A. Newton, "Puritanism in the Diocese of York (excluding Nottinghamshire), 1603–1640" (Ph.D. thesis, University of London, 1955), 61; Hunt, *Puritan Moment*, 166, 220–221; Shipps, "Lay Patronage," 134; Mather, *Magnalia*, I, 288; Waterhouse, "Reluctant Emigrants," 482; C. E. Cunningham, "John Haynes of Connecticut," *NEQ*, XII (1939), 657. For further details of gentry patronage, including the efforts of the Barnardistons, Bacons, Brewsters, Harleys, and the earl of Lincoln, see J. T. Cliffe, *The Puritan Gentry* (London, 1984), 12; Davids, *Nonconformity in Essex*, 611–613; Shipps, "Lay Patronage," 76 n.26; Come, "Cotton," 134; Cliffe, *Puritan Gentry*, 191, 226; Shipps, "Lay Patronage," 276, 153, 161–162; Shipps, "The Puritan Emigration," 95; *Winthrop Papers*, II, 88 n.3; Murray Tolmie, *The Triumph of the Saints* (Cambridge, Eng., 1977), 44–45; John Browne, *The Congregational Church at Wrentham in Suffolk* (London, 1854), 8–9; A. G. Matthews, *Calamy Revised*, 221; A. P. Newton, *The Colonizing Activities of the English Puritans* (New Haven, 1914), 177–178; McGiffert, ed., *God's Plot*, 46, 48; Donagan, "Patronage," 404; Jacqueline Eales, *Puritans and Roundheads*, 61–63.

9. Cliffe, *Puritan Gentry*, 136, 88; Richard L. Greaves, *Saints and Rebels: Seven Nonconformists in Stuart England* (Macon, Ga., 1985), 78; Hunt, *Puritan Moment*, 221; Arthur Hildersham to Lady Joan Barrington, 9 March 1629, *Barrington Family Letters, 1628–1642*, ed. Arthur Searle (London, 1983), 62; Cliffe, *Puritan Gentry*, 165, 37–38; Sir William Masham to Lady Joan Barrington, 7 February 1632, *Barrington Letters*, 227; Cliffe, *Puritan Gentry*, 152; Sir William Masham to Lady Joan Barrington, July 1629, *Barrington Letters*, 77–78; Cliffe, *Puritan Gentry*, 25; W. J. Sheils, *The Puritans in the Diocese of Peterborough, 1558–1610*, Publications of the Northampton Record Society, XXX (1979), 100. Sheils has concluded that "the strength of the local contacts were founded on a common outlook and furthered by a shared educational experience and by the patronage system" (p. 98). *Persecutio Undecima* (1648), quoted in Donagan, "Puritan Ministers," 99. Among other Puritan patrons were Sir Robert Jermyn, Drew Drury, and Lady Kydson—all in the archdeaconry of Sudbury, Essex (Rosemary O'Day, *The English Clergy: The Emergence and Consolidation of a Profession, 1558–1642* [Leicester, 1979] 86–87). Lawrence Stone has argued that in relations between Puritan clergy and peers "questions of divine law and the will of God transcended the normal respect due to a titular superior" (*The Crisis of the Aristocracy 1558–1641* [Oxford, 1965], 745).

10. Williams, "The Life of Thomas Hooker," 4; R. W. Ketton-Cremer, *Norfolk in the Civil War* (Hamden, Conn., 1970), 80; Shipps, "Lay Patronage," 176; Isabel M. Calder, ed., *Letters of John Davenport* (New Haven, Conn., 1937), 2; Come, "Cotton," 76.

11. Thomas Hill to Sir Robert Harley, 21 November 1633, *HMCR, 14,* 32; Williams, "Thomas Hooker," 4, 13 n.34; Shipps, "Lay Patronage," 305, 56 n.104; Clarke, *Thirty-Two Divines*, 238; Shipps, "Lay Patronage," 176; Cliffe, *Puritan Gentry*, 77, 78; "Mercurius Civicus" in *Somers Tracts*, IV, 583–584. Patronage could see clergy intervening for laymen as well. Thomas Dudley had been converted by the preaching

of Arthur Hildersham and became a follower of John Dod. Dod introduced Dudley to Lord Say and Lord Compton. Dudley became an attendant to Compton, who later recommended him to the earl of Lincoln, who employed him as his steward (Augustine Jones, *The Life and Work of Thomas Dudley* [Boston, 1899], 31–32).

12. See Collinson, *The Elizabethan Puritan Movement,* and "Cranbrook and the Fletchers: Popular and Unpopular Religion in the Kentish Weald," in P. N. Brooks, ed., *Reformation Principle and Practice* (London, 1980); Donagan, "Puritan Ministers," 98. R. C. Richardson, *Puritanism in North-West England* (Manchester, 1972), points out that laymen were often more vehement in their opposition to the sign of the cross than were the clergy (p. 27).

13. William Hooke, *New Englands Teares, for Old Englands Feares,* reprinted in Samuel Emery, *The Ministry of Taunton* (Boston, 1853), I, 93; Porter, *Reformation,* 270; Irvonwy Morgan, *Puritan Spirituality* (London, 1973), 187; O'Day, *English Clergy,* 168.

14. Collinson, *Elizabethan Puritan Movement,* 50; O'Day, *English Clergy,* 166; Christopher Hill, *Society and Puritanism in Pre-Revolutionary England,* 2d ed. (New York, 1967), 81; John Ley, *Defensive Doubts and Reasons for Refusall of the Oath* (London, 1641), sig. a4; Norwich, *Registrum Vagam,* quoted in Collinson, "Lectures by Combination," 182–213; Collinson, *Religion of Protestants,* 136–139 and 123–124, where he reviews evidence of such conviviality found in the records of the 1614 visitation of the Diocese of Lincoln. Collinson points out that it is wrong to assume, as some have done, that lecturers were without benefices; many combined their lecturing with a settled living in the church. Elsewhere ("Lectures by Combination") he has suggested that in some cases such combinations were a transformation of the tradition of prophesying.

15. Shipps, "Lay Patronage," 353–354; Tai Liu, *Puritan London* (Newark, Del., 1986), 86; Isabel M. Calder, "The St. Antholin's Lectures," *CQR,* CLX (1959), 52, 53; John T. Evans, *Seventeenth-Century Norwich* (Oxford, 1979), 87; Holmes, *Eastern Association,* 17; Shipps, "Lay Patronage," 286–288, 133, 131; Matthews, *Calamy Revised,* 312; Norman C. P. Tyack, "The Humbler Puritans of East Anglia and the New England Movement: Evidence from the Court Records of the 1630s," *NEHGR,* 138 (1984), 103.

16. Hunt, *Puritan Moment,* 111–112; Collinson, *Religion of Protestants,* 120 n.14; Dorothy Williams, "London Puritanism: The Parish of St. Stephen, Coleman Street, *CQR,* CLX (1959), 466; Patrick Collinson, *The Birthpangs of Protestant England* (New York, 1988), 466; Patrick Collinson, "Magistracy and Ministry: A Suffolk Minature," in R. Buick Knox, ed., *Reformation, Conformity and Dissent* (London, 1977), 76.

17. Mary Fulbrook, *Piety and Politics* (Cambridge, Eng., 1983), 107–108; Knappen, *Two Diaries,* 28; Poe, "Evangelistic Fervency," 50; C. M. Dent, "Protestants in Elizabethan Oxford" (D.Ph. thesis, Oxford University, 1980), 130; Rolph, "Emmanuel College," 93. For an example of the operations of one such conference see John H. Primus, "The Dedham Sabbath Debate: More Light on English Sabbatarianism," *The Sixteenth Century Journal,* XVII (1986), 87–102. Though the evidence is spotty, clerical conferences of various forms seem to have

continued from the formal classes of the Elizabethan era to the outbreak of the civil wars. Early in the seventeenth century Arthur Hildersham, John Dod, and others had met with John Smith in an attempt to persuade him away from the Separatist path he was taking. Unsuccessful in that case, a group of clerical friends had more succcess in dealing with Richard Bernard; see Carol Geary Schneider, "Godly Order in a Church Half-Reformed: The Disciplinarian Legacy, 1570–1641" (Ph.D. thesis, Harvard University, 1986), 217–219.

18. Collinson, *Religion of Protestants*, 135; Clarke, *Ten Divines*, 132; Morgan, *Godly Learning*, 290; Knappen, *Two Diaries*, 69; Robert Scholz, " 'The Reverend Elders': Faith, Fellowship and Politics in the Ministerial Community of Massachusetts Bay, 1630–1710" (Ph.D. thesis, University of Minnesota, 1966), 12; Schneider, "Godly Order," 240; Scholz, "Reverend Elders," 13; Stephen Foster, *Notes from the Caroline Underground* (Hamden, Conn., 1978), 4; J. A. Newton, "The Yorkshire Puritan Movement 1603–1640," *CHST*, XIX (1960–1964), 14–15; Ralph Cudworth quoted in Collinson, *Religion of Protestants*, 136. Leigh Eric Schmidt has pointed to the same relation between fasts and communion in *Holy Fairs: Scottish Communions and American Revivals in the Early Modern Period* (Princeton, 1989), 78–79.

19. Shuffleton, *Hooker*, 138; Jesse Berridge, "Thomas Hooker and John Eliot," *Essex Review*, XLI (1932), 68–69; Williams, "Thomas Hooker," 11–12, 20; Shipps, "Lay Patronage," 117; Cliffe, *Puritan Gentry*, 93; C. A. Barton, *Historical Notes and Records of the Parish of Terling, Essex* (privately printed, 1954), 88; quoted in Tyack, "Humbler Puritans," 89. Further light on Essex clerical gatherings is to be found in T. Webster, "The Godly of Goshen Scattered: An Essex Clerical Conference in the 1620s and Its Diaspora" (D.Ph. thesis, Cambridge, 1992).

20. Morgan, *Godly Learning*, 295; Thomas Edwards, *Gangraena, or, A Catalogue and Discovery of Many of the Errors, Heresies, Blasphemies, and Pernicious Practices of the Sectaries of This Time* (London, 1646), IV, 144; Hughes, "Thomas Dugard," 775; Ann Hughes, *Politics, Society and Civil War in Warwickshire 1620–1660* (Cambridge, Eng., 1989), 71–75; Clarke, *Thirty-Two Divines*, 120; Scholz, "Reverend Elders," 12; Mather, *Magnalia*, I, 311; Davids, *Nonconformity in Essex*, 166–167; Waterhouse, "Reluctant Emigrants," 481; Come, "Cotton," 132–133; Clarke, *Ten Divines*, 60; W. J. Sheils, "Religion in Provincial Towns: Innovation and Tradition," in Felicity Heal and Rosemary O'Day, eds., *Church and Society in England: Henry VIII to James I* (Hamden, Conn., 1977), 167; Shipps, "Lay Patronage," 119; Clarke, *Eminent Persons*, 106; Shipps, "Lay Patronage," 161–162; Hunt, *Puritan Moment*, 110; Brook, *Lives*, II, 417; Sir Gilbert Gerard to Lady Jane Barrington, 19 September 1631, *Barrington Letters*, 202; Porter, "Catharine Hall," 96.

21. Clarke, *Eminent Persons*, 100; Jenkyn, *A Shock of Corn*, 34; Shipps, "Lay Patronage," 111; *Winthrop Papers*, I, 245, 259; Clarke, *Eminent Persons*, 164; Shipps, "Lay Patronage," 78 n.32; [Whiston], *Mr. Henry Jessey*, 5; Porter, *Reform*, 270; Tolmie, *Triumph of Saints*, 44–45; Hughes, "Thomas Dugard," 777; Mather, *Magnalia*, I, 304, 306; Davids, *Nonconformity in Essex*, 166–167.

22. Shipps, "Lay Patronage," 234, 116–117; Shipps, "Puritan Emigration," 90 n.35; D. A. Kirby, "The Radicals of St. Stephen's, Coleman St., London,

1624–1642," *Guildhall Miscellany,* III (1970), 113; Shipps, "Lay Patronage," 39 n.51; Nancy Matthews, *William Sheppard* (Cambridge, Eng., 1984), 11; Anne Laurence, "Parliamentary Army Chaplains, 1642–51" (Ph.D. thesis, Oxford University, 1981), 289–290; Marsden, *College Life,* 138; Cliffe, *Puritan Gentry,* 44; *CSPD,* 1637, 209; *Persecutio,* 55.

23. Knappen, *Two Diaries,* 59, 53; Heywood, *Life of Angier,* 53–54; Richard Cust, "News and Politics in Early Seventeenth-Century England," *PP,* 112 (1986), 65.

24. Newton, "Puritanism," 61; Dale, *Yorkshire,* 258; Come, "Cotton," 115; Shipps, "Lay Patronage," 56 n.104.

25. Sheila Lambert, "Richard Montagu, Arminianism and Censorship," *PP,* 124 (1989), 59; William Gouge to Sir Robert Harley, 24 June 1613, in *HMCR* 14, 6; Cartwright quoted in Morgan, *Godly Learning,* 114 n.120; Jeremiah Burroughes to John Cotton, 1 November [1631], mss. in MHS Davis Papers; *CSPD: Charles I, 1633–34,* 113; Jewson, "Norfolk," 330; Shuffleton, *Hooker,* 138; Porter, *Reform,* 239; Clarke, *Thirty-Two Divines,* 121; Come, "Cotton," 173; Shuffleton, *Hooker,* 156; R. Levett to John Cotton, 3 March 1625, and Cotton's response, *MHSC,* 2d ser., X, 182–184; Clarke, *Ten Divines,* 64; *Memoir of Thomas Goodwin,* xxv–xxvii; Mather, *Magnalia,* I, 328; Fienberg, "Thomas Goodwin," 85; Robert Baillie, *A Dissuasive from the Errours of the Time* (London, 1645), 55–56; Everett Emerson, *John Cotton* (New Haven, Conn., 1965), 25; Come, "Cotton," 436; Ralph Young, "Good News from New England: The Influence of the New England Way of Church Polity on Old England, 1635–1660" (Ph.D. thesis, Michigan State University, 1971), 58 n.26; William Greenhill to Lady Jane Bacon, 18 June 1625, transcript in Shipps, "Lay Patronage," 388; Frances Rose-Troup, *John White, the Patriarch of Dorchester* (New York, 1930), 298; John Ward to William Sandcroft, British Museum Harleian Mss. 3783; John Stoughton to William Sandcroft, 4 February 1630, *MHSP,* XX, 21–22; Mather, *Magnalia,* I, 460. Sargent Bush Jr. has noted the important role that John Cotton provided as a "court of last resort for troubled ministers and lay people" and that "younger ministers, in particular, expressed their worries to Cotton, who replied with detached analysis as well as warm affection" (Bush, "John Cotton's Correspondence: A Census," *EAL,* 24 [1989], 95). See also Sargent Bush Jr., "Epistolary Counseling in the Puritan Movement: The Example of John Cotton," in Francis J. Bremer, ed., *Puritanism: Trans-Atlantic Perspectives on a Seventeenth-Century Anglo-American Faith* (Boston, 1993).

26. Knappen, *Two Diaries,* 46; Todd, "Puritan Dons," 582 n.3; Rolph, "Emmanuel College," 44, 145; Clarke, *Ten Divines,* 114; Shipps, "Lay Patronage," 191 n.64; Cust, "News and Politics," 71; Todd, "Puritan Dons," 582 n.3; Ezekiel Rogers to Lady Jane Barrington, 28 September [1626], *EIHC,* 53 (1917), 215. The Samuel Ward correspondence also reminds us that the various clusters in the larger Puritan movement or network overlapped at this time. Ward's closest associates were bishops like Bedell and Joseph Hall, all of whom formed part of a separate friendship group or cluster of prominent Calvinist churchmen rooted in Cambridge and identified and discussed by Patrick Collinson in *Religion of Protestants,* 85.

27. For Winthrop correspondence with Ward, Culverwell, Wilson,

Ames, and Jessey, see *Winthrop Papers*, especially volumes 1 and 2; B. R. White, "Henry Jessey in the Great Rebellion," in Knox, *Reformation, Conformity and Dissent*, 133; Donagan, "Patronage," 400; Come, "Cotton," 174; Shipps, "Lay Patronage," 149 n.173; John Davenport to Lady Vere, 21 July 1635, in Calder, *Letters of John Davenport*, 61. The *Barrington Letters* contain correspondence between Lady Barrington and various Puritan clergymen, including Roger Williams, Ezekiel Rogers, and William Hooke; Tolmie, *Triumph of the Saints*, 44–45.

        28. Tolmie, *Triumph of the Saints*, 44; Shipps, "Lay Patronage," 122 n.62; Tolmie, *Triumph of the Saints*, 44–45.

        29. Shipps, "Lay Patronage," 176; Davids, *Nonconformity in Essex*, 381–382; Shipps, "Lay Patronage," 56 n.104; Cliffe, *Puritan Gentry*, 186–187; Heywood, *Life of Angier*, 56–57; Thomas Ball, *Life of the Reverend Dr. Preston* (London, 1885), 103; Sprunger, *William Ames*, 73; J. C. Whitebrook, *Dr. John Stoughton, Carolian Divine, and Capt. Israel Stoughton, New England Settler* (London, 1914), 10; Shipps, "Lay Patronage," 191, 310; Clarke, *Eminent Persons*, 161; Shipps, "Lay Patronage," 122; Zakai, "Exile and Kingdom," 25; Alan Macfarlane, ed., *The Diary of Ralph Josselin* (Cambridge, Eng., 1970), 69.

        30. Williams, "London Puritanism," 474–475; *Davenport Letters*, 75 n.2; John Maidstone to John Winthrop, 4 November 1629, *Winthrop Papers*, II, 164; *Barrington Letters*, 14; Clive Holmes, *The Eastern Association in the English Civil War* (Cambridge, Eng., 1974), 19; Mather, *Magnalia*, I, 308; Holmes, *Eastern Association*, 19; Shipps, "Lay Patronage," 175; Shuffleton, *Hooker*, 138; Donagan, "Patronage," 407, 408; Jeremiah Burroughes, *A Vindication of Mr. Burroughes* (London, 1646), 19; Donagan, "Patronage," 408; Jacqueline Eales, "Robert Harley, K.B. (1579–1640) and the 'Character' of a Puritan," *The British Library Journal*, XV (1989), 143.

        31. Shuffleton, *Hooker*, 129; Tyacke, *Anti-Calvinists*, 189; Holmes, *Eastern Association*, 19; Shuffleton, *Hooker*, 132; Roger Williams, *The Bloudy Tenent, Yet More Bloudy* (London, 1652), in *The Complete Writings of Roger Williams*, 7 vols. (reprint, New York, 1963), IV, 65; Shipps, "Lay Patronage," 154; Williams, "Life of Thomas Hooker," 23; Shuffleton, *Hooker*, 159.

        32. R. Clark, "Anglicanism, Recusancy and Dissent in Derbyshire, 1603–1730" (D.Ph. thesis, Oxford, 1979), 116; Mather, *Magnalia*, I, 593; Larzer Ziff, *The Career of John Cotton* (Princeton, 1962), 44; Shipps, "Lay Patronage," 200–201; Mather, *Magnalia*, I, 310; John Horton, "Two Bishops and the Holy Brood: A Fresh Look at a Familiar Fact," *NEQ*, 40 (1967), 350–351; Come, "Cotton," 164–165, 169; Williams, "London Puritanism," 477; Williams, "Life of Thomas Hooker," 30; Esther Cope, *Politics Without Parliaments, 1629–1640* (London, 1987), 62; Shipps, "Lay Patronage," 306; Holmes, *Eastern Association*, 9; Shipps, "Lay Patronage," 178.

        33. Shipps, "Lay Patronage," 120; Shepard, "Autobiography" in *God's Plot*, 47; Barton, *Parish of Terling*, 88; Hunt, *Puritan Moment*, 197; Shepard, "Autobiography" in *God's Plot*, 50; Newton, *Colonizing Activities*, 125–126; Shepard, "Autobiography" in *God's Plot*, 56; Young, "Good News," 60–61; Shepard, "Autobiography" in *God's Plot*, 62; Shipps, "Lay Patronage," 122 n.62; Bartholomew Schiavo, "The Dissenter Connection: English Dissenters and Massachusetts Political Culture, 1630–1774" (Ph.D. thesis, Brandeis University, 1976), 109 n.74.

34. Donagan, "Patronage," 406; Clarke, *Thirty-Two Divines*, 144; Curtis, *Oxford and Cambridge*, 209. On Ward and the "moderate" Puritans see the works of Peter Lake, especially *Moderate Puritans and the Elizabethan Church* (Cambridge, Eng., 1982).

35. Hughes, "Thomas Dugard," 779; Nuttall, "John Cotton's *Keyes*," 206; Shuffleton, *Hooker*, 125; Donagan, "Godly Choice," 327; Denholm, "Thomas Hooker," 44; Shipps, "Lay Patronage," 117; Mather, *Magnalia*, I, 356; John Beadle, *The Journal and Diary of a Thankful Christian* (London, 1656), preface; Come, "Cotton," 156; Mather, *Magnalia*, I, 264. The Hartlib mss. at the University of Sheffield (29/2/46A) contain a summary of a letter from Nye to Hartlib in which the clergyman refers to the manuscript copy of the discussions with Cotton, which was evidently never printed and which does not survive (I thank Tom Webster for this reference). Ziff, *John Cotton*, 68; Baillie, *Dissuasive*, 56.

36. Mather, *Magnalia*, I, 263; Come, "Cotton," 168; Shuffleton, *Hooker*, 158; Young, "Good News," 57; Mather, *Magnalia*, I, 309.

37. Heywood, *Life of Angier*, 55–56; Come, "Cotton," 134.

38. Collinson, *Religion of Protestants*, 119; Emerson, *Cotton*, 72–73; Hughes, "Thomas Dugard," 777; Morgan, *Puritan Chaplain*, 45; Marvin Breslow, *A Mirror of England* (Cambridge, Mass., 1970), 15 n.15; Seaver, *Puritan Lectureships*, 256; Grosart, *Works of Sibbes*, xcv; Morgan, *Puritan Chaplain*, 194; Mather, *Magnalia*, I, 322; Schiavo, "Dissenter Connection," 97; Norman Petit, *The Heart Prepared* (New Haven, 1966), 67; Sprunger, *William Ames*, 251; Shipps, "Lay Patronage," 280 n.41.

39. John Cotton to Arthur Hildersham, c. 1629, in *MHSP*, vol. 42, 204; Sprunger, *William Ames*, 251.

40. Anthony Fletcher, *A County Community in Peace and War* (London, 1975), 48; Goodman, "Newbury," 67; Porter, *Reform*, 267; Morgan, *Puritan Chaplain*, 43; Shipps, "Lay Patronage," 56 n.104; Isaac Johnson's will, *Winthrop Papers*, II, 56; *DNB*, I, 1163; Shipps, "Lay Patronage," 91–92; Donagan, "Patronage," 405.

41. O'Day, *English Clergy*, 164; Fletcher, *County Community*, 73; Mather, *Magnalia*, I, 306; Wilson, *Dissenting Churches*, I, 155; Mather, *Magnalia*, I, 313; Ball, *Life of Preston*, 175; Wilson, *Dissenting Churches*, I, 155; Hunt, *Puritan Moment*, 143; Clarke, *Ten Divines*, 136, 20; Zachary Catlin, "Dr. Sibbs his Life," in J. E. B. Mayor, "Materials for a Life of Dr. Richard Sibbes," *Antiquarian Communications*, I (1859), 261.

42. Cliffe, *Puritan Gentry*, 68; Poe, "Evangelistic Fervency," 117.

43. Shepard, "Autobiography" in *God's Plot*, 152.

Chapter Three

1. Franklin Le Van Baumer, "The Church of England and the Common Corps of Christendom," *JMH*, XVI (1944), 4; Franklin Le Van Baumer, "The Conception of Christendom in Renaissance England," *JHI*, VI (1945), 145–146; Breslow, *Mirror*, 148–149; John Milton quoted in C. V. Wedgwood, *Oliver Cromwell and the Elizabethan Inheritance*, Neale Lecture in English History 1970 (London, 1970), 20; William Bradford, *Of Plymouth Plantation, 1620–1647*, ed. Samuel Eliot Morison (New York, 1967), 3; John F. Wilson, *Pulpit in Parliament* (Princeton, 1969), 20; Douglas Horton, preface to John Norton, *The Answer to the Whole Set of Questions*

of the Celebrated Mr. William Apollonious (London, 1648), trans. Douglas Horton (Cambridge, Mass., 1958), xvii; Barry Coward, "Was There an English Revolution in the Middle of the Seventeenth Century?" in Colin Jones, Malyn Newitt, and Stephen Roberts, eds., *Politics and People in Revolutionary England* (London, 1986), 18; John Cotton, "A Sermon Upon a Day of Publique Thanksgiving," mss. in MHS, 11. Anne Kibbey has commented that "Cotton's perception of the Protestant Reformation is always international in scope" (*Material Shapes,* 79); John T. McNeill, *Unitive Protestantism* (Richmond, Va., 1964), 69; see also William Haller, *The Elect Nation* (New York, 1963). Peter Lake has pointed out that the notion of England as an elect nation in the sense used by some historians simply did not exist, though he emphasizes the importance of the English awareness of the struggle against Catholicism; see Lake, "Anti-popery," in Richard Cust and Ann Hughes, eds., *Conflict in Early Stuart Religion: Studies in Religion and Politics 1603–1642* (London, 1989). Scholars have sometimes read too much into the millenarian images of this period, as Lake points out. The result has been an intensive debate over the millennial expectations of the Puritans; the latest contribution, with which I strongly disagree, is Zakai's *Exile and Kingdom.* Since the precise intent of the clerical authors does not affect the use I make of their views, I defer from engaging in that controversy at this point.

2. M. M. Knappen, *Tudor Puritanism* (Chicago, 1939), 232; Breslow, *Mirror,* 142; Ronald Van de Molen, "Anglican against Puritan: Ideological Origins during the Marian Exile," *CH,* 42 (1973), 51; Christopher Hill, *The Collected Essays of Christopher Hill,* vol. 2, 30. For contacts with "stranger" churches see Patrick Collinson, "The Elizabethan Puritans and the Foreign Reformed Churches in London," in Collinson, *Godly People* (London, 1983), essay 9. Chapter one of this study contains examples of foreign students who studied with English Puritans.

3. Baumer, "Concept of Christendom," 146; J. Minton Batten, *John Dury: Advocate of Christian Reunion* (Chicago, 1944), 12, 15–16; Gunnar Westin, *Negotiations About Church Unity 1628–1634* (Uppsala, 1932), 106–107; Batten, *John Dury,* 46; Rose-Troup, *John White,* 47; Shipps, "Lay Patronage," 92; Baumer, "Concept of Christendom," 146; Batten, *John Dury,* 25–26; John Dury, *A Summarie Account of Mr John Dury's Former and Latter Negotiations* (London, 1657), 2; Turnbull, *Hartlib, Dury and Comenius,* 133.

4. The most significant study of the anti-Catholicism of the period is Caroline M. Hibbard, *Charles I and the Popish Plot* (Chapel Hill, N.C., 1983); see also Robin Clifton, "Fear of Popery," in Conrad Russell, ed., *The Origins of the English Civil War* (New York, 1973), and Carol Wiener, "The Beleaguered Isle: A Study of Elizabethan and Early Jacobean Anti-Catholicism," *PP,* 51 (1971). For the Puritan image of Prince Henry see William Hunt, "Spectral Origins of the English Revolution: Legitimation Crisis in Early Stuart England," in Geoff Eley and William Hunt, eds., *Reviving the English Revolution* (London, 1988). Samuel Clarke, in *Ten Divines,* writes of Prynne's attendance at Fairclough's sermons.

5. See C. V. Wedgwood, *The Thirty Years War* (New York, 1961).

6. Breslow, *Mirror,* 143; Raymond P. Stearns, *The Strenuous Puritan: Hugh Peter, 1598–1660* (Urbana, Ill., 1954), 27–28; Christopher Hill, "The English Revolution and the Brotherhood of Man," in Hill, *Puritanism and Revolution* (London,

1958), 125–126; Breslow, *Mirror*, 37; Christopher Hill, *Antichrist in Seventeenth-Century England* (London, 1971), 98–100; Wedgwood, *Thirty Years War*, 106; CSPD *1619–23*, 77; Wedgwood, *Thirty Years War*, 112.

7. Thomas Cogswell, *The Blessed Revolution* (Cambridge, Eng., 1989), 21; Thomas Cogswell, "England and the Spanish Match," in Cust and Hughes, *Conflict*, 115.

8. Wedgwood, *Cromwell and the Elizabethan Inheritance*, 13; Grell, *Dutch Calvinists*, 64–70; Wedgwood, *Thirty Years War*, 182; Breslow, *Mirror*, 125, 10–11; Hill, "Brotherhood of Man," 129.

9. Leonard Trinterud, ed., *Elizabethan Puritanism* (New York, 1971), 198; Richard Sibbes, *The Soules Conflict* (London, 1635), in *The Complete Works of Richard Sibbes, D.D.*, ed. Alexander B. Grosart (Edinburgh, 1862), lix; Richard Sibbes, *The Sword of the Wicked* (London, 1639), in *Works*, I, 115–116; Richard Sibbes, *The Saints Cordial* (London, 1629), 216; Richard Sibbes, *The Bruised Reed and Smoking Flax* (London, 1630), 99; Richard Sibbes, *St. Paul's Challenge* (London, 1638), in *Works*, VII, 396–397.

10. John Preston, *Sermons Preached Before His Majesty* (London, 1630), 53; John Preston, *A Sermon Preached at a General Fast*, in Preston, *The Saints Qualification*, ed. Richard Sibbes and John Davenport (London, 1633), 293–294; Ball, *Preston*, 59–61.

11. Breslow, *Mirror*, 76; John Davenport, *A Royal Edict for Military Exercises* (London, 1629), 16–17, 24–25.

12. Breslow, *Mirror*, 41; John Cotton, *God's Promise to His Plantation* (London, 1630), 10; John Cotton, *A Brief Exposition of the Whole Book of Canticles* (London, 1642), 32, which was preached in the period 1620–1621; Todd, *Christian Humanism*, 196; Thomas Hooker, "The Church's Deliverance" (November 1626), in George H. Williams et al., eds., *Thomas Hooker, Writings in England and Holland* (Cambridge, Mass., 1975), 67; Hugh Peter quoted in George H. Williams, "Life of Thomas Hooker," in Williams et al., *Hooker*, 55 n.7; Thomas Gataker, *A Sparke toward the Kindling of Sorrow for Sion* (London, 1621), as quoted in Cogswell, *Blessed Revolution*, 29; Seaver, *Wallington's World*, 109.

13. Hill, "Brotherhood of Man," 130; Christopher Hill, *God's Englishman: Oliver Cromwell and the English Revolution* (New York, 1970), 85; Eales, *Puritans and Roundheads*, 89; Wedgwood, *Thirty Years War*, 120; Jones, *Thomas Dudley*, 34–35; Williams, "Life of Thomas Hooker," 17; *Winthrop Papers*, II, 55 n.2.

14. Sprunger, *William Ames*, 34–35; Calder, *Letters of John Davenport*, 29 n.10; Breslow, *Mirror*, 41; Stearns, *Strenuous Puritan*, 62, 64.

15. James F. Maclear, "The Influence of the Puritan Clergy on the House of Commons, 1625–1629," *CH*, XIV (1945), 273; Porter, "Catharine Hall," 96; Laurence, "Parliamentary Army Chaplains," 289–290; Cust, "News and Politics," 88; Maclear, "Influence of Clergy," 287; Todd, *Christian Humanism*, 93; Donagan, "Patronage," 400; Come, "Cotton," 174; Arthur Searle, ed., *Barrington Family Letters, 1628–1632*, Camden Society, 4th ser., 28 (London, 1983), passim; Knappen, *Two Diaries*, 46; Margo Todd, "The Samuel Ward Papers of Sidney Sussex College, Cambridge," *Transactions of the Cambridge Bibliographical Society* (1985), 582–592.

The Harley connections among the clergy are developed in Eales, *Puritans and Roundheads*. For examples of parliamentary efforts see Donagan, "Patronage," 399–400; Rich quoted in Hunt, *The Puritan Moment*, 169; Wedgwood, *Cromwell and the Elizabethan Inheritance*, 14; "Resolutions on Religion of the House of Commons, 24 February 1628/9," in Samuel Rawson Gardiner, ed., *The Constitutional Documents of the Puritan Revolution, 1625–1660* (Oxford, 1962), 77–82; Sir Edwin Sandys, *Europae Speculum* (The Hague, 1629), 214–215.

16. Turnbull, *Gleanings from Hartlib's Papers*, 34; "Circular Letter of Thomas Taylor, Richard Sibbes, John Davenport and William Gouge" in Calder, *Letters of Davenport*, 26–27; *CSPD 1627–28*, 77; see also R. M. Smuts, "The Puritan Followers of Henrietta Maria in the 1630s," *EHR*, 93 (1978), 26–45. A thorough examination of the collections for the Palatinate can be found in Grell, *Dutch Calvinists*, ch. 5.

17. Stearns, *Strenuous Puritan*, 37; Mather, *Magnalia*, I, 360; *Winthrop Papers*, I, 53; Anne Hansen, *The Dorchester Group* (Columbus, Oh., 1987), 56–57; Rose-Troup, *John White*, 43; Valerie Pearl, *London and the Outbreak of the Puritan Revolution* (Oxford, 1961), 179; Jesper Rosenmeier, " 'Clearing the Medium': A Reevaluation of the Puritan Plain Style in Light of John Cotton's *A Practical Commentary Upon the First Epistle Generall of John*," *WMQ*, XXXVII (1980), 581; Larzer Ziff, introduction to John Cotton, *John Cotton on the Churches of New England*, ed. Larzer Ziff (Cambridge, Mass., 1968), 10; Breslow, *Mirror*, 18; Kirby, "Radicals of St. Stephen's," 107; Seaver, *Puritan Lectureships*, 248; Grosart, introduction to Sibbes, *Works*, lix. Sir Robert Harley was one of many laymen who assisted in the fundraising (see Jacqueline Eales, "Robert Harley, K.B.," 141–142); Grell, *Dutch Calvinists*, ch. 5. Poe, "Evangelistic Fervency," 99, argues that Laud's opposition was not to the support of Elizabeth of Bohemia but to the "private and, therefore, political nature of the Puritans' appeal."

18. Tyacke, *Anti-Calvinists*, 4, 228–230, 2, 87, 106. Tyacke's views have been subject to attack by a number of scholars, though I think that some of their criticism is open to question because they define certain terms differently than Tyacke. On the whole I find his views persuasive, but for some evaluations that raise important points see G. W. Bernard, "The Church of England c. 1529–c. 1642," *History*, 75 (1990), 183–206; Peter White, "The Rise of Arminianism Reconsidered," *PP*, 101 (1983), 34–54, with points expanded in *Predestination, Policy and Polemic* (Cambridge, Eng., 1992); William M. Lamont, "The Rise of Arminianism Reconsidered," *PP*, 107 (1985), 227–231; Nicholas Tyacke and Peter White, "Debate: The Rise of Arminianism Reconsidered," *PP*, 115 (1987), 201–229; Jonathan Atkins, "Calvinist Bishops, Church Unity and Arminianism," *Albion*, XVIII (1986), 411–428; Julian Davies, *The Caroline Captivity of the Church* (Oxford, 1992); Lambert, "Richard Montagu," 36–68, and the relevant portions of Kevin Sharpe, *The Personal Rule of Charles I* (New Haven, Conn., 1992). In "Calvinism and the English Church 1570–1635," *PP*, 114 (1987), 32–76, Peter Lake refutes some of White's arguments and advances our understanding of the changing nature of "Calvinism" in England. Elsewhere, Lake correctly points out that whereas there was a Calvinist consensus on some of the key doctrines of faith such as predestination, there *were* theological

differences that separated individuals such as Whitgift and Cartwright; see Lake, *Anglicans and Puritans?* (London, 1988). See also Andrew Foster, "Church Policies of the 1630s," in Cust and Hughes, *Conflict,* and Peter Lake, "Defining Puritanism—Again?" in Bremer, *Puritanism: Trans-Atlantic Perspectives.*

19. Tyacke, *Anti-Calvinists,* 102–103, 123; Cogswell, *Blessed Revolution,* 32; Wallace, "Owen," 86.

20. Wallace, "Owen," 75–77, 85; Paul Christianson, "From Expectation to Militance: Reformers and Babylon in the First Two Years of the Long Parliament," *JEH,* XXIV (1973), 472; David Cressy, *Bonfires and Bells* (Berkeley, 1989), 42; Alexander, *Religion in England,* 130. Hugh Trevor-Roper, in *Catholics, Anglicans and Puritans,* 52–56, has usefully pointed to the influence of Hugo Grotius on the English anti-Calvinists and has also explored the political implications of the movement.

21. Puritan clergy did not only express their views in sermons. Ball, *Preston,* 154; Shipps, "Lay Patronage," 116; for Hugh Peter, *EIHC,* LXXI, 7–8; Shipps, "Lay Patronage," 171; Cogswell, *Blessed Revolution,* 37–38. Ketton-Cremer, *Norfolk,* 53, explains how, "in 1621, at the time of the proposed marriage between Prince Charles and the Infanta, he [Samuel Ward] produced an admirable plate entitled *The Double Deliverance.* This was printed in Amsterdam, but there was nothing furtive about its authorship 'invented by Samuel Ward, preacher at Ipswich' appeared on the plate for all to see. . . . In the centre, the Pope, the cardinals and the King of Spain are seated in solemn conclave with the Devil. On one side the Armada is dispersed by the winds. . . . On the other Guy Fawkes with his lantern approaches the Parliament House, his fell designs revealed by a beam from the eye of God. Not surprisingly the Spanish ambassador Gondomar complained, and Ward was committed to prison for a spell by the Privy Council."

22. Tyacke, *Anti-Calvinists,* 47; Shipps, "Lay Patronage," 46; J. Sears McGee, "William Laud and the Outward Face of Religion," in Richard L. DeMolen, ed., *Leaders of the Reformation* (Selinsgrove, Penn., 1984), 323; Conrad Russell, "The Parliamentary Career of John Pym, 1621–29," in Peter Clark, Alan Smith, and Nicholas Tyacke, eds., *The English Commonwealth, 1547–1640* (Leicester, Eng., 1979), 152; Montagu quoted in Lambert, "Richard Montagu," 54; Wallace, *Puritans and Predestination,* 85–86; Sprunger, "John Yates," 698.

23. Tyacke, *Anti-Calvinists,* 167, 138.

24. Wallace, *Puritans and Predestination,* 87–89; Barbara Donagan, "The York House Conference Revisited: Laymen, Calvinism and Arminianism," *HR,* LXIV (1991), 312–330.

25. John Davenport to Alexander Leighton, c. 1624, in Calder, *Letters of Davenport,* 23–24.

26. L. J. Reaves, *Charles I and the Road to Personal Rule* (Cambridge, Eng., 1989), 27; Knappen, *Two Diaries,* 122; Alan Macfarlane, *The Diary of Ralph Josselin, 1616–1683; Records of Social and Economic History,* n.s., III (London, 1976), 648; Davenport, *Military Exercises,* 14. One should take care, however, to avoid depicting all the opponents of Puritanism as anti-Calvinists. Peter Lake reminds us that Robert Sanderson and others like him were staunch Calvinists who supported Laud in the 1630s and Charles I in the 1640s because they viewed the form of

Calvinism espoused by John Cotton and others as tending toward the division of the church and society between elect and nonelect; see Lake, "Serving God and the Times: The Calvinistic Conformity of Robert Sanderson," *JBS*, 27 (1988), 81–116.

27. Isabel M. Calder, ed., *Activities of the Puritan Faction of the Church of England* (London, 1957), xi–xii; Morgan, *Puritan Chaplain*, 178; Kirby, "Radicals of St. Stephen's," 13; Shipps, "Lay Patronage," 41; Clarke, *Ten Divines*, 10, 11. Nicholas Tyacke has discussed some of the links among the Feoffees and also some other efforts to sustain godly preachers with financial assistance in *The Fortunes of English Protestantism, 1603–1640*, Friends of Dr. Williams's Library Forty-Fourth Lecture (London, 1990).

28. Hill, *Economic Problems*, 254; Kirby, "Radicals of St. Stephen's," 101; McGee, *Godly Man*, 86; O'Day, *English Clergy*, 92–93; Hugh Peter, *God's Doing and Man's Duty* (London, 1646), 39; Shipps, "Lay Patronage," 162; *CSPD 1625–1649*, 400. Shipps, "Lay Patronage," 283–284, points out that the funds of the Norwich Feoffees were not seized when the London group was prosecuted and that group continued to operate. Hill, *Economic Problems*, 267–268; *CSPD 1628–29*, 358.

29. Shipps, "Lay Patronage," 160; Calder, "St. Antholin's," 52, 53; Shipps, "Lay Patronage," 354 n.8; Calder, "St. Antholin's," 57, 53–54; Schiavo, "Dissenter Connection," 106 n.53; Calder, *Puritan Faction*, xii; Laurence, "Parliamentary Army Chaplains," 381; Hill, *Economic Problems*, 257; Eales, *Puritans and Roundheads*, 66; Pearl, *London*, 194–195.

30. Prynne quoted in Poe, "Evangelistic Fervency," 82; Laud's quoted confrontation with White in Poe, "Evangelistic Fervency," 88; Laud's views quoted in Calder, *Puritan Faction*, xxii.

31. Peter Heylyn, *Cyprianus Anglicus* (London, 1668), 211; G. E. Gorman, "A Laudian Attempt to 'Tune the Pulpit': Peter Heylin and His Sermon Against the Feoffees for the Purchase of Impropriations," *JRS*, 8 (1975), 339.

32. Heylyn, *Cyprianus Anglicus*, 210, 198; Heylyn's sermon quoted in Gorman, "Peter Heylin," 344.

33. Poe, "Evangelistic Fervency," 85; Gorman, 'Peter Heylin," 349; Thomas Hart, *The Country Clergy in Elizabethan and Stuart Times* (London, 1958), 90; Calder, *Puritan Faction*, xxiii, 26 n.1; Hill, *Economic Problems*, 264; Ethyn Kirby, "The Lay Feoffees: A Study in Militant Puritanism," *JMH*, XIV (1942), 19. *CSPD 1633–34*, 192–193, indicates that in August of 1633 the Feoffees were instructed to appoint to the advowson of All Saints Worcester a candidate designated by Dr. Juxson as per the orders of the Court of Exchequer. The Feoffees were stopped from their independent action, but they were not forgotten. The money they had held was confiscated. What remained of it in 1642 was diverted by Parliament to pay for Waller's army. The Root and Branch Petition denounced the suppression of the Feoffees. The committee that drew up the articles of Laud's impeachment (the former Feoffee Samuel Browne was a member of the committee) cited the bishop's actions against the group as one of the grounds for his trial. John White the lawyer and one-time Feoffee chaired the Commons' Committee for Preaching Ministers, which in some respects carried on the work of the Feoffees and which ordered the reversal of the Exchequer decree. See Hill, *Economic Problems*, 264–267.

34. Hill, *Economic Problems*, 261; Hunt, *Puritan Moment*, 106–107; Pearl, *London*, 164; Tyacke, *Anti-Calvinists*, 132; Shipps, "Lay Patronage," 147–149, 251; Wilson quoted in Shipps, "Lay Patronage," 108.

35. Diarmaid MacCulloch discusses some of the early efforts to mobilize support for Puritans in Suffolk elections in the late Elizabethan era in *Suffolk and the Tudors* (Oxford, 1986), 192–222. Matthews, *William Sheppard*, 17; Shipps, "Lay Patronage," 191; Hunt, *Puritan Moment*, 88; *CSPD 1639–40*, 24 March 1640; George Yule, *Puritans in Politics*, Courtney Library of Reformation Classics vol. 13 (Abingdon, Eng., 1981), 90.

36. John Gruenfelder, "The Election for Knights of the Shire for Essex in the Spring, 1640," *Essex Archaeological Society*, VII (1967), 146; account of election in Davids, *Nonconformity in Essex*, 183–184; Cliffe, *Puritan Gentry*, 214–215.

37. Hunt, *Puritan Moment*, 193; Shipps, "Lay Patronage," 81–82; Hunt, *Puritan Moment*, 202; *CSPD 1625–49*, 175. Hugh Peter quoted in David Hudson Corkran III, "The New England Colonists' English Image, 1550–1714" (Ph.D. thesis, University of California, Berkeley, 1970), 33.

38. Cope, *Politics*, 12; Commons resolution quoted in Cope, *Politics*, 44; Maclear, "Influence of Clergy," 285; Phelips quoted in Cope, *Politics*, 44; Wallace, "Owen," 67; McGee, "William Laud," 326; Commons Resolution of 24 February 1628/9 in Gardiner, *Constitutional Documents*, 77–82; Maclear, "Influence of Clergy," 274.

39. Cope, *Politics*, 45; Greenhill quoted in Cope, *Politics*, 21–22.

Chapter Four

1. McGee, "William Laud," 320; Alexander, *Religion in England*, 148–149; Carl Bridenbaugh, *Vexed and Troubled Englishmen, 1590–1642* (New York, 1968), 438; Lambert, "Richard Montagu," 50; N. R. N. Tyacke, "Arminianism in England in Religion and Politics, 1604–1640" (D.Ph. thesis, Oxford, 1968), 134. For full biographical treatments of Laud see Hugh Trevor-Roper, *Archbishop Laud, 1573–1645* (London, 1940), and Charles Carlton, *Archbishop William Laud* (London, 1987).

2. K. Sharpe, "Archbishop Laud and the University of Oxford," in Hugh Lloyd-Jones, Valerie Pearl, and Blair Worden, eds., *History and Imagination* (London, 1981), 146; Hart, *Country Clergy*, 88, 107; John Phillips, *The Reformation of Images* (Berkeley, 1973), 162–163; McGee, "William Laud," 333; Poe, "Evangelistic Fervency," 63; Hart, *Country Clergy*, 88.

3. McGee, *Godly Man*, 7; Hart, *Country Clergy*, 108; Tyacke, *Anti-Calvinists*, 85.

4. Alexander, *Religion in England*, 152; Tyack, "Humbler Puritans," 82.

5. Richard Sibbes to Thomas Goodwin, quoted in John R. Knott Jr., *The Sword of the Spirit* (Chicago, 1980), 43; account of Williams by John Hacket quoted in Poe, "Evangelistic Fervency," 114; Kenneth Fincham, "Prelacy and Politics: Archbishop Abbot's Defence of Protestant Orthodoxy," *BIHR*, 61 (1988), 133–147. Fincham points out that Abbot's views on Puritanism were shaped in part by his identification of Catholicism as the great threat to English religion. S. M. Holland takes a different view of the archbishop in "George Abbot: 'The Wanted Archbishop,' "

CH, 56 (1987), 172–187, arguing that Abbot was equally opposed to Puritans and to Catholics. I find Fincham's view more convincing.

6. John Cotton to the bishop of Lincoln, 31 January 1624, *MHSP*, 43 (1909), 206; Kirby, "Radicals of St. Stephen's," 106; Wallace, *Puritans and Predestination*, 102. Expedients were used to accommodate not only clergy but radical laity. According to Stephen Offwood, some Suffolk clergy rang a bell when the Prayer Book service was ended so that those who wished to avoid those ceremonies could enter for the exposition of the word (Michael Moody, "Trials and Troubles of a Nonconformist Layman: The Spiritual Odyssey of Stephen Offwood, 1564–ca. 1635," *CH*, 51 [1982], 159).

7. Tyacke, *Anti-Calvinists*, 224; William Gouge to Bishop Laud, 19 October 1631, *CSPD, 1631–33*, 167; Tyack, "Humbler Puritans," 105; Cliffe, *Puritan Gentry*, 157; Foster, "Church Policies," 213–214. Foster is especially critical of Kevin Sharpe's view of Laud in "Archbishop Laud," 26–30. John Beadle in his *Journal and Diary of a Thankful Christian* (1656) recollected how under previous bishops most people had accepted baptism and the Lord's Supper if the sign of the cross was not used in the former and they were not required to receive the latter at a communion rail, but that this tolerance changed with Laud.

8. Tyacke, *Anti-Calvinists*, 108; Hart, *Country Clergy*, 86–87; Laud's articles described in McGee, "William Laud," 328–329; Laud's response to the Colchester delegation quoted in Tyack, "Humbler Puritans," 93–94.

9. *CSPD, 1636–37*, 545; Cope, *Politics Without Parliament*, 59–60; Tyack, "Humbler Puritans," 95; Keith Wrightson and David Levine, *Poverty and Piety in an English Village: Terling, 1525–1700* (New York, 1979), 159–160. See also David Underdown's study of the effort to reform Dorchester, *Fire from Heaven* (New Haven, Conn., 1992), especially chapters four and five.

10. *CSPD, 1629–31*, 421; *CSPD, 1636–37*, 518–519, 545; Smith, *Ecclesiastical History*, 53; Horton, "Two Bishops," 356; Anthony Fletcher, *The Outbreak of the English Civil War* (London, 1985 ed.), 94–95; Heylyn quoted in Tyack, "Humbler Puritans," 79–80.

11. Horton, "Two Bishops," 356; Ketton-Cremer, *Norfolk*, 124; Cope, *Politics*, 52; House report quoted in Tyack, "Humbler Puritans," 80; Ketton-Cremer, *Norfolk*, 76; Samuel Rogers mss. diary quoted in Kenneth Shipps, "Puritan Emigration," 90, 69. Clement Corbet was the uncle of Miles Corbet, who was a strong supporter of the Puritans. The chancellor was particularly vehement in his views of William Greenhill and Jeremiah Burroughes.

12. The policy of depriving clergy for nonconformity was not new (see *CSPD, 1603–10*, 175), but the enforcement became more rigorous in the 1620s and 1630s; T. W. W. Smart, "A Notice of Rev. John Allin, Vicar of Rye 1653–1662, an Ejected Minister," *Sussex Archaeological Collections*, XXXI (1881), 127; Paul, *An Apologetical Narration*, 97–98; Shipps, "Lay Patronage," 133; Margaret F. Stieg, *Laud's Laboratory* (Lewisburg, Penn., 1982), 291; Jeremiah Burroughes, *A Vindication of Mr Burroughes* (London, 1646), 21.

13. Charles B. Jewson, "Return of Conventicles in Norwich Diocese, 1669," *Norfolk Archaeology*, 33 (1962), 17; *CSPD, 1635*, 489; *CSPD, 1629–31*, 233; White, "Henry Jessey," 133.

14. Waterhouse, "Reluctant Emigrants," 483; Davids, *Nonconformity in Essex*, 148; *VCH Bedfordshire*, 337; *CSPD, 1634–35*, 205; *CSPD, 1635–37*, 47; Stieg, *Laud's Laboratory*, 295–296; Waterhouse, "Reluctant Emigrants," 483.

15. McGee, *Godly Man*, 83 n.22; Clarke, *Thirty-Two Divines*, 242; *CSPD, 1635*, 504–505. (It is interesting to note in light of Congregational practice that Samuel Ward was also accused of having "contended ministers should be elected by people.") Shipps, "Lay Patronage," 206; Waterhouse, "Reluctant Emigrants," 483; Hugh Peter, *A Dying Father's Last Legacy* (London, 1659), 77.

16. Nathaniel Ward to Sir Robert Harley, 6 August 1621 in *HMCR* 14, Pt. II, vol. III (London, 1894), 14; Hart, *Country Clergy*, 159; Waterhouse, "Reluctant Emigrants," 483; *CSPD, 1619–23*, 551; Laud quoted in Todd, *Christian Humanism*, 233 n.91; *CSPD, 1625–49*, 86.

17. Collinson, "Lectures by Combination," 205–209.

18. Ogbu Uke Kalu, "Bishops and Puritans in Early Jacobean England: A Perspective on Methodology," *CH*, 45 (1976), 480; Tai Liu, *Puritan London*, 74; Ann Hughes, "Thomas Dugard," 775, 776.

19. Poe, "Evangelistic Fervency," 122; Corbet quoted in Ketton-Cremer, *Norfolk*, 80; David R. Ehalt, "The Development of Early Congregational Theory of the Church, with Special Reference to the Five 'Dissenting Brethren' at the Westminster Assembly" (Ph.D. thesis, Claremont College, 1968), 78; Paul, *An Apologetical Narration*, 98; Clive Holmes, *Seventeenth-Century Lincolnshire*, History of Lincolnshire, vol. 7 (Lincoln, 1980), 118; Wallace, "Owen," 15; *CSPD, 1628–29*, 554; Charles Ray Palmer, *Rev. William Hooke: 1601–78* (New Haven, Conn., 1912), 4; Richard A. Hasler, "The Concept of the Ministry in Puritan New England, as Exemplified in the Life and Thought of Thomas Shepard" (Ph.D. thesis, Hartford Seminary Foundation, 1964), 18; Samuel Rawson Gardiner, ed., *Reports of Cases in the Courts of Star Chamber and High Commission* (Westminster, 1886), 260; Calder, ed., *Letters of John Davenport*, 3.

20. Williams, "London Puritanism," 466; Kirby, "Radicals of St. Stephen's," 5, 9; Shipps, "Lay Patronage," 56; Kirby, "Radicals of St. Stephen's," 100.

21. Cogswell, *Blessed Revolution*, 91–92; Collinson, *Religion of Protestants*, 168 n.92; John Davenport to Secretary Conway, 17 October 1624, *CSPD, 1623–25*, 356; John Davenport to Sir Edward Conway, October 1624, in Calder, *Letters of John Davenport*, 13; Secretary Conway to the Archbishop of Canterbury, 18 October 1624, *CSPD, 1623–25*, 357; *CSPD, 1623–25*, 354–355.

22. John Davenport to Alexander Leighton, [1625], in Calder, *Letters of John Davenport*, 23–25; *CSPD, 1625–26*, 338; Kirby, "Radicals of St. Stephen's," 110, 110–111, 113; Rose-Troup, *John White*, 248; Kirby, "Radicals of St. Stephen's," 15, 16.

23. Hood's charges quoted in David Zaret, *The Heavenly Contract* (Chicago, 1985), 142–143; *CSPD, 1629–31*, 483; John Davenport to William Laud, in Calder, *Letters of John Davenport*, 33–38.

24. John Davenport to Lady Mary Vere, 30 June 1628, in Calder, *Letters of John Davenport*, 29–32; Kirby, "Radicals of St. Stephen's," 107; Mather, *Magnalia*, I, 264; Stephen Goffe to Sir William Boswell, 7 June 1633, *MHSP*, vol. 42, 221.

25. *CSPD*, 1636–37, 545; Cope, *Politics*, 214; John Davenport to Sir William Boswell, 18 March 1634, in Calder, *Letters of John Davenport*, 41.

26. Many such exchanges of advice are discussed in chapter two. Hughes, "Thomas Dugard," 787; Heywood, *Life of Angier*, 56; John Cotton to Arthur Hildersham, [1629], *MHSP*, 43 (1909), 204; Jean Beranger, *Nathaniel Ward (ca. 1578–1652)*, Études et Reserches Anglaises et Anglo–Americaines Université de Bordeaux, I (Bordeaux, 1969), 56; *CSPD*, 1635, 377–378; *CSPD*, 1633–34, 52.

27. See Thomas Shepard's "Autobiography" in McGiffert, ed., *God's Plot*; Paul, *An Apologetical Narration*, 85. Other examples of clergymen being sheltered and continuing to preach after deprivation are to be found in chapter two. The clergy were not the only Puritans to suffer. In 1607 a number of Puritans were put off the Commission of the Peace (*CSPD*, 1603–10, 368). In 1605 Northamptonshire laymen who had petitioned on behalf of deprived clergymen were targets of the government, some being jailed (*CSPD*, 1603–10, 200). The nomination of Edward Wilson (John Wilson's brother) to be lecturer in medicine at Cambridge was opposed because he was "suspected of Puritanism" (*CSPD*, 1619–23, 613).

28. Ball, *Preston*, 150–151; Beranger, *Nathaniel Ward*, 51. For background on English Puritans in the Netherlands see Raymond P. Stearns, *Congregationalism in the Dutch Netherlands* (Chicago, 1940); Keith Sprunger, *Dutch Puritanism* (Leiden, 1982); and Sprunger, *William Ames*. Sprunger, *Dutch Puritanism*, 125–126; Foster, *Caroline Underground*, 49.

29. Denholm, "Thomas Hooker," 53.

30. Sprunger, *William Ames*, 16–22; *VCH Cambridgeshire*, III, 196; Sprunger, *William Ames*, 30–31, 62–70; Douglas Horton, introduction to William Ames, *The Marrow of Theology* (London, 1629), trans. and ed. John D. Eusden (Boston, 1968), 6; Yule, *Puritans in Politics*, 95; Tolmie, *Triumph of the Saints*, 217; Sprunger, *William Ames*, 254; Sprunger, *Dutch Puritanism*, 126–133; Samuel Eliot Morison, "The Education of Thomas Parker," *CSM*, XXIII (1932), 263.

31. Stearns, *Strenuous Puritan*, ch. 3; Bryan D. Spinks, *From the Lord and the 'Best Reformed Churches'* (Rome, 1984), 132–133; Schneider, "Godly Order," 337–349.

32. Alice Carter, *The English Reformed Church in Amsterdam in the Seventeenth Century* (Amsterdam, 1964), 74–76; Stearns, *Strenuous Puritan*, 55; Stearns, *Congregationalism in the Netherlands*, 54–55; Sheffield University, Hartlib Mss., 29/2/25A, for which reference I thank Mr. Tom Webster; Sprunger, *William Ames*, ch. 10; Sprunger, *Dutch Puritanism*, 164, 325; *CSPD*, 1635, 28–29; Stearns, *Strenuous Puritan*, 75–77.

33. See Williams, "Life of Thomas Hooker"; Sprunger, *Dutch Puritanism*, 102–107; Paget's categorization of the Dutch classis's decision is quoted in Stearns, *Congregationalism in the Netherlands*, 28; Carter, *English Reformed Church*, 76–78; *CSPD*, 1633–34, 30–31; Denholm, "Thomas Hooker," 55.

34. Stearns, *Congregationalism in the Netherlands*, ch. 4.

35. Stearns, *Congregationalism in the Netherlands*, ch. 4; Stearns, *Strenuous Puritan*, 84; Sprunger, *Dutch Puritanism*, 244–245, 297; *CSPD*, 1635, 151.

36. Roger Howell, *Puritans and Radicals in North England* (Lanham, Md.,

1984), 85; Moody, "Nonconformist," *CH*, 51 (1982), 166; Sprunger, *Dutch Puritanism*, 112–118; *CSPD, 1633–34*, 324, 449–450.

37. Moody, "Nonconformist," 167; Sprunger, *Dutch Puritanism*, 118–120, 163; Carter, *English Reformed Church*, 82.

38. Jewson, "Norfolk," 332–333; Sprunger, *Dutch Puritanism*, 167; Michael R. Watts, *The Dissenters* (Oxford, 1978), 64; Jewson, "Norfolk," 333–335; Shipps, "Lay Patronage," 293, 293 n.91; Sprunger, *Dutch Puritanism*, 168–169; Watts, *Dissenters*, 64.

39. Sprunger, *Dutch Puritanism*, 169–170; Paul, *An Apologetical Narration*, 105.

40. Baillie, *Dissuasive*, 80. A number of laymen who would later be prominent in the Puritan Revolution were members of the Arnhem congregation. See Watts, *Dissenters*, 64–65; Tolmie, *Triumph of Saints*, 87; Roger Williams, *The Complete Writings of Roger Williams*, 7 vols. (New York, 1963 reprint), II, 122 n.2; Sprunger, *Dutch Puritanism*, 227; Fienberg, "Thomas Goodwin," 92, 92 n.4; Tolmie, *Triumph of Saints*, 104; Pearl, *London*, 309–311; Tolmie, *Triumph of Saints*, 105, 44–45; Sprunger, *Dutch Puritanism*, 226; Rosemary Diane Bradley, " 'Jacob and Esau Struggling in the Wombe': A Study of Presbyterian and Independent Religious Conflicts, 1640–1648, with Particular Reference to the Westminster Assembly and the Pamphlet Literature" (D.Ph. thesis, University of Kent, 1975), 16.

41. Sprunger, *Dutch Puritanism*, 188, 190, 191, 193.

42. Baillie, *Dissuasive*, 75; Clarke, *Ten Divines*, 169; Sprunger, *Dutch Puritanism*, 165, 229; Patricia Caldwell, *The Puritan Conversion Narrative* (Cambridge, Eng., 1983), 94–95; *Memoirs of the Life of Ambrose Barnes*, quoted in Caldwell, *Conversion Narrative*, 72–73; Sprunger, *Dutch Puritanism*, 333.

43. *CSPD, 1633–34*, 413, 545; *CSPD, 1635–36*, 48; *CSPD, 1633–34*, 113; Williams, "Life of Thomas Hooker," 297–298; Allen French, *Charles I and the Puritan Upheaval* (Boston, 1955), 386; Thomas Hooker, preface to William Ames, *A Fresh Suit Against Human Ceremonies* (Amsterdam, 1633), in Williams et al., *Thomas Hooker*, 334; Williams, "Life of Thomas Hooker," 274; John Davenport to Lady Mary Vere, 18 January 1627, *MHSP*, 43 (1909), 209, 206; John Davenport to Lady Mary Vere, 30 June 1628, *MHSP*, 43 (1909), 210; Calder, *Letters of John Davenport*, passim; Sprunger, *Dutch Puritanism*, 149, 126–133, 172; Turnbull, *Hartlib, Dury and Comenius*, 135.

44. Sprunger, *Dutch Puritanism*, 307; Sir William Boswell to Sec. Coke, 20 September 1633, *CSPD, 1633–34*, 213. This was perhaps a treatise on Sabbath observance that Ames wrote in cooperation with Nathaniel Eaton (Keith Sprunger, "English and Dutch Sabbatarianism and the Development of Puritan Social Theology [1600–1660]," *CH*, 51 [1982], 33); Sprunger, *Dutch Puritanism*, 311.

45. Sprunger, *Dutch Puritanism*, 149; Ketton-Cremer, *Norfolk*, 80; Smith, *Ecclesiastical History*, 54; Boswell quoted in Sprunger, *Dutch Puritanism*, 287.

46. Bridenbaugh, *Vexed and Troubled Englishmen*, 436; Rose-Troup, *John White*, 254, 61; Cliffe, *Puritan Gentry*, 191; Shipps, "Lay Patronage," 173.

47. John Pomfret, *Founding the American Colonies, 1583–1660* (New York, 1970), 151; Bridenbaugh, *Vexed and Troubled Englishmen*, 437–438; Breslow, *Mirror*, 126.

48. J. H. Hexter, *The Reign of King Pym* (Cambridge, Mass., 1941), 77; Newton, *Colonizing Activities*, 125–127. Our understanding of the Providence Island settlement is greatly enhanced with the publication of Karen O. Kupperman, *Providence Island, 1630–1641: The Other Puritan Colony* (New York, 1993).

49. Newton, *Colonizing Activities*, 242ff., 119. Showing the continuity of some of these objectives, Anthony Rous, the son of Providence Island minister Arthur Rous, later served in Cromwell's Jamaican expedition.

50. Newton, *Colonizing Activities*, 83–84; Tolmie, *Triumph of Saints*, 44–45; Newton, *Colonizing Activities*, 177–178; Hexter, *Pym*, 79–80; William Greenhill, *An Exposition of . . . the Prophet Ezekiel* (1645), 18.

51. Pomfret, *Founding*, 154; Pearl, *London*, 165, 169; Calder, "St. Antholin's," 54; Thomas Hutchinson, *The History of the Colony and Province of Massachusetts Bay*, ed. Lawrence Shaw Mayo, 3 vols. (Cambridge, Mass., 1936), 15; Bridenbaugh, *Vexed and Troubled Englishmen*, 439; William Robbins, "The Massachusetts Bay Company: An Analysis of Motives," *Historian*, 32 (1969), 97–98; Mary Frear Keeler, *The Long Parliament, 1640–1641* (Philadelphia, 1954), 390; Hexter, *Pym*, 79; Zakai, "Exile and Kingdom," 63; Pearl, *London*, 164–165; Schiavo, "Dissenter Connection," 106 n.53. For a complete list of the members of the corporation see Nathaniel B. Shurtleff, ed., *Records of the Governor and Company of the Massachusetts Bay in New England*, 5 vols. (Boston, 1853–54).

52. *Winthrop Papers*, II, 177–179; Come, "Cotton," 158; Turnbull, *Gleanings from Hartlib's Papers*, 128–129; Governor Matthew Craddock to John Endecott, 16 February 1629, *MHSC*, ser. 2, VIII, 119; Rose-Troup, *John White*, 51; Morison, *Founding of Harvard*, 400; Come, "Cotton," 153; William B. Sprague, *Annals of the American Pulpit*, vol. 1 (New York, 1857), 7; Rose-Troup, *John White*, 142; David D. Hall, "John Cotton's Letter to Samuel Skelton," *WMQ*, 22 (1965), 478–485.

53. Pomfret, *Founding*, 160; Diarmaid McCullough, "Catholic and Puritan in Elizabethan Suffolk: A County Polarizes," *AFR*, 72 (1981), 263–264; *Winthrop Papers*, II, 152; Robbins, "Massachusetts Bay," 98; Pomfret, *Founding*, 161.

Chapter Five

1. John Cotton, *The Way of the Congregational Churches Cleared* (London, 1648), in Ziff, ed., *John Cotton on the Churches of New England*, 304–305; T. H. Breen and Stephen Foster, "Moving to the New World: The Character of Early Massachusetts Immigration," *WMQ*, XXV (1973), 199–205; Bridenbaugh, *Vexed and Troubled Englishmen*, 462–463; Tyack, "Humbler Puritans," 105–106; Shipps, "Puritan Emigration," 92–93; Breen and Foster, "Moving to the New World," 205; Shipps, "Puritan Emigration," 91 n.43. For a further discussion of historians' disagreements regarding the motivations for founding Massachusetts, see Francis J. Bremer, "The English Context of New England's Seventeenth-Century History," *NEQ*, LX (1987), 323–335, and David H. Fischer, "*Albion* and the Critics: Further Evidence and Reflection," *WMQ*, XLVIII (1991), 260–308.

2. John Winthrop to his wife, 15 May 1629, *Winthrop Papers*, II, 91; Hunt, "Spectral Origins," 325; Ralph Coffman and Mary Rhinelander, "The Testament of Richard Mather and William Thompson: A New Historical and Genealogical Document of the Great Migration," *NEHGR*, CXL (1986), 4; Robert Middlekauff,

The Mathers (New York, 1971), 22, 25–26; Christopher Hill, "God and the English Revolution," *The Collected Essays of Christopher Hill*, II (Brighton, Eng., 1986), 324; Bridenbaugh, *Vexed and Troubled Englishmen*, 438. See also "God Is Leaving England," chapter 12 of Christopher Hill's *The English Bible and the Seventeenth-Century Revolution* (London, 1993).

3. Thomas Shepard and John Allin, *A Defense of the Answer Made unto the Nine Questions* (London, 1646), 5; John Cotton, preface to Norton, *Answer*, 11, 10; John Norton, *Abel Being Dead Yet Speaketh* (London, 1658), 21; Cotton, preface to Norton's *Answer*, 11.

4. John Winthrop, "A Model of Christian Charity," *Winthrop Papers*, II, 282–294; Thomas Shepard and John Allin, *A Treatise of Liturgies* (London, 1652), 3–4; Edward Johnson, *Wonder-Working Providence of Sions Saviour in New England*, ed. J. Franklin Jameson (New York, 1959), 53; Cotton, preface to Norton's *Answer*, 11.

5. Thomas Welde, *An Answer to W.R.* (London, 1644), 27; John Brock, "The Autobiographical Memoranda of John Brock, 1636–1659," ed. Clifford Shipton, AASP, LIII (1943), 97; Shepard and Allin, *Liturgies*, 3–5.

6. Lord Say and Sele to John Winthrop, 9 July 1640, *Winthrop Papers*, IV, 264; Johnson, *Wonder-Working Providence*, 29, 49; William Wilkinson referring to Colchester, Essex, in the time of Elizabeth in John Strype, *Annals of the Reformation* (Oxford, 1824), II, pt. 2, 282, as quoted in Hunt, *The Puritan Moment*, 87; William Ames, preface to Paul Baynes, *The Diocesans Trial* (1621); Samuel Rogers's mss. diary quoted in Shipps, "Puritan Emigration," 92; Seaver, *Wallington's World*," 181; John Winthrop, "Arguments for the Plantation of New England," *Winthrop Papers*, II, 106ff. See also Francis J. Bremer, "To Live Exemplary Lives: Puritans and Puritan Communities as Lofty Lights," *The Seventeenth Century*, VII (1992).

7. William Twisse to Joseph Mede, as quoted in Corkran, "New England Colonists' English Image," 36; Sibbes, *The Bruised Reed*, 100; CSPD, *1634–35*, 361–362; Sheffield University, Hartlib Mss., 29/2/53B–54A.

8. Johnson, *Wonder-Working Providence*, 61; Roger Ludlow on behalf of the General Assembly of Connecticut to the Governor and Assistants of Massachusetts, 29 May 1638, *Winthrop Papers*, IV, 36. Timothy Sehr makes a valuable comment on this subject in his "Colony or Commonwealth: Massachusetts Bay, 1649–1660" (Ph.D. thesis, Indiana University, 1977), 2: "Although a chosen people can be a paradigm for the rest of mankind, they need not see themselves in that light. The ancient Israelites did not go into Canaan in order to show the Egyptians how they should reform their social, political, and religious arrangements. The Israelites went into the wilderness in conformity to God's wishes; they did not have a broad evangelical mission. Because the New England Puritans looked to Biblical precedent in establishing Massachusetts, there was a tension between their self-image as a chosen people and as an example for England and the rest of the world. By patterning themselves too closely after the Israelites they risked turning inward and being concerned with their own purity rather than with sending their message to the rest of mankind."

9. Johnson, *Wonder-Working Providence*, 22. For the importance of this goal of recovering the ordinances of the gospel in "their primitive purity," see Theodore Dwight Bozeman, *To Live Ancient Lives* (Chapel Hill, N.C., 1988), though I have

disagreed with Bozeman's dismissal of the Puritan sense of mission in Bremer, "English Context"; Horton, "Two Bishops," 340; *CSPD, 1634–35,* 361–362; Shipps, "Lay Patronage," 354 n.8; Shipps, "Puritan Emigration," 87; Nancy Matthews, *William Sheppard,* 17; Heywood, *Life of Angier,* 55–56, 8; [Whiston], *Mr. Henry Jessey,* 7–8; Sprunger, *William Ames,* 251; Young, "Good News," 32; Newton, *The Colonizing Activities,* 177–178; Matthews, *Calamy Revised,* 369; Tyack, "Humbler Puritans," 96.

10. Norton, *Abel Being Dead,* 19–20; Shepard quoted in Horton Davies, *The Worship of the American Puritans* (New York, 1990), 56; Davies, *American Puritans,* 13.

11. Scholz, "Reverend Elders," 4, 135; Harry Stout, *The New England Soul* (Oxford, 1986), 101; Schneider, "Godly Order," 358–359.

12. Scholz, "Reverend Elders," 7, 119; John Eliot quoted in Scholz, "Reverend Elders," 54; Stout, *New England Soul,* 102; Charles Hambrick-Stowe points out that "though ministerial associations [in 17th-century New England] were not without political significance, and though they contributed to the growth of professionalism, they were intended primarily for the devotional life of the clergy" (*The Practice of Piety* [Chapel Hill, N.C., 1982]).

13. "Modell of Church and Civil Power" printed in Scholz, "Reverend Elders," 61; Scholz, "Reverend Elders," 52–53, 1; Denholm, "Thomas Hooker," 125.

14. Scholz, "Reverend Elders," 140. John Winthrop recognized in his *Journal* (I, 112–113) the importance that clerical gatherings had for those who came together, while noting that there were a few clergy who feared that such sessions would grow into a presbyterian structure for the churches.

15. Wallace, *Puritans and Predestination,* 117. On the antinomian controversy and Cotton's role in it, see Sargent Bush Jr., " 'Revising What We Have Done Amisse': John Cotton and John Wheelwright, 1640," *WMQ,* XLV (1988), 733–750.

16. Turnbull, *Hartlib, Dury and Comenius,* 187–188; Ian K. Steele, "Communicating an English Revolution to the Colonies, 1688–1689," *JBS,* 24 (1985), 333. Contacts with the international reformed community were useful not only for religious reasons. John Luce, one of the elders of the Dutch congregation in London with which many of the Bay Colony leaders had contact, negotiated a deal whereby cattle and horses were shipped to the Bay Colony from Friesland; see Grell, *Dutch Calvinists,* 183–184 n.45.

17. Schneider, "Godly Order," 9. The dualism in most interpretations of Puritanism has been cogently critiqued by Michael Finlayson in "Independency in Old and New England, 1630–1660: An Historiographical and Historical Study" (Ph.D. thesis, University of Toronto, 1968); Stephen Brachlow, *The Communion of Saints* (Oxford, 1988), 268, 271–272.

18. Schneider, "Godly Order," 13; Brachlow, *Communion,* 11; Bradley, "Jacob and Esau," 6; Schneider, "Godly Order," 82.

19. Brachlow, *Communion,* 227–228, 210–211, 223.

20. There is another dimension to the maze of English religion that Peter Lake has alerted us to. There has been a tendency to identify Calvinism with Puritanism. Although it is probably fair to conclude that Puritans in this period were Calvinists, the reverse is not the case. With their emphasis on the importance of the

godly community, Puritans seemed to some to be inherently separatists. Thus, Robert Sanderson, a neighbor in John Cotton's Lincolnshire parish, believed the formation of a core of saints encouraged by Cotton "provoked a series of local disputes that split both the congregation and the town council into warring factions." From Sanderson's point of view Puritanism—even that of those who loudly asserted their conformity and their opposition to separatism—was intrinsically separatist in its effect. A determined Calvinist, Sanderson, and those like him, was also a dedicated anti-Puritan. See Peter Lake, "Serving God," 81–116; quote from p. 101; Schneider, "Godly Order," 416–418, 399, 376–377; Bernard quoted in Schneider, "Godly Order," 364.

21. Schneider, "Godly Order," 392–393; Fienberg, "Thomas Goodwin," 94.

22. Hall, "Cotton's Letter to Skelton," 478–485.

23. John Canup, *Out of the Wilderness* (Middletown, Conn., 1990), 20; "The Humble Request of His Majesty's Loyall Subjects, the Governour and the Company late gone for *New England*; to the rest of their Brethren in and of the *Church of* ENGLAND," 7 April 1630, *Winthrop Papers*, II, 231–233; E. Brooks Holifield, "Peace, Conflict, and Ritual in Puritan Congregations," *JIH*, XXIII (1993), 555; E. Brooks Holifield, *The Covenant Sealed: The Development of Puritan Sacramental Theology* (New Haven, Conn., 1974), esp. pp. 37–38.

24. Letter from John Dod, Simeon Ashe, John Ball, and others to John Cotton [late 1630s], in Cotton Papers, Boston Public Library; Emmanuel Downing to John Winthrop Jr., 13 March 1637/8, *Winthrop Papers*, IV, 20–21; Thomas Lechford, *Notebook Kept by Thomas Lechford, Lawyer, Transactions and Collections of the American Antiquarian Society*, VII (1885), 2; Schneider, "Godly Order," 220, 234–236; Karen Ordahl Kupperman, "Definitions of Liberty on the Eve of Civil War: Lord Say and Sele, Lord Brooke, and the American Puritan Colonies," *HJ*, 32 (1989), 24 n.20; John Goodwin to Thomas Goodwin, 25 October 1639, in Thomas Goodwin, *The Works of Thomas Goodwin* (London, 1697), IV, 36; Caldwell, *Puritan Conversion*, 81.

25. Letter of John Cotton to a Puritan minister in England, 1634, in Alexander Young, *Chronicles of the First Planters* (Boston, 1846), 438–444; Sprunger, *Dutch Puritanism*, 126–133; Sprague, *American Pulpit*, vol. 1, 77; Foster, "Godly in Transit," 202; Newton, *Colonizing Activities*, 64–65; B. Richard Burg, *Richard Mather of Dorchester* (Lexington, Ky., 1976), 15; Young, "Good News," 84–85; Sprunger, *William Ames*, 236; Nathaniel Ward to William Sandcroft, [1634], in Emmanuel College Archives, Col. 9.10. When a number of Puritan peers had papers seized by the government in May 1640, Lord Brooke was found to have had in his possession manuscript copies of the exchange between Ball and Cotton (*CSPC 1574–1660*, 312).

26. Perry Miller, *The New England Mind: From Colony to Province* (Cambridge, Mass., 1953), 6; Seaver, *Wallington's World*, 68, 95; John Winthrop and John Wilson to "Our Reverend and Right Worthy Friend Mr. Dr. Stoughton," *MHSP*, ser. 1, V (1860, 1862), 128; Shipps, "Puritan Emigration," 86; Heywood, *Diary of Angier*, 101.

27. Baillie, *Dissuasive*, 55–56, 54; Young, "Good News," 30–31; Thomas Edwards, *Antapologia: Or, A Full Answer to the Apologetical Narration* (London, 1644), 38.

28. Stout, *New England Soul*, 62; Henry Jacie to John Winthrop Jr., [1631], *MHSP*, ser. 1, V, 18; Samuel Rogers manuscript diary quoted in Shipps, "Puritan Emigration," 88; White, "Henry Jessey," 133; Burg, *Richard Mather*, 173 n.33; Jeremiah Burroughes to John Cotton, 1 November [1632], with Cotton's response on back, in Davis Papers, Massachusetts Historical Society.

29. John Cotton, *A Reply to Mr Williams* in Williams, *Complete Writings*, II, 39; Thomas Shepard, *Certain Select Cases Resolved Specially* (London, 1648); Hasler, "Concept of the Ministry," 93–94; *A Letter of Many Ministers in Olde England Concerning Nine Positions* (London, 1637); John Davenport, *An Answer to the Elders of the Severall Churches in New England unto Nine Positions Sent Over to Them* (London, 1643), which circulated earlier in manuscript; John Ball, *A Trial of the New Church Way in New England and Old* (London, 1640); Shepard and Allin, *Defense of the Answer*.

30. Watts, *Dissenters*, 64; Burg, *Richard Mather*, 53.

31. Shipps, "Puritan Migration," 86, 91, including quote from Samuel Rogers's manuscript diary.

32. William Hooke, *New Englands Sence of Old Englands and Irelands Sorrowes* (London, 1645), reprinted in Emery, *Taunton*, I, 116; Lewis Bayly, *The Practice of Piety* (London, 1631), as quoted in David D. Hall, *Worlds of Wonder, Days of Judgment* (New York, 1989); William Gouge, *The Saints Sacrifice* (London, 1632), 284. For a discussion of fast days in New England see W. De Loss Love Jr., *The Fast and Thanksgiving Days of New England* (Boston, 1895), and Richard Gildrie, "The Ceremonial Puritan: Days of Humiliation and Thanksgiving," *NEHGR*, CXXXVI (1982), 3–16.

33. Winthrop, *Journal*, I, 82, 92; Love, *Fast and Thanksgiving Days*, 51; Winthrop, *Journal*, I, 208; Miller, *From Colony to Province*, 6–7; Love, *Fast and Thanksgiving Days*, 112.

34. Winthrop, *Journal*, I, 208; Love, *Fast and Thanksgiving Days*, 112.

35. Winthrop, *Journal*, I, 99, 101; Winthrop, *Journal*, I, 135, 137. For the debate over the use of the red cross in the royal ensign, see Francis J. Bremer, "Endecott and the Red Cross: Puritan Iconoclasm in the New World," *JAS*, 24 (1990), 5–22.

36. Winthrop, *Journal*, I, 145; Laud quoted in Tyack, "Humbler Puritans," 86; Winthrop, *Journal*, I, 271, 272, 274–275.

37. Winthrop, *Journal*, I, 269, 271–272.

Chapter Six

1. The events leading up to the civil wars and the early stages of the conflict can be followed in the most detail in Samuel Rawson Gardiner, *The History of the Great Civil War*, 4 vols. (London, 1893). Among the best modern narratives are Fletcher, *Outbreak*, and Conrad Russell, *The Fall of the British Monarchies 1637–1642* (Oxford, 1991). Sharpe's *The Personal Rule of Charles I* is a detailed and strongly argued defense of the monarch. Russell earlier discussed the perspective that informs his new study in "The British Problem and the English Civil War," *History*, 72 (1987), 395–415. For the ideological elements in the revolt see Glenn Burgess, *The Politics of the Ancient Constitution* (University Park, Penn., 1993), and Johann Som-

merville's *Politics and Ideology in England 1603–1640* (London, 1986), and "Ideology, Property and the Constitution," in Richard Cust and Ann Hughes, eds., *Conflict in Early Stuart England* (London, 1989). Conrad Russell gives significant attention to the religious factors in *The Causes of the English Civil War* (Oxford, 1990).

2. Cope, *Politics*, 46. Anti-Catholic feelings are examined skillfully in Caroline M. Hibbard, *Charles I and the Popish Plot* (Chapel Hill, N.C., 1983); Trevor-Roper, *Catholics, Anglicans and Puritans*, 68; Wallace, *Puritans and Predestination*, 109.

3. John Leith, *Assembly at Westminster* (Richmond, Va., 1973), 23; McNeil, *Unitive Protestantism*, 283; Samuel Rawson Gardiner, ed., *The Constitutional Documents of the Puritan Revolution, 1625–1660* (Oxford, 1962), xxvii.

4. Tyacke, *Anti-Calvinists*, 236. George Yule, *Puritans in Politics*, 103, indicates that "the elections for the Short Parliament have been analyzed and in thirty-three constituencies reasons for opposition to the government were expressed. Of the total of fifty such reasons twenty were for religion, fifteen for ship money and only fifteen for other causes." Fletcher, *Outbreak*, xxiv; Yule, *Puritans in Politics*, 106; Christopher Hill, *The Century of Revolution, 1603–1714* (New York, 1967 ed.), 13; Schneider, "Godly Order," 422–423.

5. "The Grand Remonstrance" in Gardiner, *Constitutional Documents*.

6. John Harrison Jr. to John Winthrop, 11 August 1639, *Winthrop Papers*, IV, 138; John Harrison to John Winthrop, 18 February 1640, *Winthrop Papers*, IV, 195; Matthew Craddock to John Winthrop, 27 February 1640, *Winthrop Papers*, IV, 207; Nathaniel Bourne to John Winthrop, 4 March 1640, *Winthrop Papers*, IV, 214; Benjamin Gostlin to John Winthrop, 6 March 1640, *Winthrop Papers*, IV, 216–217; Sir Nathaniel Barnardiston to John Winthrop, 15 March 1640, *Winthrop Papers*, IV, 218; Lawrence Wright to John Winthrop, 26 March 1640, *Winthrop Papers*, IV, 220; John Venn to John Winthrop, April 1640, *Winthrop Papers*, IV, 221; John Tinker to John Winthrop, 13 April 1640, *Winthrop Papers*, IV, 224–225; Brampton Gurdon to John Winthrop, 13 May 1640, *Winthrop Papers*, IV, 243–244; Edward Payne to John Winthrop, 28 May 1640, *Winthrop Papers*, IV, 248; Isaac Lovell to John Winthrop, 11 May 1640, *Winthrop Papers*, IV, 239.

7. Hugh Peter to John Winthrop, September 1640, *Winthrop Papers*, IV, 289; Roger Williams to John Winthrop, 7 August 1640, *Winthrop Papers*, IV, 273; William Bradford to John Winthrop, 16 August 1640, *Winthrop Papers*, IV, 275; Love, *Fast and Thanksgiving Days*, 147.

8. Hooke, *New Englands Teares*, repr. in Emery, *Taunton*, 85, 86, 87, 89–90, 94, 91–92. Hooke's sermon has often been interpreted as a turning away from England by historians who fail to establish it in the context of what New Englanders knew about events in England in July of 1640; Love, *Fast and Thanksgiving Days*, 149, 152; Edward Winslow to John Winthrop, 7 July 1640, *Winthrop Papers*, IV, 262.

9. Among the members of the House of Commons in the Long Parliament who were members of the Massachusetts Bay Company were Matthew Craddock, Sir Nathaniel Barnardiston, Sir William Brereton, Henry Darley, William Spurstowe, John Venn, and Samuel Vassall (Keeler, *Long Parliament*, passim); other members of the Parliament who were closely tied to New England included Thomas Barrington, Dennis Bond, John Browne, Sir John Clotworthy, Miles Corbet, Sir Walter Earle,

Nathaniel Fiennes, Sir Gilbert Gerard, Richard Long, William Rainsborough, and William Strode (Keeler, *Long Parliament,* passim). Deane Tyndal to John Winthrop, 7 April 1641, *Winthrop Papers,* IV, 329; Lucy Downing to John Winthrop Jr., 28 January 1641, *Winthrop Papers,* IV, 311; Henry Dunster to his son Henry Dunster, 20 March 1641, *MHSC,* 4th ser., vol. 2, 191–194; Joseph Davyes to Henry Dunster, 20 May 1641, *MHSP,* 2d ser., vol. 10, 306; Robert Child to John Winthrop Jr., May 1641, *Winthrop Papers,* IV, 334.

10. Robert Paul, ed. and intro., Thomas Goodwin et al., *An Apologetical Narration,* 91; Matthews, *Calamy Revised,* 178. Eaton's activities in Chesire are discussed by John Morrill in *Chesire: 1630–1660* (Oxford, 1974). Samuel Butler, a critic of the Puritans, complained of the accord given the new returnees: "If he had seen Amsterdam, or had been an adventurer to New England . . . he was a jewell," in "Letter from Mercurius Civicus to Murcurius Rusticus," 1643, in Walter Scott, ed., *A Collection of Scarce and Valuable Tracts . . . Particularly That of the Late Lord Somers* (London, 1810), 582.

11. William Lamont, *Godly Rule* (London, 1969), 112–113; Wilson, *Pulpit in Parliament,* 210; Yule, *Puritans in Politics,* 173; Hill, *Collected Essays,* II, 272–274; Noel Henning Mayfield, *Puritans and Regicide* (Lanham, Md., 1988), 55–59 (though there is much that I would disagree with in Mayfield's study); Hill, *Collected Essays,* II, 274. David Walker identifies Congregational views on the millennium as contributing to the different views of the church held by Thomas Goodwin and the other Congregationalists on one hand and the Presbyterians on the other; see Walker, "Thomas Goodwin and the Debate on Church Government," *JEH,* 34 (1983), 85–99. An important, related theme is explored by Blair Worden in "Providence and Politics in Cromwellian England," *PP,* CIX (1985), 55–59. See also K. R. Firth, *The Apocalyptic Tradition in Reformation Britain 1530–1645* (Oxford, 1979).

12. Fienberg, "Thomas Goodwin," 88; Wilson, *Pulpit in Parliament,* 227; Michael R. Watts, *The Dissenters* (Oxford, 1978) 131; Mayfield, *Regicide,* 63; Hill, *Antichrist,* 15; Wilson, *Pulpit in Parliament,* 212; B. W. Ball, *A Great Expectation: Eschatalogical Thought in English Protestantism to 1660* (Leiden, 1975), 164–165, 103; Tai Liu, *Discord in Zion* (The Hague, 1973), 5; Walker, "Thomas Goodwin," 93; Mayfield, *Regicide,* 55–59; Tai Liu, *Discord in Zion,* 5; Peter Toon, *God's Statesman* (Grand Rapids, Mich., 1971), 30. Others who expressed millennial ideas in the early stages of the revolution included Henry Burton, Nathaniel Holmes, Nicholas Lockyer, and Henry Jessey (Tolmie, *Triumph of Saints,* 87). John Eusden has pointed out, however, that before 1640 many Independents differed on the justification of resistance; see John D. Eusden, *Puritans, Lawyers and Politics in Early Seventeenth-Century England* (New Haven, Conn., 1958), 15.

13. Mayfield, *Regicide,* 65–66; Schiavo, "Dissenter Connection," 110 n.77; Ball, *Expectation,* 87, 228; Robert Keayne's notes of Cotton sermon, 19 January 1640, transcript in Alpert, "Robert Keayne," 78.

14. Davenport's sermons on Canticles were prepared by him for the press but never published, according to Increase Mather to Anthony Wood, c. 1690–1691, *MHSC,* 2d ser., VIII, 345; Zakai, "Exile and Kingdom," 140, which is substantially different from his published study of the same title; Corkran, "New

England Colonists' English Image," 61; Davenport, *Letter of Many Ministers*, n.p.; John Eliot, *The Christian Commonwealth* (London, 1660), printed in *MHSC*, 3d ser., vol. 9; Nathaniel Rogers, *A Letter Discovering the Cause of God's Continuing Wrath Against the Nation* (1644), 2, 6; Richard Mather and William Thompson, *A Modest and Brotherly Answer to Mr Charles Herle* (London, 1644), 58; Hill, *Antichrist*, 112; *Records of the First Church of Dorchester*, 160, quoted in Sehr, "Colony or Commonwealth," 27 n.32.

15. John Cotton, *Powring Out of the Seven Vials* (1642; London, 1645), 155; Stout, *New England Soul*, 49.

16. Kirby, "Radicals of St. Stephen's," 117; Tai Liu, *Puritan London*, 82. "The Attack on the Church of England in the Long Parliament, 1640–1642" has been analyzed by John Morrill in D. Beales and G. Best, eds., *History, Society and the Church* (Cambridge, Eng., 1985), 105–124.

17. George Yule, *The Independents in the English Civil War* (Cambridge, Eng., 1958), 42; Schiavo, "Dissenter Connection," 160 n.29; William Haller, *Liberty and Reformation in the Puritan Revolution, 1638–1647* (New York, 1934), 109; "Solemn League and Covenant," in Gardiner, *Constitutional Documents*, 267–270; Bradley, "Jacob and Esau," 97.

18. Alice McCampbell, "Incumbents and Patronage in London, 1640–1660," *Journal of Church and State*, 25 (1983), 301, 303; Fletcher, *Outbreak*, ch. 3.

19. Todd, "Puritan Dons," 599; J. T. Cliffe, *Puritans in Conflict* (London, 1988), 46–47.

20. "Grand Remonstrance," in Gardiner, *Historical Documents*, 229; Leith, *Assembly*, 24; W. K. Jordan, *The Development of Religious Toleration in England. III: From the Convocation of the Long Parliament to the Restoration, 1640–1660* (Cambridge, Mass., 1938), 40–41; Robert Paul, *The Assembly of the Lord* (Edinburgh, 1985), 70–71.

21. Alexander Mitchell and John Struthers, eds., *Minutes of the Sessions of the Westminster Assembly of Divines* (Edinburgh, 1874), xxviii; William Bourne to Sir Robert Harley, 19 February 1643, *HMCR* 14, *Pt. II*, vol. III (London, 1894), 164; Jordan, *Toleration*, III, 43–44; Watts, *Dissenters*, 93; William Shaw, *A History of the English Church During the Civil War and under the Commonwealth, 1640–1660* (New York, 1970 repr.), 145; Finlayson, "Independency," 267; Bradley, "Jacob and Esau," 72.

22. A full study of Puritanism would include discussion of the Presbyterian as well as the Congregationalist connection. Carol Geary Schneider has offered some excellent insights into that side of the movement in "Godly Order." She discusses some of the activities of the Presbyterian friends on pages 220–236. Those familiar with Margaret Ruth Sommerville, "Independent Thought, 1603–1649" (D.Ph. thesis, Cambridge University, 1981), will notice in the chapters to follow that there are some elements of her argument with which I am in agreement. But Sommerville, though recognizing a New England influence, fails to examine much of the colonial writing of the period as well as that emanating from the Netherlands exiles, and misses the specific affiliation between the New Englanders and the Thomas Goodwin group. Further, I feel that in treating religious Independents as a homogeneous group (and

allowing John Goodwin to speak for them) and in assuming that Independent religious views and Independent political views were held by many of the same men, she misses distinctions that I will argue are vital to make sense not only of the 1640s but of the 1650s.

23. This agreement is mentioned in Thomas Edwards, *Reasons Against Independent Government* (1641), 25; Thomas Edwards, *Antapologia*, 238; and John Vicars, *The Schismatick Sifted* (1646), 15; see also Fienberg, "Thomas Goodwin," 95, and Tai Liu, *Discord in Zion*, 9; Schneider, "Godly Order," 466–467. Schneider makes a strong case that the Aldermanbury Accord also included some who in 1640–1641 were supporters of a reformed episcopacy, though not necessarily believing it *jure divino* ("Godly Order," 444–449). Activities of the Congregationalists in London are discussed in Alan Argent, "The Independents in the Parishes of the City of London in the 1640s," *Congregational History Circle*, 2 (1991–92), 3–24.

24. Leith, *Assembly*, 25–26; Jordan, *Toleration*, III, 43–44; Paul, *Assembly*, 78.

25. Robert Baillie, *The Letters and Journals of Robert Baillie*, 3 vols. (Edinburgh, 1841), II, 107; Haller, *Liberty and Reformation*, 103; Leith, *Assembly*, 45; Paul, *Asssembly*, 116.

26. Baillie, *Letters and Journals*, I, 311; II, 117.

27. John Winthrop, *Journal*, ed. James Kendall Hosmer (New York, 1946), II, 71–72; copy of letter inviting Cotton, Hooker, and Davenport in Thomas Hutchinson, ed., *A Collection of Original Papers Relative to the History of the Colony of Massachusetts Bay* (Boston, 1769), 100–101; Winthrop, *Journal*, II, 72, 32; John Haynes to John Winthrop, 1 December 1643, *Winthrop Papers*, IV, 418; Bush, *Thomas Hooker*, 97. It has been suggested that Cotton's *True Constitution* was sent along with his declination to serve (Hanbury, *Memorials*, II, 155). Stephen Foster discussed the group that issued the invitation and their position in the Parliament in "The Presbyterian Independents Exorcized: A Ghost Story for Historians," *PP*, 44 (1969), 52–75, and "A Rejoinder," *PP*, 47 (1970).

28. Yule, *Puritans in Politics*, 267; Robert Paul, "Worship and Discipline: Context of Independent Church Order in the Westminster Assembly," in John E. Booty, ed., *The Divine Drama in History and Liturgy* (Allison Park, Penn., 1984), 150; Paul, *Assembly*, 114–115. See also Lawrence Kaplan, "Presbyterians and Independents in 1643," *EHR*, LXXXIV (1969), 244–256. Stephen Foster first pointed out to me the use of colonial authors by the Dissenting Brethren and the Scots as debating surrogates for the English groups during this period.

29. Carter quoted in Bradley, "Jacob and Esau," 56; Bridge quoted in Paul, *Assembly*, 155–156; Bradley, "Jacob and Esau," 107.

30. Bryan D. Spinks, *Freedom or Order* (Allison Park, Penn., 1984), 32, 38; Paul, *Assembly*, 363; Spinks, *Freedom*, 40–41; Paul, *Assembly*, 363.

31. Paul, *Assembly*, 322, 160–162; Baillie, *Letters and Journals*, II, 110; Paul, *Assembly*, 166, 199–200.

32. Fienberg, "Thomas Goodwin," 119–120; Paul, *Assembly*, 190–191, 192.

33. Paul, *Assembly*, 214–215; Ehalt, "Early Congregational Theory," 97–98.

34. Nye quoted in Paul, *Assembly,* 403; Baillie, *Letters and Journals,* II, 123. At this time Baillie also wrote, "We doubt not to carrie all in the Assemblie and Parliament clearlie according to our mind; but if we carrie not the Independents with us, there will be ground laid for a verie troublesome schisme. Always it's our care to use our outmost endeavor to prevent that" (*Letters and Journals,* II, 122); Paul, *Assembly,* 456.

35. Lightfoot's *Journal,* quoted in Paul, *Assembly,* 257; Ehalt, "Early Congregational Theory," 101; Paul, "Worship," 151–152.

36. Gillespie and Lightfoot quoted in Paul, *Assembly,* 259–260.

37. Paul, "Worship," 150–151; Paul, *Assembly,* 304.

38. Baillie to Buchan, 1644, in Baillie, *Letters and Journals,* II, 252.

39. Fienberg, "Thomas Goodwin," 121; Paul, *Assembly,* 229, 124–125; Robert Baillie to William Spang, 18 February 1644, in Baillie, *Letters and Journals,* II, 129–130; Perry Miller, *Orthodoxy in Massachusetts, 1630–1650* (Cambridge, Mass., 1933), 266–267.

40. Thomas Goodwin et al., *An Apologetical Narration,* 28; Fienberg, "Thomas Goodwin," 126; Haller, *Liberty and Reformation,* 116–117; Jordan, *Toleration,* III, 369; William Haller, ed., *Tracts on Liberty in the Puritan Revolution, 1638–1647* (New York, 1934), I, 49; Goodwin et al., *An Apologetical Narration,* 5.

41. Robert Baillie to William Spang, 10 August 1644, in Baillie, *Letters and Journals,* II, 218; Robert Baillie, "Letter to Scotland," 1 January 1644, in Baillie, *Letters and Journals,* I, 411; Joseph Caryl, *The Arraignment of Unbelief* (London, 1645), 47; Joseph Caryl, *England Plus Ultra* (London, 1646), 24–25; Jeremiah Burroughes, *A Sermon Preached Before the . . . House of Peers* (London, 1645), 45; Thomas Goodwin, *The Great Interest of States and Kingdomes* (London, 1645), 53; Burroughes, *Vindication,* 23.

42. Robert Baillie to the earl of Eglinton, 8 July 1645, in Baillie, *Letters and Journals,* II, 299; Yule, *Puritans in Politics,* 216; *Letter of the Ministers* quoted in Paul, *Assembly,* 490; Vicars, *Schismatick Sifted,* 15–17; Edwards, *Antapologia,* 220.

43. Yule, *Puritans in Politics,* 134; William Walwyn, *The Compassionate Samaritane* (London, 1644), 1–3, quoted in Avihu Zakai, "Religious Toleration and Its Enemies: The Independent Divines and the Issue of Toleration During the English Civil War," *Albion,* 21 (1989), 18.

44. Blair Worden, "Toleration and the Cromwellian Protectorate," in *Studies in Church History,* XXI (1984), 200; Yule, *Puritans in Politics,* 211; Schiavo, "Dissenter Connection," 95; Robert Baillie to D. Dickson, 23 July 1644, in Baillie, *Letters and Journals,* II, 211.

45. Paul, *Assembly,* 445ff.; Ehalt, "Early Congregational Theory," 102–104. It should be noted that the position on synods that the Congregationalists were willing to accept was fundamentally that which was espoused in New England, used there in the treatment of the antinomian controversy, and later incorporated in the Cambridge *Platform.*

46. Paul, *Assembly,* 249–429; Bradley, "Jacob and Esau," 23.

47. Eales, *Puritans and Roundheads,* 117–118; Winthrop, *Journal,* II, 183; Sehr, "Colony or Commonwealth," 14.

48. Rogers, *God's Continuing Wrath*, 1; Hooke, *New Englands Sence*, 109; Rogers, *God's Continuing Wrath*, 1; Bradley, "Jacob and Esau," 102–103; Rogers, *God's Continuing Wrath*, 8; Hooke, *New Englands Sence*, 115–116.

49. Benjamin Gostlin to John Winthrop, 8 May 1640, *Winthrop Papers*, IV, 238; John Venn to John Winthrop, April 1640, *Winthrop Papers*, IV, 221; John and Mary Trappe to Mary Willis, 16 May 1644, *Connecticut Historical Society Collections*, XXI, 62; Samuel Whiting, *Abraham's Humble Intercession for Sodom* (1666), 14.

50. Thomas Cobbett, *A Practical Discourse of Prayer* (London, n.d.), "To the Reader"; Hooke, *New Englands Sence*, 116–117.

51. Ezekiel Rogers to Elkena Wales, 4 December 1646, *EIHC*, 53 (1917), 223. A full discussion of the colonists' fasts can be found in Love, *Fast and Thanksgiving Days*; Winthrop, *Journal*, II, 42, 57, 67, 81; for the fast days see also Gildrie, "The Ceremonial Puritan," 3–16; John Fiske, *The Notebook of the Reverend John Fiske, 1644–1675*, edited with an introduction by Robert G. Pope (Boston, 1974), 15; Winthrop, *Journal*, II, 223–224; Stout, *New England Soul*, 51–52; *Connecticut Colonial Records*, I, 99; Love, *Fast and Thanksgiving Days*, 153; George Cleeve to John Winthrop, 27 January 1644, *Winthrop Papers*, IV, 434.

52. Winthrop, *Journal*, II, 31; John Endecott to John Winthrop, February 1641, *Winthrop Papers*, IV, 314–315; Winthrop, *Journal*, II, 24–25; see also Edmund S. Morgan, *The Puritan Dilemma: The Story of John Winthrop* (Boston, 1958), 178–179; Miller, *Orthodoxy in Massachusetts*, 276; Stearns, *Strenuous Puritan*, 148–149.

53. Winthrop, *Journal*, II, 25; Stearns, *Strenuous Puritan*, 153. The most complete discussion of the work of the agents is to be found in Raymond Phineas Stearns, "The Welde-Peter Mission to England," *CSM*, 32 (1937), 188–246; for Hartlib see G. H. Turnbull, *Hartlib, Dury and Comenius*.

54. Stearns, "Welde-Peter Mission," 218–219, 234.

55. Henry Burton, *The Grand Imposter Unmasked* (London, 1645), n.p.

56. John Cotton, *Way Cleared*, 22; Hooke, *New Englands Sence*, 113; Thomas Shepard, *The Day-Breaking, If Not the Sun-Rising of the Gospell with the Indians in New England* (London, 1647), "Epistle to the Reader"; Thomas Shepard and John Allin, *Liturgies*, 9; John Cotton quoted in Gura, *Glimpse*, 218.

57. Roger Williams, *The Bloudy Tenent of Persecution* (London, 1644), quoted in Zakai, "Exile and Kingdom," 522; Hugh Peter, preface to John Davenport, *Church Government and Church Covenant Discussed* (London, 1643).

58. Winthrop, *Journal*, I, 279; Welde, *An Answer to W.R.*, preface; Richard Mather, "A Plea for the Churches of Christ in New England," mss. in MHS; Richard Mather to "Dear brother," c. 1644, MHS, Mather Papers, Box 1 folder 11.

59. The issue of prayer was further aired by Thomas Cobbett in his *Practical Discourse of Prayer*. For a fuller discussion of this subject and of the colonial views, see Francis J. Bremer and Barbara Bremer, "Thomas Cobbet's *Practical Discourse of Prayer*," *EIHC*, 111 (1975), 138–150.

60. Edwards, *Antapologia*, 242; Isaac Backus, *A History of New England with Particular Reference to the Baptists* (New York, 1969 repr.), 150; Young, "Good News," 60; Thomas Shepard, prefatory letter to William Greenhill in *The Sound Believer* (1645; London, 1649).

61. Morgan, *Puritan Dilemma*, 179–180; William L. Sachse, "The Migration of New Englanders to England, 1640–1660," *AHR*, 53 (1948), 259; Stout, *New England Soul*, 50–51; Sachse, "New Englanders to England," 261; Samuel Eliot Morison, *Harvard in the Seventeenth Century* (Boston, 1936), 27.

62. Winthrop, *Journal*, I, 295 n.1; Sachse, "New Englanders to England," 256, 267; Hutchinson, *Massachusetts Bay*, I, 76. By focusing on the disenchanted and on those whom the colonists were glad to be rid of, Andrew Delbanco fails to recognize the larger picture in *The Puritan Ordeal* (Cambridge, Mass., 1989) and "The Puritan Errand Re-Viewed," *JAS*, 18 (1984), 343–360. I have critiqued his perspective in Bremer, "English Context," 323–335.

63. James Savage, *A Genealogical Dictionary of the First Settlers of New England*, 4 vols. (Boston, 1860), III, 411; John Browne, *History of Congregationalism in Norfolk and Suffolk* (London, 1877), 103–104; Matthews, *Calamy Revised*, 512; Fletcher, *County Community*, 112; John Sibley and Clifford Shipton, *Biographical Sketches of Those Who Attended Harvard College* (1873–), I, 93–100, 68–72; Young, "Good News," 109; Barton, *Parish of Terling*, 136; Bruce E. Steiner, "Dissension at Quinnipiac: The Authorship and Setting of *A Discourse About Civil Government in a New Plantation Whose Design is Religion*," *NEQ*, LIV (1981), 14–32. For New Englanders who served in Parliament and the army see William L. Sachse, *The Colonial American in Britain* (Madison, 1956), 142.

Chapter Seven

1. The political and military developments of the 1640s can be traced in the most detail in Samuel Rawson Gardiner's *History of the Great Civil War*.

2. The accommodation order is quoted in Jordan, *Toleration*, III, 55–56; Haller, *Liberty and Reformation*, 143; Benjamin Hanbury, *Historical Memorials Relating to the Independents, or Congregationalists*, 3 vols. (London, 1841), II, 447; Yule, *Puritans in Politics*, 140–141; Jordan, *Toleration*, III, 56–57; Yule, *Puritans in Politics*, 141. In focusing on the trans-Atlantic and national levels of the debate over the reshaping of England's religion I have neglected for reasons of space to explore in any detail the dynamics of the struggle between Congregational clergy and local parishioners. Valuable insight into local resistance to change can be found in John Morrill, *The Nature of the English Revolution* (London, 1993), esp. pp. 163–173, and in John Morrill, *The Revolt of the Provinces* (rev. ed., London, 1980).

3. Paul, *Assembly*, 232 n.47; Browne, *Congregational Church*, 10; Bradley, "Jacob and Esau," 85; Yule, *Puritans in Politics*, 141; Paul, *Assembly*, 453–456; John Morrill, "The Church in England, 1642–49," in John Morrill, ed., *Reactions to the English Civil War, 1642–1649* (New York, 1983), 93; Ehalt, "Early Congregational Theory," 108; Jordan, *Toleration*, III, 59–60; Paul, *Assembly*, 473; Thomas Goodwin et al., *A Copy of a Remonstrance Lately Delivered in to the Assembly* (London, 1645), 4; Paul, *Assembly*, 473.

4. Baillie, *Letters and Journals*, II, 266, 267; Paul, *Assembly*, 487.

5. Paul, *Assembly*, 481; Goodwin et al., *Remonstrance*, 4, 7, 8; *Grand Debate*, n.p.

6. Paul, *Assembly*, 487 ff.; Robert Baillie, Public Letter of 25 November

1645, in Baillie, *Letters and Journals*, II, 326; Robert Baillie to Robert Ramsay, 15 January 1646, in Baillie, *Letters and Journals*, II, 341.

7. Bush, *Thomas Hooker*, 100; Shuffleton, *Hooker*, 272–273. Richard Burg believes that a pair of catechisms prepared by Richard Mather were also designed to influence the Westminster Assembly; see Burg, *Richard Mather*, 61; Yule, *Independents*, 35–41; Tai Liu, *Puritan London*, 83.

8. John Bastwick, *Independency not God's Ordinance* (London, 1645), *The Second Part of That Book Call'd Independency not God's Ordinance* (London, 1645), and *The Utter Routing of the Whole Army of all the Independents and Sectaries* (London, 1646). For a discussion of Bastwick's views see Jordan, *Toleration*, III, 279–281. Vicars, *Schismatick Sifted*, 17, 5; Yule, *Puritans in Politics*, 215.

9. Edwards, *Gangraena*, 13. It is suggestive that some of the harshest criticism of the Dissenting Brethren came from Presbyterians who had known Goodwin, Nye, and their allies in the pre–civil war decades and who had perhaps at one time been tempted toward Congregational views. Edwards gives evidence in his writings of earlier meetings and discussions with the Congregationalist leaders, and Vicars had been brought before the High Commission in 1631 for gathering part of his church into a conventicle; see Foster, *Caroline Underground*, 80 n.9. For Adam Steuart's views and writings, see Jordan, *Toleration*, III, 277; Baillie quoted in Paul, *Assembly*, 441.

10. Kaplan, "Presbyterians and Independents," 251; Edwards, *Antapologia*, 11–12, 224; D. P. P., *An Antidote to the Contagious Air of Independency* (London, 1644), 21; Baillie, *Dissuasive*, 90; Baillie, *Letters and Journals*, II, 253.

11. Robert Baillie, *Errours and Induration, Are the Great Sins and the Great Judgements of the Time* (London, 1645), "To the Reader."

12. Gura, *Glimpse*, 219; Ziff, *John Cotton*, 201–202.

13. Stearns, "Welde-Peter Mission," 223 n.15; Thomas Hooker to Thomas Shepard, quoted in John Gorham Palfrey, *History of New England* (Boston, 1858), II, 173 n.1. There is another aspect of the reaction to Winthrop's *Short Story* that is worth noting. Puritanism was a faith that contained many inner tensions, one being between the pulls of an Arminian emphasis on behavior and an antinomian insistence on the possession of the saint by divine grace. The Hutchinsonian crisis had threatened to divide New England Puritanism along that fault line, but the balance was maintained—if precariously at first—when John Cotton cut himself off from his radical disciple and remained with the orthodox party. In England Cotton's friends and the Congregationalists in general tended to lean more toward the antinomian pole, whereas Presbyterianism would increasingly be characterized (especially after 1660) by Arminian leanings. These tendencies were not clearly visible in the 1640s, but the leanings of the Dissenting Brethren and the way in which Cotton and his views were presented in the *Short Story* may have contributed to the unease with which Englishmen greeted the publication.

14. John Wheelwright, *Mercurius Americanus* (London, 1645), in *John Wheelwright: His Writings*, ed. Charles H. Bell (Boston, 1876), 197; Edwards, *Antapologia*, 294; Gura, *Glimpse*, 303, 282. Another critique of the New England Way by someone who had been there was Thomas Lechford's *New Englands Advice to Old*

England (London, 1644). For a discussion of Wheelwright's tract, see Gura, *Glimpse*, 269–270. For further insight into Wheelwright's efforts to rehabilitate his reputation and to have his banishment lifted, see Sargent Bush Jr., "Revising What We Have Done Amisse," 733–750, and Sargent Bush Jr., "John Wheelwright's Forgotten *Apology:* The Last Word in the Antinomian Controversy," *NEQ*, LXIV (1991), 27–45. An important story that parallels the one this study addresses is the existence and functioning of a Presbyterian connection in the seventeenth-century Anglo-American Puritan community. Some of the problems this caused in New England are touched upon in James F. Cooper, " 'A Mixed Form': The Establishment of Church Government in Massachusetts Bay, 1629–1645," *EIHC*, 123 (1987), 254–257.

15. W. K. Jordan reports that in conducting his research, "thirty-four orthodox titles which attacked the growth of sectarianism were examined in the McAlpin Collection (Union Theological Seminary, New York, NY) for the three years, 1641–1643. Of these, twenty-nine do not dissociate between Congregationalism and the more radical and eccentric sects which were appearing in this period. The principles of Independency were held responsible for the spiritual chaos" (Jordan, *Toleration*, 355 n.1). Edwards, *Gangraena*, I, 53; III, 126.

16. Watts, *Dissenters*, 103; Robert Baillie to D. Dickson, 23 July 1644, in Baillie, *Letters and Journals*, II, 211–212; Jordan, *Toleration*, 318–319.

17. Conrad Wright, "John Cotton Washed and Made White," in F. Forester Church and Timothy George, eds., *Continuity and Discontinuity in Church History* (Leiden, 1979), 338–350; John Cotton, *Master John Cottons Answer to Master Roger Williams* (London, 1647) in Roger Williams, *The Complete Writings of Roger Williams*, 7 vols. (repr. New York, 1963), III, 89.

18. *An Attestation to the Testimony of Our Reverend Brethren of the Province of London* (London, 1648), n.p.; see Querry X in Roger Williams, *Querries of Highest Consideration, Proposed to the Five Holland Ministers and the Scottish Commissioners* (London, 1644), in Williams, *Works*, II; Williams, *Bloudy Tenent*, in *Works*, II; Williams, *Bloudy Tenent Yet More Bloudy*, in *Works*, IV, 524–525.

19. For Gorton and Clarke see Gura, *Glimpse*, 117–118 and 204–206.

20. Ephraim Pagitt, *Heresiography* (1645; 5th ed., London, 1654), 79–80, as quoted in Gura, *Glimpse*, 189; George Fenwick to John Winthrop, 17 March 1647, *Winthrop Papers*, V, 142; Sir Henry Vane quoted in Roger Williams, *Works*, IV, 53 n.1.

21. Welde, *Answer to W.R.*, 12–13; Thomas Shepard, *New Englands Lamentation for Old Englands Present Errours* (London, 1645), 4; see also Thomas Werge, *Thomas Shepard* (Boston, 1987), 71; John Davenport, *The Knowledge of Christ* (London, 1653), "To the Reader"; Welde, *Answer to W.R.*, 67; Timothy Sehr, "Colony or Commonwealth," 46–47.

22. Thomas Hooker, *A Survey of the Summe of Church Discipline* (London, 1648), Pt. 2, ch. 3; Cotton, *Way Cleared*, 186–187.

23. Thomas Shepard to Hugh Peter, 1645, *AHR*, IV, 105–106.

24. Gura, *Glimpse*, 199–200; Shepard, *Lamentation*, 5–6.

25. Cotton, *Way Cleared*, 68; Hooker, *Survey of the Summe*, preface; see also Denholm, "Hooker," 157; Winthrop, *Journal*, II, 257; Samuel Stone to Thomas

Shepard, 19 July 1647, in Sprague, *American Pulpit*, 35; Thomas Shepard, *Theses Sabaticae* (London, 1649), "To the Reader."

26. Schiavo, "The Dissenting Connection," 98; *Memoir of Thomas Goodwin*, xxix–xxx; Thomas Goodwin and Philip Nye, preface to Cotton, *Keyes of the Kingdom* (Ziff ed.), 77; Thomas Goodwin, preface to Hooker, *Survey of the Summe*; Thomas Goodwin, Philip Nye, and Sydrach Simpson, preface to Norton, *Answer*, 8; Nathaniel Holmes, preface to Cotton, *Way Cleared*, 167, 168. Among the many other examples, Joseph Caryl provided an imprimatur for Shepard's *Certain Select Cases* and for the manuscript of Richard Mather's long survey of New England church practices, which was never published. William Greenhill prefaced Shepard's *Sincere Convert* by giving thanks that "in these evil and perillous times, God hath not left us without some choice mercies." For further information see Geoffrey F. Nuttall, *Visible Saints: The Congregational Way, 1640–1660* (Oxford, 1957), 14–15, and Young, "'Good News,'" 35.

27. William Greenhill, preface to Thomas Allen, *A Chain of Scripture Chronology* (London, 1659); *Memoirs of John Owen*, 52; Hasler, "Concept of the Ministry," 224–225.

28. Paul, *Assembly*, 244; Robert Baillie to William Spang, 7 December 1643, in Baillie, *Letters and Journals*, II, 115; Schneider, "Godly Order," 349; Apollonius's letter in Norton, *Answer*, 19. Another tactic employed by Baillie in May of 1645 was to spread the rumor that the parliamentary leaders sympathetic to the Dissenting Brethren were secretly engaged in negotiations with the king; see Yule, *Puritans in Politics*, 142–143.

29. John Cotton, preface to Norton, *Answer*, 14; Goodwin, Nye, and Simpson, preface to Norton, *Answer*, 8. The effort to enlist Dutch support for the Presbyterians was countered when the English Congregationalists persuaded Gisbert Voet, a Dutch theologian at Utrecht, to write a prefatory endorsement of John Cotton's *Keyes of the Kingdom*. Robert Baillie expressed his anger at that development in a letter to William Spang (1 November 1644, in Baillie, *Letters and Journals*, II, 240).

30. Welde, *Answer to W.R.*, 11; Shepard and Allin, *Liturgies*, 1. The call for the synod is included in Williston Walker, ed., *The Creeds and Platforms of Congregationalism* (Boston, 1960), 168–170.

31. The story of the Cambridge Assembly is told in Walker, *Creeds and Platforms*, 157–188, and the text is in the same work, 194–237; Walker, "Thomas Goodwin," 87.

32. Stanley Fienberg, for instance, in his study "Thomas Goodwin" says, "The term Independent is used in this study synonymously with Congregational, as the two are today" (81 n.1). Jordan (*Toleration*, 451) and Kaplan ("Presbyterians and Independents," 253) show some awareness of the dangers of this lumping. In some cases the contemporary lumping of Congregationalists with other Independents was a reflection of honest confusion. In other cases it was a political ploy. Thomas Edwards, who in the mid-1640s was one of the most outspoken of those who tried to discredit the Congregationalists by this means, in his earlier *Reasons against the Independent Government* did distinguish between those we would label Congregationalists and those, whom he considered worse, that he referred to as Separatists.

33. Ehalt, "Early Congregational Theory," 268; Paul, *Assembly,* 124; Jordan, *Toleration,* 58. Tai Liu has argued that a distinction such as I am making between the Congregationalists and others who gathered churches in the 1640s is not clear. He believed that the position of most Puritan groups was "undefined, complex, and changing." My reading of the sources convinces me that within Independency there were gathered churches expressing views that the Dissenting Brethren would never have been comfortable tolerating, whereas those that were Congregational were identifiable by their theology, structure, and the social ties that bound their leaders (see Tai Liu, *Puritan London,* 104). Samuel C. Pearson, "The Reluctant Radicals: The Independents in the Westminster Assembly," *Journal of Church and State,* XI (1969), 485; Goodwin et al., *An Apologetical Narration,* 23–24; Hugh Peter, introduction to Davenport, *Answer of the Elders* (London, 1643); Sydrach Simpson, *The Anatomist Anatomized* (1644), whose full title refers to "the cause that is falsely called 'Independency.'" The full title of the anonymous *Reply to A.S.* refers to the position of the Apologists as known "by the nickname 'Independency'; by themselves, 'Congregational.'"

34. Jeremiah Burroughes, *Vindication,* 23–24; Paul, *Assembly,* 178; Thomas Hill, *The Trade of Truth Advanced* (London, 1642), 27–28; Burroughes, *Sermon Before Peers,* epistle; Caryl, *England Plus Ultra,* 22.

35. Peter, *Gods Doing,* prefatory letter; Simpson, *Anatomist Anatomized,* 10; Nuttall, *Visible Saints,* 126–127; Bradley, "Jacob and Esau," 83; Ehalt, "Early Congregational Theory," 165; Jeremiah Burroughes, *Irenicum to the Lovers of Truth and Peace* (London, 1646), 29; Nuttall, *Visible Saints,* 126–127.

36. Yule, *Independents,* 15; Goodwin et al., *An Apologetical Narration,* 19.

37. John Owen, *Of Schism: The True Nature of It* (London, 1657), 274; Walker quoted in *Memoir of John Owen,* 27; Cotton Mather, *Magnalia,* I, 524; John Owen, *A Vision of Unchangeable Free Mercy . . . Whereunto is Annexed, A Country Essay for the Practice of Church Government* (London, 1646), 74; John Owen, *Two Questions Concerning the Power of the Supreme Magistrate* (London, 1659), 388.

38. Owen, *Free Mercy,* 68; Owen, *Zion,* 541; Owen, *A Country Essay for the Practice of Church Government* (London, 1646), lix, lx; Owen, *Free Mercy,* 69–70.

39. Fienberg, "Thomas Goodwin," 107 n.1; Robert Baillie to William Spang, [1644], in Baillie, *Letters and Journals,* II, 181; J. W. Biggs, *John Goodwin* (London, 1961), 5, 14; Jordan, *Toleration,* III, 376; Haller, *Liberty and Reformation,* 127–128; John Vicars, *Coleman Street Conclave Visited* (London, 1648), 2; Wallace, "Owen," 167; Wallace, *Puritans and Predestination,* 151; Walwyn, *Compassionate Samaritane,* 1–2; Jordan, *Toleration,* III, 348; Haller, *Liberty and Reformation,* 118–119; Haller, *Tracts on Liberty,* I, 50; Yule, *Independents,* 45–46; Biggs, *John Goodwin,* 15.

40. William Bridge, *The Loyal Convert* (London, 1644), 6.

41. Young, "Good News," 152; Thomas Goodwin to John Goodwin, c. February 1640, in Thomas Goodwin, *Works* (1697), IV; Owen C. Watkins, *The Puritan Experience: Studies in Spiritual Autobiography* (New York, 1972), 30; Howell, *Puritans and Radicals,* 97; Surtees Society, *Evidences Illustrative of the History of Religion in Newcastle and Gateshead Between the Reformation and the Revolution* (1866),

378; Baxter quoted in Paul, *Assembly,* 154 n.81; Thomas Brooks, *Cases Considered* (London, 1653), passim; see also Caldwell, *Conversion Narrative,* 76, and Anthony Fletcher, "Oliver Cromwell and the Godly Nation," in John Morrill, ed., *Oliver Cromwell and the English Revolution* (London, 1990), 231; Stephen Ford, *Epistle to the Church* (London, 1657). See also Alan P. F. Sell, "Confessing the Faith in English Congregationalism," *Journal of the United Reformed Church History Society,* 4 (1988), 170–215, in which he discusses Ford as well as covenants employed in a variety of churches.

    42. Joseph Caryl, *The Nature, Solemnity, Grounds, Property and Benefits of a Sacred Covenant* (London, 1643), 5; Tolmie, *Triumph of Saints,* 118: Ehalt, "Early Congregational Theory," 170; Young, "Good News," 126; Stepney Church Covenant in A. T. Jones, *Notes on the Early Days of Stepney Meeting* (London, 1887), 4; the Yarmouth covenant is in *Chronicles of Great Yarmouth,* 13–14. The contrast between the brief Stepney covenant and the lengthier Yarmouth document (not all of which is quoted) was typical of New England as well as English practice. Young, "Good News," 104–105 and 127, discusses the Wrentham, Bury St. Edmunds, Woodbridge, and Beccles churches as also having New England–style covenants; Owen set forth his views in *Eschol: or, Rules of Direction for the Walking of the Saints in Fellowship* (London, 1647).

    43. Ehalt, "Early Congregational Theory," 151–153; Cliffe, *Conflict,* 99. Ralph Josselin recorded a discussion at a clerical conference in which John Owen argued for the right of the covenanted members to choose their elders (*Diary,* 48). The appointment of Thomas Goodwin as a preacher by the vestry of All Hallows, Lombard Street, is recorded in Tai Liu, *Puritan London,* 112; Sydrach Simpson defended the Congregational view of ordination in *AIATIBH,* 7; Nuttall, *Visible Saints,* 94. At the ordination of Thomas Taylor over seven neighboring East Anglian Congregational churches were represented by their clergymen or by messengers (M. H. Grieve and W. Marshall Jones, *These Three Hundred Years: Being the Story of Congregational Work and Witness in Bury St. Edmunds, 1646–1946* [London, 1946], 25). *Chronicles of Great Yarmouth,* 13–14, relates the story: In November of 1642 the organization of the congregation was begun by a group of about a dozen and the decision was made to locate the congregation in Yarmouth. In June of 1643 William Bridge and ten others took the covenant and then others were admitted. In September the congregation selected Bridge as pastor and then went on to choose other officers.

    44. Young, "Good News," 175; Wallace, "Owen," 143; Ehalt, "Early Congregational Theory," 212; Michael Finlayson, "Independency," 293. Another widespread New England practice that gained some currency in England in the late 1640s was the use of numbers to replace the names of the days and months in the calendar; see David Cressy, *Bonfires and Bells,* 46; Young, "Good News," 164, 166.

    45. Ehalt, "Early Congregational Theory," 143; Wallace, "Owen," 145–146; Wallace, *Puritanism and Predestination,* 109; Josselin, *Diary,* 81. For other examples from Josselin's *Diary* see pp. 42, 57, 61, 98, 163, 174; Young, "Good News," 92, 105–106; Gordon Rupp, *Religion in England 1688–1791* (Oxford, 1986), 120.

    46. Young, "Good News," 120–121 n.1; Josselin, *Diary,* 146; Shepard, *Theses Sabaticae,* preface; Henry Dunster to friends in Lancashire, 1651, Dunster Notebook in MHS; Come, "Cotton," 522.

47. Jordan, *Toleration*, III, 123–124; Edward Bernstein, *Cromwell and Communism* (New York, 1963), 80; tract quoted in Watts, *Dissenters*, 125.

Chapter Eight

1. John Cotton, prefatory poem to Samuel Stone, *A Congregational Church is a Catholic Visible Church* (London, 1652).

2. Mayfield, *Regicide*, 100–101; Jeremiah Burroughes quoted in Mayfield, *Regicide*, 59 n.29; the "Dissenting Ministers Vindication of Themselves from Murder of Charles I," in Scott, *Somers Tracts*. Another prominent Presbyterian, Stephen Marshall, did not take a public position on the regicide at this time and is thought to have opposed it, though he had earlier justified resistance against the king in *A Copy of a Letter Written by Mr Stephen Marshall* (London, 1643). John Canne was one of the most outspoken defenders of the regicide in *The Golden Rule* (London, 1649). It should, of course, be noted that while millennialism was characteristic of the Congregationalists, expressions of similar views could be found among other religious groups as well.

3. Clifford K. Shipton, ed., "The Autobiographical Memoranda of John Brock, 1636–1659," *AASP*, LIII (1944), 101; Roger Williams to John Winthrop Jr., 26 May 1649, *Winthrop Papers*, V, 348; Roger Williams to John Winthrop Jr., [1650], *MHSC*, 4th ser., VI, 285; John Hull, *Memoir and Diaries of John Hull, Transactions and Collections of the American Antiquarian Society*, III (1857), 172; Henry Dunster to friends in Lancashire, in Dunster Notebook, mss. in MHS. Paul Seaver has explained that letters such as this from colonists helped English Puritans to accept the developments in England (Seaver, *Wallington's World*, 101). For the text of John Cotton's sermon and an analysis of it, see Francis J. Bremer, "In Defence of Regicide: John Cotton on the Execution of Charles I," *WMQ*, 37 (1980), 103–124. Some authors have argued that New Englanders were very upset with and critical of the execution of the king; among them, Steven Crow, " 'Left at Libertie': The Effects of the English Civil War and Interregnum on the American Colonies, 1640–1660" (Ph.D. thesis, University of Wisconsin, 1974) and Sehr, "Colony or Commonwealth." I believe that though some individuals clearly did express dismay, the reaction of most who left evidence of their views—especially of the clerical leaders of the region—was supportive of the regicide. In fact, an interesting point was made by Samuel Mather, who, according to Stone, *Congregational Church*, in "To the Reader," believed that Pride's Purge and the contemporaneous events were divine vindications of New England's polity and example.

4. For discussion of Cromwell's rule see the essays in Morrill, *Cromwell*; for the major generals see Anthony Fletcher, "The Religious Motivation of Cromwell's Major-Generals," *Studies in Church History*, XV (1978). For a discussion of the foreign policy of the regime, see G. M. D. Howat, *Stuart and Cromwellian Foreign Policy* (London, 1974).

5. Correspondence across the Atlantic between lay and religious leaders continued in this period much along the lines discussed in earlier chapters. A good sampling is to be found in the manuscript collection of the Winthrop Papers, some of which material will be published in forthcoming volumes of the *Winthrop Papers*. Additional correspondence can be sampled in published collections such as Isabel M.

Calder, ed., *Letters of John Davenport,* and the *Mather Papers, MHSC,* 4th ser., VIII (1868). Massachusetts General Court instructions to Captain John Leverett, 29 November 1655, in Hutchinson, *Papers,* 273; John Cotton to Oliver Cromwell, 28 July 1651, in Hutchinson, *Papers,* 233. John Cotton's surviving correspondence, some of which is in the Cotton Papers in the Boston Public Library, will soon be published by Sargent Bush Jr. Another manuscript collection with substantial trans-Atlantic correspondence is the Wyllys Papers at the Connecticut Historical Society. *The Correspondence of Roger Williams* has copious references to letters received from English correspondents. Other evidence of such correspondence though the letters themselves no longer exist is to be found in *The Diary of Ralph Josselin, 1616–1683,* ed. Alan Macfarlane (London, 1976), and *Memoir and Diaries of John Hull.* Paul Seaver points to the importance of these trans-Atlantic exchanges of public and personal news in *Wallington's World,* especially p. 30, and David Cressy makes a similar point in *Coming Over: Migration and Communication between England and New England in the Seventeenth Century* ([Cambridge, Eng., 1987], 145) when he discusses English newssheets sent to the colonists. This brief review is only a sample of the many pieces of correspondence to be found in print and manuscript collections, many of which are cited throughout this study. Relations between the colonies and the Puritan regime in England were generally positive. In 1642 the House of Commons removed tariffs on trade between England and New England. The following May the Massachusetts General Court dropped the oath of allegiance to the king and a year later made it illegal to solicit support for the king. During the following decade special favor continued to be shown to New England by Parliament. Some of these issues can be followed in John Winthrop, *Journal: History of New England,* ed. James Kendall Hosmer (New York, 1946), II, passim; Ziff, *John Cotton,* 178; Charles J. Hoadley, ed., *Records of the Colony and Plantation of New Haven from 1638 to 1649* (Hartford, Conn., 1857), 136–137; J. Hammond Turnbull, ed., *The Public Records of the Colony of Connecticut* (Hartford, Conn., 1850), I, 163. Acceptance of parliamentary authority extended to decisions that were unpalatable, such as when the Massachusetts authorities recognized a parliamentary safe conduct given to one of the Gortonists in 1646 (Winthrop, *Journal,* II, 283–284). When the Bay Colony magistrates discovered a letter from an English correspondent who was critical of Parliament, they forwarded it to Parliament (copy of a letter from Nathaniel Briscoe to Thomas Broughton and the letter transmitting it to Secretary Lenthall are in *MHSC,* 3d ser., I, 33–36).

      6. John Eliot, *Tears of Repentance* (1653), dedicatory letter; Thomas Cobbett, *The Civil Magistrates Power* (London, 1653), "To the Reader"; John Norton, *A Discussion of the Great Point in Divinity the Sufferings of Christ* (London, 1653); see also Peter Bulkeley, Samuel Whiting, John Knowles, Thomas Cobbett, Danyel Denyson, and John Tuttell to Oliver Cromwell, 31 December 1650, *MHSC,* 4th ser., II, 115–118.

      7. Alison Gilbert Olson, *Anglo-American Politics, 1660–1775* (Oxford, 1973), 32–33; Robert Paul, *The Lord Protector, Religion and Politics in the Life of Oliver Cromwell* (London, 1955), 53; Peter Bulkeley, Samuel Whiting, Thomas Cobbett, and others to Oliver Cromwell, 31 December 1650, *MHSC,* 4th ser., II, 115–116.

      8. John Cotton to Oliver Cromwell, 28 July 1651, in Hutchinson, *Papers,*

233–234; Oliver Cromwell to John Cotton, 2 October 1651, in Hutchinson, *Papers,* 236–237; Roger Williams to John Winthrop Jr., 15 December 1654, *MHSC,* 4th ser., VI, 291.

9. John Cotton to Oliver Cromwell, 28 July 1651, Hutchinson, *Papers,* 235; John Haynes to John Winthrop Jr., *MHSC,* 4th ser., VII, 458; John Leverett to John Endecott, 20 December 1656, in Hutchinson, *Massachusetts Bay,* I, 163n; Mr. Wheelwright's letter to the church at Hampton, 20 April 1658, in Hutchinson, *Masssachusetts Bay,* I, 165n; William Hooke to John Winthrop Jr., 13 April 1657, *MHSC,* 3d ser., I, 182; Cromwell quoted in Derek Hirst, "The Lord Protector, 1653–1658," in Morrill, *Oliver Cromwell,* 123.

10. Sehr, "Colony or Commonwealth," 197, 58–59. There were a number of attempts in the 1640s and 1650s to persuade New Englanders to leave their homes and resettle elsewhere; Schiavo, "The Dissenter Connection," 92–93. A full discussion of the dispatch of Scottish prisoners and Cromwell's role is to be found in Charles Edward Banks, "Scotch Prisoners Deported to New England by Cromwell, 1651–1652," *MHSP,* 61 (1927–28). Petition of William Franklin of Boston, merchant, to Oliver Cromwell, *CSPC 1574–1600,* 46, and also in *MHSP,* VIII, 118. For further discussion of Cromwell's relations with the colonists, and especially the expedition to aid them against New Netherland, see Francis J. Bremer, *Puritan Crisis* (Westport, Conn., 1990), and Francis J. Bremer, "The New Haven Colony and Oliver Cromwell," *Bulletin of the Connecticut Historical Society,* 38 (1973).

11. Address to his Highness, Oliver Cromwell, from J. Endecott and R. Bellingham, November 1655, in Hutchinson, *Papers,* 274; see also Letter from the General Court of Massachusetts to Oliver Cromwell, 1651, in Hutchinson, *Massachusetts Bay,* I, 431; Hull, *Diaries,* 186–187; Alfred E. Young, "English Plebeian Culture and Eighteenth-Century American Radicalism," in Margaret Jacob and James Jacob, eds., *The Origins of Anglo–American Radicalism* (London, 1984), 197.

12. James Holstun in *A Rational Millennium* (Oxford, 1987) points out that Eliot's *Christian Commonwealth,* though not printed until the Restoration, was a response to a 1650 work by Edward McGee during the Engagement Controversy (p. 148). Ralph Josselin made reference to Eliot's views in a diary entry in March of 1651, indicating that the treatise may have been circulating in manuscript among Eliot's friends in England (*Diary of Ralph Josselin,* 238). Mather's *Heart-Melting Exhortation* also circulated in manuscript before its eventual publication (Burg, *Richard Mather,* 62). Johnson, *Wonder-Working Providence,* 144–145. One area of public affairs in which some Englishmen espoused imitation of New England was on the subject of law reform. This subject is explored in Matthews, *William Sheppard,* esp. pp. 146, 172–174; Hill, *God's Englishman,* 140; and Woolrych, *Commonwealth to Protectorate,* 271–273, 300. New England letters to England and English interest in colonial affairs are discussed in Seaver, *Wallington's World,* 104; Ian K. Steele, *The English Atlantic* (Oxford, 1986), 61; and Amos and Emily Jewett, *Rowley, Massachusetts, "Mr Ezechi Rogers Plantation"* (Rowley, Mass., 1946), 34–35.

13. Virginia Anderson, *New England's Generation* (New York, 1991), 122 n.69; William Hooke, *New Englands Teares,* in Emery, *Taunton,* 96; Nathaniel Mather to John Rogers, 23 March 1651, *MHSC,* 4th ser., VIII, 4. Views which downplay the

importance of return migration include Delbanco, *Puritan Ordeal* and Cressy, *Coming Over*. But see the hundreds of documented cases in Susan Mary Hardman, "Return Migration from New England to England, 1640–1660" (D.Ph. thesis, University of Kent, 1986).

14. Gura, *Glimpse*, 223; Sachse, *Colonial American in Britain*, 90; Winthrop, *Journal*, I, 95 n.1; Yule, *Independents*, 147; Young, "Good News," 93; Edwards, *Gangraena*, I, 49; Howell, *Puritans and Radicals*, 102; Matthews, *Calamy Revised*, 517; Young, "Good News," 112; Matthews, *Calamy Revised*, 367; Sprague, *American Pulpit*, I, 101; Yule, *Independents*, 137; Davids, *Nonconformity in Essex*, 451; Heard, *John Wheelwright*, 106; Sprague, *American Pulpit*, 10; John Morrill, *Chesire*, 53; Palmer, *William Hooke*, 11; A. G. Matthews, "A Censured Letter. William Hooke in England to John Davenport in New England, 1663," *CHST*, 9 (1924–26), 264. Members of the network continued to return to England from the Netherlands as well: Joseph Symonds left Rotterdam in 1647 and became rector of St. Mary Abchurch in London, and Robert Park returned to become a Congregational lecturer in Lancashire in 1649 (Sprunger, *Dutch Puritanism*, 174). Again it should be remembered that a small number of New Englanders supported the Presbyterian position and were in communication with English Presbyterian leaders; see Philip J. Anderson, "Presbyterianism and the Gathered Churches in Old and New England 1640–1662: The Struggle for Church Government in Theory and Practice" (D.Ph. thesis, Oxford University, 1979).

15. Davids, *Nonconformity in Essex*, 549–551; Geoffrey F. Nuttall, "Congregational Commonwealth Incumbents," *CHST*, XIV (1940–1944), 164–165; Yule, *Independents*, 144; Browne, *Congregationalism in Norfolk and Suffolk*; Young, "Good News," 39.

16. Sachse, *Colonial American in Britain*, 90; Young, "Good News," 102; *Works of John Owen*, I, 109; Nuttall, *Visible Saints*, 32. Some scholars, most recently Andrew Delbanco in *The Puritan Ordeal*, have depicted the colonists who went back to England as men who believed New England had failed, and the reaction of those who stayed toward their departed brethren as bitterness at being betrayed and abandoned. Whereas the departure of so many colonists—and especially of educated leaders—did raise some concerns, most of the evidence shows that members of the clerical network who stayed in the colonies did support the decision of those who went back. I have raised questions about Delbanco's interpretation in "The English Context," 323–335. In 1645 Thomas Shepard wrote to his friend Hugh Peter, "I have ever thought that it was a divine hand that sent you from us for a time, and therefore till your work be done in England I would not have you returne to New, tho' I am one of many who earnestly long to see you once agayne" (Thomas Shepard to Hugh Peter, 1645, *AHR*, IV [1898], 105). Similarly, John Eliot wrote to Peter that "I cannot wish you in N.E. so long as you are of such great use and service in old, not because I love you not, but because I love both you, and the cause of God, which you *totis viribus* pursue, & prosper in" (John Eliot to Hugh Peter, 12 October 1649, *EIHC*, LXXII [1936], 309–310).

17. Sprague, *American Pulpit*, 131; Hutchinson, *Massachusetts Bay*, I, 97; Sibley and Shipton, *Biographical Sketches*, I, 68–72, 194–195; Matthews, *Calamy*

Revised, 466; Sibley and Shipton, *Biographical Sketches*, I, 298–299, 359–360; Matthews, *Calamy Revised*, 9; Sibley and Shipton, *Biographical Sketches*, I, 352–353; Davids, *Nonconformity in Essex*, 363–364.

18. Sachse, "New Englanders to England," 258; Palmer, *William Hooke*, 10; Barton, *Parish of Terling*, 136; William L. Sachse, "Harvard Men in England, 1642–1714," *CSM* (1951), 126; Hutchinson, *Massachusetts Bay*, I, 97; Sprague, *American Pulpit*, 53.

19. Sibley and Shipton, *Biographical Sketches*, I, 163; Yule, *Independents*, 136; Sachse, "New Englanders to England," 203; Hutchinson, *Massachusetts Bay*, I, 97; Sachse, *Colonial American in Britain*, 90; Sachse, "New Englanders to England," 263; Hutchinson, *Massachusetts Bay*, I, 97.

20. Sprunger, *William Ames*, 253; Yule, *Independents*, 147; Hutchinson, *Massachusetts Bay*, I, 97; Yule, *Independents*, 131; Smith, *Ecclesiastical History*, 379; Sibley and Shipton, *Biographical Sketches*, I, 228–244, 186–190; Laurence, "Parliamentary Army Chaplains," 303; Seaver, *Puritan Lectureships*, 286; Sibley and Shipton, *Biographical Sketches*, I, 162; Matthews, *Calamy Revised*, 460; Nuttall, "Congregational Incumbents," 162; Matthews, *Calamy Revised*, 460; Sibley and Shipton, *Biographical Sketches*, I, 302–308; Yule, *Independents*, 136; Sachse, "Harvard Men," 126.

21. Sibley and Shipton, *Biographical Sketches*, I, 78–85; Robert Murray, *Dublin University and the New World* (London, 1921), 19; *CSPD, 1651–52*, 610; Laurence, "Parliamentary Army Chaplains," 424; Robert Halley, *Lancashire: Its Puritanism and Nonconformity*, 2 vols. (London, 1849), II, 182; *CSPD, 1654*, 369; Matthews, *Calamy Revised*, 344; Murray, *Dublin University*, 19, 20; Kenneth Murdock, *Increase Mather* (New York, 1966 repr.), 58; Thomas Jollie, *Notebook of the Rev Thomas Jollie, 1671–1693*, ed. Henry Fishwick, *Chetham Society Remains Historical and Literary*, new series, 33 (1895), vii; Murdock, *Increase Mather*, 60–61. Mather encouraged New England friends to join him, writing for instance in 1651 that "there is great need of good ministers & faithful men for places of trust" (Samuel Mather to Jonathan Mitchell, 26 March 1651, in MHS Miscellaneous Bound Manuscripts, I).

22. Sibley and Shipton, *Biographical Sketches*, I, 157–160; Matthews, *Calamy Revised*, 343; Murray, *Dublin University*, 27; Sachse, "Harvard Men," 127; Matthews, *Calamy Revised*, 343–344; Nathaniel Mather to John Rogers, 23 March 1651, *Mather Papers*, 3; Alexander Gordon, *Freedom after Ejection* (Manchester, Eng., 1917), 309.

23. Increase Mather, *The Autobiography of Increase Mather*, ed. Michael Hall (Worcester, Mass., 1962), 281; Morison, *Harvard*, 500; quote on humming from Calamy as quoted in Murray, *Dublin University*, 27; Mather, *Autobiography*, 282; Schiavo, "Dissenter Connection," 184; Michael Hall, *The Last American Puritan* (Middletown, Conn., 1988), 44–45; Jollie, *Notebook*, 33 n.1.

24. The task of religious reform in England in the 1650s was made easier by the prominence of lay Congregationalists from New England in positions of authority in the army and the government. Although a complete review of this element of the New England involvement in the shaping of Puritan England is not within the scope of this study, a sampling of the subject will help to set the context within which men like the Mathers, Owen, Nye, and others labored. Emmanuel Downing became

chief clerk of the Scottish Council (Sachse, "New Englanders to England," 273). George Fenwick served in the Rump and the First Protectorate Parliament (Yule, *Independents,* 97). Edward Hopkins of Connecticut also served in Parliament (Sachse, "New Englanders to England," 260). Samuel Desborough, whose brother was one of Cromwell's major generals and the Protector's brother-in-law, served in Parliament, held a seat on the Scottish Council, and was Keeper of the Great Seal in Scotland (Sachse, "New Englanders to England," 258, 273; Sachse, *Colonial American in Britain,* 141–142). Roger Ludlow served on the first Irish Commission appointed by Cromwell (Hutchinson, *Massachusetts Bay,* I, 17). Edward Winslow served as a trustee to appraise the king's goods, commissioner to compound with delinquents and to manage sequestered estates, one of the commissioners to judge all treasons, and one of the three civil commissioners accompanying the Hispaniola expedition in 1655 (Sachse, *Colonial American in Britain,* 141). Richard Saltonstall Jr. was a member of the High Court of Justice established in 1650, a trustee for settling sequestered estates in Scotland, and one of the Commissioners of the Customs (*Saltonstall Papers,* I, 37). John Winthrop's son Stephen served in the army and then represented Banff and Aberdeen in the Protectorate Parliament in 1656 (Lawrence Shaw Mayo, *The Winthrop Family in America* [Boston, 1948], 66). Many other New Englanders served in the army in addition to Winthrop, including his nephews Wait and Fitz Winthrop (Sachse, "New Englanders to England," 258). Robert Sedgwick was cocommander of the expedition Cromwell sent to assist New Englanders against the Dutch. He captured Acadia for England, led reinforcements to Jamaica, and died while serving as commander-in-chief of the English forces on that island (Sachse, *Colonial American in Britain,* 139). Francis Willoughby and Daniel Gookin also served in the parliamentary forces (Richard Johnson, *Adjustment to Empire* [New Brunswick, N.J., 1981], 67 n.145). John Leverett, later to be governor of Massachusetts, also served in Cromwell's forces and shared command of the New Netherland expedition with Sedgwick (Hutchinson, *Massachusetts Bay,* I, 153). Hezekiah Haynes rose from captain to colonel in the English army and became one of Cromwell's major generals governing England in the mid-1650s (Sachse, *Colonial American in Britain,* 138). George Fenwick commanded a regiment in the Second Civil War and served as military governor of Berwick, Edinburgh, and Leith (Sachse, "New Englanders to England," 269). Thomas Larkham served in the military and used a position of authority to assist in organizing a Congregational church at Cockermouth where his son George became pastor (Nuttall, "Congregational Incumbents," 162). George Cooke became a colonel in the army and served two years as military governor of Wexford (Sachse, *Colonial American in Britain,* 138). There was a notable concentration of New Englanders in Cromwell's old regiments. The following New Englanders were in the regiment commanded by John Winthrop's relative Colonel Thomas Rainsborough: Israel Stoughton as a lieutenant colonel, Nehemiah Bourne a major, John Leverett a captain, and William Hudson an ensign (Holmes, *Eastern Association,* 175–176; Sachse, *Colonial American in Britain,* 139).

For information on Owen's involvement with Cotton's response to Cawdrey, see Ziff, *John Cotton,* 250–251. On Shepard's *Subjection to Christ* see Thomas Werge, *Thomas Shepard,* 67. Christopher Scott was a graduate of Christ's College, Cambridge, and pastor at Great Wakering in Essex; see Davids, *Nonconformity in Essex*, 504. Pynchon's works and Norton's response are discussed in Gura, *Glimpse*, 309–311. Peter Sterry, *England's Deliverance from the Northern Presbytery* (London, 1652), 7.

25. Fienberg, "Thomas Goodwin," 267; Wallace, "Owen," 141, 245–246; Raymond P. Stearns, "Toleration as a Congregational Tactic in the English Civil Wars," *Bulletin of the American Congregational Association*, III (1956), 12; M.R., *Memoirs of the Life of Mr. Ambrose Barnes*, ed. W. H. Longstaffe, *Publications of the Surtees Society*, vol. 50 (London, 1867), 355–356. For the alienation of John Goodwin from the Calvinist Congregationalists see Ellen S. More, "Congregationalism and the Social Order: John Goodwin's Gathered Church, 1640–60," *JEH*, 38 (1987), 210–235.

26. "George Cokayne," *DNB*; Gordon Rupp, *Religion in England*, 122; J. Duncan, "William Bridge, Puritan Divine, 1600–1670," unpublished typescript in Dr. Williams's Library (1960), 16; Greaves, *Saints and Rebels*, 84; Fletcher, *County Community*, 303. Just as Quakers aroused the hostility of English Congregationalists, so they drew the opposition of the colonial clergy. Carla Pestana has made the colonial opposition to Quaker missionaries more understandable by placing their beliefs and actions in the context of the 1650s; see Pestana, "City on a Hill Under Siege: The Puritan Perception of the Quaker Threat to Massachusetts Bay 1656–1661," *NEQ*, LVI (1983), 323–333. See also Pestana, *Baptists and Quakers* (New York, 1991).

27. Letter to the Congregational churches, 9 January 1654, in Peter Toon, ed., *The Correspondence of Dr. John Owen* (Cambridge, Eng., 1970), 66–68; Sarah Cook, "The Congregational Independents and the Cromwellian Constitutions," *Church History*, 46 (1977), 342; Duncan, "William Bridge," 18; Tai Liu, *Discord*, 127.

28. An example of the sectarian anger at the Congregationalists can be found in John Canne's *The "Time of Finding"* (London, 1658): "A word likewise to our Dissenting Brethren, whose mourning of late is turned into laughter, and their heaviness to joy. . . . Here lies the difference between you and your [Independent] Brethren; you laugh and are more merry than you used to be, because of the advantages you have by these corrupt times; whereas your poor Brethren are more in tears and bitterness of soul, these three or four years, than they used to be, for the great dishonor, scandal, and reproach, which you have brought to the name of God and profession of religion, by assisting and justifying of men's interest against the interest of Christ and his people" (ch. 7). Fienberg, "Thomas Goodwin," 85; Bradley, "Jacob and Esau," 81 n.1; Leith, *Assembly*, 46; Bradley, "Jacob and Esau," 114, 81; Schneider, "Godly Order," 523; Bradley, "Jacob and Esau," 80; Paul, *Assembly*, 125 n.66; Cliffe, *Conflict*, 121; Twigg, "Cambridge," 96.

29. Paul, *Assembly*, 146, 152; Bradley, "Jacob and Esau," 80; Herle's statement in the Assembly quoted in Paul, *Assembly*, 435; license for the *Apologetical Narration* quoted in Bradley, "Jacob and Esau," 125; Charles Herle, *The Independency on Scriptures of the Independency of Churches* (London, 1643), prefatory letter; Paul, *Assembly*, 70.

30. Kaplan, "Presbyterians and Independents," 249–252; for Marshall see also Giles Firmin, *The Questions Between Conformism and Nonconformists* (London, 1681); Elisa Vaughan, *Stephen Marshall* (London, 1907); and Minna F. Weinstein,

"Stephen Marshall and the Dilemma of the Political Puritan," *Journal of Presbyterian History*, 46 (1968), 1–25.

31. Robert Baillie, letter 81, in Baillie, *Letters and Journals*, II, 60–62; Baillie quoted on Herle in Bradley, "Jacob and Esau," 80; Burroughes, *Vindication*, n.p.; Carter, *English Reformed Church*, 121; Richard Baxter quoted in Hanbury, *Historical Memorials*, III, 413; T. G. Crippen, "Nicholas Lockyer: A Half-forgotten Champion of Independency," *CHST*, 9 (1924–26); 64; Wallace, *Puritans and Predestination*.

32. McGee, *Godly Man*, 186; Howell, *Puritans and Radicals*, 97; Craddock quoted in Austin Woolrych, *Commonwealth to Protectorate*, 242; Rose-Troup, *John White*, 355; Tai Liu, *Puritan London*, 112; Orme, *Memoir of John Owen*, 199–200; Robert Horton, *John Howe* (London, 1895), 55–56; Edmund Calamy, "The Life of Mr. John Howe," in *The Works of the Rev. John Howe*, MA (New York, 1838 repr.), vi; Morrill, *Chesire*, 267; the statement of the Exeter Assembly quoted in Allan Brockett, *Nonconformity in Exeter, 1650–1875* (Manchester, 1962), 10; Matthews, *Calamy Revised*, 301, 76, 339; Tai Liu, *Puritan London*, 86. In his "Sion College and the London Provincial Assembly, 1647–1660," *JEH*, 37 (1986), Philip Anderson argues that the government's decision to execute the extreme Presbyterian Christopher Love in 1651 elicited protests from Congregationalists such as Caryl, Nye, Greenhill, and Strong, and that this "helped open lines of communication" between Congregationalist and Presbyterian leaders (pp. 83–84).

33. Orme, *Memoir of John Owen*, 42; John Owen, *An Answer to a Late Treatise of Mr. Cawdrey About the Nature of Schism* (London, 1658), 370; Richard Baxter, *Church Concord* (London, 1691), 20–22, 19, preface; John White made a call for cooperation between the two groups in his *The Troubles of Jerusalems Restauration* (London, 1646), esp. pp. 55–56.

34. Josselin, *Diary*, 119; Gura, *Glimpse*, 133–134; William Kellaway, *The New England Company* (London, 1961), 29, 20. Josselin, *Diary*, 295, mentions in 1653 "great hopes for the Heathens conversion in the West at N.E. and discourse of something in the East." Richard Lobb to Edward Winslow, 20 December 1651, *NEHGR*, 37 (1883), 392–393; Kellaway, *New England Company*, 92; White, 'Henry Jessey," 143–144. In 1650 Jessey translated a work by Caspar Sibelius that was entitled *Of the Conversion of Five Thousand and Nine Hundred East-Indians in the Isle of Formosa* (Ball, *Expectation*, 109–110). Toon, *Owen Correspondence*, 56–58; Toon, *God's Statesman*, 82 n.3. For a discussion of the work among the Indians, see Alden T. Vaughan, *New England Frontier* (Boston, 1965); Ola Winslow, *John Eliot, "Apostle to the Indians"* (Boston, 1968); and James Axtell, *The Invasion Within* (New York, 1985).

35. Jordan, *Toleration*, 111, 113–114. Blair Worden has pointed to the importance of the "distinction . . . commonly made between the holding of a belief and the propagation of it. Stephen Marshall would allow liberty to 'men who hold dissenting opinions in lesser points' provided they were 'content to have their faith in these, and to be quiet. I can be no advocate for such people, if they judge the spreading of their opinions to be a duty,' . . . a distinction which was made in the Blasphemy Act of 1648" (Worden, "Toleration," 214).

36. Cobbett, *Civil Magistrates Power*; John Owen, *Righteous Zeal Encouraged by Divine Protection* (London, 1649), in which he says, "The gospel being preached, and declared as of right it ought to be, it is the duty of the magistrate, by the power wherewith he is intrusted, to protect and defend it against all, or any persons, that by force, or violence, shall seek to hinder the progress, or stop the passage of it, under what pretence soever." John Owen, *Christ's Kingdom and the Magistrate's Power* (London, 1652); Thomas Goodwin, *The Constitution, Right Order, and Government of the Churches of Christ*, in John C. Miller and Robert Halley, eds., *Works of Thomas Goodwin* (Edinburgh, 1865), XI.

37. Wallace, "Owen," 186; Fienberg, "Thomas Goodwin," 267; Wallace, *Puritans and Predestination*, 149.

38. Crippen, "Lockyer," 64–65; Wallace, "Owen," 184, 205; Matthew, *Calamy Revised*, 252; Laurence, "Parliamentary Army Chaplains," 293; Kearney, *Scholars*, 139.

39. Toon, *God's Statesman*, 62; *DNB*, "Thomas Goodwin"; Calamy, "Life of Howe," iii; Twigg, "Cambridge," 152; Richard Slate, ed., *Select Nonconformist Remains* (London, 1814), 6; Jollie, *Notebook*, 120; Josselin, *Diary*, 45.

40. Watts, *Dissenters*, 139; Worden, "Toleration," 203; Greaves, *Saints and Rebels*, 80; Toon, *God's Statesman*, 83; Cook, "Congregational Independents," 344 n.19; Wallace, "Owen," 260.

41. Batten, *John Dury*, 130; Jordan, *Toleration*, III, 140–141; Cook, "Congregational Independents," 344; Toon, *God's Statesman*, 84; Yule, *Puritans in Politics*, 242–243; Carolyn Polizzotto, "The Campaign Against *The Humble Proposals* of 1652," *JEH*, 38 (1987).

42. Polizzotto, "Campaign," passim; Worden, "Toleration," 215; Jordan, *Toleration*, III, 142; Cook, "Congregational Independents," 340–341.

43. Polizzotto, "Campaign," passim.

44. Tai Liu, *Discord in Zion*, 120, 74, 126.

45. Toon, *God's Statesman*, 88; Orme, *Memoir of John Owen*, 109; Tai Liu, *Discord in Zion*, 130; Jordan, *Development of Toleration*, III, 150–151; Woolrych, *Commonwealth to Protectorate*, 340–341; Tai Liu, *Discord*, 106–107; Watts, *Dissenters*, 149–150; Tai Liu, *Discord*, 110 n.105; Toon, *God's Statesman*, 90–91; clergy quoted in Tai Liu, *Discord*, 141–142.

46. Jordan, *Toleration*, III, 152; Worden, "Toleration," 216–217; Fletcher, "Cromwell and Godly Nation," 211; Jordan, *Toleration*, III, 155; Cook, "Congregational Independents," 348; Jordan, *Toleration*, III, 156–157; ordinance creating Triers in Hanbury, *Historical Memorials*, III, 422; Watts, *Dissenters*, 152 n.3; N. F. Collins, "Oliver Cromwell's Protectorate Church Settlement" (Ph.D. thesis, Indiana University, 1970), 88. For general discussions of Cromwell's religious views, see Paul, *Lord Protector*; J. C. Davis, "Cromwell's Religion," in Morrill, ed., *Oliver Cromwell*, 181–208; Worden, "Toleration"; Blair Worden, "Oliver Cromwell and the Sin of Achan," in Derek Beales and Geoffrey Best, eds., *History, Society and the Churches* (Cambridge, Eng., 1985), 124–145; and Roger Howell, "Cromwell and English Liberty," in R. C. Richardson and G. M. Ridden, eds., *Freedom and the English Revolution* (Manchester, 1986), 25–44.

47. Tolmie, *Triumph of Saints*, 44–45; White, "Henry Jessey," 136; Gura, *Glimpse*, 103; Tolmie, *Triumph of Saints*, 122, 55, 120. For an indication of the concern some English Congregationalists had about the spread of Baptist views in their own congregations, see the letter from Samuel Petto in Francis Peck, *Desiderata Curiosa*, 2 vols. (London, 1779), II, 505; Fienberg, "Thomas Goodwin," 105–106; Polizzotto, "Campaign"; Christopher Hill, *The Experience of Defeat* (London, 1984), 55; Ethyn Kirby, "The Cromwellian Establishment," *CH*, X (1941), 150.

48. For an evaluation of the misdated document and the implications this has for the positions taken by Perry Miller and others, see Francis J. Bremer, "When? Who? Why? Re-evaluating a 17th-Century Source," *MHSP*, 99 (1987), 63–75; Murdock, *Increase Mather*, 142; ordinance of the General Court printed in Isaac Backus, *History of New England*, 126.

49. Gura, *Glimpse*, 113. For information on Mather's unpublished manuscript see Burg, *Richard Mather*, 126. Hall mentions the arrival of English Baptist works in the colonies during the mid-1640s in *Worlds of Wonder*, 62–63. The works arriving, and against which New England polemics were directed, tended to include non-Calvinist views and advocated believer baptism.

50. John Cotton, *The Grounds and Ends of Children's Baptism* (London, 1647), 3–4; Gura, *Glimpse*, 124; Backus, *History of New England*, 147; Gura, *Glimpse*, 120–121.

51. *Winthrop Papers*, V, 23ff.; Gura, *Glimpse*, 115–117.

52. Collins, "Protectorate Church," 42–43; Tai Liu, *Discord*, 142; Cook, "Congregational Independents," 349; Fienberg, "Thomas Goodwin," 310; John Goodwin and Richard Baxter quoted in Wallace, "Owen," 212 n.2; Collins, "Protectorate Church," 137; Oliver Cromwell to Parliament, 4 September 1654, in Hanbury, *Historical Memorials*, III, 430. See also Hill, *God's Englishman*, 188–189.

53. Worden, "Toleration," 218–219; Kirby, "Cromwellian Establishment," 152–153; Hill, *Collected Essays*, II, 311–312; Toon, *God's Statesman*, 95; Orme, *Memoir of John Owen*, 114. For an idea of the influence they wielded, Collins, "Protectorate Church," 86, puts the number of ministers approved by the Triers between 1654 and 1660 at over 5,500.

54. Document organizing the Cornwall Association in *MHSP*, I, 17, 254–255; William Cutter to Henry Dunster, 19 May 1654, *MHSC*, 4th ser., vol. 2, 195; Schiavo, "Dissenter Connection," 7; Sehr, "Colony or Commonwealth," 74–75; Johnson, *Wonder-Working Providence*, 137–139; John Norton to Giles Firmin, c. 1658, *NEHGR*, XX (1866), 229. This period was also marked by considerable cooperation by Congregationalist, Presbyterian, and Baptist clergy and magistrates in attempting to create a godly England by extensive catechizing, the spread of the gospel into the "dark corners of the land," and magisterial-enforced moral reforms. See Derek Hirst, "The Failure of Godly Rule in the English Republic," *PP*, 132 (1991), 33–66.

55. Duncan, "William Bridge," 17; Watts, *Dissenters*, 167–168; Duncan, "William Bridge," 8, 24, 19; William Bridge to Henry Scobell, 16 August 1655, in Peck, *Desiderata Curiosa*, 495–497; Duncan, "William Bridge," 20, 19. In addition to the types of cooperation discussed in reference to Bridge—and examples of advising, teaching, corresponding, and so forth could be enumerated for virtually all members

of the network—other types of activity that continued (and sources for representative examples) included recognizing a friend by preaching his funeral sermon (Wilson, *Dissenting Churches,* III, 153); cooperation in joint scholarship such as the work of Cockayn, Caryl, Venning, Barker, Mead, Jessey, and others in work on an English-Greek lexicon (Wilson, *Dissenting Churches,* III, 281); visiting one another (Josselin, *Diary,* 145); sharing books (Josselin, *Diary,* 444); exchanging pulpits (Josselin, *Diary,* 200); intermarriage (Laurence, "Parliamentary Army Chaplains," 381); and recommending each other for jobs (Hugh Peter to Henry Cromwell, 24 August 1656, *CHST,* 5 [1911–12], 122).

56. Jordan, *Toleration,* III, 220; Cook, "Congregational Independents," 339; see Fletcher, "Cromwell's Major-Generals." Though in some areas the major generals were unpopular, in Suffolk Haynes was supported by members of the county elite such as Sir Thomas Barnardiston who had been traditional supporters of the Puritan network. See Austin Woolrych, "The Cromwellian Protectorate: A Military Dictatorship?" *History,* 75 (1990), 222.

57. Jordan, *Toleration,* III, 250–251; Cook, "Congregational Independents," 355–357; "Humble Petition and Advice," in Samuel Rawson Gardiner, ed., *The Constitutional Documents of the Puritan Revolution* (Oxford, 1962 ed.), 454–455.

58. Scobell's letter to the London clergy of 15 June 1658 is printed in Orme, *Memoir of John Owen,* 175–176; A. G. Matthews, ed., *The Savoy Declaration of Faith and Order* (London, 1958), 15; Greaves, *Saints and Rebels,* 86; Toon, *God's Statesman,* 103–104; Matthews, *Savoy Declaration,* 14; Orme, *Memoir of John Owen,* 176n; W. Gordon Robinson, "The Savoy Declaration of 1658 and To-day," *CHST,* 18 (1956–59), 75.

59. *Mercurius Politicus,* 14 October 1658; Wallace, "Owen," 299; Matthews, *Savoy Declaration,* 34, 48; Jollie, *Notebook,* 129; Greaves, *Saints and Rebels,* 87 n.20; Matthews, *Calamy Revised,* 465; Sachse, *Colonial American in Britain,* 91; Matthews, *Calamy Revised,* 460; Nuttall, "Congregational Incumbents," 165; Gordon, *Freedom after Ejection,* 287; Orme, *Memoir of John Owen,* 181.

60. Slate, *Remains,* 195; Matthews, *Savoy Declaration,* 35; Orme, *Memoir of John Owen,* 176; Greaves, *Saints and Rebels,* 87; Wallace, "Owen," 300; Wallace, *Puritans and Predestination,* 150; Yule, *Independents,* 13; Savoy Declaration, in Matthews, *Savoy Declaration,* 68, 29; Wallace, "Owen," 302; Walker, *Creeds and Platforms,* 351; Matthews, *Savoy Declaration,* 37. The internationalism made explicit in the declaration's reference to other "reforming churches" marks a continuation of a theme that had long characterized the Congregational network as well as other Puritans. The internationalist thrust had not been abandoned in the 1650s. In 1655 William Greenhill's Stepney Church contributed £232 for relief of Protestant refugees from the Vaudois valley who had been persecuted by the duke of Savoy (Jones, *Stepney Meeting,* 36), and others joined in the effort. Owen and Thomas Goodwin were among many Congregationalists and Presbyterians who had renewed their support of John Dury's efforts at Protestant union in 1654 (Geoffrey Nuttall, "John Dury's Sponsors," *CHST,* XVII [1952–55], 91). Cromwell's foreign policy was applauded for its strong Protestant emphases. For further discussion see Bremer, *Puritan Crisis.*

61. *DNB,* "Thomas Goodwin"; Calamy's claim is mentioned in Mat-

thews, *Savoy Declaration*, 35; *Mercurius Politicus*, 14 October 1658. Among historians who believe that the declaration was intended as the basis for a state establishment are Woolrych, *Commonwealth to Protectorate*, 373, and Toon, *God's Statesman*, 101.

Chapter Nine

1. The statement that God had spit in their faces, occasionally attributed to Thomas Goodwin, is identified by Christopher Hill as being made by Charles Fleetwood: Hill, *Collected Essays*, II, 332. The analysis of political changes that follows is not intended to reflect the latest scholarship, but to focus on events of concern to Congregationalists and how those events were perceived by members of the network.

2. Daniel Neal, *The History of the Puritans*, 2 vols. (New York, 1844 ed.), II, 181; *Memoir of Thomas Goodwin*, xxxviii; Earle M. Hause, *Tumble Down Dick: The Fall of the House of Cromwell* (New York, 1972), 43; Robert W. Ramsey, *Richard Cromwell* (London, 1935), 44; Orme, *Memoir of John Owen*, 190; William Hooke to John Winthrop Jr., 30 March 1659, *MHSC*, 4th ser., VII, 590; Robert Horton, *John Howe*, 54; Vivian De Sola Pinto, *Peter Sterry* (Cambridge, Eng., 1934), 35; Hanbury, *Historical Memorials*, III, 551; Ronald Hutton, *The Restoration* (Oxford, 1985), 30; Orme, *Memoir of John Owen*, 212; John Maidstone to John Winthrop Jr., 24 March 1659, *MHSC*, 3d ser., I, 97; William Hooke to John Winthrop Jr., 30 March 1659, *MHSC*, 4th ser., VII, 593.

3. William Hooke to John Winthrop Jr., 30 March 1659, *MHSC*, 4th ser., VII, 593; Tai Liu, *Discord*, 149; Wallace, "Owen," 235. For an example of Richard's preferences: he appointed Samuel Annesley to the living of St. Giles, Criplegate, in 1658 (Wilson, *Dissenting Churches*, 368); Hutton, *Restoration*, 32; Jordan, *Toleration*, III, 255.

4. Factionalism had, of course, existed during Oliver Cromwell's regime, and the division between Fleetwood, Desborough, and their allies on one side and Fauconberg, Broghill, and their supporters on the other had its roots in the jockeying for influence in the last months of Oliver's life. Hutton, *Restoration*, 17; James Berry and Stephen Lee, *A Cromwellian Major-General* (Oxford, 1938), 218; W. L. F. Nuttall, "Hezekiah Haynes, Oliver Cromwell's Major General for the Eastern Counties," *Transactions of the Essex Archaeological Society*, 3d ser., I (1964), 206; Toon, *God's Statesman*, 109–110; Wallace, "Owen," 236–237, 238; Jordan, *Toleration*, III, 259; John Maidstone to John Winthrop, 24 March 1659, *MHSC*, 3d ser., I, 197; Derek Hirst, "Concord and Discord in Richard Cromwell's Parliament," *EHR*, CIII (1988), 337–358.

5. Jordan, *Toleration*, III, 263; Wilson, *Dissenting Churches*, III, 75; Matthews, *Calamy Revised*, 103; Toon, *Owen Correspondence*, 106, 114; Toon, *God's Statesman*, 116; Orme, *Memoir of Owen*, 218; Toon, *God's Statesman*, 118–119; *Chronicle of Great Yarmouth*, 27–28; Duncan, "William Bridge," 20–21; Toon, *God's Statesman*, 119. For Monck's intervention see F. M. S. McDonald, "The Timing of George Monck's March into England, 1 January 1660," *EHR*, CV (1990), 363–376.

6. Paul Seaward, *The Cavalier Parliament and the Reconstruction of the Old Regime 1661–1667* (Cambridge, Eng., 1989), 25–26; Tai Liu, *Puritan London*, 68;

Hutton, *Restoration*, 146; Seaward, *Cavalier Parliament*, 31; Richard Greaves, *Deliver Us from Evil* (Oxford, 1986), 10.

7. Hill, *Experience of Defeat*, ch. 3; Sachse, *Colonial American in Britain*, 143.

8. Seaward, *Cavalier Parliament*, 62–63, 68, 56–57; John Carswell, *The Old Cause* (London, 1954), 33 n.1; Seaward, *Cavalier Parliament*, 176; Gerald Cragg, *Puritanism in the Period of the Great Persecution, 1660–1688* (Cambridge, Eng., 1957), 35; Watts, *Dissenters*, 223.

9. Watts, *Dissenters*, 218–219; House of Lords Calendar, 7 September 1660, *HMCR*, VIII; Hutton, *Restoration*, 176–177; Greaves, *Deliver Us from Evil*, 103.

10. Harris, *London Crowds*, 59; vestry minutes of All Hallows the Great quoted in Tai Liu, *Puritan London*, 118–119; Frank Bate, *The Declaration of Indulgence* (London, 1908), 28–29.

11. Seaward, *Cavalier Parliament*, 28–31, 175, 181; Richard Davis has analyzed the Presbyterian lords in "The Presbyterian Opposition and the Emergence of Party in the House of Lords in the Reign of Charles II," in Clyde Jones, ed., *Party and Management in Parliament, 1660–1784* (Leicester, 1984); Davids, *Nonconformity in Essex*, 357n; Nuttall, "Haynes," 208; Berry, *Major General*, 266–267; Greaves, *Deliver Us from Evil*, 30–31.

12. Gura, *Glimpse*, 142–143; J. M. Sosin, *English America and the Restoration Monarchy of Charles II* (Lincoln, Nebr., 1980), 26–27; Watts, *Dissenters*, 222–223; Greaves, *Deliver Us from Evil*, 54.

13. Venner's views are discussed by Hill (*The Experience of Defeat*, 62–66), who notes the New England connection. The compiler of a contemporary narrative of the Venner uprising is quoted in Gura, *Glimpse*, 143; Greaves, *Deliver Us from Evil*, 59–60; Fienberg, "Thomas Goodwin," 341.

14. Greaves, *Deliver Us from Evil*, 88, 103, 116–117, 124; *CSPD*, LXXX, No. 101 (22 September 1663), 277–278; Greaves, *Deliver Us from Evil*, 173.

15. Greaves, *Deliver Us from Evil*, 164, 146; Hutton, *Restoration*, 232–235; Sosin, *English America*, 27; Greaves, *Deliver Us from Evil*, 203, 197–198.

16. Seaward, *Cavalier Parliament*, 57; Harris, *London Crowds*, 74–75; Greaves, *Deliver Us from Evil*, vii; Seaward, *Cavalier Parliament*, 189–190; Hutton, *Restoration*, 209; Seaward, *Cavalier Parliament*, 192; Watts, *Dissenters*, 226; Geoffrey Holmes, *Religion and Party in Late Stuart England* (London, 1975), 11. Anthony Fletcher has suggested that the enforcement of the Conventicle Acts in the countryside may not have been as rigid as in the towns and urban centers; see Fletcher, "The Enforcement of the Conventicle Acts 1664–1679," *Studies in Church History*, 21 (1984), 235–246.

17. I have dealt elsewhere with the story of New England's history and foreign relations in the Restoration period, in *The Puritan Experiment: New England Society from Bradford to Edwards* (New York, 1976), chapters 11–13, and in *Puritan Crisis*, chapters 8 and 9. For other treatments see Sosin, *English America*, though I disagree with his interpretation in many respects, and Johnson, *Adjustment to Empire*. John Davenport to John Winthrop Jr., 20 April 1660, *Davenport Letters*, 159–160; John Davenport to John Winthrop Jr., 1 August 1660, *Davenport Letters*, 169; Hutchinson,

Massachusetts Bay, I, 180; Hull, *Diaries,* 194–195; Charles Maclean Andrews, *The Colonial Period of American History: The Settlements* (New Haven, Conn., 1964 ed.), II, 37–42; Wesley Frank Craven, *The Colonies in Transition, 1660–1713* (New York, 1968), 6; Theodore Lewis, "Massachusetts and the Glorious Revolution, 1660–1692" (Ph.D. thesis, University of Wisconsin, 1967), 6–7; Hull, *Diaries,* 203–204; Hutchinson, *Massachusetts Bay,* 180n.

18. Sosin, *English America,* 5–6. For more on trading networks see Bernard Bailyn, *The New England Merchants in the Seventeenth Century* (Cambridge, Mass., 1955), "Communications and Trade: The Atlantic in the Seventeenth Century," *Journal of Economic History,* XIII (1953), and "Kinship and Trade in Seventeenth-Century New England," *Explorations in Entreprenuerial History,* VI (1954); Sehr, "Colony or Commonwealth," 272–274, 287. Richard Johnson has argued that Paul Lucas ("Colony or Commonwealth: Massachusetts Bay, 1661–1666," *WMQ,* 24 [1967], 88–107) and others have overstated the depth of the factional divisions in the colonies in the 1660s.

19. Lewis, "Glorious Revolution," 8; Sosin, *English America,* 122–123, 121. When John Eliot's *Christian Commonwealth* with its condemnation of monarchical government appeared in print after a long delay at the Restoration, the Massachusetts authorities sought to deflect criticism by having the book suppressed. See the introduction to the edition of the work in the *MHSC,* 3d ser., IX, and Sehr, "Colony or Commonwealth," 280.

20. Information on clergy in this and the next paragraph is drawn from Matthews, *Calamy Revised; DNB;* Morison, *Founding of Harvard;* James Reid, *Memoirs of the Lives and Writings of Those Eminent Divines, Who Convened in the Famous Assembly at Westminster, in the Seventeenth Century,* 2 vols. (Paisley, 1811 and 1815), one-volume reprint (Edinburgh, 1982); and Sprague, *American Pulpit,* vol. 1 (New York, 1857).

21. Joseph Caryl, "Farewell Sermon Preached 17 Aug 1662," in Edmund Calamy, *Compleat Collection of Farewell Sermons* (London, 1663), 27, 28; John Collins, "Farewell Sermon," in Calamy, *Farewell Sermons,* 266. Richard Greaves points out that the printers responsible for publication of these works were arrested; Greaves, *Deliver Us from Evil,* 220.

22. Collins, "Farewell Sermon," 266; Matthew Mead, "Farewell Sermon," in Calamy, *Farewell Sermons,* 205, 207. Like the authors of these sermons, John Owen also viewed the collapse of the Puritan regime as "God's judgement upon the failure of His saints to make the most of their opportunities and to obey His Word" (Toon, *God's Statesman,* 121). According to Christopher Hill (*Experience of Defeat,* 183), "The terrible *Discourse of the Punishments of Sin in Hell,* published posthumously in 1680 [written by Thomas Goodwin], sees 'the great God as an enraged enemy.' He and Christ 'account it a part of their glory' to execute punishment themselves." See also Cragg, *Great Persecution,* 77.

23. John Davenport, *The Saints Anchor-Hold* (London, 1661), 136, 231, 181–184. Just as New England views were printed and read in England, the colonists had access to English views. John Saffin recorded reading the volume of farewell sermons edited by Calamy (John Saffin, *The Notebook of John Saffin, 1665–1708,* ed. Caroline Hazzard [New York, 1982], 36–37).

24. Davenport, *Saints Anchor-Hold*, 231. For some writings explicitly dealing with the slaying of the witnesses, see John Davenport to William Goodwin, 2 November 1665, *MHSC*, 4th ser., VIII, 126–127; Roger Williams to John Winthrop Jr., 6 February 1660, *Writings of Roger Williams*, VI, 307; William Hooke to William Goffe, 2 August 1672, *MHSC*, 4th ser., VIII, 146–147; William Hooke, A *Discourse Concerning the Witnesses* (London, 1681).

25. Matthews, *Calamy Revised*, 301; Watts, *Dissenters*, 231; Hutton, *Restoration*, 264; Bate, *Declaration of Indulgence*, 52; Watts, *Dissenters*, 230; Hutton, *Restoration*, 211. Spurring the work of spies was the fact that, as Tim Harris points out, the revised Conventicle Act of 1670 awarded half of any fines to the informers (*London Crowds*, 71); Nathaniel Mather to Increase Mather, 31 May 1683, *Mather Papers*, 45; Harris, *London Crowds*, 66.

26. Jewson, "Return of Conventicles," 31, 17; G. Lyon Turner, ed., *Original Records of Early Nonconformity* (London, 1911), I, 88–89; Young, "Good News," 134, points out that when Greenhill died in 1671 the Stepney parish chose Mead pastor by a vote after a day of fast and prayer, in keeping with the Congregational practices of New England and England; Crippen, "Lockyer," 65; Wilson, *Dissenting Churches*, III, 71; Turner, ed., *Records of Nonconformity*, I, 85–88, 92; Greaves, *Saints and Rebels*, 90. Similar patterns existed in Ireland, where Timothy Taylor and Nathaniel Mather shared in the ministry of a conventicle (Increase Mather to Anthony Wood, c. 1691, *Mather Papers,* 347); T. C. Barnard, *Cromwellian Ireland* (Oxford, 1975), 142. There were, of course, similar conventicles of Presbyterians and other dissenting groups (see G. Lyon Turner, "The First Ten Years of Nonconformity in London," mss. in Dr. Williams's Library, 26).

27. Turner, *Records of Nonconformity*, I, 95; Bate, *Declaration of Indulgence*, 52; Nathaniel Mather to Increase Mather, 31 May 1683, *Mather Papers*, 45; William Hooke to John Davenport, 2 March 1663, *CHST*, IX, 281. Patronage by members of the nobility and gentry was not as common in the decades after the Interregnum as it had been before. The bishops complained that gentry on the local level encouraged and protected dissent, but their ability to do so was limited even if they had the will to. A notable exception was Lord Wharton, who gave lodging and money to more than two dozen clergy at various times and who had an extensive correspondence with dissenting clergy. The Ashurst family were also willing to take risks for nonconformists, visiting with them, lending their home for meetings, and contributing funds. Indirect upper-class support can be seen in the membership in conventicles of the wives of prominent political figures. But on the whole the clergy had to rely more on the zeal of humbler members of their congregations, such as the grocer who lent his home to Allen's Norwich conventicle. See Seaward, *Cavalier Parliament*, 60; Carswell, *Old Cause*, 32; Yule, "Independents," 29; Greaves, *Saints and Rebels*, 96; Heywood, *Life of Angier*, 86; Jollie, *Notebook*, 28; *CSPD, Charles II,* 93.3.

28. The information in this and following paragraphs on the residence of clergy is drawn from G. Lyon Turner, "Williamson's Spy Book," *CHST*, V (1907); Matthews, *Calamy Revised*; Gordon, *Freedom after Ejection*; Toon, *God's Statesman*; Turner, "The First Ten Years of Nonconformity"; C. Bernard Cockett, "George

Cockayne," *CHST*, 12 (1933–36); Wilson, *Dissenting Churches*; Matthews, "Censured Letter. William Hooke in England to John Davenport in New England, 1663," *CHST*, 9 (1924–26). The locations were identified in terms of their proximity to each other by consulting maps in Adrian Proctor and Robert Taylor, comps., *The A to Z of Elizabethan London*, London Topographical Society (London, 1979), 122.

29. Carswell, *Old Cause*, 33; Herbert McLachlan, *English Education under the Test Act* (Manchester, 1931), 49–51. See also J. W. Ashley Smith, *The Birth of Modern Education* (London, 1954); Samuel Eliot Morison, "Charles Morton's *Compendium Physicae*," *CSM*, XXXIII (1940), xv–xvi.

30. Urwick, *Nonconformity in Chester*, 704; McLachlan, *Education*, 106, 80; Morison, "Morton," xviii–xix.

31. Laurence, "Parliamentary Army Chaplains," 409–410; Nuttall, "Dissenters in the Netherlands," 50; Sprunger, *Dutch Puritanism*, 409, 415, 440; Quick quoted in Nuttall, "Dissenters in the Netherlands," 37–38; Sprunger, *Dutch Puritanism*, 453, 428; Nathaniel Mather to Increase Mather, 1661, *Mather Papers*, 6; Sprunger, *Dutch Puritanism*, 398 n.9; James Walker, "The English Exiles in Holland During the Reigns of Charles II and James II," *Transactions of the Royal Historical Society*, 4th ser., 30 (1948), 122–123; Nuttall, "Dissenters in the Netherlands," 50–51; English informer quoted in Sprunger, *Dutch Puritanism*, 397; Walker, "English Exiles," 114ff.; *Chronicles of Great Yarmouth*, 30–31; Greaves, *Deliver Us from Evil*, 92, 220; Sprunger, *Dutch Puritanism*, 411.

32. Matthews, *Calamy Revised*, 230; Waterhouse, "Reluctant Emigrants," 486–487; John Maidstone to John Winthrop Jr., 24 March 1659, *MHSC*, 3d ser., I, 198; Increase Mather to John Davenport, 21 June 1662, *MHSC*, 4th ser., VIII, 189; John Davenport to William Goffe, received 3 July 1662, *MHSC*, 4th ser., VIII, 198; Increase Mather to John Davenport, 21 June 1662, *MHSC*, 4th ser., VIII, 189. These letters from Mather and Davenport were both written in code.

33. Charles Hambrick-Stowe, *Practice of Piety*, 243; Eleazar Mather to John Davenport, letter in code, 6 July 1662, *MHSC*, 4th ser., VIII, 193–194; Turner, "Williamson's Spy Book," 252.

34. Sprague, *American Pulpit*, 177; Matthews, *Calamy Revised*, 5; Eleazar Mather to John Davenport, 4 July 1662, *MHSC*, 4th ser., VIII, 193; Sprague, *American Pulpit*, 163; Morison, "Morton," xxii.

35. Matthews, *Calamy Revised*, 356–357; Cragg, *Great Persecution*, 187; Sprague, *American Pulpit*, 211–212; Morison, "Morton," xix–xxv.

36. Matthews, *Calamy Revised*, 321; Sprague, *American Pulpit*, 209; Morison, "Morton," xiii.

37. Maverick quoted in Cressy, *Coming Over*, 51; *MHSC*, 4th ser., VIII, 611; Johnson, *Adjustment to Empire*, 39 n.74. A new spurt of radical immigration was touched off by the failure of Monmouth's Rebellion: see Peter Earle, *Monmouth's Rebels* (New York, 1977), 147.

38. John Davenport to John Winthrop Jr., 11 August 1660, *Davenport Letters*, 174; Ezra Stiles, *A History of the Judges of King Charles I* (Hartford, Conn., 1794), 22; "Extracts from the Journal of Colonel William Goffe," *MHSP*, VII (1864), 281–283; Chandler Robbins, "The Regicides Sheltered in New England," in *Lectures*

Delivered before the Lowell Institute (Boston, 1869), 338; Stiles, *Judges*, 23; Morison, *Harvard*, I, 335; "Journal of Goffe," 283.

39. Sosin, *English America*, 91; Lewis, "Glorious Revolution," 5–6, 26; Stiles, *Judges*, 111, 24, 26; Sprague, *American Pulpit*, 178. One 1663 report placed them with fellow conspirators in Switzerland; *CSPD, 1663–64*, LXXXVI, No. 16.

40. Robert Moody, ed., *The Saltonstall Papers, 1607–1815, Vol I: 1607–1789* (Boston, 1972), 39; Robbins, "Regicides," 343n; Stiles, *Judges*, 29; *Mather Papers*, 78; John Davenport to William Goffe, received 3 July 1662, *MHSC*, 4th ser., VIII, 198; William Goffe to Increase Mather, 8 September 1676, *Mather Papers*, 156; Stiles, *Judges*, 113, 110. There was a third regicide who fled to New England, though interest in him was not as great on either side of the Atlantic. John Dixwell resided in New Haven from 1661 until his death in 1689. He visited Whalley and Goffe on occasion and corresponded through Increase Mather and others with friends and family in England and Amsterdam. See Stiles, *Judges*, for his story.

41. D. R. Lacey, *Dissent and Parliamentary Politics in England, 1661–1689* (New Brunswick, N.J., 1969), 369. Richard Greaves makes a similar point, observing that much of the surviving material on dissenters is what was seized by the government (Greaves, *Deliver Us from Evil*, 16); Samuel Baker to Increase Mather, [1687], *Mather Papers*, 513; Joshua Churchill to Increase Mather, 25 August 1684, *Mather Papers*, 641; Matthews, "Censured Letter," 262; *CSPD 1663–64*, LXXXI, No. 12; Samuel Craddock to Increase Mather, 23 September 1684, *Mather Papers*, 642; Samuel Petto to Increase Mather, 8 October 1684, *Mather Papers*, 349.

42. Palmer, *William Hooke*, 67; William Goffe to Increase Mather, 8 September 1676, *Mather Papers*, 156; Greaves, *Deliver Us from Evil*, 203; William Hooke to William Goffe, 24 June 1663, *Mather Papers*, 125; Thomas Cobbett to Increase Mather, 13 December 1681, *Mather Papers*, 293.

43. Letter of John Allin, 20 March 1666, in Smart, "John Allin," 141; letter of John Allin, 20 June 1667, in Smart, "John Allin," 143; Thomas Jollie to Increase Mather, 2 April 1677, *Mather Papers*, 319; Jonathan Tuckney to Increase Mather, 25 February 1682, *Mather Papers*, 354; Increase Mather, mss. diary for 1688–89; Samuel Baker to Increase Mather, [1687], *Mather Papers*, 515; Increase Mather, mss. diary for 1688–89; Greaves, *Deliver Us from Evil*, 85; Randolph quoted in Olson, *Anglo-American Politics*, 73.

Chapter Ten

1. Harris, *London Crowds*, 73; Wallace, *Puritans and Predestination*, 173; Jonathan Tuckney to John Cotton Jr., 3 April 1678, MHS, Curwen Family Mss. Collection, Box 1 folder 3; Greaves, *Deliver Us from Evil*, 43–44; Harris, *London Crowds*, 69; Philip Nye, *Mr Philip Nye's Resolution of this Case of Conscience, Viz; Whether We May Lawfully Hear the Now Conforming Ministers, who are Re-ordained, and Have Renounced the Covenant* (London, n.d.), 2; Hill, *Collected Essays*, II, 316. A recent treatment of the period that is sensitive to the religious dimensions is Tim Harris, *Politics Under the Later Stuarts* (London, 1993). The intellectual crisis the Restoration posed for the Congregationalists deserves more study than it has received. The history of this Puritan group had been strongly oriented toward reformed unity, to the point where they had struggled hard early in the century to distinguish

themselves from the Separatists. The Restoration, in essence, made them Separatists by fiat.

2. Watts, *Dissenters,* 247–250; Berry and Lee, *Major-General,* 267; Bate, *Declaration of Indulgence,* 142; Richard Ashcraft, *Revolutionary Politics and Locke's Two Treatises of Government* (Princeton, N.J., 1986), 17–27. The situation of the godly in this period is put in a broader perspective by Nicholas Tyacke in "The 'Rise of Puritanism' and the Legalizing of Dissent 1571–1719," in Ole Peter Grell, Jonathan I. Israel, and Nicholas Tyacke, eds., *From Persecution to Toleration* (Oxford, 1991), 17–50, and, in the same collection, B. R. White, "The Twilight of Puritanism in the Years before and after 1688," 307–330.

3. Bate, *Declaration of Indulgence,* 109, 123, 139–141.

4. Watts, *Dissenters,* 257–259; *A Renunciation and Declaration of the Congregational Churches* (London, 1660); William Hooke to John Davenport, 2 March 1663, *CHST,* IX, 278–279; Jollie mss. in Dr. Williams's Library; Thomas Jollie to Increase Mather, 18 February 1678, *Mather Papers,* 322; Matthews, *Calamy Revised,* 359.

5. Toon, *God's Statesman,* 162. One example of advice tendered to New England is a letter to the Magistrates and Ministers of Massachusetts from John Owen, Matthew Barker, Arthur Palmer, John Rowe, Thomas Brooks, John Loder, John Collins, Philip Nye, John Knowles, Joseph Caryl, William Hooke, George Griffiths, and George Cockayn; 5 February 1672, in Toon, *Owen Correspondence,* 151–153; Jollie, *Notebook,* 25.

6. Matthews, *Calamy Revised,* 347; Joseph Green, "Matthew Mead, AM and his Sermons," *CHST,* 5 (1911–12), 117; Wilson, *Dissenting Churches,* III, 80; Browne, *Congregationalism in Norfolk and Suffolk,* 369–370; Grieve and Jones, *Bury St. Edmunds,* 29; Rupp, *Religion in England,* 121.

7. *The Records of the First Church in Boston, I, CSM,* XXXIX, 44. For an example of a private recommendation see Nathaniel Mather to Increase Mather, 9 May 1682, *Mather Papers,* 37.

8. Young, "Good News," 51; Thomas Goodwin to Robert Asty, 25 March 1675, in Goodwin, *Works,* IV, 49; John Owen to Robert Asty, 16 March 1675, in Orme, *Memoir of John Owen,* I, 376; Young, "Good News," 51; Nathaniel Guillym to Thomas Jollie, November 1690, in Jollie mss., Dr. Williams's Library; Jollie, *Notebook,* 33; Nuttall, "Dissenters in the Netherlands," 42–43; Urwick, *Nonconformity in Chester,* 639–640.

9. For Pynchon's career and views see Gura, *Glimpse,* ch. 11; Partial transcript of the Thomas Jollie Papers published in *CHST,* 6 (1913–15), 172–173.

10. Jollie, *Notebook,* 49–50; Nathaniel Guillym to Thomas Jollie, London, 1690, Jollie mss.

11. Harris, *London Crowds,* 80, 2, 79–80.

12. Samuel Mather, *A Testimony from the Scriptures Against Idolatry & Superstition* (Cambridge, Mass., 1672), 74; for a discussion of the plots in Ireland, Scotland, and England see Greaves, *Deliver Us from Evil,* and *Secrets of the Kingdom* (Stanford, 1992); Greaves, *Deliver Us from Evil,* 66; Carswell, *Old Cause,* 32–33; Hill, *Experience of Defeat,* 179; Schiavo, "The Dissenter Connection," 226–227; Lacey,

Dissent and Politics, 103; Fienberg, "Thomas Goodwin," 346–347; Cragg, *Great Persecution,* 23; Lacey, *Dissent and Politics,* 82.

13. Harris, *London Crowds,* 83–86, 93, 108, 110. The role of the London militia in preventing the capital from erupting in greater violence is examined in David Allen, "The Role of the London Trained Bands in the Exclusion Crisis, 1678–1681," *EHR,* LXXXVII (1972), 287–303. For an important discussion of the fears that underlay the hysteria, see Jonathan Scott, "England's Troubles: Exhuming the Popish Plot," in Tim Harris, Paul Seaward, and Mark Goldie, eds., *The Politics of Religion in Restoration England* (Oxford, 1990), 107–131.

14. *CSPD, 1663–64,* 442, 555–556, 678. English official quoted in Walker, "English Exiles," 122.

15. Earle, *Monmouth's Rebels,* 43; Green, "Matthew Mead," 117; Matthews, *Calamy Revised,* 348; Gordon, *Freedom after Ejection,* 304; Greaves, *Saints and Rebels,* 93; *Lord's Journal,* XI, 364a; T. Deane to Lord Preston, 28 June 1683, *HMCR, VII* (1879), 364; Lacey, *Dissent and Politics,* 162; Ashcraft, *Revolutionary Politics,* 22.

16. Schiavo, "Dissenter Connection," 263 n.60; Towgood quoted in Earle, *Monmouth's Rebels,* 65; Lacey, *Dissent and Politics,* 170–171; Earle, *Monmouth's Rebels,* 5; Basil Hall, "Daniel Defoe and Scotland," in R. Buick Knox, ed., *Reformation, Conformity and Dissent* (London, 1977), 222; Lewis, "Glorious Revolution," 195; Earle, *Monmouth's Rebels,* 175, 169–170.

17. Hull, *Diaries,* 190–191, 195; William Hooke to John Davenport, 2 March 1663, *CHST,* 9 (1924–26), 279, 266–267; John Allin to Samuel Jeakes, 5 September 1663, in Smart, "John Allin," 129–130; Hull, *Diaries,* 221. The importance of such cautionary tales, judgments, and marvels for the colonial Puritans has been brilliantly explored by Hall in *Worlds of Wonder.* Though his focus is on New England, Hall demonstrates the trans-Atlantic circulation of such tales.

18. English correspondent quoted in Corkran, "English Image," 92; Robert Atkyn to John Leverett, 18 March 1672/73, in Moody, *Saltonstall Papers Vol. I,* 161–162; William Hooke to William Goffe, 4 April 1674, *Mather Papers,* 150; John Collins to John Leverett, 19 March 1675, in Hutchinson, *Massachusetts Bay,* II, 209; Nathaniel Mather to Increase Mather, 26 February 1676, *Mather Papers,* 8; William Hooke to Increase Mather, 7 August 1677, *Mather Papers,* 582–585; Richard Blinman to Increase Mather, 14 August 1677, *Mather Papers,* 329.

19. Nathaniel Mather to Increase Mather, 19 December 1678, *Mather Papers,* 16; Samuel Petto to Increase Mather, 21 February 1679, *Mather Papers,* 347; Thomas Waterhouse to Increase Mather, 27 February 1679, *Mather Papers,* 591; Nathaniel Mather to Increase Mather, 25 August 1679, *Mather Papers,* 19–21.

20. Thomas Jollie to Increase Mather, 5 December 1681, *Mather Papers,* 327; Ichabod Chauncy to Increase Mather, 17 February 1682, *Mather Papers,* 618; Nathaniel Mather to Increase Mather, 10 May 1683, *Mather Papers,* 42; Nathaniel Mather to Increase Mather, 31 May 1683, *Mather Papers,* 45; Nathaniel Mather to Increase Mather, 25 June 1683, *Mather Papers,* 46; Nathaniel Mather to Increase Mather, 18 August 1683, *Mather Papers,* 51; Nathaniel Mather to Increase Mather, 26 March 1684, *Mather Papers,* 55; Nathaniel Mather to Increase Mather, 19 May 1684, *Mather Papers,* 57.

21. Stout, *New England Soul,* 53. Robert Middlekauff argues that it was this experience of being isolated and threatened that contributed to the shaping by Increase Mather's generation of the meaning of New England; see Middlekauff, *The Mathers,* 99–105. Although I believe that the first generation had a clear sense of having a saving mission, I do agree that the shocks of the post-Restoration period did force a reassessment and redefinition of that role. The tendency of the colonists to retreat into a kind of fortress mentality has also been noted by Craven in *Colonies in Transition,* 4.

22. Thomas Shepard, *Eye-Salve; or A Watchword from Our Lord Jesus Christ unto His Churches* (Boston, 1673), 31. For a general discussion of changes in this period and reaction to them, see Stout, *New England Soul.*

23. Sehr, "Colony or Commonwealth," 269–270; Davenport, *The Saints Anchor-Hold,* esp. pp. 181–184.

24. John Norton, *The Heart of New England Rent* (Cambridge, Mass., 1659), 78; John Norton, "Sion the Out-cast Healed of Her Wounds," in Norton, *Three Choice and Profitable Sermons* (Cambridge, Mass., 1664).

25. John Davenport to William Goodwin, 2 November 1665, in Calder, ed., *Letters of John Davenport* (New Haven, Conn., 1937), 256–257.

26. John Higginson, *The Cause of God* (Cambridge, Mass., 1663); Jonathan Mitchell, *Nehemiah on the Wall in Troublesome Times* (Cambridge, Mass., 1671), excerpted in Perry Miller and Thomas H. Johnson, eds., *The Puritans: A Sourcebook of their Writings,* 2 vols. (New York, 1963 ed.), I, 239–241; reference to the eyes of the world as quoted in Hambrick-Stowe, *Practice of Piety,* 133; Mitchell, *Nehemiah on the Wall,* 242. With the image of building a wall, Mitchell again was reflecting the conservative tide of the period. William Stoughton, *New England's True Interest; Not to Lie* (Cambridge, Mass., 1670), in Miller and Johnson, *Puritans,* I, 243–244, 245, 246.

27. John Davenport, *A Sermon Preached at the Election* (Cambridge, Mass., 1670), 15–16; Samuel Danforth, *A Brief Recognition of New England's Errand into the Wilderness* (Cambridge, Mass., 1671); Urian Oakes, *New England Pleaded With* (Cambridge, Mass., 1673), 33; Shepard, *Eye-Salve,* 37, 38, 45; Increase Mather, *The Day of Trouble* (Boston, 1674), 23; Increase Mather, *Testimony Against Severall Prophane and Superstitious Customes* (London, 1787), as quoted in Cressy, *Bonfires and Bells,* 201.

28. John Westgate to Increase Mather, 8 May 1677, *Mather Papers, MHSC,* 4th ser., VIII, 578; Joshua Churchill to Increase Mather, 25 August 1684, *Mather Papers,* 640; Samuel Craddock to Increase Mather, 23 September 1684, *Mather Papers,* 642.

29. *DNB,* "Caryl"; Nathaniel Mather to Increase Mather, 10 April 1683, *Mather Papers,* 44; William Bridge, *The Works of the Rev. William Bridge, MA,* 5 vols. (London, 1845 repr.), I, xix; Wilson, *Dissenting Churches,* III, 153, 150; Cockett, "George Cockayne," 232. For Bunyan's relations with the Congregational leaders see Christopher Hill, *A Turbulent, Seditious and Factious People* (Oxford, 1988), esp. 149–152.

30. Murdock, *Increase Mather,* 100, 94–95; Hambrick-Stowe, *Practice of Piety,* 275.

31. Samuel Petto to Increase Mather, 31 August 1677, *Mather Papers,* 341; Samuel Petto to Increase Mather, 14 May 1678, *Mather Papers,* 343; Burg, *Richard Mather,* 169. The manuscript diary of Increase Mather in the American Antiquarian Society shows an impressive familiarity with the work of contemporary English Congregationalists. Foster, "Godly in Transit," 222–223; John Richards to Increase Mather, 25 September 1682, *Mather Papers,* 498; Thomas Jollie to Increase Mather, 18 February 1678, *Mather Papers,* 319–322; Thomas Jollie to Increase Mather, 23 August 1679, *Mather Papers,* 324; Samuel Baker to Increase Mather, 30 January 1683, *Mather Papers,* 509; Samuel Petto to Increase Mather, 31 August 1677, *Mather Papers,* 341; Nathaniel Mather to Increase Mather, 31 May 1683, *Mather Papers,* 44–45; Nathaniel Mather to Increase Mather, 19 December 1678, *Mather Papers,* 16.

32. For a full discussion of Increase Mather's role see Francis J. Bremer, "Increase Mather's Friends: Personal Relations and Politics in the Trans-Atlantic Congregational Network of the Seventeenth Century," *AASP,* 94 (1984), 59–96.

33. The most complete surviving evidence of New England news being sent to England at this time is to be found in the *Mather Papers.* The collections include letters neither addressed to nor written by the Mathers but sent through the intermediary agency of Increase Mather, thus further highlighting his importance as a broker among separate clusters in the network. Letter of John Allin to an English correspondent, 4 July 1668, in Smart, "John Allin," 145; Jollie, *Notebook,* 137. For examples of exchanges of personal news of friends and relatives see John Knowles to John Leverett, April 1674, in Hutchinson, *Papers,* II, 178; Nathaniel Mather to Increase Mather, 13 February 1677, *Mather Papers,* 12; William Hooke to John Davenport, 2 March 1663, *CHST,* 9 (1924–26), 283; Robert Atkyn to John Leverett, 18 March 1672/73, in Moody, *Saltonstall Papers,* I, 161–162; John Bailey to Increase Mather, 12 June 1683, *Mather Papers,* 493; Increase Mather's Diary, *MHSP,* 2d ser., XIII, 345.

34. William Durrant Cooper, "Notices of the Last Great Plague, 1665–6, from the letters of John Allin to Philip Fryth and Samuel Jeake," *Archaeologia,* XXXVII (1857), 2–3; Matthews, *Calamy Revised,* 312; Greaves, *Saints and Rebels,* 90; diary of Increase Mather, 6–8, and 29 November 1665, mss. in Mather Family Papers, American Antiquarian Society; John Davenport to William Goodwin, 2 November 1665, *Mather Papers,* 127; Kellaway, *New England Company,* 94–95; Samuel Wakeman to Increase Mather, 27 September 1677, *Mather Papers,* 585.

35. Jollie, *Notebook,* 33; John Westgate to Increase Mather, 8 May 1677, *Mather Papers,* 577–578; Thomas Bailey to Increase Mather, 6 June 1683, *Mather Papers,* 488–489; Jane Hooke to Increase Mather, 14 April 1681, *Mather Papers,* 264; Jane Hooke to Increase Mather, 1681, *Mather Papers,* 267; Nathaniel Mather to Increase Mather, 31 December 1679, *Mather Papers,* 23; Nathaniel Mather to Increase Mather, 26 February 1676, *Mather Papers,* 9; John Eliot, James Allen, Increase Mather, and Thomas Thatcher to the Churches of Dublin, 11 February 1676, *Mather Papers,* 691–692; Jane Hooke to Increase Mather, 14 April 1681, *Mather Papers,* 265.

36. *MHSP,* 3d ser., I, 301–306; Matthews, *Calamy Revised,* 221; Magistrates and Ministers of Massachusetts to the London clergy, in Toon, *Owen Correspondence,* 149–151; London ministers to the Magistrates and Ministers of Massachusetts

Bay, 5 February 1672, in Toon, *Owen Correspondence*, 151–153; Samuel Eliot Morison reports that John Knowles was offered the Harvard presidency in 1672 (Morison, *Harvard*, 393–394); Sibley and Shipton, *Biographical Sketches*, I, 233; Hull, *Diaries*, 233; Morison, *Harvard*, 440, 382–383; Matthews, *Calamy Revised*, 464; Neal, *Puritans*, II, 290; Morison, *Harvard*, 485. For other gifts to Harvard see Morison, *Harvard*, passim, and Margery Somers Foster, *"Out of Smalle Beginnings . . .": An Economic History of Harvard College in the Puritan Period* (Cambridge, Mass., 1962).

37. Schiavo, "Dissenter Connection," 258 n.3; Olson, *Anglo-American Politics*, 48; Sosin, *English America*, 9; Kellaway, *New England Company*, 129–130, 131.

38. For examples of these types of activities see Heywood, *Life of Angier*, 32; Stanley B. Atkinson, "John Asty and the Fleetwoods," *CHST*, 3 (1907–08), 187; Heywood, *Life of Angier*, 128; Hill, *Experience of Defeat*, 211; Turner, "Williamson's Spy Book," 249; Nathaniel Mather to Increase Mather, 2 August 1687, *Mather Papers*, 67; Henry Newcome, *The Autobiography of Henry Newcome*, ed. R. Parkinson, 2 vols., Chetham Society, Remains Historical and Literary, ser. 1, 27–28 (1852), 251; Gordon, *Freedom after Ejection*, 304; Browne, *Congregationalism in Norfolk and Suffolk*, 468; Matthews, *Calamy Revised*, 501; Turner, "Williamson's Spy Book," 310; Matthews, *Calamy Revised*, 301; Green, "Mead," 117; Wilson, *Dissenting Churches*, IV: 66, II: 446, 376, I: 277, III: 87; Will of John Owen in Toon, *Owen Correspondence*, 184; Matthews, *Calamy Revised*, 229, 326; Heywood, *Life of Angier*, 30; Jollie, *Notebook*, 41.

39. Nathaniel Mather to Increase Mather, 13 February 1677, *Mather Papers*, 11; Thomas Waterhouse to Increase Mather, 24 February 1679, *Mather Papers*, 589; Nathaniel Mather to Increase Mather, 26 February 1676, *Mather Papers*, 8; Harold Keith Watkins, "The Ecclesiastical Contributions of Increase Mather to Late Seventeenth and Early Eighteenth Century Puritan Thought" (Ph.D. thesis, Pacific School of Religion, 1964), 181; Schiavo, "Dissenter Connection," 191; Toon, *Owen Correspondence*, 153–155; Orme, *Memoir of John Owen*, 269; William Hooke to John Davenport, March 1662, *Mather Papers*, 194; Daniel Hemingway to Increase Mather, 4 June 1686, *Mather Papers*, 657–659; Thomas Jollie to Increase Mather, 2 April 1677, *Mather Papers*, 318; Samuel Petto to Increase Mather, 14 May 1678, *Mather Papers*, 343. Much of the material cited is from the *Mather Papers* owing to the vagaries that determined what evidence survived to our time. However, an examination of the contents of these letters clearly reveals that others were also heavily involved in such exchanges.

40. Robert Mascall to Captain Oliver, 25 March 1669, in Backus, *History of New England*, I, 390–391; Richard Blinman to Increase Mather, 14 August 1677, *Mather Papers*, 329; John Westgate to Increase Mather, 8 May 1677, *Mather Papers*, 578.

41. Thomas Jollie to Increase Mather, 18 February 1678, *Mather Papers*, 320.

42. Watkins, "Ecclesiastical Contribution," 206; Hall, *The Last American Puritan*, 148–154; Murdock, *Increase Mather*, 151; Seymour Van Dyken, *Samuel Willard* (Grand Rapids, Mich., 1972), 38–39.

43. Thomas Jollie to Increase Mather, 5 December 1681, *Mather Papers,* 327; Samuel Baker to Increase Mather, 30 January 1683, *Mather Papers,* 510–511; Nathaniel Mather to Increase Mather, 31 December 1679, *Mather Papers,* 22.

44. Greaves, *Deliver Us from Evil,* 10; Backus, *History of New England,* I, 392; Mardina MacDonald, "London Calvinistic Baptists, 1688–1727: Tensions Within a Dissenting Community Under Toleration" (D.Ph. thesis, Oxford University, 1982), 9; Wallace, *Puritans and Predestination,* 161; Greaves, *Saints and Rebels,* 93; Cockett, "George Cockayne," 230; Wallace, *Puritans and Predestination,* 164.

45. Gould is quoted in William McLoughlin, "The Baptist Debate of April 14–15, 1664," *MHSP,* 76 (1964), 92. The remainder of the information in this paragraph is based on that article and on the general treatment of the subject in McLoughlin's *New England Dissent 1630–1833,* 2 vols. (Cambridge, Mass., 1971).

46. The letter is copied and discussed in Bremer, "When? Who? Why?" 63–75, where I have tried to show that the traditional dating of the letter to 1645 is inaccurate and that it was indeed a response to the Baptist debate of 1664 and the subsequent punishment of Gould.

47. Robert Mascall to Captain Oliver, 25 March 1669, in Backus, *History of New England,* I, 390–391; Robert Mascall quoted in John Waddington, *Congregational History, II: 1567–1700* (London, 1874), 664.

48. John Westgate to Increase Mather, 8 May 1677, *Mather Papers,* 579–580; Matthews, *Calamy Revised,* 5; John Westgate to Increase Mather, 8 May 1677, *Mather Papers,* 579–580.

49. Increase Mather, *The Divine Right of Infant-Baptism* (Boston, 1680), 20, 24–25; for Willard's views in *Ne Sutor Ultra Crepidam* (Boston, 1681), see Van Dyken, *Samuel Willard,* 138–146; Increase Mather, preface to Willard, *Ne Sutor*; Thomas Cobbett to Increase Mather, 13 December 1681, *Mather Papers,* 291–292. Cobbett was one of the more rigid New Englanders and did not want to tolerate even the most orthodox Calvinist Baptists, believing that though it might have worked in England, toleration in the colonies would mean that "they might soone flock over hither thereupon so many as would sinke our small vessel; whereas in that greater ship of England, there is no such dangers of those multitudes to founder the same."

50. Jane Hooke to Increase Mather, 14 April 1681, *Mather Papers,* 265; John Westgate to Increase Mather, 8 May 1677, *Mather Papers,* 578; Nathaniel Mather to Increase Mather, 2 March 1681, *Mather Papers,* 31; Nathaniel Mather to Increase Mather, 28 March 1682, *Mather Papers,* 35; Nathaniel Mather to Increase Mather, 26 March 1684, *Mather Papers,* 54; Nathaniel Mather wrote a treatise, "The Purity of Baptism," that criticized the practices of New England and some of his brother Increase's publications on the subject (Matthews, *Calamy Revised,* 344); Watkins, "Ecclesiastical Contribution," 372–373, 383–384.

51. For a discussion of these tendencies see David Hall, *The Faithful Shepherd* (New York, 1971) and Paul Lucas, *Valley of Discord* (Hanover, N.H., 1976).

52. Albert Peel, "Co-operation of Presbyterians and Congregationalists: Some Previous Attempts, *CHST,* XII (1937–39), 151; Watts, *Dissenters,* 289, 294; Peel, "Co-operation," 151; Neal, *Puritans,* II, 333; Gordon, *Freedom after Ejection,* 199; Watts, *Dissenters,* 289; Rupp, *Religion in England,* 115; Heywood, *Life of Angier,* 21; Bate, *Declaration of Indulgence,* 98.

53. Thomas Jollie to Increase Mather, 18 February 1678, *Mather Papers*, 321; Watts, *Dissenters*, 289; Rupp, *Religion in England*, 115; Roger Thomas, "Essay of Accommodation: An Earlier Version," Dr. Williams's Library Occasional Papers, 9 (London, 1960), 1–2; Roger Thomas, "Essay of Accommodation: Being a Scheme for Uniting Presbyterians and Congregationalists Drawn Up c. 1680," Dr. Williams's Library Occasional Papers, 6 (London, 1957), 2, 16; Toon, *God's Statesman*, 147; Thomas, "Accommodation" (1957), 2.

54. Nathaniel Mather to Increase Mather, 28 March 1682, *Mather Papers*, 35–36.

55. Harris, *London Crowds*, 69; Greaves, *Deliver Us from Evil*, 9–10. Dewey Wallace has skillfully traced the drift of many Presbyterians toward Arminian and Socinian views in the latter seventeenth century and the rift that developed between those clergy and Congregationalists such as John Owen, who were moving closer to an almost antinomian form of hyper-Calvinism; see Wallace, *Puritans and Predestination*; Peter Toon, *The Emergence of Hyper-Calvinism in English Nonconformity, 1689–1765* (London, 1967); and Peter Toon, *Puritans and Calvinism* (Swengel, Penn., 1973).

56. Raymond Phineas Stearns, "Correspondence of John Woodbridge Jr. and Richard Baxter," *NEQ*, 10 (1937), 558; Schiavo, "Dissenter Connection," 191.

57. Lewis, "Glorious Revolution," 2–3; Johnson, *Adjustment to Empire*, 67, 49. For a discussion of these new networks based on political and economic interests, see Alison Gilbert Olson, *Making the Empire Work* (Cambridge, Mass., 1992).

58. Cressy, *Bonfires and Bells*, 204; Sosin, *English America*, 293; Johnson, *Adjustment to Empire*, 52–53; Increase Mather's address quoted in Murdock, *Increase Mather*, 153–154.

59. Edward Randolph to the Archbishop of Canterbury, 1886, in Edgar Toppan, ed., *Edward Randolph, Including His Letters and Official Papers from New England*, 5 vols., Publications of the Prince Society (Boston, 1899), IV, 88. For a discussion of the politics of the period see Michael Hall, *Edward Randolph and the American Colonies, 1676–1703* (Chapel Hill, N.C., 1960), and *Last American Puritan*; Viola F. Barnes, *The Dominion of New England* (1923); David Lovejoy, *The Glorious Revolution in America* (New York, 1972).

60. Edward Randolph to William Sandcroft, Archbishop of Canterbury, 2 August 1686, in Toppan, *Randolph Papers*, IV, 104–105; Edward Randolph to Committee for Trade and Foreign Plantations, 28 July 1686, in Toppan, *Randolph Papers*, IV, 102; Edward Randolph to Lord Treasurer, 23 August 1686, Toppan, *Randolph Papers*, IV, 113; Edward Randolph to Committee for Trade and Foreign Plantations, 28 July 1686, Toppan, *Randolph Papers*, IV, 102. One of the more famous stands against the Dominion was taken by the Rev. John Wise, who did not have any direct connection with the trans-Atlantic network; see George A. Cook, *John Wise* (New York, 1966 repr.).

61. Corkran, "New England Colonists' English Image," 111–112. For the issue of the flag see Bremer, "Endecott and the Red Cross," 17, 21; Morison, "Morton," xxii.

62. Richard Lobb to Increase Mather, 7 March 1686, *Mather Papers*, 650–651; Matthews, *Calamy Revised*, 560; Samuel Baker to Increase Mather, [1687], *Mather Papers*, 514; Murdock, *Increase Mather*, 191; Nathaniel Mather to Increase Mather, 2 August 1687, *Mather Papers*, 67. Vincent Alsop's support of the Declaration of Indulgence is discussed in R. A. Beddard, "Vincent Alsop and the Emancipation of Restoration Dissent," *JEH*, XXIV (1973), 161–184.

63. Lewis, "Glorious Revolution," 217; Increase Mather, *Autobiography*, 320; Lewis, "Glorious Revolution," 220; Nathaniel Mather to Increase Mather, 31 December 1684, *Mather Papers*, 59; Lewis, "Glorious Revolution," 220–221.

64. Increase Mather, mss. diary 1688–1691, photocopy in MHS; Turner, "Nonconformity in London," mss. in Dr. Williams's Library, 235; Hall, *Increase Mather*, 213; Mather also visited prominent Puritan laymen including former General Fleetwood (Murdock, *Increase Mather*, 195) and friends of Harvard such as the Ashursts (Increase Mather diary).

65. Schiavo, "Dissenter Connection," 245; Lewis, "Glorious Revolution," 222–223.

66. Increase Mather, *Autobiography*, 326–327; Hall, *Increase Mather*, 213–217; Murdock, *Increase Mather*, 267, 215–216; Simon Bradstreet to John Hampden, 8 January 1689, *MHSC*, 4th ser., VIII, 538–539; note in unidentified hand to John Povey, 19 October 1688, in Toppan, *Randolph Papers*, IV, 245–246; Murdock, *Increase Mather*, 211–212; George Griffiths introduced Mather to Lord Wharton (Increase Mather, *Autobiography*, 327).

67. Ian Steele, "Origins of Boston's Revolutionary Declaration of 18 April 1689," *NEQ*, LXII (1989), 80. For more information on the colonial revolt and on Increase Mather's charter negotiations, see Richard Simmons, "The Massachusetts Revolution of 1689," *JAS*, 2 (1968), 1–12, and "The Massachusetts Charter of 1691," in H. C. Allen and Roger Thompson, eds., *Contrast and Connection* (Athens, Ohio, 1976); and relevant portions of Johnson, *Adjustment to Empire*; Lewis, "Glorious Revolution"; and Bremer, "Increase Mather's Friends." Increase Mather, *Autobiography*, 333; "An Extract of a Letter Written by Some of the Most Eminent Nonconformist Divines in London," in Increase Mather, *A Brief Account Concerning Several of the Agents of New England* (London, 1691).

68. Greaves, *Saints and Rebels*, 94; Murdock, *Increase Mather*, 281–282; Thomas, "Uniting Presbyterians and Congregationalists," 2. There are three letters on the subject from Noble to Jollie in the summer of 1690 that are contained in the Jollie manuscript in Dr. Williams's Library; Jollie, *Notebook*, 110; Daniel Williams, *The Answer to the Report* (London, 1698), 2; Peel, "Co-operation," 152; Watts, *Dissenters*, 290; Gordon, *Freedom after Ejection*, 155.

69. Matthew Mead to Thomas Jollie, 17 March 1691, in Jollie mss.; Jollie, *Notebook*, 104; Thomas, "Essay of Accommodation" (1957), 15–16; mss. Records of Nonconformity, Essex Assembly, 1619–1717, in Dr. Williams's Library; Jollie, *Notebook*, xxiii; Richard Baxter, *Church Concord* (London, 1691), preface.

70. Gordon, *Freedom after Ejection*, 156; Roger Thomas, "The Breakup of Nonconformity," in Geoffrey Nuttall et al., eds., *The Beginnings of Nonconformity* (London, 1964), 38; Nathaniel Mather to Thomas Jollie, 17 December 1690, Jollie

mss.; Watts, *Dissenters*, 289; Peel, "Cooperation," 155; Gary Stuart De Krey, *A Fractured Society* (Oxford, 1985), 82–83.

71. Wallace, *Puritans and Predestination*, 113 ff.; Greaves, *Saints and Rebels*, 95–96; Watts, *Dissenters*, 294–297; Gordon, *Freedom after Ejection*, 156.

72. Watts, *Dissenters*, 294–297; Greaves, *Saints and Rebels*, 95–96; Wilson, *Dissenting Churches*, III, 444–445; Stephen Lobb, *A Peaceable Enquiry into the Nature of the Present Controversie Among Our United Brethren about Justification* (London, 1693), "To the Reader," 15–16, 17–18.

73. Lobb, *Enquiry*, 17–18; Baxter quoted in Wallace, "Owen," 254; Wallace, *Puritans and Predestination*, 144, 177; Fienberg, "Thomas Goodwin," 138; Wallace, "Owen," 252; Wallace, *Puritans and Predestination*, 178; Schiavo, "Dissenter Connection," 187–188; Watts, *Dissenters*, 296–297; Sachse, "Harvard Men," 130; De Krey, *Fractured Society*, 83–84.

74. Scholz, "Reverend Elders," 223; Watkins, "Ecclesiastical Contributions," 320; records of the Cambridge Association in *MHSP*, XVII (1879–80), 254–281.

75. Watkins, "Ecclesiastical Contribution," 344–345; Murdock, *Increase Mather*, 281–282.

Epilogue

1. Norman Fiering, "The First American Enlightenment: Tillotson, Leverett, and Philosophical Anglicanism," *NEQ*, LIV (1981), 316–317.

2. Michael Crawford, *Seasons of Grace* (New York, 1991). For some examples of eighteenth-century correspondence see Kenneth Silverman, ed., *Selected Letters of Cotton Mather* (Baton Rouge, La., 1971), and Neil Caplan, "Some Unpublished Letters of Benjamin Colman," *MHSP*, 77 (1965).

3. For studies of religion and politics in the reign of Queen Anne see Holmes, *Religion and Party*; G. R. Cragg, *From Puritanism to the Age of Reason* (Cambridge, Eng., 1950); and Roger Thomas, "The Non-Subscription Controversy Amongst Dissenters in 1719: The Salter's Hall Debate," *JEH*, 4 (1953).

4. Quick's relationship with Increase and Cotton Mather, including his efforts to get the *Magnalia* published and his correspondence urging Cotton Mather to organize a clerical address to the newly crowned Queen Anne, is to be found in *Proceedings of the Colonial Society of Massachusetts*, XXVI, 301–312. Silverman, *Letters of Cotton Mather*, contains much of the correspondence regarding the "Biblia Americana." Quotes are from Cotton Mather to Sir William Ashurst, 17 November 1714, in Silverman, *Letters of Cotton Mather*, 155; Cotton Mather to Sir William Ashurst, 18 October 1715, in Silverman, *Letters of Cotton Mather*, 189–190.

5. Cotton Mather to Isaac Watts, 5 July 1720, in Silverman, *Letters of Cotton Mather*, 311; Cotton Mather to Benjamin Colman, 14 September 1722, in Silverman, *Letters of Cotton Mather*, 353–355; Kenneth Silverman, *The Life and Times of Cotton Mather* (New York, 1984), 328–332.

6. Cotton Mather to Daniel Neal, 5 July 1720, in Silverman, *Letters of Cotton Mather*, 312; Cotton Mather, unaddressed letter [July 1720], in Silverman, *Letters of Cotton Mather*, 313–315; Benjamin Colman to Robert Woodrow, 17 November 1719, in Caplan, "Unpublished Letters," 116.

7. For the role played by the political lobbies of dissent see Maurice Armstrong, "The Dissenting Deputies and the American Colonies," *CH,* XXIX (1969), and Norman Hunt, *Two Early Political Associations* (Oxford, 1968). See Charles Hambrick-Stowe, "The Spirit of the Old Writers: The Great Awakening and the Persistence of Puritan Piety," in Francis J. Bremer, ed., *Puritanism: Trans-Atlantic Perspectives on a Seventeenth-Century Anglo-American Faith* (Boston, 1993). In *Seasons of Grace* Michael Crawford points to the importance of trans-Atlantic connections in fostering revivalism in the eighteenth century. Those contacts represented a new coming together of English, Scottish, and colonial clergy who shared a common evangelical heritage and goal. Similar in some respects to the seventeenth-century Congregational communion and growing on soil prepared by earlier cooperative efforts, the connections described by Crawford were nevertheless experientially different from those of the Congregationalists in the Puritan century.

Index

Abbot, George (archbishop of Canterbury), 74, 84, 90, 282*n*5
Academies (for dissenters), 214–215, 254
Act for the Propagation of the Gospel in Wales (1650), 191
Act of Uniformity, 205
Adams, Thomas, 235
Adderley, William, 233
Admonition to Parliament (Wilcox), 89
Advowson rights, 43, 45, 62, 75–79. *See also* Livings
Aldermanbury accord, 132–135, 139, 141, 149
Aldersy, Samuel, 75, 90
Allen, James, 216, 217, 234, 241
Allen, Thomas, 87, 88, 97, 100, 164, 181, 209, 213, 236
Allin, John: and Baptists, 239; at Cambridge, 21, 22; death of, 209; deprivation of, 87; as New England emigrant, 107–108; works by, 120, 146, 147, 163, 165
Allin, John (the younger), 151, 183, 220, 228, 234–235
Alsop, Vincent, 250
Altar rails, 37, 83, 85, 87, 110, 130, 283*n*7. *See also* Altars
Altars, 37, 83, 87, 124, 127, 130
Ambrose, Nehemiah, 182
Ames, William, 150; at Cambridge, 22, 23, 29, 30–34; conversion of, 30; correspondence of, 55; death of, 95, 109, 182; as exile in Netherlands, 56–57, 65, 70, 84, 93–95, 98, 103; friendships of,

51, 62, 63, 108; as lecturer, 49; as possible New England emigrant, 102–103, 109; scholarly work of, 61; seminary work of, 37, 38; views of, 100, 114, 116
Ames, William, Jr., 182, 212
Amsterdam (Netherlands), 91, 94–98, 132, 165, 188
Anabaptists. *See* Baptists
Andrewes, Bishop Thomas, 35, 102, 183
Andros, Sir Edmund, 5, 246–248
Angier, John, 39, 109; friendships of, 53, 54, 56, 61, 92, 118, 243; seminary work of, 38
Anglesey, Lord, 226
Anglican Church. *See* Church of England
Anglo-Dutch Wars, 176–177, 179, 231
Anne (queen of England), 254
Annesley, Arthur, 204, 206
Annesley, Samuel, 205, 214, 250, 315*n*3
Anti-Calvinism: in Cambridge, 35–37; in England, 72–92, 124, 204. *See also* Cavalier Parliament; Puritan(s): persecution of
Anti-Catholicism: at Cambridge, 20, 26, 36; of Cromwell's policies, 177, 199 (*see also* Ireland); in England, 227; of Puritans, 64–66, 75, 80–81, 88, 90, 159, 170–171, 223, 246–248
Anti-Christ, 66, 72, 83, 129, 177. *See also* Anti-Catholicism
Antimonarchism, 128, 176, 246, 317*n*19
Antinomianism, 113, 153, 157, 159, 161, 167, 190, 250–251, 299*n*13, 327*n*55
Anti-Trinitarianism, 192

Apollonius, William, 165
Apologetical Narration, An (Dissenting
   Brethren), 139, 141, 150–153, 156,
   164, 167–169, 187
Apologists. See Dissenting Brethren
Archer, John, 48, 76, 98, 102, 109, 128
Arians, 255
Arminianism, 299n13, 327n55; in Bel-
   gium, 123–124; Calvinist opposition to,
   72, 78, 80–81, 88, 90, 113, 167, 169,
   186, 195–197; at Cambridge, 20, 35–
   36, 60
Arminius, Jacob, 35, 72
Arnhem (Netherlands), 98–100, 102, 118,
   123, 173
Arrowsmith, John, 22, 23, 32, 49, 56
Arundel, earl of, 124
Ashby-de-la-Zouche (England), 50, 51, 56
Ashe, Simeon: at Cambridge, 22, 29; dif-
   ferences of, with New England Puri-
   tans, 117, 118; friendships of, 53, 59,
   89; persecution of, 88, 89; as Presbyte-
   rian, 131, 190, 204; scholarly work by,
   61, 147
Ashurst, Henry, 190, 218, 236, 248
Ashurst, Sir William, 255
Ashurst family, 236, 254, 318n27, 328n64
Asseton, Ralph, 268n33
Asty, Robert, 224
Atkyn, Robert, 229
Atonement, 192, 225
Avery family, 254

Backus, Isaac, 150
Bacon, Nathaniel, 236
Bailey, John, 246
Bailey, Thomas, 235, 246
Baillie, Robert, 100, 133, 140; on Arnhem
   Puritans, 98; attacks on Congregationalists by, 156–158, 164–165, 301n28;
   on Cotton's influence, 60, 119; friendships of, 159; on millenarianism, 127;
   on Parliament, 142; as Presbyterian,
   98, 119, 188; and Westminster Assembly, 133–134, 136–138, 141, 154, 155;
   works by, 141, 156
Baker, Samuel, 219, 234, 238, 247
Ball, John, 38, 116–118; as Presbyterian,
   131, 132, 174; works by, 119–120, 147,
   148, 163

Ball, Thomas, 63, 79; at Cambridge, 22,
   29, 31; friendships of, 52, 55, 61, 187
Balliol College (Oxford University), 19
Balmford, Samuel, 96, 99, 100
Bancroft, Richard (archbishop of Canter-
   bury), 19, 32–33
Bancroft, Thomas, 35
Baptism, 98, 148, 171, 195–197, 211–
   212, 240–241. See also Baptists; Sign of
   the cross
Baptists, 148; Congregational attempts to
   include, 193–198, 217, 238–242; ques-
   tion of toleration of, 12–13, 140, 141,
   153, 162, 190, 230, 234, 238–242,
   326n49. See also Baptism
Barebone, Praisegod, 195
Barker, Matthew, 204, 213, 214, 250
Barnardiston, Arthur, 194
Barnardiston, Lady Katherine, 62
Barnardiston, Sir Nathaniel, 22, 30, 34,
   36, 62, 63, 79, 125, 134
Barnardiston, Thomas, 90, 314n56
Barnardiston family, 43
Barnes, John, 9
Barnes, Thomas, 45
Baro, Peter, 20, 35
Barrett, William, 35
Barrington, Sir Francis, 45, 46, 78, 79
Barrington, Lady Joan, 45, 46, 55, 57, 81
Barrington, Lady Judith, 63
Barrington, Sir Thomas, 45, 91, 134
Barrington family, 43, 45–46, 52, 70, 118,
   120–121, 254, 255
Barton, Henry, 171
Bastwick, John, 94, 155, 156
Bates, William, 213, 243, 250
Bawdy House Riots (1668), 227
Baxter, Richard, 171, 174, 189, 197, 204,
   243, 244, 250, 251
Bay Colony. See Massachusetts Bay Col-
   ony
Bay Psalm Book, 172
Bayly, Lewis (bishop of Bangor), 56, 121
Baynes, Paul, 6, 30, 61, 114, 116
Beadle, John, 283n7; at Cambridge, 22,
   23; death of, 209; friendships of, 52,
   60, 62, 63; persecution of, 88; seminary
   work of, 38
Beale, James, 35–36
Beard, Thomas, 80

Beccles Church (England), 172
Bedell, William, 36, 50, 54–55, 274n26
Bellingham, Richard, 62
Bergen op Zoom (Netherlands), 66, 70, 94
Bernard, Richard, 115, 118, 147, 273n17
Berry, James, 199, 206
Bill for Preventing Occasional Conformity, 254
Birden, John, 182
Bishops: in Church of England, 43, 72, 83–87, 91–92, 228; Congregationalist rejection of, 111; disapproval of Puritans by, 41, 223; in House of Lords, 130, 205. *See also* Episcopacy; Government (of churches); *names of specific bishops and archbishops*
Blackerby, Richard, 30, 37, 38, 57
Blackwood, R. G., 268n33
Blasphemy Act (1648), 190, 311n35
Blinman, Richard, 47, 229, 237
Bloody Assizes, 228
Bodleian Library (Oxford University), 54, 70
Bohemia, king of, 38
Bois, John, 50
Bond, John, 153
Book of Common Prayer, 20, 50, 83, 85, 90, 117, 124, 134, 205, 283n6
Book of Sports (King James I), 83, 86, 88
Books. *See* Censorship; Manuscripts; Pamphlet controversies; Publication; Smuggling
Boston (Lincolnshire), 3, 21, 38, 51, 89, 116
Boston (Massachusetts): Cotton in, 107, 112; fire in, 235, 237; fortification of, 122, 208
Boswell, William, 95–98, 100
Boyle, Roger, earl of Orrery, 226
Boynton, Sir Matthew, 56
Bradford, William, 64, 126
Bradshaw, William, 50, 61, 114
Bradstreet, Simon, 29
Bragge, Robert, 183, 205, 207
Brasenose College (Oxford University), 24
Brent, Sir Nicholas, 85–86, 91
Brereton, Sir William, 102
Brewster, Francis, 22, 23
Brewster, Nathaniel, 151, 181, 184
Bridge, William, 190; at Cambridge, 22,

23, 29, 33; as Congregational leader, 120; conventicle participation by, 212; correspondence of, 99; death of, 209; deprivation of, 87; as Dissenting Brethren, 109, 156, 170, 181, 191, 193; exile of, 68, 97; friendships of, 51, 55, 56, 59, 199, 215; lectureship offered by, 76; as parson, 48, 49; persecution of, 58, 85, 87; at Savoy Assembly, 200; and sects, 186, 192; sermons of, 68, 70; travels of, 39; views of, 6, 135, 172, 222; at Westminster Assembly, 138, 142; works by, 128, 192, 233, 234
Bridges, Francis, 75
Bright, Francis, 90
Brightman, Thomas, 127, 128
Briscoe, James, 243
Briscoe, Michael, 189, 206
Briscoe, Nathaniel, 148, 197
Brock, John, 107, 176
Brokers (in friendship networks), 10, 13, 342n33
Bromley, Lady Margaret, 117–118
Brooke, Lord, 40, 53, 74, 89, 290n25
Brooke, Sir Robert, 30, 46
Brooks, Thomas, 7–8, 22–23, 171, 175, 191, 204, 207, 213–214, 235, 239, 243, 251
Browne, Samuel, 75, 102, 255
Browning, Ralph, 34
Brownists, 103, 134, 138, 163
Brownrigg, Ralph, 35
Buckingham, George Villiers, duke of, 33, 36, 68, 73–74, 80
Bulkeley, John, 151, 182
Bulkeley, Peter, 62, 177–178, 182, 209
Bunyan, John, 5–6, 210, 233, 239
Burdett, George, 88, 150
Burgess, Anthony, 153
Burgess, Cornelius, 65, 133
Burnet, Gilbert, 248
Burroughs, Jeremiah: at Cambridge, 22, 23, 29, 31; as chaplain, 45; clandestine return to England by, 100; as Congregational leader, 120, 137, 138; correspondence of, 54, 119; death of, 209; deprivation of, 57, 58, 87; as Dissenting Brethren, 109, 142, 156, 160, 168, 195; friendships of, 42, 51, 52, 59, 63, 180, 182; as lecturer, 46, 47, 49, 56, 87; in

Netherlands, 97; seminary work of, 38; travels of, 39; views of, 140, 167, 188; works by, 57, 61, 128, 133, 175

Burton, Henry, 73, 131, 171

Burtt, Edward, 220

Bury St. Edmunds (England), 42, 46, 47, 49, 56, 89

Butler, Henry, 181–182

Byfield, Adoniram, 22, 23, 40, 65, 86, 192

Caius College (Cambridge University), 21, 22, 23, 35

Calamy, Edmund: conferences with, 132–135, 201; education of, 22, 23, 215; friendships of, 42, 89; as parson, 45; as Presbyterian, 174, 176; views of, 135; works by, 132, 141, 317n23

Calandrini, Cesar, 67

Calendars, 72, 303n44

Calvinism: differences within, 280n26, 289n20; tenets of orthodox, 192–193. *See also* Anti-Calvinism; Church of England; Church of Scotland; Congregationalists; Dissenting Brethren; Independents; Presbyterian(s); Protestantism; Puritan(s); Reformed churches; Sects; Separatists; *specific issues of importance in*

Cambridge Association (Massachusetts), 252

Cambridge Synod (Massachusetts), 166, 173, 201

Cambridge University (England): academic life at, 24–26; anti-Calvinism in, 35–37, 93–94, 214–215, 264n6; commencements at, 40, 92, 192; Congregationalists at, under Cromwell, 191–192; Cromwell at, 177; elections at, 32–36, 45; influence of alumni from, 33, 40; number of matriculated students at, 24; Puritan friendships in, 3, 4, 13–41, 63, 103, 174, 177, 194–195; Puritanism in, 263n1, 268n33; theology at, 26–27. *See also* Travels; *names of specific Cambridge colleges and churches*

Canne, John, 304n2, 310n28

Carleton, Bishop George, 72

Carlton, Edward, 150

Carter, John, 31, 46, 49, 62, 89, 139

Carter, William, 100, 135, 191, 194, 209

Carter, William (the younger), 153

Cartwright, Thomas, 19–20, 54, 93, 114, 279n18

Cary, Valentine, 33, 93–94

Caryl, Joseph, 139, 148, 153, 167, 171, 186, 189–191, 194, 224, 235–236, 239; conventicle worship of, 213; after Cromwell's death, 202, 204, 206, 207; death of, 209–210; at Savoy Assembly, 200; sermons of, 52, 70; views of, 251; works of, 140, 233, 234, 301n26

Catechisms, 52, 85; Geneva, 65; Racovian, 192; Shorter, 155, 187. *See also* Catechizing

Catechizing, 97; vs. sermons, 83, 88

Catholic Counter-Reformation, 65

Catholicism: under Mary I, 17, 19; under James I and Charles I, 72–73, 123, 125; James II's view of, 206, 226; under Charles II, 226. *See also* Anti-Catholicism; Mass; Papacy

Cavalier Parliament, 204–206, 226–227

Cawdrey, Daniel, 176, 185

Censorship: of books, 85, 109, 120, 147, 317n19; of correspondence, 54, 70, 92, 124, 219–220; of speech, 190, 193, 311n35. *See also* Letter drops; Manuscripts: circulation of; Seizure (of papers); Smuggling

Ceremonies, 72, 75, 88, 169. *See also names of specific ceremonies*

Chaderton, Laurence, 102; at Cambridge, 20–23, 25–28, 32, 33, 50, 98; correspondence of, 55; friendships of, 32, 47, 62; sermons by, 34

Chaplains: anti-Calvinist, 86; in Cromwell's army, 180–183, 191; to English troops in Europe, 55, 93, 94, 96; in Puritan households, 43, 45, 46, 53, 103, 178, 185, 203; at universities, 183

Charles I (king of England), 68, 80; calling of Parliaments by, 124–126; dissolution of Parliaments by, 74, 81, 101, 105, 123; Dutch influence of, 96, 104; execution of, 175–176; Massachusetts investigation by, 122; Neile and Laud's influence under, 72–75, 82–84, 96, 122; during Puritan Revolution, 131, 143, 144; Scottish troubles of, 122, 124–125; seizure of seditious papers by,

124, 126, 290n24, 320n41; succession of, 74; and Thirty Years' War, 67; trial of, 178. *See also* Henrietta Marie; Regicide

Charles II (king of England), 204, 206, 222, 226, 227. *See also* Restoration

Charnock, Stephen, 184, 188, 191, 207

Charters (for New England colonies), 5, 101, 103, 122, 208, 229, 230, 245, 249, 252. *See also* Dominion of New England

Chauncey, Charles, 21–23, 34, 37, 53, 87, 92, 183, 218

Chauncey, Ichabod, 183, 216, 227, 228, 230

Chauncey, Isaac, 183, 250, 251

Chelmsford (England), 38, 50–51, 59, 61

Chesire (England), 94, 127, 180, 181

Christ Church College (Oxford University), 191

Christian IV (king of Denmark), 66, 67

Christ's College (Cambridge University), 19, 21–23, 32–33, 52, 93–94, 127–128

Church of England: changes in, during civil wars, 170–173; Congregational exclusion from, 221–223; and Corporation Act, 205; divisions in, 72–75; exiles' departure from practices of, 95–99; fast days of, 20, 81; and the Feoffees, 77–78; Puritan clergy's vulnerability in, 47–48, 82–103, 171, 205–206; Puritan efforts to reform, 3–4, 14, 19, 40, 41, 63–81, 84–87, 100–102, 122, 124, 127, 130–138, 146–150, 174, 175, 182, 185; discouragement about, 103, 105, 208–211, 315n1, 317n22; structure of, 43. *See also* Bishops; Book of Common Prayer; Clergy; Conformity; Convocation; Lambeth Articles; State Church; Thirty-Nine Articles

Church of Scotland, 130. *See also* Scotland

Churchill, Joshua, 219, 233, 248

Civil wars, 61, 97, 129–131, 143–145, 170–174, 176, 185, 308n24

Clap, Roger, 129

Clap, Wait, 129

Clare College (Cambridge University), 21, 22

Clarendon, earl of. *See* Hyde, Edward

Clarendon Code, 207–208, 212, 216, 221, 222

Clarke, John, 193

Clarke, Samuel, 55; at Cambridge, 22, 31; as chaplain, 45; at clerical conferences, 50; friendships of, 56; views of, 51, 54, 75–76, 98–99

Classis, 95, 168; English, 93–97; of Puritans, 49, 93–95. *See also* Conferences; Government (of churches)

Cleere, Lady Elizabeth, 92

Clergy (Calvinist): in colonial ventures, 101–103; education of, 17–40; electioneering by, 79, 124, 226–227; as living model for communion, xiii, 8; postgraduate isolation of, 41–42, 46–47; post-Restoration requirements for, 205; Protestant union efforts by, 65, 84, 314n60; relations of, with laity, xiii, 51–53, 55–59, 62, 63, 68, 70–71, 78–79, 88, 100–102, 105, 118, 205–206, 254, 256, 270n6, 271n11, 304n5 (*see also* Patronage); return to England of New England, 179–190; and the Thirty Years' War, 67–71; trans-Atlantic relations between, 4, 7, 14, 134–135, 143–151, 175, 196–197, 212, 215–216, 233–238; vulnerability of, in Church of England, 47–48, 82–103, 171, 205–206. *See also* Conferences; Friendship network; Godly communion

Clinton, Theophilus, 69

Clusters (in friendship networks), 10, 12, 13, 116, 132, 274n26

Coachman, Robert, 7

Cobbett, Thomas, 144, 148, 155, 177–179, 190, 196, 220, 242, 326n49

Cockayn, George, 186, 207, 213, 214, 233, 239, 247, 250

Coddington, William, 116

Coke, Sir Edward, 79

Colchester (Essex), 49, 56, 79, 85, 108

Cole, Elisha, 233

Cole, James, 118

Cole, Thomas, 224

Collings, Samuel, 62

Collins, Edward, 59

Collins, John, 59, 183–184, 209–210, 213, 224–225, 229, 235, 236, 239, 243, 247

Colman, Benjamin, 253, 254, 255
Combination lectures. *See* Lectureships
Committee for Plundered Ministers, 171
Committee for the Propagation of the Gospel, 192
Committees of Accommodation, 142–143, 152–155
Commencements, 40, 92, 192
Common Fund, 250, 251
Communion. *See* Eucharist; Friendship network; Godly communion; Last Supper
Conferences (clerical): between Congregationalists and Baptists, 195–196; between Congregationalists and Presbyterians, 189; under Cromwell, 198–199; after Cromwell's death, 204, 223–225, 236; importance of, in shaping of belief, xii, 13, 26, 33, 42, 49–53, 60, 63, 64, 74, 82, 92, 98, 105, 107, 116, 132, 166, 172–173, 256–257, 272*n*17, 289*n*14, 303*n*43; in New England, 110–113, 163–164, 217, 252. *See also* Devon Association; Godly communion; Prophesying; Savoy Assembly
Confession of Faith. *See* Westminster Confession of Faith
Conformity: English enforcement of, 13, 82–92, 95–98, 115, 214–215, 220, 254, 283*n*6, on emigrants, 122; occasional, 222, 254. *See also* Altar rails; Altars; Book of Common Prayer; Crucifixes; Eucharist; Government (of churches); Kneeling; Marriage; Membership; Preachers; Rituals; Sabbath; Surplices
Congregational autonomy, 95, 97, 98, 111, 114–115, 138, 139, 165. *See also* Congregationalists; Covenants
"Congregational communion," xiii, 14–15. *See also* Godly communion
Congregational Fund, 251
Congregationalists: antinomian leanings of, 299*n*13; and classis, 93–95; after Cromwell's death, 202–220; as denomination, 221–223, 238–244, 254, 320*n*1; egalitarian tendency of, 7, 43, 46; figures at the center of, 120; links between churches of, 172–173; London concentrations of, 214; practices of, in Netherlands, 95, 97–99; practices of, in

New England, 103, 110–111, 113–117, 237; Presbyterian contention with, xiii, 95, 116, 132, 140–151, 174, 185–186, 250–252; Presbyterian cooperation with, 63, 187–189, 193, 194, 198–199, 236, 242–244, 249–250, 311*n*32; in Puritan Revolution, 175–176; as rising force in English religion, 152–203; sects' contention with, 174, 186, 190–193, 310*n*28; as Separatists, 320*n*1; social status of, 244; trust the basis of early, 14, 257; and Venner's Uprising, 206–207; at Westminster Assembly, 131–143, 150, 152–167. *See also* Church of England: Puritan efforts to reform; Clergy; Conformity; Congregational autonomy; Covenants; Dissenting Brethren; Friendship network; Godly communion; Heresy; Membership; New England Way; Preachers; Puritan(s); Religious toleration
Connecticut, 109, 252; clerical conferences in, 112; Dutch threats to, 179; fasts in, 144; land deeds to, 102; royal charter for, 208. *See also* New Haven Colony
Consistory Court (at universities), 35, 36
Constable, Sir William, 56
Conventicle Act (1664), 207, 212
Conventicles: Puritan, 8, 32, 82, 92, 212–213, 222, 243, 318*nn*26,27; prophesying in, 26
Conversions: to Catholicism, 123; of Indians, 100, 146, 189–190, 236; to Puritanism, xii, 5, 8, 30, 39, 59, 60, 254, and church admission, 99. *See also* Rebirth
Convocation, 124, 125, 127, 194
Conway, Sir Edward, 57, 89–90
Cooke, Charles, 220
Cooke, Elisha, 254
Cooke, George, 309*n*24
Cooper, Anthony Ashley, earl of Shaftesbury, 227, 230
Corbet, Clement, 87, 89, 283*n*11
Corbet, Miles, 21, 59, 134, 204, 283*n*11
Corbet, Mrs. John, 56, 59
Corporation Act, 205
Correspondence: between English clerics, 54–55, 63, 64, 92, 213, 225; between

English Puritans and exiles, 54, 99–100, 219–220; between European Protestants and English Puritans, 67, 99, 113; within New England, 163; between New Englanders and Cromwell, 177–178; as political tool, 70–71; relative rarity of, 261*n*7; and trans-Atlantic Puritan communion, 3, 5, 8–9, 13, 54, 113, 116–119, 156, 166, 173, 196–197, 219–220, 228–230, 234–235, 261*n*7, 304*n*5, decline of, 253–254. *See also* Censorship: of correspondence; Seizure (of papers)

Cosin, John, 36–37, 83, 85, 205

Cotton, John, 5, 65, 175; at Cambridge, 19, 21, 22, 26, 32, 33, 39; as Congregational leader in New England, 110, 112, 113, 116–117, 120, 132, 274*n*25; conversion of, 30; correspondence of, 54, 55, 70, 99, 116, 118, 119, 177–178; and Cromwell, 177–178, 179; death of, 209; emigration of, to New England, 60–61, 89, 102–103, 105, 109; friendships of, 14, 15, 42, 51, 53, 58, 60–63, 65, 69, 91, 92, 107, 130, 156, 184, 189, 257; internationalism of, 10, 65, 69, 71, 98, 177–179, 276*n*1; millenarianism of, 128, 129; persecution of, 89; Presbyterian attacks on, 185; as Puritan seminary leader, 37, 38; recommendations by, 47, 56; refusal to leave New England, 4, 131, 134–135, 150, 180; rituals practiced by, 83, 84, 98, 116–117; scholarly work by, 61; trans-Atlantic communion of, 3–4, 146, 148–149, 253; as vicar, 46, 47; views of, 6, 161–162, 69, 71, 176, 197; works by, 4, 60, 62, 94, 98, 109, 116, 118, 120, 128, 141, 148–150, 159, 163–166, 169, 173, 185, 187, 198, 224, 246, 301*n*29

Cotton, John, Jr., 222

Council for New England, 101

Council of State (England), 176, 179, 184, 191, 203

Counter-Reformation. *See* Catholic Counter-Reformation

Court of High Commission: abolition of, 130; Calvinists before, 34, 36, 57, 58, 71, 83, 86, 88, 89, 100

Covenants: between friends, 57, 116; contention over Congregational uses of, 95–99, 115, 165, 171–172, 256, 303*n*43

Craddock, Matthew, 90, 101–103, 125, 188

Craddock, Samuel, 215, 219, 233, 234

Craddock, Walter, 188–189

Crane, Sir Robert, 102

Cranfield, Edward, 230

Crew, Sir Thomas, 63, 75, 78

Crisp, Samuel, 250

Crisp, Tobias, 250

Cromwell, Henry, 181, 184–185, 207

Cromwell, Oliver, 57, 75; clerical network ties of, 80, 177, 180, 183, 185, 191–192; death of, 201–203; ecclesiastical reforms of, 194–201; education of sons of, 39; factionalism under, 315*n*4; foreign policy of, 101, 177–179, 287*n*49, 314*n*60; as House of Commons member, 126, 134; and Ireland, 177, 179, 181, 182, 184, 191; as Lord Protector, 175–179, 191–194; New England's support for, 14, 176–179; purge of Levellers by, 186; and Puritan efforts to reform Church of England, 19, 152; "western design" of, 101, 177–179, 287*n*49

Cromwell, Richard, 185, 202, 203

Crucifixes, 83, 87, 122, 124, 130, 230–231, 246. *See also* Sign of the cross

Cudworth, James, 54

Culverwell, Ezekiel, 31, 39, 52, 53, 55, 57, 73

Cutter, William, 198

Danforth, Samuel, 232

Darley, Henry, 59, 102, 129–130, 134

Darley, Sir Richard, 57, 59, 102

Davenant, Bishop John, 72

Davenport, John: career of, 46, 89–91; clandestine return to England by, 100; and colonial ventures, 102, 103; as Congregationalist leader, 120; correspondence of, 54, 55, 67, 70–71, 74, 75, 90, 91, 99, 113, 118, 119, 213, 216, 218–219, 223, 237, 254; death of, 209; electioneering by, 79; exile of, to Netherlands, 91, 96–97, to New England, 104, 109; as Feoffee, 75, 78, 102; friendships of, 50, 52, 53, 57, 58, 60, 61, 76, 95, 116, 217, 235; irenic

attempts of, 65, 84; millenarianism of,
128; persecution of, 71, 96; refusal to
leave New England, 150, 180; rituals
practiced by, 84, 98; scholarly work by,
61, 62; sermons by, 40, 68–69, 128,
210–211; trans-Atlantic contributions
of, 254; views of, 98, 161, 240; and
Westminster Assembly, 4, 131, 134;
works by, 120, 147, 163, 231–232, 234
Davenport, John, Jr., 57
Davis, Richard, 75, 102, 250
Day, Wentworth, 207
Declaration of Breda, 204
Declaration of Faith and Order (Savoy
Declaration), 200, 204, 237–239, 251,
314n60
Declarations of Indulgence, 222–223,
243, 247
Dedham (Essex), 38, 39, 56, 79; clerical
association at, 49, 51
Defoe, Daniel, 215
Denomination, Congregationalists as, xiii,
221–223, 238–244, 254, 320n1
Deprivation (of Puritan livings), 45, 57,
75, 82, 85, 87–89, 91, 101, 120, 182,
205, 285n27
Desborough, John, 178, 199, 206
Desborough, Samuel, 309n24
Devon Association, 184, 186
D'Ewes, Richard, 30
D'Ewes, Sir Symonds, 27, 28, 30, 52–53
Diocesan visitations, 36, 83, 85–87
Directory of Worship, 135–136, 139, 153,
154
Discipline (church), contention over, 72,
138. *See also* Government (of churches)
Dissenting Brethren (England), 4, 109–
110, 138–160, 179–190, 253–257; attacks on, 299n9; and Baptists, 12–13,
195; at Cambridge, 23; New England's
support for, xiii, 14, 146, 179–190,
295n28; question of tolerance by, 14,
159–161, 166–170; in Westminster Assembly, 139–143, 153–154; works by,
139, 166, 168–169. *See also* Bridge,
William; Burroughs, Jeremiah; Congregationalists; Goodwin, Thomas; Independents; Simpson, Sydrach
Dissenting Deputies, 255–256
Ditloft, Mr., 101

Dixwell, John, 204, 320n40
Dod, John: death of, 45; friendships of,
30, 46, 47, 59–62, 102, 107; positions
held by, 38, 84, 89; in Puritan Revolu-
tion, 130
Dominion of New England, 5, 208, 217,
221, 230, 246, 248, 327n60. *See also*
Charters
Dorchester Adventurers, 100–101
Downing, Emmanuel, 308n24
Downing, Lucy, 183
Drake, Francis (Mr.), 46
Drake, John, 98
Dudley, Joseph, 245–246, 254
Dudley, Thomas, 62, 69, 102, 103, 116,
271n11
Dugard, Thomas, 40, 51, 52, 60, 92,
261n8
Dunster, Henry, 176, 195, 197, 198, 239
Dury, John, 103, 192; correspondence of,
99, 113, 231; Protestant Union efforts
of, 65, 314n60; works by, 62, 187
Dury, Robert, 93
Dutch classis (Amsterdam), 95, 96
Dutch Reformed Church, 37, 93, 94,
162, 165, 171
Dutch States General, 96. *See also* Neth-
erlands

East Anglia, as center of Calvinist reform,
19, 171, 177
Eaton, Nathaniel, 90, 94
Eaton, Samuel, 97, 127, 150, 151, 180,
181, 206, 223
Eaton, Theophilus, 102
Economic issues, between England and
New England, 104, 145, 150, 208, 230,
289n16, 304n5
Edwards, Thomas, 109–110, 119, 131,
140, 141, 149–150, 155, 156, 158, 188,
299n9, 301n32
Ejectors, 197–198
Elbing (Holy Roman Empire), 93, 103
Election: Puritans' sense of, xii, 5, 6, 8,
11, 132, 254, 256, concerns about
269n1, 280n26
Eliot, John, 146, 209; advice of, 111, 257;
at Cambridge, 22, 23; correspondence
of, 307n16; friendships of, 60, 134,
232, 234, 235, 237; as millenarian, 129;

missionary efforts of, 190, 235, 236; as teacher, 39, 51; works by, 177, 179, 317*n*19

Elizabeth (princess of Bohemia), 66–67, 70, 71

Elizabeth I (queen of England), 19, 65, 72, 108

Emigration, 14, 59–61, 63, 104; attempts to reduce, 122; numbers involved in, to New England, 109. *See also* Netherlands; New England

Emmanual College (Cambridge University): as center of reform movement, 19–21, 34; number of students at, 24; prophesying at, 26, 116; Puritans at, 21–23, 27–28, 32, 36, 39, 45, 98, 195; Puritan friendships at, 3, 14, 45; theology at, 26–27

Endecott, John, 101–103, 122, 178–179, 208, 218

England: Cromwell's foreign policy for, 101, 177, 178, 287*n*49; as elect nation, 64–65, 71, 276*n*1; European volunteer regiments from, 55, 56, 66, 68–70; fears about proCatholic foreign policy of, 68, 78, 226; loss of interest in Puritan reforms in, 209; New Englanders' return migration to, 179–190, 307*n*16, 308*n*24; Puritan fears about God's wrath on, 105, 123, 127, 231–232. *See also* Church of England; Dissenting Brethren; Emigration; Forced loans; Friendship networks; Independents; News; Parliament; Protectorate; Puritan Revolution; Restoration; Ship Money case

English classis, 93–97

English Congregational Independency, 93. *See also* Congregationalists

English Society for the Propagation of the Gospel in New England, 236

English Society of Merchant Adventurers, 93, 94, 96, 98

Episcopacy: and the Church of England, 72, 83; Puritan opposition to, 111, 127, 129, 130, 132–133, 147, 169

Erastians, 142, 153, 190

Eucharist: Congregational restrictions on, 95, 99, 117, 135, 171, 237, 256; contention over, 85, 136; at Emmanuel

College, 20; in Restoration House of Commons, 205. *See also* Kneeling

Evans, Daniel, 60

Evelyn, John, 24

Everhard, Robert, 186

Exclusion Crisis, 221, 227, 229, 244, 245

Excommunication, 157, 168, 222, 225, 239

Exiles: English persecution of, in Netherlands, 95–98; importance of godly communion to, 256; Marian, 65, 107; Puritan, xiv, 3, 14, 45, 54, 58, 65, 82, 91–100, 104–105, 107, 115, 204–205, 215–216; role of, in development of new ecclesiastical order, 95–97, 174. *See also* Emigration; Friendship network; Netherlands; New England; Reformed churches

Eyre, Ralph, 75, 90

Eyre, William, 49

Fairclough, Samuel: at Cambridge, 21, 22, 30–31; electioneering by, 79; friendships of, 56; as lecturer, 49, 52; as Presbyterian, 194, 198; ritual practices of, 98–99; seminary work by, 37, 38; works by, 63

Fairfax, Thomas, 69

Faldo, John, 247, 250

Familism, 161

Fanshaw, Sir Thomas, 79

Farewell sermons, 209–210

Fast days, Church of England's, 20, 81

Fasting, Puritans' use of, 67, 80, 92, 121, 122, 126, 127, 144–145, 203, 225, 242

Fenwick, George, 22, 23, 309*n*24

Feoffees for Impropriations, 14, 75–79, 89, 90, 102, 250, 281*n*33

Ferguson, Robert, 228, 248

Field, John, 54

Fiennes, Charles, 102

Fiennes family, 43

Fifth Monarchists, 186, 193–194, 196, 206–207

Finch, Sir Henry, 127

Firmin, Giles, 180, 189, 198

First Bishops War, 124, 125, 128

Five Mile Act, 207–208, 212

Flavell, John, 212

Fleetwood, Charles, 181, 199, 203, 315*n*1, 328*n*64
Forbes, John, 93, 94, 95, 96, 99
Forced loans (England's), 46, 71, 80, 123
Ford, Stephen, 171
Foxe, John, 64, 127
Foxley, Thomas, 48, 76, 109
Franklin, William, 179
Frederick (Elector of the Palatine), 66–67
French Reformed Church, 93, 162
Friendship network (Puritan): in Cambridge, 13–40, after graduation, 41–63; in colonial venture, 102; deaths among leaders of, 209; extension of, 56; importance of, in shaping ideas of Puritans, xii, 5–6 (*see also* Conferences); in London, 214; maintenance of, from abroad, 99–100; new, based on economic interests, 245; in New England, 111–113; as placement service, 39, 45, 47, 49–51, 56–57, 59, 61, 183, 313*n*55; among Presbyterians, 294*n*22; services provided by, 313*n*55; and social status, 29–30, 43–46, 244 (*see also* Clergy: relations of, with laity); theories about, 9–13; trans-Atlantic, 5–6, 13–15, 99–100, 113, 116–117, 163–164, 173–175, 182–183, 212, 257, after Restoration, 183, 209–211, 215–216, 233–238, strains in, 238–245, weakening of, 245–253, 257; and trans-Atlantic news, 4, 113, 118, 125–126, 143, 183, 228–230, 235. *See also* Brokers; Clergy; Clusters; Conferences (clerical); Conformity; Correspondence; Godly communion; Kinship; Publication; Puritan(s): efforts of, to reform Church of England
Fund-raising: for clerical salaries, 75–79, 90, 250; for European Protestants, 14, 64, 70–71, 90, 165, 227; for Feoffees, 75–79, 90; trans-Atlantic, 145, 235–236
Funeral sermons, 62–63, 236, 313*n*55

Gale, Theophilus, 191, 214–215, 217, 233, 236, 251
Gangraena (Edwards), 141, 156
Gataker, Thomas: and Cambridge, 29, 40; at clerical conferences, 50; correspondence of, 55, 59, 67; death of, 209; as preacher, 46; as Presbyterian, 187; and

Puritan seminary leader, 37–38; sermons by, 69; works by, 62
Gateshead (England), 171, 180
Gathered (underground) churches, 120, 136–137, 155, 171, 181, 184, 193, 195, 199, 302*n*33
"General" Baptists. *See* Baptists
Geneva Bible, 72
Gerard, Sir Gilbert, 30, 51
Gering, John, 75
Germany, Puritan ties with, 19, 101, 118, 121, 125. *See also* Palatinate
Gifford, George, 15
Gilbert, Thomas, 200, 216, 236
Gillespie, George, 133, 137, 138
Glorious Revolution, 5, 221, 248, 249. *See also* William of Orange
Glover, Joseph, 88
Godly communion: as basis of trans-Atlantic Puritan relations, 5–9, 163, 173–174, 236–237, 257; and church covenants, 171; and consensus, 13–14, 256–257; in New England, 104, 107–108, 110–113, 117, 163, 172; Puritans' experience of, xii–xiii, 5–9, 17, 26–27, 31–32, 41–43, 98, 110, 132, 168, decline in, 211–212, 243–254, 257. *See also* Conferences; "Congregational communion"; Congregationalists; Friendship network; New England Way
Goffe, Stephen, 96
Goffe, William, 186, 194, 199, 204, 207, 218–220, 248
Goodwin, John, 99, 118, 131, 142, 170, 171, 174, 186, 197, 310*n*25
Goodwin, Thomas, 244; at Cambridge, 20, 22, 23, 31, 32, 34, 35, 59; career of, 181, 213; conferences with, 116, 132, 142, 239; as Congregational reform advocate, 4, 14, 98, 120, 132, 147, 169, 185, 198; conversion of, 30; correspondence of, 54, 118, 119, 171; and Cromwell, 202–203; death of, 247; as Dissenting Brethren, 109, 157, 194, 209, 222; exile of, to Netherlands, 65, 92–93, 98, 99, 100, 183; friendships of, 50–52, 58, 60, 61, 63, 84, 91, 92, 98, 102, 156, 173, 187, 189, 190, 192, 202, 217, 234, 257; irenic attempts of, 65; in London, 214, 224; millenarianism of,

128, 129; persecution of, 92–93; as preacher, 303*n*43; recommendations by, 56; resignation of lectureship by, 89; returns to England from Netherlands, 127, 132; at Savoy Assembly, 200; scholarly work by, 34, 61, 63, 149–150, 163–165; and sects, 186, 195–196; spy's report on, 86; travels of, 39, 216; views of, 109, 118, 148, 167, 172, 251, 317*n*22; at Westminster Assembly, 133–139, 141, 191; works by, 63, 128, 133, 192, 207

Goodwin, Timothy, 215

Goodyear, Hugh, 21, 22, 93, 94, 99, 118, 216

Gookin, Daniel, 309*n*24

Gorton, Samuel, 158, 160

Gouge, Edward, 216

Gouge, Thomas, 205, 215–216, 233, 251

Gouge, William: at Cambridge, 22, 27, 29, 31, 39; correspondence of, 54, 55, 70–71, 84–85; as Feoffee, 75; friendships of, 51–52, 62, 63, 90; as parson, 47, 56; persecution of, 71, 84–85, 88; recommendations of, 45; scholarly work of, 127; sermons by, 40, 53, 63, 69; skirting of conformity by, 83, 84–85; views of, 42, 121

Gould, Thomas, 239, 242

Government (of churches): contention over, 72, 83, 244, 257, at Savoy Assembly, 200–201, at Westminster Assembly, 130–135, 152–155; and friendship clusters, 116; in New England, 111, 113–114, 119, 164, 200–201. *See also* Classis; Conferences; Congregational autonomy; Covenants; Episcopacy; Magistrates; Presbyters; Synod(s)

Grace: contention over, 72, 90, 113–115, 192, 197; Puritans' experience of, xii, 5, 6, 8, 29, 42, 43, 211, 245

Grammar schools (Puritan), 38–39

Grand Remonstrance, 125, 131, 177

Great St. Andrews Church (Cambridge), 22, 34

Great St. Mary's Church, 27, 34, 36

Greenham, Richard, 37, 53

Greenhill, William, 102, 139, 171, 192; at Cambridge, 22, 23; clandestine return to England by, 100; conventicle worship

by, 212, 213; correspondence of, 54, 81; under Cromwell, 194; death of, 209, 224; friendships of, 51, 153, 190; as lecturer, 49, 76, 87; in London, 214; at Savoy Assembly, 200; scholarly work of, 150, 233, 234, 301*n*26; works by, 164, 185

Gribius, Peter, 98

Griffiths, George, 46, 186, 190, 192, 200, 204, 207, 213–214, 224, 227, 233, 239, 243, 247–248, 250–251

Grimston, Sir Harbottle, 79

Grotius, Hugo, 280*n*20

Guillym, Nathaniel, 225

Gunpowder Plot, 245

Gurdon, Brampton, 46, 52

Gustavus Adolphus (king of Sweden), 67, 70, 94, 121, 129, 165

Half-Way Covenant dispute, 211–212, 230, 232, 234, 237, 240

Hall, Joseph, 274*n*26

Hampden, John, 57, 62, 78, 124, 129

Hampden, John (the younger), 248

Harding, John, 19

Harlackenden, Richard, 59

Harlackenden, Roger, 59

Harley, Lady Brilliana Conway, 11, 46

Harley, Sir Edward, 183

Harley, Sir Robert, 11; correspondence of, 70; friendships of, 53, 54, 57, 58, 80; as Puritan patron, 21, 46, 47, 56, 76, 90

Harrison, James, 45, 52

Harrison, Thomas, 181, 184, 191–193, 213

Hartlib, Samuel, 65, 94, 99, 145, 187, 269*n*37

Harvard, John, 39

Harvard College (Massachusetts), 248; graduates of, 150–151, 179, 181–183, 216, 217; support for, 145, 146, 215, 236. *See also* Cambridge Association

Harwood, Colonel Edward, 56, 69, 70, 94

Harwood, George, 70, 75, 101–102

Harwood, John, 217

Haselrig, Arthur, 134

Haynes, Hezekiah, 194, 199, 205, 206, 309*n*24

Haynes, John, 46, 50, 178, 182

Heads of Agreement, 249–252, 253

Heidelberg (Palatinate), 66, 67, 69
Helme, Cairns, 200
Hemingway, Daniel, 237
Henderson, Alexander, 133, 139
Henrietta Marie (queen of England), 36, 57, 73, 75, 80, 123
Herbert, George, 108
Heresy, 140, 155–161, 167–170, 190. *See also* Excommunication; *names of particular sects*
Herle, Charles, 136, 143, 149, 187–188
Hewson, George, 101
Hewson, Thomas, 56
Heyes, Jonathan, 220
Heylin, Royland, 75
Heylyn, Peter, 77–79, 86
Heywood, Oliver, 39–40, 53, 192, 225
Hibbins, William, 145
Higginson, Francis, 21, 22, 47, 60, 71, 103, 180
Higginson, John, 232
High Commission. *See* Court of High Commission
Hildersham, Arthur: at Cambridge, 23, 32; correspondence of, 54, 99; friendships of, 30, 38, 46, 51, 57, 58, 60, 92, 102, 103; imprisonment of, 56; recommendations by, 47, 50, 56; reinstatement of, to living, 84; seminary work of, 37; sermons of, 78; works of, 61
Hill, John, 220
Hill, Thomas, 22, 23, 38, 47, 56, 167, 187, 192
Hoar, Leonard, 182–183, 228, 236
Hobart, Peter, 162, 166, 242
Holbech, Martin, 22, 23, 39, 45, 89
Holborne, Robert, 78
Holcroft, Francis, 224
Holdsworth, Richard, 34, 65
Holland, Henry Rich, earl of, 33–34, 36, 57, 58
Holland, Jeremiah, 181
Holmes, Nathaniel, 164
Hood, Timothy, 90–91
Hooke, Jane, 218–219, 235–236, 242
Hooke, John, 182
Hooke, William, 48, 55, 70, 73, 89, 118, 144, 146, 178–180, 182, 192, 200, 203, 209–210, 224; correspondence of, 213, 223, 228–229, 237, 254; in London,

214, 257; in New England, 218–220, 236; removal of, 205; works by, 126, 234
Hooker, Thomas, 45, 123; at Cambridge, 21–23, 26, 28, 29, 31, 33; as classis member, 93; clerical conferences of, 50–51, 112; and colonial venture, 102; as Congregational leader, 120; correspondence of, 54, 99, 118, 119; death of, 209; exile of, in Netherlands, 95, 96, 97, in New England, 104, 105, 109, 112; friendships of, 32, 51, 52, 56, 57, 59–63, 92, 95, 103, 116, 117; as lecturer, 46, 47, 51; millenarianism of, 128; persecution of, 57–58, 89; Presbyterian attacks on, 185; refusal to leave New England, 131, 150, 180; seminary work of, 37–39; sermons of, 68, 69, 73; views of, 98, 157–158, 161; and Westminster Assembly, 4, 131, 134; works by, 34, 51, 61, 62, 94, 95, 128, 148–150, 155, 163, 164, 173, 196
House of Commons (Parliament), 126, 175; Charles I's impeachment of leaders of, 129; interest of, in religious reform, 130; Montagu's impeachment by, 80–81; on religious practices after Restoration, 205, 223; Wren investigation by, 87
House of Lords (Parliament), 130, 223
Howe, John, 39, 65, 184–185, 189, 191, 200, 203, 216, 247–250
Hughes, George, 76
Hull, John, 176, 228
Humble Petition and Advice, 199
Humfry, John, 100–101, 103
Humphrey, Laurence, 19
Huntingdon, earl of, 58
Hutchinson, Anne, 112, 113, 157, 158, 168, 172, 299n13
Hutchinson, Richard, 224
Hyde, Edward, earl of Clarendon, 206, 208, 213, 218

Impropriations. *See* Livings
Independents, 246; attacks on, 155–156, 158, 193; attempts at unity among, 157, 160, 170, 174, 195; colonial discomfort with label of, 161–162; distinctions among, 166–167, 294n22, 301n32,

302*n*33; as label for opponents of Pres-
byterianism, 139–140, 147, 158. *See
also* Congregationalists; Dissenting
Brethren; Radicals; Sects
Indians, spreading gospel to, 100, 146,
189–190. *See also* King Philip's War
Ireland: clerical friends in, 146, 215; con-
venticles in, 318*n*26; Cromwell's activi-
ties in, 177, 179, 181, 182, 184, 191;
English troubles in, 123, 144; as source
of New England labor, 145
Irenic efforts, 65, 103, 314*n*60
Ireton, Henry, 174
Irish Articles (1615), 72

Jacob, Henry, 32, 93, 109, 114
James, Thomas, 180
James I (king of England): *Book of Sports*
by, 83; Calvinist orientation of, 72;
classis authorization by, 93; death of,
84; and Laud, 82; and religious obser-
vance at Cambridge, 20, 32–34; and
Thirty Years' War, 66–67
James II (king of England), 206, 226, 227,
230; accession of, 228; and Increase
Mather, 5, 247–248
Jeffreys, George, 228
Jenner, Thomas, 184
Jessey, Henry: as Baptist, 193–198; at
Cambridge, 22, 23; and colonial ven-
ture, 102; correspondence of, 55, 119;
death of, 207, 209; deprivation of, 87;
friendships of, 46, 52, 56, 190; in Lon-
don, 214; in New England, 109
Jesus College (Cambridge University), 21,
22, 23
Johnson, Edward, 107–109, 179, 198
Johnson, Isaac, 22, 23, 62, 71, 102, 116
Johnson, Robert, 49
Jollie, John, 184, 189
Jollie, Thomas, 184, 185, 189, 192, 200,
206, 207, 209, 212, 215, 220, 223–225,
228–230, 234–235, 237–238, 243, 249
Jollie, Timothy, 215
Jones, William, 218
Josselin, Ralph, 57, 59, 75, 173, 189, 190,
303*n*43
Justification by faith doctrine, 36, 195

Keach, Benjamin, 239
Keayne, Robert, 6, 112, 128–129

Kellond, Thomas, 218
Kick, Abraham, 248
Kiffin, William, 195
King Philip's War, 219, 234, 235, 237
King's College (Cambridge University),
22, 31, 39, 73
King's Lynn parish (England), 30, 47, 56
Kinship: compared to friendship, 11; and
Puritan friendship network, 29, 38, 59,
61, 63, 71, 73, 75, 89–90, 100, 102,
126, 150, 178, 181, 182, 187, 188, 192,
218, 240, 247, 255, 283*n*11
Kirke, Percy, 228
Kirke, Thomas, 218
Kneeling (to receive eucharist), 32, 83,
84, 85, 86, 87, 90–91
Knightley, Sir Richard, 63
Knollys, Hanserd, 150
Knowles, John, 209; at Cambridge, 22,
23, 29, 31, 32; friendships of, 56, 62;
fund-raising of, 227, 235; as lecturer,
49; in London, 214; as New Englander,
177–178, 181, 236; persecution of, 88;
at Savoy Assembly, 200

Laity: dangers to Puritan clergy of, 171,
205–206; relations of, to clergy, xiii,
51–53, 55–59, 62, 63, 68, 70–71, 78–
79, 88, 100–102, 105, 118, 205–206,
254, 256, 270*n*6, 271*n*11, 304*n*5; rights
of, to preach, 95, 97, 117, 172, 198.
See also Patronage; Prophesying
Lamb, Thomas, 148
Lambert, John, 194, 199
Lambeth Articles, 35, 72
Lancashire (England), 61, 76, 176, 179
Langley, Thomas, 131
Langston, John, 224
Larkham, George, 309*n*24
Larkham, Thomas, 309*n*24
Last Supper, clerical communion a version
of, 48, 85. *See also* Eucharist
Lathrop, John, 109
Laud, William (archbishop of Canter-
bury), 43, 49; agents of, 95–96 (*see also*
Spies); career of, 82–83; church innova-
tions by, 124; criticism of Puritans by,
20, 36, 74, 77, 97; impeachment and
imprisonment of, 125, 127, 145,
281*n*33; Massachusetts investigation by,
122; at Oxford, 19; as possible cardinal,

83, 123; Puritan criticism of, 34, 36, 72–75, 80; Puritan persecution by, 14, 43, 54, 57–60, 71, 78, 81–93, 104, 105, 109, 118, 256; Puritan visits to, 146

Lawrence, Richard, 219

Lechford, Thomas, 299n14

Lectures: and friendship, 13, 56, 92, in New England, 111. *See also* Lecture-ships; Sermon(s)

Lectureships: combined Presbyterian and Congregational, 243; denial of, to Puri-tans, 85, 87–89; Puritan attempts to control, 75–79; Puritans in, 21, 34–36, 43, 45, 46, 48–49, 56, 59, 63, 183, 213, 272n14

Lee, Samuel, 217, 233

Leigh, William, 22, 23

Leighton, Alexander, 74–75, 90, 93

Lenthall, William, 52, 78, 150

Leslie, Alexander, 124

Letter drops, 55, 92

Levellers, 174, 186

Leverett, John, 177–179, 219, 240, 241, 309n24

Ley, John, 48

Lincoln, earl of, 30, 55, 58, 69, 70, 100, 103, 118

Lisle, Alice, 228

Literacy, 8, 261n7

Liturgy, 72, 83, 85. *See also* Book of Com-mon Prayer

Livings, 43, 45, 46, 48, 56, 64, 118, 183, 272n14; dangers in, 171; Puritan pur-chase of, 75–79; Puritan resignation from, 89; reinstatement to, 84. *See also* Advowson rights; Deprivation

Lobb, Richard, 190, 247

Lobb, Stephen, 209, 215, 227, 233, 247, 248, 251

Lockyer, Nicholas, 188, 191, 194, 213, 215

Loder, John, 213, 248

Loeffs, Isaac, 200, 247

London, bishop of. *See* Montaigne, George

London, Great Fire of, 226, 235

London consociation, 223–225, 236, 239–240

Long Parliament, 59; electioneering for, 79; Massachusetts Bay Company mem-bers in, 292n9; New Englanders' sup-port for, 143, 144, 145; Puritans in, 125, 126, 142, 292n9; restoration of, after Cromwell's death, 204; and West-minster Assembly, 4, 131, 133–138, 142

Love, Christopher, 311n32

Love, William, 226

Lowman, Moses, 191

Luce, John, 289n16

Lucie, Mr., 35

Ludlow, Roger, 309n24

Maestricht, siege of, 70, 94

Magdalen College (Oxford University), 19, 77, 89, 181, 183–184, 191, 214

Magdalene College (Cambridge Univer-sity), 22, 23, 29, 31

Magistrates (in Massachusetts): and Bap-tists, 196, 197, 239; rights of, 110, 115, 134; role of, 138, 157, 159, 160, 166, 168–170, 190, 238

Maidstone, John, 57, 203, 216

Manchester, Henry Montagu, earl of, 57, 58

Mansfield, Count, 67, 69

Manton, Thomas, 176, 194, 205, 243

Manuscripts: circulation of, 62, 109, 118, 120, 128, 148, 255, 290n25, 301n26; of Cotton's thoughts on ritual practices, 60, 62, 99; entrusting of, 150; trans-Atlantic exchanges of, 234. *See also* Scholarly work

Manwaring, Roger, 80

Marriage, contention over rituals in, 84, 85, 172. *See also* Kinship

Marsden, Jeremiah, 189

Marshall, Stephen: at Cambridge, 22, 23; correspondence of, 54, 55; death of, 209; diocesan visitation to, 85–86; elec-tioneering by, 79; friendships of, 52, 57, 59, 62, 80, 155, 187–188, 190; irenic attempts of, 65; millenarianism of, 127; as Presbyterian, 174, 193, 194, 198; in Puritan Revolution, 130; semi-nary work of, 37; survival of, 88–89; views of, 159, 304n2, 311n35; at West-minster Assembly, 135, 136, 142, 143; works by, 132

Mary I (queen of England), 19, 65, 107, 248

Mascall, Robert, 237, 240

Masham, Sir William, 30, 46, 79

Mass, in England, 73, 75

Massachusetts Bay Colony, 254; censorship in, 317*n*19; clerical conferences in, 112, 166, 173, 201, 252; currency coining in, 178–179; delegation to England from, 145–146, 150; fasts in, 144; people banished from, 158, 160; Puritan hopes for, 107; royal investigation of, 122; settlement of, 109. *See also* Boston; Charters; Magistrates; Massachusetts General Court; Plymouth Colony; Roxbury; Salem

Massachusetts Bay Company, 101, 102, 103; members of, 69, 125, 129, 134, 292*n*9

Massachusetts General Court, 177, 196, 238, 239

Mather, Cotton, 29, 54, 169, 253–255

Mather, Eleazar, 216–217

Mather, Increase (Richard's son), 200, 209, 219; as bridge between several friendship clusters, 10, 216; on charter surrender, 245; correspondence of, 212, 217, 219, 220, 230, 236, 238, 254, 342*n*33; in England, 5, 184–185, 247, 252, 254–255, 257; and Ireland, 191; in Netherlands, 216; sermons of, 233, 235; and trans-Atlantic communion, 14, 243, 246, 253, 254, 257, 342*n*33; works by, 234, 241, 242

Mather, Nathaniel (Richard's son), 180, 184–186, 200, 209, 212–214, 216, 220, 224, 229, 230, 233, 234, 236, 238, 242, 244, 247, 248, 250, 251, 318*n*26

Mather, Richard, 116, 119; correspondence of, 54, 148; death of, 182, 209; fears of, for God's wrath on England, 105; friendships of, 56, 60, 109, 187; millenarianism of, 129; at Oxford, 24; works by, 120, 147–149, 163–165, 179, 196, 301*n*26

Mather, Samuel, 183–185, 191, 209, 304*n*3; works by, 226, 233, 244

Matthews, Marmaduke, 88, 150

Maurice (prince of Orange), 56, 94

Maverick, Samuel, 218

Mawe, Leonard, 36

Mead, Matthew, 33, 35, 65, 209, 210, 212–215, 224, 227, 228, 247–250

Mede, Joseph, 21, 22, 37, 127, 128

Medieval spirituality, and Puritans, 8

Membership (church): contention about requirements for, 98, 117, 149, 164, 165, 171, 185, 224, 303*n*43; recommendations for, 172. *See also* Rebirth

Mendlesham (Suffolk), 49, 52, 87

Middelburg (Netherlands), 37–38, 67, 98, 216

Middlekauff, Robert, 323*n*21

Mildmay, Sir Henry, 33, 51, 79, 183

Mildmay, Robert, 46

Mildmay, Sir Walter, 19–20

Millenarianism (among Puritans), 65, 127–129, 166, 175–178, 186, 193, 231, 276*n*1, 293*nn*11,12, 304*n*2

Milton, John, 25, 38, 64, 191, 193, 210

Milway, Thomas, 224

Ministers. *See* Preachers

Mitchell, J. Clyde, 9

Mitchell, Jonathan, 42, 232, 234

Monck, George, 69, 183, 203–204

Monmouth's Rebellion, 221, 228, 246, 319*n*37

Montagu, Henry, earl of Manchester, 57, 58

Montagu, Richard, 36, 73–74, 79, 80, 83, 86

Montaigne, George (bishop of London), 57, 80, 88, 90, 96, 97, 122

Morton, Charles, 198, 215, 217, 246–247, 252, 254

Morton, George, 23

Morton, Nicholas, 22, 23, 39

Morton, Bishop Thomas, 74

Mott, Thomas, 22, 23

Moulson, Lady Ann, 145

Moxon, George, 225

Munnings, William, 45

Münster (Germany), 195, 207

National church. *See* State Church

Naylor, James, 186

Neal, Daniel, 215, 255

Neile, Richard (archbishop of York), 36, 54, 72–73, 75, 82, 83, 85, 86, 88

Netherlands: discouragement about Puritan reform in, 103, 104; drain of English Calvinist leadership to, 124; English volunteer regiments in, 55, 56, 68–70; experimental church practices begin in, 94–99, 115–116, 128; Puritan exile to, xiv, 3, 4, 14, 54, 58, 82, 87, 91, 93, 95, 98, 204, 214–216, return to England from, 307n14; Puritan links with, 37, 101, 146, 165; Spanish threat to, 66–67, 96. *See also* Anglo-Dutch Wars; Dutch Reformed Church; Emigration; Reformed churches; *names of cities in*

Networks. *See* Friendship network

New England: attempts to curb autonomy of, 122, 245–246 (*see also* Charters); corporations to establish colonies in, 100–101; drain of English Calvinist leadership to, 124; intolerance in, 196–197, 230–231 (*see also* Religious toleration); as model for English Puritans, 3, 103, 104, 107–117, 119, 134–135, 139, 146–150, 160–161, 179, 190, 231–233; post-Restoration relations of, with England, 208–209; Puritan exile to, xiv, 3, 14, 45, 59, 76, 82, 87, 94, 103–122, 124, 216–219; reasons for emigration to, 104–105, 107–110; relations between Congregationalists and Presbyterians in, 162; return migrants from, 150–151, 179–190, 308n24; support for English Puritanism from, 14, 109, 125–127, 143–151, 157, 176–179, 198, 257, 295n28, 317n19 (*see also* Pamphlet controversies). *See also* Charters; Dominion of New England; Economic issues; Emigration; Indians; Magistrates; New England Way; News; Puritan(s); *names of New England colonies*

New England Company for a Plantation in Massachusetts Bay, 58, 60, 101, 235

New England Company for the Propagation of the Gospel, 190

New England Way: classic statements of, 149, 164–166; critiques of, 199n14; discussions of, 132; English Presbyterian attacks on, 156–160; origins of, 93, 116; promotion of, 120–121, 135, 146–150; 163–164; similarities of Dissenting Brethren and English reformed

churches to, 4, 159, 169–173. *See also* Congregationalists; New England

New Haven Colony, 109, 144–145, 179, 208

Newcome, Henry, 190

Newcomen, Matthew, 22, 31, 56, 62, 79, 132, 153, 216, 225

News: of European Protestants, 67, 70, 99; reliability of, 3–4, 12; trans-Atlantic, 99, 113, 118, 125–126, 143, 183, 228–230, 235, 342n33

Newton, John, 51

Nichols, Robert, 117

Noble, Isaac, 249

Nominated Parliament, 193–194

Nonconformists. *See* Baptists; Congregationalists; Dissenting Brethren; Independents; Presbyterian(s); Puritan(s); Reformed churches; Sects

Non-Separating Congregationalists. *See* Congregationalists

Norcross, Nathaniel, 180

Norfolk (England), 76, 87, 97

Norton, John, 224; at Cambridge, 22, 23, 31; as chaplain, 46; and Cromwell, 177; death of, 209; friendships of, 56, 62, 189, 198; views of, 107, 110; works by, 163–165, 185, 231

Norwich (England), 56, 76, 86–87, 89, 172

Norwood, Robert, 168

Noy, Attorney General, 78

Noyse, John, 162

Nuttall, Geoffrey, 263n1

Nye, John, 188

Nye, Philip, 102; attacks on, 156, 157; conferences with, 99, 181; conventicle worship of, 213; correspondence of, 118, 119, 237; as Dissenting Brethren, 109, 222; as English advocate of Congregational reform, 4, 120, 147, 194, 229; friendships of, 52, 56, 58, 60, 91, 173, 187, 188, 190, 199, 243; irenic attempts of, 65; in London, 214; in Netherlands, 4, 98, 100, 118; as pastor, 171; in Puritan Revolution, 130; recommendations of, 184, 191; return to England of, 127, 132; at Savoy Assembly, 200, 201; scholarly work by, 34, 61, 150, 163–165; and sects, 186, 192, 193,

195, 239; sermons by, 86; views of, 148, 172, 174, 204; at Westminster Assembly, 135–138, 141; works by, 192, 207

Oakes, Urian, 216, 232, 238
Oates, Titus, 227
Odingsell, John, 171
Offspring, Charles, 37, 48, 75
Offwood, Stephen, 283n6
Order. *See* Presbyterian(s): emphasis on order among
Ordinance for the Ejecting of Scandalous, Ignorant and Insufficient Ministers and Schoolmasters, 197
Ordination (of preachers), 95, 97, 115, 117, 137, 155, 184, 205, 224–225, 242–243
Orrery, Roger Boyle, earl of, 226
Overton, Henry, 55, 90
Owen, John, 40, 124, 172, 173, 181, 184, 196, 222, 224, 251; under Cromwell, 191, 193, 194, 198, 200, 202, 203, 206; death of, 247; friendships of, 189, 190, 199, 233, 235, 239; hiding of, 227, 228; millenarianism of, 175; persecution of, 213, 214; recommendations of, 183, 224–225; removal of, 205; resignation of, 89; Restoration reform efforts of, 226; as vicar, 171, 182; views of, 6, 8, 15, 169–170, 192, 303n43, 317n22; works by, 185, 186, 190, 192, 233, 234, 244
Owen, Thankful, 191, 194, 214
Oxenbridge, John, 199, 216, 217, 241
Oxford University (England): academic life at, 24–26; anti-Calvinism at, 36, 83, 89, 214; Congregationalists at, under Cromwell, 191–192; Puritanism at, 19, 24, 41, 195. *See also names of colleges and churches in*

Paget, John: Congregational responses to, 62, 99, 119, 163; in Netherlands, 94–97, 132, 165, 188
Pagitt, Ephraim, 160
Palatinate: Puritan support for, 14, 66–67, 69–71; refugees from, 14, 70–71, 101, 103, 165
Palmer, Anthony, 187, 214
Palmer, Herbert, 136, 142

Pamphlet controversies, 97, 146–150, 155–160, 163–164, 185–190, 196–197, 226–227. *See also* Publication
Papacy, 66, 72–73
Parker, Thomas, 94, 158, 162, 242
Parker, William, 171
Parliament: alliance of, with Scots, 129–130; appointment of clerical synod by, 131; Cavalier, 204–206, 226–227; Charles I forced to call, 124–126; Charles I's dissolution of, 74, 81, 101, 105, 123; Congregationalist appeals to, 138–139, 152–155; fusion between dissent in, and Puritan dissent, 78; and heresy, 190, 203; Laud's sermons to, 83; Nominated, 193–194; Puritan pressure on, 70, 73, 74, 77–79, 226–227; Puritan support for Cromwell's, 175–176; Rump, 176, 191–193, 203; Short, 79, 124, 126. *See also* Council of State; House of Commons; House of Lords; Long Parliament
Parliamentary Commission for Foreign Plantations, 160
Particular Baptists. *See* Baptists
Pastors (in Congregational churches), 114, 136, 172, 224
Patronage, 30, 43, 45–46, 57–58, 78, 88, 271n11, 318n27. *See also* Clergy: relations of, with laity; Friendship network: and social status
Peck, Robert, 49, 150, 180
Pelagian doctrines, 36, 72
Pemberton, William, 22, 32
Pembroke College (Cambridge University), 22, 23, 35, 36
Penhallow, Samuel, 217
Pennington, Isaac, 71, 130, 134
Pensioners (at British universities), 25
Perkins, William: attacks on, 35; censorship of works by, 85; as Chaderton's student, 26; conversions by, 30; friendships of, 51, 61, 108; as Puritan leader at Cambridge, 19, 22, 31, 32, 38, 59; sermons by, 34, 35, 128; will of, 62; works by, 85, 114
Persecution. *See* Puritan(s): persecution of; Religious toleration
Peter, Hugh: at Cambridge, 22, 23, 29; as classis member, 93; and colonial ven-

ture, 101, 102; as Congregational
leader, 120, 139, 191, 194–196; correspondence of, 54, 67, 92, 99, 118, 134,
307n16; as delegate to England from
Massachusetts, 145–146, 150, 153,
180; execution of, as regicide, 204, 209;
exile of, to Netherlands, 65, 92, 94–99,
119, to New England, 104; as Feoffee,
102; friendships of, 50–52, 60, 63, 134,
162, 173; leaves Netherlands, 97; as
parson, 45; persecution of, 57, 58; plots
by, 206; scholarly work of, 61, 147,
150; seminary work of, 37–38; sermons
of, 68, 69, 73, 80, 86, 176; support for
Netherlands by, 70, 71; views of, 76,
88, 167, 168; works of, 70
Peter, Thomas, 180
Peterhouse College (Cambridge University), 22, 23, 35, 36
Petition(s): about clerical abuses, 130;
about need for New England Reformation, 238; as political tool, 70, 73, 226–
227; Root and Branch, 125, 130,
281n33
Petto, Samuel, 191, 213, 219, 224, 229,
233, 234, 248
Phelips, Sir Roger, 80
Phillips, George, 51, 57, 148, 181, 196
Phillips, John (of Wrentham), 54, 92, 99,
139, 150, 153, 171, 173, 181, 182, 209
Pickering, Sir Gilbert, 79
Piers, Bishop (of Bath and Wells), 87
Pierson, Thomas, 21, 22, 47, 61, 70
Plymouth Colony (Massachusetts), 160,
162
Pockocke, John, 171
Popish Plot, 221, 227, 229, 248–249
Postmasters, 220
Prayer(s): Puritan opposition to set, 118,
148; as Puritan weapon, 68–69, 92,
121–122, 126, 144–145, 178, 226. *See
also* Prayer groups
Prayer Book. *See* Book of Common Prayer
Prayer groups: at Cambridge, 26–27, 31,
191; congregational, 98, 225, 236
Preachers: ordination of, 95, 97, 115,
117, 137, 155, 184, 205, 224, 225, 242,
243, 254, 303n43; radical, 130, 131;
selection of, 114, 117, 136, 164, 172,

284n15, 303n43. *See also* Laity: rights
of, to preach; Prophesying
Predestination, 20, 35, 36, 72, 73, 83, 85,
279n18
Presbyterian(s): Arminian leanings of,
299n13; and classis, 93; conferences of,
50; Congregational contention with,
xiii, 95, 97, 116, 132–167, 174, 185–
186, 250–252; Congregational cooperation with, 63, 187–189, 193, 194, 198–
199, 236, 242–244, 249–250, 311n32;
disassociation of, from regicide, 176;
emphasis on order among, xiii, 99, 114,
117, 132, 139, 174; friendship network
among, 294n22, 307n14; friendships of,
with Dissenting Brethren, 187; and
millenarianism, 127; in New England,
113–114; Puritans who became, 117–
118, 132, 133; rise of, in England, 152–
174, 203; social status of, 244; and
Westminster Assembly, 131–143, 152–
167. *See also* Presbyters; Scotland
Presbyterian Fund, 251
Presbyters, 111, 114, 130, 132, 136, 142–
143, 154, 168, 244, 289n14
Preston, John: considers emigrating, 93;
conversion of, 30; correspondence of,
54, 55; death of, 62, 63; friendships of,
6, 42, 46, 50, 51, 56, 57, 62, 69, 73; as
master at Emmanuel College, 32, 33,
38, 98, 191; patrons of, 36, 89–90; as
Puritan leader, 68–70, 73–74, 80, at
Cambridge, 19, 21, 22, 26, 29–31, 59;
recommendations by, 39, 45, 56; sermons by, 34–35, 52, 53, 61, 68, 70, 73,
80, 187; skirting of conformity by, 83;
will of, 62
Price, Nicholas, 30
Pride's Purge, 178, 304n3
Prince, Thomas, 253, 254
Proost, Jonas, 67
Prophesying, 26, 95, 97, 111, 116, 117,
165, 172, 198, 223, 272n14
Protectorate: ecclesiastical Triers during,
31, 194–195; establishment of, 176;
New England's support for, 14. *See also*
Cromwell, Oliver
Protestantism: international, 14, 40, 48,
64–72, 74–75, 101, 121, 125, 165, 231–

232, 314*n*60; martyrs for, 19. *See also* Calvinism; Puritan(s)

Providence Island Company, 101–102

Prynne, William, 46, 52, 55, 76, 78, 83, 87

Publication (of treatises): Puritans' involvement with, 61–63, 94, 96, 127–128, 132–133, 135, 139, 146–150, 157–160, 163–166, 185–190, 215, 301*n*26, 317*n*19; trans-Atlantic, 4, 119–120, 126, 166, 233–234, 255. *See also* Pamphlet controversies

Pullen, John, 36

Puritan(s): at Cambridge, 17–20; basis of self-definition by, xii, 5; criticism of, 20, 36, 46, 74, 77, 97; disagreements among, 111–118, 131, 203, 238–253; divergence between New England and England, 238–253; efforts of, to reform Church of England, 19, 40, 41, 63–81, 84–87, 101–102, 122, 124, 127, 130–138, 146–150, 174, 175, 182, 185, discouragement about, 103, 105, 208–211, 315*n*1, 317*n*22; evolution of views of, 113–116; growth of power in England, 43–46, 152–203; intolerance by, 112, 113, 158–163, 166–170, 174, 178, 180, 195–196, 234 (*see also* Religious toleration); millenarianism of, 65, 127–129, 166, 175–178, 186, 193, 231, 276*n*1, 293*nn*11,12, 304*n*2; persecution of, 14, 41, 43, 54, 57–60, 71, 78, 82–93, 104, 105, 109, 118, 125; plan for society of, in New England, 101, 105, 107–117; vulnerability of clerical, 47–48, 82–103, 171, 202. *See also* Anti-Catholicism; Conformity; Congregationalists; Dissenting Brethren; Election; Friendship network; Gathered churches; Grace; New England; New England Way; Presbyterian(s); Protestantism; Reformed churches

Puritan Revolution, 61, 97, 129–131, 143–145, 170–174, 176, 185, 308*n*24

Pym, John, 51, 62, 73, 74, 101, 116, 124, 129

Pynchon, John, 218

Pynchon, William, 102, 185, 225

Quakers (Society of Friends), xiii, 180, 186, 190, 199, 230, 234, 241, 310*n*26

Queens' College (Cambridge University), 21, 22, 28, 30–32, 34, 45

Quick, John, 99, 216, 255

Radicals, 283*n*6; criticism of Puritan clergy by, 47, 157, 158; discouraged Dissenters become, 227–228; plots against government by, 221, 226. *See also* Independents; Preachers: radical; Sects

Rainsborough, Thomas, 309*n*24

Randolph, Edward, 218, 220

Randolph, Thomas, 309*n*24

Ranew, Nathaniel, 22, 23

Rathband, William, 117–118, 131, 143, 147–148, 163

Rawson, Edward, 182

Rebirth, xii, 11, 43, 117

Redich, Katherine, 58

Reformed churches, 65, 67, 69, 74–75, 80, 115–116, 118, 128, 130, 140, 141, 216, 314*n*60; attempts to alienate, from Congregationalists, 164–165. *See also* Dutch Reformed Church; French Reformed Church; Gathered churches; "Stranger" churches

Reforming Synod, 238

Refugees (Palatinate), 14, 70–71, 101, 103, 165

Regicide, 175–176, 304*nn*2,3

Regicides, 59, 101, 103–104, 218–220, 320*n*40

Religious toleration, 12–14, 73, 75, 112, 113, 138–141, 154–156, 158–164, 166–170, 174, 178, 180, 193–201, 221, 226, 230–231, 234, 238–242, 247, 326*n*49; by Charles II, 206, 207. *See also* Clarendon Code; Conventicle Act; Spies

Restoration: censorship after, 54; as end of Puritan efforts to reform England, 14, 257; trans-Atlantic friendships after, 183

Reynolds, Thomas, 255

Rhode Island, 208

Rich, Henry, earl of Holland, 33–34, 36, 57, 58

Rich, Sir Nathaniel, 33, 45, 55, 62, 70, 267*n*29

Rich, Robert, 2nd earl of Warwick: at
Cambridge, 29–30, 33; electioneering
by, 78, 79–80; friendships of, 51, 52,
57–58, 118; and New England colonies,
101, 102; as patron, 39, 43, 45–46, 89;
seizure of papers of, 124; and Westmin-
ster Assembly, 134; and York House
conference, 74
Rich family, 43, 45, 62
Richardson, Alexander, 37
Ringley (Lancashire), 61, 92, 109
Rituals, contention over, 36–37, 84–87,
90–91. *See also* Conformity
Roberts, Richard, 31, 32
Roberts, Sir William, 30
Robinson, John, 116, 264*n*8
Rogers, Daniel, 38, 52, 59, 62, 79, 120
Rogers, Ezekiel, 45, 47, 53, 55, 57, 70,
88, 144, 209
Rogers, John, 38–40, 47, 50–51, 56, 58,
61, 62
Rogers, Nathaniel: at Cambridge, 22, 23;
death of, 209; deprivation of, 87–88;
friendships of, 52, 58, 60, 92, 144; mil-
lenarianism of, 129; seminary work of,
38
Rogers, Richard, 30, 49, 50, 52, 53, 57
Rogers, Samuel, 39, 52, 108, 119, 120
Root and Branch Petition, 125, 130,
281*n*33
Rotterdam (Netherlands), 110, 173, 215,
216; Hugh Peter in, 54, 70, 94–95, 97,
99, 119
Rous, Anthony, 287*n*49
Rous, Arthur, 101
Rous, Francis, 101, 194
Rous, John, 53, 74, 267*n*29
Rowe, John, 51, 200, 218, 233
Rowe, Owen, 90, 102
Rowe, Thomas, 215
Roxbury (Massachusetts), 134
Rulice, John, 38, 67, 71
Rump Parliament, 176, 191–193, 203
Rupert (Prince), 179
Russell, John (regicide harborer), 218–219
Russell, John (Massachusetts Baptist),
241–242
Russell family, 43
Ruth (Biblical figure), 7

Rutherford, Samuel, 133, 149, 163
Rye House Plot, 215, 221, 227, 229, 247

Sabbath, Puritan observance of, 110, 119
Sacheverell, Henry, 254
Sacraments: Anglicans' emphasis on, 72–
73; Congregational requirements for,
95–97, 99. *See also* Baptism; Eucharist;
Marriage
Saffin, John, 317*n*23
St. Andrew's Church (Norwich), 47
St. Anne's Blackfriars Church, 47, 56, 75
St. Antholin's Church (London), 37, 48,
49, 75, 76, 183
St. Botolph's Church (Cambridge), 22, 34
St. Botolph's parish (Boston, Lincoln-
shire), 3, 21, 46, 53, 89, 91, 187
St. Catharine's College (Cambridge Uni-
versity), 22, 23, 30, 32, 34, 195
St. Clement's Church (Cambridge), 22,
34
St. George's Tombland Church, 49, 87
St. John, Oliver, 52, 134, 142
St. John's College (Cambridge University),
20, 21, 22, 23, 27, 31, 34, 50
St. Lawrence, Jewry, 89, 90
St. Margaret's Church (London), 81
St. Mary the Virgin Church (Oxford Uni-
versity), 77
St. Mary's Aldermanbury Church, 53, 89
St. Mary's Church (Cambridge Univer-
sity), 37, 191
St. Mary's Church (Chelmsford, Essex),
46, 51
St. Peter Hungate Church, 48, 76
St. Peter Mancroft Church (Norwich),
46, 89
St. Saviour's Church (Southwark, Lon-
don), 39
St. Sepulchre Church (London), 36
St. Stephen's Coleman Street Church
(London), 46, 49, 52, 53, 57, 75, 84,
89–91, 98, 102, 129
Saints (Puritan). *See* Election; Godly com-
munion
Salem (Massachusetts), 103, 112, 113,
122, 134
Saltonstall, Henry, 182
Saltonstall, Sir Richard, 56, 90, 102, 103,
219

Saltonstall, Richard, Jr., 309*n*24
Sammes, John, 182
Sandcroft, William, 21, 22, 31, 33–35, 45, 54
Sanderson, Robert, 280*n*26, 289*n*20
Savoy Assembly, 183, 185, 199–201, 203, 204, 223, 244
Savoy Declaration. *See* Declaration of Faith and Order
Sawbridge, Anthony, 45
Saxton, Peter, 88
Say and Sele, Lord, 53, 74, 108, 116, 118, 124, 134
Saybrook Adventurers, 102
Saybrook Platform, 252
Schism Act, 254
Schneider, Carol Geary, 113–114, 294*n*22
Scholarly work, Puritan help with, 59–62. *See also* Manuscripts; Pamphlet controversies; Publication
Schools. *See* Academies (for dissenters); Cambridge University; Grammar schools; Oxford University; Seminaries
Scobell, Henry, 200, 201
Scotland, 82; English troubles in, 122–125, 129–130, 152; prisoners from, as New England labor, 179; representatives of, at Westminster Assembly, 133–139, 142–143, 152. *See also* Church of Scotland; Presbyterian(s)
Scott, Christopher, 185
Scottish Confession of 1616, 72
Scottish National Covenant, 124
Sects: contention between Congregationalists and, 174, 186, 190–193, 310*n*28; Presbyterian linking of Congregationalists with, 156, 158, 162, 166–167; Puritan alliances with, 139–142, 148, 170; Puritan opposition to, 132, 136–137, 157, 167–168, 178. *See also* Antinomianism; Arminianism; Baptists; Brownists; Erastians; Heresy; Independents; Levellers; Pelagian doctrines; Quakers; Radicals; Separatists; Socinianism
Sedgwick, Obadiah, 45, 70, 99, 194
Sedgwick, Robert, 179, 309*n*24
Seizure (of papers), 124, 126, 290*n*24, 320*n*41
Seminaries (Puritan), 37–38
Separatists (from a national church), 84,

91, 93, 95, 98, 114–116, 134, 135, 138, 141–142, 264*n*8, 273*n*17, 289*n*20, 301*n*32; Congregationalists as de facto, 320*n*1; fears about New Englanders becoming, 113–118, 120
Sergeant, Peter, 218
Sermon(s): farewell, 209–210; for friends' funerals, 62–63, 236, 313*n*55; in Oxford and Cambridge, 27; political uses of, 67–70, 78–80, 128; significance of, 34–35; travel to hear, 39–40, 45, 48–52. *See also* Catechizing: vs. sermons; Sermon notes
Sermon notes, 6, 62, 111–112, 128–129
Sewall, Samuel, 217, 246
Shaftesbury, Anthony Ashley Cooper, earl of, 227, 230
Shaw, John, 39, 52, 76
Sheldon, Gilbert (archbishop of Canterbury), 204, 205
Shepard, Thomas, 39, 161; at Cambridge, 22, 23, 28, 29, 31, 59; correspondence of, 118, 162–163, 307*n*16; death of, 209; friendships of, 52, 56–57, 59, 60, 63, 92, 102; reasons of, for emigrating to New England, 107; recommendations by, 47; refusal to leave New England, 180; resignation of living by, 89, 92; on Sabbath worship, 110; sermons of, 128; works by, 120, 146, 147, 149, 150, 163, 165, 173, 185, 196, 301*n*26
Shepard, Thomas, Jr., 230–231, 232
Sheppard, William, 52
Sherfield, Henry, 79
Sherland, Christopher, 75, 79
Sherland, Thomas, 63
Ship Money case, 78, 101, 123, 124
Short Parliament, 79, 124, 126
Shute, Samuel, 255
Sibbes, Richard: at Cambridge, 19, 21, 30–32, 34; conversion of, 30; correspondence of, 54, 70–71; as Feoffee, 75, 78; friendships of, 32, 45, 46, 50, 58, 59, 62, 63, 90; irenic attempts of, 65; persecution of, 70–71; recommendations by, 56; scholarly work by, 61; sermons of, 34, 45, 51, 52, 63, 67–68, 70, 128; skirting of conformity by, 83–84; views of, 6, 42, 108; will of, 62

Sidney Sussex College (Cambridge University), 20–22, 36, 40

Sign of the cross, 84, 85, 88, 90, 283n7

Simpson, Sydrach, 121, 191, 192; at Cambridge, 22, 23, 29, 192; death of, 209; as Dissenting Brethren, 109–110, 150, 154, 164, 168, 183, 186, 190; irenic attempts of, 65; in Netherlands, 97, 99; reform efforts of, 198; resignation of post by, 89; scholarly work by, 165; and sects, 194; works by, 167, 192

Singing, 117, 170–171, 172

Skelton, Samuel, 21, 51, 58, 103, 112, 116–117

Skippon, Philip, 69

Slater, Samuel, 194

Smectymnians, 31, 132, 133. *See also* Presbyterian(s)

"Smectymnuus," 132

Smith, John, 273n17

Smuggling: of dissenters abroad, 217; of Puritan propaganda into England, 96, 100

Social status, and Puritan friendship, 29–30, 43–46, 244. *See also* Clergy: relations of, with laity; Patronage

Society of Friends. *See* Quakers

Socinianism, 167, 186, 192, 327n55

Solemn League and Covenant, 129–130, 133, 144

Sommerville, Margaret Ruth, 294n22

Sowerby Plot, 206

Spain: Armada from, 129; mercenaries from, in Bishops War, 124; possible English royal match with, 66, 67, 73; Puritan interest in blocking, in America, 101, 177–179, 287n49; as threat to Netherlands, 66–67, 96

Spang, William, 165

Sparrowhawke, Edward, 22, 23

Spies, 86, 100, 173, 212–214, 248. *See also* Seizure (of papers)

Spilsbury, John, 148, 196

Spinola, Ambrogio, 66

Sports: at university, 28. *See also Book of Sports* (James I); Sabbath

Spring, Sir William, 6, 7, 79

Spurstowe, Sir William, 102, 132, 176

Star Chamber, 83, 86, 87

Starr, Comfort, 183, 184, 200, 251

State Church: Congregationalists' eventual exclusion from, 221–223; contention about jurisdiction of, 138–141; efforts to found a new English, 4, 140, 190–201; Puritans' commitment to, 98, 135, 159, 160, 164. *See also* Church of England; Church of Scotland; Conformity; Separatists

Stephens, Nathaniel, 79

Sterry, Peter, 53, 153, 186, 191, 202, 203, 213, 243

Stock, Richard, 29, 51, 62, 75, 102

Stockton, Owen, 236

Stone, John, 182

Stone, Samuel, 22, 23, 29, 37, 47, 58, 163, 185, 209

Stonestreet, John, 200

Stoughton, Israel, 54, 309n24

Stoughton, John, 65; at Cambridge, 22, 31; correspondence of, 54, 70, 92, 99; friendships of, 56, 57, 58, 92, 118

Stoughton, William, 181, 217, 232

Strafford, Thomas Wentworth, earl of, 124–125, 145

"Stranger" churches (in London), 65, 67, 70, 83, 164. *See also* Reformed churches

Strong, William, 31, 34, 36, 153, 190, 192, 194, 209, 233

Stuteville, Sir Martin, 33

Surplices, 19, 20, 60, 82, 84–88, 90, 92, 93, 127

Swallow, Matthew, 49

Swinnock, Josph, 182

Switzerland, 19, 93

Sydenham, Cuthbert, 188

Symmes, Zachariah, 22, 23, 29, 48, 54, 76, 109, 209

Symonds, John, 87

Symonds, Joseph, 38, 307n14

Synod(s): contention over, 95, 114–115, 137–141, 154, 165, 244, 252, 296n45; in New England, 157, 166, 238; post-Restoration lack of, 223; Puritan calls for, 131; work of, compared to clerical conferences, 112. *See also* Synod of Dort; Westminster Assembly

Synod of Dort, 35, 72, 73

Tayler, Francis, 59
Taylor, Edward, 217
Taylor, Nathaniel, 216
Taylor, Thomas, 38, 53, 62, 65, 70–71, 89, 199, 303*n*43
Taylor, Timothy, 184, 318*n*26
Teachers (church), 114, 136, 172, 224
Teelinck, Maximilian, 38
Teelinck, Willem, 37–38, 67
Terling (Essex), 46, 59, 86
Thilenius, Wilhelm, 37, 67
Thirty-Nine Articles (of the Church of England), 19, 20, 133, 198
Thirty Years' War, 66–70, 73, 118, 121, 129
Thompson, John, 191
Thompson, Robert, 248
Thompson, William, 149
Thomson, Sir William, 226
Thorne, George, 219
Thorner, Robert, 236
Thornton, Thomas, 216
Tilly, Johann Tserclaes, Count, 66
Tombes, John, 46, 148, 194, 196, 197, 239
Tourney, John, 36
Towgood, Stephen, 228
Townshend, Sir Roger, 79
Trainbands, 79, 122
Travels: between New England and England, 113, 120–121, 236, 253–254; clandestine, of exiles to England, 100; of English preachers to hear each other, 51–53; of English students to hear preachers, 39–40, 49, 51; of New England preachers to hear each other, 111. *See also* Conferences
Travers, Walter, 19, 114
Treatises, colonial, 4. *See also* Pamphlet controversies; Publication
Triers (ecclesiastical), 31; Puritans as, 183, 184, 194–198
Trinity Church (Cambridge), 21, 22, 34, 92
Trinity College (Cambridge University), 20–23, 25–26, 29, 38
Trinity College (Dublin), 29, 32, 50, 184, 191
Tserclaes, Johann, Count Tilly, 66
Tuby, Job, 199

Tuckney, Anthony, 21–23, 29, 33, 38, 53, 55, 187
Tuckney, Jonathan, 220, 222
Twisse, William, 108, 133, 188

University of Franeker (Netherlands), 38, 56, 94, 98
University of Leiden (Netherlands), 93, 94
Ussher, James, 32, 109

Vane, Sir Henry, 129–130, 142, 157, 160, 193, 204, 206
Vassall, Samuel, 102
Veal, Edward, 215
Venn, John, 101, 102
Venner, Thomas, 206–207, 223
Venning, Ralph, 190
Vere, Sir Horace, Baron, 45, 69, 70, 94, 89, 118
Vere, Lady Mary, 55, 57, 89–91, 118, 130
Vernon, George, 226
Vestments. *See* Surplices
Vicars, John, 141, 155–156, 299*n*9
Villiers, George. *See* Buckingham, earl of
Vincent, Thomas, 235
Vines, Richard, 22, 23, 29, 142, 143, 187, 209
Visitations. *See* Diocesan visitations
Visits, to clergy. *See* Travels
Voet, Gisbert, 301*n*29

Wakeman, Samuel, 235
Walley, Thomas, 216
Wallington, Nehemiah, 118
Walwyn, William, 141–142, 170
War, Baptist position on, 196. *See also* Puritan Revolution
Ward, Jacob, 182
Ward, John (Nathaniel's son), 45
Ward, John (Norwich preacher), 21, 22, 54, 73, 97
Ward, Nathaniel: at Cambridge, 29, 33; correspondence of, 54, 55, 118; deprivation of, 45, 88; exile of, 93, 94; friendships of, 57, 59, 92; as pastor, 45; petitions by, 73
Ward, Samuel, 65, 75, 284*n*15; at clerical conferences, 50; correspondence of, 54–55, 70, 92, 267*n*29, 274*n*26; friendships

of, 59–60, 92; as master of Sidney Sussex College, 20, 29, 31, 33, 36, 37; in Puritan Revolution, 130

Ward, Samuel (of Ipswich), 62, 79, 88, 108, 110, 280*n*21

Warwick, 2nd earl of. *See* Rich, Robert

Watson, Thomas, 213, 243

Watts, Isaac, 183, 215, 255

Welde, Edmund, 182

Welde, John, 151, 180

Welde, Thomas, 96, 139, 161; at Cambridge, 21, 22, 29; at clerical conferences, 50, 173; correspondence of, 118, 134; death of, 209; friendships of, 56–59, 63, 86, 89, 92, 134, 182, 188; as Massachusetts delegate to England, 145–146, 150, 153, 157; as parson, 39, 46, 171; reasons of, for emigrating to New England, 107; return migration of, 171, 180; and sects, 186; sermons of, 52; works by, 147–148, 150, 161, 165, 186

Wellman, Barry, 9

Wentworth, Thomas, earl of Strafford, 124–125, 145

Wesley, Samuel, 215

West Indies, 101, 177–179, 287*n*49

Westgate, John, 233, 235, 237–238, 241

Westminster Abbey (London), 81

Westminster Assembly, 4, 131, 133–143, 150, 152–155, 165–166, 168, 191

Westminster Confession of Faith, 139, 153, 154, 155, 200, 239

Whalley, Edward, 192, 194, 199, 204, 207, 218–219, 248

Wharton, Goodwin, 248

Wharton, Lord, 142, 215, 226, 248, 318*n*27

Wharton, Richard, 245

Wharton, Samuel, 59, 62, 63

Wheelwright, John, 21, 22, 28, 113, 158, 178, 180

Whig party, 226–227, 254

Whitaker, Alexander, 54

Whitaker, William, 20

White, John (lawyer), 75–78, 101, 102, 130, 281*n*33

White, John (minister from Dorchester), 47, 54, 65, 71, 86, 88, 100–103, 133, 189

White, Peter, 279*n*18

Whitefield, Henry, 54, 56, 58, 60, 88, 180, 190

Whitgift, John (archbishop of Canterbury), 35, 279*n*18

Whiting, Anthony, 58

Whiting, John, 220

Whiting, Samuel, 21–23, 29, 51, 177–178

Wilcox, Thomas, 89

Willard, Samuel, 238, 241–242, 247

William of Orange, 5, 215, 216, 247–249

Williams, Daniel, 250–251

Williams, John (bishop of Lincoln), 84, 86

Williams, Roger, 58, 169; absence of, from New England clerical conferences, 112; banishment of, from Bay Colony, 158–160, 168; as chaplain, 46; correspondence of, 55, 70, 126, 176; friendships of, 60, 92, 158; and religious tolerance, 170; views of, 142, 147, 178; works by, 159, 160, 193

Willington, John, 36

Willoughby, Francis, 309*n*24

Wills, 62, 112, 215, 236

Wilson, John, 23, 39; anti-Catholicism of, 88; at Cambridge, 21, 22, 31; correspondence of, 54, 55; death of, 62; electioneering by, 79; friendships of, 52, 60, 62, 197, 236; jailing of, 80; in New England, 109, 112, 180; persecution of, 57, 58; sermons of, 51; visits to England by, 120; works by, 245

Wilson, Mrs. John, 61, 120

Wilson, Thomas, 187

Winslow, Edward, 160, 162, 166, 170, 309*n*24

Winstanly, Ellen, 38

Winter, Josiah, 184

Winter, Samuel, 22, 31, 38, 47, 53, 92, 184, 191

Winthrop, Fitz, 309*n*24

Winthrop, John, 45, 75, 181; correspondence of, 54, 55, 117, 125, 203; friendships of, 52, 56, 59, 62, 76, 160, 196; in New England, 103, 110; on trans-Atlantic communion, xiii–xiv, 145; views of, 6–7, 20, 41–43, 105, 108, 122, 134, 143, 163, 289*n*13; works by, 7, 157–158, 232

Winthrop, John, Jr., 8–9, 102, 145, 214;

correspondence of, 176, 178, 202, 216, 218
Winthrop, Wait, 309n24
Wise, John, 327n60
Wood, Seth, 218
Woodbridge, Benjamin, 181
Woodcock, Thomas, 216
Woodrop, Nicholas, 216
Worcester House Declaration, 204
Wren, Matthew, 35, 36, 49, 58, 86–88, 97, 127, 188

Wrentham (Suffolk), 54, 92, 99, 150, 171, 182
Wroth, William, 120

Yarmouth (England), 58, 59, 172, 186
Yates, John, 21, 22, 29, 35, 37, 47, 61, 73, 233
Yelverton, Henry (Sir), 51, 62
Yonge, John, 22, 23, 101, 102
York House Conference, 74, 80, 93
Young, Thomas, 38, 132, 136